SOCIETY TODAY AND TOMORROW

SOCIETY
TODAY
AND
TOMORROW

READINGS IN SOCIAL SCIENCE

EDITED BY

Elgin F. Hunt and Jules Karlin

SECOND EDITION

THE MACMILLAN COMPANY
New York

COLLIER-MACMILLAN LIMITED
London

To Agnete and Dorothy

First Printing

Earlier edition © 1961 by The Macmillan Company

Library of Congress catalog card number: 67–11282

The Macmillan Company, New York
Collier-Macmillan Canada, Ltd., Toronto, Ontario

Printed in the United States of America

PREFACE

IN PREPARING THIS second edition of *Society Today and Tomorrow* the editors have made every effort to retain those characteristics which resulted in a wide use of the first edition. At the same time they have sought to take advantage of the experience of the instructors and students who used the earlier book. Although the main outline remains the same, almost half the selections are new. Most of the changes have been made for one of two reasons: first, to bring the book up to date; second, to substitute for old material new material which is better, or at least better adapted to the needs of most of those who will use the book.

Society Today and Tomorrow was planned primarily as a book of readings for the introductory college course in social science, but the wide variety of selections in the second edition will, it is hoped, also interest the adult layman and students of the various disciplines within the social sciences. Some of the selections are short, some are rather long; some expound more fully than the average textbook certain important concepts; some present unusual or controversial points of view, and some are written with a light touch and leavened by a sense of humor. Always in choosing readings the editors have tried to keep in mind not only their readability, relevance, clarity, and interest, but also the quality of the insights which they provide into the nature of society and its problems.

Social science is a relatively new approach to the understanding of man and society, one which involves learning to think in terms of relationships, and in terms of process and change. As the social scientist sees it, human life itself is made up of countless active relationships of individuals to other people and to things, and the notion of the single, wholly self-contained individual, a prisoner within himself, is a myth. Further-

v

more, the social scientist views the human personality as a plastic, changing entity which emerges gradually from a complex network of relationships, the most important of which are those with other people.

The ancient Greek maxim "Know thyself," which formerly meant probing inward introspectively to "our very depths," has been reinterpreted by the social scientist to mean a search into the motives, the values, the ideas, the institutions, and the general social forces which have become a part of the individual person. Hence when he looks for the source of our major troubles, the social scientist seeks it in some weakness, disturbance, or distortion of our human relations.

Through complex historical processes, the social system has become subject to increasingly rapid change. We have witnessed unprecedented advances in science and technology, and we have seen the United States transformed from a rural society to a predominantly urban mass society. But our failure to grasp cause and effect relationships and to foresee social trends has left us largely unprepared for such disastrous events of the twentieth century as two world wars, a major depression, numerous revolutions, and the protracted period of world tension which we call the "cold war." These immense developments demand reorganization of our lives, but we are not at all sure of the direction in which we should move. Today we are genuinely troubled about the uncertainties of the future.

If we could see the future more clearly in a broad social and historical context some of our doubts and fears might be allayed. In the present volume we draw on the work of outstanding social scientists for the purpose of developing greater social understanding and a more adequate image of our changing society. We emphasize social change, and we believe that the material of this book, as we have organized it, will enable and encourage the reader to perceive order and form in the drift of events. The title of our volume is intended to suggest continuity among past, present, and future; we have therefore attempted, in various parts of the book, to include selections which indicate what lies ahead.

While we have covered the main areas of social life, we have tried at the same time to produce a work which is compact and manageable. Further, it has been our aim to offer a reasonably integrated body of facts and ideas without glossing over conflicting opinions or overextending favored ideas. Though man's social life is a unity, it is a very complex unity, and we do not believe that anything is gained by attempting to disregard or to "scramble" such traditional social science disciplines as history, sociology, economics, and political science. Each has a contribution to make to the understanding of human society. We do believe, however, that their interrelations should be emphasized, and we have drawn upon all of them for integrating concepts.

In its organization this book is divided into an introduction and six major parts. The first part offers up-to-date analyses of such basic concepts as man and animal, community and society, culture and cultural relativity, and technological and social change. The second part continues with discussions of some of the important problems of personal and social adjustment. The problems of family living, juvenile delinquency and crime, racial prejudice, and mental illness are dealt with in terms of difficulties in interpersonal relations. It is shown that serious problems arise when these relations become either too limited and harsh, or are distorted by dread, hate, and intolerance. Later parts of the book deal with the economy, government, and the quest for peace within the sphere of international relations. The major problems within the areas of our economic and political life and our international relations are linked to rapid social change in an industrial society. The sixth and final part of the book is devoted to readings which consider vitally significant social trends and attempt to glimpse and to prophesy the emerging shape of the future.

The editors wish to express their appreciation to all who have aided them in preparing this book. Recognition is given in footnotes to the authors and publishers of individual selections, but it is not possible to mention all the individuals who have made useful criticisms of the old edition or useful suggestions for the new one. However, special recognition should be given to Mrs. Elgin F. Hunt. Her services were invaluable in handling the great volume of necessary correspondence and the many other details connected with preparing the manuscript for the publisher.

E. F. H.
J. K.

Chicago

CONTENTS

INTRODUCTION

P A R T

II

SOCIAL ADJUSTMENT AND SOCIAL PROBLEMS   133

P A R T

III

ECONOMIC ORGANIZATION AND SOCIAL PROBLEMS 247

PART

IV

POLITICAL ORGANIZATION AND
SOCIAL PROBLEMS 359

P A R T
V
INTERNATIONAL RELATIONS   445

P A R T
VI
THE SHAPE OF THE FUTURE   499

Introduction

I

Talk with a Stranger

by Robert Redfield

One day last month as I sat on an old bench near my house on the outskirts of Chicago, a stranger appeared and sat down beside me.

"Do you mind if I join you?" he asked. "There is some information I want very much to get. But perhaps I interrupt your thoughts?"

I told him that my thoughts were at the moment not much—I had been trying to think of an address I was to give to some college students.

He asked me what I would say to them.

"Give them good advice," I replied. "That is the usual thing to do."

"About what?" He seemed really interested.

"I don't quite know," was my answer, "but the usual thing is to tell them about the importance of the free mind and the privilege they enjoy in getting an education. And that sort of thing. You know—exhort them and commend them and encourage them."

"If you can advise them," said the stranger, "perhaps you can advise me."

I remembered that he had said he wanted information. My first thought had been that he would ask me about what kind of dogfood I bought for my dog—you know, market research—or that perhaps he was making a political canvass of our neighborhood. But his first question showed me that these guesses were very wrong.

"I wish you would explain to me about this war that I hear is going on—the war that is now cold and might get hot. Are you people at war with each other?"

That didn't seem to me the way to put it. I started to explain. "The Russians want to conquer everybody, by propaganda if they can and by force if they have to. So they make monstrous weapons that threaten us and that force us to make monstrous weapons to threaten them. We have some bombs big enough to kill millions of people that we carry around in airplanes in case the Russians begin to drop bombs on us. For the

Robert Redfield, "Talk with a Stranger," An Occasional Paper on the Free Society (New York: The Fund for the Republic, 1958). Reprinted by permission of the Center for the Study of Democratic Institutions, Santa Barbara, California.

The late Robert Redfield was Distinguished Service Professor at the University of Chicago, and Chairman of the Department of Anthropology.

Russians have bombs just as big, and now they are learning how to shoot them over to us with rockets or maybe pretty soon from space-ships circling overhead. So of course there is a kind of war—two sides all ready to shoot at each other."

He didn't say anything for a while. He seemed to be thinking. Then he said, "Tell me, do you, yourself, know anything about war?"

"Well, yes." I tried to sound modest. "I had some personal connection with a war in 1917 and I saw something of another one in the 1940's."

"And this cold war you speak of," he continued, "when it becomes hot, when the monster bombs are dropped, will it be like those old wars you knew?"

At once I understood that it would be quite different. But I found it hard to get out the words that would describe the new thing we were calling war. I thought of the sober estimates of scientific advisors to our President that if the bombs are set off, whether by design or by accident, about sixty million Americans would be killed, our greater cities would be reduced to ruin, and the survivors—in whatever appalling chaos they might find themselves—as well as their children and children's children would be poisoned and distorted to an extent impossible to predict. I thought of this and knew that the provincial little massacre I witnessed on the Aisne River in 1917 was something else again. I thought, but I could say little.

"No, it would be a new kind of experience," I said.

"Then," said the stranger, "it should have a different name. Not 'war.' 'Mutual suicide,' perhaps. Or maybe I should put it down that you people are getting ready for your own partial extermination. Is that it?"

I felt I was becoming confused. And a little annoyed with my visitor. I didn't like the way he kept saying "you people." What did he mean by "you people"? I asked him that in so many words.

"Oh," he said, "you people—you, and Khrushchev and the young college people you are going to talk to and John Foster Dulles and the boys down at the corner in Brooklyn and those fishermen drawing up their nets on the Malabar coast."

He did talk in a strange way. Where had he come from? I tried to get our conversation back into easier paths.

"Do *you* come from India?" I asked.

"No," he said, "no. I come from farther away than that."

He sat silent and I tried to get a good look at him. But although he sat close to me on the bench, I could not see him well because the sun was setting just behind him. It was he who took up the conversation. "I suppose you people want to go on living?"

I said that most of us did.

"Then," he said, "I suppose you people are doing what you can to prevent this thing that you call a war but would not be a war but a kind of suicide?"

"We are doing what we can," I replied. "In this country we are spending more money for missiles and maybe we can get the Europeans to put our missiles on their land nearer to the Russians and maybe we can build space-ships before the Russians do and so get the drop on them that way. We have been working pretty hard to make our weapons as big or bigger than the Russians' weapons. You know we were the first to kill people with atomic bombs and we were the first to make bombs one thousand times bigger than the little ones that killed only about seventy-five thousand people apiece in Japan. We had to make the very big bombs because if we hadn't the Russians would have made them first and then we wouldn't have had security. Neither side wants to start a war when it is clear that the starter would be destroyed also. Of course it is true that the Russians made the very big bombs too and now they are going after space and the moon and we have to go after these things too. Two-thirds of the national budget for next year will be used for military purposes of one kind or another. So we *are* trying to prevent it from happening."

He made a gesture of interruption. "You go too fast," he said. "I can't quite follow. You say you Americans are doing these things for security? And you Russians are doing these things too?"

You Russians! He addressed *me* as "you Russians"! I took him up. "I can't speak for the Russians," I said. "We can't trust the Russians."

"Why not?" he asked. "Don't they want to live too? And can't you trust their common interest with you in continuing to live? It seems to me quite a basis for getting together on some arrangement not to shoot at each other. Two men with firebrands in a room of explosives share one very immediate common interest. But there is something else in what you just said that puzzles me. I think you told me that you went ahead with making more monstrous weapons in order to have security. Tell me, now that you have the thousand-times-bigger bombs, do you feel more secure?"

My impatience had subsided, and, besides, I saw that he had a point or two. I tried to answer his question honestly.

"No," I said, "I don't really feel more secure now than before we had the hydrogen bomb. For at least two reasons. The destruction that could be done now is very much greater—all civilization could be blown to bits. And also, so many countries are getting the weapons and their management is getting so difficult and complicated that the decisions whether or not to fire a missile or drop a bomb must be left to many different people—base commanders, airplane pilots and so on—so that the chance that the first big explosion might occur through a misunderstanding or a rash act grows greater and greater. We might more and more easily have a catastrophe by a sort of inevitable accident. No, I don't feel more secure."

He was thoughtful. Then he spoke again. "I shouldn't express an opinion. But I can say I am confused. You seem to be telling me that you are working hard to prevent this mutual suicide by making bigger and bigger weapons to shoot at each other, and that the more you make, the more likely they will go off of themselves. It is like piling more and more explosives into this room with the two waving firebrands. It seems a strange way to seek security."

Again there was a slience. Then he asked me if I thought that the young college people would continue to choose the same way to security when they took over matters. I told him that I could not predict as to that.

"They might find some other way," he said. "They might call the thing that you are trying to prevent not war but mutual destruction. They might become less bellicose about that struggle that is now going on between some of you and others of you. They might talk less about how each wants to destroy the other and fears to be destroyed by the other and talk more with each other about your common interests—in keeping alive, in keeping down the cost of threatening each other. They might even move some of the explosives out of the room—what difference would that make to mutual security if each can destroy the other several times over with the explosives that are left? They might even stamp out the firebrands and walk away from the explosives.

"These young people don't *have* to do just what you have been doing," he continued. "They will do better. They are more experienced than you."

"*Less* experienced, I think you mean," said I.

"No, I mean more experienced. They start knowing not only what you know but also what you did—which is more than you knew when you started. So they are a more experienced people than you. And I suppose I am at liberty to believe that you people learn by experience? That you do things better as you go along?"

"Yes," said I. "That is progress. Progress is something we all believe in. Or maybe used to believe in. There seem to be doubts now about progress. Progress, it appears, is not going forward step by step, or leap by leap, to the better and better. It seems to me like going ahead and backward at one and the same time, by the same effort of movement. Or like—"

"Like what?" he asked.

"Like a strange dream in which one opens door after door down a corridor with a light at the end of it only to find that each door opened makes the light brighter and the darkness darker. There is more light all the time: the antibiotics and the good music that comes out of my loudspeaker and the old slums torn down. And there is also more darkness: people living longer to suffer from other diseases, and many wasted hours in front of the TV, and the new slums growing up around the over-crowded cities. Progress seems to me very untrustworthy. She can't just be believed in. She has somehow to be managed."

"You are becoming eloquent," he said. "If I may say so without offense, eloquence is like progress—bright and shining, but untrustworthy. Let us try again to understand the problem of how to go forward without going backward, to let new light shine undarkened. May I ask how you people are doing with space control?"

"Not much—yet," I said. "We have put some satellites into orbit and our President proposed that space be controlled internationally—an inter-planetary police force, some day—"

He interrupted. "You misunderstand me. I referred not to interplanetary space—which by the way seems to me a very poor place to be—but to space right here, on your own planet, where you people live. How are you people doing with respect to control of your own terrestrial space?"

I remembered a piece I had been reading by Paul H. Sears about how badly we had been doing, and I recalled some facts about occupation of terrestrial space. So I began at once to provide the stranger with in-formation about the topic he had just raised.

"The population of our planet is increasing at a rate of about 40,000,000 a year. By 1987, when college students of today are putting their children through college, at the present rate of growth there will be about six and a half billion people. The world will then be more than twice as crowded as it is now. China will have a population of five bil-lion people in a hundred years if the present rate of growth continues. Indeed, stranger, if your wish was to get to know us, you have come at a favorable time, for about twenty per cent of all the people who ever lived are alive now. But more important than this great number of us is the fact that the rate of increase overcomes much of the advantages we think we give ourselves by modern medicine and technology. The Egyptians are probably poorer than ever because there are so many more of them. Most of the increase that India has achieved by better technology and planning is no real increase at all because medicine and hygiene have caused the number of people who eat the food to increase as rapidly as the food has."

"You do indeed go forward backward toward a darkened light," said he. "However," he continued, "you don't look so badly off right around here—on this American patch of your terrestrial space."

"We are very proud, we Americans, of our standard of living. I will give you another statistic. It is estimated that with present technology this planet of ours could support, with the standard of living enjoyed by Americans, less than one-third of the people who are now on it. So some of us are doing pretty well. And we shall probably do better. Gunnar Myrdal says that on this earth the rich nations are getting richer. Of course he also says that the poor ones are getting poorer."

"That does not sound like a very desirable arrangement," went on the stranger. "It must cause some hard feelings. And I suppose you people who are Americans do pretty well by making and consuming things? Don't you ever use up any of the things you need for getting along better?"

I had still another statistic for him. "The people of my nation, with about seven per cent of the world's population, are now absorbing about sixty per cent of the world's minerals—mostly irreplaceable. We are indeed great consumers. We consume raw materials, use up water so it sometimes has to be rationed in cities, pollute air and rivers with waste products, and almost take pride in the piles of junked automobiles. It all goes to make the American standard of living the highest on earth. Now that I understand that it is the control of terrestrial space in which you are interested, I can say that we overrun it rather than control it."

He was silent and thoughtful. "What is that great wall of earth over there?" he suddenly asked. I followed the line of his gaze.

"That is a superhighway under construction. It will get more people around places faster."

"It certainly overruns space," he remarked. This time I did not say what was on my mind—that industry and highways take out of agricultural use about a million acres of American land yearly, and Sears' prediction that the agricultural surpluses that are now so troublesome will be only a memory twenty years from now. Instead I said that Chicago was growing very fast and needed better transportation.

"You are indeed an odd people," he said. "In your efforts to get security from war you make yourselves more and more insecure; in your efforts to get a good life, you rather mess up much of the life you are busy improving. This is indeed a darkened light."

The sun had set now and the twilight made that wall of earth loom larger against the amber sky. My mind, perhaps tired by the effort to explain how things are on this earth, relaxed into reminiscence, into dreamy consideration of times past. I said something like this to the stranger.

"Where that superhighway runs, there used to be a cornfield. In June the unfolding leaves made a neat, fresh carpet there—nine acres of it. In August one walked slowly between the rows of stalks, taller than one's head. When we went into the corn on very hot nights and stood still and listened, we used to tell ourselves that we heard the corn growing. And over there farther, there was a piece of aboriginal prairie that had never been broken by the plow. Only native plants grew there, prairie dock and tickseed, downy phlox, and bluegrass. And up there where there are so many houses, the oaks stood very old and tall, and I used to find yellow adder's tongue growing beneath some of them.

"Do you know what I miss? I am thinking just now, although the season of the year is not appropriate, that I miss very much the sound of the whetstone on the scythe—a good, clean sound. Oh, and many other things I miss—the voice of the bobwhite, the flight of the red-headed woodpecker as he flashed along the dirt road to fling himself like a painted dart against a telephone pole. And I miss the fields filled with shooting stars. And the clang and rattle of the windmill when the vanes swung around in a shift of breeze, and the puddles of water at the well where the wasps came in summer.

"Excuse me," I said. "This must bore you. Older people tend to look back on things that are gone and were good to them. If now you were talking to a young person, he would not have on his mind these changes that are losses to me. It is a great and necessary thing about young people that they look forward with a confidence unshaken by such regrets. It is a good thing that some things are unremembered as the generations pass. Really you should be talking to the young people. Why don't you go to some college town and talk to young people?"

He told me that he might do just that. I could see that indeed he was growing tired of me. Neither of us spoke for a time and in the growing dusk I thought I could see him looking through the pages of a notebook.

"Young people," he said. "I do have some notes on the topic. I have been looking into some of the authorities you have on young people, at least young people who are Americans. The matter has been investigated by *The Nation,* David Riesman, William Whyte, Alan Harrington, and others. I have here a summary of the results of research on this subject. Yes, here it is: 'American young people are uncommitted and other-directed; they have no heroes and few illusions; they seek security and togetherness; they want only to find places in the slots of employment and safe advancement; after comfortable years in college they become organization men and succumb slowly to creeping contentment.' "

His words stirred me to a disagreement, even resentment, that I could not at once express. Was this true of our young people? I wanted to argue the matter with him but could not find the words. But my resentment was growing. Somehow I felt that the view of us people that he was developing was incomplete. He saw us, but in a queer, unnatural light, a light from firebrands and neon signs. It was true, and yet it was not true. Or not all the truth, and my resentment was directed also at myself, for had I not been telling him things, true things yet not all the truth, about us? Somehow I had responded to him in such a way as to help him to form this true yet not quite true view of us. I wanted to turn upon him, to make *him* say something, make some observations that I could contradict. He had risen and I saw he was about to leave me.

"Stranger," I said, "before you go won't you tell me what your impressions are, on the whole, thinking over what you know about us, all of us here?"

When he did speak his words were only one more question. "How do *you* know all these things you have been telling me, about war and space control and the multiplication of people and so on?"

"I read things," I said, "and then we have many studies of these matters. And commissions and reports and committees and conferences."

"I see," he said. "You have commissions and reports and conferences. Tell me, did you ever have a conference on the good life?"

"On what?"

"On the good life. On what a good life would be for all you people. Just in case you stamp out the firebrands and go on living with yourselves. A conference as to what would be a good life, for everybody, given the limitations of earth and space and the nature, whatever it is, of all of you."

"It seems a large subject. And not too definite. How would such a conference be organized?"

"I think I could make some suggestions," said the stranger. "I could propose a tentative agenda. The topics could be formulated for group discussion in the form of a list of questions. Like this:

ITEM ONE: Do you want more and more people existing together somehow or do you want not quite so many people living well?

ITEM TWO: What is growth—is it getting bigger or getting better?

ITEM THREE: What is a good standard of living, more things to consume or better things to appreciate and discriminate? This third item on the agenda would require much subdivision and consideration of particular subtopics. You could appoint a subcommittee for each subtopic, you know. For example, Subtopic 37, Production and Consumption, Subsubtopic 49, division b, 3: Do you want to buy the car of tomorrow today only to find that tomorrow it is already the car of yesterday and you are expected to buy another? And so on. Oh, it could be quite an agenda.

ITEM FOUR: What is the right relation of man to the cosmos? Again, a subtopic: Which is the better use of the moon: to hit it with a rocket or just to look at it?

ITEM FIVE: Where are the frontiers of human enterprise? That item could be put in different ways, for example: Should people build and pioneer always outward or sometimes inward?

He must have seen that I still looked puzzled. So he tried again. "Item Five could be put more concretely," he said. "Like this: To take risks, make adventures, create and add to human life, is it necessary to climb a mountain or build a space-ship, or could one also adventure and create within a limited world? Find new good things within the limits of earth-space, production and consumption? Exercise restraints to free one's self for the making of new things for enjoyment, improved experience, wiser and finer judgments? Where is freedom? In always doing more and more or in doing fewer things to do them better? That, of course, amounts to asking if the very abundance of material goods may not result in a loss of freedom."

I was trying to take this in. "It would certainly be a difficult conference to organize," I said. "And it would make some people very uneasy. It seems to ask questions that are somehow, where I live, not quite the sort of question to ask. And so different from what is discussed at the conferences that I do go to! Those conferences are concerned with how to do things. Your conference would be concerned with why one should do them at all. And with what is good to do and why."

"Just so," he said. "And now I say goodbye. It has been nice knowing you people. You *are* odd, and, from what I have seen of you, pretty mixed up. But I wish you well. Goodbye."

He was gone, and I have not seen him since. But what he said is much in my mind. It troubles me a good deal. Somehow the conversation was unsatisfactory. I didn't like being asked so many questions. And such questions! As an anthropologist, I am used to being the one who asks the questions; I find out about other people. With this stranger I felt that somehow I had caught hold of the wrong end of the stick. And I felt that I had held up my end badly. I hadn't said things about us that he ought to know, if he really wanted to understand us. Ever since he went away my mind has been full of what is called "staircase wit"—those clever or right things you didn't say and wish you had as you go down the stairway jamming your hat on your head and getting angrier and angrier with yourself.

I had told him truly things that indeed show that mankind is confused. I could not deny that we are in a terrible predicament. It had to be admitted that we waste our substance and threaten ourselves with a perhaps ultimate destruction. It is so that at least locally, here in America, we are inclined to trust too much in technology to get us out of trouble, pretty complacent about ourselves, and unwilling to look the human tragedy in the face. So much of the worst about us he had got out of me with his unexpected questions. If you come to us, just like that, from somewhere outside of our human affairs, we do appear a mixed-up lot of people leading a totteringly precarious existence, and doing much that is both stupid and base. And yet that is not all that is true and important about us. What had I failed to say?

As I turned it over in my mind and struggled to understand my dissatisfaction with the interview, one clarifying thought came to me. So far as I could tell, the stranger had found out nothing about our past. He had asked about us now, what we were doing now, what we are like now. Can a stranger come really to understand a man by asking some questions about his present situation only? I might meet a man at a moment of crisis, when his affairs were confused and his very existence endangered; learning this about him I might conclude: This is a hopeless incompetent on his way to immediate destruction through his own folly. But, if I had the story of his life, if I saw how he had acted in other crises, if I came to know not only his present predicament but his character, I might change my judgment of him and his prospects; I might come to see that in spite of his current mistakes he had managed to deal with earlier difficulties and, perhaps, had shown that he did indeed learn by experience; that he had been growing, adding to his capacities, making some judgments more wisely than he had been able to at an earlier stage in his career. So, I thought, it was with this interviewing stranger: he showed no knowledge of the human career; he gave no indication that he had looked into the story of the collective human life from the days of the cave man to today. I just wished I had kept him with me long enough to take him to a performance of Thornton Wilder's play, *The Skin of Our Teeth.*

I began to say to myself some of the things I should have said to him. A phrase came into my mind, a phrase used by Albert Camus when he replied not long ago to some questions put to him by another French novelist. The phrase was, "the spirit matures." Yes, it does. Our human career is growing up. Though our follies continue and our dangers increase, it is also true that if not century by century then millennium by millennium we grow more worth saving. We learn to put some bad things behind us and we make new good things that we could not make before. Slavery and legal torture are no longer respectable. We learn to write books, and good books! The cave man could not give us the Platonic dialogues. Once there was no Bach, no Tolstoi and no Einstein, and then, after the spirit had further matured, there were these men. That stranger, coming to us at one moment, could not know these things.

Yes, I went on saying to myself and as it were to him: On the whole we people are busy making a living, keeping house, and avoiding boredom. We might seem to be so many ants, living and dying one after another in an eternal, changeless anthill. But it is not so. Over and beyond the eating and the sleeping, the mere living and dying one after another, the spirit adds, invents, creates what is better than what was before. Other words spoken by Camus came to me and I imagined myself saying them to the stranger. It was plain that he had thought us a pretty poor lot. But I wished that I had spoken as Camus spoke; then I would have caused him, I thought, to pay "homage to the miserable, magnificent life we live."

How badly I had replied, or how I had not replied at all, to his remarks about the young people of America! He had been led to form a judgment that they are complacent seekers of a mean society. I thought of the replies I should have made. I should have doubted that this is the full truth about them. There are so many of them, and among the many are some, I might have said, who will take the risks of being truly themselves, who will speak and act for the common good though it be to their own injury. There have always been such, and there will be such again. I should also have said that the people of a generation change, become something different from what they were, as they grow older and as the terrible demands of the human predicament press upon them. The young people of today will be a different kind of people. Now we are all in a condition of shock from abrupt realization of the human predicament. But these young people of today will later have borne with the shock, and will have found the strength to deal with the predicament.

And then I should have recognized my own limited, parochial mind in responding, with silent resentment, to his succinct report on American youth. American young people so described are not all of us. We people are composed of many kinds, and each kind has its virtues and its weaknesses. If Americans are complacent and shelter themselves with an unconsidered optimisim, others of us are basely cynical, and still others of us are more resolute in confronting tragedy. If, in my own country, there is an aversion from or denial of suffering, some others of us have seen the necessary part of suffering in the maturing of the human spirit. Dostoevsky wrote it, and it is heard in the great music of Beethoven. We are many, of many kinds, and though today each kind tends to think of itself and for itself, one may venture to recognize a growing tendency, as yet small, for the different strains of the common humanity to affect one another, and perhaps one day to develop a mankind whose best men and women speak not for just one kind of us, here in America, or somewhere else, but for all of us.

And then I had responded badly to the stranger's easy lumping of all mankind into one kind of thing. I had resented his calling me "you Russians." I should not have resented it; I should have thought about how I can and do speak also for Russians, and yet cannot and do not always speak for them. I am one with them because they and I are human, because we live and love and work and laugh and feel tender or unhappy as do all men. They and I share this earth and whatever annexes to it come about in outer space; and we share the responsibility of making it a decent place to live for us all. Further, Americans are like Russians in particular respects in which others—say the people of India or the South Sea Islanders—are not like Russians or Americans. We both like to make big things; both look for material results and probably make too much of technology; both have a class of managers to run most of their affairs. In these respects we join in a common effort to give the growth of mankind a bias, a bent toward one side that may not, in the very long judgment of human kind, prove to be a wise deflection.

On the other hand, we who are Americans are different from the Russians in ways that place upon us special responsibilities, that give us, in these respects, the larger share of power and duty to extricate us all from the predicament. We mean this difference when we say that we are free, and they are not. We are a people all of whom have some power and responsibility to think and speak and act as to what ought to be changed, as to what measures to take, as to what new lines of effort to pursue to avoid the mutual suicide and to work upon the good life. The Russians today, the common, ordinary, on-the-street Russians, cannot stand up and say, "This we do is wrong. The right lies there." But we, in America, can. In this we *are* different; here I can speak only for a Russian who is silenced and perhaps waiting; but we in America have made a society in which differences and dissensions are the very stuff of public life. Every one of us can, if he will, speak, strive, persuade, decry, and insist. So, though we on this earth are, in the stranger's words, "we people," we are a diversity within our unity, and to each kind falls the responsibility to make strong, to put to work for all on earth the virtue and the power special to his own kind.

I thought I might have said these things and then I thought of the immediate peril to us all, the threat, the still-increasing threat, of an ultimate destruction. In answering his questions about the peril, I had told the truth; I could not, in the second thoughts, imagine myself denying that peril. I had to admit that the growth of the human spirit might, by destruction, come to an end. It could end in nuclear violence; it could end in abasement to a nihilism of values, a tyranny of doctrine, police power, or material things. What a fragile thing is human spirit! So threatened are we that a stranger might well conclude his investigations of us with a judgment that we are neither able to save ourselves nor worth saving.

And again I found my mind imagining that he had not spoken with me but with some stronger and wiser one of us. I thought once more of the words of Camus: "We suffocate and we survive; we think we will die of grief and life triumphs . . . Anyway, we have no choice . . . wherever we are and to the best of our abilities we must do what has to be done so that everyone can live together once again." "The very fact that atomic warfare would make the future meaningless gives us back our freedom of action." These things he said. And he said, "We have nothing to lose—except everything. So let's go forward. . . . If we fail, it will be better to have taken our stand at the side of those who want to live rather than with those who destroy."

What words! As I remembered them, I wanted to recall the stranger so that he could hear them. Those words were spoken from the maturing human spirit. It will speak, like that, from this one or that, no matter how great the peril. We are indeed an odd people, but odd in ways that I fear the stranger did not fully understand. We are a thrust upward amid dangers and darknesses of our own making. We have no promise from the universe that we shall survive. We live for the growing of the human spirit, and in spite of all, we strive toward that growth, up to the last moment of possiblity.

Basic Factors in Social Life

I

MAN AND SOCIETY

WHAT DISTINGUISHES MAN from animal? Although accepting the theory of evolution, Susanne K. Langer finds a deep gulf between the two forms of life. An entirely new process in the human brain has made possible the use of symbols, especially words, for things and ideas. Man is defined as a symbol-making and symbol-using animal. Entering into communication with each other through words, human beings have created their own peculiar environment consisting of symbols, tools, rules, patterns of life and thought. Man remains a creature of biological needs, but he is not strictly confined to the narrow limits of animal existence. Through the social world he has created, man can strive for self-realization and individuation: "We are not the masses (of the beehive): we are the Public."

In every society there must be basic agreement on the norms of social behavior and on essential social values. Only a limited amount of deviation can be permitted. What then is the relationship between man and society? In their treatment of the primary concepts in terms of which society can be understood, MacIver and Page make a number of distinctions between society as a web of relationships, community as the matrix or ground of social life, and associations as specific organizations which grow within the matrix. They emphasize the essential harmony between society and man, believing, along with Langer, that the social world is so organized as to afford individuals the conditions under which they can develop individuality and freedom.

2

Society: Primary Concepts

by Robert M. MacIver and Charles H. Page

Society

WHAT WE MEAN BY SOCIETY. Our first, the most general of our terms, is *society* itself. Social beings, men, express their nature by creating and re-creating an organization which guides and controls their behavior in myriad ways. This organization, society, liberates and limits the activities of men, sets up standards for them to follow and maintain: whatever the imperfections and tyrannies it has exhibited in human history, it is a necessary condition of every fulfillment of life. Society is a system of usages and procedures, of authority and mutual aid, of many groupings and divisions, of controls of human behavior and of liberties. This ever-changing, complex system we call society. It is the web of social relationships. And it is always changing.

THE PSYCHICAL CONDITION OF SOCIAL RELATIONSHIPS. Society, we have said, is the changing pattern of social relationships. What do we mean by social relationship? We may approach the answer by contrasting the social with the physical. There is a relationship between a typewriter and a desk, between the earth and the sun, between fire and smoke, between two chemical constitutents. Each of these is affected by the existence of the other, but the relationship is not a social one. The psychical condition is lacking. The typewriter and the desk are in no intelligible sense *aware* of the presence of one another. Their relationship is not in any way determined by mutual awareness. Without this recognition there is no social relationship, no society. Society exists only where social beings "behave" toward one another in ways determined by their recognition of one another. Any relations so determined we may broadly name "social."

From *Society: An Introductory Analysis,* by MacIver and Page, copyright 1949 by Robert M. MacIver and Charles H. Page. Reprinted by permission of Holt, Rinehart and Winston, Inc.

Robert M. MacIver is Emeritus Professor of Political Science at Columbia University.

Charles H. Page is Professor of Sociology at Princeton University.

THE RANGE OF SOCIAL RELATIONSHIPS. Social relationships are as varied as society is complex. The relations of voter to candidate, mother to child, employee to employer, friend to friend, are but a few of the varying types. The generality of the concept of "social" is borne out when we note the almost countless terms our language employs to name the many kinds of social relationships between men. Some of them we label "economic," some "political," some "personal," some "impersonal," some "friendly," some "antagonistic," and so on. But they are all *social* relationships when they are grounded in mutual recognition.

Among such relationships there are some which express mere conflict or unmitigated hostility, such as those between two armies in time of war. Armies in the field are certainly aware of nothing so much, and their activities are animated by nothing so much, as the presence of one another. Such relationships are "social." However, the great majority of social relationships involve a principle which the example of the armies expressly denies. This is the sense of community or belonging together. As sociologists, we study both the conditions that unite and those that separate human beings. But if there were no sense of community, if there were no co-operative undertakings by man, there would be no social systems, no society or societies—there would be practically nothing for sociologists to study. Hence the relationships which are central to sociology are those which involve both mutual recognition and the sense of something held or shared in common.

SOCIETY NOT CONFINED TO MAN. From our definition it should be clear that society is not limited to human beings. There are animal societies of many degrees. The remarkable social organizations of the insects, such as the ant, the bee, the hornet, are known to most school children. It has been contended that wherever there is life there is society, because life means heredity and, so far as we know, can arise only out of and in the presence of other life. But in the lowest stages of life, social awareness, if it exists, is extremely dim and the social contact often extremely fleeting. Among all higher animals at least there is a very definite society, arising out of the requirements of their nature and the conditions involved in the perpetuation of their species.

As above defined, there may be society also between animals of different species, as between a man and a horse or dog or, say, between sheep and their shepherd dog. Our concern is with society among the human species.

SOCIETY INVOLVES BOTH LIKENESS AND DIFFERENCE. It is often said that the family, in some form, was the first society. It is certainly true that the sex relationship is a primary and essential type of social relationship. It is clear that this relationship involves *both* likeness and difference in the beings whom it relates. So with society in its various manifestations. . . .

Without likeness and the sense of likeness there could be no mutual recognition of "belonging together" and therefore no society. Society exists among those who resemble one another in some degree, in body and in mind, and who are near enough or intelligent enough to appreciate the fact. Society, as F. H. Giddings expressed it, rests on "consciousness of kind." In early society and among some of our "primitive contemporaries," the sense of likeness is focused on kin-membership, that is, real or supposed blood relationships. The conditions of social likeness have broadened out in modern societies. But the basic conception of likeness that primitive man identified with the kin remains in even so extensive a principle of union as nationality. And if the struggling principle of "one world" is to win out it must necessarily rest upon the recognition of the fundamental *likeness* of the entire human race.

Society, however, depends on difference as well as on likeness. If people were all exactly alike, merely alike, their social relationships would be as limited, perhaps, as those of the ant or bee. There would be little give-and-take, little reciprocity. They would contribute very little to one another. What we have noted above to be true of the sex relationship is present, in various forms, in all social systems. For they all involve relationships in which differences complement one another, in which exchange takes place. In society each member seeks something and gives something. . . .

MAN AS A SOCIAL ANIMAL.   We have still to mention the fundamental attribute, fundamental beyond even the sense of likeness, on which society depends. It was expressed by Aristotle when he said that man was a social animal.[1] It is evidenced in man's reflection on society ever since the beginnings of recorded thought, the reflection that it was not good for man to be alone. Man is dependent on society for protection, comfort, nurture, education, equipment, opportunity, and the multitude of definite services which society provides. He is dependent on society for the content of his thoughts, his dreams, his aspirations, even many of his maladies of mind and body. His birth in society brings with it the absolute need of society itself.

No wonder, then, that solitary confinement is one of the most fearful of all punishments, for it prevents the satisfaction of this fundamental need. Whatever the claims of "independence" we may hear from some persons, no man is free of the need of society. When the hermit leaves the society of men he imagines he can find another society in communion with God or with "Nature," or he is driven by some obsession to a kind of self-punishment. If he is not mad at the outset he becomes so in the end. For normal humanity must have social relationships to make life livable.

---

[1] Aristotle significantly adds that the person who is incapable of sharing a common life is either below or above humanity, "either a beast or a god."

Community

DEFINITION OF COMMUNITY. The second of our primary concepts is that of *community*. Let us begin with examples. It is the term we apply to a pioneer settlement, a village, a city, a tribe, or a nation. Wherever the members of any group, small or large, live together in such a way that they share, not this or that particular interest, but the basic conditions of a common life, we call that group a community. The mark of a community is that one's life *may* be lived wholly within it. One cannot live wholly within a business organization or a church; one can live wholly within a tribe or a city. The basic criterion of community, then, is that all of one's social relationships may be found within it.

COMMUNITIES NEED NOT BE SELF-SUFFICIENT. Some communities are all-inclusive and independent of others. Among primitive peoples we sometimes find communities of no more than a hundred persons, as, for example, among the Yurok tribes of California, which are almost or altogether isolated. But modern communities, even very large ones, are much less self-contained. Economic and, increasingly so, political interdependence is a major characteristic of our great modern communities.

We may live in a metropolis and yet be members of a very small community because our interests are circumscribed within a narrow area. Or we may live in a village and yet belong to a community as wide as the whole area of our civilization or even wider. No civilized community has walls around it to cut it completely off from a larger one, whatever "iron curtains" may be drawn by the rulers of this nation or that. Communities exist within greater communities: the town within a region, the region within a nation, and the nation within the world community which, perhaps, is in the process of development.

THE BASES OF COMMUNITY. A community then is an area of social living marked by some degree of *social coherence*. The bases of community are *locality* and *community sentiment*.

[1] *Locality.* A community always occupies a territorial area. Even a nomad community, a band of gypsies, for example, has a local, though changing, habitation. At every moment its members occupy together a definite place on the earth's surface. Most communities are settled and derive from the conditions of their locality a strong bond of solidarity. To some extent this local bond has been weakened in the modern world by the extending facilities of communication; this is especially apparent in the penetration into rural areas of dominant urban patterns. But the extension of communication is itself the condition of a larger but still territorial community.

The importance of the conception of community is in large measure that it underscores the relation between social coherence and the geographical area. This relation is easily revealed in such examples as an Eskimo village or a frontier town or the semi-isolated communities of French Quebec. Whatever modifications in the relation of social bonds and territorial abode have been introduced by civilization, yet the basic character of locality as a social classifier has never been transcended.

[2] _Community Sentiment._ Today we find, what never existed in primitive societies, people occupying specific local areas which lack the social coherence necessary to give them a community character. For example, the residents of a ward or district of a large city may lack sufficient contacts or common interests to instill conscious identification with the area. Such a "neighborhood" is not a community because it does not possess a feeling of belonging together—it lacks community sentiment. Later we shall analyze the various elements of community sentiment. Here it is sufficient to stress that locality, though a necessary condition, is not enough to create a community. A community, to repeat, is an area of common living. There must be the common living with its _awareness_ of sharing a way of life as well as the common earth. . . .

THE SPREAD OF CIVILIZATION AND THE WORLD COMMUNITY. The wholly self-contained community belongs to the primitive world. In the modern world the nearest approach to it is found in the huge nation-community included within the frontiers of a single state. This has been especially the case when the state has sought to "co-ordinate" the whole national life as did National Socialist Germany, or when, as in Soviet Russia, it establishes a form of economy very different from that of most other nations. But Nazi Germany was never self-sufficient, nor is the U.S.S.R., as American exporters of heavy machinery will testify. Modern civilization, we know, unleashes forces which break down the self-containedness of communities great or small.

These forces are partly _technological,_ such as the improvement of the means of communication and transportation; partly _economic,_ such as the demand for markets and for wider areas of economic exchange necessitated by the newer processes of industrial production; and partly _cultural,_ since the thought and art and science of one country are, whatever the temporary barriers of "ideological" and political construction, inevitably carried on the wings of civilization to others. In the face of these forces, there are no national "secrets," atomic or otherwise, of permanent duration.

Certainly Wendell Willkie's _One World_ has been in the making for centuries. We have been approaching a stage where no completely self-contained community can be found on any scale unless we extend the limits of community to include the whole earth. Men's current efforts to develop political agencies of world scope are consistent with the trend of the spread of civilization. In our view, the counterefforts of some men ignore the realities of expanding community itself.

THE GREAT AND SMALL COMMUNITIES.   We have noted the historical expansion of community to the dimensions of the nation and, perhaps, the world. The smaller communities, however, still remain, though only in degree. The nation or the world-state does not eliminate the village or neighborhood, though they may be changed in character. As civilized beings, we need the smaller as well as the larger circles of community. The great community brings us opportunity, stability, economy, the constant stimulus of a richer, more varied culture. But living in the smaller community we find the nearer, more intimate satisfactions. The larger community provides peace and protection, patriotism and sometimes war, automobiles and the radio. The smaller provides friends and friendship, gossip and face-to-face rivalry, local pride and abode. Both are essential to the full life process. . . . The significance of the term "community" is more clearly brought out when we contrast it with our next major concept, association.

Associations

ASSOCIATIONS AS MEANS OF PURSUING ENDS.   There are three ways in which men seek the fulfillment of their ends. First, they may act independently, each following his own way without thought of his fellows or their actions. However seemingly desirable, this unsocial way has narrow limitations wherever men live together. Second, they may seek them through conflict with one another, each striving to wrest from the others the objects that he prizes. But this method, if not channeled strictly by regulation, is precarious and wasteful and is opposed to the very existence of society. True, as we shall see later, conflict is an ever-present part of social life, but for the most part it is, like economic competition, socially limited and regulated. Finally, men may pursue their ends in company, on some co-operative basis, so that each is in some degree and manner contributing to the ends of his fellows.

This last method, co-operative pursuit, may be spontaneous, such as the offering of a helping hand to a stranger. It may be casual. It may be determined by the customs of a community, as in the case of farmers assisting their neighbors at harvest time. On the other hand, a group may organize itself expressly for the purpose of pursuing certain of its interests together. When this happens, an *association* is born.

We define an association, then, as a group organized for the pursuit of an *interest or group of interests* in common.

ASSOCIATION AND COMMUNITY.   It follows from our definition that an association is not a community, but an organization within a community. A community is more than any specific organizations that rise within it. Contrast, for example, the business or the church or the club with the village or city or nation. With respect to the business or church or club, we can ask such questions as why they exist and what they stand for. And we can answer in terms of the particular *interests* around which they are organized. But if we ask *why* communities exist, we can expect no such definite answer. (We can ask why a community, say a city, exists *where it is situated,* but this is a different question.)

Another contrast between the community and the association is revealed by considering the interest aspect of associations. Because the association is organized for particular purposes, for the pursuit of specific interests, we belong to it only by virtue of these interests. We belong to an athletic club for purposes of physical recreation or sport, to a business for livelihood or profits, to a social club for fellowship. Membership in an association has a limited significance. It is true that an association may engage our whole devotion. Or the interests of an association may be wider than or different from those officially professed. But we belong to associations only by virtue of some *specific* interests that we possess. Consequently, there can be a multitude of associations within the same community. And the individual, of course, may belong to many. The late President Butler of Columbia University reported membership in twenty clubs in addition to dozens of other associations.[2]

Associations may become communities, at least temporarily. There are the examples of seventeenth-century trading company outposts which became communities in every respect, or of military units compelled to create their own communities when isolated for a period of time. And there are borderline cases between community and association, such as the monasteries, convents, and prisons discussed in the previous section. The two major social organizations which may seem to lie on the borderline between associations and communities are the family and the state. We shall consider these two at length later, but each demands brief comment in this introductory treatment of primary concepts.

THE FAMILY AS AN ASSOCIATION.   In some of its forms, especially in some primitive and extremely rural societies, the family has many of the attributes of a community. In these cases, people toil, play, and even worship almost wholly within the orbit of the family. It circumscribes largely or even wholly the lives of its members.

However, in modern society, as in all complex civilizations, the family becomes definitely an association, so far as its adult members are concerned. For the original contracting parties it is an association specifically established with certain ends in view. These interests are vastly important but nevertheless limited. The functions of the family are more and more limited and defined as the social division of labor increases.

But even in the most complex society, the family, for the new lives that arise within it, is more than an association. To the child the family is a

[2] W. F. Ogburn and M. F. Nimkoff, *Sociology* (Boston, 1940), pp. 258–260.

preliminary community which prepares him for the greater community. .
By imperceptible degrees it is transformed for him also, as he grows up,
into an association of, often intense, but *limited* interest. Eventually he
will normally leave it to establish a new family.

THE STATE AS AN ASSOCIATION.   The state is frequently confused with
the community. In reality the state is *one* form of social organization, not
the whole community in all its aspects. We distinguish, for example, the
state from the church, the political from the religious organization. The confusion of community and state is increased by the usage of the same term
to indicate either. Thus "United States" refers either to our national state
association with its governmental apparatus or to the national community
which it governs.

It is highly important, for the understanding of social structure and particularly of the evolution of that structure, that we should realize the
associational character of the state. The state is an agency of peculiarly
wide range, but nevertheless an agency. The state may assume at times
absolutist or "totalitarian" form, claiming to control every aspect of human life. Even if this claim were *fully* realized—which never could be the
case—the state would not become the community, but an association controlling the community.

Human beings are, without choice to be sure, citizens or subjects of the
state. But they are also members of families and churches and clubs, they
are friends or lovers, scientists or laborers or artists associating with their
kind. However significant the citizen role may be, it is only *one* of many
roles that each man exercises as a social being.

The state, we must recognize, is different in important respects from all
other associations . . . [but] the state as a form of social organization is,
like the church or business or club, an association.

3

Man and Animal: The City
and the Hive

by Susanne K. Langer

Within the past five or six decades, the human scene has probably changed more radically than ever before in history. The outward changes in our setting are already an old story: the disappearance of horse-drawn vehicles, riders, children walking to school, and the advent of the long, low, powerful Thing in their stead; the transformation of the mile-wide farm into a tic-tac-toe of lots, each sprouting a split-level dream home. These are the obvious changes, more apparent in the country than in the city. The great cities have grown greater, brighter, more mechanized, but their basic patterns seem less shaken by the new power and speed in which the long industrial revolution culminates.

The deepest change, however, is really a change in our picture of mankind; and that is most spectacular where mankind is teeming and concentrated—in the city. Our old picture of human life was a picture of local groups, each speaking its mother-tongue, observing some established religion, following its own customs. It might be a civilized community or a savage tribe, but it had its distinct traditions. And in it were subdivisions, usually families, with their more special local ties and human relations.

Today, natural tribes and isolated communities have all but disappeared. The ease and speed of travel, the swift economic changes that send people in search of new kinds of work, the two wars that swept over all boundaries, have wiped out most of our traditions. The old family structure is tottering. Society tends to break up into new and smaller units—in fact, into its ultimate units, the human individuals that compose it.

This atomization of society is most obvious in a great cosmopolitan city. The city seems to be composed of millions of unrelated individuals, each scrambling for himself, yet each caught in the stream of all the

Reprinted from *The Antioch Review*, Fall, 1958 (Vol. 18, No. 3). Antioch Press, Yellow Springs, Ohio. By permission of the publishers and the author.

Susanne K. Langer is a philosopher who has taught at Radcliffe College and Connecticut College. She has a special interest in the philosophy of art and has written a pioneer textbook on symbolic logic.

others. Ever since this shakeup in society began, a new picture of society has been in the making—the picture of *human masses,* brought together by some outside force, some imposed function, into a super-personal unit; masses of people, each representing an atom of "manpower" in a new sort of organism, the industrial State.

The idea of the State as a higher organism—the State as a super-individual—is old. But the old picture was not one of the masses driven by some imposed economic power, or any other outside power. The super-individual was a rational being, directed by a mind within it. The guardians of the State, the rulers, were its mind. Plato described the State as "the man writ large." Hobbes, two thousand years later, called it "Leviathan," the great Creature. A city-state like ancient Athens or Sparta might be "a man writ large," but England was too big for that. It was the big fish in the pond. The mind of Hobbes's fish was perhaps subhuman, but it was still single and sovereign in the organism.

Another couple of centuries later, Rudyard Kipling, faced with a democratic, industrialized civilization, called his allegory of England "The Mother Hive." Here, a common will, dictated by complicated instincts, replaced even Leviathan's mind; each individual was kept in line by the blind forces of the collective life.

The image of the hive has had a great success as an ideal of collaborative social action. Every modern Utopia (except the completely wishful Shangri-La) reflects the beehive ideal. Even a statesman of highest caliber, Jan Smuts, has praised it as a pattern for industrial society. Plato's personified State and Hobbes's sea monster impress us as fantasies, but the hive looks like more than a poetic figure; it seems really to buzz around us.

I think the concept of the State as a collective organism, composed of multitudes of little workers, guided by social forces that none of the little workers can fathom, and accomplishing some greater destiny, is supported by another factor than our mechanized industry; that other factor is a momentous event in our intellectual history: the spread of the theory of evolution.

First biologists, then psychologists, and finally sociologists and moralists have become newly aware that man belongs to the animal kingdom. The impact of the concept of evolution on scientific discovery has been immense. Gradually the notion of the human animal became common currency, questioned only by some religious minds. This in turn has made it natural for social theorists with scientific leanings to model their concepts of human society on animal societies, the ant hill and the beehive. . . .

Despite man's zoölogical status, which I wholeheartedly accept, there is a deep gulf between the highest animal and the most primitive normal human being: a difference in mentality that is fundamental. It stems from the development of one new process in the human brain—a process that seems to be entirely peculiar to that brain: the use of *symbols for ideas*. By "symbols" I mean all kinds of signs that can be used and understood whether the things they refer to are there or not. The word "symbol" has, unfortunately, many different meanings for different people. Some people reserve it for mystic signs, like Rosicrucian symbols; some mean by it *significant images,* such as Keats' "Huge cloudy symbols of a high romance"; some use it quite the opposite way and speak of "mere symbols," meaning empty gestures, signs that have lost their meanings; and some, notably logicians, use the term for mathematical signs, marks that constitute a code, a brief, concise language. In their sense, ordinary words are symbols, too. Ordinary language is a symbolism.

When I say that the distinctive function of the human brain is the use of symbols, I mean any and all of these kinds. They are all different from signs that animals use. Animals interpret signs, too, but only as pointers to actual things and events: cues to action or expectation, threats and promises, landmarks and earmarks in the world. Human beings use such signs, too; but above all they use symbols—especially words—to think and talk about things that are neither present nor expected. The words convey *ideas,* that may or may not have counterparts in actuality. This power of thinking *about* things expresses itself in language, imagination, and speculation—the chief products of human mentality that animals do not share.

Language, the most versatile and indispensable of all symbolisms, has put its stamp on all our mental functions, so that I think they always differ from even their closest analogues in animal life. Language has invaded our feeling and dreaming and action, as well as our reasoning, which is really a product of it. The greatest change wrought by language is the increased scope of awareness in speech-gifted beings. An animal's awareness is always of things in its own place and life. In human awareness, the present, actual situation is often the least part. We have not only memories and expectations; we have a *past* in which we locate our memories, and a *future* that vastly over-reaches our own anticipations. Our past is a story, our future a piece of imagination. Likewise our ambient is a place in a wider, symbolically conceived place, the universe. We live in *a world*.

This difference of mentality between man and animal seems to me to make a cleft between them almost as great as the division between animals and plants. There is continuity between the orders, but the division is real nevertheless. Human life differs radically from animal life. By virtue of our incomparably wider awareness, our power of envisagement of things and events beyond any actual perception, we have acquired needs and aims that animals do not have; and even the most savage human society, having to meet those needs and implement those aims, is not really comparable to any animal society. The two may have some analogous functions, but the essential structure must be different, because man and beast live differently in every way.

Probably the profoundest difference between human and animal needs is made by one piece of human awareness, one fact that is not present to animals, because it is never learned in any direct experience: that is our foreknowledge of Death. The fact that we ourselves must die is not a simple and isolated fact. It is built on a wide survey of facts, that discloses the structure of history as a succession of overlapping brief lives, the patterns of youth and age, growth and decline; and above all that, it is built on the logical insight that *one's own life is a case in point*. Only a creature that can think symbolically *about* life can conceive of its own death. Our knowledge of death is part of our knowledge of life.

What, then, do we—all of us—know about life?

Every life that we know is generated from other life. Each living thing springs from some other living thing or things. Its birth is a process of new individuation, in a life-stream whose beginning we do know.

Individuation is a word we do not often meet. We hear about individuality, sometimes spoken in praise, sometimes as an excuse for being slightly crazy. We hear and read about "the Individual," a being that is forever adjusting, like a problem child, to something called "Society." But how does individuality arise? What makes an individual? A fundamental, biological process of *individuation,* that marks the life of every stock, plant or animal. Life is a series of individuations, and these can be of various sorts, and reach various degrees. . . .

Our power of symbolic conception has given us each a glimpse of himself as one final individuation from the great human stock. We do not know when or what the end will be, but we know that there will be one. We also envisage a past and future, a stretch of time so vastly longer than any creature's memory, and a world so much richer than any world of sense, that it makes our time in that world seem infinitesimal. This is the price of the great gift of symbolism.

In the face of such uncomfortable prospects (probably conceived long before the dawn of any religious ideas), human beings have evolved aims different from any other creatures. Since we cannot have our fill of existence by going on and on, we want to have *as much life as possible* in our short span. If our individuation must be brief, we want to make it complete; so we are inspired to think, act, dream our desires, create things, express our ideas, and in all sorts of ways make up by concentration what we cannot have by length of days. We seek the greatest possible individuation, or development of personality. In doing this, we have set up a new demand, not for mere continuity of existence, but for *self-realization*. That is a uniquely human aim. . . .

The greatest possible individuation is usually taken to mean, "as much as is possible without curtailing the rights of others." But that is not the real measure of how much is possible. The measure is provided in the individual himself, and is as fundamental as his knowledge of death. It is the other part of his insight into nature—his knowledge of life, of the great unbroken stream, the life of the stock from which his individuation stems.

One individual life, however rich, still looks infinitesimal: no matter how much self-realization is concentrated in it, it is a tiny atom—and we don't like to be tiny atoms, not even hydrogen atoms. We need more than fullness of personal life to counter our terrible knowledge of all it implies. And we have more; we have our history, our commitments made for us before we were born, our relatedness to the rest of mankind. The counterpart of individuation from the great life of the stock is our rootedness in that life, our involvement with the whole human race, past and present.

Each person is not only a free, single end, like the green palm leaf that unfolds, grows in a curve of beauty, and dies in its season; he is like the whole palm leaf, the part inside the trunk, too. He is the culmination of his entire ancestry, and *represents* that whole human past. In his brief individuation he is an *expression* of all humanity. That is what makes each person's life sacred and all-important. A single ruined life is the bankruptcy of a long line. This is what I mean by the individual's involvement with all mankind.

All animals are unconsciously involved with their kind. Heredity governs not only their growth, color and form, but their actions, too. They carry their past about with them in everything they do. But they do not know it. They don't need to, because they never could lose it. Their involvement with the greater life of the race is implicit in their limited selfhood.

Our knowledge that life is finite and, in fact, precarious and brief, drives us on to greater individuation than animals attain. Our mental talents have largely freed us from that built-in behavior called instinct. The scope of our imagination gives each of us a separate world, and a separate consciousness, and threatens to break the instinctual ties of brotherhood that make all the herrings swim into one net, and all the geese turn their heads at the same moment. Yet we cannot afford to lose the feeling of involvement with our kind; for if we do, personal life shrinks up to nothingness.

The sense of involvement is our social sense. We have it by nature, originally just as animals do, and just as unconsciously. It is the direct feeling of needing our own kind, caring what happens. Social sense is an instinctive sense of being somehow one with all other people—a feeling that reflects the rootedness of our existence in a human past. Human society rests on this feeling. It is often said to rest on the need of collaboration, or on domination of the weak by the strong, or some other circumstance, but I think such theories deal with its modes, and ignore its deeper structure; at the bottom of it is the feeling of involvement, or social sense. If we lose that, no coercion will hold us to our duties, because they do not feel like commitments; and no achievements will matter, because they are doomed to be snuffed out with the individual, without being laid to account in the continuity of life.

Great individual development, such as human beings are driven by their intellectual insights to seek, does of course always threaten to break the bonds of direct social involvement, that give animal life its happy unconscious continuity. When the strain gets hard, we have social turmoil, anarchy, irresponsibility, and in private lives the sense of loneliness and infinite smallness that lands some people in nihilism and cynicism, and leads others to existentialism or less intellectual cults.

It is then that social philosophers look upon animal societies as models for human society. There is no revolt, no strike, no competition, no anti-anything party, in a beehive. As Kipling, fifty years or more ago, represented his British Utopia that he called the Mother Hive, that ideal State had a completely cooperative economy, an army that went into action without a murmur, each man with the same impulse, the moment an enemy threatened to intrude, and a populace of such tribal solidarity that it would promptly run out any stranger that tried to become established in the State and disrupt its traditions. Any native individual that could not fit into the whole had to be liquidated; the loss was regrettable, but couldn't be helped, and would be made up.

Yet the beehive really has no possible bearing on human affairs; for it owes its harmonious existence to the fact that its members are *incompletely individuated,* even as animals go. None of them perform all of a creature's essential functions: feeding, food-getting, nest-building, mating, and procreating. . . . So there is not only division of labor, but division of organs, functional and physical incompleteness. This direct involvement of each bee with the whole lets the hive function with an organic rhythm that makes its members appear wonderfully socialized. But they are really not socialized at all, any more than the cells in our tissues are socialized; they are associated, by being un-individuated.

That is as far away from a human ideal as one can get. We need, above all, a world in which we can realize our capacities, develop and act as personalities. That means giving up our instinctive patterns of habit and prejudice, our herd-instincts. Yet we need the emotional security of the greater, continuous life—the awareness of our involvement with all mankind. How can we eat that cake, and have it, too?

The same mental talent that makes us need so much individuation, comes to the rescue of our social involvement: I mean the peculiarly human talent of holding ideas in the mind by means of symbols. Human life, even in the simplest forms we know, is shot through and through with *social symbols. . . .*

Most people have some religious ritual that supports their knowledge of a greater life; but even in purely secular affairs we constantly express our faith in the continuity of human existence. Animals provide lairs or nests for their immediate offspring. Man builds for the future—often for nothing else; his earliest great buildings were not mansions, but monuments. And not only physical edifices, but above all, laws and institutions are intended for the future, and often justified by showing that they have a precedent, or are in accord with the past. They are conveniences of their day, but symbols of more than their day. They are symbols of Society, and of each individual's inalienable membership in Society.

What, then, is the measure of our possible individuation, without loss of social sense? It is the power of social symbolism. We can give up our actual, instinctual involvements with our kind just to the extent that we can replace them by symbolic ones. This is the prime function of social symbols, from a handshake, to the assembly of robed judges in a Supreme Court. In protocol and ritual, in the investment of authority, in sanctions and honors, lies our security against loss of involvement with mankind; in such bonds lies our freedom to be individuals.

It has been said that an animal society, like a beehive, is really an organism, and the separate bees its organic parts. I think this statement requires many reservations, but it contains some truth. The hive is an organic structure, a super-individual, something like an organism. A human city, however, is an *organization*. It is above all a symbolic structure, a mental reality. Its citizens are the whole and only individuals. They are not a "living mass," like a swarm of semi-individuated bees. The model of the hive has brought with it the concept of human masses, to be cared for in times of peace, deployed in times of war, educated for use or sacrificed for the higher good of their state. In the specious analogy of animal and human society, the hive and the city, lies, I think, the basic philosophical fallacy of all totalitarian theory, even the most sincere and idealistic— even the thoroughly noble political thought of Plato.

We are like leaves of the palm tree, each deeply embedded in the tree, a part of the trunk, each opening to the light in a final, separate life. Our world is a human world, organized to implement our highest individuation. There may be ten thousand of us working in one factory. There are several millions of us living in a city like New York. But we are not the Masses: we are the Public.

2

SOCIAL SCIENCE AND ITS METHODS

HISTORY IS OFTEN CLASSIFIED as a social science, though some regard as dubious its claims to such a designation. Professor Eisenstadt analyzes the relationship of history to social science, and discusses differences in their methods. He concludes that "history is *with* the social sciences but not really *of* them."

What ought social scientists to do, and what is their function in society? C. Wright Mills expresses strong dissatisfaction with what most present-day social scientists are doing. He accuses them of being preoccupied with trivial factual studies in the form of "abstract empiricism" or with vague generalities in the form of "grand theory."

There is too little concern with making man aware of mankind through cultivation of the sociological imagination. To Mills this means the ability to relate parts to wholes, to see individual lives and problems in terms of history and institutional changes—it means viewing the "present as history." Knowledge of the sort provided by the use of the sociological imagination promises to make it possible for people to guide their social destinies.

(In selection number 10, in Chapter 5, Clyde Kluckhohn throws light on the methods used by anthropologists in their study of human societies.)

4

American History and Social Science

by A. S. Eisenstadt

What uses are our historians making of the newer perspectives afforded by the social sciences? The question is more than academic. It touches upon the uses of knowledge in an age of crisis. The constraint of human events turns the kaleidoscope of knowledge to the sight of a particular configuration. A particular type of serviceability dictates to knowledge, defining both what it will be and how it will serve. With respect to what men study and seek to master, an age of crisis is almost necessarily an age of science. Social science models itself upon the forms of science, trying thereby to perform the services of science. It would seem reasonable to expect that historians, who are entrusted with the remembrance of things past, would suit their remembrance to the patterns and formulas of social science. The interesting thing is that, for the larger part, they do not. There are many reasons why they do not, and the reasons reveal not merely the differences between history and social science but also the nature and uses of knowledge in an age such as ours.

That social science has been undergoing a change during the past few decades, and particularly since World War II, there can be little doubt. The change may be analyzed into three separate components: first, the substance with which social science is concerned; second, the method it uses to comprehend that substance; and third, the larger social theory which serves as a frame for housing both the newer substance and the newer method of social science.

As to its subject matter and substance: social science is becoming more concerned with understanding the regularities in human experience rather than what is unique. It is increasingly concerned with process rather than simply with institutions. It is trying to understand the complexities of the whole social process and to see the various activities of human life in constant interplay with each other. Social science is trying to comprehend the many ways in which an advanced industrial society, caught up in the toils

Reprinted from *Centennial Review*, Vol. VII, No. 3, 1963, pp. 255–272. Portions reprinted are from pp. 255–266 and p. 272. By permission of *Centennial Review of Arts & Sciences* and the author.

A. S. Eisenstadt is Professor of History at Brooklyn College of the City University of New York.

of crisis, articulates its problems and seeks to fulfill its purposes. The social scientist is concerned with dissecting and anatomizing the social process. He is concerned with the structure of society, with various social roles—particularly those of the leader and of the entrepreneur, with the composition and function of groups, with social mobility and stratification, with status and caste, with the emergence of new classes, with the urbanization of life and the rise of the megalopolis, with ethnic and racial minorities, with the growth and forms of mass culture, with the changing sociology of knowledge, with the psychology of leaders and of the led, with economic organization and activity, with the influence of industrialization upon the whole social process, with new cultures in formation and with the reciprocal impact of new cultures and old ones. The social scientist is concerned with the impact of each form and function of human experience upon another and upon a complex of forms and functions, and the permutations and combinations of problems which he contemplates are without number.

No less important than the wide view which social science takes of modern society is the method by which it seeks to insure that the view is accurate and objective. "Indeed," says Robert Bierstedt, Chairman of the Department of Sociology of the City College of New York; ". . . the methods and techniques of empirical research . . . have received perhaps an extra share of attention in recent decades." The newer social science postulates hypotheses about a phase of human activity. It defines rigorous criteria for testing these hypotheses. It uses a variety of devices to insure that its tests are impersonal and valid. These devices include sample surveys, panel studies, projective techniques, interviews, content analysis, and models. The words which recur as the *leitmotif* of the newer method are sociometry and quantification. Sociometry summarizes the whole current desire to measure various aspects of the social process by valid means. Quantification summarizes the desire to insure the validity of those means by getting tangibly measured data.

In speaking of the newer social science, one would not halt at the line of its newer areas of interest and of its newer methodology. The perspective and method of social science are informed by suggestions deriving from the great social scientists of modern times, from Max Weber, from Sigmund Freud, from Emile Durkheim, Ferdinand Tönnies, John Dewey, Ruth Benedict, David Riesman, and a score of others. It would be absurd to suggest that the contributions of these notable minds are used by modern social science as an integrated whole, in which the various parts fit perfectly and complement each other. And yet it is true enough to say that the precepts of these men and women, in one way or another, are taken into consideration in the attempts of social science to analyze human behavior and that these precepts form, whatever modification or alteration has been made upon them, a theoretical frame for the newer house of social science.

In trying to understand how far and why historians are using the insights of social science, let me at this point define terms and set limits to my analysis. First, a consideration of the social sciences as a set of disciplines does not imply that they have an organic unity. The social sciences not only differ among themselves but each of them also has serious differences within itself. If the social sciences are considered here as a unit, it is because the path they are taking and the role they are playing differ substantially from those being taken and played by history. Secondly, while I am interested in the question of whether or not history should use the social sciences, my principal interest is in whether or not it does. I am not so much concerned to propose an interdisciplinary alliance as to explain why the proposals for alliance have, in actual practice, not been realized. Third, in talking about history's use of social science I am not talking about social science's use of history. We are all familiar, for example, with the historical orientation of the contribution of David Riesman, Erich Fromm, and C. Wright Mills. My concern here is with the use of social science by professional historians in their regular and continuing researches. Finally, I am confining my analysis to research and writing in the field of American history, which is the field I have myself cultivated and am most familiar with. Much of what I say will no doubt apply to research and writing in other areas of history. This is true, certainly, of my explanation of the relation between American history and social science: since the explanation is itself historical, it deals necessarily with conditions which affected the whole discipline of history (as it arose and developed) rather than with merely one part of it. Yet it is recent work in American history which served me as my vantage ground in arriving at my observations and it is this work which frames the views I am presenting.

The changing conditions of modern American life have altered both the subjects with which social science deals and the purposes which it serves. Inevitably, of course, these changing conditions have raised a question about history's use of social science in dealing with the newer subjects and in serving the newer needs. In its book on *The Social Science in Historical Study,* which appeared in 1954, the Committee on Historiography of the Social Science Research Council argued that historians ought to embrace the teachings of the social sciences. In his presidential address to the American Historical Association a few years ago, William L. Langer sustained this argument by designating the application of psychoanalytic knowledge to history as "the next assignment" for historians. Richard Hofstadter has urged his fellow historians to use the new approaches of social science to add "to the speculative richness of history." The liaison between history and social science is the subject of many conferences and is encouraged by many grants. Indeed, some writers assert that history's use of social science has gone beyond the stage of preaching, that it has indeed passed into actual practice. John T. Marcus, in a recent and very stimulating article on "The Changing Consciousness of History," in

The South Atlantic Quarterly contends that the historical approach has been changing from one that is linear, positivistic, and interested above all in causation, to one that is—as he puts it—configurational, Gestaltist, and multi-directional. Evidences abound that historians are facing up to the problems of history's use of the social sciences.

I

Conspicuous instances may indeed be cited of a new departure in recent American historical writing. Seeking to canvass the whole expanse of the American past, David M. Potter's *People of Plenty* (1954) is almost in a class by itself. Using the tools of behavioral science, Potter shows how economic abundance contributed to the shaping of the American character. Historians have, moreover, been making a goodly use of the insights of social psychology in their recent studies of groups and of regions, focusing these insights on such questions as status consciousness, social mobility, the relation of minorities to the values of the majority, and the family as a factor in social and political developments. Notable contributions in this realm include: Bernard Bailyn's *The New England Merchants in the Seventeenth Century* (1955), Forrest McDonald's *We The People: The Economic Origins of the Constitution* (1958), John Hope Franklin's *The Militant South, 1800–1861* (1956), Thomas C. Cochran's *Railroad Leaders, 1845–1890: The Business Mind in Action* (1953), Oscar Handlin's *The Uprooted* (1951), and Richard Hofstadter's *The Age of Reform* (1955). Mention ought to be made of at least one further area in which history is using the insight of social science: biography. A most conspicuous example here is David Donald's *Charles Sumner and the Coming of the Civil War* (1960) which has availed itself of psychoanalytic knowledge to arrive at a deeper understanding of central episodes in the life of its protagonist.

It would be erroneous to pretend that these examples represent completely the uses of social science by writers of American history. But it would also be erroneous to pretend that there are many more important examples to cite, or that these represent the rule rather than the exception. This is not to deny that the insights of modern social science do filter into current writing on the American past. But one ought not to confuse scattered intelligences gleaned from the social science with a social science intelligence. A history which approaches some aspects of American society is far from being a sociological approach to American history. Whatever the preachment of American historians at interdisciplinary colloquia on the social sciences, their practice remains relatively traditional. Indeed, the very fact of the continuing preachment is its own testimony to the continuing absence of the practice. For proof of this, one has but to peruse the last decade's issues of the two principal professional journals in the

United States devoted to writings on American history: *The American Historical Review* and *The Mississippi Valley Historical Review.*

No comment is more relevant or pointed here than that of Thomas C. Cochran, of the University of Pennsylvania, who, as much as any other contemporary American historian, has been pleading the case of social science to his fellow guildsmen. "In the field of American history," submits Professor Cochran, ". . . the past fifty years of rapid progress in the development of social science methods and hypotheses have had surprisingly little effect on historical interests, content, or forms of syntheses. This statement applies to American history either as taught in universities and colleges, as presented in textbooks, or as reflected in general literature. The main props of a synthetic structure, erected more or less unconsciously by such gifted pioneers as Channing, Hart, McMaster, and Turner, are still securely in place."

If historians are not, for the larger part, using the approaches of social science, what approaches are they using? What are the principal features of contemporary writing on the American past? To begin with, the form in which the writing is cast remains fairly traditional. It is what Cochran calls "narrative synthesis," and by this he means a story centering on great men, generally the major American presidents, and on important events. H. Stuart Hughes of Harvard further suggests that historians still offer simple causal explanations, which they arrive at intuitively. Secondly, the interest in political developments remains the dominant one. Evidence for this could be offered in profusion. A commentary on the vistas of our historiography is afforded by what is clearly the most grandiose and indeed the most important writing venture of our times: Allan Nevins's *Ordeal of the Union,* a ten-volume history of the republic before and during the Civil War. However much he concerns himself with social and intellectual matters, Nevins is principally concerned with politics, and with politics in the traditional sense of the word. Probably the second most important work of our times is Arthur M. Schlesinger, Jr.'s *The Age of Franklin D. Roosevelt.* Here too the primary interest is political and the form of the account narrative.

A third feature of present-day writing is what I would call "the cult of biography." The foremost younger historians of our generation are devoting their talents to this form and are using the form in fairly conventional ways. I am thinking in particular of such luminaries as Frank Freidel of Harvard and his multi-volume work on Franklin D. Roosevelt; John M. Blum of Yale and his work on Tumulty, Theodore Roosevelt, Wilson and the Morgenthau diaries; and Arthur S. Link of Princeton and his distinguished work on Woodrow Wilson. A fourth feature, if not historical writing then at least of historical effort, is what might be called "the cult of the Founding Fathers." We are passing through an age of spectacular editions of the papers of the founders of the American republic; of Thomas Jefferson,

Alexander Hamilton, John Adams, and Benjamin Franklin. From a list of these features it seems fair enough to conclude that the orientation underlying present American historiography is conventional and conservative. For whatever reasons, writers of American history have not walked down the newer paths of social science. For whatever reasons, they seem, as much as ever before, to be abiding by the older canons and interests of their profession.

II

The big question, of course, is why. What are the reasons for which research and writing in the field of American history has tended, for the larger part, to pass by the teachings of social science? I should like to offer some suggestions, which, while they do not apply to all of the social sciences, will surely touch upon some of them. In answering our question about history's use of social science, we shall inevitably have to deal with the nature of history and its relation to the other disciplines. In the process, we may come upon deeper differences between them, differences in their function, their premises, and their methods.

The social sciences grew out of an attempt to find a science of society. Their purposes were practical, their goals utilitarian. They were designed to be an instrument for social understanding and, by means of that understanding, for social improvement. It is only in this light that we understand the great work of Auguste Comte, the French "Utopian" socialists, Herbert Spencer, the classical economists, Marx and Engels, the Fabians, and the whole school of late nineteenth-century American sociology. The continuing interest of social science has been with analyzing the human condition and with taking action based upon that analysis. As Robert K. Merton of Columbia University puts it: sociology seeks ". . . to acquire the knowledge needed to cope with the many social ills man has the inveterate capacity to contract." The social sciences are under the dictate of current events, they have an immediate goal, they serve a social need. If they are not useful, they are nothing.

History also plays a social role, but it is less immediate and practical. In the sociology of knowledge, the role of history might be considered both ideological and utopian. It is ideological in the respect that it conforms to the social myth, to the convention of values by which society lives. It is utopian in the respect that it always second guesses the past, it arraigns the past on a charge of what should have been, it always proceeds in terms of the difference between the imperfections of actual reality and the consummate reality so devoutly to be wish'd. In performing their role, historians often play tricks with the dead. For the larger part, they tell the fables which convention requires for the pursuit of social life.

If the service of social science is to set up a program of action for society, that of history is to serve the national myth. The service of social science is performed by analysis, by studies in arrested motion. That of history is performed by narrative. Historians may aspire to science, but their highest calling is that of troubadours and of bards, of minnesingers and of Homers, recalling to the folk the present meaning of earlier deeds, the heroism and cowardice of earlier men, the nobility or baseness of earlier generations. A folk-singer and myth-maker tells stories; he tells them personally; he commits himself to the narrative. He does not quantify; he does not set up models; he cannot remain uncommitted. He uses the records of the past—which center, for the larger part, on the unusual and the unique—to serve his cause. Citing the unusual, the historian teaches by example. Drawn from the unique, his portrait is an idealization of social behavior rather than a representation of it.

Differing substantially in their respective uses, it is inevitable that history and social science will differ too in method and theory.

The historian works under the sense that truth is less self-evident and less certain than the social scientist may consider it to be, beset as the latter always is with society's cry for functional truth, the whole functional truth, and nothing but functional truth. Moreover, because the historian cannot possibly know all the social interrelations of a whole scene or of a whole age, and because he cannot presume to deal with less, his account can be little more than (as one historian has put it) an imprecise and impressionistic "explanation sketch." Canvassing the larger frame of experience with which he is perforce concerned, he could not possibly use the narrower and more controlled methods of social science. In their quest for practical truth, social scientists are understandably concerned with how truth is to be found out. They postulate hypotheses, define areas for inspection, set up charts, classify IBM cards, make the chemistry of human action a matter of quantitative analysis. The historian is both impressed and depressed. If he sees method in their madness, he also suspects madness in their method.

In exploring why history makes only a limited use of social science, we must consider that the social scientist proceeds from the premise that out of a limited sampling of human experience one can arrive at larger generalizations. He proceeds from the instance to the rule. The historian's premises regarding human experience are different. He accepts the uniqueness of experience, the difference of individuals and groups. If the social scientist is looking for rules and laws, the historian has long since come to doubt that they can be found. He is concerned with variables, with the uniqueness of what he is dealing with, with the improbabilities of abstracting a universal out of an instance.

The focal points of history and social science are in many respects different. Social science concentrates on regularities in human experience, on norms, on the usual. History concentrates on irregularities, on leaders, on unique events, on the exceptional. The language difference between history and social science both reflects and explains their different approaches and concerns. Writers of books on freshman English descend zestfully, looking for evidences of what Orwell would probably have called nonspeak, upon the rich, alluvial lands of sociologese. Sociology is considered the worst of the offenders here, but psychology, political science, and economics are often almost as guilty. The sharp difference between history and social science in their uses of language as a means of communication lies deeply in the respective image which each has of its function. The language of social science is impersonal. Talking in ponderous and magisterial tones, using the passive voice instead of the active, it lays claim to the remove of science. By its language shall ye know it. Social science is valid only to the degree that it is above the play and noise of human experience. Any experience is a commentary on all experience, and the language is made bloodless enough to accord with that axiom. But if your premise is, as the historian believes it to be, that any experience is self-sufficient, that it is at best relevant to others, but not as the basis of a model, a norm, a larger hypothesis, or a law, then language must convey the reality of that particular experience, its self-sufficiency, its vitality, dramatic uniqueness. The experience is not an example of life but life itself, and the historian's language seeks to express that very basic difference. My point here is not to enter into an empty argument about the way some social scientists write or speak. It is rather to get beneath the surface of the different uses of language and to see that there is a very fundamental difference in approach to discipline.

III

The difference between social science and history is the difference between a method which pretends to philosophy and a method which has given philosophy up. Both history and social science are rooted in positivism. Both began in the nineteenth century as quests for certain truth, to be achieved by certain methods. Both appealed to the example of science, and like science, both were to serve society: history by showing the road society had thus far come in its march toward progress and perfection, social science by showing the road it had yet to march. But nineteenth century philosophy has had some very rude shocks. The mythology of the liberal world came clattering down under the assault of two world wars. Western man's sense of his destiny is less of progress than of poverty, less of a certain goal in life than of muddling through. The grand social philosophy of the nineteenth century has found no sequel. Where today is the over-arching ideological structure of Hegel, of Marx, of Darwin, of Spencer? As H. Stuart Hughes of Harvard University puts it: "The chair of speculative social thought stands vacant."

We are living in a world of gods that have failed. We have run the gamut of the grand ideas, of positivistic faith, of belief in science, of conviction about progress, of programs for social reforms, of hopes for human perfectibility and Utopia. But the recent past of man has disabused us of hopes for his present and future. We are not so sure, we do not know, and we do not readily venture into metaphysical systems which, as we now realize, may be more the products of our psyches—whether as projections or as wish fulfillments—than they are of the real world around us. In such a condition of mankind, philosophy cannot flourish. Ideas yield to techniques, metaphysics to methods, ends to means.

All of this has a close relevance to the issue of history's use of social science. If historians still use the methods of positivism, they have long since abandoned a certain belief in its goals. . . . Disbelieving in regularities, uniformities, and laws, historians have lost their earlier rapport with social science. The problem of communication between history and social science has arisen, suggests Professor Oscar Handlin of Harvard University, ". . . because historians claimed there was no such thing as a historical 'law' and because many social scientists believed that history conceived in such terms had no utility for them. . . ."

My own conviction is that history is *with* the social sciences but not really *of* them. History stands between the social sciences and the humanities. It canvasses both the real world of man and the world of his imagination. In this poise, history inclines toward the sense that our view of reality is also an imaginative one. In getting that view of reality, historians must, even as a condition of their art, seek the insight afforded by the best of social science. But, having done this, they will have qualified only as apprentices and journeymen. For their masterpiece, they must rise ultimately to the challenge of literature and philosophy. The most notable of our historians are men of letters and men who argued, without really proving, a set of values. In these attainments may be found the claim to greatness of George Bancroft, Francis Parkman, Henry Adams, and Charles Beard, to name the irrefutably outstanding among the American historians.

5

The Sociological Imagination: The Promise

by C. Wright Mills

Nowadays men often feel that their private lives are a series of traps. They sense that within their everyday worlds, they cannot overcome their troubles, and in this feeling, they are often quite correct: What ordinary men are directly aware of and what they try to do are bounded by the private orbits in which they live; their visions and their powers are limited to the close-up scenes of job, family, neighborhood; in other milieux, they move vicariously and remain spectators. And the more aware they become, however vaguely, of ambitions and threats which transcend their immediate locales, the more trapped they seem to feel.

Underlying this sense of being trapped are seemingly impersonal changes in the very structure of continent-wide societies. The facts of contemporary history are also facts about the success and the failure of individual men and women. When a society is industrialized, a peasant becomes a worker; a feudal lord is liquidated or becomes a businessman. When classes rise or fall, a man is employed or unemployed; when the rate of investment goes up or down, a man takes new heart or goes broke. When wars happen, an insurance salesman becomes a rocket launcher, a store clerk, a radar man; a wife lives alone; a child grows up without a father. Neither the life of an individual nor the history of a society can be understood without understanding both.

Yet men do not usually define the troubles they endure in terms of historical change and institutional contradiction. The well-being they enjoy, they do not usually impute to the big ups and downs of the societies in which they live. Seldom aware of the intricate connection between the patterns of their own lives and the course of world history, ordinary men do not usually know what this connection means for the kinds of men they are becoming and for the kinds of history-making in which they might take part. They do not possess the quality of mind essential to grasp the

From *The Sociological Imagination,* by C. Wright Mills, pp. 3–24, 132–134 *passim.* © 1959 by Oxford University Press, Inc. Reprinted by permission.
The late C. Wright Mills was Professor of Sociology at Columbia University.

interplay of man and society, of biography and history, of self and world. They cannot cope with their personal troubles in such ways as to control the structural transformations that usually lie behind them. . . .

The very shaping of history now outpaces the ability of men to orient themselves in accordance with cherished values. And which values? Even when they do not panic, men often sense that older ways of feeling and thinking have collapsed and that newer beginnings are ambiguous to the point of moral stasis. Is it any wonder that ordinary men feel they cannot cope with the larger worlds with which they are so suddenly confronted? That they cannot understand the meaning of their epoch for their own lives? That—in defense of selfhood—they become morally insensible, trying to remain altogether private men? Is it any wonder that they come to be possessed by a sense of the trap?

It is not only information that they need—in this Age of Fact, information often dominates their attention and overwhelms their capacities to assimilate it. It is not only the skills of reason that they need—although their struggles to acquire these often exhaust their limited moral energy. What they need, and what they feel they need, is a quality of mind that will help them to use information and to develop reason in order to achieve lucid summations of what is going on in the world and of what may be happening within themselves. It is this quality, I am going to contend, that journalists and scholars, artists and publics, scientists and editors are coming to expect of what may be called the sociological imagination.

The sociological imagination enables its possessor to understand the larger historical scene in terms of its meaning for the inner life and the external career of a variety of individuals. It enables him to take into account how individuals, in the welter of their daily experience, often become falsely conscious of their social positions. Within that welter, the framework of modern society is sought, and within that framework the psychologies of a variety of men and women are formulated. By such means, the personal uneasiness of individuals is focused upon explicit troubles and the indifference of publics is transformed into involvement with public issues.

The first fruit of this imagination—and the first lesson of the social science that embodies it—is the idea that the individual can understand his own experience and gauge his own fate only by locating himself within his period, that he can know his own chances in life only by becoming aware of those of all individuals in his circumstances. In many ways it is a terrible lesson; in many ways, a magnificent one. We do not know the limits of man's capacities for supreme effort or willing degradation, for agony or glee, for pleasurable brutality or the sweetness of reason. But in our time we have come to know that the limits of "human nature" are frighteningly broad. We have come to know that every individual lives, from one generation to the next, in some society; that he lives out a biography, and that he lives it out within some historical sequence. By the fact of his living, he contributes, however minutely, to the shaping of this society and to the course of its history, even as he is made by society and by its historical push and shove.

The sociological imagination enables us to grasp history and biography and the relations between the two within society. That is its task and its promise. . . . No social study that does not come back to the problems of biography, of history and of their intersections within a society has completed its intellectual journey. . . .

That, in brief, is why it is by means of the sociological imagination that men now hope to grasp what is going on in the world, and to understand what is happening in themselves as minute points of the intersections of biography and history within society. In large part, contemporary man's self-conscious view of himself as at least an outsider, if not a permanent stranger, rests upon an absorbed realization of social relativity and of the transformative power of history. The sociological imagination is the most fruitful form of this self-consciousness. By its use men whose mentalities have swept only a series of limited orbits often come to feel as if suddenly awakened in a house with which they had only supposed themselves to be familiar. Correctly or incorrectly, they often come to feel that they can now provide themselves with adequate summations, cohesive assessments, comprehensive orientations. Older decisions that once appeared sound now seem to them products of a mind unaccountably dense. Their capacity for astonishment is made lively again. They acquire a new way of thinking, they experience a transvaluation of values; in a word, by their reflection and by their sensibility, they realize the cultural meaning of the social sciences.

Perhaps the most fruitful distinction with which the sociological imagination works is between "the personal troubles of milieu" and "the public issues of social structure." This distinction is an essential tool of the sociological imagination and a feature of all classic work in social science.

Troubles occurs within the character of the individual and within the range of his immediate relations with others; they have to do with his self and with those limited areas of social life of which he is directly and personally aware. Accordingly, the statement and the resolution of troubles properly lie within the individual as a biographical entity and within the scope of his immediate milieu—the social setting that is directly open to his personal experience and to some extent his willful activity. A trouble is a private matter: values cherished by an individual are felt by him to be threatened.

Issues have to do with matters that transcend these local environments of the individual and the range of his inner life. They have to do with the organization of many such milieux into the institutions of an historical society as a whole, with the ways in which various milieux overlap and interpenetrate to form the larger structure of social and historical life. An issue is a public matter: some value cherished by publics is felt to be threatened. Often there is a debate about what that value really is and about what it is that really threatens it. This debate is often without focus if only because it is the very nature of an issue, unlike even widespread trouble, that it cannot very well be defined in terms of the immediate and everyday environments of ordinary men. An issue, in fact, often involves a crisis in institutional arrangements, and often too it involves what Marxists call "contradictions" or "antagonisms."

In these terms, consider unemployment. When, in a city of 100,000, only one man is unemployed, that is his personal trouble, and for its relief we properly look to the character of the man, his skills, and his immediate opportunities. But when in a nation of 50 million employees, 15 million men are unemployed, that is an issue and we may not hope to find its solution within the range of opportunities open to any one individual. The very structure of opportunities has collapsed. Both the correct statement of the problem and range of possible solutions require us to consider the economic and political institutions of the society, and not merely the personal situation and character of a scatter of individuals.

Consider war. The personal problem of war, when it occurs, may be how to survive it or how to die in it with honor; how to make money out of it; how to climb into the higher safety of the military apparatus; or how to contribute to the war's termination. In short, according to one's values, to find a set of milieux and within it to survive the war or make one's death in it meaningful. But the structural issues of war have to do with its causes; with what types of men it throws up into command; with its effects upon economic and political, family and religious institutions, with the unorganized irresponsibility of a world of nation-states. . . .

In so far as an economy is so arranged that slumps occur, the problem of unemployment becomes incapable of personal solution. In so far as war is inherent in the nation-state system and in the uneven industrialization of the world, the ordinary individual in his restricted milieu will be powerless—with or without psychiatric aid—to solve the troubles this system or lack of system imposes upon him. In so far as the family as an institution turns women into darling little slaves and men into their chief providers and unweaned dependents, the problem of a satisfactory marriage remains incapable of purely private solution. In so far as the overdeveloped megalopolis and the overdeveloped automobile are built-in features of the overdeveloped society, the issues of urban living will not be solved by personal ingenuity and private wealth.

What we experience in various and specific milieux, I have noted, is often caused by structural changes. Accordingly, to understand the changes of many personal milieux we are required to look beyond them.

And the number and variety of such structural changes increase as the institutions within which we live become more embracing and more intricately connected with one another. To be aware of the idea of social structure and to use it with sensibility is to be capable of tracing such linkages among a great variety of milieux. To be able to do that is to possess the sociological imagination. . . .

In every intellectual age some one style of reflection tends to become a common denominator of cultural life. Nowadays, it is true, many intellectual fads are widely taken up before they are dropped for new ones in the course of a year or two. Such enthusiasms may add spice to cultural play, but leave little or no intellectual trace. That is not true of such ways of thinking as "Newtonian physics" or "Darwinian biology." Each of these intellectual universes became an influence that reached far beyond any special sphere of idea and imagery. In terms of them, or in terms derived from them, unknown scholars as well as fashionable commentators came to re-focus their observations and re-formulate their concerns.

During the modern era, physical and biological science has been the major common denominator of serious reflection and popular metaphysics in Western societies. "The technique of the laboratory" has been the accepted mode of procedure and the source of intellectual security. That is one meaning of the idea of an intellectual common denominator: men can state their strongest convictions in its terms; other terms and other styles of reflection seem mere vehicles of escape and obscurity.

That a common denominator prevails does not of course mean that no other styles of thought or modes of sensibility exist. But it does mean that more general intellectual interests tend to slide into this area, to be formulated there most sharply, and when so formulated, to be thought somehow to have reached, if not a solution, at least a profitable way of being carried along.

The sociological imagination is becoming, I believe, the major common denominator of our cultural life and its signal feature. . . . By means of it, orientation to the present as history is sought. As images of "human nature" become more problematic, an increasing need is felt to pay closer yet more imaginative attention to the social routines and catastrophes which reveal (and which shape) man's nature in this time of civil unrest and ideological conflict. Although fashion is often revealed by attempts to use it, the sociological imagination is not merely a fashion. It is a quality of mind that seems most dramatically to promise an understanding of the intimate realities of ourselves in connection with larger social realities. It is not merely one quality of mind among the contemporary range of cultural sensibilities—it is *the* quality whose wider and more adroit use offers the promise that all such sensibilities—and in fact, human reason itself—will come to play a greater role in human affairs. . . .

In the absence of an adequate social science, critics and novelists, dramatists and poets have been the major, and often the only, formulators of private troubles and even of public issues. Art does express such feelings and often focuses them—at its best with dramatic sharpness—but still not with the intellectual clarity required for their understanding or relief today. Art does not and cannot formulate these feelings as problems containing the troubles and issues men must now confront if they are to overcome their uneasiness and indifference and the intractable miseries to which these lead. The artist, indeed, does not often try to do this. Moreover, the serious artist is himself in much trouble, and could well do with some intellectual and cultural aid from a social science made sprightly by the sociological imagination. . . .

Of late the conception of social science I hold has not been ascendant. My conception stands opposed to social science as a set of bureaucratic techniques which inhibit social inquiry by "methodological" pretensions, which congest such work by obscurantist conceptions, or which trivialize it by concern with minor problems unconnected with publicly relevant issues. These inhibitions, obscurities, and trivialities have created a crisis in the social studies today without suggesting, in the least, a way out of that crisis.

Some social scientists stress the need for "research teams of technicians," others for the primacy of the individual scholar. Some expend great energy upon refinements of methods and techniques of investigation; others think the scholarly ways of the intellectual craftsmen are being abandoned and ought now to be rehabilitated. Some go about their work in accordance with a rigid set of mechanical procedures; others seek to develop, to invite, and to use the sociological imagination. Some —being addicts of the high formalism of "theory"—associate and disassociate concepts in what seems to others a curious manner; these others urge the elaboration of terms only when it is clear that it enlarges the scope of sensibility and furthers the reach of reasoning. Some narrowly study only small-scale milieux, in the hope of "building up" to conceptions of larger structures; others examine social structures in which they try "to locate" many smaller milieux. Some, neglecting comparative studies altogether, study one small community in one society at a time; others in a fully comparative way work directly on the national social structures of the world. Some confine their exact research to very short-run sequences of human affairs; others are concerned with issues which are only apparent in long historical perspective. Some specialize their work according to academic departments; others, drawing upon all departments, specialize according to topic or problem, regardless of where these lie academically. Some confront the variety of history, biography, society; others do not. . . .

I believe that what may be called classic social analysis is a definable and usable set of traditions; that its essential feature is the concern with historical social structures; and that its problems are of direct relevance to urgent public issues and insistent human troubles. I also believe that there are now great obstacles in the way of this tradition's continuing— both within the social sciences and in their academic and political settings —but that nevertheless the qualities of mind that constitute it are becoming a common denominator of our general cultural life and that, however vaguely and in however a confusing variety of disguises, they are coming to be felt as a need.

Many practitioners of social science, especially in America, seem to me curiously reluctant to take up the challenge that now confronts them. Many in fact abdicate the intellectual and the political tasks of social analysis; others no doubt are simply not up to the role for which they are nevertheless being cast. At times they seem almost deliberately to have brought forth old ruses and developed new timidities. Yet despite this reluctance, intellectual as well as public attention is now so obviously upon the social worlds which they presumably study that it must be agreed that they are uniquely confronted with an opportunity. In this opportunity there is revealed the intellectual promise of the social sciences, the cultural uses of the sociological imagination, and the political meaning of studies of man and society. . . . A truly remarkable variety of intellectual work has entered into the development of the sociological tradition. To interpret this variety as A Tradition is in itself audacious. Yet perhaps it will be generally agreed that what is now recognized as sociological work has tended to move in one or more of three general directions, each of which is subject to distortion, to being run into the ground.

Tendency I.   Toward a theory of history. For example, in the hands of Comte, as in those of Marx, Spencer, and Weber, sociology is an encyclopedic endeavor, concerned with the whole of man's social life. It is at once historical and systematic-historical, because it deals with and uses the materials of the past; systematic, because it does so in order to discern "the stages" of the course of history and the regularities of social life.

The theory of man's history can all too readily become distorted into a trans-historical strait-jacket into which the materials of human history are forced and out of which issue prophetic views (usually gloomy ones) of the future. The works of Arnold Toynbee and of Oswald Spengler are well-known examples.

Tendency II.   Toward a systematic theory of "the nature of man and society." For example, in the works of the formalists, notably Simmel and Von Weise, sociology comes to deal in conceptions intended to be of use in classifying all social relations and providing insight into their supposedly invariant features. It is, in short, concerned with a rather static and abstract view of the components of social structure on a quite high level of generality.

Perhaps in reaction to the distortion of Tendency I, history can be altogether abandoned: the systematic theory of the nature of man and of
society all too readily becomes an elaborate and arid formalism in which
the splitting of Concepts and their endless rearrangement becomes the
central endeavor. Among what I shall call Grand Theorists, conceptions
have indeed become Concepts. The work of Talcott Parsons is the leading
contemporary example in American sociology.

Tendency III.   Toward empirical studies of contemporary social facts
and problems. Although Comte and Spencer were mainstays of American
social science until 1914 or thereabout, and German theoretical influence
was heavy, the empirical survey became central in the United States at
an early time. In part this resulted from the prior academic establishment of economics and political science. Given this, in so far as sociology is defined as a study of some special area of society, it readily
becomes a sort of odd job man among the social sciences, consisting of
miscellaneous studies of academic leftovers. There are studies of cities
and families, racial and ethnic relations, and of course "small groups."
As we shall see, the resulting miscellany was transformed into a style of
thought, which I shall examine under the term "liberal practicality."

Studies of contemporary fact can easily become a series of rather unrelated and often insignificant facts of milieu. Many course offerings in
American sociology illustrate this; perhaps textbooks in the field of social
disorganization reveal it best. On the other hand, sociologists have tended
to become specialists in the technique of research into almost anything;
among them methods have become Methodology. Much of the work—
and more of the ethos—of George Lundberg, Samuel Stouffer, Stuart
Dodd, Paul F. Lazarsfeld are present-day examples. These tendencies—
to scatter one's attention and to cultivate method for its own sake—are
fit companions, although they do not necessarily occur together.

The peculiarities of sociology may be understood as distortions of one
or more of its traditional tendencies. But its promises may also be understood in terms of these tendencies. . . .

What social science is properly about is the human variety, which
consists of all the social worlds in which men have lived, are living, and
might live. These worlds contain primitive communities that, so far as
we know, have changed little in a thousand years; but also great power
states that have, as it were, come suddenly into violent being. Byzantine
and Europe, classical China and ancient Rome, the city of Los Angeles
and the empire of ancient Peru—all the worlds men have known now
lie before us, open to our scrutiny.

Within these worlds there are open-country settlements and pressure
groups and boys' gangs and Navajo oil men; air forces pointed to demol-
ish metropolitan areas a hundred miles wide; policemen on a corner; intimate circles and publics seated in a room; criminal syndicates; masses

thronged one night at the crossroads and squares of the cities of the world; Hopi children and slave dealers in Arabia and German parties and Polish classes and Mennonite schools and the mentally deranged in Tibet and radio networks reaching around the world. Racial stocks and ethnic groups are jumbled up in movie houses and also segregated; married happily and also hating systematically; a thousand detailed occupations are seated in businesses and industries, in governments and localities, in near-continent-wide nations. A million little bargains are transacted every day, and everywhere there are more "small groups" than anyone could ever count.

The human variety also includes the variety of individual human beings; these too the sociological imagination must grasp and understand. In this imagination an Indian Brahmin of 1850 stands alongside a pioneer farmer of Illinois; an eighteenth-century English gentleman alongside an Australian aboriginal, together with a Chinese peasant of one hundred years ago, a politician in Bolivia today, a feudal knight of France, an English suffragette on hunger strike in 1914, a Hollywood starlet, a Roman patrician. To write of "man" is to write of all these men and women—also of Goethe, and of the girl next door.

The social scientist seeks to understand the human variety in an orderly way, but considering the range and depth of this variety, he might well be asked: Is this really possible? Is not the confusion of the social sciences an inevitable reflection of what their practitioners are trying to study? My answer is that perhaps the variety is not as "disorderly" as the mere listing of a small part of it makes it seem; perhaps not even as disorderly as it is often made to seem by the courses of study offered in colleges and universities. Order as well as disorder is relative to viewpoint: to come to an orderly understanding of men and societies requires a set of viewpoints that are simple enough to make understanding possible, yet comprehensive enough to permit us to include in our views the range and depth of the human variety. The struggle for such viewpoints is the first and continuing struggle of social science.

Any viewpoint, of course, rests upon a set of questions, and the overall questions of the social sciences come readily to the mind that has firm hold of the orienting conception of social science as the study of biography, of history, and of the problems of their intersection within social structure. To study these problems, to realize the human variety, requires that our work be continuously and closely related to the level of historical reality—and to the meanings of this reality for individual men and women. Our aim is to define this reality and to discern these meanings; it is in terms of them that the problems of classic social science are formulated, and thus the issues and troubles these problems incorporate are confronted. It requires that we seek a fully comparative understanding of the social structures that have appeared and do now exist in world history. It requires that smaller-scale milieux be selected and studied in terms of larger-scale historical structures. It requires that we avoid the arbitrary specialization of academic departments, that we specialize our work variously according to topic and above all according to problem, and that in doing so we draw upon the perspectives and ideas, the materials and the methods, of any and all suitable studies of man as an historical actor. . . .

3

THE ROLE OF CULTURE

THE CONCEPT of culture is a key concept of social science. Culture was first defined as that complex whole which includes knowledge, belief, art, morals, law, custom, and any other capabilities and habits acquired by man as a member of society. Today culture is defined more briefly as a way of life of a people, a legacy of tradition handed down from generation to generation—it is that part of the environment created by man. Because of the accumulation of tradition, even the simple things that people as animals want are expressed in cultural patterns—an animal eats when it is hungry, a human being waits for lunch. In the selections which follow Robert Redfield criticizes the doctrine of "cultural relativity." If everything is right in terms of its own logic, then nothing including tyranny can be condemned. Murdock finds broad similarities as well as diversities in culture. He describes those aspects of culture found wherever men are found. The third selection offers an American Indian's judgments on our way of life.

6

Universals of Culture

by George P. Murdock

Early reports of peoples lacking language or fire, morals or religion, marriage or government, have been proved erroneous in every instance. Nevertheless, even today it is not generally recognized how numerous and diverse are the elements common to all known cultures. The following is a partial list of items, arranged in alphabetical order to emphasize their variety, which occur, so far as the author's knowledge goes, in every culture known to history or ethnography: age-grading, athletic sports, bodily adornment, calendar, cleanliness training, community organization, cooking, cooperative labor, cosmology, courtship, dancing, decorative art, divination, division of labor, dream interpretation, education, eschatology, ethics, ethnobotany, etiquette, faith healing, family, feasting, fire making, folklore, food taboos, funeral rites, games, gestures, gift giving, government, greetings, hair styles, hospitality, housing, hygiene, incest taboos, inheritance rules, joking, kin-groups, kinship nomenclature, language, law, luck superstitions, magic, marriage, mealtimes, medicine, modesty concerning natural functions, mourning, music, mythology, numerals, obstetrics, penal sanctions, personal names, population policy, postnatal care, pregnancy usages, property rights, propitiation of supernatural beings, puberty customs, religious ritual, residence rules, sexual restrictions, soul concepts, status differentiation, surgery, tool making, trade, visiting, weaning, and weather control.

Cross-cultural similarities appear even more far-reaching when individual items in such a list are subjected to further analysis. For example, not only does every culture have a language, but all languages are resolvable into identical kinds of components, such as phonemes or conventional sound units, words or meaningful combinations of phonemes, grammar or standard rules for combining words into sentences. Similarly funeral rites always include expressions of grief, a means of disposing of the corpse, rituals designed to protect the participants from supernatural harm, and

From *The Science of Man in the World Crisis,* edited by Ralph Linton, pp. 123–125, *passim.* New York, Columbia University Press, copyright 1945. Reprinted by permission.

George P. Murdock is Mellon Professor of Anthropology at the University of Pittsburgh, and a former president of the American Sociological Society.

the like. When thus analyzed in detail, the resemblances between all cultures are found to be exceedingly numerous. . . .

The true universals of culture, then, are not identities in habit, in definable behavior. They are similarities in classification, not in content. They represent categories of historically and behaviorally diverse elements which nevertheless have so much in common that competent observers feel compelled to classify them together. There can be no question, for example, that the actual behavior exhibited in acquiring a spouse, teaching a child, or treating a sick person differs enormously from society to society. Few would hesitate, however, to group such divergent acts under the unifying categories of marriage, education, and medicine. All of the genuinely widespread or universal resemblances between cultures resolve themselves upon analysis into a series of such generally recognized categories. What cultures are found to have in common is a uniform system of classification, not a fund of identical elements. Despite immense diversity in behavioristic detail, all cultures are constructed according to a single fundamental plan—the "universal culture pattern" as Wissler has so aptly termed it.

The essential unanimity with which the universal culture pattern is accepted by competent authorities, irrespective of theoretical divergencies on other issues, suggests that it is not a mere artifact of classificatory ingenuity but rests upon some substantial foundation. This basis cannot be sought in history, or geography, or race, or any other factor limited in time or space, since the universal pattern links all known cultures, simple and complex, ancient and modern. It can only be sought, therefore, in the fundamental biological and psychological nature of man and in the universal conditions of human existence. . . .

7

Cultural Relativism and Social Values

by Robert Redfield

In this . . . chapter I will consider some of the questions that arise when we look at all the primitive or the precivilized cultures with a view to the goodness or the badness of them. My own behavior, as an anthropologist, is relevant to the subject now to be discussed, for I am interested here in the way anthropologists do or do not place values on the things they see in prehistoric or in contemporary nonliterate or illiterate societies, and what comes of it if they do. I shall venture to anthropologize the anthropologists, and shall not leave myself out of their number.

. . . Writing of Petalesharoo, the Pawnee Indian who in the face of the customs of his tribe rescued a woman prisoner about to be put to death ceremonially and strove to end human sacrifice among his people, I called him "a hint of human goodness." Plainly I placed a value on his conduct. Looking back twenty-five years, I recall when as a student I first heard the story of Petalesharoo from Professor Fay-Cooper Cole, anthropologist. He told the story with great human warmth, and I know that then I responded sympathetically. Now I begin to wonder if he or I *could* tell the tale barely, neutrally, without implying admiration of the deed.

In the course of these pages, I have not infrequently indicated my admiration for some act, my approval of some turn in human events. The long story of human affairs which I have been sketchily recounting is a story in which I have not pretended to be disinterested. It is the human biography; it is your story and mine; how can we help but care? I have not tried to conceal a certain sense of satisfaction that in the childhood of our race, before there were cities, precivilized men, like the preliterates of today, recognized moral obligations, even if the moral rules were not my rules. I think this better than the unrestrained selfishness which Hobbes imagined wrongly to characterize the behavior of men before political society developed. So when in the course of these discussions I

From *The Primitive World and Its Transformations* by Robert Redfield, pp. 139–165, *passim*. Ithaca, N. Y., Cornell University Press. © 1953 by Cornell University. Reprinted by permission.

The late Robert Redfield was Distinguished Service Professor at the University of Chicago, and Chairman of the Department of Anthropology.

have encountered in some uncivilized society a custom which I liked or disliked, I think I have in many cases shown how I felt about it. I regret that the Siriono in the Bolivian forest abandon their dying kinsmen without a word, while I come to understand the rigors of their life that make such conduct excusable. I am pleased that the Yagua in their big communal houses respect even a child's desire to be alone, and refrain from speaking to him when he turns his face to the wall. . . .

This is, perhaps, a shocking admission. What right have I, who admit to caring about the human career, to speak as an anthropologist? For are not anthropologists enjoined to adopt in their work a rigid objectivity? Professor Kroeber has written that "there is no room in anthropology for a shred of ethnocentricity, of homino-centricity." My ethnocentricity appears in the positive valuations I have placed on the increase and widening of humane standards, for are not such standards a special pride of Euro-American civilization? And my homini-centricity is patent: I have placed myself squarely on the side of mankind, and have not shamed to wish mankind well.

My predicament stimulates an examination of some of the problems of objectivity and value judgment that arise in anthropology. There are a good many of these problems, and I shall try to sort them out and to reach at least the first points of understanding as to what is involved in some of them. . . .

Since Westermarck wrote two books to show that it is not possible to establish one way of thought or action as better than another, if not before that time, anthropologists have taken this position. It has come to have a name: cultural relativism. Most anthropologists would, I think, accept the term as naming their position, or would take the position without perhaps accepting the name. Cultural relativism means that the values expressed in any culture are to be both understood and themselves valued only according to the way people who carry that culture see things. In looking at a polygamous society and a monogamous society, we have no valid way to assert that one is better than the other. Both systems provide for human needs; each has values discoverable only when we look at marriage from the point of view of the man who lives under the one system or the other. This is, necessarily then, also to be said in comparing cultures which practice torture, infanticide, in-group sorcery, and homosexuality with those that do not. The gist of cultural relativism as stated by Professor Herskovits, who has discussed the concept at length, is that "judgments are based on experience, and experience is interpreted by each individual in terms of his own enculturation."

With this proposition I do not disagree. I fail to see that having accepted it one finds it necessary to accept everything else that Professor Herskovits says about cultural relativism. It is possible, I think, to agree that everybody passes judgments as guided by the experience he was brought up to have and recognize, and yet to assert some reasonable basis for preferring one thought or action to another. . . .

However this may be, I am persuaded that cultural relativism is in for some difficult times. Anthropologists are likely to find the doctrine a hard one to maintain. The criticisms of philosophers will be directed more sharply against it. Moreover, the experiences of anthropologists are changing, and these changed experiences will work changes in their judgments as to the relativity of values. (It occurs to me that this proposition is itself an application of the principle!) It was easy to look with equal benevolence upon all sorts of value systems as long as the values were those of unimportant little people remote from our own concerns. But the equal benevolence is harder to maintain when one is asked to anthropologize the Nazis, or to help a Point Four administrator decide what to do for those people he is committed to help. The Point Four man is committed to do something to change that people, for he cannot help them without changing them, and what is the anthropologist to say when the Point Four man asks him just what he ought to do? Perhaps the anthropologist can keep on saying: "Do A, and X will result, but Y will result from doing B—*you* choose which to do." But I doubt that if the anthropologist says only this, he and the administrator will get on very well together. And perhaps the anthropologist, if he continues this neutrality, and yet sees a smash coming, will be just a little restless at night.

At any rate, I should like to point out that the doctrine of cultural relativism does enjoin the benevolence. It is a doctrine of ethical neutralism, but it is not a doctrine of ethical indifference. Ruth Benedict's *Patterns of Culture* is an exemplification of cultural relativism. She wrote in large part to tell us that all cultures are "equally valid." But this meant, for her, not that we are to value none of them, but that we are to value all of them. The book is a call to positive sympathetic valuation of other ways of life than our own. Malinowski has gone so far as to write of "the respect due even to savages." And Herskovits states the positive element in the doctrine very clearly. He is not confused into supposing that cultural relativism is a mere scientific method, a procedure instrumental in reaching statements as to fact. No, he says, "cultural relativism is a *philosophy* which, in recognizing the values set up by every society to guide its own life, lays stress on the dignity inherent in every body of custom, and on the need for tolerance of conventions though they may differ from one's own." And again: "Emphasis on the worth of many ways of life, not one, is an affirmation of the values of each culture."

However, the two parts of this doctrine are not logically or necessarily interdependent. The first part says that people are brought up to see the value in things that their local experience has suggested. The second part says that we should respect all cultures. But there is no true "therefore" between these two parts. It cannot be proved, from the proposition that values are relative, that we ought to respect all systems of values. We might just as well hate them all. It is Professor Herskovits who has intruded upon the objectivity of science a moral judgment, which I personally admire, but for which he can show no demonstration of proof.

The anthropologist is, then, ethically neutral, but unlike him of whom the partisan demanded, "Just who are you neutral *for*?", the anthropologist is neutral for everybody. This, at least, is the way anthropologists represent their position. It seems to me that their success in living up to their doctrine may be questioned.

The difficulties of doing so were remarked by not a few of the anthropologists themselves when in 1947 the Executive Board of their American professional association submitted a statement to the Commission on Human Rights of the United Nations. The statement urged the Commission to recognize that, not only should the personality of the individual be accorded respect, but that "respect for the cultures of differing human groups is equally important." It declared the principle of cultural relativity and told the UN Commission that therefore any attempt it might make to write something about human rights ("formulate postulates") "that grow out of the beliefs or moral codes of one culture must to that extent detract from the applicability of any declaration of Human Rights to mankind as a whole." So the Commission was advised to incorporate in the Declaration of Human Rights a statement of the right of men to live in terms of their own traditions.

I understand that the UN Commission did not follow this advice. I imagine that some anthropologists are rather relieved that they did not. Such a declaration might seem to authorize the head-hunting peoples to continue head hunting, for would they not, by continuing head hunting, be living in terms of their own traditions? Of course the anthropologists who drafted this statement were not thinking of the head hunters. They knew, as well as you or I, that the head hunters and the cannibals will not be permitted to live in terms of these particular traditions if it is our heads and bodies they go for. They were thinking of the great and influential world civilizations—Indonesian, Indian, Chinese, African, Euro-American. But even here it is not clear just what the writers of the declaration expected to guarantee to these traditional ways of life—the right of a Mississippi human group to maintain its traditional white supremacy, of Russia to maintain a dehumanizing, fear-ridden way of life? At the time the anthropologists wrote their statement it was perhaps nazism that presented to their minds most plainly the difficulties with their statement, for they wrote the following sentence: "Even where political systems exist that deny citizens the right of participation in their government, or seek to conquer weaker peoples, underlying cultural values may be called on to bring the people of such states to a realization of the consequences of the acts of their governments." If we call upon underlying values to save us, it is we, on the outside of the culture, who are making them effective. And what if the underlying approved values are not there? The sentence is, to put it bluntly, a weasel; by including it, the declaration was made self-contradictory. You either respect all values or you do not. If the Nazis had come to have values approving the subjugation of everybody else, we, or the United Nations, would have either to respect this traditional way of life or not respect it. . . .

As soon as the anthropologist puts his attention on the particular human individuals in a primitive society, it becomes difficult to avoid the suggestion if not the fact that he is valuing one culture, or cultural situation, as better than another. It is not uncommon for an anthropologist, now studying a primitive culture disorganized by its contact with civilization, to see that the people he is studying are less comfortable than they were. Some of them, indeed, as those Oceanic natives whom Rivers described, appear now on their way to extinction just because they do not find life worth living any more. The anthropologist can hardly convince us—or himself—that so far as he is concerned a disorganized culture that fails to provide a desire to live is as valid as any other. Equal validity can be safely attributed only to cultures that arrange it so people can do what they want to do and are convinced that it is the right thing to do.

But even among such cultures, the well-integrated and the motive-providing, it is not always possible for the anthropologist to avoid at least the suggestion that he is preferring one of them to another. Ruth Benedict was a cultural relativist who told us that cultures are equally valid. Nevertheless, in reading some of her pages, one doubts that she found them equally good. In the seventh chapter of *Patterns of Culture* she introduces the concept of "social waste." Here she leads the reader to see a resemblance between the values of Kwakiutl society and those of his own (Middletown); both emphasize rivalry. But rivalry, wrote Benedict, is "notoriously wasteful. It ranks low in the scale of human values." One asks, Whose scale? Is there a universal scale of values which ranks rivalry low? She goes on to point out not only that "Kwakiutl rivalry produces a waste of material goods," but also that "the social waste is obvious." In Middletown, also, rivalry is "obsessive." Thus she is led to the conclusion that "it is possible to scrutinize different institutions and cast up their cost in terms of social capital, in terms of the less desirable behavior traits they stimulate, and in terms of human suffering and frustration." Apparently "social waste" includes a poor choice of desired behavior traits, human suffering, and frustration. In this passage Benedict is saying how, within one society (that of Middletown) one might make an evaluation, a sort of scoring, of the social waste that follows from one set of institutions rather than another. . . .

It is that disturbing fellow, the living human individual, who makes trouble for the scientist's stern principle of perfect objectivity. Whenever the anthropologist looks at him, something human inside the anthropologist stirs and responds. It is easy to be objective toward objects; but the human individual refuses to be only an object. When he is there before you, he insists on being judged as human beings are judged in life, if not in science. While the anthropologist is looking at the bones of the dead, at flint implements, or at institutions formally conceived and named—the Omaha kinship system or the tribal ideology—he is not much distracted by these claims upon his own human nature. But when the anthropologist meets and talks with some particular Indian or Oceanic islander, then he is apt to feel for that native while he is trying to describe him objectively. If the society is one that is running along the traditional ways of life, the field ethnologist is apt to respond with sympathy and indeed with favor toward the culture that keeps men's lives going in directions that they find good. If the ethnologist is himself gifted in communicating the human warmth of an exotic scene, as was Malinowski, an account results which communicates not only the humanity of the life described, but something of the enjoyment and satisfactions which the ethnologist himself experienced in coming to know that life. If the culture is one which puts the people who live by it into constant and fearful anxieties, the anthropologist is apt to show the disfavor he feels toward such a life. Reo Fortune's Dobuans are familiar; so I mention here instead the Tzeltal Indians of Chiapas, where Alfonso Villa Rojas found a people often sick, always believing that each sickness was the result of some moral transgression committed by the sufferer or, more terribly, by some one of his near kinsmen, and who are continually ridden by anxiety and compulsions to confess sins. Villa has described this people objectively, in the sense that his report is well documented and obviously trustworthy. But it would be untrue to assert that he has not shown, strongly in conversation and of course much more reservedly in his written description, his own unfavorable view of such a life. Furthermore, if one reads such an account of a people whose traditional ways of life have been disrupted, as, for example, McGregor's account of a reservation community of Sioux Indians, one finds oneself making value judgments that seem to reflect those of the writer, as to the somewhat unhappy predicament in which these people find themselves.

I think that the objectivity claimed by the anthropologist must admit of difficulties and qualifications. Professor Herskovits declares that "a basic necessity of ethnographic research . . . calls for a rigid exclusion of value judgments." This seems a little too strongly put. Rather, I should say, ethnographic research calls for as much objectivity as can be combined with the necessity to come to know the values of the people one is studying. The exception to allow the ethnographer to respect—i.e., value positively—all cultures, has already been noted. Professor R. H. Tawney is then expressing an opinion with which we may suppose that Professor Herskovits would agree when he writes that the student of a society must bring to his study "respect and affection." The necessity to understand the values of the people one is studying requires, I should say, the projection into unfamiliar words and action of human qualities—sympathy, pride, wish to be appreciated, and so on. Otherwise the ethnologist will not find out what the people he is studying are proud about or what, for them, deserves appreciation. My own opinion is that it is not possible to make use of these human qualities in field work, as I think one must, without also valuing what one sees. In the very necessity to describe the native, one must feel for him—or perhaps against him. The feelings are mixed with valuations. In Indian communities in which I have worked, I have found myself constantly liking and disliking some people as compared with others, some customs as compared with others, and some aspects of the total culture as compared with others. I remember, after having spent a good deal of time in Chan Kom, Yucatan, how I had come to admire a certain quality of decency and dignity about the people, and how bored I had become with their—to me—overemphasis on the prudent and the practical. If they would only once admire a sunset or report a mystic experience, I used to hear myself thinking. I would not know how to find out about a culture without this sort of valuing. Objectivity requires that I hold in suspense each formulation I make about the native life. It requires me to become aware of the values I have that may lead me in one direction rather than another. It demands that I subject my descriptions to the tests of documentation, internal consistency, and if possible the evidence and judgments of other observers. But I do not think that it asks of me that I divest myself of the human qualities, including valuing. I could not do my work without them. . . .

Perhaps we should ask of the field ethnologist, not that he divest himself of values, for that is impossible, nor that he emphasize in every case values predominating in his own times with regard to applied science, increased production, and adjusted personalities, but that he make plain what he does find that is good or bad about the people he reports. And then, also, perhaps he can help to bring it about that he is followed in the same community to be studied by an ethnologist with a contrasting value emphasis! It was *The New Yorker* that suggested that we do not want balanced textbooks; we want balanced libraries. We do not want ethnologists so balanced that they have no humanity. We want a balanced profession, a varied lot of anthropologists. . . .

My praise of Petalesharoo here receives explanation, if not justification. Petalesharoo acted against the customary practice of his people. It is a little easier to do that after civilization than before; in precivilized societies it was harder. So Petalesharoo gets my praise on that count. And when he acted, he acted in conformity with the trend of the human career of which he was ignorant, but which I know about, being some thousands of years older in civilization than was he. So it is not remarkable that I praise him. Perhaps also you, my reader, do too.

If you do, and you are not an anthropologist, no one will scold. But I am an anthropologist, and have taken the oath of objectivity. Somehow the broken pledge—if it is broken—sits lightly on my conscience. In me, man and anthropologist do not separate themselves sharply. I used to think I could bring about that separation in scientific work about humanity. Now I have come to confess that I have not effected it, and indeed to think that it is not possible to do so. All the rules of objectivity I should maintain: the marshaling of evidence that may be confirmed by others, the persistent doubting and testing of all important descriptive formulations that I make, the humility before the facts, and the willingness to confess oneself wrong and begin over. I hope I may always strive to obey these rules. But I think now that what I see men do, and understand as something that human beings do, is seen often with a valuing of it. I like or dislike as I go. This is how I reach understanding of it. The double standard of ethical judgment toward primitive peoples is a part of my version of cultural relativity. It is because I am a product of civilization that I value as I do. It is because I am a product of civilization that I have both a range of experience within which to do my understanding-valuing and the scientific disciplines that help me to describe what I value so that others will accept it, or, recognizing it as not near enough the truth, will correct it. And if, in this too I am wrong, those others will correct me here also.

8

An Indian's Soliloquy

by Burt W. Aginsky

While doing field research in northern California with an Indian group which had suffered a great deal under the disruptive influences of Spanish and Americans, I became familiar with an old Indian man well over one hundred years of age. He had lived through a period which encompassed the days before any whites had come into his territory, the Spanish raids, the white massacres, the herding of his people upon reservations, and the variegated civilized tortures accompanying these deprivations. One day after a long period of discussion concerning the changing family situation he talked eloquently for a period of about two hours. As soon as it was possible I returned to my headquarters and recorded what he had said in as close an approximation as I could.

An old Pomo Indian once said to me: "What is a man? A man is nothing. Without his family he is of less importance than that bug crossing the trail, of less importance than the sputum or exuviae. At least they can be used to help poison a man. A man must be with his family to amount to anything with us. If he had nobody else to help him, the first trouble he got into he would be killed by his enemies because there would be no relatives to help him fight the poison of the other group. No woman would marry him because her family would not let her marry a man with no family. He would be poorer than a newborn child; he would be poorer than a worm, and the family would not consider him worth anything. He would not bring renown or glory with him. He would not bring support or other relatives either. The family is important. If a man has a large family and a profession and upbringing by a family that is known to produce good children, then he is somebody and every family is willing to have him marry a woman of their group. It is the family that is important. In the white ways of doing things the family is not so important. The police and soldiers take care of protecting you, the courts give you justice, the post office carries messages for you, the school teaches you.

From *The American Journal of Sociology,* Vol. XLVI, pp. 43–44, published by The University of Chicago Press. Reprinted by permission.

Burt W. Aginsky is Associate Professor of Sociology and Anthropology at City College, New York.

Everything is taken care of, even your children, if you die; but with us the family must do all of that.

"Without the family we are nothing, and in the old days before the white people came the family was given the first consideration by anyone who was about to do anything at all. That is why we got along. We had no courts, judges, schools, and the other things you have, but we got along better than you. We had poison, but if we minded our own business and restrained ourselves we lived well. We were taught to leave people alone. We were taught to consider that other people had to live. We were taught that we would suffer from the devil, spirits, ghosts, or other people if we did not support one another. The family was everything, and no man ever forgot that. Each person was nothing, but as a group joined by blood the individual knew that he would get the support of all his relatives if anything happened. He also knew that if he was a bad person the head man of his family would pay another tribe to kill him so that there would be no trouble afterward and so that he would not get the family into trouble all of the time.

"That is why we were good people and why we were friends with the white people when they came. But the white people were different from us. They wanted to take the world for themselves. My grandfather told me that the white people were homeless and had no families. They came by themselves and settled on our property. They had no manners. They did not know how to get along with other people. They were strangers who were rough and common and did not know how to behave. But I have seen these people of yours are even worse. They have taken everything away from the Indians, and they take everything away from one another. They do not help one another when they are in trouble, and they do not care what happens to other people. We were not like that. We would not let a person die of starvation when we had plenty of food. We would not bury our dead with no show. We would kill another person by poisoning him if he was an enemy, but we would not treat a stranger the way they treat their own brothers and sisters. Your people are hard to understand. My brother lived with your people for twenty years, and he said that he was used to you; but he cannot understand yet why you people act as you do. You are all the same in one way. We are all the same in another. What is wrong with you? The white people have the land. They own the courts, they own everything, but they will not give the Indians enough money to live on. It is hard to understand.

"With us the family was everything. Now it is nothing. We are getting like the white people, and it is bad for the old people. We had no old people's homes like you. The old people were important. They were wise. Your old people must be fools."

4

CULTURE AND THE NATURAL ENVIRONMENT

BETTY J. MEGGERS considers the relations of environment to culture. The evidence she examines suggests that the environment exerts a limiting effect on the cultures it supports. This limiting effect is insurmountable in relation to hunting and subsistence food-gathering patterns of life. In the case of agricultural economies a breakthrough is achieved and culture becomes progressive; but the level to which a culture can develop is still dependent on the agricultural potentialities of the environment it occupies. However, when these potentialities are relatively great, cultural evolution is largely freed from the limitations placed upon it by environment. The concept of differential potential is offered as an explanation of both the regional distribution of cultures and the lack of stability of certain culture areas through time.

9

Environmental Limitation on the Development of Culture

by Betty J. Meggers

The relationship of culture to environment is one of the oldest problems in the science of anthropology and has provided a leading source of controversy. Early students, impressed with the ways in which cultures were adjusted to unique features of their local environments, developed the concept of environmental determinism. As more field work was done by trained observers, the variability in culture patterns became more evident and the idea of determinism was rejected. Then, as individual cultures were grouped into culture areas and recognized as specific manifestations of a general pattern, the role of environment once again compelled attention. . . .

There are few anthropologists today who would disagree with the general statement that environment is an important conditioner of culture. However, efforts to establish the relationship more specifically seem to give negative results. The potentialities of a particular habitat can be seen reflected in the subsistence pattern, the material culture, and by extension, in the social and religious aspects of the culture that is exploiting it, but when cultures of similar subsistence patterns or general features are compared they are not found to occupy similar environments. Hunting tribes, for example, may live in semi-deserts, swamps, forests, grasslands, or mountains, and in the arctic, the tropics or the temperate zone. Conversely, areas that seem similar geographically may differ greatly culturally. This has led to the conclusion expressed by Forde: [1]

> Physical conditions enter intimately into every cultural development and pattern, not excluding the most abstract and non-material; they enter not as determinants, however, but as one category of the raw

From "Environmental Limitation on the Development of Culture," by Betty J. Meggers. *American Anthropologist,* LVI (1954), pp. 801–824, *passim.* Reprinted by permission of the author and publisher.

Betty J. Meggers is an anthropologist who is a Research Associate at the Smithsonian Institution, Washington, D.C.

[1] Daryll Forde, *Habitat, Economy and Society* (London, 1934), p. 464.

material of cultural elaboration. The study of the relations between cultural patterns and physical conditions is of the greatest importance for an understanding of human society, but it cannot be undertaken in terms of simple geographical controls alleged to be identifiable on sight. It must proceed inductively from the minute analysis of each actual society.

Given the traditional conceptions of environment, no other conclusion is possible. However, in view of the very definite evidence that cultures have an ecological aspect, which can be shown to have a determinative character particularly on the lower levels, it does not seem likely that no more general relationship exists. It is more probable that, in attempting to discover it, we have not been distinguishing the fundamental factors involved. All the efforts to correlate culture with environment have utilized the landscape classifications set up by geographers. James, for example, has summarized world environments under eight principal types: (dry lands or deserts, tropical forests, Mediterranean scrub forests, mid-latitude mixed forests, grasslands, boreal forests, polar lands and mountain lands.) It has frequently been noted that these categories do not represent cultural uniformities or even similarities. Desert cultures range from food gatherers to high civilizations; both polar lands and boreal forests, on the other hand, are exploited by food gatherers. Since environment does have an important effect on culture, and since the usual geographical classifications fail to discriminate culturally significant units, it is logical to search for some other basis for distinction.

Definition of Environment

The primary point of interaction between a culture and its environment is in terms of subsistence, and the most vital aspect of environment from the point of view of culture is its suitability for food production. Until the discovery of agriculture, this was relatively equal over the major portion of the earth's surface. In some areas game, wild plants or fish were more abundant than in others, but the range of variation was slight in comparison with what it became following the adoption of agriculture. The cultivation of cereals was designated by Tylor as "the great moving power of civilization," and the cultural revolution that followed in its wake has since been commented upon frequently. Most anthropologists, however, do not carry the analysis beyond the effect that agriculture has had on culture, to the effect that environment has on the productivity of agriculture. Differences in soil fertility, climate and other elements determine the productivity of agriculture, which, in turn, regulates population size and concentration and though this influences the sociopolitical and even the technological development of the culture. Once this point is raised, it is evident that differential suitability of the environment for agricultural exploitation provides a potential explanation for differences in cultural development attained around the world.

To be culturally significant, a classification of environment must recognize differences in agricultural potential. Areas that permit only limited, shifting cultivation because of the poverty of the soil must be distinguished from those of enduring fertility where intensive agriculture can be practised over long periods of time. An examination of the methods of food production suggests that four types of environment can be recognized, each with a distinct agricultural and cultural implication:

TYPE 1.—AREAS OF NO AGRICULTURAL POTENTIAL. This includes the greatest variety of natural landscapes because only one of the many components necessary for agriculture need be absent for the area to be unsuitable. The defective element may be soil composition, temperature, rainfall, short growing season, elevation, terrain, etc. Type 1 regions include tundra, some deserts, tropical savannas, swamps, some mountain ranges, and similarly uncultivable types of land.

A few areas with no agricultural potential are suitable for a pastoral economy. These constitute a special category of Type 1 because food gathering is replaced by food production and a higher level of cultural development can be attained than is typical of Type 1 areas. Some Type 3 areas have also supported pastoral cultures on the aboriginal level. However, since pastoralism is a minor source of food production compared to agriculture among the cultures of the world, and lacks both the environmental adaptability and the variety of potentiality for cultural development characteristic of agriculture, it will receive only brief mention in this discussion.

TYPE 2.—AREAS OF LIMITED AGRICULTURAL POTENTIAL. Here agriculture can be undertaken, but its productivity is minimized by limited soil fertility, which cannot economically be improved or conserved. When the natural vegetation cycle is broken by clearing, planting and harvesting, the delicate balance between what is taken from and what is returned to the soil is upset. The soil is poor to begin with, and exposed fully to the detrimental effects of the climate, it is quickly exhausted of plant nutrients. The addition of fertilizer is not feasible on a primitive level or economically practical on a modern one. Since the major cause of this condition is abundant rainfall and high humidity, Type 2 environments may be restricted to the tropics, and a good example is the South American tropical forest and selva. This does not mean, however, that all tropical environments are necessarily Type 2.

Up to the present time, no method of maintaining such areas in continuously profitable, intensive food production has been found, in spite of our extensive knowledge of plants and soils. Permanent and intensive production has been achieved in some places by the introduction of tree crops (cacao, coffee, bananas, citrus, etc.) and jute, but with the possible exception of the banana, none of these could provide an adequate subsistence base. Should a solution appear in the future, the "limited" designation for Type 2 might have to be modified, but since the obstacles to the increased productivity of food crops are infinitely greater than in Type 3, a distinction between the two should still be made.

TYPE 3.—AREAS OF INCREASABLE (IMPROVABLE) AGRICULTURAL PO-TENTIAL. Areas of this type contain all the essentials for agricultural production that exist in Type 2. However, being in more temperate climates where rainfall and humidity are less detrimental, soil exhaustion is caused mainly by the raising of food crops. Under a slash-and-burn type of utilization, the productivity of the land is not much greater than that of Type 2 areas. However, crop returns can be appreciably increased by techniques such as rotation, fallow and fertilization, and the same fields can be kept in almost constant production over long periods of time if not permanently. Temperate forest zones like Europe and the eastern United States belong in this category.

Other Type 3 environments are less readily improved because the deficient element is not soil fertility, but water. The Imperial Valley of California is such a case, where agriculture is made possible by water brought long distances over mountains.

Further methods of increasing agricultural potential are by the introduction of more suitable plants, such as the replacement of dry rice by wet rice in Madagascar, and the introduction of new or improved tools like the animal-drawn plow in the North American plains.

TYPE 4.—AREAS OF UNLIMITED AGRICULTURAL POTENTIAL. Here the natural environment approximates as closely as possible the ideal conditions for agriculture. Climate, water and terrain are suitable and soil fertility is for the purposes of this discussion inexhaustible, so that the land can support intensive food production indefinitely. The "cradles of civilization" all belong to Type 4.

The classification of an area into one of these types is theoretically independent of the time factor. Since the introduction of agriculture in most of the world, there has been little alteration in climate or topography that has affected the agricultural potentiality of the environment. Where changes have occurred because of climatic shifts, such as the gradual northward extension of the limit of agriculture in North America, the area can be reclassified in accord with its new potential.

For purposes of practical ease in identifying an area as to type, the year 1950 can be taken as a base line. If an area is improvable by modern agricultural techniques, it is Type 3, regardless of what might have been its primitive or aboriginal usage. If it cannot be shown to have been so improved, or to be comparable to some area where similar natural deficiencies in agricultural potential have been compensated for with modern knowledge and techniques, then it is Type 2 or Type 1, depending on whether agriculture is feasible or impossible. Type 3 areas, as will be seen, are most dependent on such technical advances to develop their potential. Type 4 areas are highly productive even with relatively primitive means of exploitation. . . .

If we accept as a working hypothesis the existence of a definite cause and effect relationship between these four kinds of environment and the maximum cultural development they can continuously support, the next step is to examine from this point of view some of the evidence that has been assembled about cultures. Since limitations of space do not permit coverage of the world, the greatest temporal, spatial and cultural variety may be included by using South America as a test area. . . .

Culture and Environment in South America

. . . The evidence suggests that the environment exerts an insurmountable limiting effect on the cultures it supports as long as it permits only a hunting and gathering subsistence pattern, and that this limitation extends to all areas of the culture, even those that seem remotely or not at all related to the subsistence requirements. No amount of inventive genius or receptivity to borrowing that might be theoretically attributable to the people psychologically is sufficient to overcome this barrier. . . .

In the Andean culture area with a Type 3 and Type 4 environment, the highest cultural development in South America was achieved. The Peruvian coastal valleys furnish the longest uninterrupted prehistoric sequence, partly because favorable conditions for preservation accompany favorable conditions for human occupancy. Art and crafts, social organization, and religion were elaborated to an extent that rivaled what had been achieved in Europe in the same centuries. Cotton and woolen textiles were produced by a variety of techniques, some so complex that they cannot be duplicated on modern machine looms, and often ornamented with elaborate designs. Pottery was mass-produced and of high quality. Metallurgy included casting, alloying, plating of gold, silver and copper. Massive fortifications, agricultural terraces, palaces, temples and lesser buildings were constructed of carefully fitted stone masonry or adobe. Minor arts and crafts existed in profusion. Settlements ranged from small villages to cities, some of which were administrative centers attaining an estimated population of 100,000. A network of roads facilitated communication and transportation of goods between towns.

The functions of government were handled by a hierarchy of officials of increasing rank and responsibility, culminating in the divine and absolute monarch. Class distinctions were clearly defined and hereditary, with distinctive garments, insignia and other privileges for individuals of the upper class. Governmental supervision touched all aspects of life; the duties and obligations of each individual were fixed, all activities were regulated. It is almost superfluous to add that occupational division of labor was advanced to modern proportions. The religious organization paralleled the governmental one, with a hierarchy of priests headed by a close relative of the ruler. These presided over temples dedicated to gods of varying importance and housing images and ceremonial parapher-nalia. The gods were approached with blood sacrifice, fasting, prayer and offerings, and ceremonies were held in accord with the ritual calendar.

The existence of so elaborate a civilization depends upon the intensive production of food and its effective distribution. Large irrigation works increased cultivatable land in the valleys on the coast, and terracing with fertilization was employed in the highlands. Specialization in crops per-mitted each region to grow what was best suited to its climate, altitude and soil. The surplus of one year or area were stored for distribution in time of need. These methods were so productive that many thousands of commoners could be levied for military service, labor on public works or similar specialized tasks that contributed nothing to the basic subsis-tence. The closeness of the correlation between these advanced techno-logical and sociological features and the highly productive subsistence base is demonstrated by the failure of the Inca Empire to extend its boundaries into regions with lesser agricultural potential. The failure to expand farther north or south might be laid to the slow communication and consequent difficulties in maintaining control, which were com-pounded as distance from the center increased. This could not excuse lack of expansion to the east, however, nor would it have prevented the dif-fusion of advanced pottery and weaving techniques, which were not adopted to any extent by neighboring tribes.

The evidence summarized above leads to the following conclusion: In determining the degree of evolution that a culture or culture area can attain, geographical location (in terms of proximity to centers of dif-fusion), intelligence (or genius) and psychological receptivity to new ideas are not as important as environment as it is reflected in the subsis-tence resources. If the temperature, soil, altitude, rainfall, growing season, terrain or some other factor will not permit agricultural production, then only unusual circumstances in the form of a bountiful and permanent supply of wild food (as on the Northwest Coast), or the adoption of a pas-toral food production (as in parts of Asia) will permit the cultural adapta-tion to go beyond nomadic family bands with a minimum of material equipment and social organization. Where other factors are favorable, but the soils are of limited natural fertility that cannot be artificially in-creased, agriculture can be carried on although it requires constant clear-ing of new fields to be maintained. Even with such limitations, the effect on culture is remarkable, bringing a radically altered settlement pattern and an increase in the inventory of material traits. However, unless a method of continuing fields under permanent production is found, the culture can never proceed beyond a simple level. Where soils are of in-creasable or unlimited fertility and capable of permanent productivity, cultural evolution has no environmental limitation.

5

PRIMITIVE SOCIETIES

IN OUR FIRST SELECTION Clyde Kluckhohn describes the nature of anthropology and the methods it employs in studying human societies. He puts special emphasis on the value of studying relatively simple primitive societies for the light which they throw on human nature and on some of the basic problems which we face in our modern complex societies.

In our second selection Peter Freuchen, from a lifetime of close association with the Eskimos, gives us an insight into their attitudes toward love and marriage, their ways of life, their hardships, the recent changes in their culture patterns, and the outlook for their future. Though contacts with modern civilization are breaking down the traditional patterns of Eskimo culture, Freuchen believes that the Eskimos are gaining from these contacts much more than they are losing.

10

Queer Customs, Potsherds, and Skulls

by Clyde Kluckhohn

Anthropology provides a scientific basis for dealing with the crucial dilemma of the world today: how can peoples of different appearance, mutually unintelligible languages, and dissimilar ways of life get along peaceably together? Of course, no branch of knowledge constitutes a cure-all for the ills of mankind. If any statement in this book seems to support such messianic pretensions, put this absurd claim down as a slip of an enthusiast who really knows better. Anthropology is, however, an overlapping study with bridges into the physical, biological, and social sciences and into the humanities.

Because of its breadth, the variety of its methods, and its mediating position, anthropology is sure to play a central role in the integration of the human sciences. A comprehensive science of man, however, must encompass additional skills, interests, and knowledge. Certain aspects of psychology, medicine and human biology, economics, sociology, and human geography must be fused with anthropology in a general science which must likewise embrace the tools of historical and statistical methods and draw data from history and the other humanities.

Present-day anthropology, then, cannot pretend to be the whole study of man, though perhaps it comes closer than any other branch of science. Some of the discoveries that will here be spoken of as anthropological have been possible only by collaboration with workers in other fields. Yet even the traditional anthropology has a special right to be heard by those who are deeply concerned with the problem of achieving one world. This is because it has been anthropology that has explored the gamut of human variability and can best answer the questions: what common ground is there between human beings of all tribes and nations? What differences exist? what is their source? how deep-going are they?

By the beginning of the twentieth century the scholars who interested themselves in the unusual, dramatic, and puzzling aspects of man's history

From *Mirror for Man*, by C. Kluckhohn. Copyright, 1949, McGraw-Hill Book Company. Used by permission.
The late Clyde Kluckhohn was Professor of Anthropology at Harvard University and a past president of the American Anthropological Association.

were known as anthropologists. They were the men who were searching for man's most remote ancestors; for Homer's Troy; for the original home of the American Indian; for the relationship between bright sunlight and skin color; for the origin of the wheel, safety pins, and pottery. They wanted to know "how modern man got this way": why some people are ruled by a king, some by old men, others by warriors, and none by women; why some peoples pass on property in the male line, others in the female, still others equally to heirs of both sexes; why some people fall sick and die when they think they are bewitched, and others laugh at the idea. They sought for the universals in human biology and in human conduct. They proved that men of different continents and regions were physically much more alike than they were different. They discovered many parallels in human customs, some of which could be explained by historical contact. In other words, anthropology had become the science of human similarities and differences.

In one sense anthropology is an old study. The Greek historian, Herodotus, sometimes called the "father of anthropology" as well as the "father of history," described at length the physique and customs of the Scythians, Egyptians, and other "barbarians." Chinese scholars of the Han dynasty wrote monographs upon the Hiung-Nu, à light-eyed tribe wandering near China's northwestern frontier. The Roman historian, Tacitus, produced his famous study of the Germans. Long before Herodotus, even, the Babylonians of the time of Hammurabi collected in museums objects made by the Sumerians, their predecessors in Mesopotamia.

Although ancients here and there showed that they thought types and manners of men worth talking about, it was the voyages and explorations from the fifteenth century onward that stimulated the study of human variability. The observed contrasts with the tight little medieval world made anthropology necessary. Useful though the writings of this period are (for example, the travelogues of Peter Martyr) they cannot be ranked as scientific documents. Often fanciful, they were written to amuse or for narrowly practical purposes. Careful accounts of firsthand observation were mixed up with embellished and frequently secondhand anecdotes. Neither authors or observers had any special training for recording or interpreting what they saw. They looked at other peoples and their habits through crude and distorting lenses manufactured of all the prejudices and preconceptions of Christian Europeans.

It was not until the late eighteenth and nineteenth centuries, that scientific anthropology began to develop. The discovery of the relationship between Sanskrit, Latin, Greek, and the Germanic languages gave a great impetus to the comparative point of view. The first systematic anthropologists were gifted amateurs—physicians, natural historians, lawyers, businessmen to whom anthropology was a hobby. They applied common sense, the habits they had learned in their professions, and the fashionable scientific doctrines of their day to growing knowledge about "primitive" peoples.

What did they study? They devoted themselves to oddities, to matters which appeared to be so trivial or so specialized that the fields of study which had been established earlier failed to bother with them. The forms of human hair, the variations in skull formation, shades of skin color did not seem very important to anatomists or to practicing physicians. The physical remains of cultures other than the Greco-Roman were beneath the notice of classical scholars. Languages unrelated to Greek and Sanskrit had no interest for the comparative linguists of the nineteenth century. Primitive rites interested only a few of the curious until the elegant prose and respectable classical scholarship of Sir James Frazer's *Golden Bough* won a wide audience. Not without justification has anthropology been termed "the science of leftovers."

It would be going too far to call the nineteeth-century anthropology "the investigation of oddments by the eccentric." The English Tylor, the American Morgan, the German Bastian, and other leading figures were respected citizens. Nevertheless, we shall understand the growth of the subject better if we admit that many of the first anthropologists were, from the point of view of their contemporaries, eccentrics. They were interested in bizarre things with which the average person had no serious concern and even the ordinary intellectual felt to be inconsequential.

If one does not confuse the results of intellectual activities with the motives leading to these activities, it is useful to ask what sort of people would be curious about these questions. Archaeology and museum anthropology provide an obvious happy hunting ground for those who are driven by that passion for finding and arranging which is common to collectors of everything from stamps to suits of armor. Anthropology has also always had with it the romantics, those who have taken it up because the lure of distant places and exotic people was strong upon them. The lure of the strange and far has a peculiar appeal for those who are dissatisfied with themselves or who do not feel at home in their own society. Consciously or unconsciously, they seek other ways of life where their characteristics are understood and accepted or at any rate, not criticized. Like many historians, the historical anthropologist has an urge to escape from the present by crawling back into the womb of the cultural past. Because the study had something of the romantic aroma about it and because it was not an easy way to make a living, it drew an unusual number of students who had independent means.

The beginnings do not sound very promising, either from the point of view of the students who were attracted to the subject or of what they were drawn to study. Nevertheless these very liabilities provided what are the greatest advantages of anthropology as compared with other approaches to the study of human life. Because nineteenth-century anthropologists studied the things they did out of pure interest and not either to earn a living or to reform the world, a tradition of relative objectivity grew up. The philosophers were shackled by the weighty history of their subject and by the vested interests of their profession. Auguste Comte, the founder of sociology, was a philosopher, but he tried to model sociology after the natural sciences. However, many of his followers, who were only slightly disguised philosophers of history, had a bias in favor of reasoning as opposed to observation. Many of the first American sociologists were Christian ministers, more eager to improve the world than to study it with detachment. The field of political science was also tinged with the philosophic point of view and with reformist zeal. The psychologists became so absorbed in brass instruments and the laboratory that they found little time to study man as one really wants to know him—not in the laboratory but in his daily life. Because anthropology was the science of leftovers and because leftovers were many and varied, it avoided the preoccupation with only one aspect of life that stamped, for instance, economics.

The eagerness and energy of the amateurs gradually won a place for their subject as an independent science. A museum of ethnology was established in Hamburg in 1850; the Peabody Museum of Archaeology and Ethnology at Harvard was founded in 1866; the Royal Anthropological Institute in 1873; the Bureau of American Ethnology in 1879. Tylor was made Reader in Anthropology at Oxford in 1884. The first American professor was appointed in 1886. But in the nineteenth century there were not a hundred anthropologists in the whole world.

The total number of anthropological Ph.D.'s granted in the United States prior to 1920 was only 53. Before 1930 four American universities gave the doctorate in anthropology. Even today there are a bare dozen. Nor has anthropology become in any sense a staple of the undergraduate curriculum. In only two or three secondary schools is instruction regularly given.

The astonishing thing, considering the trifling number of anthropologists and the minute fraction of the population that has been exposed to formal instruction in the subject is that during the last decade or so the word "anthropology" and some of its terms have come out of hiding in recondite literature to appear with increasing frequency in *The New Yorker, Life, The Saturday Evening Post,* detective stories, and even in moving pictures. It is also symptomatic of a trend that many colleges and universities and some secondary schools have indicated their intention of introducing anthropology in their revised courses of study. Although anthropologists —like psychiatrists and psychologists—are still regarded with a bit of suspicion, present-day society is beginning to feel they have something useful as well as diverting to offer.

In the American Southwest one of the signs of summer is the arrival of many "-ologists" who disrupt the quiet of the countryside. They dig up ruins with all the enthusiasm of small boys hunting for "Indian curios" or of delayed adolescents seeking buried treasure. They pry into the business of peaceful Indians and make a nuisance of themselves generally with a lot of queer-looking gadgets. The kind who dig into ruins are technically called "archaeologists," those who dig into the minds of Indians, "ethnologists" or "social anthropologists," those who measure heads, "physical anthropologists," but all are varieties of the more inclusive breed term "anthropologists."

Now what are they really up to? Is it just sheer curiosity about "ye beastly devices of ye heathen" or do the diggings, questionings, and measurings really have something to do with the world today? Do anthropologists merely produce exotic and amusing facts which have nothing to do with the problems of here and now?

Anthropology is something more than brooding over skulls or hunting for "the missing link," and it has a greater usefulness than providing means to tell one's friends from the apes. Seen from the outside, anthropological activities look, at best, harmlessly amusing, at worst, pretty idiotic. No wonder many a Southwesterner quips, "The Indians are going to start putting a bounty on you fellows." The lay reaction is well summed up by the remark of an army officer. We had met socially and were getting along very well until he asked me how I made my living. When I told him I was an anthropologist he drew away and said, "Well, you don't have to be crazy to be an anthropologist, but I guess it helps."

An anthropologist is a person who is crazy to study his fellow man. The scientific study of ourselves is relatively new. In England in 1936 there were over 600 persons who earned their living as students of one specialized branch (bio-chemistry) of the science of things, but fewer than 10 were employed as anthropologists. There are less than a dozen jobs for physical anthropologists in the United States today.

Yet nothing is more certain than that men ought to see whether the scientific methods which have given such stupendous results in unlocking the secrets of the physical universe might not help them understand themselves and their neighbors in this rapidly shrinking world. Men build machines that are truly wonderful, only to find themselves next to helpless when it comes to treating the social disorders that often follow the introduction of these machines.

Ways of making a living have changed with such bewildering rapidity that we are all a bit confused most of the time. Our ways of life have altered too—but not symmetrically. Our economic, political, and social institutions have not caught up with our technology. Our religious beliefs and practices and our other idea systems have much in them that is not appropriate to our present way of life and to our scientific knowledge of the physical and biological world. Part of us lives in the "modern" age—another part in medieval or even Greek times.

In the realm of treating social ills we are still living in the age of magic. We often act as if revolutionary and disturbing ideas could be exorcised by a verbal rite—like evil spirits. We hunt for witches to blame for our troubles: Roosevelt, Hitler, Stalin. We resist changing our inner selves even when altered conditions make this clearly necessary. We are aggrieved if other peoples misunderstand us or our motives; but if we try to understand them at all, we insist on doing so only in terms of our own assumptions about life which we take to be infallibly correct. We are still looking for the philosopher's stone—some magic formula (perhaps a mechanical scheme for international organization) that will make the world orderly and peaceful without other than external adaptions on our part.

We don't know ourselves very well. We talk about a rather vague thing called "human nature." We vehemently assert that it is "human nature" to do this and not to do that. Yet anybody who has lived in the American Southwest, to cite but one instance, knows from ordinary experience that the laws of this mysterious "human nature" do not seem to work out exactly the same way for the Spanish-speaking people of New Mexico, for the English-speaking population, and for the various Indian tribes. This is where the anthropologists come in. It is their task to record the variations and the similarities in human physique, in the things people make, in ways of life. Only when we find out just how men who have had different upbringing, who come from different physical stocks, who speak different languages, who live under different physical conditions, meet their problems, can we be sure as to what all human beings have in common. Only then can we claim scientific knowledge of raw human nature.

It will be a long job. But perhaps before it is too late we will come close to knowing what "human nature" really is—that is, what the reactions are that men inevitably have as human beings, regardless of their particular biological or social heritage. To discover human nature, the scientific adventurers of anthropolgy have been exploring the byways of time and of space. It is an absorbing task—so absorbing that anthropologists have tended to write only for each other or for scholars in other professions. Most of the literature of anthropology consists of articles in scienitfic journals and of forbidding monographs. The writing bristles with strange names and unfamiliar terms and is too detailed for the general reader. Some anthropologists may have had an obsession for detail as such. At any rate there are many whole monographs devoted to such subjects as "An Analysis of Three Hair-nets from the Pachacamac Area." Even to other students of man the great mass of anthropological endeavor has appeared, as Robert Lynd says, "aloof and preoccupied."

Though some research thus appears to leave the "anthropos" (man) off to one side, still the main trends of anthropological thought have been

focused on a few questions of broad human interest, such as: what has been
the course of human evolution, both biologically and culturally? Are there
any general principles or "laws" governing this evolution? What necessary
connections, if any, exist between the physical type, the speech, and the
customs of the peoples of past and present? What generalizations can be
made about human beings in groups? How plastic is man? How much can
he be molded by training or by necessity to adapt to environmental pressures? Why are certain personality types more characteristic of some
societies than of others?

To most people, however, anthropology still means measuring skulls,
treating little pieces of broken pottery with fantastic care, and reporting
the outlandish customs of savage tribes. The anthropologist is the grave
robber, the collector of Indian arrowheads, the queer fellow who lives with
unwashed cannibals. As Sol Tax remarks, the anthropologist has had a
function in society "something between that of an Einstein dealing with
the mysterious and that of an entertainer." His specimens, his pictures, or
his tales may serve for an hour's diversion but are pretty dull stuff compared to the world of grotesque monsters from distant ages which the
paleontologist can recreate, the wonders of modern plant and animal life
described by the biologist, the excitement of unimaginably far-off universes
and cosmic processes roused by the astronomer. Surely anthropology seems
the most useless and impractical of all the "-ologies." In a world of rocket
ships and international organizations, what can the study of the obscure
and primitive offer to the solution of today's problems?

"The longest way round is often the shortest way home." The preoccupation with insignificant nonliterate peoples that is an outstanding feature of
anthropological work is the key to its significance today. Anthropology
grew out of experience with primitives and the tools of the trade are unusual because they were forged in this peculiar workshop.

Studying primitives enables us to see ourselves better. Ordinarily we are
unaware of the special lens through which we look at life. It would hardly
be fish who discovered the existence of water. Students who had not gone
beyond the hoizon of their own society could not be expected to perceive
custom which was the stuff of their own thinking. The scientist of human
affairs needs to know as much about the eye that sees as the object seen.
*Anthropology holds up a great mirror to man and lets him look at himself
in his infinite variety.* This, and not the satisfaction of idle curiosity nor
romantic quest, is the meaning of the anthropologist's work in nonliterate
societies.

Picture the field worker in a remote island of the South Seas or among
a tribe of the Amazon jungle. He is usually alone. But he is expected to
bring back a report on both the physique and the total round of the people's
activities. He is forced to see human life as a whole. He must become a
Jack-of-all-trades and acquire enough diverse knowledge to describe such

varying things as head shape, health practices, motor habits, agriculture, animal husbandry, music, language, and the way baskets are made.

Since there are no published accounts of the tribe, or only spotty or inadequate ones, he depends more on his eyes and his ears than upon books. Compared with the average sociologist, he is almost illiterate. The time that the sociologist spends in the library, the anthropologist spends in the field. Moreover, his seeing and his listening take on a special character. The ways of life he observes are so unfamiliar that it is next to impossible to interpret them through his own values. He cannot analyze in terms of the things he had decided in advance were important, because everything is out of pattern. It is easier for him to view the scene with detachment and relative objectivity just because it is remote and unfamiliar, because he himself is not emotionally involved. Finally, since the language has to be learned or interpreters found, the anthropologist is compelled to pay more attention to deeds than to words. When he cannot understand what is being said, the only thing he can do is devote himself to the humble but very useful task of noting who lives with whom, who works with whom in what activities, who talks loudly and who talks softly, who wears what when.

A perfectly legitimate question at this point would be: "Well, perhaps anthropologists in working in nonliterate societies did happen to pick up some skills that have given good results when applied to studies of our society. But in the name of everything, why, if you anthropologists are really interested in modern life, do you keep on bothering with these inconsequential little tribes?"

The anthropologist's first answer would be that the life ways of these tribes are part of the human record and that it is his job to see that these things get recorded. Indeed anthropologists have felt this responsibility very keenly. They have felt that they had no time to write general books when each year saw the extinction of aboriginal cultures that had not yet been described. The descriptive character of most anthropological literature and the overpowering mass of detail are to be traced to the anthropologist's obsession with getting down the facts before it is too late.

The traditional scientific attitude is that knowledge is an end in itself. There is much to be said for this point of view. Probably the applications that have been made possible by pure science have been richer and more numerous because scientists did not narrow their interest to fields that promised immediate practical utility. But in these troublous times many scientists are also concerned about the social justification of their work. There is such a thing as scientific dilettantism. It is nice that a few rich museums can afford to pay a few men to spend their lives in the intensive study of medieval armor, but the life careers of some anthropologists do remind one of Aldous Huxley's character who consecrated his existence to writing the history of the three-tined fork. Society cannot afford, in a period like the present, to support many specialists in highly esoteric studies unless they show promise of practical usefulness. Fortunately, the detailed study of primitive peoples falls into the useful category.

I may decide that what is really needed is knowledge of urban communities like Cambridge, Massachusetts. But, in the present situation of social science, a host of practical difficulties confront me. In the first place, to do a comprehensive job, I should need more collaborators than could be paid for under existing arrangements for the support of research on human behavior. Then I should have to ask: in terms of actual human interactions, where does Cambridge leave off and where do Boston, Watertown, and Somerville begin? Many people living in Cambridge grew up in different parts of the United States and in foreign countries. I should always be in danger of attributing to conditions in Cambridge ways of behavior which in fact should be explained as results of upbringing in far-distant places. Finally, I should be dealing with dozens of different biological stocks and mixtures between them. L. J. Henderson used to say, "When I go into my laboratory and try an experiment in which there are five or six unknowns, I can sometimes solve the problem if I work long enough. But I know better than even to try when there are twenty or more unknowns."

This is not to argue that it is useless to study Cambridge at the present time. Far from it. Certain small problems can be defined and answers of a high degree of validity obtained. Something of scientific and practical benefit could be learned about the workings of the whole community. The issue is not: Shall the scientific student of man work in our own society *or* among primitives? It is rather: Does the anthropologist by working in the simpler scene isolate certain crucial factors which can then be investigated more effectively in the complex picture? The right questions to ask and the right techniques for getting the answers to them can best be discovered by work on smaller canvases, that is, in more homogeneous societies that have been by-passed by civilization.

The primitive society is the closest to laboratory conditions the student of man can ever hope to get. Such groups are usually small and can be studied intensively by few people at slight expense. They are ordinarily rather isolated so that the question does not arise as to where one social system begins and another ends. The members of the group have lived their lives within a small area and have been exposed continually to the pressure of the same natural forces. They have had an almost identical education. All of their experiences have much more in common than is the case with members of complex societies. Their ways of life are comparatively stable. Commonly there is a high degree of biological inbreeding so that any member of the society chosen at random has about the same biological inheritance as any other. In short, many factors can be regarded as more or less constant, and the anthropologist is free to study a few variables in detail with real hope of ferreting out the connections between them.

This can be made clearer by an analogy. How much would we know today of human physiology if we had been able to study the physiological processes only among human beings? The fact that we would have been blocked at every turn is due partly to the humanitarian limitations we place upon using humans as guinea pigs, but it must also be traced to the complexity of the human organism. There are so many variables that it would have been enormously difficult to isolate the decisive ones had we not been able to study physiological processes in simpler settings. A reflex could be speedily isolated in the frog, then studied with more complications in the simpler mammals. Once these complexities had been mastered, it was possible to go successfully to monkeys and apes and then to mankind. This is, of course, the essential method of science: the method of successive steps, the method of going from the known to the unknown, from the simple to the ever more and more complex.

Nonliterate societies represent the end results of many different experiments carried out by nature. Groups that have largely gone their way without being absorbed in the great civilizations of the West and the East show us the variety of solutions which men have worked out for perennial human problems and the variety of meanings that peoples attach to the same and to different cultural forms. Contemplation of this vast tableau gives us perspective and detachment. By analyzing the results of these experiments, the anthropologist also gives us practical information on what works and what doesn't.

A nonanthropologist, Grace de Laguna, has luminously summed up the advantages of a view of ourselves from the anthropological angle:

> It is indeed precisely with regard to standards of life and thought that the intimate studies of primitive peoples have cast more light on human nature than all the reflections of sages or the painstaking investigations of laboratory scientists. On the one hand, they have shown concretely and vividly the universal kinship of mankind, abstractly recognized by the Stoics and accepted as an article of Christian faith; on the other hand, they have revealed a wealth of human diversity and a variety of human standards and of modes of feeling and thinking hitherto unimagined. The horrid practices of the savage have shown themselves to the intimate and unprejudiced study of the field ethnologist at once more amazing and more understandable than romance had painted them. The wider sympathy with men and the deeper insight into human nature which these studies have brought have done much to shake our complacent estimate of ourselves and our attainments. We have come to suspect that even our own deepest beliefs and our most cherished convictions may be as much the expression of an unconscious provincialism as are the fantastic superstitions of the savage.

From The Book of the Eskimos

by Peter Freuchen

The Eskimos have for centuries been the object of much interest and admiration from all peoples of the civilized world, and the reason for this is obvious: Alone of all primitive people, they live permanently in the inhospitable Arctic zone, and have there established a way of life and an economic culture independent of many things millions consider necessary for survival. To put it briefly, the Eskimos possess an extraordinary hardiness which enables them to live where nobody else can.

It is true that there are other people living in the Arctic, as for instance the Samoyeds and Chukchi of northern Siberia, but these are seasonal dwellers who live on the Arctic tundras and coasts in summer, but retire to the forests of the temperate zone in winter. Only the Eskimos confine themselves to the Arctic the year round, and they alone have adapted themselves completely to it. . . .

Love and Marriage Among the Eskimos

Life is so hard for the Eskimos, and the different chores they must perform are so specialized, that each man must always have one woman to take care of his skins, his clothes, and his food. Through necessity as well as an ancient custom, which in many cases amounts to a taboo, all work is rigorously divided between man and woman. Even so, both of them have plenty to do.

The man has the more heroic tasks of fighting the polar bear, harpooning the fierce walrus, or outsmarting the tricky seal. Sometimes he must endure the long wait at the seal's blowhole for many hours during the cold nights. In the springtime, when the sun is in the sky day and night, the man must seek out every opportunity to catch game. Not only must daily

The late Peter Freuchen was a Dane who achieved fame as a trader, explorer, and writer. He spent a large part of his life among the Eskimos, and probably knew them better than any other white man.

needs be taken care of, but meat caches must be built and filled for the coming winter. So when the weather permits, he hunts continually, sleeping and resting as little as possible, wandering around in the open with the dog team.

The woman with her children and her needlework stays at home. She has to scrape the animal skins and prepare them while they are still fresh. She sews the clothes of the entire family, cooks, and keeps the house warm. Also, meat must be laid out on the sunbaked rods and dried for traveling provisions. . . . If a man loses his wife, he is immediately destitute. He can no longer claim a household of his own, and has to move into the home of a married couple to have his clothes dried and mended, his boots softened by a woman's chewing the soles, and his stockings turned inside out every night, and to be supplied with fresh dried grass in the morning. In return for taking care of his needs in such a case, his hosts claim all his catch.

On the other hand, a woman who loses her husband, and who is not taken to wife by another hunter, is reduced to the state of a beggar. She must live on the mercy of other people, only now and then trapping a fox or fishing some trout. She has never learned hunting since, Eskimos believe, "the great animals would be offended and go away from our shores if they were hunted by women." And if the woman happens to lose her husband during travel in desolate places, she frequently starves to death along with all her children.

Thus man and woman stick together as a close unit, and the woman's work is considered just as essential as the man's. This of course is not official; the man is reputed the stronger one, and his physical prowess makes him feel far superior. To regard a woman as having anything to say would make a man ridiculous, and he never lowers himself to mention his wife when he is out hunting with his fellows. . . . The fact remains that man and woman are indispensable to each other; they form a basic economic unit. Consequently, marriage between Eskimos is usually a matter of mutual interest and sheer necessity rather than of love in the sense in which we use the term. On the other hand, married people are generally very devoted to each other and as a rule remain faithful to each other throughout life. But Eskimo love for—or rather devotion to—each other has very little to do with sex. It is considered rather ludicrous if a man can find pleasure in only one woman; as for the woman, it is considered a great honor if she is desired by many men and can give them pleasure. For this reason, Eskimos have never understood why white people put so much significance on their so-called *wife-trading*. . . .

When an Eskimo goes on a hunting trip, it is essential to his success that he take a woman along with him. When I drove with Eskimos from Thule across to Ellesmereland to hunt musk oxen, in my earlier days, women were absolutely essential as traveling partners. For musk oxen are hunted early in the spring when it is still cold; and it was very practical, when we came to the place where we intended to camp during the hunt, to build an igloo and install women to make it habitable, if not comfortable. When we returned from the hunt to get food and rest, they would have ice chopped and melted for fresh water, and the igloo was warmed by their blubber lamps. Further, they had dry stockings, mended mittens, and other clothes completely ready. And if we were lucky enough to bring in the raw skins, they stretched them on a frame, scraped them, and dried them. In this manner, we were able to bring thirty or forty large musk-ox skins home on our sleds after each trip.

If, however, we had been alone, we would have had to stop hunting early at night to return to the igloo to light our fires, melt ice for water, and boil meat. We would have had to bring spare boots and mittens from home, as there would be no time for drying them. The musk-ox hides could not be scraped or thawed out; they would have had to be brought home raw and frozen, and we could have carried only ten or so in our sleds, as they weigh so much more in that condition.

Now perhaps a man intends to go musk-ox hunting, but his wife is unable to go along. She might be advanced in pregnancy or have a very small baby, or she might be sick. In such a case, the problem is solved by leaving her with a neighbor, who graciously consents to let his wife go along on the hunting trip. Another case might be that a woman wants to visit some relatives far away, and for some reason or other her husband has other plans. It might then be arranged that she go with some other man who is headed that way—provided that this other man will leave his wife behind to do the housework. . . .

I myself, during one of my first visits to Thule, had occasion to appreciate this Eskimoic tact. I was expecting my Danish girl friend, Michella, to join me. But the ship that summer brought no Michella, only one of those clumsy letters it is as embarrassing to write as to receive. She was not coming, and I hardly found life worth living any more. But then, some weeks later, I was active again, trying to forget as I made plans for a trip up north to hunt walrus. An Eskimo, Tatianguaq, came and wanted a word with me.

"It appears that you are without woman's companionship," he said. "My poor wife wishes to see her family up north. It is not impossible that one would benefit a little bit from her company. It is supposed that she knows the best way to travel; she can help set up camp and dry clothes. Also, a man's pleasure at night is increased by the presence of a sensuous woman in his sleeping skins!"

In this modest way, Tatianguaq let me know that he knew my problem and wanted to help. There was of course another side to the coin: he had for some time been having a little difficulty with Ivalu, his beautiful wife. She had been on board Peary's ship and there learned to like the white men's form of courtship. A temporary separation might set matters straight. As for me, I was more than ever—due to my keen disappointment—feeling akin to these kind and carefree people, and I was ready to adopt their way of life. So Ivalu and I started north. . . .

Visiting a wife behind her husband's back just isn't done. It should be clearly understood that, in each case of wife trading or wife borrowing, it is strictly an arrangement made between the men. The wives have little or nothing to say in the matter. The man who dares to visit a woman without her husband's express consent not only delivers a mortal insult to the husband, he also becomes an eyesore to his tribesmen, being guilty of a serious breach of all good rules. His behavior is related with the utmost contempt and, in many cases, it calls for decisive action by the husband. In order to save his honor, he might drag his wife out and beat her in public—whether the affair be her fault or not. He might seek out her paramour and take his revenge upon him. Among some Canadian Eskimos, fist fights take care of the matter, but in other tribes—as the Polar Eskimos —blood revenge was quite common, and everybody would consider such a killing justified when there was no other way of saving the husband's honor.

But, conversely, it could also be a dangerous insult to a man to refuse to partake of his wife's embraces when he had clearly indicated that it was permitted. It was like saying that what the house had to offer was not good enough. . . .

The Eskimos: Past and Present

I traveled in and out of the Arctic for almost three quarters of a century, though when I look back on it, this does not seem like a long time. Nevertheless, I can see the tremendous change that took place during these years. I experienced the advance of civilization and I saw the natives slowly accept the ideas of the outside world—for the arctic regions are by no means immune to progress and new developments.

It has been maintained over and over again by certain thoughtless people that the native man was far better and happier before he met the white man with his inventions and tools. I have seen any number of films and read countless books with the same theme, whether the native in question was a Negro or a Polynesian, an Indian or an Eskimo. The story is always the same: The native tribe was happy and carefree, innocent and well off until the evil day when the white men arrived. That day marked the beginning of their inevitable doom. They were torn from their native Eden, infested with disease and vices, and soon the tribe broke up and perished.

I have never been able to understand why the white man should insist on seeing himself in such an unfavorable light. I know from personal experience that this picture is entirely wrong in the case of the Eskimos and the Indians in the Far North. I know them both quite well, and I have a certain right to speak about them, for I am one of the last civilized men who met the Eskimos when they still lived like men in the Stone Age. In Committee Bay I have met Eskimos who had no knives. The only cutting instruments they had were made of old metal straps from barrels. For flensing they used sharp stones or knives made of bone. They were walrus hunters, and it would take them days to flense and cut up one single walrus. While they worked with their miserable tools, hundreds of walrus would pass by their camp. If they had had steel knives, as they do now, the whole job could be done in half an hour and they could get out again while the hunting was still good and maybe get a whole winter's supply in a day or two.

I have gone reindeer hunting with the natives on the tundra in the Northwest Territories. Hunting is not easy on the tundra—the endless, barren, flat land where there is no rock, no bush, nothing to hide behind. When the reindeer stay together in herds, they are safe, because they have a clear view in all directions. To get at them, one has to sneak up to them from a great distance, against the wind. After a while one has to crawl on the snow, and finally one has to lie down flat on the stomach without moving and wait until the animals come close enough for the range of the weapons at hand. The reindeer have very poor eyes, but an excellent sense of smell. They get no clear pictures of fairly close objects as long as these are stationary. As long as the Eskimos don't move, the animals may come within their range, but if they make one careless movement the reindeer are gone.

The Eskimos had a very hard job in the days when they did their hunting with bow and arrow. In winter they might wait for days and days until the animal came close enough for the very limited range of their arrows, and they often had to return empty-handed—not because they were lazy or careless but simply because their primitive weapons did not go far enough and their aim could never be sure enough. Today the Eskimos all have rifles. They can get more meat, more furs, more supplies of every kind. Their life is more secure and less frustrating than before. . . .

Or consider the importance of the humble match. Like most people, I have read countless stories of explorers running out of matches. But that never bothered them as long as the natives were there to help them. In a short while the natives—whether Indian, Eskimo, or whatever—would provide a roaring fire by rubbing sticks of wood together. The people who write such stories have obviously never been the ones who were compelled to make fire in this primitive way.

I have tried it myself. During the first world war I was the only white man living in Thule. From Thule we made long trips across Smith Sound to Ellsmereland, where it was then still permitted to go hunting. . . .

On one such trip we ran out of matches. We all knew the old method of making fire by rubbing two sticks of wood together, but we had no idea just how slow and difficult it was. Two men sit facing each other, pulling as fast as possible the string which is attached to the vertical stick grinding back and forth in the same spot on the horizontal stick. There must be no slackening of the speed. If the arm gets tired, which it always does, and one stops for a second or two for a rest or to change position, the sticks cool off, and one has to start all over again. If there is the least breath of wind it is impossible to produce a flame, the whole struggle has been in vain, and in the end one eats frozen, raw meat for supper and breakfast. No, it's a pretty good thing to be able to pull a box of matches out of a pocket and get fire at any time.

Think of the old cooking utensils made of stone. One needed time and patience to prepare food in those old pots. Among the Eskimos, there grew up a class of people whose job it was to tell stories and make the impatiently waiting people forget the food which never boiled.

The Hudson Bay Company has done more than any other company in the world to make life simpler and easier for the people living in the Far North. True enough, I have heard stories about the Hudson Bay Company exploiting the "innocent" native population, but such tales always proved to originate with people who had no personal knowledge of the facts. Such accusations have never been made by people who have been able to observe the actual situation objectively. . . . The Hudson Bay Company moved into remote regions where nobody else could or would invest capital, and the name became synonymous with security and comfort to the natives. The establishment of regular trade routes meant a revolution in the arctic form of life. One of the results was an improvement in health which an outsider can hardly believe. Those who talk so glibly of conditions in the Arctic, after spending a month or two there, have virtually no idea how vastly the life of the Eskimos has changed since the arrival of the Hudson Bay Company.

I want to stress that it is the *regular* exchange of trade which has been so important. There have been many so-called "free traders" who had no scruples in their dealings with the natives. They grabbed what they could, not caring that the Eskimos might be much worse off than before once the trader left, once they could no longer get what they had learned to depend on for their comfort. When a native has had some tool which made life a little easier, it is much harder for him to do without it than if he had never known anything but his old primitive way of life. . . . Perhaps a true-life story will show better than many words what the "native bliss" really was like.

There used to be a small settlement of Eskimos on an island called Igloolik in the eastern part of the Fury and Hecla straits. The place is a veritable wildlife paradise. There were seals and walrus and caribou. In spring there is an overabundance of eggs. There are polar bears and foxes and wolverines, and plenty of salmon in the lakes. I don't think I have seen better hunting any other place in the world. No wonder these Eskimos settled there permanently.

The following events took place there in 1921, when there was no such thing as commercial flying in the Arctic. Motorboats could not get through the heavy ice of Hudson Bay, and no regular traffic by sea was possible. Igloolik was nearly inaccessible, but a wonderful place for people who felt independent of civilization and trading posts.

Once in a long while these Eskimos made a shopping expedition to Fullerton, the nearest place to the south, or up to Ponds Inlet, where a Hudson Bay post had just been established. In previous years the natives had sometimes gone up to the eastern tip of Bylot Island to wait for the whalers, but it was a hazardous undertaking. Sometimes the whalers did not show up and sometimes they could just be seen far out at sea while ice kept them from approaching the coast. By then the Eskimos might have to wait until the next year before they could cross Baffin Island. The Eskimos said that the establishment of the new post at Ponds Inlet meant the opening of a whole new era of security, since they could go there, do their shopping, and return again, all in the span of one year.

They had more fox furs than they knew what to do with in Igloolik, but they had none of the things they could get in exchange for their furs. At last a group of the Eskimos on the island decided to make the long trip to Ponds Inlet. There was great excitement in the village, since they would be gone a whole year. Their friends and neighbors gave them commissions of every kind as they prepared for the long journey by sewing new clothes—a strenuous job, since sewing needles were among the most sorely needed objects. As soon as daylight was beginning to return to Igloolik after the dark winter, the travelers set out on the road to Ponds Inlet. Their equipment was very primitive and they were all used to spending their days on dog sleighs and their nights in a snowhut, so they made slow progress. One of the things they had to do without was wood for making sleighs. In the village there were two wooden sleighs, but since the traveling party were going to a region where they could get more wood, they had decided to let their friends who stayed behind keep the precious sleighs.

These sleighs were made in the same ancient way it has always been done in these treeless regions. First several reindeer skins were tightly rolled together. Next the long, narrow roll was pushed through a hole in the ice of a lake and left in the water until it was thoroughly soaked. Finally the dripping roll was put on the ice, covered with heavy ice-blocks and left there to freeze in the right shape. Soon the Eskimos had two stiff, strong —even if somewhat heavy—runners which would last the whole trip.

For crossbars they used large salmon which had been frozen in the same way, or walrus meat which had been cut to the right size and shape. The result was not very snappy-looking, but a useful and serviceable sleigh with the extra advantage that it contained spare supplies for an emergency. And they set off happily with these sleighs for the long run across Baffin Island.

The island is very well suited for this primitive means of transportation, except for some large stretches of deep, soft snow which slow down the sleighs. The people from Igloolik made fairly good progress, but not as rapid as expected, since the snow was exceptionally deep that year. They didn't mind, however, since they were in no great hurry. And building their snowhuts at night was an easy and quick job with all that soft snow.

One night they were all asleep in their warm huts when something which is feared above all the hard arctic winter took place outside in the darkness: the mild weather set in. Most people who have traveled in the Arctic know this phenomenon, which usually takes place twice during each winter. In the bitter cold a warm wind will suddenly send the temperature above the freezing point, and everything starts dripping. Clothes get soaking wet, and a great part of one's food may get ruined. It is most unpleasant when it occurs, but to the Eskimos from Igloolik it was much worse than unpleasant. It spelled disaster for all of them.

In their three huts they were sound asleep, oblivious of the outside world. But their dogs did not sleep, they knew what was happening. They had been let loose to keep them from eating their harness. Every evening the Eskimos put sleighs, harness and all the supplies on top of very high snowpiles, beyond the reach of the constantly hungry dogs. The people slept. They were exhausted from a long day's driving; a change of weather was not enough to wake them up. They did not know that their sleighs were thawing, getting soft, slipping off the snow. In their sleep they had no idea of the terrible thing that took place outside. In no time the hungry animals had eaten the sleighs—runners, crossbars, and all. The food supplies, harness, clothes—all went the same way. The Eskimo dog knows how to hurry when unexpected food comes within his reach.

The Eskimos did not wake up until some of them felt the roof of the igloo sinking. Then it was too late. The dogs had left nothing. There was no food, there was no means of transportation left. And as their bad luck would have it, the mild weather had met them in a district where the hunting was exceptionally poor. There was hardly a chance of catching anything to eat—and no possibility of going on without sleighs.

They were soon tortured by hunger. The dogs were rationed, eaten one by one, but they did not last long. The Eskimos ate all the clothes they could do without. Any hope they may have had of being rescued in time rapidly dwindled. Soon death claimed its first victim, then another. The living ate the flesh of their dead friends. Eskimos are not cannibals, but they may be forced to commit acts beyond human judgment.

Nobody knew of the fate which befell the lonely travelers. Nobody expected to see them again until nearly a year had passed, and there was no cause for alarm. Even if people in the outside world had known what had happened to them, there was little chance of coming to their aid in time.

Later on in spring, when the sunshine lasted all through the night, an Eskimo named Patlok crossed the island with his wife. He was a prosperous man, had his own beautiful wooden sleigh, and could visit the trading post every other year if he wanted to. It was Patlok who discovered the lost travelers. One morning his dogs behaved strangely. After a great deal of sniffing in the air, they changed their course and began speeding up. Patlok thought they would lead him to a flock of reindeer or some other game, and let them follow their own course.

At last he found a tiny, broken-down snowhut. And he found two women. At first he could hardly believe that they were human beings. They were too weak to move and they could hardly talk. They had eaten their clothes until there was hardly a thread left on them. He carried them into his sleigh and began questioning the stronger of the two, a woman called Atakutaluk.

"Where are the others?" Patlok asked.

"One does not know," was the answer.

After a long pause Patlok asked again, "Have human beings been eaten here?"

"One knows nothing," the old woman answered, but she pointed to a big snowpile behind the remnants of an igloo. When Patlok looked further, he found the bones of the other people, those who had starved to death. Some of the larger bones had been split in two to remove the marrow.

Patlok offered food to the two women, but he warned them. After a long period of starvation, the sufferer actually feels no pain any more, and it takes quite an effort to swallow food. Once the starved person begins eating again, the pains come, and then the dreadful hunger returns. The first few days are very critical, since it is easy to eat more than the starved system can take.

Atakutaluk was a wise and strong woman; she controlled her hunger, eating only a little at a time and not very often. But the other woman could not resist the temptation. She jumped on the food, and when the others warned her against overeating she cried and screamed for more food. Patlok had food enough, and he did not have the strength to keep it away from her. But she did not eat for long. After a short while she began vomiting and complained of sharp pains in the stomach. She did not gain much from her rescue for she died within a few days.

Atakutaluk, who knew the art of self-control, lived to a ripe old age. It was she who told me of the whole tragedy.

What can one say to a woman calmly describing such a disaster? I listened to her and found no words. But Atakutaluk was an Eskimo. She saw that I was deeply shocked when she told of eating her husband and her three children. It is considered very impolite for an Eskimo to "remove the smile from the face of a guest," so Atakutaluk hastened to reassure me. She had found herself a new husband, she told me. And she had had a child with him and was the stepmother of his other two children, so she no longer had any debt to the "Great Being."

Such a story was not unique in the old days. A great many similar tragedies took place among the Eskimos, but they do not happen any more. The arctic life is growing ever more secure and the population is increasing year by year. Eskimos in places like Igloolik all have wooden sleighs these days, and a pot made of stone is only a curiosity. There is hardly an Eskimo who does not have the most modern tools and weapons.

. . . I have seen many things in the Arctic and I have done many things there, and my body is tired, yearning for rest and relaxation. But my soul is still young and more adventurous than ever at the sight of the marvelous developments that are taking place in Hudson Bay, Greenland, and Alaska. The hope I have always entertained for the backward and under-privileged people of these places has been greatly satisfied in what I notice each time I visit my friends anew. Far from being discouraged at the changes I see and yearning for a return to times that are past, I look forward to the day when the Arctic will help man to realize his dreams of making the earth a better and more happy place in which to live.

6

SOCIAL CHANGE AND
SOCIAL PROBLEMS

SOCIETIES, like all other phenomena of nature, are in incessant change. What is the direction of social change? Are we moving toward some desired goal, or toward catastrophe? Does social change possess form and regularity, depending upon certain laws of change? Can the causes and sources of social change be discerned and, perhaps, be controlled for the great benefit of mankind? These are questions Kingsley Davis considers. They are most important questions. Since men are social creatures, social change means change in people—to change society is to change man.

The rapidity of social change in modern times raises the important problem of social adjustment. This is the issue which concerns Ogburn. His thesis is that the various parts of modern culture are not changing at the same rate, some are changing rapidly, some more slowly. Since the various parts of culture are interdependent, the result is often seen in dislocation, maladjustment of parts, and social problems. Material conditions and material culture change most rapidly, while the non-material, the adaptive part of culture often changes slowly—thus a lag develops which may last for years.

12

The Meaning of Social Change

by Kingsley Davis

To see a picture of the strange clothes that were worn only yesterday, to read the history of the queer customs and ideas that once were current, to hear predictions of the marvels that are destined for tomorrow—to do these things is to realize the incessant changeability of human society. Individuals may strive for stability and security; societies may foster the illusion of permanence; the quest for certainty may continue unabated and the belief in eternity persist unshaken, yet the fact remains that societies, like all other phenomena, unremittingly and inevitably change.

This fact of change has long fascinated the keenest minds and still poses some of the great unsolved problems in social science. What, for instance, is the *direction* of social change? Is it toward some goal, toward some catastrophe, or toward mere extinction? . . . What is the *form* of social change? Is it more rapid now than in the past, and will it be more rapid in the future? . . . What is the *source* of social change? Is it a matter of borrowing or a matter of independent invention? . . . What is the *cause* of social change? Is it some key factor that explains all change, a prime mover that sets everything else in motion, or is it many different factors operating together? . . . And finally, what is necessary for the *control* of social change? Can we regulate and guide it in the direction of our heart's desire? . . . These are the tantalizing questions—tantalizing not only because of their difficulty but because of their human significance. Since men are social creatures, social change means human change. To change society is to change man.

For obvious reasons social change has been a perennial happy hunting ground for spurious theories and illogical beliefs. It has been approached too often with the reformer's zeal and with a philosophical or religious question uppermost. The strictly scientific literature on it is scant indeed, and none too good. If the following discussion can clarify some of the issues and suggest a few truths, it will have achieved its purpose. Necessarily social change has been discussed in various connections in early

From Kingsley Davis, *Human Society,* pp. 621–631. Copyright 1948 and 1949 by The Macmillan Company, and used with their permission.
Kingsley Davis is Professor of Sociology at the University of California, Berkeley.

parts of the book. The present chapter aims merely to state the problem and define the major theoretical issues.

SOCIAL VERSUS CULTURAL CHANGE.   By "social change" is meant only such alterations as occur in social organization—that is, the structure and functions of society. Social change thus forms only a part of what is essentially a broader category called "cultural change." The latter embraces all changes occurring in any branch of culture, including art, science, technology, philosophy, etc. as well as changes in the forms and rules of social organization.

To illustrate, let us cite on the one hand the rise of organized labor in capitalistic society and, on the other, the occurrence of systematic sound shifts in the Indo-European languages. The first represents a basic alteration in the relation of employer and employee, and has had repercussions throughout the economic and political organization of modern civilization. The second is just as definitely a change. The sound shifts in the various languages after separation from the original and long extinct Aryan mother-tongue were strikingly regular and parallel, so that the philologists could reduce them to a few basic principles such as Grimm's Law. But this phonetic change neither arose from nor affected the social organization of the peoples who spoke the Indo-European languages. It was purely a linguistic phenomenon, a cultural rather than a social change.

Cultural change is thus much broader than social change. Since our interest is focused on the narrowed topic we shall not become involved in such matters as the evolution of phonetic sounds, the history of art forms, the transition of musical styles, or the development of mathematical theory. Of course, no part of culture is totally unrelated to the social order, but it remains true that changes may occur in these branches without noticeably affecting the social system. Sociologically, therefore, we are interested in cultural change only to the extent that it arises from or has an effect on social organization. We are not interested in it for itself apart from social change.

CHANGE VERSUS INTERACTION.   From the standpoint of atomic physics an iron bar is not quiescent. Instead its protons and electrons are constantly active. Yet the shape of the bar remains relatively fixed, altering only when it is smelted, bent, rusted, broken, welded, etc. Similarly the individuals in a society are constantly interacting, yet the structure governing such activity—the forms and rules of interaction—may remain relatively stable for long periods of time. The activity itself should not be confused with changes in the structure, which alone comprise social change.

For example, the principle of monogamous wedlock has remained fixed in American law from the beginning. Marriage has changed in many ways but not in this one particular. Yet many millions of Americans have entered wedlock under this principle and have left it through death or divorce. Each such step has meant an important change to them as indi-

normative what ought to be
positive beh. what is.

viduals but not a change in the social order. Just as linguistic change does not refer to the activity of speaking but rather to the forms of speech, so social change does not refer to social interaction but rather to the normative conditions of interaction.

Certainly there is a close connection between social interaction and social change, for it is mainly through interaction that change comes about. The development of organized labor occurred, in part at least, because of strains in the interaction of employer and employees under the old system. In other words interaction is possible because there is a structure, and change is possible because there is interaction.

The distinction between interaction and change may seem elementary, but in practice it is not always clear. For instance, where does the phenomenon called "the circulation of the elite" belong? Pareto, who has discussed this phenomenon at great length, seems to believe he is discussing social change. Yet if the conditions by which the elite are recruited remain the same, there is no social change but merely social circulation or "metabolism." If, on the other hand, as Pareto seems to intimate, the displacement of one elite by another alters the social structure, it is social change—even though it may occur in cycles.

SHORT- VERSUS LONG-RUN CHANGES.   It seems wise to emphasize fairly long periods—generations or centuries at least—in first approaching the topic of social change. This helps to eliminate the confusion between interaction and change, and saves us from too great a preoccupation with the ephemeral present. What seems important today, what seems a vital change, may be nothing more than a temporary oscillation having nothing to do with essential trends. This is what historians mean when they say that time alone can place the events of the day in their true perspective. In any case, in discussing social change, one should specify the length of time one has in mind.

WHOLE SOCIETIES VERSUS PARTS.   Any social system differs in different epochs. Some of its parts may remain virtually stable but as a whole it changes. This fact has led many authors to try to delineate types of societies and to interpret social change as the successive shifting from one type to another. The task has proved extremely difficult, because societies differ in such myriad ways that any typology seems rough and vague. Scholars have been forced to talk about the "spirit," the general "ethos," or the "essence" of one society as against another. The very names they have given the alleged types disclose the nebulous and sometimes metaphorical character of their speculations. For instance Spengler distinguishes "Faustian," "Apollonian," and "Magian" cultures; Sorokin, "Ideational," "Sensate," and "Idealistic"; and Ruth Benedict, "Apollonian" and "Dionysian." MacIver points out that these terms are so indefinite that the same ones are applied to the most advanced societies (e.g. by Spengler) and to the most primitive ones (e.g. by Ruth Benedict). In addition different scholars looking at the same society are apt to characterize it differently, according to which particular traits they emphasize.

Perhaps the analysis of change in the parts of society may throw light on changes in the whole. As we shall see later, the way the different parts of society figure in the process of change is by no means clear, however.

DESCRIPTION VERSUS ANALYSIS. The poorest way to understand social change is simply to recapitulate all past changes. Twenty tomes would not suffice for such recapitulation, nor would any amount of repetition give it relevance.

> Information, no matter how reliable or extensive, which consists of a set of isolated propositions is not science. A telephone book, a dictionary, a cookbook, or a well-ordered catalogue of goods sold in a general store may contain accurate knowledge, organized in some convenient order, but we do not regard these as works of science. Science requires that our propositions form a logical *system*, that is, that they stand to each other in some one or other of the relations of equivalence and opposition already discussed.[1]

If a mere narrative were adequate for an understanding of social change the best means would be a moving picture of everything that happens. This film could then be run off whenever the subject of social change arose. The only trouble would be that showing the picture would take as long as it took the events to happen in the first place. We would have to repeat life in order to understand life.

The study of social change has often tended in the direction of sheer history, with no real light on causation; or, discouraged by the avalanche of facts, it has tended in the direction of sheer generalization, with mere citation of examples instead of systematic proof or disproof. To strike a golden mean requires that the facts be marshalled, organized, and dealt with in terms of theoretical propositions susceptible of verification. Only in this way, by a *method* of analysis, can this kaleidoscopic phenomena of history be reduced to scientific order.

THE RATE OF CHANGE. One must conceive of a balance of opposed forces, some favoring change, others opposing it. To the extent that they cancel each other, stability reigns. To the extent that forces favoring change prevail, a rate of change results.

But the "rate of change" has two different applications according to whether one thinks of whole societies or of parts. In the first application the rate refers to the rapidity of change in different societies or in the same society at different times. Thus modern Europe is commonly believed to have changed more rapidly than Medieval Europe and, in the

---

[1] Morris R. Cohen and Ernest Nagel, *An Introduction to Logic and Scientific Method* (New York: Harcourt, Brace, 1934), p. 128.

nineteenth century, the United States more rapidly than Latin America. In the second application the rate refers to the rapidity of change in various parts of the same society, usually in the same period. Thus it is a disputed question as to whether in Western civilization during the last three centuries, economic and political institutions have changed more rapidly than familial and religous institutions.

No matter in which context, the comparison of rates of change is exceedingly difficult. To begin with, there are few ways of measuring change in an entire society. By what procedure, for example, can one prove statistically that the Roman society of the first century A.D. was changing more or less rapidly than the Greek society of the fifth century B.C.? It seems best to break the problem down into component parts. One may compare the changes in religion in the two places at the specified times, and also the changes in government, kinship, business, and what not. This has the advantage that in each case things of the same order are being compared—government with government, business with business, etc. In the end one may arrive at a tentative summation of the relative rates of change in the two societies during the two periods, although the techniques of measurement in the various fields would be hard to contrive.

When a comparison is made between different parts of society, an important basis of comparability is lost. How can it be proved, for instance, that the replacement of private by public ownership of railroads is a greater or lesser change than the passage of a prohibition amendment, or that the development of air transportation is a greater or lesser change than the spread of college education? It may seem absurd to speak of relative rates of change in such noncomparable matters—like asking if a giraffe moves faster than a cell divides—but it is sometimes done.

It is extremely difficult if not impossible to prove that in fact the rate of change in a particular part of culture is faster than the rate in other parts. On logical grounds we suspect that any such diversity of rate, if it occurs at all, occurs for a very limited time. The notion of "lag" implies that in order to have an "adjusted society" all parts of culture must eventually "catch up" with the most rapidly changing parts; and since a society must be fairly well "adjusted" in order to keep going, the size of the lag cannot grow continually larger. If there were a permanent difference in the rate of change, no matter how small, it would eventually produce a gap that would be intolerably wide. This reasoning suggests that over a long period the rate of change in two different parts of culture cannot be very different. We must conclude, therefore, that comparisons of rates of change between different parts of social organization have at best a dubious validity, and that comparisons between different whole societies, though difficult, may have a better claim to validity.

THE DIRECTION OF CHANGE. Though it appears difficult to say that

within a given period a change from believing in three gods to believing
in one is faster or slower than a change from horse-drawn to motor-drawn
vehicles, one possible way of making the two comparable is to take into
account the direction of change. If the ultimate result is going to be a
belief in six gods, a change from a belief in three to a belief in one is
not speed at all but retrogression. If in the same society the ultimate
vehicle is to be a sun-driven motorcar, a change from horse-powered to
gasoline-powered vehicles may be a step toward that result and therefore "faster" than the other change. Thus changes in different parts of
culture could be compared with respect to the rapidity with which they
approach the eventual result.

In most discussions of social change some direction is assumed. Often,
however, this assumption is not inherent in the facts but is contributed by
the wishes of the observer. The direction is interpreted as tending towards
some goal that the individual would like to see reached, and it is against
this goal (not the actual end-result) that "speed" or "slowness" is measured. Frequently it *is* possible to discern a consistent trend in changes
that have taken place in the past—for example, the trend of modern
technology toward greater productivity. But such a trend may not continue forever. It may reverse itself, in which case there would still be
change but in the opposite direction. Again, the length of time under
discussion must be kept in mind.

Attempting to take account of the direction of change is necessary procedure both in organizing the facts and in arriving at causal principles.
But a trend cannot be extrapolated unless there are logical and empirical
grounds lying outside the given phenomenon for expecting a continuation
of the trend. For instance, the fact that a given population has been growing rapidly does not mean that it will continue to grow at the same rate.
An analysis of the various demographic and social factors affecting population growth may indicate that it will grow even more rapidly or considerably less so. When "factors" are mentioned we are obviously in the
realm of causal analysis, which is fundamental both for a consideration
of rates and for a consideration of direction.

THE FORMS OF SOCIAL CHANGE. Closely linked with the question of
direction is the problem of the *form* of social change. This seemingly
boils down to a single issue—namely, whether change is cyclical or linear.
An extreme statement of the cyclical hypothesis would be that social
phenomena of whatever sort (whether specific traits or whole civilizations) recur again and again, exactly as they were before. An equally extreme statement of the linear hypothesis would be that all aspects of
society change continually in a certain direction, never faltering, never
repeating themselves. Put so baldly, neither of these statements would
prove acceptable to most people. Yet what sort of an answer can be
given? Is there any sort of compromise? Yes, if we confine ourselves to

what is known rather than to the eternal, there is a possible compromise.

It is quite obvious that any trend will show minor fluctuations, for nothing changes at identically the same rate from one year to the next; and it is equally obvious that recurrences will not be absolutely perfect, for nothing returns to exactly its original state. Proponents of the linear or the cyclical view really take refuge in the unknown. They argue that although fluctuations and trends are both observable, social change is "ultimately" one or the other. Their opinions thus become philosophical dogmas rather than scientific hypotheses.

We cannot know anything about *all* of social change. We can know only about the social change that is observable. At best we have reasonably full data concerning a few thousand years of human history, out of millions of past years and no telling how many future ones. Any claim that a mode of change has always persisted and always will persist clearly goes beyond empirical knowledge. The question of what is the ultimate nature of social change is therefore simply a philosophical puzzle that has no place in social science. When we confine ourselves to what is knowable, we find both trends and fluctuations. Indeed, whether a given change is cyclical or linear depends largely on the span of time under consideration. A decline in business appears as a trend if only a few years are taken, whereas in a larger time context it appears as merely one phase of the business cycle.

THE SOURCE OF SOCIAL CHANGE. For a long time a controversy raged in cultural anthropology as to which is the more important, invention or diffusion. Though not quite dead, it is a dying controversy—not because one side is winning but because the question is proving pointless.

The emphasis on diffusion was in the main a protest against the evolutionary point of view, which had implied that culture develops through a series of self-generating stages. The diffusionists pointed out that independent invention occurs with extreme rarity. The fact that a particular society has a given cultural trait is not usually due to its having evolved to that stage, but to the fact that it borrowed the trait from another society. Indeed, by the simple process of borrowing, a primitive society may become civilized within a century or so (as the Maori are doing today in New Zealand) and thus jump across a cultural chasm that took thousands of years to bridge by independent invention.

The diffusionists were correct in their criticism of the extreme evolutionary point of view. Yet they too overstated their case. Some of them went so far as to claim that two similar traits in two different societies could not possibly be due to invention in both places. The civilizations of South and Central America, for example, could not have arisen by themselves, but must have obtained their civilized traits from Egypt by way of India, Java, and Polynesia.

Obviously, the opposition between these two points of view is much

like that between environmentalists and hereditarians, or linear and cyclical theorists.[2]

> As usually happens in the perpetration of scientific fallacies, the error
> has been introduced into the framing of the question. Hence we are
> tempted at first sight to jump to the erroneous answer. The correct reply
> to the . . . question, however, must insist that the very opposition, sharp
> and precise though it appears, between diffusion and invention, is really
> misleading.
>
> Let us inquire, then, what precisely an "invention" is. In the case of
> every modern invention, we know that it is invariably made and re-made
> time after time in different places, by different men along slightly differ-
> ent roads, independently of one another. It is enough to mention the
> famous disputes about the discovery of the infinitesimal calculus, the
> steam engine, the telephone, the turbine, the wireless; the endless priority
> wrangles in science; the difficulties of establishing rights to a patent; and
> so on. The fact is that each invention is arrived at piece-meal, by infinitely
> many, infinitely small steps, a process in which it is impossible to assign
> a precise share to any one worker or still less to connect a definite object
> and a definite idea with a single contribution. In the wireless, for instance,
> the man to whom the invention is popularly ascribed has little more than
> commercialized the already existing practical appliances. The real work
> can be traced back through Righi, Braun, Hertz, Clerk-Maxwell, Faraday,
> Ampere, and so on back to Galvani and Galileo. But these are only the
> summits—illuminated by the flash-light of sensational coincidence and the
> limelight of success as well as by the elevation of their genius. The real
> pathway of ideas and achievements goes through hundreds and thousands
> of humbler workers and laboratory mechanics, and mathematicians and
> engineers who jointly make the final success possible. Thus the invention
> of the wireless can be treated as a single event and ascribed to one man
> or another only after its nature has been completely misconceived.
>
> In the same way "diffusion" turns out to be a complex abstraction, not
> a separate entity. No idea, no practice, no technique ever passed from
> one society to another without some modification being added to it. The
> borrowed culture trait must be somehow modified and adapted so as to
> fit into the existing cultural context. It follows that diffusion and inven-
> tion are always inseparably mixed. To oppose them as if they were mu-
> tually exclusive is to raise a false issue.

[2] Reprinted from *Culture: The Diffusion Controversy* by G. Elliott Smith *et al.*, by
permission of W. W. Norton & Company, Inc. Copyright 1927, 1955, by W. W. Norton & Company, Inc.

13

The Hypothesis of Cultural Lag

by William F. Ogburn

This rapidity of change in modern times raises the very important question of social adjustment. Problems of social adjustment are of two sorts. One concerns the adaptation of man to culture or perhaps preferably the adapting of culture to man. The other problem is the question of adjustments, occasioned as a result of these rapid social changes, between the different parts of culture, which no doubt means ultimately the adaptation of culture to man. This second problem of adjustment between the different parts of culture is the immediate subject of our inquiry.

The thesis is that the various parts of modern culture are not changing at the same rate, some parts are changing much more rapidly than others; and since there is a correlation and interdependence of parts, a rapid change in one part of our culture requires readjustments through other changes in the various correlated parts of culture. For instance, industry and education are correlated, hence a change in industry makes adjustments necessary through changes in the educational system. Industry and education are two variables, and if the change in industry occurs first and the adjustment through education follows, industry may be referred to as the <u>independent variable</u> and education as the <u>dependent variable</u>. Where one part of culture changes first, through some discovery or invention and occasions changes in some part of culture dependent upon it, there frequently is a delay in the changes occasioned in the dependent part of culture. The extent of this lag will vary according to the nature of the cultural material, but may exist for a considerable number of years, during which time there may be said to be a maladjustment. It is desirable to reduce the period of maladjustment, to make the cultural adjustments as quickly as possible.

The foregoing account sets forth a problem that occurs when there is a rapid change in a culture of interdependent parts and when the rates of

From *Social Change* by William Fielding Ogburn. Copyright 1922 by B. W. Huebsch, Inc., 1950 by William Fielding Ogburn. Reprinted by permission of The Viking Press, Inc., New York.

The late William Fielding Ogburn was the Sewell Avery Distinguished Service Professor of Sociology at the University of Chicago.

change in the parts are unequal. The discussion will be presented according to the following outlines. First the hypothesis will be presented, then examined and tested by a rather full consideration of the facts of a single instance, to be followed by several illustrations. Next the nature and cause of the phenomenon of cultural maladjustment in general will be analyzed. The extent of such cultural lags will be estimated, and finally the significance for society will be set forth.

A first simple statement of the hypothesis we wish to investigate now follows. A large part of our environment consists of the material conditions of life and a large part of our social heritage is our material culture. These material things consist of houses, factories, machines, raw materials, manufactured products, foodstuffs and other material objects. In using these material things we employ certain methods. Some of these methods are as simple as the technique of handling a tool. But a good many of the ways of using material objects of culture involve rather larger usages and adjustments, such as customs, beliefs, philosophies, laws, governments. One important function of government, for instance, is the adjustment of the population to the material conditions of life, although there are other governmental functions. Sumner has called many of these processes of adjustment, mores. The cultural adjustments to material conditions, however, include a larger body of processes than the mores; certainly they include the folkways and social institutions. These ways of adjustment may be called, for purposes of this particular analysis, the adaptive culture. The adaptive culture is therefore that portion of the nonmaterial culture which is adjusted or adapted to the material conditions. Some parts of the nonmaterial culture are thoroughly adaptive culture such as certain rules involved in handling technical appliances, and some parts are only indirectly or partially so, as for instance, religion. The family makes some adjustments to fit changed material conditions, while some of its functions remain constant. The family, therefore, under the terminology used here is a part of the nonmaterial culture that is only partly adaptive. When the material conditions change, changes are occasioned in the adaptive culture. But these changes in the adaptive culture do not synchronize exactly with the change in the material culture. There is a lag which may last for varying lengths of time, sometimes indeed, for many years.

An illustration will serve to make the hypothesis more clearly understood. One class of material objects to which we adjust ourselves is the forests. The material conditions of forestry have changed a good deal in the United States during the past century. At one time the forests were quite plentiful for the needs of the small population. There was plenty of wood easily accessible for fuel, building and manufacture. The forests were sufficiently extensive to prevent in many large areas the washing of the soil, and the streams were clear. In fact, at one time, the forests seemed to be too plentiful, from the point of view of the needs of the people. Food and agricultural products were at one time the first need of the people and the clearing of land of trees and stumps was a common undertaking of the community in the days of the early settlers. In some places, the quickest procedure was to kill and burn the trees and plant between the stumps. When the material conditions were like these, the method of adjustment to the forests was characterized by a policy which has been called exploitation. Exploitation in regard to the forests was indeed a part of the mores of the time, and describes a part of the adaptive culture in relation to forests.

As time went on, however, the population grew, manufacturing became highly developed, and the need for forests increased. But the forests were being destroyed. This was particularly true in the Appalachian, Great Lakes and Gulf regions. The policy of exploitation continued. Then rather suddenly it began to be realized in certain centers of thought that if the policy of cutting timber continued at the same rate and in the same manner the forests would in a short time be gone and very soon indeed they would be inadequate to supply the needs of the population. It was realized that the custom in regard to using the forests must be changed and a policy of conservation was advocated. The new policy of conservation means not only a restriction in the amount of cutting down of trees, but it means a more scientific method of cutting, and also reforestation. Forests may be cut in such a way, by selecting trees according to their size, age and location, as to yield a large quantity of timber and yet not diminish the forest area. Also by the proper distribution of cutting plots in a particular area, the cutting can be so timed that by the time the last plot is cut the young trees on the plot first cut will be grown. Some areas when cut leave a land which is well adapted to farming, whereas such sections as mountainous regions when denuded of forests are poorly suited to agriculture. There of course are many other methods of conservation of forests. The science of forestry is, indeed, fairly highly developed in principle, though not in practice in the United States. A new adaptive culture, one of conservation, is therefore suited to the changed material conditions.

That the conservation of forests in the United States should have been earlier is quite generally admitted. We may say, therefore, that the old policy of exploitation has hung over longer than it should before the institution of the new policy. In other words, the material conditions in regard to our forests have changed but the old customs of the use of forests which once fitted the material conditions very well have hung over into a period of changed conditions. These old customs are not only not satisfactorily adapted, but are really socially harmful. These customs of course have a utility, since they meet certain human needs; but methods of greater utility are needed. There seems to be a lag in the mores in regard to forestry after the material conditions have changed.

The foregoing discussion of forestry illustrates the hypothesis which it is proposed to discuss. It is desirable to state more clearly and fully the points involved in the analysis. The first point concerns the degree of adjustment or correlation between the material conditions and the adaptive nonmaterial culture. The degree of this adjustment may be only more or less perfect or satisfactory; but we do adjust ourselves to the material conditions through some form of culture; that is, we live, we get along, through this adjustment. The particular culture which is adjusted to the material conditions may be very complex, and, indeed, quite a number of widely different parts of culture may be adjusted to a fairly homogeneous material condition. Of a particular cultural form, such as the family or government, relationship to a particular material culture is only one of its purposes or functions. Not all functions of family organization, as, for instance, the affectional function, are primarily adaptive to material conditions.

Another point to observe is that the changes in the material culture precede changes in the adaptive culture. This statement is not in the form of a universal dictum. Conceivably, forms of adaptation might be worked out prior to a change in the material situation and the adaptation might be applied practically at the same time as the change in the material conditions. But such a situation presumes a very high degree of planning, prediction and control. The collection of data, it is thought, will show that at the present time there are a very large number of cases where the material conditions change and the changes in the adaptive culture follow later. There are certain general theoretical reasons why this is so; but it is not desirable to discuss these until later. For the present, the analysis will only concern those cases where changes in the adaptive culture do not precede changes in the material culture. Furthermore, it is not implied that changes may not occur in nonmaterial culture while the material culture remains the same. Art or education, for instance, may undergo many changes with a constant material culture. Still another point in the analysis is that the old, unchanged, adaptive culture is not adjusted to the new, changed, material conditions. It may be true that the old adaptive culture is never wholly unadjusted to the new conditions. There may be some degree of adjustment. But the thesis is that the unchanged adaptive culture was more harmoniously related to the old than to the new material conditions and that a new adaptive culture will be better suited to the new material conditions than was the old adaptive culture. Adjustment is therefore a relative term, and perhaps only in a few cases would there be a situation which might be called perfect adjustment or perfect lack of adjustment.

It is desirable, however, not to make the analysis too general until there has been a more careful consideration of particular instances. We now propose, therefore, to test the hypothesis by the facts in a definite case of social change. In attempting to verify the hypothesis in a particular case by measurement, the following series of steps will be followed. The old material conditions will be described, that part of the adaptive culture under consideration will be described, and the degree of adjustment between these two parts of culture shown. Then the changed material conditions and the changed adaptive culture will be defined and the degree of adaptation shown. It is necessary also to show that the unchanged adaptive culture is not as harmoniously adjusted to the new conditions as to the old and not as harmoniously adjusted to the new conditions as is a changed adaptive culture.

7

TECHNOLOGY AND SOCIAL CHANGE

TECHNOLOGICAL CHANGE and mechanization are the most novel and pervasive aspects of our civilization. Every major problem that confronts man today either has its origin in or is strongly affected by technological change. Modern capitalism, important as it is in its effects on social life, may be a mere by-product of the growth of technology. The selection from MacIver and Page well illustrates how profoundly mechanization has altered our mode of life and our habits of thought.

Ever since the beginning of the Industrial Revolution many people have believed that machines, by replacing men, would result in a persistent, long-continued rise of unemployment. Although no such rise has ever occurred, today some writers are sure that modern automation will bring it about. Brozen, however, argues that automation creates more employment than it destroys. At present high wage rates employers can afford to hire the millions of men who now have jobs only because technological progress, including automation, has kept raising the productivity of the average worker. What we need, says Brozen, is still more automation to provide both more jobs and higher standards of living.

14

Technology and Social Change

by Robert M. MacIver and Charles H. Page

Modern Society and the Machine Age

The approach to social change through technology has . . . a particular appeal and significance for our own age. The rapid changes of our society are obviously related to and somehow dependent upon the development of new techniques, new inventions, new modes of production, new standards of living. We live more and more in cities, and "in the city—and particularly in great cities—the external conditions of life are so evidently contrived to meet man's clearly organized needs that the least intellectual . . . are led to think in deterministic and mechanistic terms." [1] *The most novel and pervasive phenomenon of our age is not capitalism but mechanization,* of which modern capitalism may be merely a by-product. We realize now that this mechanization has profoundly altered our modes of life and also of thought.

[1] MECHANIZATION AND SOCIAL CHANGES.   Attitudes, beliefs, traditions, which once were thought to be the very expression of essential human nature, have crumbled before its advance. Monarchy, the divine ordering of social classes, the prestige of birth, the spirit of craftsmanship, the insulation of the neighborhood, traditions regarding the spheres of the sexes, regarding religion, regarding politics and war, have felt the shock. The process, beginning with the external change and ending with the social response, is easy to follow and to understand. Take, for example, the profound changes which have occurred in the social life and status of women in the industrial age. Industrialism destroyed the domestic system of production, brought women from the home to the factory and the office, differentiated their tasks and distinguished their earnings.

From *Society: An Introductory Analysis* by Robert M. MacIver and Charles H. Page, pp. 553–557. Reprinted by permission by Holt, Rinehart and Winston Inc. Copyright 1949 by Robert M. MacIver and Charles H. Page.

Robert M. MacIver is Emeritus Professor of Political Science at Columbia University.

Charles H. Page is Professor of Sociology at Princeton University.

[1] R. E. Park, chapter on "Magic, Mentality, and City Life," in Park and E. W. Burgess, *The City* (Chicago, 1925).

Here is the new environment, and the new social life of women is the response. The rapid transitions of modern civilization offer a myriad of other illustrations.

The swift transitions of our industrial mechanized civilization have not only been followed by far-reaching social changes, but very many of these changes are such as appear either necessary accommodations or congenial responses to the world of the machine. In the former category come the higher specialization of all tasks, the exact time-prescribed routine of work, the acceleration of the general tempo of living, the intensification of competition, the obsolescence of the older craftsmanship, the development, on the one hand, of the technician and, on the other, of the machine operative, the expansion of economic frontiers, and the complicated, extending network of political controls. In the latter may be included the various accompaniments of a higher standard of living, the transformation of class structures and of class standards, the undermining of local folkways and the disintegration of the neighborhood, the breaking up of the old family system, the building of vast changeful associations in the pursuit of new wealth or power, the increasing dominance of urban ways over those of the country, the spread of fashion, the growth of democracy and of plutocracy, the challenge of industrial organized groups, particularly the organizations of labor, to the older forms of authority.

[2] MECHANIZATION AND CHANGES IN VALUES.   With these conditions are bred corresponding attitudes, beliefs, philosophies, A great mass of contemporary social criticism seeks to depict and often to arraign the cultural concomitants of the machine age. Its tenor is generally as follows: Different qualities are now esteemed because the qualities which make for success, for wealth, and for power are different. Success is measured more in pecuniary terms, as possession is more detachable from social and cultural status. A form of democratization has developed which measures everything by units or by quantities and admits no differences in personal values save as they are attached to external goods or are the means of their acquisition. Men grow more devoted to quantity than to quality, to measurement than to appreciation. The desire for speed dominates, for immediate results, for quick speculative advantages, for superficial excitations. The life of reflection, the slow ripening of qualitative judgments, is at a discount. Hence novelty is sought everywhere, and transient interests give a corresponding character to social relationships. The changing interests of civilization absorb men to the relative exclusion of the more permanent interests of culture. Men grow pragmatic in their philosophies. "Things are in the saddle and ride mankind." The mechanistic outlook explains life itself in behavioristic terms, as a series of predetermined responses to successive stimuli. The unity of life is dissipated, since from the mechanistic point of view all things are

means to means and to no final ends, functions of functions and of no values beyond.

[3] DIRECT AND INDIRECT EFFECTS OF TECHNOLOGICAL CHANGE. That the tendencies thus described are at least accentuated by the mechanization both of work and of the means and conditions of recreation is clearly established by a great mass of evidence. It can scarcely be a mere coincidence that in the periods and in the countries of rapid technological advance there should have developed corresponding or congenial ways of thinking and of living. Nevertheless we should be wary of concluding too hastily that social relations are in all important respects predominantly determined by technological changes. This conclusion would hold only if culture also, the values men set before them as ends for which to live, were essentially the product of technology. But culture in turn seeks to direct technology to its own ends. Man may be the master as well as the slave of the machine. He has already rejected many of the conditions that accompanied and seemed to be imposed by the earlier technology of the industrial revolution. He has taken some steps in all civilized countries to place a variety of controls on factory toil, on the squalor of factory towns, on the shoddiness and ugliness of many factory-made goods, on the risks and fatigues of many factory operations. Man is a critic as well as a creature of circumstance.

Therefore we should distinguish between the more direct and less direct social consequences of mechanization or other technological process. Certain social consequences are the inevitable results of technological change, such as a new organization of labor, the expansion of the range of social contacts, the specialization of function, and the encroachment of urban influences on rural life. Other concomitants, not being inevitable conditions of the operation of the new techniques, are more provisional or more precarious, such as the increase of unemployment, the intensified distinction between an employing and a wage-earning class, the heightening of competition, and the prevalence of mechanistic creeds. In the remaining sections of this chapter we shall endeavor to show that the deterministic theories which make technological change the dominant or overruling cause of social change are one-sided or misleading. But first it is well to insist on the positive aspect, and show by citing some recent developments how real and how important an agency of social change is the quest of modern man to discover and to utilize new techniques, new and more efficient methods of accomplishing his ends.

How Technological Advance Initiates Social Change

Every technological advance, by making it possible for men to achieve certain results with less effort or at less cost, at the same time provides new opportunities and establishes new conditions of life. The opportunities, or some of them, are frequently anticipated in the development or exploitation of the new devices; the new conditions of life are in large measure the necessary and unanticipated adjustments to the new opportunities. A few illustrations will bring out the distinction.

[1] NEW AGRICULTURAL TECHNIQUES AND SOCIAL CHANGE. Take, for example, the advance of agricultural technology. The improvements in the breeds of cattle, in the use of fertilizers, in the varieties of seed, in mechanical laborsaving devices, and so forth, have had as their direct objective the increase in the quantity and quality of agricultural production. But as concomitants of the attainment of this objective there have gone changes in farm economy and in the manner of life of the farming household. And beyond these again there have gone changes in the relation of agriculture to industry, migrations from the farm to the city because of the lessened numbers required to supply the agricultural needs of the whole community, the decay or abandonment of marginal farm lands, tendencies to agricultural depression, new struggles for foreign markets and new tariff barriers. And these changes in turn have stimulated new and difficult economic problems. Thus the achievement of the immediate objective of agricultural technology has led by an inevitable nexus to changes of an entirely different order.

[2] ADVANCES IN COMMUNICATION AND SOCIAL CHANGE. Even more far reaching and complex are the social changes that spring from the development of the techniques of communication. For communication is at once a primary condition of social relations and a basis of nearly all other forms of technological advance. The course of civilization has been marked by a constant development of the means of communication, but never so rapidly as in our own days, when electricity is not only being adopted as motive power in place of steam, not only is a factor in the improvement of automobile and airplane, not only makes the motion picture a vast commercial enterprise and television a promising adventure, but also, resuming its distance-annihilating range, becomes in the radio a voice that is heard simultaneously by millions over the face of the earth. The impact of these changes on society is too enormous and too multifarious to be dealt with here except by way of incidental illustration. Every step of technological advance inaugurates a series of changes that interact with others emanating from the whole technological system. The radio, for example, affects a family situation already greatly influenced by modern technology, so that its impetus toward the restoration of leisure enjoyment within the home is in part counteracted or limited by opposing tendencies. Again, the radio combines with other technological changes to reduce the cultural differentiation of social classes and of urban and rural communities. On the other hand, by enabling an individual speaker to address great multitudes, it makes possible the rapid rise of new parties or social movements, provided the broadcasting system is

not itself politically controlled. In the latter event it tends to produce the opposite result, becoming a most powerful agency of propaganda monopolized by the ruling power. This last illustration should serve to show that what we call the "effects" of invention are in large measure dependent variables of the social situation into which they are introduced.

[3] THE CONTROL OF ATOMIC ENERGY AND SOCIAL CHANGE. The most spectacular illustration, however, is that afforded by the epoch-making discovery of a way to make atomic energy serviceable to human objectives. Like so many other discoveries of modern science, this new agency is available equally for destructive or for constructive purposes. As an agent of war it forebodes the most appalling annihilation of all the works of man. As an agent of peace it may ultimately bring an unprecedented era of plenty.

The General Direction of Social Change with Advancing Technology

Bearing in mind the caution contained in the last paragraphs we may still ask whether there is any major direction in which society moves under the continual impact of technological change.

[1] SPECIALIZATION. We have seen that technology itself tends always in the same direction, attaining ever greater efficiency in the performance of *each* of the various functions to which its devices are applied. In doing so it specializes functions more and more, and thus tends to create an ever-increasing division of labor, with whatever social consequences depend thereon. The social significance of this growing division of labor has been given classic treatment by Durkheim, though some of his conclusions, such as that greater liberty and a diminution of class differences are concomitants of specialization, are stated in too sweeping and universal a form. More certain is the correlation between technological advance and a more elaborate social organization with higher interdependence between its parts, greater mobility of the members with respect to location and to occupation, more elaborate systems of laws and of governmental controls, new concentrations both of economic and of political power, greater instability of the institutional order, greater leisure and generally higher standards of living for large numbers. These conditions seem to be directly bound up with growing technological efficiency, and they in turn have further repercussions on every aspect of social life. They also create some extremely important social problems, one being the unbalance of the economic system that accompanies the accelerated processes of technological change. But within our limits we can do no more than suggest some of the immediate social concomitants of technological advance.

[2] THE MODERN SIGNIFICANCE OF THE TECHNOLOGICAL FACTOR. It

is scarcely too much to say that every major problem of modern society is either initiated by or at least strongly affected by technological change. Conflicts between states, as they strive for dominance, for security, or for prosperity, are in no small measure concerned with competing ambitions to secure or control areas rich in oil, coal, or other resources of crucial importance to modern industry. Again, the specialization of functions in a modern economy gives rise to a multitude of organized groups, each of which seeks its own economic advantage and each of which has the power of withholding a service that modern interdependence renders indispensable. On the other hand, these groups are affiliated with or incorporated into massive federations or combinations. These in turn exercise a correspondingly greater power, so that the disputes arising out of their clashing interests sometimes threaten to disrupt the whole social order.

15

Automation: A New Look at an Old Problem

by Yale Brozen

The mathematician who developed much of the logic underlying computer design predicted, in 1949, that we faced "a decade or more of ruin and despair." He forecast wholesale unemployment because automation, he felt, would abolish jobs on an unprecedented scale.[1] Despite his expectations, the number of people gainfully occupied in civilian pursuits increased from 59 million in 1949 to 63 million in 1955.

From Yale Brozen, *Automation and Jobs,* Selected Paper No. 18, pp. 1–11, 18–20 *passim,* Graduate School of Business, University of Chicago. Reprinted by permission of the author and the Graduate School of Business.

Yale Brozen is Professor of Economics at the Graduate School of Business of the University of Chicago, and is internationally known for his work in the economics of technological change.

[1] Norbert Wiener, *The Human Use of Human Beings: Cybernetics and Society* (Boston: Houghton Mifflin Company, 1950), p. 189.

In 1955, a parade of witnesses testified before the Congressional Sub-committee on Automation that intolerable unemployment was in prospect unless automation was used wisely and well. Since 1955, the number of people with jobs has increased from 63 million to 71 million—a record number. In addition, four million people now hold second jobs—an increase of almost two million.

During this period in which the number of civilian job holders increased by twelve million and the number of jobs by 14 million—the period predicted to include "a decade or more of ruin and despair"—real wage rates and per capita income also increased. . . .

In the face of this data, why do some cry that doomsday is coming? What is it about automation that causes alarm? Why is it that workers asked about their attitude toward mechanization feel no threat, yet appear frightened when asked about their feelings toward automation?

The hallmarks of automation, to distinguish it from mechanization or automatic methods, are its sensing, feed-back, and self-adjusting character-istics. Because it senses changing requirements and adjusts without human intervention, it presumably does away with the need for human attendants or human labor. This is very fearful indeed to those who depend upon jobs for their livelihood.

Fear of automation can be traced to four sources. One is based upon the assumption that there is a fixed amount of goods which buyers want. Any new method which enables us to turn out more goods per man-hour will, it is believed, enable us to turn out the fixed amount of goods and services with fewer men. If a man helped by an automatic machine can produce twice as many widgets per hour as he formerly did, then, presumably, only half as many hours of work will be available for each man to do. If work weeks are not shortened, only half as many jobs could, it is asserted, be provided in these circumstances. The President of the United States used this sort of logic when he said "that approximately 1.8 million persons holding jobs are replaced every year by machines."

The second source of fear springs from the idea that automation or cybernation is something more than the latest stage in the long evolution of technology. Automation is said to be so different in degree that it is profoundly different in its effect. Automated machines controlled by computers do not simply augment muscle power as previous machines did. They replace and outperform human intelligence. In the future, machines will not only run machines; they will repair machines, program production, run governments and even rule men. Union leaders will collect no dues and business will have no customers because, supposedly, there will be no production workers required. Human beings, it is believed, will be made as obsolete by these machines as horses were by the tractor and the automobile.

The third source of fear is our greater awareness of the people displaced by automation than of the other unemployed and a greater concern for these people. Among the more than three million unemployed are several thousand persons laid off because their skills are not usable by concerns installing automated processes to replace previously used technology. . . .

A fourth source of fear is the high incidence of joblessness among the unskilled. It is felt that the unskilled are unemployed because automated production reduces the demand for unskilled workers. Any increases in the demand for labor occurring because of automation are believed to be concentrated on highly skilled workers.

Automation causes displacement. Some people do become unemployed because of it, although most firms retrain and place employees in new jobs when eliminating old jobs. However, automation does not create unemployment. The number of jobless men is not greater than it would have been if no automation had occurred.

It may seem paradoxical to argue that automation causes displacement but does not cause unemployment. Many observers point to specific persons unemployed as a result of this phenomenon. They fail, however, to point to the unemployed who found jobs because of automation. They fail to recognize those who would have joined the jobless if new technology had not been developed and applied. . . .

Although automation has displaced some employees, the total number unemployed is smaller today than it would have been without automation, *given the present wage structure.* There are, certainly, some people among the unemployed who would not have been jobless but for these innovations. However, a larger number are among the employed who would not have been but for automation.

We may grant that automation differs from other kinds of technology. Yet, we should not blind ourselves to history to the point of saying it is completely new. . . .

During the eighteenth century, several types of automatic regulators were applied to windmills. An automatic, card-programmed loom was devised by Jacquard over 150 years ago. An automatic flour mill was built in 1741. Eighteenth century steam engines were controlled by governors which had sensing, feedback, and resetting characteristics which are the hallmarks of automation. Despite increasing automation in the last two centuries, employment has risen continually.

In terms of a very recent type of automation, the use of electronic data processing equipment, a United States Department of Labor study of large firms which introduced such equipment concluded that:

> Despite the reduction in labor requirements for the tasks performed by the computers, total employment of the offices as a whole rose. . . . Although the immediate effect of electronic data processing suggests some

retardation in the growth of office employment, particularly part-time work, the experience of some offices suggests the possibility of expanding employment in new areas of office activity to handle information which had previously been uneconomical to acquire.

This experience of increasing office employment despite reduced labor requirements per unit of output is a specific instance of what has been going on generally in our economy. From 1919 to 1962, man-hours required per unit of output in the American economy dropped by 67 per cent, yet total number of jobs rose from 42 million to 68 million. . . .

The primary effect of automation is not a reduction in the number of jobs available. Rather, it makes it possible for us to do many things which otherwise could not and would not be done. Automation enables us to earn larger incomes and lead fuller lives. It will, in the future, literally make it possible to travel to the moon. It saves lives through the aid it gives doctors. By controlling traffic signals in response to traffic flows and reducing traffic congestion, it adds hours to the free time of commuters every week. It helps scientists, with the aid of high-speed data processing, to develop new knowledge that otherwise would not be available in our lifetimes. We are increasing the scale of educational activities because mechanization, automation, cybernation, or whatever we choose to call our new technology, makes it possible to do more than we could formerly. With the coming of automation, men are able to do more and have more. Both sublime and mundane activities are being enlarged.

Types of Jobs Change

Technological change does tend to change the nature of work. We know from experience that automation in the factory turns machine operators into machine tenders and maintainers. This has already occurred in the textile industry, to name one example. Upon walking into the loom room of a modern mill, the first impression is that of a vast space filled with busy machinery and no people in sight. (Yet employment in textile mills totals nearly 900,000 workers.) Controls on individual machines enable one man to supervise a dozen or more looms. The chemical and petroleum refining industries use automatically controlled, continuous processes. (They, too, provide employment on large scale amounting to more than 1,000,000 jobs.) Instead of men running to distant points in a refinery to twist valve wheels, they now monitor instrument panels.

The effect of automation has been to increase the relative number of maintenance men, engineers, office employees, production control specialists, and other non-machine operators that are required. (These are the people the U.S. Census Bureau calls non-production workers.) This is simply a continuation of a trend which has been going on for decades. In 1899, only 7 per cent of the manufacturing industry labor force consisted of persons other than production workers. Today 26 per cent of manufacturing employees are non-production or indirect workers. Since 1939, production worker employment in manufacturing has increased 65 per cent, while that of other workers has increased by over 160 per cent. . . .

In addition to changing the balance among occupations in a given industry such as manufacturing, technological progress is also changing the balance among industries. Only a century ago, fifty out of every one hundred workers toiled on farms producing the nation's supply of food and fiber. Only two to three out of every one hundred workers were producing educational, medical, recreational, and other services which contribute to a richer, fuller, healthier life. Today, the number of workers in these life-enriching occupations is relatively five times as great. Those toiling on farms have been reduced relatively to one-sixth their former number. They now direct machines instead of using animal power and their own muscles. The quality of life has been improved and brute toil has been reduced because technology has increased our incomes to the point where we can afford these services and these machines.

Those who are concerned about unemployment should welcome rather than fear automation. If it were not for the technical advances of the past decade, unemployment, at present wage levels, would be above the astronomical levels of the early 1930's. Many workers would produce so little that employers simply could not afford to hire them at present wage rates. Alternatively, if real wage rates were at levels consistent with full employment using the same technology as that available a decade ago, wage rates would be lower by about $8.00 a week (or 20 cents an hour) than they are now. . . .

If automation creates jobs and raises the productivity of those with jobs sufficiently to make it possible for them to earn more, then why is unemployment among teen-agers now at the 14 per cent level, four times the unemployment rate of adults? Are we faced with a situation in which jobs for the unskilled and the inexperienced are being wiped out by automation?

In this case, the primary cause of unemployment is the over-pricing of many jobs which would normally be filled by inexperienced, unskilled new entrants to the labor force. The unemployment among teen-agers is a consequence of arbitrarily determined wage rates for certain groups of jobs which have caused a contraction of employment opportunities for the unskilled, inexperienced worker. These arbitrarily high rates are set by unions or by minimum wage laws.

The situation of elevators in Chicago provides an example of unemployment caused by arbitrarily determined wage rates. There is a high incidence of unemployment among male juveniles in Chicago. Many of these boys would be happy to accept jobs as elevator operators at $1.25 to $1.50 an hour. The elevator operators' union, however, imposes a minimum wage rate of $2.40 an hour for operators in downtown Chicago buildings. In this circumstance, owners of the buildings find it economic to spend $40,000 per elevator to automate their lifts and make them self-operating. The tax, insurance, depreciation, maintenance, and interest costs of automating an elevator amount to $8,000 per year. It did not pay to automate when two shifts of operators cost only $5,000 per year. The union has driven the two-shift cost of operation to $10,000 per year. The result is elevator automation, a drain of capital from expansion of production where it would provide more jobs, fewer jobs for elevator operators, and problems of unskilled teen-agers finding tasks to keep themselves occupied. The decreased demand for unskilled teen-agers resulting from the high minimum wage rates set in jobs which they might take forecloses the opportunity for the acquisition of personal characteristics and skills which would equip them for more productive, better paying jobs in later years.

CHAPTER

8

POPULATION

WORLD POPULATION is now about three and a quarter billion and is multiplying at the compound interest rate of one-and-three-quarters per cent a year. This is producing an increase of over sixty million human beings a year, and most of this increase is taking place in nations which at present are industrially underdeveloped. In 1900 these countries had less than two-thirds of the world's population, but if current trends continue their proportion will increase to about four-fifths by the year 2000, and at that time total world population will be about 7 billion. Obviously such a rate of growth could not continue indefinitely. But Hauser is optimistic that man can control population growth. He points out that a number of nations have already formulated population policies and are developing programs intended to make sure that the Malthusian checks on population growth—vice, misery, war, and famine—will not operate.

16

The Population of the World: Recent Trends and Prospects

by Philip M. Hauser

Knowledge about population in the past, the present, and the future enables a person to see himself as an element in world population. It provides perspective of one's self in relation to fellow men in the same manner that astronomy provides one with perspective about this earth as an element in the solar system, the galaxy and the universe. Four numbers summarizing the population history of the world help to provide such a perspective.

Although the first complete census of mankind has yet to be taken, it is possible to reconstruct, within reasonable error limits, the estimated population of the world from the end of the Neolithic period (the new Stone Age) in Europe (8000–7000 B.C.). World population at that time is estimated to have been some ten million, and perhaps was as low as five million. At the beginning of the Christian Era the population of the world probably numbered between 200 and 300 million. At the beginning of the Modern Era (1650) world population had reached about 500 million. In 1962 world population totaled three billion. A relatively simple analysis of these numbers discloses that an enormous increase in the rate of world population growth has occurred, especially during the past three centuries.

Man or very close kin to man has been on the face of the earth for perhaps two million years. Although it is not known exactly when Homo sapiens, the present version of man, first appeared, he was much in evidence in Europe something like 25,000 to 30,000 years ago. It is estimated that for the some six hundred thousand years of the Paleolithic Age (the old Stone Age) population growth perhaps approximated .02 per thousand per year. During the three centuries of the Modern Era, population growth increased from about 4 per thousand to 10 per thousand per year

"The Population of the World," by Philip M. Hauser, from the book *Population: the Vital Revolution,* edited by Ronald Freedman, pp. 15–28. Copyright 1964 by Doubleday & Company, Inc. Reprinted by permission of the publisher.

Philip M. Hauser is Professor of Sociology at the University of Chicago, and an authority on population.

during the interwar years. The rate of world population growth continued to accelerate after World War II, so that in 1963 it approximated 20 per 1000 per year.

In the course of man's inhabitation of this globe, then, his rate of population growth has increased from about 2 per cent per millennium to 2 per cent per year, a thousandfold increase in growth rate.

If man's precursors prior to the old Stone Age are ignored, it has been estimated that since the beginning of that era there have been perhaps 77 billion births. Of this number only 12 billion, or less than 16 per cent of the total, occurred during the approximately 8000 years encompassing the Neolithic period and history up to the middle of the seventeenth century. Some 23 billion births, or 30 per cent of the total, occurred during the three centuries of the Modern Era. Of the total number of persons that have ever been born, according to these estimates, about 4 per cent, therefore, are now living.

Population data prior to the Modern Era are admittedly speculative as are, also, the inferences and conclusions which are drawn. But they provide a reasonably sound perspective and permit a very firm conclusion— namely, that whatever the precise numbers may be, there can be no doubt that in his habitation of this planet, man has experienced tremendous acceleration in his rate of growth.

This conclusion is supported by placing in perspective the present rate of world population increase, estimated by the United Nations as approximating 2 per cent per year. Although 2 per cent per year may seem like a small return on investment to persons fortunate enough to have funds out at interest, it turns out to be a truly astonishing rate of world population growth. For example, to produce the present population of the world, about three billion, one dozen persons increasing at the rate of 2 per cent per year would have required only 976 years. Yet Homo sapiens alone has been on this earth at least twenty-five to thirty thousand years and some form of man perhaps as long as two million years. Similarly, the same one dozen persons reproducing at the rate of 2 per cent per year since the beginning of the Christian Era could by 1962 have had 300 million descendants for each one actually present on the face of the earth.

Further appreciation of the meaning of a 2 per cent rate of increase per year is gained by observing the population that this growth rate would produce in the future. With an initial population of three billion, the present rate of world population growth would give a population of fifty billion in 142 years. This is the highest estimate of the population-carrying capacity of the globe ever calculated by a responsible scholar. This estimate, by geochemist Harrison Brown, is based on two extreme assumptions: first, that solar or nuclear energy will be developed to a point where the cost of power is so low that it approximates zero. Under this condition it would be possible to obtain the "things" we need from rock, sea, and air to support a population of this size indefinitely. The second assumption is that mankind would be content to forego not only meat, as the Hindu has already done, but also vegetables, and be content to subsist on food products from "algae farms and yeast factories."

A continuation of the 2 per cent rate of world population growth from the present population of about three billion would provide enough people, in lock step, to reach from the earth to the sun in 237 years. It would give one person for every square foot of land surface on the globe, including mountains, deserts and the arctic wastes, in about six and one-half centuries. It would generate a population which would weigh as much as the earth itself in 1,566 years. These periods of time may seem long when measured by the length of the individual lifetime, but they are but small intervals of time measured in the time perspective of the evolutionary development of man.

Projections of this type, of course, are not to be interpreted as predictions. They merely help to indicate the meaning of the present rate of growth. They also permit another firm conclusion—namely, that the present rate of world population growth cannot possibly persist for very long into the future. As a matter of fact, in the long run, given a finite globe and excluding the possibilities of exporting human population to outer space, any rate of population growth would in time saturate the globe and exhaust space itself. In the long run, man will necessarily be faced with the problem of restricting his rate of increase to maintain some balance between his numbers and the finite dimensions of this planet.

It is possible quickly to summarize the remarkable acceleration of his growth rate which man has experienced. It took most of the millennia of man's habitation of this planet to produce a population as great as one billion persons simultaneously alive. This population was not achieved until approximately 1850. To produce a population of two billion persons simultaneously alive required only an additional seventy-five years, for this number was achieved by 1925. To reach a population of three billion persons required only an additional thirty-seven years, for this was the total in 1962. Continuation of the trend would produce a fourth billion in about fifteen years and a fifth billion in less than an additional ten years.

Analyses of this type have led the student of population, the demographer, to use emotional and unscientific language on occasion to describe population developments. Such a phrase as "the population explosion" is admittedly non-scientific language, but it serves to emphasize the dramatic increase in man's rate of growth and to call attention to its many implications.

Why has the rate of world population growth increased so greatly? The answer may be found by analyzing the great differences in rates of population growth among the continental regions of the world and examining the reasons for these differences. Although the data are subject to error, it is possible to reproduce with reasonable accuracy the populations of the continents over the three centuries of the Modern Era.

Examination of these data discloses that for the three centuries between 1650 and 1950 the population of the world as a whole increased fivefold, from about 500 million to about 2.5 billion. The population of Europe (including Asiatic U.S.S.R.), however, increased almost sixfold. The population of Northern America (north of the Rio Grande) increased 168-fold, from about 1 to 168 million. The population of Latin America (south of the Rio Grande) increased about 23-fold, from about 7 to 163 million. Oceania increased more than sixfold, from about 2 to 13 million; Asia, showing a fivefold increase, grew at a rate close to the average for the world, of which it constitutes the greatest portion. In contrast, Africa, the slowest-growing region of the world, merely doubled its population during these three centuries, increasing from about 100 to about 200 million. The regions which experienced the most rapid growth during the three centuries of the Modern Era were Europe and the areas of European settlement. The population of Europe and the areas of European settlement combined increased about sevenfold; the areas of European settlement alone, the Americas and Oceania, increased eight- to nine-fold between 1650 and 1950.

Why did the rate of population growth increase so spectacularly in Europe and areas of European settlement? The answer is to be found of course in the technological, economic, and social developments within these regions during the Modern Era. Acceleration in growth rate may be traced to the impact of the many technological, economic, and social changes which are summarized by the expressions the "agricultural revolution," the "technological revolution," the "commercial revolution," and the "industrial revolution," climaxed by the "scientific revolution." The profound changes in man's way of life and in the social order generated by these developments produced the "demographic revolution." More specifically, the combination of developments accelerated the rate of population growth because it brought about a sharp and unprecedented decline in death rates, with a corresponding great increase in average length of life.

Precise information is not available, but in all probability the expectation of life at birth in Egypt, Greece, and Rome around the beginning of the Christian Era was not above thirty years. During the first half century of the Modern Era, 1650 to 1700, life expectation at birth in Western Europe and North America was at a level of about thirty-three years, and probably had not changed much during the preceding three or four centuries. By 1900 death rates had declined to a point where expectation of life at birth in Western Europe and North America had increased by fifteen or twenty years, reaching a level of forty-five to fifty years. By 1960 another twenty years of life had been gained. Life expectation in Western Europe and North America reached a level of about seventy years.

Although some changes in birth rates were also involved, it is clear that the major factor in the great acceleration of population growth, first evident in Europe and areas of European settlement, was the decline in the death rate. Three factors contributed to this decline. The first was the general increase in level of living resulting from technological advances and increased productivity and the achievement of relatively long periods of peace and tranquillity by reason of the emergence of relatively powerful and stable central government. The second major factor accounting for the decrease in mortality was the achievement of environmental sanitation and improved personal hygiene. During the nineteenth century great strides were made in purifying food and water and improving personal cleanliness, which contributed materially to the elimination of parasitic and infectious diseases. The third major factor is of course to be found in the great and growing contribution of modern medicine, enhanced by the recent progress in chemotherapy and the insecticides.

These developments during the Modern Era upset the equilibrium between the birth rate and the death rate that had characterized most of the millennia of human existence. In eighteenth-century France, for example, of 1000 infants born, 233 had died before they reached age one, 498 had died before they reached age twenty, and 786 had died before they reached age sixty. In contrast, in present-day France, of 1000 infants born only 40 had died before age one, only 60 had died before age twenty, and only 246 had died before age sixty. In eighteenth-century France, of the original 1000 infants only 214 survived to age sixty. In contemporary France, 754 of the original 1000 infants were still alive at age sixty. As a result of such a decrease in death rates, the 100 million Europeans in 1650 three centuries later had about 940 million descendants.

The acceleration in rate of total population growth was the result of sharp declines in mortality while fertility remained at relatively high levels. This pattern, an example of which is given for England and Wales, characterized the demographic transition in Europe and in areas colonized by European stock. At mid-eighteenth century the birth rate in England was at a level of about 37—that is, 37 births per 1000 persons per year. The death rate stood at a level of about 33–33 deaths per 1000 persons per year. Natural increase, the excess of births over deaths, approximated 4 persons per 1000 per year, or a .4 of 1 per cent per year rate of population growth. A century later, by 1850, the death rate had declined to a level of 21, while the birth rate remained at the relatively high level of approximately 34. Natural increase with this fertiilty and mortality was therefore 13, producing a population growth of 1.3 per cent per year, more than three times the rate of increase a century earlier. As in the case of England and Wales, mortality in Western Europe began its relatively rapid descent toward the end of the eighteenth and early part of the nineteenth century, while fertility still remained at relatively high levels. It is only with considerable lag that the birth rate began to decline and, therefore, to dampen rates of population increase. This is the manner in which the "demographic transition" occurred.

Prior to World War II, the spectacular decrease in the death rate of the economically advanced nations had not been shared by most of the population of the world. Of the peoples of non-European stock, only Japan had managed appreciably to increase longevity. The two thirds of the world's people who live in the economically underdeveloped regions—Asia, Latin America, and Africa—before World War II had achieved some decrease in mortality, largely through contact with advanced nations. But most of the world's people prior to World War II were characterized by an expectation of life at birth no greater than that which Western Europeans had during the Middle Ages.

This situation has dramatically changed since the end of World War II. A combination of factors, including the advent of the United Nations and the specialized agencies with programs emphasizing economic development and improved health conditions, "the revolution of rising expectations," the development and dissemination of chemotherapy and insecticides, have opened up to the mass of the world's people the achievement of the twentieth-century death rates. Since the end of World War II, declines in mortality among the economically underdeveloped areas of the world have been more dramatic than those in the industrialized areas.

Longevity is increasing much more rapidly in the less developed areas than it did among Europeans and European stock, because of the much more efficient means now available for eliminating causes of mortality. For example, the death rate of the Moslem population in Algeria in 1946–47 was higher than that of Sweden in 1771–80, more than a century and a half earlier. By 1955, however, in eight years the decrease in the death rate in Algeria was greater than that Sweden experienced during the century from 1775 to 1875. Between 1940 and 1960 Mexico, Costa Rica, Venezuela, Ceylon, Malaya, and Singapore were among the nations which decreased their death rates by more than 50 per cent. Ceylon's death rate was decreased by more than 50 per cent in less than a decade.

Without question the most important population development in the twentieth century is the spectacular decline which is taking place in the death rates of the people in the less developed areas. As a result of the decline in mortality rates, population growth among the two thirds of the world's people in the less developed areas is now greater than that previously experienced by European stock. Whereas annual rates of population growth among the industrialized nations rarely exceeded 1 per cent per year through natural increase during most of the Modern Era, populations in the present less developed areas of Asia, Latin America, and Africa are increasing at rates from 2 to 3 per cent per year. The reason for the more rapid rate of population growth in the less developed areas today than was experienced by the economically advanced nations during their period of rapid population growth is to be found of course in relation between the death rate and the birth rate. In the experience of economically advanced countries a decline in mortality was spread out over the entire three centuries of the Modern Era, during the latter part of which, over periods ranging from half a century to perhaps a century and a half, the birth rate also began to decline.

Precise statistics are not available for birth and death rates of the less developed regions of the world. Reasonably good estimates are available through the United Nations which, from the time it was first organized, has devoted considerable attention to population trends. Birth rates in the less developed regions of the world tend to average 40 or more (births per 1000 persons per year), a level little lower, if any, than it was centuries ago. In contrast the birth rates in the economically advanced regions in Europe, North America and Oceania range from below 15 to 25 (births per 1000 persons per year).

The great acceleration in the rate of population growth in the less developed regions is brought about by the retention of their high birth rates while they are experiencing precipitous decline in death rates. The death rates in the less developed continents, although higher than those which obtain in the more developed regions, have now fallen to levels (deaths per 1000 persons per year) from below 10 to about 20 (per 1000 persons per year). This difference between the death rate and the birth rate gives a natural increase of about 20 to 30—a population growth rate of 2 to 3 per cent per year.

At the present time a number of the industrialized countries of the world, largely European nations and Japan, are growing relatively slowly at rates which would double their populations in from fifty to 100 years. Some of the industrialized countries, including the United States, the Soviet Union, Australia, New Zealand, Canada and Argentina are growing somewhat more rapidly, at rates which would double their populations in about thirty to forty years, about the average for the world.

The less developed areas of the world, containing two thirds of the total population, are now the most rapidly growing regions of the world. They are increasing at rates which would double their population in from twenty to forty years.

The less developed areas are now experiencing the demographic transition already experienced by the industrialized nations, but at a much more rapid pace. The implications of the present patterns of fertility and mortality for future population have great significance, particularly in view of the national aspirations of the less developed areas for improving levels of living. To achieve higher levels of living, income per capita must, of course, be increased. Planners must, therefore, be aware of what the prospects are for future population so as to be in a position to set desired economic goals and lay plans for their achievement. The United Nations has made population projections for the world and for individual nations as well as for its various regions. The projections made before the new censuses were taken, in or around 1960, are already too conservative. That is, the acceleration in growth rates of the less developed areas has been so rapid as to have outmoded the population projections since they were constructed in the late 1950's. The United Nations "high" projections serve, however, to illustrate what the present trend would produce by the end of the century.

Should the trends continue, the population of the world as a whole would increase from about 3 billion in 1960 to approximately 7 billion by the year 2000. World population would more than double during the remainder of this century. The effect of declining mortality in the less developed areas may be readily seen by comparing anticipated growth in the second half of this century with actual growth during the first half. Between 1900 and 1950 world population increased by less than 1 billion persons. Between 1950 and 2000 present trends indicate an increase of 4.4 billion persons. That is, the absolute increase in the population of the world during the second half of this century will be almost four and a half times as great as that during the first half of the century. During the second half of this century, there will be a greater increase in world population than was achieved in all the millennia of human existence up to the present time.

Between 1960 and the end of the century, Latin America will have the most rapidly growing population—more than tripling, to reach a total of 650 millions from a level of about 200 million. Asia and Africa will each increase by two and a half-fold. Africa's population will rise from 250 million in 1960 to 660 million by 2000. Asia's population will increase to 4.3 billion in 2000 from a level of 1.7 billion in 1960. The slowest-growing regions of the world between now and the end of this century will be the industrialized areas. North America and Europe will each increase by about 50 per cent while Oceania will less than double during the remainder of this century. The population of Europe will total about 1 billion in 2000, compared with 640 million in 1960; that of North America will number 330 million in 2000, as compared with 200 million in 1960. Oceania will have about 30 million persons in 2000 as compared with 17 million in 1960. These projections, it must be emphasized, are estimates of what would happen if the trends observed were to continue for the remainder of the century.

An interesting shift has occurred, and is again in prospect, in the population relationships of North and Latin America. Latin America contained more people than did North America before European colonization. The more rapid economic development of North America gave that continent a larger population than Latin America during the course of the nineteenth century. In 1960 the number of persons in Latin America exceeded the number in North America for the first time in more than a century. Despite the postwar boom in marriages and babies in North America, the population in Latin America is now growing so much more rapidly that by the end of this century Latin America will contain about twice as large a population as North America.

It is difficult to comprehend the significance of the population increase during the remainder of this century which present trends indicate. Some understanding of what lies ahead may be gained by historical comparisons. The absolute increase in the population of Latin America during the last half of this century may equal the total increase in the population of the world in all the millennia which man has inhabited this globe up until 1650 when the first colonists in the United States were settling New England. The projected increase in the population of Asia during the second half of this century is as great as the total population of the world in 1958.

The world's population is unevenly distributed over the surface of the globe. About two thirds of the people on the earth live on about 7 per cent of the land area. There are four areas of great population concentration—Eastern Asia, South Central Asia, Europe and Northeastern United States. This distribution of the world's peoples is, of course, the result of the adjustment of population to world resources that has taken place over the millennia.

Differences in rates of population growth, historically and in prospect, alter the distribution of the world's population by regions. In 1650 Asia contained 61 per cent of the world's people. Africa and Europe each had 18 per cent, and the remaining continents—North America, Latin America, and Oceania combined—had less than 3 per cent of the world's total population. By 1950 the effects of the demographic transition in Europe and the areas colonized by Europe were clearly visible. Asia's share of the world's total population had shrunk to 54 per cent and Africa's to only 8 per cent of the total. Europe's share had increased to 23 per cent, and the areas of European colonization, North America, South America and Oceania had increased their share of the world's total to over 14 per cent.

Differential growth rates during the remainder of this century, reflecting the demographic transition in the less developed areas, will reverse the previous pattern of change in population distribution by world regions. The economically less developed continents—Asia, Africa and Latin America—will increase their share of the world's total population at the expense of North America and Europe. Asia's share of the world's total will increase to about 62 per cent, Latin America to over 9 per cent, Africa's to close to 10 per cent. In contrast, Europe's share of total population will decrease to less than 15 per cent, while North America's will shrink to less than 5 per cent.

At mid-twentieth century, the industrialized continents—North America, Europe and Oceania—contained over 30 per cent of the world's total population. The less developed continents—Asia, Africa and Latin America—contained the remainder. In the course of the twentieth century, the proportion of the world's population in the less developed continents will have increased from less than two thirds in 1900 to about four fifths by 2000. Conversely, the share of the world's total population contained in the more economically developed continents will have declined from 36 per cent of the world's total in 1900 to 21 per cent in 2000.

Acceleration in the rate of the world's population growth is still under way. But it is clear that even present rates of world population growth cannot continue for very long into the future. Man is the only culture-building animal on the face of the earth. He not only adapts to environment but creates environment to which to adapt. In developing his culture and precipitating the technological, the industrial and the scientific revolutions, man has profoundly altered the rhythm of his own reproduction. He has destroyed the equilibrium between the birth rate and the death rate which existed for most of the millennia he has been on this globe.

Man has the capacity, however, not only to build culture but also to perceive the consequences of his handiwork. It is because he is becoming increasingly aware of the implications of accelerating population growth that so much attention is now being paid to population problems. It is because of the increasing awareness of population trends and their implications that the United Nations and its specialized agencies and an increasing number of individual nations are facing up to the population problem. A number of nations, including India, Pakistan, Egypt, Tunisia, Korea and Japan, have formulated population policies and are developing programs to make sure that the Malthusian checks to population growth —vice, misery, famine and war—do not provide the solution to their increasing numbers.

Social Adjustment
and Social Problems

9

PERSONAL ADJUSTMENT

OUR AGE has been called the "Age of Anxiety." Rollo May accepts this characterization, but adds that anxiety has now become overt. During the past two decades it has emerged as a most pervasive and explicit social problem. This is partly evidenced in the large number of emotional disturbances and behavioral disorders which afflict our people. May explores the fields of literature, philosophy, religion, psychology, sociology, and economic and political thought for authentic insights as to how anxiety has come to be regarded as the "nodal" or central problem of our times.

Flowerman describes the authoritarian personality. He finds that "authoritarians see the world and its people as menacing and unfriendly." They tend to be extreme conformists, undemocratic, and to have strong prejudices against "outgroups" such as Mexicans and Negroes.

17

Centrality of the Problem of
Anxiety in Our Day

by Rollo May

Now there are times when a whole generation is caught . . .
between two ages, two modes of life, with the consequence that it
loses all power to understand itself and has no standards, no security,
no simple acquiescence.

HERMAN HESSE, *Steppenwolf.*

Every alert citizen of our society realizes, on the basis of his own experience as well as his observation of his fellow-men, that anxiety is a
pervasive and profound phenomenon in the middle of the twentieth century. The alert citizen, we may assume, would be aware not only of the
more obvious anxiety-creating situations in our day, such as the threats of
war, of the uncontrolled atom bomb, and of radical political and economic
upheaval; but also of the less obvious, deeper, and more personal sources
of anxiety in himself as well as in his fellow-men—namely, the inner
confusion, psychological disorientation, and uncertainty with respect to
values and acceptable standards of conduct. Hence to endeavor to "prove"
the pervasiveness of anxiety in our day is as unnecessary as the proverbial
carrying of coals to Newcastle.

Since the implicit sources of anxiety in our society are generally recognized, our task in this introductory chapter is somewhat more specific.
We shall point out how anxiety has emerged, and has to some slight extent
been defined, as an *explicit* problem in many different areas in our culture.
It is as though in the present decade the explorations and investigations in
such diverse fields as poetry and science, or religion and politics, were
converging on this central problem, anxiety. Whereas the period of two
decades ago might have been termed the "age of covert anxiety"—as we
hope to demonstrate later in this chapter—the present phase of our century may well be called, as Auden and Camus call it, the "age of overt

---

From *The Meaning of Anxiety* by Rollo May, pp. 3–15 *passim*. Copyright 1950,
The Ronald Press Company. Reprinted by permission.

Rollo May is on the faculty of the William Alanson White Institute of Psychoanalysis, Psychiatry, and Psychology, Washington, D.C.

anxiety." This emergence of anxiety from an implicit to an explicit problem in our society, this change from anxiety as a matter of "mood" to a recognition that it is an urgent issue which we must at all costs try to define and clarify, are, in the judgment of the present writer, the significant phenomena at the moment. Not only in the understanding and treatment of emotional disturbances and behavioral disorders has anxiety become recognized as the "nodal problem," in Freud's words; but it is now seen likewise to be nodal in such different areas as literature, sociology, political and economic thought, education, religion, and philosophy. We shall cite examples of testimony from these fields, beginning with the more general and proceeding to the more specific concern with anxiety as a scientific problem.

IN LITERATURE. If one were to inquire into anxiety as exhibited in the American literature, say, of 1920 or 1930, one would be forced in all probability to occupy oneself with symptoms of anxiety rather than overt anxiety itself. But though signs of open, manifest anxiety were not plentiful in that period, certainly the student could find plenty of symptomatic indications of underlying anxiety. *Vide,* for example, the pronounced sense of loneliness, the quality of persistent searching—frantically and compulsively pursued but always frustrated—in the writings of a novelist like Thomas Wolfe.

In 1950, however, our inquiry is simpler because anxiety has now emerged into overt statement in contemporaneous literature. W. H. Auden has entitled his latest poem with the phrase which he believes most accurately characterizes our period, namely, *The Age of Anxiety.* Though Auden's profound interpretation of the inner experience of the four persons in this poem is set in the time of war—when "necessity is associated with horror and freedom with boredom"—he makes it very clear that the underlying causes of the anxiety of his characters, as well as of others of this age, must be sought on deeper levels than merely the occasion of war. The four characters in the poem, though different in temperament and in background, have in common certain characteristics of our times: loneliness, the feeling of not being of value as persons, and the experience of not being able to love and be loved, despite the common need, the common effort, and the common but temporary respite provided by alcohol. The sources of the anxiety are to be found in certain basic trends in our culture, one of which, for Auden, is the pressure toward conformity which occurs in a world where commercial and mechanical values are apotheosized. . . . *What has been lost is the capacity to experience and have faith in one's self as a worthy and unique being, and at the same time the capacity for faith in, and meaningful communication with, other selves, namely one's fellow-men.*

The French author, Albert Camus, . . . designates this age as "the century of fear," in comparison with the seventeenth century as the age of mathematics, the eighteenth as the age of the physical sciences, and the nineteenth as that of biology. Camus realizes that these characterizations are not logically parallel, that fear is not a science, but "science must be somewhat involved, since its latest theoretical advances have brought it to the point of negating itself while its perfected technology threatens the globe itself with destruction. Moreover, although fear itself cannot be considered a science, it is certainly a technique."

Another writer who graphically expresses the anxiety and anxiety-like states of people in our period is Franz Kafka. The remarkable surge of interest in the 1940's in the writings of Kafka is important for our purposes here because of what it shows in the changing temper of our time; the fact that increasing numbers of people are finding that Kafka speaks significantly to them must indicate that he is expressing some profound aspects of the prevailing experience of many members of our society. In Kafka's novel *The Castle,* the chief character devotes his life to a frantic and desperate endeavor to communicate with the authorities in the castle who control all aspects of the life in the village, and who have the power to tell him his *vocation* and give some meaning to his life. *Kafka's hero is driven "by a need for the most primitive requisites of life, the need to be rooted in a home and a calling, and to become a member of a community."* But the authorities in the castle remain inscrutable and inaccessible, and Kafka's character is as a result without direction and unity in his own life and remains isolated from his fellows. What the castle specifically symbolizes could be debated at length, but since the authorities in the castle are represented as the epitome of a bureaucratic efficiency which exercises such power that it quenches both individual autonomy and meaningful interpersonal relations, it may confidently be assumed that Kafka is in general writing of those aspects of his bourgeois culture of the late nineteenth and early twentieth centuries which so elevated technical efficiency that personal values were largely destroyed.

Herman Hesse, writing less in literary symbols than Kafka, is more explicit about the sources of modern man's anxiety. He presents the story of Haller, his chief character in the novel *Steppenwolf,* as a parable of our period. Hesse holds that Haller's—and his contemporaries'—isolation and anxiety arise from the fact that the bourgeois culture in the late nineteenth and early twentieth centuries emphasized mechanical, rationalistic "balance" at the price of the suppression of the dynamic, irrational elements in experience. Haller tries to overcome his isolation and loneliness by giving free rein to his previously suppressed sensuous and irrational urges (the "wolf"), but this reactive method yields only a temporary relief. Indeed, Hesse presents no thoroughgoing solution to the problem of the anxiety of contemporaneous Western man, for he believes the present period to be one of those "times when a whole generation is caught

. . . between two ages." That is to say, bourgeois standards and controls have been broken down, but there are as yet no social standards to take their place. Hesse sees Haller's record "as a document of the times, for Haller's sickness of the soul, as I now know, is not the eccentricity of a single individual, but the sickness of the times themselves, the neurosis of that generation to which Haller belongs . . . a sickness which attacks . . . precisely those who are strongest in spirit and richest in gifts."

IN SOCIOLOGICAL STUDIES. The emergence of awareness of anxiety as an overt sociological problem in an American community during the third and fourth decades of our century is seen when we compare the Lynds' two studies of Middletown. In the first study, made in the 1920's, anxiety is not an overt problem to the people of Middletown, and the topic does not appear in the Lynds' volume in any of its explicit forms. But anyone reading this study from a psychological viewpoint would suspect that much of the behavior of the citizens of Middletown was symptomatic of *covert anxiety*—for example, the compulsive work ("businessmen and workingmen seem to be running for dear life" in the endeavor to make money), the pervasive struggle to conform, the compulsive gregariousness (*vide* the great emphasis on "joining" clubs), and the frantic endeavors of the people in the community to keep their leisure time crammed with activity (such as "motoring"), however purposeless this activity might be in itself. But only one citizen—whom the Lynds describe as a "perspicacious" observer—looked below these symptoms and sensed the presence of covert apprehension: of his fellow townsmen he observed, "These people are all afraid of something; what is it?"

But the later study of the same community made in the 1930's presents a very different picture: *overt anxiety is now present.* "One thing everybody in Middletown has in common," the Lynds observe, "is insecurity in the face of a complicated world." To be sure, the immediate, outward occasion of anxiety was the economic depression; but it would be an error to conclude that the inclusive *cause* of the emerging anxiety was economic insecurity. The Lynds accurately relate this insecurity in Middletown to the *confusion of role* which the individual was then experiencing; the citizen of Middletown, they write, "is caught in a chaos of conflicting patterns, none of them wholly condemned, but no one of them clearly approved and free from confusion; or, where the group sanctions are clear in demanding a certain role of a man or woman, the individual encounters cultural requirements with no immediate means of meeting them." This "chaos of conflicting patterns" in Middletown is one expression of the pervasive social changes occurring in our culture, which are intimately connected with the widespread anxiety of our times. The Lynds observe that, since "most people are incapable of tolerating change and uncertainty in all sectors of life at once," the tendency in Middletown was toward a retrenchment into more rigid and conservative economic and social ideologies. This ominous development as a symptom of, and defense against, anxiety points toward the discussion of the relation between anxiety and political authoritarianism in the next section.

IN THE POLITICAL SCENE. Turning to the political scene, we again find pronounced anxiety evidenced both in symptomatic and in overt forms. Without going into the complex determinants of fascism, we wish to note that it is born and gains its power in periods of widespread anxiety. Tillich describes the situation in Europe in the 1930's out of which German fascism developed:

> First of all a feeling of *fear* or, more exactly, of indefinite anxiety was prevailing. Not only the economic and political, but also the cultural and religious, security seemed to be lost. There was nothing on which one could build; everything was without foundation. A catastrophic breakdown was expected every moment. Consequently, a longing for security was growing in everybody. A freedom that leads to fear and anxiety has lost its value; better authority with security than freedom with fear!

In such periods, people grasp at political authoritarianism in the desperate need to be relieved of anxiety. *Totalitarianism in this sense may be viewed as serving a purpose on a cultural scale parallel to that in which a neurotic symptom protects an individual from a situation of unbearable anxiety.* With some very significant differences, communistic totalitarianism fulfills a similar function. As we shall endeavor to indicate later in this study, fascism and communism are not only economic phenomena, but are also the product of the spiritual, ethical, and psychological vacuum which characterized the breakdown of the bourgeois tradition in Western Europe. As Martin Ebon phrases it, communism is a product of "the desperate wish to find a purpose in what seems confusion and emptiness." In this confusion and emptiness one thing did exist, namely anxiety; and we are submitting that totalitarianism gains its foothold to a considerable extent because, like a symptom, it "binds" and provides some relief from the anxiety.

In addition to anxiety in the above symptomatic forms, *unsystematized* anxiety has been increasingly evident in the sociopolitical scene in the past decade. The frequent references to Roosevelt's sentence in his first inaugural, "The only thing we have to fear is fear itself," testify to the fact that large numbers of people have become increasingly aware of "fear of fear," or more accurately, anxiety, in the face of the radical sociopolitical changes in our day. The emergence of the atom bomb brought the previously inchoate and "free-floating" anxiety of many people into sharp focus. The stark possibilities of modern man's situation are stated in an impassioned expression of the crystallization of anxiety at that moment by Norman Cousins:

> The beginning of the Atomic Age has brought less hope than fear. It is a primitive fear, the fear of the unknown, the fear of forces man can neither channel nor comprehend. This fear is not new; in its classical form it is the fear of irrational death. But overnight it has become intensified, magnified. It has burst out of the subconscious into the conscious, filling the mind with primordial apprehensions. . . . Where man can find no answer, he will find fear.

Even if we should escape being confronted with actual death in a shooting and atomic war, the anxiety inhering in our portentous world situation would still be with us. The historian Arnold Toynbee has stated his belief that overt warfare on a world scale is not probable in our lifetime, but that we shall remain in a "cold" war for a generation, which will mean a perpetual condition of tension and worry. To live in a state of anxiety for a generation is, indeed, a horrendous prospect! But the picture is not inevitably black: Toynbee holds that the tension in the persistent cold war can be used constructively as our motivation for bettering our own socioeconomic standards in the West. The present writer agrees with Toynbee that our political and social survival depends both on our capacity for tolerating the anxiety inherent in the threatening world situation (and thus not irrationally precipitating war as a way out of the painful uncertainty) and also on our capacity for turning this anxiety to constructive uses.

IN PHILOSOPHY AND RELIGION.   The fact that anxiety has emerged as a central problem in contemporaneous philosophy and religion is not only a general, but also a specific indication of the prevalence of anxiety in our culture. It is a specific indication in the respect that anxiety has become most prominent in the thought of those theologians, like R. Niebuhr, who are most intimately concerned with the economic and political issues of our day; and in those philosophers, like Tillich and M. Heidegger, who have experienced in their own lives the cultural crises and upheavals of Western society in the past three decades.

Tillich describes anxiety as man's reaction to the threat of *nonbeing*. Man is the creature who has self-conscious awareness of his being, but he is also aware that at any moment he might cease to exist. Thus in philosophical terms anxiety arises as the individual is aware of being as over against the ever present possibility of nonbeing. "Nonbeing" does not mean simply the threat of physical death—though probably death is the most common form and symbol of this anxiety. The threat of nonbeing lies in the psychological and spiritual realms as well, namely the threat of *meaninglessness* in one's existence. Generally the threat of meaninglessness is experienced negatively as a threat to the existence of the self (the experience of the "dissolution of the self" in Goldstein's term). But when this form of anxiety is confronted affirmatively—when the individual both realizes the threat of meaninglessness and takes a stand against the threat

—the result is a strengthening of the individual's feeling of being a self, a strengthening of his perception of himself as distinct from the world of nonbeing, of objects.

Niebuhr makes anxiety the central concept of his theological doctrine of man. To Niebuhr every act of man, creative or destructive, involves some element of anxiety. Anxiety has its source in the fact that man is on one hand finite, involved like the animals in the contingencies and necessities of nature; but on the other hand has freedom. Unlike "the animals he sees this situation [of contingency] and anticipates its perils," and to this extent man transcends his finiteness. "In short, man, being both bound and free, both limited and limitless, is anxious. Anxiety is the inevitable concomitant of the paradox of freedom and finiteness in which man is involved." Much will be said later in the present study about anxiety as the precondition of neurosis; it is significant that Niebuhr, in parallel theological terms, makes anxiety "the internal precondition of sin. . . . Anxiety is the internal description of the state of temptation."

IN PSYCHOLOGY. "Anxiety is the most prominent mental characteristic of Occidental civilization," R. R. Willoughby asserts. He then presents statistical evidence for this assertion in the form of the rising incidences in three fields of social pathology which he believes may reasonably be understood as reactions to anxiety, namely *sucide,* the *functional forms of mental disorder,* and *divorce.* Suicide rates for the last 75 to 100 years show a steady increase in the majority of the countries of continental Europe. With regard to the functional forms of mental illness, Willoughby holds, "it seems probable . . . that there is a real rise in incidence of mental disease even when the greatest reasonable allowance is made for increasing facilities for hospitalization and insight in diagnosis." The divorce rates for every country except Japan have shown a steady upward trend in the twentieth century. Willoughby believes the incidence of divorce is a measure of the inability of the members of the culture to tolerate the additional stress of the critical marital adjustment, and the higher incidence must presuppose a considerable load of anxiety in the culture.

We would not question Willoughby's purpose in introducing these statistics, namely, to substantiate the "commonsense proposition that there is in our civilization a large and increasing incidence of anxiety." But there might rightly be considerable question as to whether the relation between these statistical evidences and anxiety is as direct as he holds. Suicide can be due to other motivations than anxiety—revenge is one example. And the rising incidence of divorce would seem to be due to changing social attitudes toward divorce as well as to the prevalence of anxiety. But certainly the three groups of statistics Willoughby presents indicate radical social upheavals in our society which involve psychological and emotional trauma. To the present writer it seems more logical to regard rising divorce, suicide, and mental disease rates as symptoms and products of the traumatically changing state of our culture, and to regard anxiety also as a symptom and product of that cultural state. And certainly a culture described by these statistics would be a culture which generates much anxiety.

Anxiety has gradually come to be seen as a central problem in learning theory, in dynamic psychology, and specifically in psychoanalysis and other forms of psychotherapy. While it long has been recognized that apprehensions and fears, particularly those related to approval or punishment from parents and teachers, exerted much power over the child in school, not until recently have there been scientific recognitions of the innumerable subtle expressions and influences of anxiety permeating the child's educational and classroom experience. For this appreciation of anxiety as a focal problem in learning theory, and the scientific formulation thereof, we are indebted to such learned psychologists as Mowrer, Miller, and Dollard.

More than three decades ago, Freud singled out anxiety as the crucial problem of emotional and behavioral disorders. Further development of psychoanalysis has only substantiated his proposition, until it is now recognized on all sides that anxiety is the "fundamental phenomenon of neurosis," or in Horney's term, the "dynamic center of neuroses." But not only in psychopathology; in the actions of "normal" people as well as "abnormal," it is now recognized that anxiety is much more prevalent than was suspected several decades ago. From the viewpoint of dynamic psychology, Symonds accurately notes that "it would surprise most persons to realize how much of their behavior is motivated by a desire to escape anxiety by either reducing it or disguising it in one way or another." Whether we are concerned with "normal" or pathological behavior, Freud was correct in saying that the solution to the "riddle" of anxiety "must cast a flood of light upon our whole mental life."

18

The Authoritarian Personality

by Samuel H. Flowerman

Findings of recent scientific investigations reveal that the real menace to democracy is not the brutal dictator but the anonymous man-in-the-crowd on whose support the dictator depends for power. Social scientists have found that this nameless individual is not a creation of the dictator but a ready-made "authoritarian personality"—a person whose family background and social environment have made him peculiarly attuned to antidemocratic beliefs. It requires authoritarian personalities to take hold of authoritarian ideas; it takes authoritarian personalities—thousands and even millions of them—to build an authoritarian state.

Concern about authority and the relationship between the ruler and the ruled is not new. It runs through the fabric of recorded history of civilization. Philosophers and poets—from at least as far back as ancient Egypt and Greece to present-day Existentialists—have wrestled with the dilemma of how to attain the highest level of development of the individual within some system of order governing man's relation to man. In the United States a spate of studies about various aspects of personality development has been going forward for several decades. And research workers, most of them trained here, have been conducting studies in postwar Germany in an effort to understand why a people will produce, nurture and follow a dictator. The bulk of these inquiries tend to yield somewhat consistent results: there is something special, something different about the "authoritarian man."

Perhaps the most detailed study of all time in this field was made by a team of social psychologists in California, working for almost five years. They recently completed an investigation of the democratic and antidemocratic ideas and attitudes of the American man-in-the-crowd, seeking keys to their origin. Teams from other parts of the country have added to their findings. The California group—T. W. Adorno, Else Frenkel-Brunswik, Max Horkheimer, Daniel Levinson and R. Nevitt Sanford—

From "Portrait of the Authoritarian Man," by Samuel H. Flowerman, *The New York Times Magazine,* April 23, 1950, pp. 9, 28–31. Reprinted by permission.

The late Samuel H. Flowerman was a consulting psychologist, and from time to time a visiting professor at several leading colleges and universities.

interviewed and tested more than two thousand persons in the San Francisco Bay area, Los Angeles, Portland, Ore., and Washington, D.C.

Among the groups tested were factory workers, officer candidates in a maritime training school, veterans, members of service clubs (Rotarians and Kiwanis), office workers, male inmates of a prison, members of parent-teacher associations, out-patients in a psychiatric clinic, church groups, and college students.

While the California study is not a statistical study but rather examines various groups psychologically, it was found that authoritarian men did exist in many groups and in many places. Based on the California study and other readings and observations over a number of years, social scientists feel that it can be said that about 10 percent of the population of the United States probably consists of "authoritarian men and women" while as many as another 20 percent have within them the seeds that grow into authoritarianism.

Lest the conclusion be drawn that there are only two kinds of people, authoritarians and anti-authoritarians, it should be said that the social scientists' findings rate persons on a scale from very low to very high, as regards their authoritarian tendencies, with perhaps the bulk of the population clustered around the middle.

From the findings of the California study has emerged this composite psychological portrait of the Authoritarian Man:

HE IS A SUPREME CONFORMIST. The Authoritarian Man conforms to the nth degree to middle-class ideas and ideals and to authority. But conforming is no voluntary act for him; it is compulsive and irrational. It is an attempt to find security by merging with the herd, by submitting to some higher power or authority. Not only does he feel compelled to submit; he wants others to submit, too. He cannot run the risk of being different and cannot tolerate difference in anyone else.

In a mild form, such compulsive submission to authority may find a Casper Milquetoast chewing each mouthful of food thirty times because some bogus health expert has said he should. In its extreme form it finds people reduced to sheep, herded into marking "yes" on ballots that do not have "no," bleating "Heil!" to the commands of a Hitler, and doing his bidding even when it means oppressing, even killing, other people.

Authoritarians see the world and its inhabitants as menacing and unfriendly. Being so threatened, so anxiety ridden, they must seek security somehow, somewhere. The best security for the authoritarian is to surrender to a powerful authority. He agrees, for example, that "What the world needs is a strong leader"; and "There are two kinds of people, the weak and the strong."

To him, life is a power system into which he must fit. He doesn't have to wield the power himself so long as he can be near power, sharing it vicariously. It is this latter tendency which makes the authoritarian such a good camp-follower.

But the authoritarian is a loyal camp-follower only so long as the leader remains strong. Let the leader falter, let him be defeated; then, "Down with the old, up with the new."

So today in Germany many people agree that Hitler was bad, but only because he was unsuccessful in the long run; their basic way of life is still authoritarian—they simply await a new, stronger, more powerful leader.

HE IS RIGID AND SHOWS LIMITED IMAGINATION.   He is a mechanical man, a kind of robot who reacts to only a limited number of ideas and can't be budged out of the channels in which he has been conditioned to operate. This doesn't mean that the Authoritarian Man is a person of low intelligence; but it does mean that his personality restricts his intelligence and imagination. He is generally incapable of figuring out alternate solutions to problems.

The extent to which this rigidity operates was demonstrated by Dr. Milton Rokeach, a junior member of the California team and now at Michigan State College. Dr. Rokeach worked out a series of simple problems in arithmetic and map reading. He presented these problems to groups of adults and children, whose authoritarianism had already been determined. All the people in the experiment were taught to solve the problems by using a complicated method, but nothing was said about other, easier, solutions; they were simply instructed to get the right answers. As Dr. Rokeach's guinea pigs continued to work down the list of problems they soon reached a series of examples that could be solved either the hard way or very simply. Authoritarians continued to solve the problems the hard way. The non-authoritarians shifted readily to the easy solutions— they were able to use more channels.

HE IS HERD-MINDED.   And to be herd-minded—"ethnocentric" is the scientists' term—implies being prejudiced. To the authoritarian, people who are—or seem to be—different are strange, uncanny and threatening, although they may be few in number and unimportant in influence. He tends to exalt his own group and reject members of other groups. (To be sure, there are some exceptions to this praise of one's own group. Sometimes members of minority groups take over the prejudices of the majority groups and engage in what psychologists call "self-hate.")

The person who dislikes one "out-group" generally dislikes many other "out-groups." In this respect he is like the hay-fever victim, who is usually allergic to more than one kind of pollen.

The authoritarian puts neat—and often false—labels on people. In his group he may see individuals; outside his own group he sees only masses or types. So he will frequently say of members of "minority" groups that "that kind" is "lazy," "sex-crazy," "dishonest in business," "money-mad," "smelly," and so on. What is more, he tends to see "them" everywhere.

HE IS A PHONY CONSERVATIVE. He waves the flag, he sounds like a patriot, but at heart hates the very traditions and institutions he professes to love. In his most rabid form the phony conservative is the anti-democratic agitator who is more destructively radical than the radicals he claims he is attacking.

The California team distinguishes between the true conservative and the phony conservative. The true conservative may be patriotic, believe in American traditions and institutions, and support their continued existence; he may also believe in a laissez-faire economy. But he is also for giving every individual an equal "break" regardless of his group membership. And it is in regard to this last point that the true conservative can be distinguished from the counterfeit flag-waver.

HE IS A MORAL PURIST. The authoritarian frowns on sensuality, a trait he is ready to find in members of other groups. He regards his own group as morally pure. Authoritarian men—and women—tend to agree, for example, that no "decent man" would marry an unchaste woman. Even male prisoners jailed for sex crimes support statements condemning sex crimes; and they are also more conforming, more anti-Semitic, more anti-Negro, and more pseudo-conservative than their fellow-prisoners.

It would be a grave mistake to regard the authoritarian as a lunatic or freak, although doubtless there are such extreme cases. If anything, the democratic person may appear outwardly to be less well-adjusted because he "internalizes" his problems to a greater degree and blames himself for many of his difficulties. The authoritarian "externalizes" his problems and blames other people and other forces. On the surface, the authoritarian may seem to be less troubled, but this is often because he has buried his smoldering resentment and hostility within himself.

By contrast with his opposite the extremely democratic personality is a man with a mind of his own; he is a flexible individual, adjusting readily to new situations. He is sensitive to the part he plays in conflicting situations and he is ready to take responsibility for his own behavior.

The model anti-authoritarian tends to like all sorts of people regardless of whether they are members of his group. He is without prejudice against religious or racial minorities. He regards persons as individuals, not types. Nor is he inclined to judge the moral standards of others. It is easy for him to see some good in the world and some hope for its future. Most important, he refuses to surrender his individuality to a "big shot," although he may submit to rational authority by choice when he believes that such authority is based upon equality, superior ability, and co-operation, and that it is subject to dismissal for a job badly done.

The findings of these studies suggest that people are not deliberately and systematically taught the ABC's of authoritarianism. Authoritarianism is a term which describes personality; and personality is developed in the crucible of inter-personal relationships, the most important of which is the relationship between parent and child.

As a child the typical authoritarian was usually subjected to harsh discipline and was given little affection in a home in which the father was a tough boss. In such a home children must "knuckle under" and submit. There is little opportunity to act as an individual. Fear rules, and parents and other figures of authority are regarded as menacing, punitive and overpowering. This fear, based on the inability to disagree, is carried over into adult life; when the opportunity to assert one's self occurs, it is seized by way of compensation. The slave of one generation becomes the domineering master of the next generation.

On the other hand, as a child the democratic individual most often grew up in a home where the mother had much to say. Children in these families knew affection and had a feeling that they counted as individuals. They exercised the right to disagree, although often not without conflict and guilt. As adults they regard their parents as flesh-and-blood characters with the traits of real people. In childhood, the democratic person was able to choose equality and independence instead of blind, passive submission. As an adult, the democratic person is not so easily pushed around because he has no compulsive need, based on fear, to submit to the authority of the "big shot."

To be sure, there are reasons for the development of authoritarian personalities which are not to be found in the home. There are the major environmental upheavals—depressions and unemployment, inflations, wars, earthquakes, revolutions, floods—which alter ways of living and believing. There are also the chance experiences which an individual encounters in a lifetime. Sometimes the harshness of a child's home may be offset by kindly teachers, decent playmates, and other significant figures who treat the child affectionately as an individual. Sometimes a child grows up in such a way as to be able to throw off the effects of his slavery.

But these rebels are perhaps the exception, whereas the slave personality occurs more often when childhood has been spent in an authoritarian house. Certainly research findings indicate that so far the key to the difference between the authoritarian and democratic personalities lies in the relationship between parents and children. Learning to disagree with one's parents may be the capstone of a democratic personality.

How great is the threat of authoritarian development in this country? There are several deeply ingrained trends in American culture which probably offset to a considerable degree the spread of authoritarianism.

Americans traditionally scoff at authority. An American President reads a State of the Union message before Congress and is heckled, only to answer right back. Prize-fight referees are booed when they award unfair decisions against Negro boxers in favor of white boxers. Players and spectators "razz" baseball umpires. Radio programs and movies make fun of cops, school teachers, and principals, and especially fathers.

American homes are mother-oriented—and if anything—child-dominated. Women control the family purse strings of America, handle immediate problems of discipline, and are favored by over-sentimentality in a Victorian sense.

We have an American creed of fair play, of equality, and of upward mobility among social and economic classes. We are an individualistic, freedom-loving, rational, practical people. Americans are suspicious of flag-waving and of military authority.

Yet there are those who note that our American creed is "honored more in the breach than in the observance." Wide gaps separate what we claim to believe and what we feel and do. Like any national group, we are susceptible to anti-democratic ideologies; we have authoritarian personalities among us.

10

THE FAMILY

HOWEVER WIDELY it may differ in form, it is generally agreed that the family as an institution for regulating sexual relations and rearing children is found in all human societies. In modern societies the patriarchal family of the past has given way before the swift onrush of economic and social change. Technological advance has reduced the economic functions of the family, while the state has taken over in part certain other functions, including education. Thus the family has come gradually to play a less dominant role in the life of individuals. This process has gone farthest in urban areas.

In this chapter Benedict deals with hazards confronting the American family, but she is optimistic about its ability to meet them. Moore, on the other hand, raises certain questions which have a bearing on the very survival of the family. The major theme of sociologists has been that the family is making up for the lost or weakened functions by strengthening certain other functions such as companionship and the fulfilling of emotional needs. To Moore this seems little more than a middle-class hope. The crucial question is, To what extent does the modern family perform the essential function of developing in children healthy personalities?

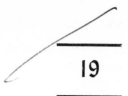

19

The Family: Genus Americanum

by Ruth Benedict

A great many people today speak as if the family were in some special sort of danger in our times. We hear a great deal about "saving the family" and about "preserving the home." Authors and lecturers describe how the family is threatened by divorce, or by mothers who work outside of the home, or by unemployment, or by lack of religious training of children. Each of them, depending on his experience in his own home and on his observations in the families he knows, selects something which he thinks should be changed—or should be preserved—and says that, if this or that were done, the family would be "saved."

To an anthropologist such phrasings are dangerously misleading. He has studied the family among naked savages and in contemporary civilizations and he knows that it has survived in all human societies known in the record of mankind. Just as surely he knows that the family takes all kinds of different forms. It is not merely that unlettered primitive nomads have family arrangements different from Western industrial nations; even in Western nations around the Atlantic shores the family differs profoundly. The ethics of marriage, the specific close emotional ties which the family fosters, the disciplines and freedoms for the child, the nature of the dependency of the children upon the parents, even the personnel which makes up the family—all these differ in Western civilized nations. The anthropologist knows that the changes taking place in the home in any decade in any country do not mean that the family is now about to disintegrate under our eyes unless we do something about it. The problem as he states it is quite different: how do legal and customary arrangements in the family tally with the arrangements and premises of the whole way of life which is valued in any tribe or nation? If, for instance, the father has a heavy, authoritarian hand upon his children, the anthropologist asks: Is this in keeping with authoritarianism in the state and in industry? Or is it at odds with a society which values non-authoritarianism and the pursuit of happiness? He asks the same kind of question about a nation's

From *The Family: Its Function and Destiny,* edited by Ruth Nanda Anshen, pp. 159–166. Copyright 1949 by Harper & Brothers, New York. Reprinted by permission. The late Ruth Benedict was Professor of Anthropology at Columbia University.

laws of inheritance from father to son, about the divorce laws, about the architectural layout of the house, about the reasons that are given to children when they are told to be good.

Customs enshrined in the family in any tribe or nation are likely to be sensitively adjusted to the values and customs of each particular people. This is no mystic correspondence; the persons who make up the family are the same people who are the citizens of that nation—the business men, the farmers, the churchgoers or non-churchgoers, the readers of newspapers, and the listeners to the radio. In all their roles they are molded more or less surely into a people with certain habits, certain hopes, and a certain *esprit de corps*. Americans come to share certain slogans, behavior, and judgments which differ from those of Frenchmen or Czechs. This is inevitable. And in the process the role of the family also becomes different. By the same token, just as economic and political changes occur over a period of time in the United States or in France or in Czechoslovakia, the family also changes.

An anthropologist, therefore, when he reads about the failure of the family, finds in such criticism a somewhat special meaning. He remembers how often the family is made a convenient whipping boy among many peoples who disapprove of the way their world is going. He has seen it in Amazon jungles and on the islands of the Pacific. The author remembers an American Indian tribe which used to talk about the family in a most uncomplimentary fashion. They were a people who, not long before, had roamed over the great plains hunting buffalo and proving their courage by war exploits. Now they lived on a reservation, and tending crops was no adequate substitute for their old way of life. Their old economic arrangements of boastful gift giving, their political life, and their religious practices had either been destroyed by circumstances or had lost their meaningfulness. Life had become pointless to them. These men talked with gusto about the failure of the family. They said that in the family the children no longer learned manners, or religion, or generosity, or whatever it was the individual Indian favored as a cure-all. The family, too, weighed a man down, they said; it was a burden to him.

To the anthropologist studying this tribe, however, the family was precisely the best arranged, most trustworthy institution in their whole culture. It was hard beset and it had not escaped the tragic effects of the general disintegration of tribal life, but it was what provided the warm, human ties and the dependable security which were left in that Indian tribe. The children were loved and cared for, the husbands and wives often had comfortable relations with each other, and the family hospitality had a graciousness that was absent in more public life. At birth and marriage and death the family still functioned as an effective institution. And there seemed to be no man or woman of childbearing age who was not married or would not have preferred to be.

The writer thinks of this Indian tribe when she hears Americans talk about the decay of the family. Instead of viewing the family with such alarm, suppose we look at it as it exists in this decade in this country and see how it is arranged to fulfill its functions in American schemes of life. Let us leave aside for the moment the questions of whether conditions are provided that would keep it from preventable overstrain and of whether as human beings we are able to get all the satisfaction we might out of this institution; let us consider only the arrangements of the family as we know it and how these fit in with our values and with the way we should like to plan our lives.

Suppose we take marriage first. Marriage sets up the new family, and it seems to make a great deal of difference whether a society dictates that the new home shall be begun in tears and heartache or with rejoicing. Many human societies would not recognize a marriage without a wailing bride and a sullen groom. Often the bride has to be surrounded by her mourning women, who lament her coming lifelong separation from her parents and her brothers and sisters, as well as her future misery as she goes to work for her mother-in-law. Often they cut her long hair and remove her jewelry as a sign that she is now a worker and no longer alluring. The groom's role, too, may be that of an unwilling victim. Often marriages are arranged by the parents without giving the two young people any chance to know each other.

All these circumstances are absent in marriage in the United States. The young people are hardly hampered in their choice of a mate; if occasionally parents deplore their choice, public opinion allows the young couple to outface them and expects the parents to accept the inevitable with as much decency as they can muster. We expect that the bride and groom will be in love or will have chosen each other for reasons known to themselves. Whether they marry for love or for money or to show they can win a sought-after mate from a rival, in any case they are making a personal choice and are not acting on command. Because in every field of life American culture puts such a high value on this kind of freedom and so bitterly resents its curtailment in peace time, the fact that the young people do make their own choice of a mate is an important and auspicious arrangement. The arranged marriage which is traditional in France or the careful class restrictions which have been observed in Holland would be difficult to manage in the United States. The wide range of choice of a mate and the fact that the young people make their own selection are conditions which could hardly be made more satisfactory for Americans with their particular habits and demands.

After marriage, too, the new family has a wide range of choices about where to live, how the wife shall occupy herself, when to start a family, and a host of other important matters. Such freedom is extremely unusual in the world. Sometimes the couple must live with the husband's family, sometimes with the wife's. Often in other countries, until one or two children are born, the young man continues to work for his father and has no say about the farm or the flock and no money which he can control. But in the United States a young couple plans the family budget before the wedding and what they earn is theirs to spend.

The way the new family in this country sets up its own separate home makes possible a rare and delightful circumstance: the two of them can have an incomparable privacy. No matter how hard it has been to arrange for privacy before marriage, as soon as the wedding is over everybody expects them to have their own latch key and their own possessions around them. If they cannot manage this, they feel cheated and other people think something is wrong. It is the same if they have to give a home to a parent. In most civilized countries this is a duty to which as a good son and good daughter they are bound, but if it is necessary in the United States their friends and neighbors will regard them as exceptionally burdened. Even the scarcity and high wages of domestic servants give the young family a greater privacy. Considering that they have chosen each other to their own liking, this privacy in the home is made in order to gratify them; the only problem is whether they can use it to their own happiness.

When they cannot, and when they find that their choice of a mate was not fool-proof just because they made it on their own, there is in the United States great freedom to get a divorce. Our growing divorce rate is the subject of much viewing-with-alarm; yet in a culture built as ours is on ever expanding personal choice, an important goal of which is the pursuit of happiness, the right to terminate an unhappy marriage is the other side of the coin of which the fair side is the right to choose one's spouse. Weak and stunted individuals will of course abuse both privileges, yet it is difficult to see how divorce could consistently be denied in a culture like ours. Certainly if we accepted it more honestly as a necessary phase of our way of life, however sorrowful, and put honest effort and sympathy into not penalizing the divorced, we should be acting more appropriately and in our best interests. At any rate, the high divorce rate in the United States is no attack on marriage, for it is precisely the divorced —those who have failed in one or two attempts—who have the highest rate of marriage. Between the ages of twenty-five and thirty-five not even the unmarried or the widowed marry at so great a rate as the divorced.

Besides free choice and privacy, the American family has unusual potential leisure because of the labor-saving devices, prepared foods, and ready-made clothes available under modern conditions. The basic labor-saver is running water in the sink, and Americans have little idea how many millions of homes in civilized countries do not have it. Thus we are saved an endless round of drudgery that ties down women—and men also—in countries where homes have no running water, no gas and electricity, no farm tools but those which are driven into the earth by human hands or are swung in human arms, and no use of ready-made soaps and foods and clothes. Americans put high value on lessened drudgery, but they deprecate having free spaces of truly leisure time; the more time they save the more they fill up their days and nights with a round of engagements and complications. They are unwilling to admit that they have leisure, but the schedules of their lives prove clearly how much they have.

Universal schooling in the United States also frees the family of many duties when children have come. It is hard for Americans to imagine the difference which regular school hours make in a mother's role. For a great part of the working day, American children are the responsibility of the teacher and not the mother. As nursery schools spread over the country, younger and younger children get trained care outside the home and the mother's labors are correspondingly relieved. As the children grow older the mother's leisure increases, until finally she reaches that middle age with its round of card parties and clubs and window shopping and movies which engross and waste the energy of so many millions of American women. Her husband is earning more money now than when he was younger, and her children have flown; she has a plethora of privileges and freedom and leisure. In one sense she has everything.

It is obviously unfair to talk about the incomparable freedom from drudgery which the American home offers without emphasizing that interval of a few years when there is no leisure for the mother in the home —the years when the babies are little. In our great cities where each family is strange to all the others, a mother is likely to have to be a baby tender every hour of the day, with no one to relieve her. Along with these duties she must do all her cooking and washing and cleaning. And, as all our magazines and women's pages reiterate, she must make efforts to keep her husband. She must keep herself looking attractive, must keep up social contacts, and be a companion to him. To European wives this program looks formidable. "I was always told that American women were so free," a Polish woman said to me, "but when I came here and saw how they had to manage with the babies and the house without any older women of the family to help, and then how they had to play around with their husbands in the evening to keep them happy, I decided I wouldn't change places with them for anything. In Poland a woman doesn't have to 'keep' her husband; it's all settled when they're married."

The striking fact about the nursery years in the United States is that in comparison with those in other countries they are so short and that nevertheless we do not really treat them as an interim. Mothers who are going through this period give remarkably little thought to the leisure that will come soon. They are often vocal enough about the turmoil of their present lives, and sometimes bitter, but the fact that the nursery years last so short a time in the United States and could be treated as an interim—like a professor's going into the government during war time

—is all too seldom part of their thinking. No doubt this is due in part to a lag in our culture, since even with our grandparents conditions were different; but in part it is a result of the sentiment which selects this period, no matter how short, as the fulfillment of a woman's chief duty in life. A social engineer looking at the family, however, would certainly put his major effort into better arrangements for the overburdened mother during these years and into thinking about effecting some transition from this period into that next one during which, in the United States, millions of women become idle parasites upon society—and dull and unhappy into the bargain.

Another notable feature of the American family is its peculiarly non-authoritarian character. The old rules that a child should be seen and not heard and the adage, "Spare the rod and spoil the child," are anachronistic in the United States; they are dispensed with even in immigrant groups which honored them in their native country. The rule of the father over the family is still a reality in some European nations, but in the United States the mother is the chief responsible agent in bringing up her children; here the father's opinions are something the children are more likely to play off against the mother's, to their own advantage, rather than a court of last authority from which there is no appeal. Children take the noisy center of the stage at the breakfast table and in the living room in a way that is quite impossible in European countries. The fact that they are expected to know right from wrong in their tenderest years and to act upon it on their own is often commented on by European mothers who have lived here. A Dutch mother once spoke to the author about how hard we are on our children because we expect this of them; she said, "I don't expect it of my children before they are seven; until then, I am there to see that they act correctly." But an American mother expects a child of three or four to be a responsible moral agent, and she gives him great latitude in which to prove that he can manage his little affairs by himself.

All this lack of strong authoritarianism in American families accords well with the values that are chiefly sought after in this country. No strong father image is compatible with our politics or our economics. We seek the opportunity to prove that we are as good as the next person, and we do not find comfort in following an authoritarian voice—in the state or in the home, from landowner or the priest—which will issue a command from on high. We learn as children to measure ourselves against Johnny next door, or against Mildred whose mother our mother knows in church, and this prepares us for living in a society with strongly egalitarian ideals. We do not learn the necessity of submitting to unquestioned commands as the children of many countries do. The family in the United States has become democratic.

These free-choice and non-authoritarian aspects of the family, along with its privacy and potential leisure, evidence only a few of the many ways in which it has become consistent with major emphases in our national life. They seem, when one compares them with arrangements in other civilized nations, to be quite well fitted to the role the family must play in a culture like the United States. . . .

20

Thoughts on the Future of the Family

by Barrington Moore, Jr.

Among social scientists it is almost axiomatic that the family is a universally necessary social institution and will remain such through any foreseeable future. Changes in its structure, to be sure, receive wide recognition. The major theme, however, in the appraisal American sociologists present is that the family is making up for lost economic functions by providing better emotional service. One work announces as its central thesis that "the family in historical times has been, and at present is, in transition from an institution to a companionship." In the past, the authors explain, the forces holding the family together were external, formal, and authoritarian, such as law, public opinion, and the authority of the father. Now, it is claimed, unity inheres in the mutual affection and comradeship of its members. Another recent work by a leading American sociologist makes a similar point. The trend under industrialism, we are told, does not constitute a decline of the family as such, but mainly a decline of its importance in the performance of economic functions. Meanwhile, the author tells us, the family has become a more specialized agency for the performance of other functions, namely, the socialization of children and

Reprinted by permission of the publishers from Barrington Moore, Jr., *Political Power and Social Theory,* Cambridge, Mass.: Harvard University Press, Ch. V, pp. 160–178. © Copyright 1958, by The President and Fellows of Harvard College.

Barrington Moore, Jr., is a writer on social and political topics. He became associated with the Russian Research Center at Harvard University after it was established by the Carnegie Foundation in 1949. His book, *Soviet Politics: The Dilemma of Power,* resulted from his study of modern Russia, a study which was one of the projects sponsored by the Center.

the stabilization of adult personalities. For this reason, the author continues, social arrangements corresponding rather closely to the modern family may be expected to remain with us indefinitely.

In reading these and similar statements by American sociologists about other aspects of American society, I have the uncomfortable feeling that the authors, despite all their elaborate theories and technical research devices, are doing little more than projecting certain middle-class hopes and ideals onto a refractory reality. If they just looked a little more carefully at what was going on around them, I think they might come to different conclusions. This is, of course, a very difficult point to prove, though C. Wright Mills, in a brilliant essay, has shown how one area of American sociology, the study of crime, is suffused with such preconceptions. While personal observations have some value, one can always argue that a single observer is biased. Here all I propose to do, therefore, is to raise certain questions about the current sociological assessment of the family on the basis of such evidence as has come my way rather casually. In addition, I should like to set this evidence in the framework of an intellectual tradition, represented, so far as the family is concerned, by Bertrand Russell's *Marriage and Morals,* that sees the family in an evolutionary perspective, and raises the possibility that it may be an obsolete institution or become one before long. I would suggest then that conditions have arisen which, in many cases, prevent the family from performing the social and psychological functions ascribed to it by modern sociologists. The same conditions may also make it possible for the advanced industrial societies of the world to do away with the family and substitute other social arrangements that impose fewer unnecessary and painful restrictions on humanity. Whether or not society actually would take advantage of such an opportunity is, of course, another question.

It may be best to begin with one observation that is not in itself conclusive but at least opens the door to considering these possibilities. In discussions of the family, one frequently encounters the argument that Soviet experience demonstrates the necessity of this institution in modern society. The Soviets, so the argument runs, were compelled to adopt the family as a device to carry part of the burden of making Soviet citizens, especially after they perceived the undesirable consequences of savage homeless children, largely the outcome of the Civil War. This explanation is probably an accurate one as far as it goes. But it needs to be filled out by at least two further considerations that greatly reduce its force as a general argument. In the first place, the Soviets, I think, adopted their conservative policy toward the family *faute de mieux*. That is to say, with their very limited resources, and with other more pressing objectives, they had no genuine alternatives. Steel mills had to be built before crèches, or at least before crèches on a large enough scale to make any real difference in regard to child care. In the meantime the services of the family, and especially of grandma (*babushka*), had to be called upon. In the second place, with the consolidation of the regime in the middle thirties, Soviet totalitarianism may have succeeded in capturing the family and subverting this institution to its own uses. At any rate the confidence and vigor with which the regime supported this institution from the early thirties onward suggests such an explanation. Thus the Soviet experience does not constitute by itself very strong evidence in favor of the "functional necessity" of the family.

If the Soviet case does not dispose of the possibility that the family may be obsolete, we may examine other considerations with greater confidence, and begin by widening our historical perspective. By now it is a familiar observation that the stricter Puritan ethics of productive work and productive sex have accomplished their historical purposes in the more advanced sections of the Western world. These developments have rendered other earlier elements of Western culture and society, such as slavery, quite obsolete, and constitute at least prima facie evidence for a similar argument concerning the family. Let us ask then to what extent may we regard the family as a repressive survival under the conditions of an advanced technology? And to what extent does the modern family perform the function of making human beings out of babies and small children either badly or not at all?

One of the most obviously obsolete features of the family is the obligation to give affection as a duty to a particular set of persons on account of the accident of birth. This is a true relic of barbarism. It is a survival from human prehistory, when kinship was the basic form of social organization. In early times it was expedient to organize the division of labor and affection in human society through real or imagined kinship bonds. As civilization became technically more advanced, there has been less and less of a tendency to allocate both labor and affection according to slots in a kinship system, and an increasing tendency to award them on the basis of the actual qualities and capacities that the individual possesses.

Popular consciousness is at least dimly aware of the barbaric nature of the duty of family affection and the pain it produces, as shown by the familiar remark, "You can choose your friends, but you can't choose your relatives." Even if partly concealed by ethical imperatives with the weight of age-old traditions, the strain is nevertheless real and visible. Children are often a burden to their parents. One absolutely un-Bohemian couple I know agreed in the privacy of their own home that if people ever talked to each other openly about the sufferings brought on by raising a family today, the birth rate would drop to zero. It is, of course, legitimate to wonder how widespread such sentiments are. But this couple is in no sense "abnormal." Furthermore, a revealing remark like this made to a friend is worth more as evidence than reams of scientific questionnaires subjected to elaborate statistical analyses. Again, how many young couples, harassed by the problems of getting started in life, have not wished that their parents could be quietly and cheaply taken care of in some institution for the aged? Such facts are readily accessible to anyone who listens to the conversations in his own home or among the neighbors.

The exploitation of socially sanctioned demands for gratitude, when the existing social situation no longer generates any genuine feeling of warmth, is a subtle and heavily tabooed result of this barbaric heritage. It is also one of the most painful. Perhaps no feeling is more excruciating than the feeling that we ought to love a person whom we actually detest. The Greek tragedians knew about the problem, but veiled it under religion and mythology, perhaps because the men and women of that time felt there was no escape. In the nineteenth century the theme again became a dominant one in European literature, but with the clear implication that the situation was unnecessary. Even these authors, Tolstoi, Samuel Butler, Strindberg, and Ibsen, in exposing the horrors and hypocrisies of family life, wove most of their stories around the marital relationship, where there is an element of free choice in the partner selected. Kafka's little gem, *Das Urteil,* is a significant exception. With magnificent insight into the tragedy on both sides, it treats the frustrations of a grown-up son forced to cherish a helpless but domineering father. Henry James' short story, *Europe,* is an effective treatment of the same relationship between a mother and her daughters. Despite some blind spots and limitations, the artists, it appears, have seen vital aspects of the family that have largely escaped the sociologists.

In addition to these obsolete and barbaric features one can point to certain trends in modern society that have sharply reduced rather than increased the effectiveness of the home as an agency for bringing up children. In former times the family was a visibly coherent economic unit, as well as the group that served to produce and raise legitimate children. The father had definite and visible economic tasks, before the household became separated from the place of work. When the children could see what he did, the father had a role to be copied and envied. The source and justification of his authority was clear. Internal conflicts had to be resolved. This is much less the case now.

It is reasonably plain that today's children are much less willing than those of pre-industrial society to take their parents as models for conduct. Today they take them from the mass media and from gangs. Radio and television heroes, with their copies among neighborhood gangs, now play a vital part in the socialization process. Parents have an uphill and none too successful struggle against these sources. Like adult mobs, children's groups readily adopt the sensational, the cruel, and the most easily understood for their models and standards. These influences then corrupt and lower adult standards, as parents become increasingly afraid to assert their own authority for fear of turning out "maladjusted" children.[1]

The mass media have largely succeeded in battering down the walls of the social cell the family once constituted in the larger structure of society. Privacy has greatly diminished. Newspapers, radios, and television have very largely destroyed the flow of private communications within the family that were once the basis of socialization. Even meals are now much less of a family affair. Small children are frequently plumped down in front of the television set with their supper on a tray before them to keep them quiet. Since the family does less as a unit, genuine emotional ties among its members do not spring up so readily. The advertising campaign for "togetherness" provides rather concrete evidence that family members would rather not be together.

The mother, at least in American society, is generally supposed to be the homemaker and the center of the family. Has she been able to take up the slack produced by the change in the father's role? Is she, perhaps, the happy person whose face smiles at us from every advertisement and whose arts justify the sociologists' case? A more accurate assessment may be that the wife suffers most in the modern middle-class family, because the demands our culture puts upon her are impossible to meet. As indicated by advertisements, fiction, and even the theories of sociologists, the wife is expected to be companion, confidante, and ever youthful mistress of her husband.

If the demands could be met, many wives might feel very happy in this fulfillment of their personality. The actual situation is very different. The father is out of the house all day and therefore can be neither overlord nor companion. With the father absent, radio and television provide the mother with a watery substitute for adult companionship. A young colleague told me recently that his wife leaves the radio on all day merely to hear the sound of a grown-up voice. The continual chatter of little children can be profoundly irritating, even to a naturally affectionate person. The absence of servants from nearly all American middle-class households brings the wife face to face with the brutalizing features of motherhood and housework. If she had the mentality of a peasant, she might be able to cope with them more easily. Then, however, she could not fulfill the decorative functions her husband expects. As it is now, diapers, dishes, and the state of the baby's bowels absorb the day's quota of energy. There is scarcely any strength left for sharing emotions and

[1] It is sometimes claimed that the modern family still represents a bulwark against mass and totalitarian pressures. No doubt this is true in the best cases, those few where parents are still able to combine authority and affection. These are, however, mainly a relic of Victorian times. By and large it seems more likely that the family constitutes the "transmission belt" through which totalitarian pressures toward conformity are transmitted to the parents through the influence of the children.

experiences with the husband, for which there is often no opportunity until the late hours of the evening. It is hardly a wonder that the psychiatrists' anterooms are crowded, or that both husband and wife seek escapes from psychological and sexual boredom, the cabin fever of the modern family. For the wife, either a job or an affair may serve equally well as a release from domesticity.

A further sign of the modern family's inadequacy in stabilizing the human personality may be seen in the troubled times of adolescence. This stage of growing up has been interpreted as a rejection of adult standards of responsibility and work by youngsters who are about to enter adult life. It seems to me that this period is more significantly one of pseudo-rebellion, when the youngsters copy what they see to be the real values of adult life instead of the professed ones. Even in the more extreme forms of youthful rebellion, relatively rare among respectable middle-class children, such as roaring around in noisy cars to drinking and seduction parties, the adolescents are aping actual adult behavior. Adolescents then do things they know many grown-ups do when the latter think they are escaping the observant eyes of the young. A "hot-rod" is, after all, nothing but an immature Cadillac. Where the Cadillac is the symbol of success, what else could be expected? Adult standards too are made tolerable through commercialized eroticism that lures us on to greater efforts and greater consumption from every billboard and magazine cover. Thus the whole miasma of sexual and psychological boredom in the older generation, pseudo-rebellion and brutality in the younger one, is covered over by a sentimental and suggestive genre art based on commercial sentiment.

No doubt many will think that these lines paint too black a picture. Statistics could perhaps be accumulated to show that families such as the type sketched here are far from a representative cross-section of American middle-class life. Such facts, however, would not be relevant to the argument. As pointed out elsewhere in these essays, the representative character of certain types of social behavior is not necessarily relevant to estimates of current and future trends. This kind of statistical defense of the status quo represents that of a certain maiden's virtue by the claim, "After all, she is only a little bit pregnant."

To refute the appraisal offered in these pages it would be necessary to demonstrate that they misrepresent basic structural trends in the family in advanced industrial countries. The most important argument of this type that I have encountered asserts that the proportion of married people in the population has steadily risen while the proportion of single individuals has steadily dropped. Therefore, people obviously prefer family life to bachelorhood, and the gloomy picture sketched above must be nothing more than vaporings of sour-bellied intellectuals thrown on the dumpheap by the advance of American society.

Before discussing the question further, let us look at some of the relevant facts. The table below shows changes in the proportions of single, married, and divorced persons in the United States from the age of fourteen onward. The source, an authoritative and very recent statistical survey of the American family, has standardized the proportions for age, using the 1940 age distribution as a standard, in order to eliminate changes due merely to shifts in the age composition of our population, which would merely confuse the issue.

Percentage Distribution of Persons 14 Years and Over by Marital Status and Sex in the Civilian Population 1890–1954

Year	MALE Single	Married	Divorced	FEMALE Single	Married	Divorced
1954	28.4	66.7	1.8	22	65.8	2.2
1950	29.4	65.5	1.5	22.5	64.8	2.1
1940	34.8	59.7	1.2	27.6	59.5	1.6
1930	34.7	59.1	1.1	26.9	59.7	1.3
1890	36.7	57.9	0.2	27.8	57.7	0.4

The figures do show a rise in the proportion of married persons and a decline in the proportion of single ones. They also show that the proportion of married persons is overwhelmingly larger than the number of divorced ones. But the biggest change has been in the proportion of divorced people. For men it has risen ninefold since 1890 and for women more than fivefold. A bigger proportion of people are married now than in 1890, but a *much* bigger proportion have abandoned the marital state. In the long run, the latter change might turn out to be the more important one.

Even the statistical evidence, in other words, does not uphold in a completely unambiguous manner the sociologists' argument for the family. Sometimes an attempt to save the case is made by interpreting the rise in divorce as something that allows greater freedom for the individual to choose marital partners on the basis of congeniality. Thereby divorce allegedly strengthens the family's function as a source of emotional support. By talking about greater freedom for the individual in this fashion one has already taken a long step toward the opponents' view that marriage as such may be superfluous.

The point cannot be considered merely in the light of the facts as they exist now or have existed in the past. To do this in social questions is basically unscientific. Those who dismiss negative appraisals of the family with the crude observation that they reflect personal bias or mere "European decadence" deserve an equally crude reply: "So what if Americans prefer to get married! That simply shows how stupid they are."

Acrimony here unfortunately conceals a genuine issue. It is perfectly possible that conditions exist, perhaps even now, that permit better institutional arrangements than most people would be willing to accept. The word better, of course, implies a definite standard of judgment. One can debate such standards endlessly, and perhaps cannot reach agreement without at some point making arbitrary assumptions. I shall not enter this debate here except to say that any social institution is a bad one that imposes more suffering on people than is necessary when they have sufficient material resources and scientific knowledge to do away with this suffering. This standard, anthropologists tell us, is that not only of Western culture, but of all culture.

What then, are the prospects for the future? We need not take a completely determinist view. Indeed, the perceptions that both plain people and opinion makers have about the present enter in as a significant component among the forces shaping the future and thereby provide an entering wedge for rational adaptation.

Among those who accept a substantial part of the preceding image of the family as basically correct, one frequently hears the prescription that what American culture really needs is a higher evaluation of the social role of the housewife and of motherhood. The trouble with this prescription, I would suggest, is that it merely increases the element of self-deception already so prevalent in our culture. Under present conditions motherhood *is* frequently a degrading experience. There is nothing to be gained by concealing the facts in the manner of an advertising campaign designed to raise the prestige of a particular occupation. We would not think of trying to eliminate the hazards of coal mining in this way. Why should we try to do it with motherhood? If it is true that under present circumstances the experience of motherhood narrows and cramps the personality rather than promotes the development of its capacities, some other way will have to be found if it is to be a real solution.

The trend towards a continually more efficient technology and greater specialization, which dominates the rest of our culture, may conceivably provide an answer. In regard to the division of labor it is important to recall one widely known but neglected fact. In the past, whenever human beings have acquired sufficient resources and power, as among aristocracies, they have put the burden of child-rearing on other shoulders. Twenty years ago Ralph Linton pointed out that "aristocrats the world over . . . are reluctant to take care of their own children. Anyone who has had to take care of two or three infants simultaneously will understand why. This arduous business is turned over to slaves or servants. . . ."

Since the decline of slavery, a basic trend in European society has been to transfer to machines more and more tasks formerly carried out by slaves. By and large, this change has been accompanied by the growth of large organizations to perform tasks formerly scattered among many small groups. This trend may well affect the family. Specialized human agencies, developing from such contemporary forms as the crèche, play school, and boarding school, might assume a much larger share of the burden of child-rearing, a task that could in any case be greatly lightened by machinery for feeding and the removal of waste products. Can one sensibly argue that the technical ingenuity and resources required to solve this problem are greater than those necessary for nuclear warfare? Are we to regard as permanent and "natural" a civilization that develops its most advanced technology for killing people and leaves their replacement to the methods of the Stone Age?

Against this viewpoint it is usually argued that human infants require some minimum of human affection, even fondling, if they are to survive, and that therefore some form of the family is bound to remain. The premises may be correct, but the conclusion does not follow. A nurse can perform these tasks of giving affection and early socialization just as well as the parents, often better. The argument does not prove anything therefore about the inevitable necessity of the family.

At the same time this point of view does call attention to certain important problems. Industrial society is not likely to produce household nurses, or any form of "servant class" in abundance. On of the other hand, as everyone knows who has been in a hospital, nurses in a bureaucratic setting have a strong tendency to treat persons under their care "by the book," without much regard for their individual tasks and requirements. This is a well-known trait of bureaucracy, which tends to treat people and situations alike in order to achieve precision and efficiency. Infants and small children on the contrary require individual attention. For some years they may need to feel that they are the center of the universe. How then can the characteristics of bureaucracy be brought in line with those of maternal affection?

Though this may be the most difficult problem facing any qualitative transformation of the family, it is not necessarily insoluble. In the first place, as Bertrand Russell points out, a good institutional environment may be better for the development of the human personality than a bad family one. In the second place, an increase in the resources allocated to a bureaucratic organization can greatly increase its flexibility and capacity to satisfy variations in individual temperament. Any first-class hotel knows how to cope with this problem. In a few of the best ones in Europe the guest can have privacy and the illusion of being the center of the universe. Finally, one might legitimately expect that the persons who are drawn to serve in any such child-rearing institutions of the future would have more than the average amount of fondness for children, as well as general human warmth and kindliness. Under proper circumstances and management such institutions could give full scope to these benevolent sentiments.

Certain other considerations suggest an alternative that has at least the merit of being much more palatable to the vast majority of people today, since it is more in line with our deep-rooted cultural traditions. These considerations are essentially two. One is the possibility of some innate biological trait roughly resembling the "maternal instinct." The other lies in technological developments that might allow for wider dissemination of machinery to lighten household tasks and to take over the more routine aspects of child-rearing. The dish-washing machine, laundromat, and, as a much more extreme device, the "Skinner box" represent prototypes of this technological development that could strengthen decentralized arrangements for rearing children.

I do not know what students of human physiology now believe about the maternal instinct. Common observation is enough to show that it cannot be an instinct like sex or hunger. There are many women who never become fond of children, or who soon cease to be fond of them. For them the institutional outlet just sketched would be the most satisfactory way of providing for their offspring. But for others, possibly the majority, the gestation period with its trials and burdens may be enough to create in the mother a desire to retain the infant under her care, after which she could become reluctant to give it up. If machinery were available to lighten child-rearing and household tasks on a far wider scale than is now the case, mothers might be able to satisfy the more positive desires of motherhood. One that seems to be quite important in the middle class is the desire to mold the child according to some ideal image, though it is now contradicted by fears of damaging the child that derive from superficial popularizations of Freud.

For the home to become again the place where human beings take the first important steps toward realizing their creative potentialities, parents would have to become willing once more to assert their authority. In turn this authority would have to acquire a rational and objective basis, freed of current attempts to revive religious taboos. Thus there would have to be a philosophical as well as a social revolution whose implications we cannot here pursue. One aspect, nevertheless, deserves to be stressed. Rational arguments can be given only to persons competent to understand them. For obvious reasons children are not able to absorb all rational arguments at once, though the present system of education undoubtedly postpones the development of this faculty where it does not destroy it altogether. Therefore parents will have to learn not to be afraid of saying to a child, "You are not old enough yet to understand why you have to do this. But you must do it anyway." The "progressive" family, where every decision turns into an incoherent and rancorous debate, actually contributes to reactionary tendencies in society by failing to equip the next generation with adequate standards of judgment.

There are, however, some grounds for doubting that this conservative solution will eventually prevail as the dominant one. The disappearance of the wider economic functions of the family would make it very difficult, and probably impossible, to restore the emotional atmosphere of a co-operative group in which the father has a respected authority. Furthermore, the bureaucratic division of labor has proved the most effective way of solving recurring and routine problems in other areas of life. Though a considerable part of the task of raising children is not routine, a very great portion is repetitive. For these reasons one may expect that semi-bureaucratic arrangements will continue to encroach on the traditional structure of the family. No doubt many individual variations, combinations, and compromises will remain for some time to come. Yet one fine day human society may realize that the part-time family, already a prominent part of our social landscape, has undergone a qualitative transformation into a system of mechanized and bureaucratized child-rearing, cleansed of the standardized overtones these words now imply. As already pointed out, an institutional environment can be warm and supporting, often warmer than a family torn by obligations its members resent.

Such a state of affairs, if it comes at all, is well over the visible horizon now. Quite possibly it may never come at all. If it does come, there is not the slightest guarantee that it will solve all personal problems and land us in a state of airconditioned euphoria. Values that many people hold high today may go by the board, such as the affection older couples show for one another who have shared the same pains in life until they have grown but a single scar. It is also possible that a world of reduced family burdens might be one of shallow and fleeting erotic intrigues, based really on commercial interests. Hollywood could conceivably be the ugly prototype of such a future world, especially in its earlier transitional phases. The most that might be claimed by any future apologist for such institutions, if they ever come to pass, is that they gave greater scope to the development of the creative aspects of the human personality than did the family, which had begun to damage rather than develop this personality under advancing industrialism. And the most that can be claimed for the arguments supporting this possibility is that they correspond to some important trends visible in the family itself as well as in the rest of society. Nevertheless, it would appear that the burden of proof falls on those who maintain that the family is a social institution whose fate will differ in its essentials from that which has befallen all the others.

II

RURAL AND URBAN COMMUNITIES

THE TERM CITY has a variety of meanings: statistical, political, and sociological, and hence it can be regarded from a number of perspectives and levels of understanding. Statistically, the city is an aggregation of people living within a comparatively small area, merely a matter of numbers. Politically, it is a unit of government recognized by some state. Sociologically, the city is a mode of life created by man: the product, Hauser suggests, of the cumulative effects of various revolutions ranging from the neolithic to the industrial. Urban areas today face further revolution. Hauser surveys the possible impact of the changes in our cities upon human nature and society.

Silberman deals with the efforts of the people of a slum neighborhood —the Woodlawn community in Chicago—*to help themselves* by taking concerted action to achieve a variety of goals. Those who organized the Woodlawn community assumed that most efforts at improving slum neighborhoods fail—not because of the nature of the community, but because of the objectives and methods of the planners and their failure to enlist the active support of the people.

21

On the Impact of Urbanism on Society

by Philip M. Hauser

Man as the only culture-building animal on the globe not only adapts to environment but creates environment to which to adapt. The urban or metropolitan area is one of man's more complex cultural constructs which, on the one hand, is an impressive symbol of achievement and, on the other, the matrix of serious and pressing problems. Product of the cumulative effects of the various "revolutions," ranging from the "neolithic" to the "industrial" the urban area today faces the prospect of adjustment to still further revolutions. These revolutions are being generated by electronic and atomic technology, which together with developing rocketry may produce new and as yet unvisualized dimensions of change, or even result in the annihilation of the metropolis altogether.

It is generally believed that the neolithic revolution with its invention of domesticated plants produced the first relatively widespread and fixed human settlements. The emergence of an agricultural economy and increasing dependence on its products led gradually to the abandonment of the nomadic existence. Neolithic settlements were relatively small population groupings, villages rather than towns, whose size was limited by technological, economic, social and political factors. The appearance of larger population aggregations, the town and the city, depended on developments which did not appear until the metal ages. The emergence of a metropolitan area of a million or more is probably a modern phenomenon dependent on the technology and the economic, social and political organization identified with the industrial revolution.

Since the first city of one million or more inhabitants was probably nineteenth century London, it may be said, in broad perspective, that it took man, or closely related ancestors, some one hundred thousand to one million years to produce the modern metropolis. But the metropolis not only is the consequent of such developments; it is also a determinant of further development. Urbanism has profoundly affected the social order;

From *Confluence: An International Forum*, Spring 1958, Vol. 7, No. 1, pp. 57–69, *passim*. Reprinted by permission.
Philip M. Hauser is Professor of Sociology at the University of Chicago.

has modified the nature of human nature and has produced vast changes in the political order.

It is to the consideration of aspects of these changes, or aspects of "urbanism as a way of life," that this essay is addressed.

I

The fact that living in the city makes a difference in the way of life has been noted by the writers of antiquity, as well as by more recent observers. . . . Increased size and destiny of population produce the equivalent of a mutation in social structure and organization. Great variations in physical spacing and accessibility of people to one another lead to quite different social orders. In the most abstract documentation of this observation, it may be indicated that in a density situation of 35 persons per square mile (common in non-urban areas) the individual can, within a 3 mile radius, reach fewer than 1,000 persons. If the population density is 10,000 persons per square mile (a common figure in cities) the person has access within a 3 mile radius to over 280,000 people. . . .

The urban social order is the opposite of the folk society which Redfield described as small, isolated, homogeneous, with simple technology, with simple division of labor, largely independent economically, characterized by strong organization of conventional understanding with no systematic knowledge in books and with no "market" complex. Wirth, in describing the "urban mode of life," emphasized the way in which the physical mechanism of the city, including the pattern of land use, land values, transport and communication facilities, influenced urban living. He emphasized the dominance of the city over its hinterland. He pointed to the way in which the essential abstract characteristics of the city—"size," "density" and "heterogeneity" resulted in "the substitution of secondary for primary contacts, the weakening in the bonds of kinship and the declining social significance of the family, the disappearance of the neighborhood, and the undermining of the traditional bases of social solidarity."

In connection with the general impact of urbanism on the social order as described above, it must be noted that in the United States "heterogeneity" played a peculiarly important role because this nation has been largely peopled by diverse ethnic groups from Europe and by the Negro from Africa. Our cities during the nineteenth and early part of the twentieth century were made up predominantly of the foreign born and their immediate descendants. During the last four or five decades, and especially since the onset of World War II, our cities have been subject to relatively large streams of Negro migrants, shifting from the South to the North and to the West. Thus the emergence of the urban mode of life in the United States has, in comparison with most other Western nations, been more vitally affected by the admixture of diverse ethnic and racial groups. This process is by no means complete. In Chicago, in 1950, for example—and this is not an atypical situation—the "foreign white stock" as defined by the United States Census (that is, the foreign born plus native of foreign or mixed parentage) made up about 45% of the population; and the non-white made up an additional 15%. Thus the third generation or [more] white population of Chicago, and of many of our large metropolitan areas, constitute a minority.

The changes described are of course reflected in changes in social institutions. Because the family has in our society traditionally been recognized as the primary social unit, it is a convenient unit through which to trace many of the influences of urbanism on social institutions. The colonial family in early American history was the keystone of social organization. For example, it was a basic and largely self-sufficient economic unit; it provided for the security and protection of its members; and it was the center for their affectional and recreational life.

Even this most solidly rooted of our social institutions, however, has not been able to withstand the impact of urbanization. Compared with the colonial family, the modern urban family is smaller; it is more often childless and has fewer children, if fertile. The urban family collectively and individually is much more mobile; it possesses comparatively little economic or social unity; is much more frequently broken by separation or divorce; and, as my collegeaue William F. Ogburn demonstrated some time ago, has long since lost many of its various historic functions, or shared them with new, specialized, urban institutions. The relationship of husband and wife, parents to children, children to each other and of the "small" to the "large" family have been redefined in the urban setting. The relations of family members to one another compete in depth, range, influence and satisfaction with extra-family relationships.

As old institutions, including the family, were modified, new institutions emerged in response to new needs. These have given rise to specialized types of agencies such as the police department, public health services, insurance, workmen's compensation laws, unemployment compensation, labor unions and civilian defense organizations. In brief, the urban environment has forced modification of our inherited institutions and has precipitated the need for the formation and development of new institutions.

One of the most important differences between the urban and "folk" environment as it affects the conduct of the person is to be found in the extent to which he is faced with the necessity of exercising choice, of substituting rational for traditional ways of doing things. In the "folk" setting there is generally a prescribed way of dealing with most situations, certainly with the most important recurrent situations in life. In the city there are almost always alternatives—and the person is forced to make a choice.

These basic changes in the nature of human nature in the urban setting are expressed, of course, in changes in modes of thought and action and in personality types. . . .

Enforced rationalism and urban living, together with rapid social change, provide the matrix for social and personal disorganization, blatant manifestations of the frictions of urbanism as a way life. . . .

The juvenile delinquent and the criminal are manifestations of the breakdown of inherited social controls. They are symptoms of the deteriorating influence in the urban environment of such social institutions as the family and the church, of the waning grip of our mores, of the inadequacy, as yet, of the emergent new controls represented by such substitute institutions as the school, the court, the prison and the reformatory. The pauper, early industrial sweated labor, the radical and revolutionist, the unemployed, the aged dependent and the striker are some of the by-products of rapid change and its attendant frictions in our economic organization and in its impact on other aspects of total social organization. The corrupt political boss, the "big fix," the grafter, the "short pencil" operator and the unscrupulous lobbyist mirror the disorganization of political institutions caught in the vortex of rapid social change. Modern war, as a symptom of social disorganization, can be described largely as an outgrowth of the new forms of international contact and international economic, social and political interdependence which precipitate new frictions and problems for the peaceful resolution of which an adequate international social heritage—adequate international institutions, processes and patterns of conduct and thought—have not yet emerged.

Urban existence in breaking down the inherited vestiges of a "folk" order is producing many forms of disorganization. But it has also opened up new vistas for self-expression and new opportunities for shaping both man's environment and his destiny. For the same processes of social change that produce social and personal disorganization free man's mind from the constraints of the past and promote the exercise of ingenuity and creativity. It is not merely a coincidence that the great centers of learning, invention, innovation, art and culture have historically been located in urban areas.

In the new urban matrix of social interaction, a new human nature has been bred which is still in process of social evolution. The "city mentality," characterized by its sophistication, objectivity, utilitarianism and rationalism, is on the one hand a product of the urban environment, and on the other a major force producing and influencing changes in our social heritage, in our economic, social and political intsitutions and in the urban environment itself.

II

Many of our pressing contemporary problems in government and in politics are symptoms of the strains arising from the anachronism represented by our twentieth century industrial, urban, economic and social order and eighteenth and nineteenth century forms of government and political structure.

The city as the symbol of the twentieth century order is the nub of the many sore political problems of the day. The great metropolitan areas of the country have long since outgrown their inherited governmental structures. Arising as geographic, economic, demographic and social entities, they are nevertheless subjected to layer upon layer of local governmental structure. The 168 Standard Metropolitan Areas delineated by the Federal government in 1950 contained over 16,000 governmental units (including school districts) with powers to tax and to spend. They thus averaged some 100 governmental units per Standard Metropolitan Area; and the larger SMA's had about a thousand governmental units.

The city in the United States is usually the corporate creature of a state, with boundaries rigidly defined by a state charter. In contrast, the economic, population and social phenomena which it symbolizes, but of which the metropolitan area rather than the city is the expression, are not so rigidly defined.

As a result chaos is evident in many of our metropolitan areas in respect to problems with which prevalent forms of governmental structure are ill-equipped to deal. These include such area-wide problems as traffic control, highways, public transport, water and air ports, water supply, sanitation, housing, crime, recreation, health and welfare and the like. The pressures created by the area-wide problems may be expected to mount. It may be anticipated in the coming decades that new governmental mechanisms will emerge to complement or to supplant present forms of local government.

An acute aspect of problems of local government is evident in the conflict of interests between central cities and the metropolitan rings or suburbs. Mayor Zeidler of Milwaukee in a recent paper has predicted increasing political cleavage between central cities and their suburban areas, and has suggested that suburban areas may unite with downstate areas in coalition against central cities.

Certainly there is a basis for drawing such a generalization in recent voting behavior. But such projections overlook at least several factors which may conceivably produce a quite different situation, perhaps even within the next two decades.

For one thing, by 1975, of a total possible population of 228 million in the United States, about two-thirds—or about 150 million persons—are likely to be resident in Standard Metropolitan Areas, with only a third of the population in the remaining areas of the country. Of the population within the Standard Metropolitan Areas, only half will be resident in central cities and the remainder will live in suburban areas. Certainly it will be true that suburban area populations together with non-standard metropolitan area populations will greatly surpass central city populations, in fact surpass them by a ratio of two to one. But the community of interest between metropolitan suburban populations and non-metropolitan area populations is easily exaggerated. The following are among the considerations that indicate that community of interest between suburban and central city populations will grow closer rather than further apart, and tend to preclude suburban-non-metropolitan area coalition.

Standard Metropolitan Areas are at present absorbing 97 per cent of the total population increase of the nation, with disproportionate increases in outlying suburban areas which, between 1950 and 1955, grew 7 times as rapidly as central cities (28 per cent as compared with 4 per cent). The rapidity of metropolitan area growth, especially suburban growth, together with the fact that a relatively large proportion of suburban growth is derived from the central cities through migration, is likely to mean that suburban areas will more closely resemble central cities in the next two decades than they have in the past decade. That is, the continued process of metropolitan area growth is extending so far beyond central city boundaries that large parts of suburban areas will contain working-class and lower-middle-class populations of the type which was previously located in inner zones of central cities when metropolitan areas as a whole were smaller. Many political analysts tend to assume that migrants from central cities to suburbs become conservative and Republican when they come in association with the higher social-economic strata previously associated with suburban living. But these political analysts fail to recognize that by the time the suburbs contain 50 to 56 per cent of the population in Standard Metropolitan Areas, which may be the case by 1975, they will no longer be made up entirely of upper- and upper-middle-class groups.

Another acute aspect of contemporary problems in local government and politics is evident in the widespread concern about the growing Negro population in central cities. Some political analysts assume that the Negro migrant to the central cities will retain his low social-economic characteristics and previous political behavior; and visualize that "a kind of economic caste system will develop." They believe that lower-class Negroes will remain in central cities with the suburbs containing the white upper-income groups.

This assumption completely ignores the past history of migration to cities and the processes by which migrants have been absorbed into "urbanism as a way of life." The Negro migrant to the central city will, without question, follow the same patterns of social mobility blazed by the successive waves of immigrants who settled in our central cities. Just as the immigrant underwent a process of "Americanization," the in-migrant Negro is undergoing a process of "urbanization." The Negro is already rising and will continue to rise on the social-economic scale as measured by education, occupation, income and the amenities of urban existence.

Furthermore, the Negro, in time, will diffuse through the metropolitan area and occupy outlying suburban as well as central city areas.

These observations should not be construed to deny the possibility, in the short run, of central cities becoming vast non-white areas of lower economic status than the suburbs. The forces described above, however, are likely, in the longer run, to produce an admixture of low and high economic status and white and non-white populations both in the central cities and in the suburbs. . . .

Quite apart from the problems of governmental structure and levels of government, urbanism has greatly affected the role of government itself, the character of public administration, the nature of representative government, the political party system and the substance of political issues.

There is no doubt that the complex of technological, economic and social changes which constitute "urbanism" is the major factor in the rapidity with which governmental functions have proliferated, often despite the express intent of administrations. The urban way of life, the increasing interdependence of the elements of the social order and the increasing inability of traditional and inherited social institutions to cope with the new problems of urban living have led inexorably to the multiplication of government functions, powers and personnel; and the process is still under way.

The complex and often technical character of the urban problems has changed the requirements of "governing." In the urban setting, public administration requires many technical and professional skills. The "expert" has emerged as a new and powerful element in government, and bureaucracy has become an indispensable tool in the functioning of society.

Urbanization has also brought great changes in the nature of representative government. Representative government as provided for in the United States was an adaptation of the "democracy" of the Greek city state. It is one thing, however, for a representative to speak for a small, homogeneous, rural, agricultural constituency; and quite another thing to "represent" a heterogeneous population of one-quarter to one-half million persons with diverse and sometimes conflicting interests. The emergence of the public opinion poll may be regarded as an invention in the urban scene for the measurement of the "will" of the urban population. It may play an increasingly important role in representative government in the years to come.

Urbanism is also increasing the strains to which our two party system is being subjected. The historic differences which led to the formation of our political parties are more and more obscured by the problems of our complex urban order. As a result there is a wider range of interests, political philosophies and policies within each of our great political parties than between them. The increased choice forced upon the urbanite, discussed above, extends also to the choice of political parties. The urban voter is more apt to choose than to inherit his political preferences; therefore the increasing importance of the "independent" vote. In the state of transition in which we still find ourselves, the citizen, in voting, often has little notion of just what men, principles and policies he is supporting; and the elected official often operates with no better awareness of the policy preferences of the electorate. . . .

III

The problems of urbanization—social, personal and political—are but symptoms of the frictions produced by the differential rates of change in our social heritage. But reorganization can never be achieved without a certain amount of disorganization. We can be comforted by the many obvious advantages and advances which the industrial revolution and the city have brought with them, including an ever-rising standard of living and an unprecedented opportunity for personal expression and creativity.

The adjustments necessary to achieve an integrated and consistent social heritage can conceivably be attained in time through "natural" processes—through the forces which produce the "strain toward consistency" in our culture. This process of social evolution perhaps parallels the biological "struggle for existence" and the "survival of the fittest," but in the area of culture traits and culture complexes.

Unlike the rest of the animal kingdom, however, man has it within his power to speed up the social evolutionary process—to accelerate the adjustment of social and political institutions and ideologies to the new requirements forced by technological and structural change. Indeed, one of the most important influences of urbanization lies in the emancipation of the person from the rigidities and restraints imposed upon him by tradition, in the new opportunity—in large measure forced upon him by the nature of urban existence—to be a rational animal and to intervene in the processes of social change so as to exert some control over its tempo and its direction.

22

Up from Apathy—The Woodlawn Experiment

by Charles E. Silberman

In recent years a growing number of liberals—reflecting the wistful American notion that with enough money any problem can be solved— have been pushing for a federal "crash program" to remove the disabilities and deprivations that bar Negroes from full participation in American society. Yet expenditures for welfare assistance have been rising at a rapid rate in every large city, and without making a dent in the problem. Many of these expenditures, in fact, have either been wasted or have proved to be a positive disservice to the dependent poor.

One need not agree with Julius Horwitz, the novelist who was once a welfare worker, that the whole system of public assistance is an "ugly, diseased social growth [that] must be removed from American life." But few can argue with the studied judgment of Professor S. M. Miller of Syracuse University that "Welfare assistance in its present form tends to encourage dependence, withdrawal, diffused hostility, indifference, ennui." For there is mounting evidence that the present welfare system is self-perpetuating—that far from relieving dependency, it *encourages* dependency.

Nor does the answer lie in expanding the number of social workers, settlement houses, mental-health clinics, and the like. In New York City, the *Directory of Social and Health Agencies* runs to 721 pages; social work is one of the city's major industries. In the Harlem-Upper Manhattan area alone there are, according to a study by the Protestant Council of the City of New York, some 156 separate agencies serving an estimated 240,-000 people—roughly 40 per cent of the total population of the area. Without question, there are gaps here and there in the services offered, and many existing services are grossly inadequate. But it seems clear that the solution to Harlem's problems does not lie in any extension of the present system.

What has gone wrong? First of all, social agencies and social workers have concentrated more on symptoms than on causes—and on symptoms seen and treated individually rather than in connection with other symptoms. This concern with symptoms has been a reflection, in good measure, of the social-work profession's preoccupation with case work and the study and treatment of individual maladjustment.

Unlike the early sociologists, many of whom were reformers, contemporary sociologists and social workers, as Lewis Coser points out, have focused their attention "predominantly upon problems of adjustment rather than upon conflict." Their goal, that is, has been to teach maladjusted individuals to adjust to society as it is, rather than to change those aspects of society that make the individuals what they are. Social workers in particular have religiously followed Freud when they should have been listening to Emile Durkheim. For the troubles of the slum arise far less from individual neurosis (though certainly there is plenty of that) than from an objective lack of opportunity, from a social system that denies dignity and status to the individual. . . .

Ultimately, however, the failure of the enormous American social welfare effort stems from the same factor that has produced the political strain between Negroes and white liberals: the idea of doing things *for* Negroes instead of *with* them—an approach that destroys the dignity and arouses the hostility of the people who are supposed to be helped.

A particularly candid expression of this patronizing frame of mind— "welfare colonialism," as some critics call it—is found in a report published two years ago by Raymond M. Hilliard, director of the Cook County (Chicago) Department of Public Aid. In proposing that those on relief be deprived of their benefits unless they go to school, the report asserts: "Society stands in the same relation to them as that of parent to child. . . . Just as the child is expected to attend classes, so also the 'child-adult' must be expected to meet his responsibility to the community. In short, 'social uplifting'—even if begun on the adult level—cannot expect to meet with success unless it is combined with a certain amount of 'social disciplining'—just as it is on the pre-adult level."

Small wonder, then, that these "child-adults" should hate the colonial administrators who come to "uplift" them through "social discipline," or that they try to sabotage the disciplinarians' program. One typical East Harlem adolescent put it as follows to Richard Hammer of *The New York Times Magazine:*

> Most of them are rat fink types. They act like they think we're not human. They think they've got all there is, and all they've got to do is to convert us to think and do what they think and do. . . . Man, these jerks pop up in the morning with their little briefcases, and they cut out

for their homes a hell of a way away around 5 or 6 at night, and tha's it.
If you are ever nuts enough to go to one of them they hand you the old
crap, "Now, son, you shouldn't feel that way."

In general, the social workers and administrators remain aliens in a world
they cannot understand and frequently do not even see. There is a large
"youth center" in Harlem, for example, which provides counseling to some
5,000 adolescents a year. Unknown to the staff, the center was also a major
contact point for the sale of narcotics—a fact discovered with ease by
the Negro interviewers of HARYOU (Harlem Youth Opportunities Unlimited Inc., a federally supported research and demonstration program)
when they began talking to the neighborhood kids. . . .

What all this means is that Negroes, like any other group, can be
helped in only one way: by giving them the means with which to help
themselves. In the last analysis, the rejection by Negroes of the conventional offers of help—the resentment they show—springs less from injustice per se than from their sense of inadequacy and impotence. White
philanthropy, white liberalism, white sympathy and support, no less than
white bigotry and discrimination, have had the effect of preventing Negroes
from standing on their own feet, from "exercising their full manhood
rights," to use W. E. B. DuBois's phrase. What Negroes need more than
anything else is to be treated like men—and to believe in their hearts that
they *are* men—who can stand on their own feet and control their own
destinies. Consequently, Negroes will not be able to climb out of their
slums *en masse* until they can act in their own behalf—until they are in a
position to make or to influence the decisions that affect them—until, in a
word, they acquire power.

But can this be done? Can Negroes be mobilized in the face of the apathy
and anomie of the Negro slum? The answer, quite simply, is that is *has*
been done—in the Chicago slum of Woodlawn. Created in 1960, The
Woodlawn Organization is a federation of some eighty-five or ninety
groups, including thirteen churches (virtually all those with any influence
in the community); three businessmen's associations, and an assortment
of block clubs, neighborhood associations, and social groups of one kind
or another; all told, the organizations represented in TWO have a membership of about 30,000. As the first broadly representative organization to be created in a Negro neighborhood, TWO is probably the most
significant social experiment going on among Negroes in America today.

The existence of any coherent organization in Woodlawn would seem
to be a complete anomaly. An oblong slum directly to the south of the
University of Chicago campus, it contains between 80,000 and 150,000
people, depending on how the area is defined. Until the 1930's, Woodlawn
was part of the university community—a desirable residential area with

broad shady streets, excellent transportation facilities, and a respectable admixture of private homes and apartment houses.

The decline of the neighborhood began during the Great Depression, and accelerated during the postwar rush to the suburbs. Around 1950, Negroes from the neighboring Black Belt started moving in, and the trickle soon turned into a torrent as Woodlawn became the "port-of-entry" for Negroes migrating to Chicago from the South. Within a decade Woodlawn had become a virtually all-Negro slum. Today nearly 25 per cent of the area's residents receive some form of welfare. They also pay an average of eighty-four dollars a month in rent—more than ten dollars above the city average—for an average housing unit of 2.2 rooms. There is a flourishing traffic in gambling, narcotics, and prostitution. The commercial business district is active but declining, with large numbers of vacant stories. In short, Woodlawn is precisely the sort of crowded, decaying, anomic neighborhood which social workers and urban planners assume can never help itself.

Yet Woodlawn *is* helping itself; it is taking concerted action toward a variety of goals. The impetus for The Woodlawn Organization came from three Protestant ministers and a Catholic priest who had "worn out the seats of several good pairs of trousers attending an uncountable number of meetings held to 'do something about Woodlawn'." After investigating various approaches to community organization, the clergymen "took the plunge," as two of them put it, and invited Saul D. Alinsky, executive director of the Industrial Areas Foundation, to help organize the Woodlawn community.

A sociologist and criminologist by training, Alinsky is a specialist in creating mass organizations that enable "the so-called 'little man' [to] gather into his hands the power he needs to make and shape his life." In the late 1930's he was a leading force in the creation of Chicago's Back-of-the-Yards Neighborhood Council, which turned the stockyards area into one of the most desirable working-class neighborhoods in the city. Subsequently he established the Industrial Areas Foundation, a nonprofit organization which has by now been called in by some forty-four groups across the country.

Though George N. Shuster is president of IAF, and other notable figures from labor, management, politics, and religious affairs sit on its board of directors, Alinsky himself is nothing if not controversial. At various times, Alinsky (who is Jewish) has been attacked as a Communist, as a fascist, as a dupe of the Catholic Church and the mastermind of a Catholic conspiracy, as a racist, as a segregationist, and as an integrationist whose aim is to "mongrelize" Chicago. Certainly no one in recent memory has had as great an impact as Alinsky on the city of Chicago; and no one in the United States has proposed a program of action better calculated to rescue slum dwellers—Negroes or whites—from poverty and degradation. For Alinsky is that rarity in American life, a superlative organizer, strategist, and tactician who is also a social philosopher.

Alinsky really believes that the helpless, the poor, the badly educated can solve their own problems if given the chance and the means—that they have the right to decide how their lives should be run and what services they require. "I don't believe that democracy can survive, except as a formality," he has written, "if the ordinary citizen's part is limited to voting —if he is incapable of initiative and unable to influence the political, social, and economic structures surrounding him."

The individual, however, can influence these structures in his own behalf only if he has power. As Alinsky sees it, there are two sources of power: money and people. Since the residents of Woodlawn and similar areas do not have money, their only source of power is themselves—and the only way they can draw on that power is by organizing. . . .

Most efforts at organizing slum neighborhoods fail, Alinsky argues, not because of the nature of the community but because of the objectives and methods of the planners. The conventional appeal to the interests of homeowners in conserving property values, for instance, is useless in a community like Woodlawn, and even "civil rights" is too abstract. "The daily lives of Woodlawn people," an early Alinsky memo suggested, "leave them with little energy or enthusiasm for realizing principles from which they themselves will derive little practical benefit. They know that with their educational and economic handicaps they will be exceptions indeed if they can struggle into a middle-class neighborhood or a white collar job." Instead of the conventional middle-class incentives, then, Alinsky uses the traditional appeal of trade-union organization: that is, to the self-interest of the local residents and to their resentment and distrust of the outside world. And following union practice, he seeks out and develops a local leadership to embody and direct this appeal.

But just as no factory could ever be organized without pressure and guidance from the outside, so no slum can be organized without a good deal of outside assistance. The mean and difficult job of building the organization must be handled by professionals who know how to deal with the apathy of the slum and who can find a way of bringing its disparate fragments together into a working whole. For, more often than not, the indigenous leaders of the slum area are out of touch with one another and only very rarely do they possess the skills to set up a large organization and keep it running.

At the same time, however, the Industrial Areas Foundation is out to make the local community self-sufficient: Alinsky will not enter a community until he is assured that a workable cross-section of the population wants him, and he invariably insists that the community itself, no matter how poor, take over full responsibility for financing the new organization within a period of three years.

Alinsky has a standard way of dramatizing the importance of financial independence. There is usually a convention at which the new group formally approves the constitution that has finally been hammered out. Alinsky will take a copy of the document, look at it briefly, and then flick it to the floor. "This constitution doesn't mean a damned thing. As long as the IAF organizers are on my payroll they'll do what I damn well tell them to do and not what it says on any paper like that." After a shocked silence, someone in the audience will inevitably protest: "I thought you were on our side!" "I am," Alinsky answers back. "But think of the number of people who've come down here telling you the same thing, and how many turned out to be two-timing, double-crossing s.o.b.'s. Why should you trust me? The only way you can be sure that the aims in that constitution are carried out is to get the organizers off my payroll and on to your payroll. Then *you* can tell them what to do; and if they don't do it, you can fire them and get someone who will."

The actual work of creating The Woodlawn Organization began in the spring and summer of 1960, eighteen months after the four ministers had called on Alinsky for help. A formal request to IAF now came from the Greater Woodlawn Pastors Alliance supported by most other groups of any significance in the community, and subsidized by grants from the Catholic Archdiocese of Chicago, the Presbyterian church of Chicago, and the Schwartzhaupt Foundation.

How do you begin organizing an area like Woodlawn? Nicholas von Hoffman, chief organizer at the time for the IAF, says with studied casualness, "I found myself at the corner of 63rd and Kimbark and I looked around." What he was looking for were grievances—the basic agent in the Alinsky process of community organization. It didn't take much looking or listening to discover that a major source of complaints was the cheating and exploitation suffered in some of the neighborhood stores.

In Woodlawn, as in most low-income areas, credit-purchasing is a pervasive trap. According to Dr. Leber, there were instances of customers being charged interest rates as high as 200 per cent; second-hand merchandise was sold as new; and prices bordered on outright piracy—for example, a six-dollar diamond chip in a gaudy ring setting would be sold for two-hundred-and-fifty dollars, with a "Certificate of Guarantee" attesting that it was a real diamond. Other merchants also took whatever advantage they could of their ignorant customers: thus, food stores regularly gave short weight, overcharged, and in a few cases even rigged their cash register to produce false totals.

Before very long, enough such complaints had piled up to create an issue —one, moreover, on which the legitimate businessmen in the area could unite with the consumers. TWO promptly set up a committee of prominent members of the Businessmen's Association, several ministers, and some of the indigenous leaders of the Woodlawn area. (A leader, in Alinsky's definition, is anyone with a following—anyone, be he bookie, barber, minister, or businessman, to whom residents turn for help.) Together they worked out a Code of Business Ethics covering credit practices, pricing, and advertising. To implement the Code, TWO set up a Board of Arbitration made up of four representatives from the Businessmen's Association and four from consumer groups, with an impartial chairman from outside the community.

The next stage was to publicize the Code and the new organization. To these ends a big parade was staged in which nearly one thousand people, singing and carrying signs, marched through the Woodlawn business section; the demonstration created enough of a stir to make the front pages of most of the Chicago newspapers. The following Saturday a registered scale and an adding machine were set up at a nearby Catholic church. Shoppers from the suspected markets brought their packages directly to the church, with the result that false weights and false totals were exposed, and most of the offending merchants agreed to comply with the "Square Deal" code. Those who did not were harassed by leaflets distributed throughout the communty.

Within a few weeks the "Square Deal" campaign had succeeded in eliminating a considerable amount of exploitation and chicanery. More importantly, it had made the residents of Woodlawn aware that the new organization indeed existed and that it *could* improve some of the circumstances of their lives.

Moving quickly to harness the enthusiasm they had aroused, the IAF staff next began to organize rent strikes. A tenants' group was formed wherever a substantial majority of tenants could be persuaded to act together against building code violations—broken windows, defective plumbing work, creaky staircases, inadequate heat, vermin, and so on. In each case the owner was given a period of time to make repairs; if it ran out before action had been taken, TWO called a rent strike: rents were withheld from the landlord and deposited in escrow in a special bank account. If a landlord still remained recalcitrant, groups of pickets were dispatched to his own home, where they marched with placards that read: "Your Neighbor is a Slum Lord."

The picketing provided an outlet for anger and also gave the Woodlawn residents concerned a rare opportunity to use their color in an affirmative way. For as soon as the Negro pickets appeared in a white suburban block, the landlord would be deluged with phone calls from angry neighbors demanding that he do something to call off the pickets. In response to such pressure, some landlords agreed within a matter of hours to make repairs.

Another early focus for action were overcrowded and segregated schools.

When William G. Caples, president of the Board of Education, refused to meet with TWO to discuss their complaints—he denounced the organization as "the lunatic fringe"—a delegation of eighteen Protestant and Catholic pastors staged a sit-in at the executive offices of Inland Steel, where Caples was vice-president in charge of public relations; other TWO members circled the building carrying placards denouncing Caples as a segregationist. (Caples resigned from the Board of Education the following month "because of the pressure of company business.")

When the Superintendent of Schools, Benjamin Willis, denied that overcrowding could be relieved by transferring Negro students to all-white schools, TWO sent "truth squads" of mothers into neighboring white schools to photograph half-empty classrooms. TWO members also staged a "death watch" at Board of Education meetings, which they attended in long black capes to symbolize their "mourning" over the plight of their children.

Such programs and tactics soon provoked denunciations of Alinsky as an agitator who dealt in hate and incited conflict. "The fact that a community may be stirred and organized by 'sharpening dormant hostilities' and 'rubbing raw the sores of discontent' is not new," said Julian Levi, in quoting from a TWO memorandum. "The technique has been proved in practice in the assembling of lynch mobs." Levi is executive director of the South East Chicago Commission and the key figure in the vast urban renewal activities of the University of Chicago, which once had plans of its own for Woodlawn.

Specifically, Levi objected to a TWO leaflet naming a local food store and warning people to "watch out" for short weights, spoiled food, and short changing. "If this is what this merchant is really doing," Levi argued, "he should be punished by the court—but with all the safeguards the law provides. This is not the way people should be taught to protect themselves." They should be taught instead, Levi said, to register complaints about spoiled food with the Department of Health, about short weights with the Department of Weights and Measures, and about short change with the Police Department.

Levi similarly objected to the tactic of rent strikes. If landlords were violating the building code, TWO should have brought action through the Building Department, following the practice of his South East Chicago Commission, instead of taking the law into its own hands.

But slum dwellers have been complaining to the Building Department and to other city agencies for years, usually to no avail. The reason the South East Chicago Commission has been able to get rapid action on its complaints from the Building Department or any other city agency is that it has political "clout": the Commission is the urban renewal arm of the University of Chicago, whose trustees include some of the most influential businessmen and politicians in the city. Alinsky and TWO do not have these discreet but powerful influences at their disposal and perforce must rely upon more overt pressures.

Levi's criticism, moreover, misses the further point that Alinsky's tactics are designed to serve other purposes besides the exerting of pressure. In TWO the most urgent need was not to persuade the local entrepreneurs to change their ways, but to convince the local population that it could solve some of its own problems through organized action.

The basic characteristic of the Negro slum—and the basic problem in organizing it—is that its "life style" is one of apathy. No organization can be created unless this apathy is overcome, but the slum residents will not be stirred until they see evidence that they *can* change things for the better. This reluctance to act contains a deep element of fear as well as hopelessness, for it is simply not true that the very poor have nothing to lose; in some respects, they have more to lose in their struggles with prevailing authority than the middle class does. They face the danger of having a relief check taken away, of being fired from an unskilled patronage job, of having a son on probation remanded to jail—and these are only a few of the reprisals that a politically powerful bureaucracy can impose.

Indeed, one of the differences between lower-class Negro communities and middle-class white ones is that while the latter clamor for more protection *by* the police, the former frequently need protection *from* the police. Residents of a place like Woodlawn are often treated brutally and illegally by the police; and it is obvious that the traffic in narcotics, gambling, and prostitution that flourishes in most Negro slums could not go on without the active cooperation of the local police.

The net effect is that a community like Woodlawn seethes with inarticulate resentments and with muffled, dormant hostilities. The slum dwellers are incapable of acting, or even of joining, until these resentments and hostilities are brought to the surface and seen as problems, i.e., conditions they can do something about. Thus Alinsky calmly admits to the charge of being an agitator. "The community organizer," he writes, "digs into a morass of resignation, hopelessness, and despair, and works with the local people in articulating (or 'rubbing raw') their resentments." His job is to "agitate to the point of conflict," to formulate grievances and persuade the people to speak out, to hope, and to move—in short to develop and harness the power needed to change the prevailing patterns.

Agitation in itself, however, is not sufficient. To use the language of war (for that is what TWO is conducting), the only way to build an army from scratch is by winning a few victories. But how do you gain a victory before you have an army? The only method is guerilla warfare: to avoid major battles and concentrate on hit-and-run tactics designed to gain the small but measurable triumphs which can create a sense of solidarity and elan.

Once guerilla warfare begins the best organizing help of all comes from "the enemy"—the established institutions which feel threatened by the new organization. Thus what really welded the Woodlawn community together was the University of Chicago's announcement on July 19, 1960, that it planned to extend its "South Campus" in Woodlawn by annexing a strip of land a block wide and a mile long. Woodlawn residents had no particular attachment to this strip, in which university buildings extended into a dreary amalgam of warehouses, tenements, and empty lots. But they suspected that annexation was the prelude to clearing a large part of Woodlawn itself for middle- and upper-income apartment and town houses.

There was ample basis for these fears: the huge urban renewal projects which the university was sponsoring in the Hyde Park-Kenwood district to the north had in fact been designed in good measure to remove Negroes along with "crime" and "blight." Unless they acted quickly to establish the principle that no plan should be adopted for Woodlawn without active participation by Woodlawn residents in the planning process itself, the Negro community might wake up one morning to find bulldozers in every front yard.

According to Rossi and Dentler, "the characteristic mode of action of the University and of the South East Chicago Commission, was to develop plans quickly, announce proposals in general terms, and then obtain quick approval through political leverage downtown." Almost immediately and quite loudly, TWO therefore demanded that the city defer approval until university and city-planning officials had met with TWO and negotiated a long-term plan for Woodlawn. Otherwise, the organization warned, its members would lie down in front of the bulldozers and wrecking equipment. Some three hundred TWO members crowded into a City Planning Commission hearing and succeeded in blocking the quick approval the university had expected. . . .

. . . The Chicago planners showed no eagerness to engage the Woodlawn residents in any active role. In March 1962 the City Commission presented a comprehensive plan for Woodlawn which included a huge program of urban renewal clearance, conservation, and rehabilitation; a massive investigation of illiteracy, ill health, crime, and unemployment; and a pilot attack on these problems to be financed by government and foundation grants. When asked if the planning committee had been guided by opinions from the community, the committee's coordinating consultant replied that "There is nobody to speak for the community. A community does not exist in Woodlawn." Philip Hauser, a University of Chicago sociologist and another consultant, remarked that "the people there have only one common bond, opposition to the University of Chicago," and added gratuitously, "this is a community that reads nothing."

The two consultants were quickly disabused of these views. In conjunction with the Woodlawn Businessmen's Association, TWO employed its own firm of city planners to analyze the City Commission's plan and present alternate proposals. Besides issuing a detailed critique of the commission's urban renewal plan for Woodlawn, TWO affirmed the principle that "self-determination applies in the field of social welfare. Therefore the best programs are the ones that we develop, pay for and direct ourselves. . . . Our aim is to lessen burdens in practical ways, but in ways that also guarantee we will keep our personal and community independence. We go on record as unqualifiedly opposing all notions of 'social planning' by either government or private groups. We will not be planned for as though we were children."

This radical assertion of independence did not please the planners. "Some of their resolutions against welfare are singularly unfortunate," Philip Hauser was moved to say. "What would they do without welfare?" Other of his colleagues regarded the resolutions as "revolutionary" and even "subversive"—much to the bemusement of the Negroes of Woodlawn. "They've been calling us 'welfare chiselers' and 'dependent' and everything else," said one TWO member. "Now they distrust us for trying things for ourselves."

The University of Chicago sociologists and the professional planners may have resisted the message, but the Chicago politicians did not. Mayor Richard Daley brought the reluctant Chancellor of the University to his office to meet with TWO representatives. Eventually negotiators from both sides agreed on a compromise which called for construction of low-income housing on vacant land *before* any existing buildings were torn down. Thus for the first time in the history of urban renewal people displaced by demolition will have new homes waiting for them in the same neighborhood.

Instead of the usual wholesale replacement of lower-class housing by "middle-income" units, Woodlawn will be renewed in stages. Only houses beyond salvage will be torn down, and units to be rehabilitated will be repaired without evicting tenants. City officials also agreed to give TWO majority representation on the citizens' planning committee that will draw up further plans and supervise their execution, and Mayor Daley asked Dr. Blakely, one of the founders of TWO, to serve as chairman of the committee. . . .

It would be fatuous to pretend that Woodlawn has become a model community; it remains a slum, and it is still largely sunk in poverty and crime. However, it is a slum with hope—a slum that is developing the means of raising itself "by its own bootstraps." "We've learned to live together and act as a community," a TWO activist says, and adds, "Two years ago I didn't know a soul." Most of the problems that make Woodlawn what it is—high unemployment, lack of education, family disorganization, poor health—cannot be solved by a community organization alone.

Enormous resources must still be poured into Woodlawn in the form of compensatory education, job retraining, advice on child-rearing, and preventive medicine. But experience in every city in the nation has also demonstrated that any paternalistic program imposed from above will be resisted and resented as "welfare colonialism." The greatest contribution of an organization like TWO is its most subtle: it gives the slum residents the sense of dignity that makes it possible for them to accept help. For help now comes not as charity, but as a response to their own initiative and power: *they* have decided what services they need and want. Hence social programs which the community would in the past have contemptuously ignored as one more instance of "Mr. Charlie's brainwashing" are now eagerly sought after.

Recent negotiations between TWO and the University of Chicago produced a nursery school program designed to reverse the effects of "cultural deprivation," while cooperation between TWO and a team of psychiatrists has led to the setting up of some promising experiments in group therapy. And so, throughout this once completely depressed and deprived area, a new sense of energy and possibility is at work, and a new conception of social welfare has begun to take form in America.

CHAPTER

12

SOCIAL STRATIFICATION

MANY PEOPLE are troubled because they feel that social classes are inconsistent with the democratic ideal of human equality; yet social classes are found in all complex societies, even in those that, like Russia and China, claim to have abolished them. Warner explains the nature of social class and why it is necessary. He also emphasizes the importance of keeping our society as democratic as possible by opening to all citizens the doors of opportunity to move upward in the social scale.

Malloy describes briefly the rigid caste system of India and its gradual disintegration under modern industrialism and the efforts of the government to establish a democratic society.

Swados is concerned with the myth of the "happy worker," the belief that the man on the assembly line is satisfied with his social status and with the work he is doing; and he subjects this myth to severe criticism.

23

Social Classes and Why We Have Them

by W. Lloyd Warner

The American Dream and Social Class

In the bright glow and warm presence of the American Dream all men are born free and equal. Everyone in the American Dream has the right, and often the duty, to try to succeed and to do his best to reach the top. Its two fundamental themes and propositions, that all of us are equal and that each of us has the right to the chance of reaching the top, are mutually contradictory, for if all men are equal there can be no top level to aim for, no bottom one to get away from; there can be no superior or inferior positions, but only one common level into which all Americans are born and in which all of them will spend their lives. We all know such perfect equality of position and opportunity does not exist. All Americans are not born into families of equal position: some are born into a rich man's aristocracy on the Gold Coast; some into the solid comfort of Suburbia's middle classes; and others into a mean existence among the slum families living on the wrong side of the tracks. It is common knowledge that the sons and daughters of the Gold Coasts, the Main Lines, and Park Avenues of America are more likely to receive recognition for their efforts than the children of the slums. The distance these fortunate young people travel to achieve success is shorter, and the route up easier, than the long hard pull necessary for the ambitious children of the less fortunate middle class. Though everyone has the common right to succeed, it is not an equal "right"; though there is equality of rank for some of us, there is not equality of rank for all of us.

When some men learn that *all* the American Dream does not fit *all* that is true about the realities of our life, they denounce the Dream and deny the truth of *any* of it. Fortunately, most of us are wiser and better adjusted to social reality; we recognize that, though it is called a Dream and though some of it is false, by virtue of our firm belief in it we have made some

From *Social Class in America* by W. Lloyd Warner and others, Harper and Row, Publishers, 1960 (Harper Torchbook edition), pp. 3–7 *passim*. Copyright 1949 by Science Research Associates, Inc. Reprinted by permission of Harper and Row, Publishers, and the author.

W. Lloyd Warner is a Professor of Sociology at Michigan State University who gained fame through his studies of social stratification.

of it true. Despite the presence of social hierarchies which place people at higher and lower levels in American communities, the principles of democracy do operate; the Christian dogma that all men are equal in the sight of God because He is our Father and we are His spiritual children, buttressed by the democratic faith in the equality of men and the insistence on their equal rights as citizens, is a powerful influence in the daily life of America.

From grade school on, we have learned to cite chapter and verse proving from the lives of many of the great men of American history that we can start at the bottom and climb to the highest peaks of achievement when we have a few brains and a will to do. Our mass magazines and newspapers print and reprint the legendary story of rags to riches and tell over and over again the Ellis-Island-to-Park-Avenue saga in the actual lives of contemporary successful immigrant men and women. From mere repetition, it might be thought the public would tire of the theme; the names are all that vary and the stories, like those of children, remain the same. But we never do tire of this theme, for it says what we need to know and what we want to hear.

Among people around us, we sometimes recognize men who have got ahead, who have been successfully upward-mobile, and who have reached levels of achievement beyond even the dreams of most men. Many Americans by their own success have learned that, for them, enough of the Dream is true to make all of it real. The examples from history, from the world around us, and from our own experience provide convincing evidence that, although full equality is absent, opportunity for advancement is present sufficiently to permit the rise of a few from the bottom and a still larger number from the middle to the higher economic and social levels. Although we know the statement that everyone is equal but that some men are higher than others is contradictory, and although some of us smile or become angry when we hear that "all of us are equal but some are more equal than others," we still accept both parts of this proposition either by understressing one part of the proposition or by letting all of it go as a paradox we feel to be true.

Our society does an excellent job in giving us an explicit knowledge of, and good argument for, the equalitarian aspects of our life. We have much scholarly knowledge about the workings of democracy, but we have little scientific knowledge about the powerful presence of social status and how it works for good and evil in the lives of all of us. Yet to live successfully and adaptively in America, every one of us must adjust his life to each of these contradictions, not just one of them, and we must make the most of each. Our knowledge of the democratic aspects of America is learned directly as part of our social heritage, but our understanding of the principle of social status tends to be implicit and to be learned obliquely and through hard and sometimes bitter experience. The lives of many are destroyed because they do not understand the workings of social class. . . .

Although well aware of social class, social scientists have been more concerned with their theories and with quarreling among themselves about what social class is than with studying its realities in the daily lives of the people. Until recently, they have lagged behind the novelists in investigating what our classes are, how they operate in our social life, and what effect they have on our individual lives.

But recent scientific studies of social class in the several regions of the United States demonstrate that it is a major determinant of individual decisions and social actions; that every major area of American life is directly and indirectly influenced by our class order; and that the major decisions of most individuals are partly controlled by it. To act intelligently and know consciously how this basic factor in American life affects us and our society, it is essential and necessary that we have an explicit understanding of what our class order is, how it works, and what it does to the lives and personalities who live in it. Our most democratic institutions, including our schools, churches, business organizations, government, and even our family life, are molded by its all-pervading and exceedingly subtle but powerful influence. . . .

The Structural Imperative—Why We Have a Class System

The recognition of social class and other status hierarchies in this country comes as no surprise to students of society. Research on the social life of the tribes and civilizations of the world clearly demonstrates that some form of rank is always present and a necessity for our kind of society.

Just as students of comparative biology have demonstrated that the physical structure of the higher animals must have certain organs to survive, so students of social anthropology have shown that the social structures of the "higher," the more complex, societies must have rank orders to perform functions necessary for group survival.

When societies are complex and service large populations, they always possess some kind of status system which, by its own values, places people in higher or lower positions. Only the very simple hunting and gathering tribes, with very small populations and very simple social problems, are without systems of rank; but when a society is complex, when there are large numbers of individuals in it pursuing diverse and complex activities and functioning in a multiplicity of ways, individual positions and behaviors are evaluated and ranked. This happens primarily because, to maintain itself, the society must co-ordinate the efforts of all its members into common enterprises necessary for the preservation of the group, and it must solidify and integrate all these enterprises into a working whole. In other words, as the division of labor increases and the social units become more numerous and diverse, the need for co-ordination and integration also increases and, when satisfied, enables the larger group to survive and develop.

Those who occupy co-ordinating positions acquire power and prestige. They do so because their actions partly control the behavior of the individuals who look to them for direction. Within this simple control there is simple power. Those who exercise such power either acquire prestige directly from it or have gained prestige from other sources sufficiently to be raised to a co-ordinating position. For example, among many primitive peoples a simple fishing expedition may be organized so that the men who fish and handle each boat are under the direction of one leader. The efforts of each boat are directed by the leader and, in turn, each boat is integrated into the total enterprise by its leader's taking orders from his superior. The same situation prevails in a modern factory. Small plants with a small working force and simple problems possess a limited hierarchy, perhaps no more than an owner who bosses all the workers. But a large industrial enterprise, with complex activities and problems, like General Motors, needs an elaborate hierarchy of supervision. The position in a great industrial empire which integrates and co-ordinates all the positions beneath it throughout all the supervising levels down to the workers has great power and prestige. The same holds true for political, religious, educational, and other social institutions; the more complex the group and the more diverse the functions and activities, the more elaborate its status system is likely to be. [We will amplify this point later.]

The studies of other societies have demonstrated one other basic point: the more complex the technological and economic structure, the more complex the social structure; so that some argue (the Marxians and many classical economists) that technological advancement is the cause of social complexity and all class and status systems. It cannot be denied that economic and technological factors are important in the determination of class and status orders. We must not lose sight of the fact, however, that the social system, with its beliefs, values, and rules, which governs human behavior may well determine what kind of technology and what kind of economic institutions will survive or thrive in any given tribe or nation. In any case, social complexity is necessary for economic advancement. Furthermore, social complexity is a basic factor determining the presence or absence of class.

The Marxians have argued that the economic changes our society is undergoing always result in a class war in which "the proletariat" will be triumphant and out of which a "classless society" will result. The authors do not agree with them for several reasons. The principal reasons are: (1) the presence of a class or order does not necessarily mean class conflict—the relations of the classes can be and often are amiable and peaceful; (2) classless societies (without differential status systems) are impossible where there is complexity for the reasons previously given. Russia's communistic system, supposedly designed to produce a pure equalitarian society, necessarily has citizens who are ranked above and below each other. Generals, there, outrank privates; commissars, the rank and file; and members of the Politburo, the ordinary comrade. Occupants of these higher ranks in Russia tend to associate together; those of the lower ranks form their own groups. Their children are trained according to the rank of their parents. This means that the younger generation learns these status differences, thereby strengthening status differences between levels and fostering the further development of social class in Communistic Russia.

All this has occurred despite the fact the Russians have removed the means of production from private hands and placed them under the control of the State ("the people"). The economic factor which by Marxian doctrine produced social classes is largely absent; yet social hierarchies and social classes are present for the reason that Russia is a complex society and needs them to survive.

These status trends in Russia will undoubtedly continue, for her population is vast, her peoples diverse, her problems immensely complex; and elaborate systems of co-ordination and control are necessary for such a nation to maintain itself. The Communist ideals of economic and political equality cannot produce perfect equality within the complexities of Russian life.

But let us return to the United States. We, too, have a complex, highly diverse society. We, too, possess an elaborate division of labor and a ramified technology. And we, too, possess a variety of rank orders built on the need of maintaining unity and cohesion in making our common enterprises successful. Men occupying high and low positions possess families. Their families and their activities are identified with their social position. Families of the same position tend to associate together. They do this informally or through cliques, associations, or other institutions. This social matrix provides the structure of our class system. Children are always born to their families' position. Through life they may increase or decrease their status. The family thereby strengthens and helps maintain our class order. Social status in America is somewhat like man's alimentary canal; he may not like the way it works and he may want to forget that certain parts of it are part of him, but he knows it is necessary for his very existence. So a status system, often an object of our disapproval, is present and necessary in our complex social world.

If we cannot eliminate the system of status, we can and must work to keep it as democratic and equalitarian as possible. To be successful we must see to it that each American is given his chance to move in the social scale. This ideal of equality of opportunity is essential for our democracy. . . .

24

Untouchability Fades in India

by Michael T. Malloy

The ancient practice of untouchability is dying out in the cities of India.

But in the countryside its cruel grip persists and its "unclean" victims are barred from the village temple, the well, and the tea shop.

The government has taken measures to educate the 40 million untouchables, find them jobs, and punish orthodox Hindus who still openly discriminate against them.

The measures have been successful in the cities where everybody mixes on crowded buses and at public drinking fountains.

Untouchability dies hard in the countryside, but even there, with courts, police, education, and the conditions of modern life all combined against it, the practice of formal untouchability will eventually die out.

The caste system itself, which created untouchability, seems actually to be enjoying a new lease on life. Many observers believe it is changing from a religious system to a modern political force.

Caste is as old as India. Most authorities believe it grew up when Aryan invaders poured out of central Asia, three or four thousand years ago, and conquered the river valleys of Hindustan.

The Aryans were faced with the job of organizing and ruling a hodgepodge of racially different people who ranged from naked jungle savages to the cultivated merchants of highly developed city states.

Each group had something to contribute to the evolving new culture, but each group was different. So the different peoples were organized into four varnas, or colors.

From the top down, the varnas were:

The holy *Brahmins,* who taught, preached, studied the laws and sacrificed to the gods to keep their people from harm.

The bold *Kshatriyas,* who enforced the law, fought the enemy, and collected taxes.

The wily *Vaishyas,* who bought, sold, lent money, and ran the economy with their talent and wealth.

From *The Chicago Tribune,* February 2, 1964. Reprinted by permission of United Press International.

Michael T. Malloy is a foreign correspondent for United Press International.

The sturdy *Sudras,* who tilled the soil, paid the taxes, and uncomplainingly did the work that kept the rest of society in motion.

The Brahmins explained the system with a myth about the great god Brahma, who created the universe. When Brahma created man, they said, the Brahmins sprang from his head, the Kshatriyas from his hands, the Vaishyas from his thighs, and the Sudras from his feet.

At the fringes of society, or mixed with the Sudras, were the lowly untouchables. They were probably the original forest dwellers of the country. Their primitive skills were neither needed nor wanted by the elaborate civilization of Hindustan.

The untouchables could come into the village, perhaps, but only to do the work that was too unpleasant or too dirty for anyone else. They carried away the garbage and swept the streets. They watched their step to see that their shadows did not fall upon and pollute the holy Brahmins. They avoided defiling the wells and temples with their presence.

The system was the most highly-organized society of its time. It flourished and grew, taming the original inhabitants of the land and absorbing wave after wave of invaders.

The varnas cut themselves off from each other through the ritual of pollution. To marry or eat with an inferior could mean being turned out and stoned by one's friends and family.

The penalty was a severe one, and nobody took any chances.

Fear of pollution split the original varnas into separate castes and the castes into separate subcastes.

The steam engine knocked the first big hole in the caste system. You couldn't work in a factory and keep all the little rituals in mind. You couldn't run a railroad with a different car for each caste. The industrial towns couldn't have a separate restaurant for all the thousands of microscopic subcastes.

Mahatma Gandhi took the next big whack at caste. He coined the word *harijan* (god's people) for the untouchables. He deliberately associated with them, drank from their wells, and did such untouchable chores as sweeping floors.

Even the most ignorant peasant could see that Gandhi was pure and holy, despite the way he defied pollution. The British-educated intellectuals could use his example as an excuse for breaking the annoying restrictions of the old system.

The British government had never recognized untouchability, but the new government went a step further when India became independent. The constitution flatly outlaws untouchability; you could go to jail for refusing to serve a Harijan in a public restaurant, or for chasing him away from a village well.

Even the Brahmins faced a day in court, if they refused to let a Harijan worship in their temple.

But in the countryside peasants still lynch occasional Harijans who have the gall to furnish their homes with rugs or to beat drums at a son's wedding.

Each incident usually ends in a Harijan victory. Judges order jail sentences, and heavy-handed Indian police break up orthodox mobs with rifle fire.

But jails and laws are not enough to raise the Harijans to equality. Most of them know only the humble trades of their fathers and have no way of earning money that could eventually make them the economic equals of the other castes.

The Indian government has tried to remedy this with a program of benefits for the 64 million deprived persons listed as "scheduled castes" and the 30 million backward forest dwellers who qualify as "scheduled tribes."

A certain proportion of university scholarships, government jobs, and classroom seats are reserved for the scheduled people, in a program of positive discrimination in their favor.

These programs are increasing the stature of the backward classes, and helping talented individuals get jobs, but this official recognition of caste differences has heightened the system's new role as a political force.

The new caste lineup grew as modern life broke down the barriers between subcastes.

In each great language area, the biggest caste groups have discovered that they can swing elections by voting as a bloc. Some of the lower castes have to get themselves "scheduled" [in order to qualify for special benefits].

Parties balance their tickets among castes in the same way an American political machine divides offices among ethnic groups.

25

The Myth of the Happy Worker

by Harvey Swados

*"From where we sit in the company," says one of the best per-
sonnel men in the country, "we have to look at only the aspects of
work that cut across all sorts of jobs—administration and human
relations. Now these are aspects of work, abstractions, but it's easy
for personnel people to get so hipped on their importance that they
look on the specific tasks of making things and selling them as
secondary. . . ."*

—*The Organization Man,*
by WILLIAM H. WHYTE, JR.

The personnel man who made this remark to Mr. Whyte differed from
his brothers only in that he had a moment of insight. Actually, "the specific tasks of making things" are now not only regarded by his white-collar
fellows as "secondary," but as irrelevant to the vaguer but more "challenging" tasks of the man at the desk. This is true not just of the personnel
man, who places workers, replaces them, displaces them—in brief, manipulates them. The union leader also, who represents workers and sometimes
manipulates them, seems increasingly to regard what his workers do as
merely subsidiary to the job he himself is doing in the larger community.
This job may be building the Red Cross or the Community Chest, or it
may sometimes be—as the Senate hearings suggest—participating in such
communal endeavors as gambling, prostitution, and improving the breed.
In any case, the impression is left that the problems of the workers in the
background (or underground) have been stabilized, if not permanently
solved.

With the personnel man and the union leader, both of whom presumably
see the worker from day to day, growing so far away from him, it is hardly
to be wondered at that the middle class in general, and articulate middle-
class intellectuals in particular, see the worker vaguely, as through a cloud.

Reprinted from the *Nation,* CLXXXV, No. 4 (1957), 65–68, by permission.
(Copyright 1957, by Harvey Swados.)

Harvey Swados is a novelist, a freelance writer, and a member of the faculty of
Sarah Lawrence College.

One gets the impression that when they do consider him, they operate from one of two unspoken assumptions: (1) the worker has died out like the passenger pigeon, or is dying out, or becoming acculturated, like the Navajo; (2) if he *is* still around, he is just like the rest of us—fat, satisfied, smug, a little restless, but hardly distinguishable from his fellow TV-viewers of the middle class.

Lest it be thought that (1) is somewhat exaggerated, I hasten to quote from a recently published article apparently dedicated to the laudable task of urging slothful middle-class intellectuals to wake up and live: "The old-style sweatshop crippled mainly the working people. Now there are no workers left in America; we are almost all middle class as to income and expectations." I do not believe the writer meant to state—although he comes perilously close to it—that nobody works any more. If I understand him correctly, he is referring to the fact that the worker's rise in real income over the last decade, plus the diffusion of middle-class tastes and values throughout a large part of the underlying population, have made it increasingly difficult to tell blue-collar from white-collar worker without a program. In short, if the worker earns like the middle class, votes like the middle class, dresses like the middle class, dreams like the middle class, then he ceases to exist as a worker.

But there is one thing that the worker doesn't do like the middle class: he works like a worker. The steel-mill puddler does not yet sort memos, the coal miner does not yet sit in conferences, the cotton millhand does not yet sip martinis from his lunchbox. The worker's attitude toward his work is generally compounded of hatred, shame, and resignation.

Before I spell out what I think this means, I should like first to examine some of the implications of the widely held belief that "we are almost all middle-class as to income and expectations." I am neither economist, sociologist, nor politician, and I hold in my hand no doctored statistics to be haggled over. I am by profession a writer who has had occasion to work in factories at various times during the thirties, forties, and fifties. The following observations are simply impressions based on my last period of factory servitude, in 1956.

The average automobile worker gets a little better than two dollars an hour. As such he is one of the best-paid factory workers in the country. After twenty years of militant struggle led by the union that I believe to be still the finest and most democratic labor organization in the United States, he is earning less than the starting salaries offered to inexperienced and often semi-literate college graduates without dependents. After compulsory deductions for taxes, social security, old-age insurance, and union dues, and optional deductions for hospitalization and assorted charities, his paycheck for forty hours of work is going to be closer to seventy than to eighty dollars a week. Does this make him middle class as to income? Does it rate with the weekly take of a dentist, an accountant, a salesman, a draftsman, a journalist? Surely it would be more to the point to ask how a family man can get by in the fifties on that kind of income. I know how he does it, and I should think the answers would be a little disconcerting to those who wax glib on the satisfactory status of the "formerly" underprivileged.

For one thing, he works a lot longer than forty hours a week—when he can. Since no automobile company is as yet in a position to guarantee its workers anything like fifty weeks of steady forty-hour paychecks, the auto worker knows he has to make it while he can. During peak production periods he therefore puts in nine, ten, eleven, and often twelve hours a day on the assembly line for weeks on end. And that's not all. If he has dependents, as like as not he also holds down a "spare-time" job. I have worked on the line with men who doubled as mechanics, repairmen, salesmen, contractors, builders, farmers, cab-drivers, lumberyard workers, countermen. I would guess that there are many more of these than show up in the official statistics: often a man will work for less if he can be paid under the counter with tax-free dollars.

Nor is that all. The factory worker with dependents cannot carry the debt load he now shoulders—the middle-class debt load, if you like, of nagging payments on car, washer, dryer, TV, clothing, house itself—without family help. Even if he puts in fifty, sixty, or seventy hours a week at one or two jobs, he has to count on his wife's paycheck, or his son's, his daughter's, his brother-in-law's; or on his mother's social security, or his father's veteran's pension. The working-class family today is not typically held together by the male wage earner, but by multiple wage earners often of several generations who club together to get the things they want and need—or are pressured into believing they must have. It is at best a precarious arrangement; as for its toll on the physical organism and the psyche, that is a question perhaps worthy of further investigation by those who currently pronounce themselves bored with Utopia Unlimited in the Fat Fifties.

But what of the worker's middle-class expectations? I had been under the impression that this was the rock on which Socialist agitation had foundered for generations: it proved useless to tell the proletarian that he had a world to win when he was reasonably certain that with a few breaks he could have his own gas station. If these expectations have changed at all in recent years, they would seem to have narrowed rather than expanded, leaving a psychological increment of resignation rather than of unbounded optimism (except among the very young—and even among them the optimism focuses more often on better-paying opportunities elsewhere in the labor market than on illusory hopes of swift status advancement). The worker's expectations are for better pay, more humane working conditions, more job security. As long as he feels that he is going to achieve them through an extension of existing conditions, for that long he is going to continue to be a middle-class conservative in temper. But only for that long.

I suspect that what middle-class writers mean by the worker's middle-class expectations are his cravings for commodities—his determination to have not only fin-tailed cars and single-unit washer-dryers, but butterfly chairs in the rumpus room, African masks on the wall, and power boats in the garage. Before the middle-class intellectuals condemn these expectations too harshly, let them consider, first, who has been utilizing every known technique of suasion and propaganda to convert luxuries into necessities, and second, at what cost these new necessities are acquired by the American working-class family.

Now I should like to return to the second image of the American worker: satisfied, doped by TV, essentially middle class in outlook. This is an image bred not of communication with workers (except as mediated by hired interviewers sent "into the field" like anthropologists or entomologists), but of contempt for people, based perhaps on self-contempt and on a feeling among intellectuals that the worker has let them down. In order to see this clearly, we have to place it against the intellectual's changing attitudes toward the worker since the thirties.

At the time of the organization of the C.I.O., the middle-class intellectual saw the proletarian as society's figure of virtue—heroic, magnanimous, bearing in his loins the seeds of a better future; he would have found ludicrous the suggestion that a sit-down striker might harbor anti-Semitic feelings. After Pearl Harbor, the glamorization of the worker was taken over as a function of government. Then, however, he was no longer the builder of the future good society; instead he was second only to the fighting man as the vital winner of the war. Many intellectuals, as government employees, found themselves helping to create this new portrait of the worker as patriot.

But in the decade following the war, intellectuals have discovered that workers are no longer either building socialism or forging the tools of victory. All they are doing is making the things that other people buy. That, and participating in the great commodity scramble. The disillusionment, it would seem, is almost too terrible to bear. Word has gotten around among the highbrows that the worker is not heroic or idealistic; public-opinion polls prove that he wants barbecue pits more than foreign aid and air-conditioning more than desegregation, that he doesn't particularly want to go on strike, that he is reluctant to form a Labor Party, that he votes for Stevenson and often even for Eisenhower and Nixon—that he is, in short, animated by the same aspirations as drive the middle class onward and upward in suburbia.

There is of course a certain admixture of self-delusion in the middle-class attitude that workers are now the same as everybody else. For me it was expressed most precisely last year in the dismay and sympathy with which middle-class friends greeted the news that I had gone back to work in a factory. If workers are now full-fledged members of the middle class, why the dismay? What difference whether one sits in an office or stands in a shop? The answer is so obvious that one feels shame at laboring the point. But I have news for my friends among the intellectuals. The answer is obvious to workers, too.

They know that there is a difference between working with your back and working with your behind. (I do not make the distinction between hand-work and brain-work, since we are all learning that white-collar work is becoming less and less brain-work.) They know that they work harder than the middle class for less money. Nor is it simply a question of status, that magic word so dear to the hearts of the sociologues, the new anatomizers of the American corpus. It is not simply status-hunger that makes a man hate work which pays *less* than other work he knows about, if *more* than any other work he has been trained for (the only reason my fellow-workers stayed on the assembly line, they told me again and again). It is not simply status-hunger that makes a man hate work that is mindless, endless, stupefying, sweaty, filthy, noisy, exhausting, insecure in its prospects, and practically without hope of advancement.

The plain truth is that factory work is degrading. It is degrading to any man who ever dreams of doing something worthwhile with his life; and it is about time we faced the fact. The more a man is exposed to middle-class values, the more sophisticated he becomes and the more production-line work is degrading to him. The immigrant who slaved in the poorly lighted, foul, vermin-ridden sweatshop found his work less degrading than the native-born high school graduate who reads "Judge Parker," "Rex Morgan, M.D.," and "Judd Saxon, Business Executive," in the funnies, and works in a fluorescent factory with ticker-tape production-control machines. For the immigrant laborer, even the one who did not dream of socialism, his long hours were going to buy him freedom. For the factory worker of the fifties, his long hours are going to buy him commodities . . . and maybe reduce a few of his debts.

Almost without exception, the men with whom I worked on the assembly line last year felt like trapped animals. Depending on their age and personal circumstances, they were either resigned to their fate, furiously angry at *themselves* for what they were doing, or desperately hunting other work that would pay as well and in addition offer some variety, some prospect of change and betterment. They were sick of being pushed around by harried foremen (themselves more pitied than hated), sick of working like blinkered donkeys, sick of being dependent for their livelihood on a maniacal production-merchandising setup, sick of working in a place where there was no spot to relax during the twelve-minute rest period. (Some day—let us hope—we will marvel that production was still so worshiped in the fifties that new factories could be built with every splendid facility for the storage and movement of essential parts, but with no place for a resting worker to sit down for a moment but on a fire plug, the edge of a packing case, or the sputum- and oil-stained stairway of a toilet.)

The older men stay put and wait for their vacations. But since the assembly line demands young blood (you will have a hard time getting hired if you are over thirty-five), the factory in which I worked was aswarm with new faces every day; labor turnover was so fantastic and absenteeism so rampant, with the young men knocking off a day or two every week to hunt up other jobs, that the company was forced to overhire in order to have sufficient workers on hand at the starting siren.

To those who will object—fortified by their readings in C. Wright Mills and A. C. Spectorsky—that the white-collar commuter, too, dislikes his work, accepts it only because it buys his family commodities, and is constantly on the prowl for other work, I can only reply that for me at any rate this is proof not of the disappearance of the working-class but of the proletarianization of the middle class. Perhaps it is not taking place quite in the way that Marx envisaged it, but the alienation of the white-collar man (like that of the laborer) from both his tools and whatever he produces, the slavery that chains the exurbanite to the commuting timetable (as the worker is still chained to the time-clock), the anxiety that sends the white-collar man home with his briefcase for an evening's work (as it degrades the workingman into pleading for long hours of overtime), the displacement of the white-collar slum from the wrong side of the tracks to the suburbs (just as the working-class slum is moved from old-law tenements to skyscraper barracks)—all these mean to me that the white-collar man is entering (though his arms may be loaded with commodities) the grey world of the working man.

Three quotations from men with whom I worked may help to bring my view into focus:

Before starting work: "Come on, suckers, they say the Foundation wants to give away *more* than half a billion this year. Let's do and die for the old Foundation."

During rest period: "Ever stop to think how we crawl here bumper to bumper, and crawl home bumper to bumper, and we've got to turn out more every minute to keep our jobs, when there isn't even any room for them on the highways?"

At quitting time (this from older foremen, whose job is not only to keep things moving, but by extension to serve as company spokesmen): "You're smart to get out of here. . . . I curse the day I ever started, now I'm stuck: any man with brains that stays here ought to have his head examined. This is no place for an intelligent human being."

Such is the attitude toward the work. And towards the product? On the one hand it is admired and desired as a symbol of freedom, almost a substitute for freedom, not because the worker participated in making it, but because our whole culture is dedicated to the proposition that the automobile is both necessary and beautiful. On the other hand it is hated and despised—so much that if your new car smells bad it may be due to a banana peel crammed down its gullet and sealed up thereafter, so much so that if your dealer can't locate the rattle in your new car you might ask him to open the welds on one of those tail fins and vacuum out the nuts and bolts thrown in by workers sabotaging their own product.

Sooner or later, if we want a decent society—by which I do not mean a society glutted with commodities or one maintained in precarious equilibrium by over-buying and forced premature obsolescence—we are going to have to come face to face with the problem of work. Apparently the Russians have committed themselves to the replenishment of their labor force through automatic recruitment of those intellectually incapable of keeping up with severe scholastic requirements in the public educational system. Apparently we, too, are heading in the same direction: although our economy is not directed, and although college education is as yet far from free, we seem to be operating in this capitalist economy on the totalitarian assumption that we can funnel the underprivileged, under-educated, or just plain underequipped, into the factory, where we can proceed to forget about them once we have posted the minimum fair labor standards on the factory wall.

If this is what we want, let's be honest enough to say so. If we conclude that there is nothing noble about repetitive work, but that it is nevertheless good enough for the lower orders, let's say that, too, so we will at least know where we stand. But if we cling to the belief that other men are our brothers, not just Egyptians, or Israelis, or Hungarians, but *all* men, including millions of Americans who grind their lives away on an insane treadmill, then we will have to start thinking about how their work and their lives can be made meaningful. That is what I assume the Hungarians, both workers and intellectuals, have been thinking about. Since no one has been ordering us what to think, since no one has been forbidding our intellectuals to fraternize with our workers, shouldn't it be a little easier for us to admit, first, that our problems exist, then to state them, and then to see if we can resolve them?

13

RACIAL AND CULTURAL GROUPS

RACIAL PREJUDICE, discrimination, and conflict have become a major problem in many parts of the world. A factor contributing to this problem is the widely held belief that some races are biologically inferior to others. Such a belief has little or no scientific foundation. In "Biology Looks at Race" Georghi F. Debetz presents the major conclusions of twenty-two biologists at a UNESCO meeting on race.

Next Louis E. Lomax discusses the Negro revolt in the United States, what it means, why it has come now in spite of great progress by Negroes in recent years, and how it affects the traditional Negro leadership in education, politics, and in other fields. Lomax believes that the American Negro has no future except as a part of American society, and he looks forward hopefully to the day when the Negro will be fully integrated into that society.

Finally, Al Capp describes the amusing problems of a handsome and capable Negro with a degree from Harvard, who is offered numerous good jobs and invited to many parties by people who want to prove that they do not discriminate against Negroes.

26

Biology Looks at Race

by Georghi F. Debetz

[At a Unesco meeting in Moscow, twenty-two scientists drew up and unanimously adopted, on August 18, 1964, a 13-point statement on the biological aspects of the race question. Here the chairman of the meeting reviews its work and conclusions.]

Racism is the expression of a system of thought which is fundamentally anti-rational. Hate and racial strife feed on scientifically false ideas, and live on ignorance. They can also derive from scientifically sound ideas which have been distorted or taken out of context, leading to false implications. To demonstrate these errors of fact and of reasoning, and to spread knowledge of the conclusions reached by different scientific disciplines, Unesco convened in 1949 a meeting of scientists from different countries to draw up a declaration on the nature and significance of racial differences.

The text prepared by these experts and published by Unesco in 1950 was well received by the public, but drew some criticism from anthropologists and geneticists who considered that it caused confusion between race as a biological fact and the idea of race as a social phenomenon.

Unesco therefore called a second conference in 1951, this time exclusively for specialists in physical anthropology and in human genetics. This group drew up a new text in which the main conclusions of the earlier declaration were maintained, others amended and certain deletions made. The text of this new declaration was sent to fifty geneticists and anthropologists for their comments, and the results of this inquiry, including favourable comments and adverse criticisms, were published in book form under the title "The Race Concept."

Since then Unesco's action has been focused more on the social aspects of race than on the biological ones. On the other hand, scientific advances in the field of human biology during the past fifteen years have clearly shown the need for a fresh study of the 1951 declaration and its revision in the light of the latest biological discoveries. It has also been felt that

Reprinted by permission from *The Unesco Courier,* April, 1965, pp. 4–7.
Georghi F. Debetz, a Soviet biologist, is a professor at the Institute of Ethnography of the Academy of Sciences in Moscow.

its scope should be enlarged by encompassing several points, dealing with the nature and forms of racial prejudice in inter-racial situations, that were not previously covered.

Unesco therefore decided to hold two successive meetings: one in 1964 to cover the biological aspects, and a second, in 1966, to deal with the social and ethical aspects of the problem and to draft a statement which . . . would englobe both the biological and social aspects of the problem of race.

The first of these meetings was held in Moscow in August 1964 immediately after the VII Congress of Anthropological and Ethnological Sciences which had taken place in that city. It was attended by anthropologists and ethnologists from 17 countries.

During eight sessions twenty-five reports devoted to the main scientific problems related to the study of human races were discussed. At the last two sessions a 13-point declaration was drafted and adopted unanimously. This text will provide the biological elements for the new declaration on race and racial prejudice to be drawn up in 1966.

At one time the essential object of discussions between anthropologists was to decide whether man had one or several ancestors, whether the various races derived from a single species of monkey or from a variety of species. Today, this question can be regarded as finally settled. It was not even raised during the 1964 Moscow meeting. The declaration merely notes, as if to sum up earlier discussions, that "all living human beings belong to a single species, known as 'Homo Sapiens' and are derived from a common stock origin."

The keenest discussion was concerned with the nature of the concept of race as applied to human beings and with the scientific evidence for this concept. It might be thought that no discussion is called for on this question. Everyone knows that, so far as many physical features are concerned, the people in various parts of the world frequently differ—as regards colour of skin, type of hair, facial characteristics, etc. It is true that the number of features which all men have in common is very much greater, and it is equally true that such common features are biologically of much greater importance than the divergent features. At the same time differences do exist and are evident at a glance. If, for instance, we were to compare groups made up of Congolese, Swedes, and Mongols selected at random, we would have no trouble in identifying each of the three groups. They would not even need to be dressed differently, or to speak. Their physical features alone would distinguish them.

While everyone is agreed on this point, many anthropologists are now calling attention to another equally indisputable fact. If, for example, one were to go on foot from the sources of the Nile to the Nile delta, then across the Arab countries of Asia, through Turkey, Bulgaria, Rumania and the Ukraine to northern Russia and finally towards Mongolia via the homes of the Udmurt, Bashkir and Kazakh peoples, no difference of physical type would be apparent between the inhabitants of any neighbouring points on this route.

However, if one were to compare the people encountered at the beginning, middle and end of the journey, the differences between them would be manifest. It is for this reason, say the opponents of racial classification, that the division of mankind into rigidly distinct categories is scientifically unsound and results in a completely unacceptable schematic approach.

On the other hand, those who believe that human races should be recognized as distinct entities argue that the existence of transitional stages between any kind of phenomena should not lead us to deny the reality of such phenomena. The hypothetical traveller would not observe any difference in climate between two adjoining points on the route nor between the local fauna, yet classification by regions is useful and even essential to a knowledge of climate and fauna. "Where is the dividing line between the mountain and the valley?" ask the defenders of classification. "Nobody denies the existence of valleys and mountains simply because they cannot point to such a line."

Opponents of classification point out that physical features change not only in space but, even more, in time. In central Europe as in other regions, the human head has become much rounder over the last eight centuries but more recently has tended to lengthen again; the average height in certain countries has risen by 10 centimetres in the last 100 years; and so on. Those opposed to classification likewise emphasize the considerable degree of individual variation in regard to all physical features.

The average width of face among the people of Azerbaijan, for instance, is one cm. less than in the case of the Kazakhs; but this measurement varies from one individual to another and some of the former have broader faces than some of the latter. Supporters of classification admit this, but argue that sometimes—and even fairly frequently—women are taller than men. Is this a reason, they ask, for denying the obvious fact that men are generally bigger than women?

Having noted that opinions differed as to the importance of racial classifications, participants in the Moscow meeting nonetheless unanimously felt able to reach certain conclusions which, while not wholly eliminating the disagreements, did indicate that opinions might be brought more into harmony with each other.

One of the points in their declaration was that "as entities defined by sets of distinctive traits, human races are at any time in a process of emergence and dissolution." Still more important is another point in the declaration, contending that "certain physical characters have a universal biological value for the survival of the human species, irrespective of the environment. The differences on which racial classifications are based do not affect these characters and therefore it is not possible from the biological point of view to speak in any way whatsoever of a general inferiority or superiority of this or that race."

All the experts attending the Moscow meeting were specialists in the field of biological science. But a genuinely scientific survey cannot be kept within the framework of a single science. Biologists dealing with human beings cannot bypass the phenomena of social existence. It is indeed because of social existence, as the declaration points out, that "human evolution presents attributes of capital importance which are specific to the species." "As a consequence," the declaration adds, "general adaptability to the most diverse environments is in man more pronounced than his adaptations to specific environments."

This is one of the most important biological differences between man and all other biological species and derives from the very nature of man and his social life. The following point in the declaration should also be noted: "For long millenia, progress made by man, in any field, seems to have been increasingly, if not exclusively, based on culture and the transmission of cultural achievements and not on the transmission of genetic endowment. This implies a modification in the role of natural selection in man today."

Racism, a system which falsifies scientific facts, automatically ascribes to men all those phenomena observed among animals.

The biological elements in the declaration adopted by the 1964 Moscow meeting are therefore a barrier raised against racism. Man is primarily a social being and the fundamental nature of his history is determined by social phenomena.

As is well known, wherever racists are in power they seek to set men of differing races against each other and to use every possible means of preventing the natural intermingling process of the human race. One of the racists' favourite techniques for falsifying science is to assert that interracial marriages are harmful and that the children of such marriages are physically and psychically "deficient."

Here, the declaration is clear and categorical: "It has never been proved that interbreeding has biological disadvantages for mankind as a whole. On the contrary, it contributes to the maintenance of biological ties between human groups and thus to the unity of the species in its diversity." Noting that the individual hereditary characteristics of the parents naturally influence their offspring (it may happen that the combination of certain such characteristics has undesirable consequences), the declaration emphasizes that this is not a question of racial differences and that "therefore, no biological justification exists for prohibiting intermarriage between persons of different races, or for advising against it on racial grounds."

The declaration once again stresses that racial differences do not coincide with national, religious, linguistic or cultural differences. Here again, social phenomena exercise an influence on the formation of racial, i.e.

biological, differences. "Human beings who speak the same language and share the same culture have a tendency to intermarry, and often there is as a result a certain degree of coincidence between physical traits on the one hand, and linguistic and cultural traits on the other," says the declaration. "But there is no known causal nexus between these and therefore it is not justifiable to attribute cultural characteristics to the influence of the genetic inheritance."

Racists claim that races are not equal in respect of psychic qualities. The psychologists who help to draw up the 1966 declaration will be dealing with this point. However, the biologists meeting in Moscow could naturally not pass over this important aspect of the race question.

Like certain major anatomical traits in the human species, the genetic capacity for intellectual development belongs to those biological characteristics which are universally valid, because of its importance for the survival of the species in any natural or cultural environment. The peoples of the world today appear to possess equal biological potentialities for attaining any level of civilization. Differences in the achievements of different peoples must be attributed solely to their cultural history:

"Certain psychological traits are at times attributed to particular peoples. Whether or not such assertions are valid, we do not find any basis for ascribing such traits to hereditary factors, until proof to the contrary is given.

"Neither in the field of hereditary potentialities concerning the over-all intelligence and the capacity for cultural development, nor in that of physical traits, is there any justification for the concept of 'inferior' and 'superior' races."

The anthropologists and other biologists who unanimously adopted the biological elements of the declaration did not do so solely as scientists but also as men. In their desire to emphasize this aspect of their work, participants in the Moscow meeting concluded their declaration in the following words: "The biological data given above stand in open contradiction to the tenets of racism. Racist theories can in no way pretend to have any scientific foundation and the anthropologists should endeavour to prevent the results of their researches from being used in such a biased way that they would serve non-scientific ends."

27

The Negro Revolt

by Louis E. Lomax

The Britannica World Language Dictionary defines a revolt, among other things, as an extensive or drastic change in a condition, method or idea. And it is in this precise sense that I contend that the American Negro has been in a state of revolt for more than five years.

The Negro revolt involves a drastic change in our methods and ideas concerning segregation and established Negro leadership organizations.

Concerning segregation, the revolt lies in the fact that we not only have decided that the last vestige of that evil must be eliminated, but have embraced a new methodology, and armed ourselves with new weapons in our war against segregation and all of its concomitants.

And the revolt against the established Negro leadership organizations has come about because these organizations are wed to weapons which, though they accomplished some gains, have proved incapable of dealing segregation a final death blow.

To say that we have revolted against certain methods and the civil rights organizations that sponsored them is not to say that we have completely abandoned or turned against them; rather, it means that we Negroes have demanded tactical changes, that our traditional leadership organizations have debated, rather than acted upon, our demands, and that while the established Negro leaders were still locked in the methodological debate, rank-and-file Negroes have moved on their own, employed new tactics and achieved incomparable results. As a result, established Negro leadership is in the position of the oddly dressed man who said to a bystander, "Please tell me which way the parade went; after all, I'm leading it." . . .

The American Negro revolt is one of the nonwhite uprisings now sweeping the world. In every single case, the black man has a grievance against the white man; these grievances are already couched in bitterness, and many serious thinkers, Negro and white, believe they could one day soon burst into open and bloody conflict. In a very real sense, the American

Negro holds the key to the rise of nonwhite peoples all over the world. And to the degree that the question of the American Negro is admitted and resolved, the probability of a world free from racial strife is increased. . . .

Why has the Negro revolt come *now*? The late fifties and early sixties have been good years, relatively speaking, for Negroes; and even white liberals are hard pressed to understand why better conditions for Negroes have served only to usher in a new Negro militancy. This new militancy jars when seen against the surface appearance of Negro life in this country. One sees the Negro in his well-furnished home in suburbia, indolent and idle along the streets of the Negro ghetto, or hustling in the commercial centers of our great cities, and concludes that, though deprived, these are not very angry people after all. And if one goes South to visit the Negro middle class and then the black masses that support the Black Bourgeoisie in their comfort, it is more than easy to conclude that although Negroes want civil rights they are not going to work up a real sweat about it. More than once it has been suggested to me that the voices one hears in the current revolt are false, that the Negro is not really mad, that he is only frightened and anguished and thrashing about.

This, I feel, is a valid surface view of the Negro. But the fact of segregation has decreed that the dynamics of Negro life always be subliminal. And when the true nature of our own feelings emerges into our consciousness and we admit such feelings exist, we articulate them in a jargon peculiar to our anguish and fright. Our greatest protection is the white man's indifference; he seldom stops to notice us, and, when he does, he doesn't realize what he is looking at.

Few white people have more than a headline acquaintance with the Negro, and even white liberals share the general white population's total ignorance of Negro history. And it is for this very reason that all white people are at a total loss concerning the current racial unrest. Through the liberal eye, things are better than they were in, say, 1950, and they cannot understand why the courageous Negro leadership organizations that have played such a magnificent role in the past decade are now under bitter and open attack. Yet the attack is there, and its existence can no longer be doubted.

The white population's confusion about what Negroes are up to is understandable, for, if the truth is told, Negroes are fairly confused about themselves. I would wager that more than half of the Negro population has deep psychological problems over the apparently simple ethnic question, "Who and what am I?" I would go on to wager even more that Negroes are incapable of articulating just what it is they seek under the catch-all label of integration.

There are scores of easy answers to what the American Negro is and what it is he is up to, but these replies beg too much and tell too little. One must pause, at least so it seems to me, to isolate and understand the forces that have shaped the Negro into what he is today. Until we do this, we are dealing in nothing but comfortable presumptions.

The American Negro is a man- not God-made race. We are the result of alliances between slave masters and their female slaves. (There were liaisons between Negro men and white women of the pre-Civil War era but all scholars agree that the white man-Negro woman relationship was, by far, the more frequent.) This indisputable historical and biological fact has caused Southern states to spend thousands of dollars and millions of man-hours trying to determine just who among them are Negroes. Prior to 1910, the state of Virginia decreed that a Negro was anyone with one-fourth or more Negro blood in him. By 1910 the burgeoning number of non-negroid Negroes caused the keepers of white purity to revise their thinking and declare that one was Negro if he had as much as one-sixteenth Negro blood in his veins. By 1930 this definition was not sufficient to maintain the bastions of white supremacy and it was enacted into Virginia law that anyone having "any quantum of Negro blood whatsoever" was a Negro.

Blood sampling aside, the fact remains that few of today's Negroes are of pure African descent. Biologically, then, we were fashioned in the New World; every conceivable blood flows in our veins. We speak an Anglo-Saxon tongue, worship the Christian God, and our political ideals are identical with those of this nation's founding fathers.

Thus the American Negro does not have a culture in the precise and classic sense of that word. Although we are socially and economically segregated from the American mainstream, we are culturally integrated with it. We speak the language of the majority and, when allowed to, we participate in majority institutions. When not allowed, we form our own institutions and pattern them after those of the majority. Thus the only difference between the Negro Baptist Church and the Baptist Church proper is that Negroes attend the former and white people attend the latter.

This, of course, is a sore point with Negroes as well as white people. Since the general histories of this nation omit the deeds and contributions of the Negro, there is a tendency on the part of many Negroes to isolate their contribution to the nation and cite it as a culture. Only in the loosest sense can it be called that. Rather the Negro, like America itself, is a participant in and contributor to what the late Professor Solomon Bloom of Brooklyn College called "Atlantic Civilization." We are a product of the hammering out of a way of life that has been going on in "Atlantic" countries—in the Old World and the New—for centuries.

The American Negro has been fashioned, body, mind and spirit, in the New World. Unlike other "minorities" in American society, we Negroes do not share a positive sense of identity. Alas, the only thing one Negro has exclusively in common with another Negro is the animus of the white man.

There is no denying that, historically, the white majority is the founder of Atlantic Civilization, nor can it be questioned that our African ancestors were introduced into this culture as handymen. Once here, however, the Negro not only absorbed the culture but made remarkable contributions to its evolution. We have remained marginal members of this civilization because only doors on the periphery have been opened to us. We cannot change our color; instead, our efforts have been directed toward achieving what must be called "cultural whiteness," although we and our ancestors made substantial contributions to that culture. We sought this cultural whiteness in the now apparently ill-fated hope that acquiring the manners and value system of the majority would merit us the rights and the freedoms enjoyed by white people.

This cultural confusion has everything to do with the current Negro revolt. It explains the deep schism within the Negro race and it accounts for the fact that the Negro individual has no hope of final and secure identification except with the general American social structure. And so it is that the American Negro is the only American who, as an individual, must reach beyond his own group for absolute identification; therefore we Negroes are the only Americans unwilling to make even the slightest compromise with the American creed as stated by the founding fathers. We have an ultimate and final stake in the triumph of Atlantic Civilization, intact, without reservations and with all the chaotic possibilities involved in the proposition that the voice of the people, rightly heard, is the voice of God and that, indeed, all men are created free and, in that sense, equal.

To understand the Negro one must reread *The Federalist,* come to grips anew with the basic assumptions about man, God and government that guided Jefferson, Washington, Jay and Adams. These are the political ideals that drive the Negro as he seeks integration or "cultural whiteness," and Negro history is but our continuing efforts to escape the boundaries placed upon us by the white majority and to find identification in the American mainstream. We have made some progress, but, on the whole, our every effort toward majority identification, regardless of the tool we employed, has been thwarted. Now we are employing a new weapon, or at least an old weapon with a new militancy in our hearts. This, in essence, is what the Negro revolt is about. . . .

Pain and progress are inseparable. The severest pain brought on by the Negro revolt stems from the cleavages that have developed within the Negro group; not the disaffection toward the established Negro leadership class . . . but the Negro institutions that served their time well but have now fallen into disfavor because they are inextricably tied to the *status quo*.

The Negro college, the Negro press, the Negro politician and the Negro church all have this flaw in common: they were born into a segregated world and set out to serve us with the view that our separate world would someday be equal. As a result, each of these, in a different way, has a stake in the *status quo*. And, needless to say, *status quo* is now anathema to most Negroes.

Ten years ago, in 1952, a Negro college president who was able to talk some white philanthropist into giving him, say, a hundred thousand dollars for a new library was a hero and a highly respected race leader. Now the Negroe college president must spend much of his time explaining himself, saying why he still heads a "Negro" college, trying to tell a skeptical world about the future of the "Negro" college, attempting to soothe the restless Negro students, who are embarrassingly aware that they are receiving an inferior education while being surrounded by all the trappings of segregation.

"Intellectual Uncle Tom!" That's the phrase one hears throughout the South nowadays. It is uttered by college students and their supporters, and it is used in the open, at public meetings and rallies. This is the students' way of talking about the "failure" of Southern Negro intellectuals—schoolteachers, for the most part—to support the Negro revolt in clear, open terms. . . .

The Negro politician is also racked by the pains of progress. In the early days of this century, the Negro politician, particularly if elected to office, held a position of great stature and respect. Now, alas, he is just another politician, a ghetto politician at that. Although all the Negro politicians make speeches calling for justice and equality, they are not in the front ranks of the Negro revolt for they owe their existence to segregation. Men like Congressman Adam Clayton Powell will be undone by the Negro's growing demand that he be freed from the ghetto. Powell, to be sure, is for integration, but it is certain that he does not want to see his district integrated right out from under him, and his constituents dispersed. Indeed, one of the arguments one hears as new, expensive apartments go up in Harlem is that there is a sinister plot afoot to reclaim Harlem "for the white man," that white people are building these expensive apartment buildings in the full knowledge that low-salaried Negroes cannot afford the rent and, thus, will be forced to move elsewhere.

This, of course, is the thorny issue raised by the revolt: Will the Negro become another "tribe," like the Jews and the Poles, in America, or is it his ambition to be absorbed and dispersed? For the Negro politician this boils down to whether he can maintain his power and get "Negro" patronage and "Negro" power at city hall. This is more than just a theoretical matter; in a few years Manhattan Island, as well as several other "central cities" in America, will be predominantly Negro. There is reason to believe that New York City may have a Negro mayor by 1975. Negro politicians feel strongly on this point.

"The Irish had their day in City Hall," one of them told me, "the Jews have theirs, the Catholics have theirs. Now it is time for the Negro to have his day."

This argument assumes that American politics will continue to mirror the emergence of the nation's various ethnic groups. . . .

As far as the Negro individual in politics is concerned, the day has not quite dawned that a Negro candidate can get elected from a district that is not predominantly Negro. This day will come soon; I predict it will break over a suburban community of liberals, more than likely predominantly Jewish with a sprinkling of Negroes. When this day arrives, a giant step will have been taken toward the ultimate goal of the Negro revolt: that golden day when a Negro will stand or fall on his own merits, neither hindered nor helped by the fact that he is a Negro. . . .

The Negro press—and this includes all forms of "Negro" communication —also pains as the Negro revolt continues. The problem of the Negro press arises from the fact that, like all other news media, it depends upon advertising for its existence. . . . Negroes own very little business even in their own communities. As a result the Negro press must depend upon white businessmen for their advertising revenue. In the North, for example, the Negro press can afford to be very militant about integration and Southern police brutality, but it cannot expose sharp business practices and loan-shark dealings that keep the masses of Negroes in perpetual debt. I know of one Negro editor who has a fat folder full of evidence—pictures, affidavits, etc.—showing just how Negroes are swindled by some of his best advertisers. These articles will never be run. . . .

The Negro press as a whole is walking a tightrope. To date they have been successful in reflecting the interests of their readers, but this success has been due largely to the assumption that there is a separate "Negro" audience with special interests that can be appealed to and exploited. This is true now, but there will come a time when the Negro revolt will make it less true. And it is against this day that the Negro individual who is a publisher must begin now to make his plans.

The Negro church is in something of the same fix. By nature and organization it is "Negro." Born, as it was, out of the refusal of white people to let Negroes worship in dignity in the "white" churches of the slavery era, the Negro church was not constructed against the day when Negroes would seek to remove all barriers. . . . Like the NAACP and CORE, the Negro church will enjoy its greatest and final success the day it destroys itself. This does not mean that the "Negro" church will die and the "white" church will survive; rather it foresees that one day America will become what it swears it already is, a truly democratic society. When that occurs we will be a nation with churches, schools, newspapers and politicians without an ethnic prefix. This, of course, is a long way off; but the day is not nearly so removed as it was when the inexplicable Rosa Parks sat down on a bus seat in Montgomery, Alabama.

The key factor in the future of all these people and organizations—the Negro politician, the Negro press, the Negro schoolteacher, the Negro church—is whether they will be able to make the shift from ethnic to general institutions. Under the able guidance of Dr. William J. Trent, Jr., executive director of the United Negro College Fund, many of the better private Negro colleges have already begun to work toward just such a shift. All of the Fund's member colleges have dropped the designation "Negro" from their charters and many of them have white students. There is no doubt that schools such as Spelman and Morehouse will attract white students once the air settles in Atlanta. . . .

Whatever else the Negro is, he is American. Whatever he is to become —integrated, unintegrated, or disintegrated—he will become it in America. Only a minority of Negroes have ever succumbed to the temptation to seek greener pastures in another country or another ideology. Our lot is irrevocably cast, and whatever future awaits America awaits the Negro; whatever future awaits the Negro, awaits America.

And the Negroes' total commitment to America indicates that the prospect ahead seems bright. It is true that we are angry about our present plight, for we measure America by her potential rather than by her achievements: like a schoolboy genius with a consistent B average, America is too good not to be better. I have talked to scores of Negroes in the months of research involved in this book. What has impressed me is that although they were angry and often bitter, although they were discouraged at what could be done in a lifetime to rectify the effects of generations of oppression and servitude, not a single Negro doubted that we would one day get our full freedom. It has just never occurred to us that the Negro revolt will not, in the end, succeed. This fundamental optimism is, I submit, a resounding statement of faith in the American dream.

Dr. Kenneth Clark goes to what I feel is the heart and truth of the matter when he says, "there is no point in talk, regardless of how poetic it may be, about whether the Negro wants to integrate with America. He has no choice. He is involved, inextricably so, with America and he knows it. And the sensible Negro is the man who takes pride in this involvement and accepts it as a mandate to work for the change that is written in the way of things."

America is the latest outpost in man's journey away from provincialism. From here man will go forward, not backward, and he will be less encumbered by dividedness than he was when he spread from the old world to the new. The art of being a Negro consists in the realization of this central fact; the act of being a Negro in America consists in joining in every way the liberal forces who enjoy the challenge of tomorrow more than they do the comfortable provincialism of yesterday.

And so the hydrogen thing ticks. It may go off; then again it may not. I hope and pray it will not. But in either case man will survive; in either case provincialism is doomed. And if it is the lot of surviving man to probe the ashes of war in search of the will to carry on, he will know that America was once here. And if surviving man studies the evidence well, taking pains to blow away the dust of time, he will know that a disturbed, lonely, yet inspired, American black people once walked this way.

28

The Problems of a Fortunate Negro

by Al Capp

"There seem to be only two kinds of Negroes who get attention in your country," my friend from London said, looking up from his American paper.

"The adored—such as, Lena Horne, Ralph Bunche and Sammy Davis, Jr.—and the submerged—the kids who want to go to school in Virginia, and the people who want lunch at counters in Alabama. Aren't there any undramatic Negroes here, those who have quietly become an honored part of American life and are content?"

I realized that I had never actually met a perfectly content Negro, either adored or submerged, so I sent my secretary out to find one.

She could have found 20 Caucasians who qualified in 20 minutes. But it took her two days to find the tall, handsome man of 30 whom I interviewed.

"Life's been fine for me," he grinned. "No complaints. My father, who began as a bootblack in a Westchester country club, ran the valet service in a dozen country clubs. He sent me to Cornell and the Harvard Business School."

From *The Chicago Daily News*, May 31, 1961, p. 14. Reprinted by permission of the author.

Al Capp is a well-known cartoonist, writer, lecturer, and radio-TV personality.

"Any social problems?" I asked.

"Just finding time to attend all the social functions I was invited to," he said. "I couldn't embarrass my white friends by refusing. There were so many parties to go to, and so few of us Negroes around. One of us just had to be included to prove we weren't excluded."

"Any problem finding a job after graduation?"

"Same problem as the social one," he said. "I got twice as many offers as my white friends. My offers were all from big companies. It was hard turning down all but the best offer. I know how much they needed to include at least one Negro to prove they don't exclude any."

"Has being the lone Negro created any problems in your career?"

"Yes. Whenever I do anything just as well as the whites around me, I get praised twice as much, and get salary raises twice as fast."

"Hasn't being a Negro created any difficult moments at all?"

"Just once," he said. "Our kids were growing up, so we decided to move to the suburbs. We would have preferred a Negro community, but there aren't enough Negroes of our education—my wife is a Radcliffe graduate—and our income—$15,000 a year—to form one yet. So we looked for a community where young people of our economic class lived.

"I found a suitable development, advertising apartments ready for immediate occupancy. While my wife watched the kids in the car, I looked at the apartment. It was perfect. Then the agent said, 'Ready For Immediate Occupancy was misleading. Call us again in six months, in a year.' He said he wouldn't forget me.

"I was sure he wouldn't. We rode around town for a while, then my wife—who is so light-skinned she could pass—went back to the development without me, and got an apartment. I stayed out of sight until the day we moved in."

"What happened then?" I asked.

"There were a couple of double-takes. But no incidents. We've been there over a year now."

"Has it been a happy year?"

"Yes, but terribly exhausting. The same old problems fortunate Negroes will have to face. My wife is asked to join every club, not just those she's interested in. My kids are invited to all the other kids' parties. And they have to go, or the parents are embarrassed. Being Negroes is ruining our kids' stomachs."

CHAPTER

14

CRIME AND DELINQUENCY

H. ASHLEY WEEKS gives an interesting account of the treatment of criminals in the past, and of the development of modern prisons and reformatories. But he concludes that we have not succeeded in developing institutions which prepare criminals for a successful social adjustment when they are released. He describes, however, several interesting experiments which have this objective and which seem to provide hope for the future.

Margolis attaches special importance to the larger social aspects of combatting delinquency and crime. As he sees it, the problem with juveniles is to maintain their allegiance to the values of adult society. From this point of view punishment is a force often misapplied, for it aims at restraining the juvenile and not at recovering his allegiance; yet it is precisely this allegiance that the adult world must win back.

29

Treatment of Criminals: Past, Present and Possible

by H. Ashley Weeks

From the days of Hammurabi (ca. 1955–1913 B.C.) to the present we know pretty well how man has regarded and treated deviant behavior. We can infer from Hammurabi's code as well as from other early writings that treatment of deviant behavior (there was no distinction during those early days between mental aberration of one kind or another and delinquent or criminal behavior as it is defined today) was then essentially revengeful—"an eye for an eye, a tooth for a tooth." If a person slandered another, his tongue was cut out; if he took what did not belong to him, his fingers or hands were removed; if he killed, he was killed in turn. A large number of specific offenses were enumerated with specific punishments to go with them, and not only was the offender subject to punishment, but if he was not caught or available for punishment other members of his family could be punished in his stead.

Concurrent with such thinking was the belief that aberrant behavior was the work of the devil or evil spirits. Among many different peoples even ordinary illnesses were attributed to evil spirits, and the way to change or cure the behavior was to exorcise these evil spirits which were in possession. Christ cast out demons into swine and they were so affected that they ran into a river and were drowned. Even as late as the nineteenth century an indictment used by judges in the English courts not only accused the defendant of violating the law, but also of "being prompted and instigated by the devil and not having the fear of God before his eyes." And about the time of the War between the States, the North Carolina Supreme Court declared: "To know the right and still the wrong pursue proceeds from a perverse will brought about by the seduction of the evil one."

It was not until relatively modern times that more rational and philo-

---

Reprinted by permission from *Key Issues: A Journal of Controversial Issues in Criminology,* Vol. 2, 1965: The Future of Imprisonment in a Free Society, pp. 57–62, published by St. Leonard's House, Chicago 60612.

H. Ashley Weeks is professor of sociology in the School of Public Health, University of Michigan.

sophical theories of crime causation, and controls resulting from such theoretical ideas, were developed. Cesare Beccaria in 1764 is credited with the first application of a theory of crime causation to punishment. Beccaria believed in a hedonistic philosophy, that man acted solely on a pleasure-pain principle. From this premise he argued that in order to control crime it was necessary to devise a system of punishment which would inflict at least a little more pain to an individual who committed a delinquent or criminal act than the pleasure he derived from committing the act. According to Beccaria, the exact punishment for each criminal act should be made known to all; and each person, regardless of age, wealth, social status, circumstances, sanity, or whatnot should receive the same punishment for the same crime.

Jeremy Bentham, in England, accepting the hedonistic philosophy, applied the theory to recommended legislation. From England Beccaria's ideas, modified and elucidated by Bentham, spread to other European countries and to America. Although there has been some modification of the absolute equality of punishment, particularly as applied to children and "lunatics" because such persons were incapable of calculating pleasures and pains intelligently, and some small amount of judicial discretion so far as the penalties were concerned, the ideas of Beccaria and Bentham became the prevailing body of criminal law and have persisted to the present.

Even though the psychology underlying the theories is now generally questioned, the ideas are still applied almost automatically. When a particularly heinous offense is publicized there is an immediate demand to stiffen the penalty, as though this action would curtail similar offenses. Actually there has been no evidence that increased penalties of any kind have acted as deterrents of criminal or delinquent behavior. It is difficult to understand why there is still so much faith in this kind of simple expedient when there seems to be increasing evidence that very little, if any, relationship exists between the number and nature of offenses committed and the severity of the punishment meted out. In fact, there appears to be evidence to the contrary. There is a positive relationship between the length of time a person stays in a custodial facility and the rate of recidivism. The longer the institutional stay the greater the chance of failure on parole or the greater the chance of a new offense with a return to the same or a different institution.

A striking example of this is the abolition of capital punishment for relatively minor offenses. No one argues that a person should be hanged for stealing a loaf of bread as was once the case in England. In fact, one hears more arguments against capital punishment than for it regardless of the enormity of the offense.

The more that is learned about human behavior the greater the evidence that all behavior, whether law-abiding or the opposite, results from what happens in the course of the socialization of the individual. If a child has love, understanding, good adult figures to identify with and emulate, he will usually grow into adulthood as a law-abiding citizen, whereas the reverse is likely when these elements are lacking. This is not to say, of course, that this is a simple one-to-one relationship. Behavior of any kind, at any one time, is the complex resultant of a multiplicity of interrelated factors, but the basic ingredients of socialization must be present. Much of the law enforcement machinery, in the long run, serves to hinder the socialization process.

Let us examine some of the historical theories and ideas underlying the correctional system as it has developed and exists at present. One of the earliest prison systems which was founded on a philosophy of reform, or at least attempted rehabilitation, was the so-called Pennsylvania system, brought about by demands by the Quakers for reform. This system held the belief that more than simple confinement or punishment must take place if an individual was to return to society at the expiration of his sentence as a law-abiding citizen. The Quakers, being a religious sect, believed that a man who was arrested, tried, and sentenced must realize that he had done wrong and must want to be better. Their way to assure his betterment was for him to be penitent. They therefore recommended and established between 1791 and 1801 in the Walnut Street Jail, Philadelphia, solitary cells where hardened inmates were incarcerated and remained alone to meditate and be penitent over their sins and wrongdoing. Although there were some other long-term prisons before this, such as the Maison de Force in Ghent and the Hospice of Saint Michael in Rome, Harry Elmer Barnes credits the Walnut Street Jail as being the "practical birth place" of the prison system, not only in the United States but throughout the world. There seems to be no doubt that it was the first institution to which the name "penitentiary" could be applied.

About the same time as the Quakers were creating their reforms, New York established a new prison at Auburn, where solitary cells were built for the oldest and most hardened criminals as a test of the Pennsylvania system. It was a dismal failure. Some Frenchmen, observing this test at first hand, condemned it outright as conducive to depression and insanity and endangering life.

As the result of the test at Auburn, prison policies were modified and inmates, although still confined in solitary cells at night, were allowed to work together and eat together though they were not allowed to communicate with one another. This latter system prevailed and became the dominant system in the United States until recently. Now, possibly because of overcrowding and newer theories, solitary confinement has been abandoned except as further punishment for some drastic violation of prison rules and regulations.

Late in the nineteenth century another innovation in the "treatment"

of offenders had world-wide ramifications. The State of New York established a new institution for adolescent and young adult offenders up to
the age of 30. It was a graded system. Each inmate, on admission, was
placed in second grade. If he behaved and gave no trouble for six months,
he graduated to first grade. After another six months in this grade without trouble, he became eligible for parole. If, at any time during his stay,
there was misconduct he was placed in a third grade in which he had to
demonstrate "good behavior" for a month before being returned to second
grade and then again to first after the required lapse of time. In addition
to the grade system, the Elmira Reformatory emphasized physical training,
military training, schooling, and training for a trade. For the first time the
length of stay became a function of an observable reformation, at least
according to prison keepers and supervisors. Along with such reform went
the indeterminate sentence and parole, so that those who made the grade
got out earlier. Unquestionably, as the system developed, some inmates
learned to "do time" and "keep their noses clean," and so got out quicker
than others, without any fundamental change in their behavior or reformation of their characters. Nonetheless, ideally it was a step forward and
influenced the establishment of the Borstal System in England where Sir
Evelyn Ruggles-Brice during 1897 set apart a specialized institution at
Borstal prison modeled after that at Elmira.

Reformatories and industrial or vocational schools for even younger
offenders were established subsequently as the Juvenile Court idea expanded and need developed for some kind of institution to confine those
who most needed "help" from the state. Many juvenile facilities, reformatories and prisons have put work programs into effect. The work was
rationalized as training for outside vocations, but no one, so far as is
known, ever tried to ascertain how many entered or even tried to get jobs
similar to those they had engaged in while in the facility. For example,
almost every state industrial school has a farm on which a high proportion
of the boys work, despite the fact that most inmates are from urban environments and return to such communities upon discharge.

Although some changes have taken place over the years, which have
made the punishment of offenders more humane and less brutal, the fact
remains that for most adults and juveniles incarcerated in institutions there
is no real program of treatment or understanding of the behavioral manifestations which brought them before the courts and into the various kinds
of institutions. Punishment for wrongdoing still remains the basic philosophy with an almost blind faith that enough punishment will remold behavior, and because of fear of more punishment inmates will subsequently
refrain from criminal and delinquent acts. But most institutions for juvenile
delinquents and adult criminals show high recidivist rates.

We should not, however, be too quick to condemn those who manage
our correctional institutions. In some ways their tasks have become almost

impossible. Institutions have grown ever more crowded until today practically all of them are housing many more persons than they were built to accommodate. It is no wonder that many institutional workers ask resignedly, "What can we do? How can we carry on any treatment program under such conditions?" Treatment implies knowledge of the individual, and to get such knowledge there must be adequate professional staff. Then training or retraining of many non-professional workers is necessary so that they will be capable of carrying out a therapeutic program for the individual once knowledge of his needs is gained, and all this must be done within limited budgets.

What can we say to these persons? What can we do? Is there any hope? In very recent years there have been a few experiments which offer much promise. There have also been a number of studies which seem to indicate that perhaps we should begin to move in a different direction. First, it seems clear that a great many persons now housed in the larger maximum security institutions do not need to be kept in such places at all. It has been estimated by Robert D. Barnes, the famous Senior Architect of the Federal Bureau of Prisons, that only one-third of the prisoner population in state penal and correctional institutions need maximum security facilities, and only a small proportion of these would need to be confined in an inside cell in a walled institution.

Philosophically it can be argued that the more we confine individuals the less likely they are to make a go of it when they are released to take their places once again in society. Any large institution requires regimentation. Once an offender enters a large institution he loses most of his individual responsibility. Instead of building personal responsibility the institution removes it. The individual has no choices. He rises when a bell rings, he goes to the bathroom and to eat when other bells ring, he eats what is put on a tray, he goes to work at another bell and he does what he is told. He engages in what recreation he is allowed at a specific time. He is locked into his cell and lights are turned off according to institutional regulations. After years of such a regime is it any wonder that so many have difficulty in adjusting to the outside world?

Thus any attempts to break up the larger institutions into smaller units are all to the good. Such newer facilities as work camps, and places with more freedoms of choice and opportunities of socializing with family and friends at picnic-style visiting grounds, such as those at the California Institution for Men at Chino, seem to offer great possibilities. Parole prediction studies have shown that one of the most effective indicators of success on parole is the number of letters the inmate received from family and friends while in the institution. This shows the value of keeping up the offenders' most important social contacts.

Such short-term facilities as Highfields, established by the State of New Jersey for boys, have been demonstrated to be tremendously successful in terms of reducing the number of boys who become recidivists after their three to four months' stay.[1] Highfields is a small therapeutically oriented facility begun in 1950 for a maximum of twenty boys who voluntarily go there, at the discretion of the judge, while still on probation. There the boys engage in what are called "social group interaction sessions" five nights a week. The sessions go by this name to emphasize the fact that they attempt to uncover the individual's social problems rather than any deep-seated psychotic ones. The boys work during the day at a nearby state institution for which they are paid a minimum amount. They are allowed at least one furlough home during their stay. While at the facility the boys discover their problems and attempt to do something about them. When this happens the boys may return home regardless of how long they have been at the facility.

The original Highfields was considered so successful that similar facilities, including one for girls, have been established in New Jersey.

Another successful experiment is the one carried out by BARO under the auspices of Kings County Court in Brooklyn, New York. Two probation officers, Drs. Alexander Bassin and Alexander Smith, undertook to conduct non-directed group psycho-therapy sessions with a randomly selected group of young adult offenders, with great success. Later they conducted similar successful sessions with groups of narcotic offenders, sex offenders and alcoholics.

A third experiment using a different method but with the same underlying philosophy was also successful. Dr. Martin Haskel carried out role-training sessions with a randomly selected group of Riker's Island inmates about to be released on parole. The role-training sessions were organized around the problems of getting and keeping a job and getting along with one's family. Not only did the tests given show an improvement for the treatment group when compared with a control group, but a follow-up study three months after release showed a much larger number of those undergoing the role-training sessions still successfully on parole than was the case in the control group.

These three examples of successful treatment programs based on modern conceptions of changing human behavior into more socialized ways are not offered as the only ones being carried on or offering the most chance of successful outcomes. Other treatment programs could be cited. The ones discussed are those which the author of this essay has been close to in one capacity or another and therefore knows about at first hand.

It should be made clear that such programs as those discussed are not set forth as cure-alls, any more than a doctor would claim that he is successful in treating all sick patients who come to him for help. It is felt that these three examples of treatment programs do show possibilities of

[1] Weeks, H. Ashley, *Youthful Offenders at Highfields,* University of Michigan Press, Ann Arbor, Michigan, 1958.

what can be accomplished when programs are carefully conceived and carried through. Some offenders should probably always be kept under custody. It does not make sense to release a criminal just because he has served his sentence when nothing has been done to resocialize him or change the behavior which got him into trouble in the first place. No one wants to mollycoddle offenders, or be sickly sentimental about the poor lads and lassies who get into trouble with the law. But what is being done at present in most prisons, penitentiaries, reformatories, and industrial schools is not really protecting society. It is time we tried sound treatment programs based on what we know of human behavior, and as we learn more about what works, modify the programs and keep trying.

30

Juvenile Delinquents:
The Latter-Day Knights

by Joseph Margolis

No one can hope to discover the cause of juvenile delinquency, just as no one can hope to discover the cause of crime. These are labels applied to large clusters of acts that may have in common nothing more than the breaching of the law by minors or merely the breaching of the law. If we fasten on such fractional uniformities, we are inevitably led to expect simple and adequate causal correlations. We speak, accurately enough, of an upsurge in juvenile delinquency, which, because it is an isolable trend, we expect to be assigned an equally isolable source. But if we asked instead for the cause of crime, we should at once realize that "crime" is an umbrella term held over the heads of some extraordinarily different kinds of things. And even if we invented a term to cover criminal activity committed between the ages of thirty and thirty-nine (say, "trigintennial criminality"), we would still find it odd to inquire into its causes.

From *The American Scholar,* Vol. 29, No. 2, Spring 1960. © Copyright 1960 by the United Chapters of Phi Beta Kappa. Reprinted by permission of the publisher. Joseph Margolis is Professor of Philosophy at the University of Cincinnati.

This does not mean that it is pointless to search out as many correlations as the traffic will bear between juvenile delinquency and the kinds of lives delinquents actually lead. The trends are clear enough and ugly, and they excite our honest hopes for corrective action. Nothing is lost, for instance, in noticing that delinquency is very highly correlated with the various patterns of the "broken home." But one senses that delinquency is too amorphous a phenomenon to respond to the specific of patching homes. And the causally relevant sequences may even come to minimize the juvenile condition of the delinquents and the delinquent condition of the juveniles. Our concern is, properly, with the fact that it is juveniles, in mounting numbers, who are responsible for our crime records. But this, after all, is an outcome completely detached from any insight into the kinds of careers offending juveniles have come to prefer.

I think we are nowadays shocked by delinquency. We are startled and horrified by certain of the most dramatic aspects of much juvenile delinquency. But, above all, we are puzzled by it, failing to find its core of sense and purpose. We notice apparently unmotivated crimes, attacks on total strangers, inordinate punishment for seemingly trivial and imagined slights, bloodthirstiness and excessive violence, the exhilarated state of delinquents during their exploits, their disdain of, and relative independence from, the legal and ethical codes of society. Much of the special bravado that we associate with this kind of delinquency, I admit, collapses when the law uses its teeth; but this is not significant, since the delinquent simply behaves as a hostile captive isolated from the little world in which he finds his former conduct appropriate.

I shall not attempt to isolate the causes of juvenile delinquency. I wish only to make the well-known facts about a certain kind of delinquency fall into place in a coherent pattern whose causal analysis would prove more fruitful than the steady, piecemeal accumulation of statistical data. What we require at the present time is a promising model for interpreting the various patterns of delinquent behavior. Perhaps the model I propose is inadequate; it is, however, at least an attempt at correcting our conception of what the delinquents in question think they are doing in carrying on the way they do. Apparently, we don't understand them, for it is perfectly clear that we regard their behavior as senseless, pointless, unprovoked, inexplicable. But we must be mistaken, from their point of view, since there is among them as much seriousness, devotion to imagined duties, sense of honor and trust and co-operation (however perverse), even heroism and self-sacrifice, industry, incentive and reward, foresight and planning as can be found in any legitimate group endeavor. There is among them, moreover, an impressive enthusiasm, *esprit,* solidarity and even pride that would be genuinely hard to duplicate.

Let me exaggerate somewhat the description of two important features that regularly appear in these delinquency patterns. The first is that "there is a war on." The second is that "there must be witnesses." Although I say these are exaggerations, they would not be unlikely first impressions. The sense of a war stems partly from the quite regular skirmishes ("rumbles") between highly organized, usually well-armed, and even territorially distinct rival gangs. It stems also from the understandable hatred (however unpardonable) of this juvenile underworld toward law-enforcement agencies, a hatred that spills over not infrequently into overt hostilities. And it stems finally from the cruel and usually senseless victimization of random members of the law-abiding community.

But in fact there is no war, there are only patterns that strongly resemble warfare. Even the skirmishes between rival gangs are initiated largely by invitation (although it may not be possible to refuse it): "Do you want a rumble?" is, apparently, a common announcement that sufficient reason has been found for a skirmish to be staged. Nevertheless, there seems to be an understanding between warring companies that a return engagement is always to be expected and that no surrender or compensation could establish peace; moreover, each group seems primarily occupied with the way its owns champions conduct themselves. The police are simply a perpetual threat, for the activities of these gangs happen typically to be criminal. That is, I do not believe these delinquents wish merely to be law-breakers; they are fully prepared to break the law and, hence, permanently alienate the police. And again, the victims meaninglessly selected from the law-abiding community are merely victims, the unfortunate innocent bystanders of a gang code that affects them in an altogether contingent way. The code imposes obligations on the membership; compliance leads inevitably to the violence we know so well. But the important matter is compliance and not the breach of law. We, within our adult, law-abiding world, are struck by the frequent horror of these acts; whereas the juveniles themselves have hardly considered the victim's personal plight or the anguish of society at large. They are genuinely thoughtless in this respect, so engrossed are they (apart from their immaturity) in leading lives dictated by their own intimate society and in assessing, by their own standards, the talents and reliability and loyalty of their comrades.

I have said also that there must be witnesses. But in a sense, there always are witnesses, because these delinquents specialize in forays, in group adventures in which more than two boys participate. It is important, apparently, that accredited observers attest the prowess, hardness, strength, courage, cruelty, imagination of any single participant. It would be an absolutely idle waste of energy to commit any of the crimes that are committed and to go unnoticed.

I should like to approach this observation in another way. In my opinion, in the large urban centers in which delinquency is most flagrant (and somewhat less noticeably in smaller cities), juvenile gangs constitute the most coherent, publicly self-conscious, and vigorous communities that can be found. I discount businesses, churches, schools, the police and other similar groups as not, properly, forming neighborhoods. The gangs actually live together as social ensembles, the perfection of their communities marred here and there by the impinging adult world. The city is the locale of disintegrating neighborhoods (in the traditional sense) and, conversely, the locale of a rising, novel and peculiarly mobile neighborhood. In short, increasingly in our cities (as well as in certain of the cities of Europe and Asia) the most effective and powerful neighborhoods that exist are juvenile neighborhoods. They are the ones, ironically, that preserve some measure of face-to-face community living. And they are themselves aware of it, at least in that revealing lapse by which their members boldly attack innocent people without fear of reprisal. The law-abiding adult world is distinctly inert, from their point of view, providing only an endless variety of occasions and targets for the exhibition of the skills that are prized within the gang. Even the unfriendly press provides gratuitous and welcome confirmation of the gang's own chronicles. And, periodically, the forays themselves lead to large-scale rumbles, which, as is well known, are advertised to all except the police and others interested in law enforcement.

So the adult world is abdicating in large part its neighborhood responsibility and authority and, by its increasing inertia, has allowed control to pass into the hands of vigorous and ardent youngsters, whose code, however, does not promise to preserve the law-abiding values of the old neighborhood. It also happens that cities spring up without ever having had the experience of the old neighborhood solidarity; but this hardly is designed to prevent the rise of the new gangs.

I have put forward what I take to be two important clues for any suitable interpretive model of the sort required. I should like to say something now about such a model. The adult world thinks of these delinquents as deviants, outlaws, irresponsibles; and it is baffled by its inability to contain them. But the juveniles themselves actually form a string of genuine and relatively stable neighborhoods, with a day-to-day code of conduct, a system of sanctions and rewards, a calendar of community life, an educational program, and facilities for communications and the provision and distribution of goods and services. It is a simple society in which everyone is known by name and face and accomplishment; it is an aristocratic society —frequently monarchical—but in any case ruled by the most talented persons (discounting the perversity of the talents preferred). It is in fact *the* society to which these juveniles belong. The adult world, from their point of view, is vaguely defined and alien, usually threatening in its intermittent contact with their own; although, of course, the juvenile cannot ever be entirely free of a subordinate participation in that adult world.

The juvenile neighborhood has, I should say, two principal rituals to perform. It is, as a matter of fact, overwhelmingly concerned with ritual forms. But the two I have in mind bear most directly on the terror and violence that have so shocked the adult world. One is the initiation ritual, and the other is what I can only call the ritual sortie. They are essentially indistinguishable as far as overt behavior is concerned; they are different only in their purpose. The initiation ritual has to do with recruitment, the selection of suitable members of an elite society. The ritual sortie has to do with status and prestige within that society, both a requirement of members in good standing and an opportunity for the advancement of the ambitious and the talented. The society is usually, at its most audacious, a society of warriors and "free" souls who accept only those limitations upon conduct that, as a corporation, they themselves impose. But it is also a society of pranksters, gaming companions, exhibitionists, children, concerned as much with extremities of style in dress and speech as with murder and theft. It is always, however, a loyal brotherhood provided with a more or less clear schedule of honors. And it leads what is essentially a public life, protected as far as possible from the eyes of law-enforcement agencies.

If we are to understand this model, we shall find that we must look to some surprising parallels. I should suggest, because of its familiarity, that of the Knights of the Round Table, without at all ignoring the willingness of our own juvenile gangs to give themselves—in all candor and accuracy —sinister and evil and even repugnant names. It is important to notice that there are no ready models (even models that they might pervert) to be found in the law-abiding adult world. And it is important also to isolate that critical feature of their own way of life that is so entirely alien to the more or less official ideology of the adult world.

The feature in question may perhaps most succinctly be described as "climax-technique" (I borrow the term from the accounts of the code of life of the pagan Teutonic knights). I submit that our juvenile gangs implicitly subscribe to this significant principle, however corrupt their particular values may be said to be. Briefly, the routine of ordinary, unadventurous life is quite worthless, boring, idle to our juveniles; it is made supportable only by celebrating previous sorties and by preparation for others. In an odd sense, then, the juvenile does not wish to be idle—idleness is death to him. But, curiously, he considers the life of the adult world (and his submission to it) an idle life and, correspondingly, the adult world views his exploits also as a species of idling. The significance of his life lies exclusively in the climactic and perilous mountain peaks of the adventures he enters into so wholeheartedly (an important inversion of the purity of the soul we associate with, say, the devotion of the Round Table Knights). So he proves himself from episode to episode—whether by torture, theft, sexual liberties, murder, fighting, vandalism, drinking—always in accord with the strict code of his own society.

The values of the adult world have to do with docility and safety and, most important, with the merits of prolonged routine work. It is here, therefore, that we have the most dramatic evidence of the breakdown in the educational apparatus of the adult world, of the autonomy of the juvenile: we must acknowledge the existence of a subsociety that effectively recruits and instructs novices (willing or not) in a way of life that, in the most fundamental manner possible, is opposed to the values of an otherwise incredibly powerful society. The juvenile world is simply slipping through very strong nets; but, as it does, it is also managing to get control of the vital neighborhood. It repudiates the declared values of the adult world and, finding itself potentially in control of an unorganized neighborhood, simply reinforces the quite naturally intimate and sustained society of the young and moves to institutionalize its own values. It is necessarily parasitic, feeding on the wealth and skills and goods of the adult world, relieved therefore of any positive concern with the maintenance of the requisite routines; and thus relieved, it is almost entirely free to pursue those special ritual adventures by which it distinguishes itself.

The phenomenon of the delinquent gang is not an altogether new one. Gang and quasi-tribal patterns are quite familiar among adolescents, patterns at once compulsive and inclined toward outlawry. Still, we cannot fail to notice certain distinctive features of the current delinquency: the advanced decline in adult participation in the forming and maintaining of neighborhood policy, particularly with respect to the hour-to-hour activities of the adolescent, and the apparently easy accessibility of dangerous weapons. We may also remark the juvenile's interest in the publicized exploits of otherwise unfamiliar criminal "heroes." Delinquency appears to have taken on an epidemic quality, and the criminal achievements of newly discovered offenders invite appraisal and emulation. In fact, the ever-efficient press actually facilitates the standardization of juvenile conduct, hence that of juvenile crime. It has, for example, become altogether common for informal, small and inexperienced groups of juveniles spontaneously to attempt dangerous, violent sorties of the kind formerly reserved for the most desperate criminals: we hear every day of unbelievable crimes motivated by pure whim.

Although it would be madness to refuse to admit the threat posed by juvenile gangs and their responsibility for their own crimes, it would be a serious blunder to imagine that increasing the severity of penalties for juvenile criminals will in any way reduce their activity. Similar measures have not affected senior crime. Given the mentality of the juvenile types I have been trying to describe, such measures can only serve to make their lives more daring and more exciting, without at all disturbing the solidarity of their society. Punishment, then, is a force somewhat misapplied, since it aims at restraining the juvenile and not at recovering his allegiance. But it is precisely this allegiance that the adult world has lost.

15

EDUCATION

EDUCATION, like any other social institution, is sensitive to social change. Havighurst points out that this relationship has three aspects: (1) education helps to transmit traditional culture patterns; (2) it is an instrument for bringing about changes which society desires; and (3) in its search for truth it initiates change.

"The Big Federal Move Into Education" deals with the significance of the law that is titled *The Elementary and Secondary Education Act of 1965*. This Act authorized the spending of 1.3 billion dollars. Though such an amount is not a large sum in relation to our total expenditure on education, its authorization did mark an important breakthrough in overcoming a long-standing taboo against any broad program of federal aid to grade school and secondary education, whether public or private.

31

How Education Changes Society

by Robert J. Havighurst

When the future historian writes of the twentieth century, he will probably call it the century of world-wide social change. He will describe the hopes and frustrations, the visions and bewilderment of people who were caught up in the process, some desiring change and some resisting it.

While change is not a new thing in the world, there is a new modern element, which did not play an important role in the processes of social change in previous times. This new element is education. The notion of education as productive of change is a modern notion. This paper will explore some of the relations of education to change in the modern world, and touch on the basic question of the degree and manner of the *causal* action of education in the processes of change.

In discussing the influence of education on a society it would be well to begin by defining education broadly as that which the society teaches its young so as to enable them to be successful adults. Thus every society has a system of education, though it may not have specific educational institutions like our own schools and universities.

Education is carried on in all societies by the family and by religious, political and economic institutions; these will be called the "basic social institutions" in this discussion. Generally, as societies become more complex, they develop specific educational institutions to carry on some of the educational functions which in simpler societies were fulfilled by the basic social institutions. The education provided by schools, colleges and universities will be called *formal* education to distinguish it from the *informal* education carried on by these other institutions.

Education, when seen in relation to society, has two general aspects. First, it is a stabilizer or perpetuator of the society, and second, it is an agent for change. As a stabilizer, education mirrors what is already in the society and reflects it into the lives of the next generation. As an agent of change, education acts under the direction of technological or ideological forces to make each generation different from its parent.

Reprinted from *Confluence: An International Forum,* Spring, 1957 (Vol. VI, No. 1), pp. 85–96 *passim*. By permission of the publisher.
Robert J. Havighurst is Professor of Education at the University of Chicago.

The stabilizing, culture-perpetuating function of education is best seen in the simple societies which have not developed specialized educational institutions. Examples are to be found in the American Southwest, where the ancient and almost unchanging Pueblo Indian cultures exist side by side with the dynamic American culture, and where many of the Pueblo Indians participate in both cultures. One of these Pueblo Indians, a member of the Hopi tribe who was born about 1890, has given us his autobiography.[1] This man received the traditional Hopi education as a young boy and then was sent to a government board school where he got a white man's education. He speaks of his early education, obtained through his family and the other basic social institutions, as follows:

> Learning to work was like play. We children tagged around with our elders and copied what they did. We followed our fathers to the fields and helped plant and weed. The old men took us for walks and taught us the uses of plants and how to collect them. We joined the women in gathering rabbitweed for baskets, and went with them to dig clay for pots. We would taste this clay as the women did to test it. We watched the fields to drive out the birds and rodents, helped pick peaches to dry in the sun, and gathered melons to lug up the mesa. We rode the burros to harvest corn, gather fuel, or herd sheep. In house-buildings we helped a little by bringing dirt to cover the roofs. In this way we grew up doing things. All the old people said that it was a disgrace to be idle and that a lazy boy should be whipped.

The boy, who was later to fill the important position of Sun Chief, when he was six or seven years old went through the first initiation, in which all Hopi children learn the simplest of the religious mysteries. Before that he had received some of his early moral education through the visits of Katcinas (villagers disguised as supernatural beings). Of this he says:

> I saw some giantlike Katcinas stalking into the village with long black bills and big sawlike teeth. One carried a rope to lasso disobedient children. He stopped at a certain house and called for a boy. "You have been naughty" he scolded. "You fight with other children. You kill chickens. You pay no attention to the old people. We have come to get you and eat you." The boy cried and promised to behave better. The giant became angrier and threatened to tie him up and take him away. But the boy's parents begged for his life and offered fresh meat in his place. The giant reached out his hand as if to grab the boy but took the meat instead. Placing it in his basket, he warned the boy that he would get just one more chance to change his conduct. I was frightened and got out of sight. I heard that sometimes these giants captured boys and really ate them.

[1] L. W. Simmons, Editor, *Sun Chief* (New Haven, Conn., Yale University Press, 1942), pp. 45, 51–2.

We can see how deeply the traditional, non-changing Hopi culture was implanted in the boy by the family and the other basic social institutions, thereby enabling him to do his share in carrying on the culture unchanged.

The same culture-perpetuating function is present in the highly-developed educational systems of modern societies, and especially in the elementary schools, which teach the traditional reading, writing and arithmetic, and the basic loyalties to family, community and nation.

Education is seen most clearly in its other aspect—as an agent of change —after a successful revolution, when the revolutionary government seeks to use it to re-form the society in its own revolutionary image. For instance, the Russian Revolution of 1917 was followed by a widespread use of adult education and by a reformation of the schools. Since the Communist regime did not trust the Church and to some extent mistrusted the Russian family, it removed the teaching function entirely from the Church and as far as possible from the family. The State, collaborating with the Labor Unions, reorganized the formal education of the country and supplied a corps of teachers who were in sympathy with the revolutionary purposes.

A society that is changing in a slower, evolutionary way also uses education to promote change; in fact, it relies on education more fully than does a revolutionary society, which has other more drastic means of bringing about the desired changes. To see how formal education is related to these various aspects of change in the basic social institutions, we will have to modify the simple distinction already made between education as a perpetuator of society and education as an agent for change. Formal education in a contemporary society is not one or the other of these—it is both of them at the same time. In some areas of culture education works for change, while in other areas it may resist or ignore change.

The kinds of social change most effectively promoted by education are those (1) which can be taught readily, and (2) which the society generally approves. Therefore new kinds of techical skills and knowledge and new occupational techniques are readily introduced through education into a society, as also are new material modes of living. For instance, the training of engineers and medical practitioners has changed greatly, with general social approval. And the use of automobiles, of electrical gadgets in the home and of vitamin pills are examples of social changes for which education is effectively used.

The areas of social change least open to educational influence are those in which there is (1) a taboo, or (2) a controversy. As an example of taboo, let us take sex relations. It seems clear that social and physical relations between the sexes have changed a great deal in the past century in the Western civilization, and are changing rapidly now. But formal education has generally either neglected this area or has taught conservatively so as to preserve the older forms of sex relations.

An example of the difficulty of using education to promote social change in areas of controversy is seen in the conflict over foreign policy in the United States. This is an area in which education could and should play a large part; certainly there have been major efforts to use education as an agent of change, especially through adult education projects such as those of the American Foreign Policy Association and through courses given in universities and colleges. But the secondary schools in many communities have been prevented from being entirely candid in their treatment of international relations because the subject is controversial. As a result, the teacher either ignores this area or treats it "safely"—which generally means conservatively and in such a way as to avoid change. . . ."

The modern national State uses education to change itself—and this, too, is a comparatively recent phenomenon. The nation-states which began to arise in the sixteenth century in Europe achieved unity through political and military rather than educational means. Then, with the coming of the industrial revolution, the national states were caught up in vast social changes profoundly affecting their rapidly growing populations. This was the signal for the development of national systems of education, aimed to make the people literate and more efficient both as workers and citizens, and to inculcate national loyalties. At first the national governments ventured gingerly into the field of formal education, limiting themselves to assisting the Church and various philanthropic educational organizations to provide a free education for the children of the poor. This was the practice of the British Government in the first half of the nineteenth century, and was eloquently supported by John Stuart Mill in his Essay on Liberty, where he argued that the State should limit itself so far as possible to enforcing universal education, while the family and the Church provided this education in a wide variety of ways which would guarantee individual liberty. He cited objections against State education, saying, "that the whole or any large part of the education of the people should be in State hands, I go as far as any one deprecating. All that has been said of the importance of individuality of character and diversity of opinions and modes of conduct, involves, as of the same unspeakable importance, diversity of education. A general State education is a mere contrivance for making people to be exactly like one another: and as the mould in which it casts them is that which pleases the predominant power in the government, whether this be a monarch, a priesthood, an aristocracy, or the majority of the existing generation, in proportion as it is efficient and successful, it establishes a despotism over the mind leading by natural tendency to one over the body." [2]

Despite the logic of this reasoning, it seems quaint today, when every national state provides a general State education which is regarded as an

[2] John Stuart Mill, edited by R. B. McCallum, *On Liberty* (Oxford, Basil Blackwell, 1946), p. 95.

essential part of the task of maintaining a successful government, whether it be a democracy or some other type. The national state operates within a changing society, and uses education to adapt its people to change and to control change in favor of the values of the society. . . .

The economic institutions of a society also use education to effect change. Industry looks to the educational system for the training of workers who will be adaptable to change and for the education of its professional workers—engineers, scientists and business administrators who are the key personnel in modern industrial development. Furthermore, industry uses educational means to train its own personnel for the specific jobs they will perform. Thus a giant corporation like the International Harvester Company, doing business throughout the world, maintains a kind of private university for training its employees for important executive and sales positions.

It is clear that formal education, in school or university, is an essential instrument for the promotion of change in a changing society, and is so used by the basic institutions of family, church, government and economy. On the other hand, a society which is not changing rapidly, such as that of Medieval Europe, employs education primarily as a stabilizer to perpetuate the status quo. Such a society has less use for formal education than does the society which is "on the march."

Formal education is most fully used to promote social change in the modern urban industrial societies. To see the reason for this it is useful to look at Brazil, a great nation passing through changes which Europe and North America have already known. From its colonization in the early sixteenth century until it became a republic at the close of the nineteenth century, Brazil made its living by extracting things from the earth and exporting them—brazil wood, sugar, gold, diamonds, coffee, rubber, cotton. This was done by a small aristocracy and a large working class consisting mainly of slaves. During all that time, education tended to preserve this type of social structure. About 1900, Brazil began to industrialize rapidly, a process which was hastened by the two World Wars. With this came the growth of large cities, the movement of population from the country to the industrial centers, and most important of all, the development of a middle class of professional and managerial people who were *educated* for their leading roles. Thus a modern system of education became essential to Brazil's development into a modern industrial nation. In Russia there is a variation on the same theme in the rise of a class of educated managers and technical experts who spearhead the social changes. The political structure in which the changes operate is different from that of most other countries, but the goal is the same. . . .

The argument so far has tended to indicate that the forces making for change in a society operate *through* education but not as a planned result of it. For instance, when technology develops to the point where it needs more engineers, the educational system produces more engineers. But the educators do not of their own accord get together with the industrialists and decide whether in the interest of society there should be more engineers at some future date.

Generally speaking, the formal education of a society mirrors and reflects what is already in the society, including those forces and movements making for change. Thus one might think of education as simply an instrumentality, a set of processes that go on in schools and universities and the minds of men in response to the decisions of powerful people who themselves are moved by changes which demand action.

This seems to be very true of the Technical Assistance programs by which a number of nations are now changing themselves. Through the Technical Assistance Program of the United Nations, and the analogous programs of various nations including England, Russia and the United States, the leaders of the less developed countries are deliberately creating change in their own societies. Much "technical assistance" is essentially education: either training people to carry on certain new methods of working or educating the general public to follow new modes of living. The government of Puerto Rico, for example, in planning major improvements in the lives of its people, uses education to help achieve them. . . .

Yet it is not the whole truth to say that education operates as an instrumentality for change after the decision has already been taken that change is desirable. There is also a drive for change implicit in education as we know it today. Schools and universities present facts and ideas to their students; ideas are active. Research workers discover new knowledge; knowledge gives power. Who can say that the idea of an electromagnetic field which occurred to physicists in the early nineteenth century and gave rise to the electric generator was not more influential in promoting social change than any act of government or the formation of any great industrial enterprise? Einstein's equation which asserts the equivalence of energy and matter was only an idea for a good many years, but it was a necessary idea on the road to the discovery of the secret of releasing atomic energy. These great and fruitful ideas were at one and the same time the products of changing times and the products of men's minds. They were not produced through any planned process.

Education certainly is capable of originating change as well as of promoting changes already planned. But perhaps it must always originate change blindly, as seems to have been the case in the past. The human intellect, when working in an educational milieu and focussing either on the physical world, the social world or the world of ideas, has always come out with some new truth, and the new truth has very often worked to change the society. It seems a reasonable conclusion that under present conditions education will always work for change, whether in the industrial processes of a society, its religious beliefs, its esthetic standards or other areas of life.

In working for material improvement, education will be performing a well-accepted and relatively well-understood function in society. But in discovering new truth which makes for change in the non-material aspects of life, education will operate somewhat blindly, the results of its influence will not be easily foreseen, and it will enter into controversial areas.

Can education be so organized and directed as to prevent social change and to perpetuate or stabilize a particular social order or social structure?

Education certainly is used successfully to conserve traditional values. But in modern society this very act of conserving values seems to require changes in society which are fostered by education. For example, to conserve certain values of the family in a changing society it may be necessary to change certain things in the family. To conserve and to achieve the values of democracy it may be necessary to change modern societies in far-reaching ways.

Two general statements can be made about education in relation to social change. First, education is a powerful instrument for social change in a society which knows what kinds of changes it wants. Generally, such changes are in technology and in material modes of living. The contemporary Technical Assistance programs work for such changes in the less-developed countries.

Second, education as the search for truth also results in social change, but generally such changes are not planned in advance, and sometimes they are not welcomed by the people and groups of people who are in power.

There seems to be no place in the world today where education is simply a perpetuator of traditional ways of behaving and believing. The world is caught up in a vast and varied process of change, in which education may be either instrument or originator.

32

The Big Federal Move into Education

A TIME Essay

"I will never do anything in my entire life that excites me more, or benefits the nation I serve more, or makes the land and all of its people better and wiser and stronger, or anything that I think means more to freedom and justice in the world than what we have done v⁻th this education bill."

So said Lyndon Johnson in his rambling pastoral prose, and many U.S. educators agree with him about the historic importance of the new law that is formally titled the Elementary and Secondary Education Act of 1965. . . .

The bill authorizes the spending of $1.3 billion—a relatively small sum considering the fact that public education in the U.S. is an annual $34 billion business. The real breakthrough lies in the fact that the Federal Government has overcome a longstanding taboo and become a full-scale partner in grade-school education, both public and private. Thomas Braden, chairman of California's State Board of Education, sums it up this way: "With the rapid moving of families in our nation, the interlocking economy, the sense of a national community, it is archaic to think that education is not a national task."

Historic Shift

Not since the Northwest Ordinance of 1787, which set aside new lands for public schools, has the national government been formally committed to broad support of education at the precollege level. Explained the Ordinance: "Religion, morality and knowledge being necessary to good government and the happiness of mankind, schools and the means of education shall forever be encouraged." Yet the U.S. Constitution, drafted the same year, said nothing at all about education, reserving that function to the states—which assumed the task so conscientiously that, even without federal direction, the uniquely American drive toward universal education

TIME, April 30, 1965, pp. 44–45. Reprinted by permission from *TIME, The Weekly Newsmagazine;* copyright Time Inc., 1965.

soon became a key strength of the nation. In fact, education became almost synonymous with democracy.

As the cost of education increased, the Federal Government was repeatedly urged to act, but it did so only in response to specific crises and with relatively narrow, mostly vocational aims. Thus the Morrill Act of 1862, which helped set up 68 land-grant colleges to promote agriculture and "mechanic arts," was partly a Civil War tactic. Each war inspired similar federal action, from support of vocational training in high schools during World War I to aid for school districts with heavy concentrations of defense workers and the famed G.I. Bill of Rights of World War II. The Soviet Sputnik in 1957 scared Congress into enacting the National Defense Education Act, which supports science, math and language instruction in public schools and provides loans to college students. Defense and space needs sent federal research grants pouring into colleges—and chased many a good teacher out of his classroom and into his lab. Total federal aid to education now runs to about $5 billion a year.

Yet this aid has had little impact on the bulk of the nation's 26,000 public-school districts. Bills for general aid to education have been pending in all but twelve of the last 96 sessions of Congress, dating back to 1867. Their backers have generally argued that the wide differences between and within states in expenditures on education frustrate equal opportunity. Example: Mississippi spends $273 per pupil, New York $790; within Connecticut, Darien spends $697, Montville $298. Real estate is often overtaxed for local school support, and states risk driving away industry if they raise local taxes; federal aid should ease these problems. Yet all previous general-aid bills died because they became mired in three issues: aid to church-supported schools, aid to racially segregated schools, the fear of federal control.

Lyndon Johnson succeeded because he avoided the mistakes of his predecessors and produced an ingenious bill that neatly defused the explosive issues. It is a bill that combines local autonomy with a great deal of federal initiative and leaves remarkable latitude for the play of creative ideas.

The Poor & Operation Bootstrap

TITLE I, which draws most of the attention and most of the money ($1.06 billion), is designed to aid local school-district projects which help "educationally deprived children." The money will flow to state education officials, who will decide what specific projects originated by local public-school districts qualify. The U.S. Office of Education can veto a project, but its decision could be appealed in the courts. Each district can request a maximum amount equal to half of what the state spends to educate each child, multiplied by the number of children of all families in its district with incomes under $2,000. This will mean, for example, a 25% increase in Mississippi's public-school funds, a 4% hike for New York. No district can use the money to lower the level of its local support of education.

The funds may not be used for such general purposes as raising teachers' salaries or building classrooms, but otherwise the only limitation is the extent of local imagination. A Senate report lists 50 possibilities, ranging from hiring additional teachers in order to reduce the size of classes, to providing clothing and shoes for the needy, to assigning social workers to work with parents of the poor. Georgia expects to finance kindergartens, which have proved invaluable in easing the transition from a bad home environment; only half of U.S. public-school districts now maintain them. Cleveland plans to extend its school day past 3:30 p.m. to permit an array of remedial reading and arithmetic classes, individual tutoring, personal and vocational counseling. Atlanta hopes to set up workshops for the teachers who will teach the poor, since most are from middle-class backgrounds and may be out of touch with such children.

Public schools holding special classes for children with special environmental problems will be required to accept similar students from private schools on a "shared-time" basis—already a longstanding practice in some communities, where parochial-school students attend certain classes in public schools. Since Title I is pegged to state levels of school support, it is expected to have a bootstrap effect as states realize that each dollar they add to their own support will bring more federal funds. Beginning in 1966, districts that increase their own spending by at least 105% per pupil can apply for a matching amount from Washington for each pupil; this program is expected to cost some $400 million next year.

Libraries & Far-Out Projects

TITLE II provides an even $100 million to buy textbooks and expand school libraries, including the purchase of books, periodicals, phonograph records. The money will go directly to state agencies, will be handled entirely by the states, but distribution of the materials must be made equitably to private- as well as public-school students "to the extent consistent with" state law. To avoid legal complications, ownership of the materials will be retained by the public agency. The program is not tied to the poor; funds will be split among the states according to their percentage of all the nation's elementary- and secondary-school pupils.

This money will be eagerly snapped up: only about one-third of U.S. lower schools now have libraries. Boston's 55,000 public-elementary-school pupils have no library at all, nor do some 100 elementary schools in Philadelphia. . . .

TITLE III has brought most enthusiasm from educators, since it involves no strings at all, aims at uplifting educational services to all students in public or private schools, in any way a local district sees fit. The first-year authorization of $100 million is certain to set off a keen competition for approval of local projects. Under this section of the bill, local districts will deal directly with Washington. . . . Of the available funds, $200,000 must be set aside for each state, and the rest, roughly $90 million, will be split among the states in two ways: half on the basis of their school-age population, half on the basis of their total population.

The purposely vague wording of the title calls for "supplementary centers and services," and the bill carries only three broad hints as to what these would do: provide new communitywide services to schoolchildren, raise the quality of such existing services, and set up model programs. . . .

The most obvious possible services are bookmobiles and portable science laboratories to reach isolated students, special classes for the gifted or the handicapped. Yet it will probably take more than the obvious to meet the competition, and such an imaginative project as New York's Harkness Center, operated by 18 school districts near Buffalo seems a likely candidate. The center develops courses, trains teachers, keeps a library of 2,400 films, has a computer that does payrolls and report cards for all the member schools. St. Paul hopes to qualify with its "Operation Fresh Start," which tries to lure high school dropouts back for vocational training.

Rockland Community College in New York plans a cultural center with library, museum, planetarium and closed-circuit educational television for the benefit of neighboring towns. Cleveland's Superintendent Paul W. Briggs has plans for a center offering "almost limitless innovation, looking like no school building ever constructed before—where most talented elementary-school violinists might work in small groups with top players of the Cleveland Orchestra, where top industrial researchers could work in labs with talented children."

Fading Fears

TITLE IV provides $100 million for research contracts . . . with any "university, college or other appropriate public or nonprofit private agency." Reason behind this provision: of the $34 billion now spent on public education, less than one-fifth of 1% is going into basic research to find new techniques and new teaching concepts.

TITLE V is designed to cope with the danger that in many cases the new bill might fall short for lack of direction at the state level. Many of the state departments of education are woefully understaffed, underpaid and incompetent. Since the workload will increase sharply under the bill, $25 million will go to states to strengthen such state agencies.

The act seeks to evoke, rather than force, improvement in local districts and the states. This responsibility should stimulate rather than stifle them. There will be fiscal safeguards against flagrant mishandling of money, but the only hint that Washington's hand could become heavy lies in a requirement that Title I projects be reviewed annually to see whether the money is having a beneficial effect. This could lead to some type of national testing so that progress can be evaluated, a specter that always frightens school superintendents. Yet one eventual result of the act may well be some form of national minimum educational standards. . . .

The bill avoided any racial flare-up because the Civil Rights Act of 1964 had already decreed that no federal funds can aid any project operated on a discriminatory basis. But the law will put heavy pressure on the nation's public-school districts to file assurances that they do comply with the Civil Rights Act. . . .

Religious controversy was avoided partly because the bill offers only indirect aid to parochial schools and because much of this aid benefits poor children—a feature difficult to attack. But parochial schools were also included in the wide-open Title III, which particularly pleases Catholic educators since it constitutes a sharp thrust toward broadly based general aid. To a great extent, this was made possible by the ecumenical trend in the U.S. today, which has eased religious tensions. . . .

There still are practical religious problems to be worked out in shared-time programs. Asks Sam Hamerman, a Los Angeles public-school official: "Will the nuns appear in their habits in public-school classes? Will the parochial children be kept together or split up in public-school classes?" Undoubtedly there are many court tests ahead, but Washington is confident that little will come of them.

The U.S. faces a new age of education. On even the simplest levels of life, learning is the key to survival; standing on the edge of space, witnessing the dizzying extension of the human brain by the computer, Americans more than ever require an extension of knowledge and the right kind of learning. The new education bill does not by itself provide this. It does not contain an ideology of education and would have neither shocked nor necessarily cheered educators from Horace Mann to John Dewey. It does not and cannot answer the question of what shape U.S. education should take in the wake of its long era of permissiveness and mass-production methods; but it does greatly stimulate the search for answers. In short, if it does not guarantee excellence, it promises improvement. And it begins to fulfill the goal set forth in the 1830s by Pennsylvania Congressman Thaddeus Stevens, who said: "We must teach our citizens to dread ignorance more than they dread taxation."

Economic Organization and Social Problems

16

THE ORGANIZATION OF ECONOMIC ACTIVITIES

IN ANY COMPLEX SOCIETY a high degree of organization is required to meet the needs of people for food, clothing, shelter, and other economic goods. Paul A. Samuelson, in excerpts from the early chapters of his well-known textbook, *Economics,* states the basic problems which economic organization must solve in any economy. He then explains how a free enterprise economy solves these problems by means of markets, competition, and the price system.

In "The New Russian Revolution" Margaret Miller describes the new Charter for Industrialists, recently approved by Russia's Council of Ministers, and she argues that it represents a "revolution" in Russian economic policies because it proposes to apply capitalist methods to stimulate production in the Russian economy. Though the term "revolution" may be too strong, the Charter does indicate that the Russian leaders are seeking new approaches to the problems of operating a socialized economy.

33

Economic Organization and
Free Enterprise

by Paul A. Samuelson

Problems of Economic Organization

Any society, whether it consists of a totally collectivized communistic state, a tribe of South Sea Islanders, a capitalistic industrial nation, a Swiss Family Robinson, a Robinson Crusoe—or, one might almost add, a colony of bees—must somehow confront three fundamental and interdependent economic problems.

1. WHAT commodities shall be produced and in what quantities? That is, how much and which of alternative goods and services shall be produced? Food or clothing? Much food and little clothing, or vice versa? Bread and butter today, or bread and grape plantings today with bread, butter, and jam next year?

2. How shall goods be produced? That is, by whom and with what resources and in what technological manner are they to be produced? Who hunts, who fishes? Electricity from steam or from waterfall?

3. FOR WHOM shall goods be produced? That is, who is to enjoy and get the benefit of the goods and services provided? Or, to put the same thing in another way, how is the total of national product to be *distributed* [1] among different individuals and families? A few rich and many poor? Or most people in modest comfort?

These three questions are fundamental and common to all economies, but different economic systems try to solve them differently. In a primitive

From *Economics: An Introductory Analysis,* by Paul A. Samuelson. 6th ed., pp. 14–17, 37–40, 42–45, *passim.* Copyright © 1964 McGraw-Hill, Inc. Used by permission of McGraw-Hill Book Company.

Paul A. Samuelson is Professor of Economics at the Massachusetts Institute of Technology.

---

[1] WARNING: Usually when an economist is talking about "distribution," he means the distribution of incomes—the principles which determine labor's wage, land's rent, capital's interest, and the whole FOR WHOM process. The man on the street usually means, by distribution, wholesaling and retailing—how goods once produced get into the hands of the consumer. Try to avoid this last usage, which can cause confusion.

civilization, custom may rule every facet of behavior. WHAT, HOW, and FOR WHOM may be decided by reference to traditional ways of doing things. To members of another culture, the practices followed may seem bizarre and unreasonable; the members of the tribe or clan may themselves be so familiar with existing practices as to be surprised, and perhaps offended, if asked the reason for their behavior. Thus, the Kwakiutl Indians consider it desirable not to accumulate wealth but to give it away in the *potlach*—a roisterous celebration. This deviation from acquisitive behavior will not surprise anthropologists; from their studies they know that what is correct behavior in one culture is often the greatest crime in another.

In the bee colony, all such problems, even those involving an extraordinarily elaborate cooperative division of labor, are solved automatically by means of so-called "biological instincts."

At the other extreme we can imagine an omnipotent benevolent or malevolent dictator who by arbitrary decree and fiat decides WHAT, HOW, and FOR WHOM. Or we might imagine economic organization by decree, but with decrees drawn up by democratic vote or by selected legislative authorities.

As Chapter 3 develops at length, the WHAT, HOW, and FOR WHOM questions in a so-called "capitalist free enterprise economy" are determined primarily [2] by a system of prices (of markets, of profits and losses).

THE LAW OF SCARCITY. WHAT to produce, HOW, and FOR WHOM would not be problems if resources were unlimited: if an infinite amount of every good could be produced, or if human wants were fully satisfied, it would not then matter if too much of any particular good were produced. Nor would it then matter if labor and materials were combined unwisely. Since everyone could have as much as he pleased, it would not matter how goods and incomes were distributed among different individuals and families.

There would then be no *economic goods,* i.e., no goods that are relatively scarce; and there would hardly be any need for a study of economics or "economizing." All goods would be *free goods,* like air.

In the world as it is, even children learn in growing up that "both" is not an admissible answer to a choice of "which one." Compared with backward nations or previous centuries, modern industrial societies seem very wealthy indeed. But higher production levels seem to bring in their train higher consumption standards. People feel that they want and "need" steam heat, indoor plumbing, refrigerators, education, movies, radios, television, books, autos, travel, music, chic clothes, and so forth. The biological scientist may tell them that they can be well nourished on a thin porridge for a few cents a day, but that possibility leaves them as cold as the information that the

---

[2] There has never been a 100 per cent purely automatic enterprise system. Even in our capitalistic system, the government has an important role in modifying the workings of the price system. We live in what may be called a "mixed economy."

chemicals in their bodies are worth only a couple of dollars. Anyone who has kept a family budget knows that the necessities of life—the absolute musts—have little to do with the minimum *physiological* needs of food, clothing, and shelter.

In *The Affluent Society,* Harvard's Galbraith has eloquently pointed out that Americans today have for the most part gone beyond the level of physiological necessity; that often the consumer flits from one purchase to another in response to pressures of fashion and advertising. Without challenging Galbraith's thesis that the time has come to spend more on public needs and less on private needs, one may properly point out that our total product would have to become many times higher than its present level if everyone were to become able to live at the level of a moderately well-off doctor, lawyer, professor, or advertising man—to say nothing of the really well-to-do.

Whether or not people would be genuinely happier spending twice as much as now, observation suggests that folks in the suburbs now act as if they want more income to spend: they take on extra work; they resist tax increases; they end up saving much the same fraction of their incomes as in 1900; and middle-class mothers seem to work harder than their mothers did. Even if the national income were divided up equally between every man, woman, and child—and it clearly cannot be—there would be only about $50 per week to go around. Therefore, while it recognizes the important germ of truth in the notion that America has become an affluent society, economics must still contend with scarcity as a basic fact of life. . . .

How a Free Enterprise System Solves the Basic Economic Problems

In a system of free private enterprise, no individual or organization is consciously concerned with the triad of economic problems set forth [earlier]: WHAT, HOW, and FOR WHOM. This fact is really remarkable.

To paraphrase a famous economic example, let us consider the city of New York. Without a constant flow of goods in and out of the city, it would be on the verge of starvation within a week. A variety of the right kinds and amounts of food is involved. From the surrounding counties, from 50 states, and from the far corners of the world, goods have been traveling for days and months with New York as their destination.

How is it that nearly 10 million people are able to sleep easily at night, without living in mortal terror of a breakdown in the elaborate economic processes upon which the city's existence depends? For all this is undertaken without coercion or centralized direction by any conscious body!

Everyone notices how much the government does to control economic activity—tariff legislation, pure-food laws, utility and railroad regulations, minimum-wage regulations, fair-labor-practice acts, social security, price ceilings and floors, public works, national defense, national and local taxation, police protection and judicial redress, zoning ordinances, municipal water or gas works, and so forth. What goes unnoted is how much of economic life proceeds *without* direct government intervention. Hundreds of thousands of commodities are produced by millions of people more or less of their own volition and without central direction or master plan.

NOT CHAOS BUT ECONOMIC ORDER. This functioning alone is convincing proof that a competitive system of markets and prices—whatever else it may be, however imperfectly it may function—is not a system of chaos and anarchy. There is in it a certain order and orderliness. It works.

A competitive system is an elaborate mechanism for unconscious coordination through a system of prices and markets, a communication device for pooling the knowledge and actions of millions of diverse individuals. Without a central intelligence it solves one of the most complex problems imaginable, involving thousands of unknown variables and relations. Nobody designed it. It just evolved, and like human nature, it is changing; but at least it meets the first test of any social organization—it is able to survive.

A dramatic example of the importance of a pricing system is postwar Germany. In 1946–1947 production and consumption had dropped to a low level. Neither bombing damage nor postwar reparation payments could account for this breakdown. Paralysis of the price mechanism was clearly to blame: Money was worthless; factories closed down for lack of materials; trains could not run for lack of coal; coal could not be mined because miners were hungry; miners were hungry because peasants would not sell food for money and no industrial goods were available to give them in return. Prices were legally fixed, but little could be bought at such prices; a black market characterized by barter or fantastically high prices existed. Then in 1948 a "miracle" happened. A thoroughgoing currency reform set the price mechanism back into effective operation. Immediately production and consumption soared; again the WHAT, HOW, and FOR WHOM were being resolved by markets and prices.

The fact to emphasize is that such so-called miracles are going on all around us all the time—if only we look around and alert ourselves to the everyday functioning of the market. A revolutionist out to destroy the capitalistic system could ask nothing better than a great inflation or deflation that would paralyze the price mechanism.[3]

THE INVISIBLE HAND AND "PERFECT COMPETITION." Students of economics have to avoid the error of thinking that a price mechanism must work chaotically if it is not controlled by somebody. Having learned this lesson, they must not go to the other extreme and become enamored of

[3] In the 1960s writers in the Soviet and Satellite countries are rediscovering some virtues of a pricing system. Imitation is the sincerest form of flattery.

the beauty of a pricing mechanism, regarding it as perfection itself, the essence of providential harmony and beyond the touch of human hands.

Adam Smith, whose *Wealth of Nations* (1776) is the germinal book of modern economics or political economy, was thrilled by the recognition of an order in the economic system. Smith proclaimed the principle of the "Invisible Hand"; every individual, in pursuing only his own selfish good, was led, as if by an invisible hand, to achieve the best good for all, so that any interference with free competition by government was almost certain to be injurious. While Smith did recognize some of the realistic limitations on this doctrine, it was not until later that economists discovered this truth: The virtues claimed for free enterprise are fully realized only when the complete checks and balances of "perfect competition" are present.

Perfect competition is defined by the economist as a technical term denoting the case where no farmer, businessman, or laborer has any personal influence on market price; on the other hand, when his grain, merchandise, or labor is large enough in size to produce depressing or elevating effects on market prices, some degree of monopolistic imperfection has set in, and the virtues of the Invisible Hand must be that much discounted.

Actually, some of the praise of perfect competition is beside the point. As discussed earlier, ours is a mixed system of government and private enterprise; as will be discussed later, it is also a mixed system of monopoly and competition. A cynic might say of perfect competition what Bernard Shaw said of Christianity: The only trouble with it is that it has never been tried.

Historians quarrel over whether there ever was a golden age of free competition. And certainly, competition is not now perfect in the economist's sense. We do not even know whether, because of the fundamental nature of large-scale production and technology, consumers' tastes, and business organization, competition is becoming less or more intense. The statistics suggest at least a slight weakening of monopolistic concentration of power.

In any case, society need not accept as inevitable any trend toward big business, mergers, trusts, and cartels such as began to swell in the 1890s. The challenge is to work out laws and customs that help to improve the working of our less-than-perfect competitive system. The polar cases— *laissez faire* and totalitarian dictatorship of production—dramatize economic principles. Yet the relevant choice for policy today is not a decision between these extremes, but rather the degree to which public policy should do *less* or *more* in modifying the operation of particular private economic activities.

THE PRICE SYSTEM.   Just how does the unconscious automatic price mechanism operate? The bare outlines of a *competitive* profit-and-loss system are simple to describe.

Everything has a price—each commodity and each service. Even the different kinds of human labor have prices, usually called "wage rates." Everybody receives money for what he sells, and uses this money to buy what he wishes.

If more is wanted of any one good—say, shoes—a flood of new orders will be given for it. This will cause its price to rise and more to be produced.

Similarly, if more becomes available of a commodity such as tea than people want to buy at the last-quoted market price, its price will be marked down by competition. At the lower price people will drink more tea, and producers will no longer produce quite so much. Thus equilibrium of supply and demand will be restored.

What is true of the markets of consumers' goods is also true of markets for *factors of production* such as labor, land, and capital inputs. If welders rather than glass blowers are needed, job opportunities will be more favorable in the welding field. The price of welders, their hourly wage, will tend to rise, while that of glass blowers will tend to fall. Other things being equal, this will cause a shift into the desired occupation. Likewise, an acre of land will go into sugar cultivation if sugar producers bid the most for its use. In the same way, machine-tool production will be determined by supply and demand.

In other words, we have a vast system of trial and error, of successive approximation to an *equilibrium system of prices and production.* We shall see later that the matching of supply and demand and of prices and costs helps solve our three problems simultaneously. Here are the bare outlines:

1. WHAT things will be produced is determined by the votes of consumers—not every two years at the polls, but every day in their decisions to purchase this item and not that. Of course, the money that they put into business cash-registers ultimately provides the payrolls, rents, and dividends that consumers receive in weekly income. Thus the circle is a complete one.

2. How things are produced is determined by the competition of different producers. The method that is cheapest at any one time, because of both physical efficiency and cost efficiency, will displace a more costly method.

The only way for producers to meet price competition and maximize profits is to keep costs at a minimum by adopting the most efficient methods. For example, synthetic rubber will be made from oil rather than alcohol if the price of the one is in a certain relation to the price of the other; or electric power will be generated by steam rather than atomic power if the price of coal is below some critical level. The large tractor-operated farm will displace the family-size farm if this leads to lower costs of production. . . .

3. FOR WHOM things are produced is determined by supply and demand

in the markets for productive services: by wage rates, land rents, interest rates, and profits, all of which go to make up everybody's income—relative to everyone else and relative to the whole. (Of course, the character of the resulting distribution of income is highly dependent upon the *initial* distribution of property ownership and on acquired or inherited abilities.)

Note this: Consumer votes do not by themselves determine WHAT goods are produced. Demand has to meet with a supply of goods; so business cost and supply decisions along with consumer demand help to determine WHAT. Just as a broker may help arrange a match between buyer and seller, the auctioneer in the commodity market acts as the go-between who reconciles the consumer votes and business supplies that impinge on the market. . . . The profit seeker is society's agent to determine How, seeking least factor-costs for producing each good and being punished by ruthless competition if he fails to use best methods. . . .

ETHICAL ASPECTS OF INCOME DISTRIBUTION. The above picture of competition tending toward ideal efficiency, toward being on the production-possibility frontier and not inside it, is a highly over-simplified one. But even if the system worked perfectly as described above—which everybody knows not to be the case—many would not consider it ideal. In the first place, goods go where there are the most votes or dollars. A rich man's dog may receive the milk that a poor child needs to avoid rickets. Why? Because supply and demand are working badly? No. Because auction markets are doing what they are designed to do—putting goods in the hands of those who can pay the most, who have the most money votes. Defenders and critics of the price mechanism should recognize this fact.

Or suppose the invention of automatic machines should cause the competitive price of labor to fall, thereby reducing incomes of the poor. Would all ethical observers regard that as necessarily right or ideal?

Should the fact that a man inherited 500 square miles of range land, for which oil companies offer a million dollars per year, necessarily justify so large an income?

These questions are discussed repeatedly in Congress. Whether incomes should be completely determined by a competitive struggle—the survival of the survivors—is an ethical question that goes beyond the mechanics of economics. . . .

IMPERFECTIONS OF COMPETITION. As we said earlier, one drawback to the picture of the price system as described above is the fact that, in the real world, competition is nowhere near "perfect." Firms do not know when consumer tastes will change; therefore they may overproduce in one field and underproduce in another. By the time they are ready to learn from experience, the situation may have changed again. Also, in a competitive system many producers simply do not know the methods of other producers, and costs do not fall to a minimum. In the competitive struggle one can sometimes succeed as much by keeping knowledge scarce as by keeping production high.

An even more serious deviation from perfect competition comes from *monopoly elements*. These—as we shall see later on—may result in wrong pricing, incorrect and wasteful resource allocation, and monopoly profits. We shall be reminded again and again how strict is the economist's definition of a "perfect competitor"; the mere presence of a few rivals is not enough for perfect competition. The economic definition of "imperfect competitor" is *anyone who buys or sells a good in large enough quantities to be able to affect the price of that good.* To some degree that means almost all businessmen, except possibly the millions of farmers who individually produce a negligible fraction of the total crop. All economic life is a blend of competitive and monopoly elements. Imperfect (monopolistic) competition is the prevailing mode, not perfect competition. This is a fact, not a moral condemnation. A good approximation of perfect competition may be all one need hope for.

Of course, as we shall later see, a businessman cannot set his prices completely as he pleases and still make profits. He must take into account the prices of goods that are substitutes for his own. Even if he produces a trademarked coal with unique properties, he must reckon with the prices charged for other coals, for oil and gas, and for house insulation.

Businessmen, farmers, and workers both like and dislike competition. We all like it when it enables us to expand our market, but we label it as "chiseling," "unfair," or "ruinous" when the knife cuts the other way. The worker whose livelihood depends on how the market prices his labor may be the first to howl when competition threatens to depress wages. Farm groups, aware of what competition can do to agricultural prices, constantly bring pressure to bear on the state to restrict production and thereby raise prices.

Some of the basic factors responsible for monopoly-creating bigness in business may be inherent in the economies of large-scale production. This is especially true in a dynamic world of technological change. Competition by numerous producers would simply not be efficient in many fields and could not last. Trademarks, patents, and advertising are often responsible for still other market imperfections. It would be humanly impossible, therefore, to attempt to create *perfect* competition by law. The problem is one of achieving reasonably effective "workable competition."

We shall proceed later to a more microscopic examination of supply and demand. After that discussion we shall be in a position to appraise the workings of the price system more judiciously. A competitive price system is one way of organizing an economy, but not the only way. Still it is of interest that some socialists plan to continue to use a price mechanism as part of their new society. A price system is not perfect, but neither are its alternatives.

Economic Role of Government.   An outline of [government] influence can be briefly indicated here. Democratic countries are not satisfied with the answers to What, How, and For Whom given by a perfectly unrestrained market system. Such a system might dictate that certain people starve from lack of income and that others receive inadequate or excessive incomes.

Therefore the citizenry through their government step in with expenditure to supplement the real or money incomes of some individuals. Thus, government may provide hospital beds for citizens or may present the more needy with monthly allowances in times of unemployment or old age. Minimum standards of life are widespread modern goals.

More than this, government provides certain indispensable *public* services without which community life would be unthinkable and which by their nature cannot appropriately be left to private enterprises. Government came into existence once people realized, "Everybody's business is nobody's business." Obvious examples are the maintenance of national defense, of internal law and order, and the administration of justice and of contracts.

By and large, in its expenditure of money, government is behaving exactly like any other large spender. By casting sufficient votes in the form of dollar bids in certain directions, it causes resources to flow there. The price system then works much as if these were private rather than public needs.

Actually, most government expenditure is paid for out of taxes collected. It is here that an important element of *coercion* enters. It is true that the citizenry as a whole imposes the tax burden upon itself; also, each citizen is sharing in the collective benefits of government. But there is not the same close connection between benefits and tax payments as holds when the individual citizen puts a nickel into a gum machine or makes an ordinary purchase. I need not smoke Luckies or buy nylon stockings, but I must pay my taxes.

Moreover, a second important form of coercion is involved in the universal custom of passing governmental laws: thou shalt not sell false weight, thou shalt not employ child labor, thou shalt not burn houses, thou shalt not pour out smoke from thy factory chimney, thou shalt not sell or smoke opium, thou shalt not charge more than the ceiling price for food, and so forth. This set of rules gives the framework within which private enterprise functions; it also modifies the direction of that functioning. Together with government expenditure and taxation, the decrees of government supplement the price system in determining the economic fate of the nation.

It would be fruitless to debate whether public enterprise or private enterprise is the more important—as fruitless as to debate heredity versus environment. Without either, our economic world would be an entirely different one.

Finally, it is part of the government's function to help stabilize acute and chronic cycles of unemployment and inflation and to help achieve economic growth.

34

The New Russian Revolution

by Margaret Miller

On October 4, 1965, Russia's Council of Ministers approved the new Charter for Industrialists which had been promised by Premier Khrushchev as long ago as November, 1962. This was the final step in the sweeping economic reforms initiated by Mr. Khrushchev and continued by his successors. The highlights of the new law give practical details of the way it affects plant management.

The manager must still operate within the general limits of the state plan, as decided by the government and conveyed to him in the form of "control figures" by the body to which his enterprise is directly subordinated. But within this framework he is free to work out his own plan according to the capacity and resources of his plant. It is the duty of the supervisory body to insure that the plan finally given to the enterprise provides the director with the labor, finance and materials he needs to carry out the duties assigned to him, and also that these duties are mutually coordinated. Once the plan is set, the higher body is specifically debarred from making any changes during the course of the planned period, unless the enterprise is first consulted, and corresponding changes are made in the amount to be produced, planning indicators and budget allocations. A factory which has successfully fulfilled its plan and has materials and by-products left over is given a new freedom to use these for further production, at its own discretion. The aim of this section is to give the director fewer and more general planning directives, and to let him work out the executive details himself.

From "The New Russian Revolution" by Margaret Miller, *The Nation,* December 6, 1965, pp. 437–439, 453–456. Reprinted by permission.

Margaret Miller is an English writer who has a special interest in Soviet affairs.

The new charter shows definite indications of a desire to strengthen local initiative in these matters. The plant director confirms the contracts entered into with building organizations in the case of capital construction and repairs, and with research institutes when improvements in technology are concerned. Part of the central funds allotted for these purposes can, at the discretion of the director, be used for construction that benefits his staff: housing, children's nurseries, medical buildings, etc.

The provisions here also strengthen local initiative by leaving at the disposal of the enterprise a much larger proportion of the profits accruing from its work, and from allowances for depreciation, instead of directing the bulk of these to central funds as hitherto. The director thus gains considerable scope for ploughing money back into his own concern. For example, the production fund could be used to finance technical improvements, modernize equipment, expand production, in ways he decides would do most good. Evidently such resources had been very sparse in the past. In commenting on this part of the law, Premier Kosygin said that they had amounted to only 700 million rubles in 1964, but would rise to more than 4 billion rubles in 1967.

An incentive fund, also built up out of profits, would enable the director to pay efficiency bonuses, to construct welfare amenities, notably housing, for his workers. Here again, Mr. Kosygin revealed the inadequacy of previous provision when he said that only half of Russia's industrial enterprises had had special funds of this kind, and of these only a few were adequate. Bonuses had had to be paid out of the general wages fund, which meant that there was simply not enough money to give the workers effective monetary and welfare incentives. Specific provisions prohibit the supervisory body from alienating or redistributing the money in these funds.

Increased freedom is counterbalanced by new responsibilities. The director no longer gets his fixed and working capital as "handouts" from the state. They are allocated to him as long- and short-term credits on which he pays the equivalent of a rate of interest. Thus he is encouraged to "mobilize his internal reserves" and make the most economic use of his resources. Some of the provisions of the act relate directly to "internal reserves" that exist in most factories in the shape of temporarily unused or surplus equipment, buildings, machines, and so on. The director may now dispose of these, either by selling them or renting them to other bodies at prevailing local rates. He is also empowered to write off obsolete equipment, bad debts and minor losses due to spoilage. His personal interest in doing all this is secured by allowing him to use the sums accruing as additional working capital or above-plan capital investment, according to the source of the income.

An impressive list of new powers is accorded to the manager in recruiting, handling and paying his employees. Previously he was told how many workers, of what grades, he was to hire, how much and in what way they were to be paid, what their rate of productivity should be, and the percentage by which it should increase. Now, in place of all these separate indicators on labor, the factory plan will contain only one, the general wages fund. Within this, the manager can "hire and fire," decide the proportion between administrative, technical and manual workers of all grades, set up time and piece rates, bonus systems, including special bonuses of up to 30 per cent of normal salaries for highly qualified personnel.

One's first reaction to this long-awaited piece of legislation is an astonishment that three years of intensive work behind the scenes, accompanied by an avalanche of speeches by Soviet leaders, proposals and counterproposals by economists, industrialists, government officials, should have done no more than confer upon Soviet managers executive powers that are taken for granted by their counterparts in free-enterprise societies. In fact, any Western director who failed to exercise them would be held to be in grave dereliction of duty. Against the background of Soviet conditions, however, the changes are tremendous, indeed revolutionary.

The key to their significance lies in the frequency with which the charter intervenes between the supervisory and the subordinate body, with the aim of giving the latter genuine freedom of action. The highly centralized, detailed control from above, characteristic of industrial management in the days of Stalin's "command" economy, has definitely been put aside. Mr. Kosygin's deputy, K. T. Mazurov, spoke of the former passivity, irresponsibility, even negligence, of some factory managers. Under the new dispensation they are expected to display "boldness" and "independence" in decision making. He did not mention that they had exercised these qualities unofficially in the past; but if they had not done so, the "command" system would have broken down much sooner than it did. Faced with unrealistic and frequently inconsistent orders from above, Russia's practical men had for many years banded together in an "economic resistance movement." They evaded the worst unreason of planning techniques by hoarding labor and materials, employing their own agents to secure needed supplies on the ubiquitous free market, setting up an extensive system of personal extra-plan contacts. An easily recognizable object of the charter is to make such activities unnecessary.

The charter also reveals the disappearance of the doctrinaire insistence on the inherent superiority of Socialist planning over the market mechanism, on the Marxist belief that, labor being the sole source of value, there could be no need for the automatic economic regulators employed in Western communities: profit, rate of interest for capital, rent for land, adequate depreciation rates, rational price fixing, credits, economic self-interest. Today's Soviet leaders never tire of emphasizing the necessity for using these same economic regulators, of denouncing the undue attention paid to quantity at the expense of other planning indices, and of insisting that economic laws must take the place of administrative fiat in the conduct of industry. The new attitude also marks the passing of the "new Soviet man," who used to be prominently featured as the builder of the coming Communist society. The official theory was that, with the disappearance of the "exploiting classes," this paragon would labor as devotedly for the interests of the state as he would for his own interests. The image has had to be replaced by the familiar figure of "economic man" who makes no bones about the fact that he will give of his best only if assured of adequate rewards. . . .

Irreversible change is no less clear in the people who carry out the government's plans. Industrialization has created an entirely new class in Russia—technicians, engineers, scientists, economists, specialists in automation and cybernetics. There are more than 2 million of them working in industry alone, and they are essential to the running of an economy that is vastly larger and more complex than it was before the war. They demand a climate of opinion in which they can freely exercise their skills, and refuse to be dominated by methods and dogma that are at variance with the facts of economic life. Nothing has been more striking throughout the conferences and debates on the reforms than the new note of boldness and confidence in the speeches of the practical men and women who are faced with the day-to-day problems of getting things done.

Progress in the neglected sectors of agriculture and distribution is likely to be slower than in industry, mainly because of the difficulty of channeling funds into these spheres of operation with sufficient speed and in sufficient quantities to make up for past deficiencies. Russia's resources are not unlimited, and the weight of defense expenditure, including the cost of its technically brilliant achievements in space, reduces the area within which those in charge of economic policy are able to maneuver. But the penalties for failure have political as well as economic implications. From the inception of the revolution, Russia has been proclaiming that socialism is able to provide a higher standard of living for the population than capitalism can hope to do. So far practice has lagged notably behind theory. Promises of a better life for its much-deprived citizens cannot be indefinitely postponed without unfortunate repercussions both within and outside Russia's borders.

For the managerial class the reforms represent an immense improvement in the conditions under which they previously worked, and a degree of freedom which probably feels to them as great as that enjoyed by their opposite numbers in capitalist societies. What impact this freedom will have on industrial efficiency remains to be seen, but it is bound to be considerable. There is no mention of competition as an economic regulator: it is believed, presumably, that the new material and moral incentives will stimulate Soviet economy as competition stimulates capitalist economies. For consumers in general, the reforms hold out the prospect of a slow but steady movement toward a more comfortable life which, again against the background of their own experience, must eventually act as a powerful incentive to greater efficiency.

The difficulties and limitations with which Russia's economic reforms are beset will make for uneven progress, but will do nothing to turn back the tide. Insofar as the changes infuse rationality into the working of the economy, and enthrone reason in place of doctrine, they may be expected to remove many barriers to understanding between East and West. At the same time they will sharpen the economic rivalry between the two systems by striking off many of the shackles that have prevented Russia's citizens from contributing their full share to the fulfillment of national aspirations.

CHAPTER

17

THE AMERICAN ECONOMY

HOW MUCH COMPETITION and how much monopoly is there in the American economy? What policies should the government follow in dealing with industrial concentration and monopoly? Do administered prices endanger competition? On the basis of long study and research George Stigler attempts to answer these and related questions. On the whole his answers are reassuring, though he sees potential dangers to competition from the side of both government and business.

Hans Morgenthau sees our most important economic problems as political rather than strictly economic, because he believes that government is playing an ever-increasing role in economic affairs. What we need is a government strong enough to restrain the private power of the economic giants and at the same time protect the liberties of the individual.

35

Competition, Concentration, and Government Policy

by George J. Stigler

Q *Dr. Stigler, most people believe that a company which dominates a large share of its market is bound to end up with a higher return on its investment than a firm operating in a highly competitive market. But in your recent book, "Capital and Rates of Return in Manufacturing Industries," you indicated that there was no evidence of appreciably higher returns in concentrated industries. What conclusions can be drawn from this regarding competition in concentrated industries?*

A Unfortunately, like most economic research, mine led to results which were ambiguous on the most interesting questions. I did find that in the peacetime years between 1938 and 1957 there was less than a one per cent difference in profit rates in concentrated and unconcentrated industries, and when certain plausible corrections are made in the data, even this difference vanishes. But one cannot conclude that concentrated industries are fully competitive. I also found that high profit industries keep their preferred position much longer if they are concentrated. This suggests that concentration does not necessarily allow monopoly profits, but that under fortunate market conditions they can be obtained for long periods. Finally, in an article soon to appear in the *Journal of Political Economy,* I find a substantial correlation between concentration in more precisely defined industries and the ratio of market value of stocks to book value of corporation assets.

Q *What are the major yardsticks by which a modern economist measures competition?*

A It is a lot easier to describe clear, significant persistent *departures* from competition than it is to define competition itself. Indeed, we have experienced over time a progressive refinement in our concept of

Reprinted from *Challenge,* The Magazine of Economic Affairs, January, 1964, pp. 18–21, a publication of Challenge Communications, Inc., 475 Fifth Avenue, New York 10017. Reprinted by permission.

George J. Stigler is Walgreen Professor of American Institutions at The University of Chicago and a former president of the American Economic Association.

competition. For example, in 1890 almost every economist looking at the steel industry in the United States would say that of course it is a competitive industry. Any industry with dozens and dozens of firms in which the largest firm has only 30 per cent of the industry's output was believed to be obviously competitive. Nowadays a large number of economists would say it is an oligopolistic industry and thus expect some significant departures from a perfectly competitive situation. So I would answer your question by asking how does one prove the absence of competition? I would say that we haven't done too well in this respect. The basic measure, of course, is the share of the output of an industry that is in a few hands. But that isn't enough. The precise scope of a particular industry may have been misdefined. And so we look for other things, the two most common being high rates of return on investment, and price rigidity.

Q *Can we measure departures from competition accurately enough so that public policies with respect to it can have a reasonably sound factual basis?*

A We can sometimes recognize an outright collusive structure such as existed in the electrical equipment industry, and there is no real doubt of the need for certain kinds of public policy to cope with it. We can recognize the so-called natural monopoly of a public utility and consider what policies are necessary to deal with it. On the other hand, the dividing line between what is a serious and what is a trifling departure from competition is open to dispute. There are, for example, many disinterested and competent academic economists who think that the decision in the Brown Shoe case, which forbade a merger that involved trifling percentages of the shoe industry's output, was overzealous, and other economists who think that it was a far-sighted precaution to avoid eventual overconcentration in a basic industry. As with most things in life, we can deal on a reasonably informed basis with a substantial number of problems, and in a fair number of cases we are just guessing.

How Much Monopoly?

Q *Sen. Paul H. Douglas, in a recent interview in* CHALLENGE *("Evaluating the Employment Act," October, 1963), stated: "There is a tremendous amount of monopoly and oligopoly throughout our economy." Do you agree?*

A Sen. Douglas certainly has the right to use the phrase "tremendous amount," but I don't know exactly how to interpret it. That we have a good deal of monopoly and oligopoly in the American economy seems to me beyond dispute and should be a source of serious concern for public policy. There is a very common view that American manufacturing is preponderantly organized in oligopolistic industries. Using the word oligopoly in its proper sense—an industry sufficiently concentrated so that there is a substantial probability of noncompetitive behavior—I disagree with that statement. I would estimate that in manufacturing something like one-tenth to two-tenths of our industries, whether measured by employment or income originating in them, do have a degree of concentration which I hope does not become permanent. The rest of our manufacturing industries, on the other hand, are sufficiently deconcentrated. We have every reason to believe that the normal form of behavior will be essentially competitive, and that the departures from competitive behavior will be relatively short run and of very little consequence. As for Sen. Douglas' statement that we have a *tremendous* amount of monopoly and oligopoly, I would say that we have a *serious* amount in our economy, but that the economy itself is still predominantly competitive.

Q *Dr. Stigler, in terms of the general effectiveness of present-day competition, are we overregulating or underregulating our economy in this area, or are our antitrust policies generally correct?*

A Well, one should draw a distinction between two kinds of regulation of our competitive business system. On the one hand, there is traditional antitrust policy, the purpose of which is to maintain a competitive structure and then allow the business system to operate relatively freely. On the other hand, we have a set of industries which we believe cannot economically or for other reasons be restored to a competitive situation. Therefore, they require continuing regulation. Let me put aside for a moment the traditional antitrust policies and say that so far as our other regulatory policies go, I think that we are in general overregulating, and by a substantial amount. I think we have gotten much too deeply committed as a government in the solution of labor disputes and at a very substantial long-run cost to the community. I think we have regulated such areas as motor trucking and agriculture far too long and far too much in detail. Both are capable of viable and effective existence in the long run without detailed governmental control. As for underregulating, I find it harder to give you a good answer since my own tastes clearly run in the direction of a decentralized economic system in which there is a minimum both of private monopoly power and direct public control.

Present Antitrust Policy

Q *How, in general, would you evaluate our present policies in the antitrust area?*

A On the whole, I am quite complacent about our progress and satisfied
with the effectiveness of our policies. There has been a very substantial
reorientation of antitrust policy since I served on the Attorney General's Antitrust Committee in 1954–55. The control over mergers has
come to be the major part of antitrust enforcement in both the Justice
Department and the Federal Trade Commission. This, in my opinion,
is a highly desirable development. Of course, we cannot allow old-
fashioned collusive practices to become respectable or widespread.
While I deplore the long-run effect on the reputation of our economy
of things like the General Electric-Westinghouse case of several years
ago, I think that they have served as a therapeutic reminder to the
American business community that it is engaged in a competitive system and it should stay that way. We have never been very effective in
dealing with a highly concentrated industry—let us say a traditional
monopoly of the type that at one time was held by the Aluminum Company of America. We have always felt—and by we I mean both the
Antitrust Division and the federal judges who render the decisions—
that one should be very loath to dismember an enterprise and that therefore the remedy of dissolution or divestiture should be used only in
the most extreme occasions. This has led, I think, to a great deal of
ineffectual pursuit of certain highly concentrated industries. This has
been the long-standing weakness in our antitrust policy. I think our
policy with respect to the mergers will eventually correct that. The law
as now interpreted and enforced seems to make it virtually impossible
for any major producer in any major industry to acquire a substantial
rival in that industry. Indeed, we have gone farther than that—maybe
too far. Thus it is not clear to me whether General Motors could successfully merge with a bootblack in Detroit without bringing down antitrust sanctions. So that as I look at the long-run outlook in the area of
competition, I feel rather complacent.

Defining a Concentrated Industry

Q *How would you define a concentrated industry?*

A There is, of course, no unique definition. It is an industry in which one,
two, three or four firms—a small number, in any case—control a very
large fraction of the industry's output. Whether it be 100 per cent or
80 per cent or 70 per cent is not important. The concentrated industry
is best illustrated, I suppose, by, say, the American automobile industry, where the Big Three account for well over 90 per cent of our
domestic output and have accounted for over 90 per cent for a good
many years. This is simply a matter of fact and calls for no moral
reprobation or denunciation. The crucial question is always whether that

concentrated industry will behave in a competitive fashion. Can we quickly say, as soon as we know that there are two or three dominant firms, that there is high probability of important departures from competition? And here I must say there is a major split in the economics profession. There is a substantial group that embraces the doctrine of "workable competition"—which was invented by my former colleague at Columbia University, John Maurice Clark. Looking at things broadly and wisely—and they have considerable confidence in their ability to do both—they are satisfied with the performance of a great many industries which are relatively concentrated. I, myself, am much more iconoclastic in this matter, and I find it very hard to know precisely how, proceeding on such a basis, one reaches a definite conclusion. What is the precise distinction between an industry that is behaving satisfactorily and one that is not? In my view, the doctrine of workable competition in effect says that the way in which to decide whether an industry is acting satisfactorily in the public interest is to have a young man write a Ph.D. thesis on the subject and accept his verdict. And while that is obviously an employment-increasing activity from the viewpoint of professors, I can't believe that it is a tenable basic solution. But it is also reasonably certain that not every concentrated industry is seriously uncompetitive.

Q *Does the rate of return on investment after taxes offer a reliable clue as to the degree of competition in a particular industry?*

A No. The reasons a firm makes a high rate of return on an investment are numerous. One perfectly good reason is that the entrepreneur himself is a man of prodigious ability, so that, even without any monopolistic advantages, he sets profits records that are hard to match. Mr. Sears of Sears, Roebuck made colossal sums of money without having any monopolistic powers at all—having indeed only one little thing: genius in business organization. Henry Ford's great success was obviously not due to monopolistic powers but to a genius in the production of inexpensive automobiles.

Q *How valid are the oft-repeated charges of the Senate Antitrust and Monopoly Subcommittee to the effect that administered prices in the concentrated industries have led to oligopolistic profits which in turn have spurred inflation?*

A I am a great admirer of much of what the late Sen. Estes Kefauver did during his long years in Congress, but I would say that this was not among the most important and lasting works which we shall associate with his name. I do think that there are oligopolistic profits in some industries. The real question, however, is whether the presence of concentration or of oligopoly has led to a more rapid rise of prices over time than would have occurred with a more competitive industrial structure. There are three broad schools here. The traditional school says that monetary inflation has been the basic source of price rises, and that fiscal and monetary restraints are the only method of coping with the persistent rise of prices. There is a second school, very widespread in the profession, which believes that wage increases have been a major factor and that only a system of increasing sanctions or controls over labor disputes and wage settlements is likely to prevent the constant outstripping of productivity increases by wage increases. And there is a third, smaller group, which, however, was dominant in the Kefauver Committee. This last group argued that oligopolistic profits were rising over time and the desire for these profits was the force making for price rises.

Administered Prices

Q *Can any case be made for the latter view?*

A I have done a fair amount of statistical work in this area, partly as the result of my chairmanship two years ago of the Committee to Review the Price Statistics Program of the Federal Government—a committee created by a contract between the Bureau of the Budget and the National Bureau of Economic Research. Our investigations convinced me that there is grave doubt that so-called administered prices—by which I think we mean primarily prices which are unresponsive to falls in demand but are often quite sensitive to increases in demand, so that like a ratchet they work in only one direction—exist on any important scale in the industrial sector of the American economy. The empirical evidence seems quite strong that this is a blind alley and that the Senate Antitrust Subcommittee did a disservice in creating a suspicion of oligopoly as a source of inflation. This certainly contributed somewhat to 1962's unfortunate steel price embroglio.

Productivity Gains

Q *Dr. Stigler, do you believe that in the future business shall again pass on productivity gains to the consumer through lower prices rather than to itself in the form of higher profits?*

A In many instances business is doing so now and will continue to do so in the future. There are other instances, of course, in which business is not doing so, and I am afraid won't do so in the future. When a new industry emerges and shifts over from small- to large-scale production with immense increases in efficiency, there are, of course, declines in prices, and of a very major magnitude. You will recall that ball-point pens that used to sell for $12.50 are now six for 25¢. The color television set has dropped 50 per cent in price in the last few years. Indeed, this is the only way in which new products can make their way into new markets and drive old products out of existence. But there is a separate question. Putting aside large differences in productivity increase in one industry as compared to another, what about the average upward drift of efficiency throughout the economy as a whole—a figure that is commonly put somewhere in the two to four per cent range. Here one almost has to get nostalgic in discussing the possibility of an economy in which dividends and wages are held stable while prices of finished products drift downward through time and, therefore, *real* incomes rise steadily for workers, investors and, indeed, everyone in the community. Unless prices drift down as efficiency in production increases, however, pensioners and others who live on fixed incomes will not share the gains. But I think that this argument has lost some merit because, after 20 years of price instability, fewer and fewer people are allowing themselves to get into the position where they are totally dependent on a fixed income. We all know, for example, that a major price level change would probably lead to changes in the level of benefits under the social security program.

Q *What forces in our economy do you see as potential threats to competition?*

A The threats to competition can come either from the business side in a desire to suppress competition as an obnoxious and troublesome phenomenon, or from the governmental side. On the whole, I think that the threats usually originate from the business side. They are, of course, ineffective unless they are accepted by the government. To give an example, I think it would be quite impossible for the domestic petroleum industry—and I refer to the crude oil branch—effectively to restrain competition without government assistance. The way in which they achieve their result is by persuading the government to institute a system of oil embargoes with quotas on imports which protect, at very substantial cost to the consumer, the domestic crude oil industry against foreign competition. Too many sectors of the business community are eager to run to Washington and seek shelter against competition when the slightest wave of competitive activity appears. The current endeavor, for example, to restrict the rate that is paid by savings and loan associations to depositors is an indication of how sensitive many people are to price competition.

Q *What about the threat from the government side?*

A This usually stems from a mistaken impression of the importance of monopoly, and of the proper methods for dealing with it. More and more we find the government seeking to counter what it thinks are unsound price moves in the economy. Mr. Kennedy's intervention in the steel price increases in the spring of 1962 is an obvious example. While this particular incident was highly dramatic, the attitude behind it was certainly nothing new. Mr. Eisenhower, during his eight years in the White House, was persistently striving to persuade business and labor to act in what he characterized as a "statesmanlike manner"— that is, to sacrifice their own interests to those of the community at large. I think that kind of exhortation is a most undesirable one. On the one hand, it exaggerates the power of these people to do harm, and seriously underestimates the degree of competition in the economy. On the other hand, the remedy of men acting together in a statesmanlike manner or being pushed into it by strong governmental pressures leads to a seriously inefficient working of our economy. We are not going to get the right prices with the proper degree of flexibility, the right places for investment and the right kinds of innovation if we have to clear these steps through a Congressional committee or through a Cabinet officer. I believe that if we could rekindle the idea that the primary task of the central government is to preserve competition, to widen economic opportunity for all people and to protect only those people who need protection, there would be no serious threat to the viability of the competitive system.

Q *Thank you, Dr. Stigler.*

36

The State and the Economic System

by Hans Morgenthau

The most important economic problem which the United States is likely to face in the next twenty years is political rather than economic in the strict technical sense. This seeming paradox results from the decisive influence which political factors exert, and are likely to exert in the foreseeable future, upon the economic life of the nation. We are in the presence of the revival of a truly political economy, whose major economic problems are political in nature.

This interconnectedness of the political and economic spheres is not peculiar to our age. Even in the hey-day of nineteenth-century liberalism, the strict separation of the two spheres was in the nature of a political ideal rather than the reflection of observable reality. The monetary, tax, and tariff policies of the government had then, as they have now, a direct bearing upon the economic life; and so had the outlawry of the association of working men as criminal conspiracy. Yet the ideal of strict separation served the political purpose of protecting the economic forces from political control without impeding the former's influence in the political sphere.

What is peculiar to our age is not the interconnectedness of politics and economics but its positive philosophic justification and its all-persuasiveness. The State is no longer looked upon solely as the umpire who sees to it that the rules of the game are observed and who intervenes actively only if, as in the case of the railroads, the rules of the game favor one player to excess and thereby threaten to disrupt the game itself. In our age, the State, aside from still being the umpire, has also become the most powerful player, who, in order to make sure of the outcome, in good measure rewrites the rules of the game as he goes along. Neither the government nor society at large rely any more exclusively upon the mechanisms of the market to keep the game going. Both deem it the continuing duty of the government to see to it that it does.

The State pursues three main purposes in the economic sphere: obser-

Reprinted from *Problems of United States Economic Development,* Vol. I, January, 1958. Published by The Committee for Economic Development, 711 Fifth Ave., New York 22, N. Y.

Hans Morgenthau is Professor of Political Science at the University of Chicago.

vance of the rules of the game, maintenance of economic stability, and national defense.

The rules of the game are oriented toward the pluralistic objectives of American society. Thus they seek to prevent any sector of the economy from gaining absolute power vis-à-vis other sectors of the economy, competitors, or the individuals as such, by controlling and limiting its power. Regulatory commissions, legislation controlling and limiting the strong and supporting the weak, tariff and monetary policies serve this purpose.

While the State started to assume responsibility for the rules of the game in the last decades of the nineteenth century, it made itself responsible for economic stability in the nineteen thirties. Economic stability, in this context, signifies the mitigation, if not the elimination in certain sectors, of the business cycle. Its main positive characteristics, as conceived by the government of the United States, are stability of employment, of the value of the dollar, and of agricultural prices. A plethora of legislative and administrative devices serve this purpose.

Since the end of the Second World War, technological research and industrial production have become to an ever increasing extent the backbone of military defense. The regular annual expenditure by the government of close to forty billion dollars on national defense, its decrease or increase from year to year, its shift from one sector of the economy to another, all exert a sometimes drastic influence upon the economic life of the nation. They have made the government the most important single customer for the products of the national economy. In addition, many tax and monetary, price and wage policies are determined by considerations of national defense.

With the government thus exerting an enormous controlling, limiting, and stimulating influence upon the economic life, the ability to influence the economic decisions of the government becomes an indispensable element in the competition for economic advantage. Economic competition manifests itself inevitably in competition for political influence. This political influence is exerted through two channels: control of, and pressure upon, government personnel.

The most effective political influence is exerted by the direct control of government personnel. The economic organization which has its representatives elected to the legislature or appointed to the relevant administrative and executive positions exerts its political influence as far as the political influence of its representatives reaches. Insofar as the latter cannot decide the issue by themselves, the competition for political influence and, through it, economic advantage will be fought out within the collective bodies of the government by the representatives of different economic interests. While this relationship of direct control is typical in Europe, it is by no means unknown in the United States. State legislatures have been controlled by mining companies, public utilities, and railroads, and many individual members of Congress represent specific economic interests. Independent administrative agencies have come under the sway of the economic forces which they were intended to control. The large-scale interchange of top personnel between business and the executive branch of the government cannot help but influence, however subtly and intangibly, decisions of the government relevant to the economic sphere.

However, in the United States the most important political influence is exerted through the influence of pressure groups. The decision of the government agent—legislator, independent administrator, member of the executive branch—is here not a foregone conclusion by virtue of the economic control to which he is subject. His decision is in doubt, for he is still open to divergent economic pressures. The competition for determining the decisions of the government takes place not among the government agents themselves, but between the government agent, on the one hand, and several economic pressure groups, on the other. Only after this latter competition has been settled one way or another, the former will take place, provided the issue is still in doubt.

The political struggle, ostensibly fought for victory in periodical elections by political parties, reveals itself in good measure as a contest of economic forces for the control of government action. In consequence, the decision of the government and, more particularly, of legislatures ostensibly rendered "on the merits of the case," tends to reflect the weight of economic influence and, at worst, to give political sanction to decisions taken elsewhere. Legislators and administrators tend to transform themselves into ambassadors of economic forces, defending and promoting the interests of their mandatories in dealing with each other on behalf of them. The result is a new feudalism which, like that of the Middle Ages, diminishes the authority of the civil government and threatens it with extinction by parcelling its several functions out among economic organizations to be appropriated and used as private property. And just like the feudalism of the Middle Ages, these new concentrations of private power tend to command the primary loyalties of the individual citizens who owe them their livelihood and security. In the end, the constitutionally established government tends to become, in the words of Chief Justice Marshall, a "solemn mockery," glossing over the loss of political vitality with the performance of political rituals.

If giant concentrations of economic power, in the form of corporations and labor unions, were thus to become laws unto themselves, deciding with finality the matters vital to them and using the government only for the purpose of ratifying these decisions, they would not only have drained the life blood from the body politic but also destroyed the vital energies of the economic system. For the vitality of the American economic system has resided in its ability to renew itself on new technological opportunities, unfettered by the interests identified with an obsolescent technology.

Seen from the vantage point of the individual enterprise, this is what we call freedom of competition. This freedom of competition has been a function of the rules of the economic game, as formulated and enforced by the State.

Yet the new feudalism, if it is not controlled and restrained, must inevitably tend to abrogate these rules of the game in order to assure the survival of the economic giants which, in turn, tend to take over the functions of the State. The consummation of this development, possible but not inevitable, would be a state of affairs in which for those giants the rule of life would not be freedom of competition, which might jeopardize their survival, but freedom from competition in order to secure their survival. The dynamics of the American economic system, continually destroying and creating as life itself, would then give way to a gigantic system of vested interests in which the established giants would use the State to make themselves secure from competitive displacement, only to die the slow death of attrition.

It is the measure of the quandary which American society faces in this problem, insoluble by any simple formula, that the only visible cure raises issues as brave as the disease. That cure is a State strong enough to hold its own against the concentrations of private power. In good measure, such a State already exists. It is the State whose importance for the economic life of the nation we have referred to above. Insofar as this State is able to act as an independent political force, controlling, restraining, and re-directing economic activities, it is indeed the strong State, capable of keeping the concentrations of private power in check. Yet such a State, by being strong enough for this task, cannot fail being also strong enough to control, restrain, and re-direct the economic activities of everybody. In other words, as the American political tradition correctly assumes, a strong government, whatever else it may be able to accomplish, threatens the liberties of the individual, especially in the economic sphere.

Thus America is faced with a real dilemma: a government which is too weak to threaten the freedom of the individual is also too weak to hold its own against the new feudalism, and a government which is strong enough to keep the new feudalism in check is also strong enough to destroy the liberties of all. What, then, must it be: the new feudalism of private power or the new despotism of the public power? Or is there a third way in the form of an intricate system of checks and balances within the economic sphere, within the political sphere, and between both—combining, in the spirit of *The Federalist,* the ability to perform the functions of government, private and public, with those restraints upon government action upon which the liberties of all depend?

The next twenty years are likely to pose these questions in different guises, but with ever increasing urgency. The answers we are able to give to these questions will determine both the political and economic system under which we shall live.

18

STABILITY, GROWTH, AND EMPLOYMENT

JOHN MAYNARD KEYNES was the outstanding economist of the first half of the twentieth century. As Slichter notes, he "contributed invaluable tools of analysis" to economics. However, he did his most important writing during the period of the great depression, and he was unduly influenced by it. His belief that highly developed industrial societies would increasingly suffer from unemployment because of a chronic shortage of consumer demand, along with too much saving and inadequate opportunities for investment, has not been borne out by experience. Slichter explains why, but he overstates his case when he speaks of the "passing" of Keynesian economics. Some of Keynes's basic concepts continue to be a powerful force in shaping economic theories and policies.

Our second selection is a debate. In it Braverman, a Socialist, argues that major depressions cannot be avoided in a capitalist economy. Lerner, an economist who employs Keynesian techniques of analysis, maintains that we not only can but will prevent them and explains the reasons for this belief.

In our third selection, W. W. Rostow outlines the developments he thinks are necessary to start a country along the road of sustained economic growth.

37

The Passing of Keynesian Economics

by Sumner H. Slichter

John Maynard Keynes ranks with Adam Smith and Karl Marx among economists in the influence that his views have exerted on the general public. He had the vision to see that economics lacked a general theory of demand, and he proceeded with boldness and brilliance to construct one.

False! His theory produced the startling conclusion that highly developed industrial countries suffer from a chronic deficiency of demand, and that this deficiency is bound to grow worse as countries become richer. Hence, Keynes called upon government to assume a new responsibility and a new function—that of closing the growing gap between the power of progressive economies to produce and the size of effective private demand. Keynes suggested two general lines of action—that of controlling the size of the gap through changes in the distribution of income and that of offsetting the gap through greater government spending.

Keynes's theory contributed invaluable tools of analysis to economics and started hundreds of able economists in many lands studying the important problems that the theory opened up. No one in the history of economics has done as much as Keynes to stimulate good work. But Keynes's theory has turned out to have been wrong in all its essentials. Although intended to be a "general" theory, applicable to all conditions, it was unduly molded by the depressed thirties, the period when Keynes composed it. Advanced economies do not suffer from a chronic deficiency of demand—they suffer from a chronic *excess* of demand. It would be hard today to find an advanced economy that is not struggling to control demand, and most of them are having only partial success.

It is among the undeveloped economies, precisely where Keynes did not expect to find a chronic shortage of demand, that unemployment is endemic and most severe. Keynes's theory that unemployment is caused by an excessive disposition to save obviously does not explain the high

From *The Atlantic Monthly,* November, 1959. Reprinted by permission.
The late Sumner H. Slichter was for many years Professor of Economics at Harvard University. He had a special interest in the relation of economics to the problems of business.

unemployment in countries which are too poor to have any savings at all. The high unemployment in undeveloped countries is best explained by Marx's theory of unemployment—that men lack work because savings are insufficient to provide the growing labor force with the tools of production.

THE CONSUMER'S ROLE. Why has Keynes turned out to have been so completely wrong? He made two basic mistakes. In the first place, he assigned to consumers a relatively passive role in determining the demand for goods. In the second place, he overlooked the fact that the development of investment opportunities is itself an expanding industry carried on for profit and able to supply the community with a rapidly growing number of investment outlets.

Keynes thought that consumers play a rather passive role in determining the demand for goods because he believed that the amount spent on consumption depends pretty completely upon the size of the national income. Hence, the dynamic influences in the economy, the influences that make the national income and the total demand for goods change, must be found, according to Keynes, outside the spending habits of consumers. Keynes found a single dominant dynamic influence in the rate of investment, which by rising and falling determines whether the economy expands or contracts. As business increases or cuts its buying of investment goods, incomes will rise or fall, and as they rise or fall consumption too will rise or fall.

Had Keynes lived in the United States, he would perhaps have seen that consumers do not let their consumption be determined so completely by the size of their incomes. American consumers, with their strong desire to live better and with their freedom from customs and traditions that decree what ways of living are suitable for people in certain stations, have always been ready to cut their rate of saving, to draw on their capital, or to go into debt in order to buy new things.

Particularly in recent years, consumers have developed a growing willingness to incur short-term debts in order to buy goods. Since the boom year of 1929 there has been an almost sevenfold increase in consumer credit, from a mere $6.4 billion at the end of 1929 to a whopping $41.9 billion at the end of 1956. During this period consumers were obviously not limiting their spending by their incomes. Their spending was being determined, as one would expect it to be, by their total resources, which include their credit, not merely by their incomes. Instead of playing the passive role ascribed to them by Keynes, consumers have been a powerful dynamic influence accelerating the expansion of the economy.

THE ETHICS OF BORROWING. Consumers have been encouraged to play a dynamic role in the economy by the rapidly growing consumer credit industry. This industry is based upon the discovery, only recently made, that consumers are far better credit risks than anyone had dreamed them to be. As a result, there has been a rush by finance companies, banks, mail order houses, automobile dealers, department stores, airplane and steamship lines, and many others to persuade consumers to buy goods on credit. At first consumer credit was limited to tangible goods with a rather definite resale value, such as automobiles or household appliances, but now one may finance trips and vacations on the installment plan. And the proportion of sales made on credit steadily rises. Sears, Roebuck reports that in 1954, 39 per cent of its sales were made on credit. Last year the proportion was 44 per cent. With consumers behaving as American consumers are accustomed to behave, Keynes's fear that people will insist on saving too much seems farfetched.

Incidentally, with the discovery that consumers are better risks than had been previously suspected, there has developed a marked change in attitudes toward personal loans—a real change in the ethics of borrowing. Time was when personal indebtedness, except for a few emergencies and to provide the necessary furnishings for a home, was regarded as imprudent or reckless. Today it is seen that debt is a stabilizing and stimulating influence, and that it is a good thing for most young men, particularly married men, to have at least a moderate volume of debts that they are paying off.

THE DEMAND FOR CAPITAL.   Although Keynes thought that the dominant dynamic influence in the economy is investment, he conceived of businessmen as a surprisingly unenterprising and helpless lot—unable to do much about the scale of investment. Keynes was obsessed with the fear that, as the country's stock of capital became larger and larger, outlets for savings would be harder to find, and he expressed his fears quite eloquently. He said that he felt sure that the demand for capital is strictly limited in the sense that it would not be difficult to increase the stock of capital to the point where its ability to produce a return would fall to a very low figure.

Keynes's belief that the return on capital would drop very drastically as the stock of capital increased must be ascribed to his failure to appreciate the significance of modern technology. Though a man of affairs, and a highly successful one at that, he failed to see what others saw, the large and growing capacity of industry to discover investment opportunities— a capacity that is far greater in highly developed countries than in undeveloped ones and that grows as the economy becomes richer and more industrial. Technological discoveries are the most important single influence on investment in advanced industrial economies, and yet Keynes's brilliant work contains no discussion of technological research.

THE INDUSTRY OF DISCOVERY.   It is ironic that at the very time that Keynes was proclaiming his pessimistic views on the shortage of investment opportunities, the rise of technological research was producing a revolutionary change in the economy. Technological research was becoming an industry. It is convenient to call it the industry of discovery. It consists of many captive laboratories which work only for the company which owns them and a rapidly growing number of firms which do research under contract. The <u>industry of discovery is one of the most rapidly growing industries in the country</u>. Industry spent $116 million of its own money on research and development in 1930, $234 million in 1940, and about $1.5 billion in 1953, and it has been making even larger outlays under government research contracts. Outlays on research and development would grow even faster were they not limited by the shortage of engineers and scientists.

The revolutionary nature of the rise of the industry of discovery is not appreciated even by economists. Until recently, discoveries have been made mainly in two ways: by the efforts of <u>operating men</u> (incidental to their regular work), who have seen opportunities to improve methods of production or products, and by the efforts of "<u>inventors</u>" who, using their own resources and often driven by much stronger motives than hope of gain, have made industrial applications of scientific knowledge. The revolutionary change is that it has become possible to find a large number of problems or areas of investigation on which money may be spent with a reasonable expectation that the outlay will produce enough useful information and understanding to justify the expense. This means that it has become possible to apply the economic calculus—the balancing of expected expenses against expected gains—to an important new area of human activity, and to have the organized pursuit of gain take over a field of activity where formerly there had only been haphazard individual activities. . . .

Many thousands of able men now make their living by disturbing our lives and by forcing us to discard old equipment, old methods, and old ways of doing things. The more they disturb us, the better living they make. And the vested interests of the people who live by making discoveries cause them to strive to improve the methods and instruments of investigation, thus steadily raising the capacity of the economy to develop investment opportunities. The danger that Keynes feared—namely, that we shall run out of investment opportunities—grows more remote every day, and it becomes most remote in the highly developed economies, precisely where Keynes erroneously believed that it would be greatest.

THE OUTLOOK FOR PRODUCTION. How does the world look when Keynes's theory of demand, constructed in the midst of the great depression, is replaced with one based on the developments of the last twenty years? On the whole, it appears to be a far better world than the one described by Keynes's theory—though not a world from which tough economic problems are absent. The specter of chronic unemployment, slowly growing as wealth increases and as the rate of saving rises, has pretty completely disappeared, at least as far as the industrially developed countries are concerned. Only a series of major blunders in policy could produce the chronic unemployment that Keynes dreaded. Consumers are a far more dynamic influence than Keynes ever suspected, and industry has far greater power to create demand for goods, mainly through technological discoveries, than anyone a generation or so ago dreamed it might have —and this power is growing. . . .

NEW CONFIDENCE IN FREE ENTERPRISE. The discovery that our economy has far greater capacity to increase the demand for goods than Keynes suspected has naturally produced a great resurgence of confidence in capitalism and private enterprise. Rising confidence in the effectiveness of capitalistic institutions has had the interesting result of causing radicals and conservatives alike to abandon extreme positions. As attacks on capitalism have moderated, the defense of capitalism has become less doctrinaire. In the United States there has been a marked growth of "middle-of-the-road" opinion. The same thing has happened in Western Europe where the Labor and Socialist parties have shifted from advocating nationalization of industry to championing the welfare state—the operation of private enterprise within a comprehensive framework of public policies— and where the principal conservative parties have also accepted the welfare state.

We should be grateful that the world is what it is rather than what Keynes pictured it as being. It is a world in which the energies and aspirations of men are stimulated by expanding opportunities rather than depressed by the constant threat of chronic unemployment. Most important of all, it is a world in which the rapidly growing industry of discovery is creating the possibility of a great cultural revolution. For the first time in history, the high productivity of some countries is enabling their people to have sufficient income, sufficient education, and sufficient leisure so that the good life is ceasing to be the privilege of a favored few and is being brought within the reach of all members of the community.

38

Can We Cure Depressions?

a debate between
Abba P. Lerner and Harry Braverman

Harry Braverman:

It's pretty widely agreed that there is an instability in a capitalist economy. That wasn't something that was agreed upon twenty-five years ago. At that time, most economists went on the theory that there couldn't be a serious and prolonged depression, as the economy was guided by some kind of "invisible hand," a set of laws which saw to it that things turned out right. With the Great Crash of 1929, that point of view was pretty decisively repudiated. So I don't believe Dr. Lerner and I will have a lot of argument about that point.

Now, I'll state why I think the economy tends to get out of whack. The very dynamics of the capitalist system when it's in a period of boom, the drive to produce an ever larger amount with less and less labor per unit of production, alters the proportions of the parts of the economy to each other. There is a tendency to expand production and capacity as though the sky were the limit, while on the other side expanding consumption and purchasing power in a relatively limited way. That disproportion leads to a bust in the boom. That's been the history of every big upswing in the business cycle up to now, and I believe that that's the tendency in the economy at the present time.

The government spent during the war some $180 billion more than it took in in taxes, giving a terrific stimulus to the economy by throwing in purchasing power that wouldn't otherwise have been there. Then consumer credit in the eight years following the war added another $200 billion, this time in private indebtedness. In the decade and a half after 1940, some $400 billion of additional debt was piled up in this country that hasn't been repaid. I know we've all gotten badly jaded by many of the astronomical figures, but if you stop to think what $400 billion of credit buying means, you can quickly see that, measured against our average national income during that same period, it represents roughly an

Reprinted from *The American Socialist*, April 1958, Vol. 5, No. 4, pp. 6–8.
Abba P. Lerner is Professor of Economics at Michigan State University.
Harry Braverman was, for many years, an active member of the Socialist Party.

additional year's purchasing power for every ten; within ten years, there was about eleven years of buying, by borrowing ahead on future income.

If you see this picture clearly, you must realize how lame our formerly self-reliant capitalism is getting, and the kind of props it needs. The question also arises whether this kind of a credit splurge can be repeated every 15 years. Even if the government could repeat, the consumer cannot add much more to his credit load.

That is what I think is a chief defect in Dr. Lerner's theory of functional finance. Perhaps I should leave this to Dr. Lerner to explain, as he is the originator of the theory, but it's necessary for my presentation to say a few words about it. The thought is that a national debt is a useful proposition. In times of depression, the government should spend what it hasn't got, or in other words borrow. Business gets an impetus to pick up. Then when you have a major boom going on, the government can repay some of its indebtedness, and in that way it will prevent the boom from getting too exuberant. In theory, the valleys and peaks of the business cycle get leveled off somewhat. That, at any rate, was the hope.

Well, if symmetry is a virtue in a theory, this is one that has great beauty. But the symmetry has not been displayed in real life. Instead of being able to pay off a good part of our indebtedness during the boom, even in this time of prosperity after the war, the government had to pile up another $30 billion of debt. Now what that means to me, is that the mechanism which Dr. Lerner or other followers of John Maynard Keynes speak of does tend to work if it is applied in massive enough doses, *but these economists have underestimated the downward trend of the capitalist economy.* The way their theory actually worked out in practice has required continual spending—for armaments, as we all know—to keep the boom going.

This big flow of government and consumer spending set off an investment boom—which has been historically the last stage in all our major upswings. There was a great stimulus to investment in new plant and equipment. Because the whole effort is, quite naturally, to turn out more with less labor, there was no comparable stimulus to consuming power. Consumption has been growing at a slow and leveling-off rate, and has begun to decline recently. Over the last year or two, Leon Keyserling calculated, expansion of plant and equipment was about eight times as fast as the increase of consuming power.

This jibes with the theory I presented at the start. The McGraw-Hill Department of Economics has done some surveys of this and come up with startling results. Where, in the first six, seven years after the war, the economy was running at well over 90 percent of capacity—with the exception only of the slump year of 1949—the economy was operating at

82 percent of capacity in 1953. 81 percent in 1954, 84 percent in 1955 (our top boom year), 80 percent in 1956 and at the end of 1957. They revised these figures somewhat upwards later, but the revisions were just a point or two.

As distinguished from the twenties, there are certain stabilizers in the economy, cushions to consumer income. Economists, government officials, businessmen have some confidence in these shock absorbers to *slow* a decline, but they don't expect them to *prevent* a decline. These stabilizers have one important feature in common, that they have less effect the deeper a recession gets and the longer it goes on.

A major argument of the "new economists" is that they today know a great deal more than we used to. They know how income and investment ought to be shifted, how the different forces in the economy ought to be balanced to prevent or cure a depression. Admittedly, if you have the power to shift anything in the economy any way you wanted, you can readjust the proportions to get it working again. That all goes on the assumption that the only thing we were lacking in the past was knowledge. But can anyone tell me of a capitalist country where disinterested political scientists are running the government, and economists are running the economy? The major decisions in our economy are still being made in the same old way: *by the self-interest calculations of private firms.* Politics and economics encompass fierce struggles between contending interests. That is why it is foolish to predict an end to depressions because of the growth in economic knowledge.

The subtitle for this debate is: "Can America Avoid Depression and Maintain Free Enterprise?" and I'll answer that question this way: First I would alter the question to read "capitalism," or "private enterprise," as we don't have any such thing as the free enterprise this country used to know a century or more ago. It's a highly trustified, cartelized, monopolized economy. With that correction, I would answer to the question that, in the long run, we cannot maintain capitalism and enjoy prosperity.

That is the conclusion that emerges no matter from what angle you choose to view the technical-economic debate. Look at the experience of the last twenty-five years: We went into the deepest depression in our history, we finally climbed out of it, not by any ordinary government intervention, not by welfare spending, but when the big military spending started. We wound up then with a government sector of the economy amounting to some 20 percent of the total—mostly tied to the military. Now, how many more depressions or recessions can we climb out of that way and still maintain a capitalist system? Mind you, I'm not saying that's the way this country will get socialism—I doubt it very much, but that's another discussion. But I am saying that even this method of curing depression is one that bodes ill for the future of capitalism. So even the

Keynesian theory, when tested against the experience of the past quarter century, tends to show that capitalism is not a viable or desirable proposition for the people of this country.

Abba P. Lerner:

I want to thank Mr. Braverman for a very pleasant, polite, patient, and clear discussion, with about nine-tenths of which I find myself in agreement. But unfortunately the one-tenth with which I find myself in disagreement rather spoils what comes out at the end.

The essential part of Mr. Braverman's argument is that there is "an inherent instability." That's a very nice-sounding word, but I think we ought to try to look at it a little more closely and deal with it in more ordinary language. Economists used to believe that it isn't necessary to have any policy to prevent depressions; that they will cure themselves. But it is no longer believed, as Mr. Braverman clearly pointed out, that depressions can't happen—that an "invisible hand" looks after these things. The "invisible hand" doesn't prevent depressions and we need to have a policy.

The essentials of this policy are very simple. If depressions are caused by people not spending enough money—and this is the only kind of depression which we have discussed so far—the cure is to see to it that enough money is spent. The government can always do that by spending money itself. It's no use telling me, or Mr. Braverman, to spend more money because we haven't got the money to spend. And we are not in the position of printing more money to spend because if we do they'll put us in jail. But the government can print as much money as it likes—nobody can put the government in jail—and so the government can provide all the money that is necessary to keep people spending, and if the government wants to do that, nobody can stop it. Such a policy is "functional finance."

Mr. Braverman correctly described functional finance as a policy by which the government undertakes action to maintain spending at the required level, but he imposed a limitation which I never recognized. It is therefore, I'm afraid, necessary for me to give Mr. Braverman a further lesson on functional finance. The essential point about functional finance is that the *only* judgment as to whether the government should or shouldn't provide more money is: how it works—how it functions. If more money is needed to maintain full employment, why then it should provide more, and if not, then it shouldn't, and if a reduction in money spending is required to prevent inflation then there should be a reduction.

Actually a lot of people have made exactly the same mistake as Mr. Braverman though they didn't call it functional finance and did not attribute it to me. The Swedish economists in particular made the same mistake when they went part of the way towards functional finance. They very properly said: The idea of balancing the budget every year is not a very sensible one. Why should the necessity of the government to encourage and discourage spending just balance out in the 365¼ days that it takes the earth to go round the sun? Spending is a matter of economics, not of astronomy. And indeed 365¼ days is no more relevant than the ninety minutes it takes the sputnik to go around the earth. Nobody thus far has been suggesting that we balance our budget every ninety minutes, nor should we balance it every year. But the Swedes slipped when they said: "Maybe it should be balanced every ten years." And they had long-term budgets. This is just like Mr. Braverman's "limitations." However they soon realized that ten years made no more sense than one year, and so they wiggled themselves out of the error in a very complicated way. They spoke about having a "cyclical budget," and a "capital budget," and other kinds of budgets; then they had a lot of footnotes saying that if necessary, something else can be done—which means they didn't really believe in any of these budget balancings but just left them in for window-dressing so that people like Mr. Braverman who felt strongly the budget should be some way, somehow, or sometime brought into balance, shouldn't feel too bad about it.

Functional finance says clearly that there are no such limits, and that is why all of the argument Mr. Braverman made here just disappears. There is no reason why the government should stop spending short of achieving and maintaining full employment. I once wrote an article, called "Functional Finance and the Federal Debt," on what happens if the government keeps on increasing federal debt. Will the debt grow so big that it would destroy the economy? It wouldn't because in the first place we owe the debt to ourselves, not to any other nation. If we owed the debt to the Germans or to the Japanese the payments on its interest and principal could ruin us. But since we owe it to ourselves we also get the payments, and so we are not impoverished. We can still consume all that we produce and that's what really matters; as long as we can produce a great deal, we're all right.

In the second place the debt will not grow indefinitely. Supposing the government found there wasn't enough spending—people didn't invest enough or consume enough—and so the government had to provide some more spending. Then either the national debt would increase, or the volume of money would increase, or more probably both would increase. As the amount of money in the economy grew larger and larger, the public would have more and more money in their pockets. As the amount of debt grew larger and larger, the public would own more U.S. bonds and government debt certificates. These people look at their bankbooks and debt certificates and they feel rich. As the growth goes on, they feel richer and richer, and they can afford to spend more. And since they spend more, *they* fill the gap in spending and it isn't necessary for the *government* to come in. So *the debt automatically stops growing* when people have become sufficiently rich in cash and in government debt certificates. If this is overdone and causes *too much* spending, then you apply functional finance in reverse, create a budget surplus and pay off some of the debt. But there is no need to get to that point, because the government doesn't need to keep on increasing spending if people are spending enough. So there is no need to worry about the difficulty or danger of debt growth.

There's only one more point which I think is important here, and that is the last point that was made by Mr. Braverman; namely: Even if the economists know what ought to be done, will the government do it? If the government doesn't, then all this knowledge, I agree, is of no use. However, I think the government is extremely interested in doing it, because—one peculiar thing about governments—they like to be re-elected. And no government is going to be re-elected if it has a depression. You can find much better reasons why we shouldn't have depressions: People shouldn't be out of work and hungry; a depression would make more people believe that the Russian system is better than the American system. But even if our politicians didn't care about the people, and didn't care about America and Russia, they still care about being re-elected, and so they will do whatever they can to stop a depression. Even politicians who are worried about an unbalanced budget and who think functional finance is wicked, find themselves pressured in deficits, because, if there is unemployment, not only the politicians and the economists, but everybody, almost, in America knows, that the government can provide jobs by spending money—they've seen it happen.

When the war broke out, as Mr. Braverman pointed out, in spite of the New Deal, in spite of Keynes, we still had many millions of people unemployed, because, when Keynes said you should spend $30 billion, the government said, $30 billion is too much, let's try $3 billion, and so we got some reduction in unemployment, but we didn't effect a cure. And then the war came, and the government spent $30 billion and $50 billion and $100 billion, and everybody saw what happened. Everybody was working; we were able to produce all the goods we wanted, we were able to maintain our standards of living and still produce all the airplanes and armaments and guns for ourselves, for our allies, for Russia, because we were spending enough money. Having seen this happen the public knows that government spending can prevent depression and governments cannot avoid their responsibility for providing enough spending and still be re-elected. I am confident we are not going to have a bust; mainly because I have great confidence in the eagerness of politicians to be re-elected.

39

"Take-off" into Economic Growth

interview with W. W. Rostow

Q *Professor Rostow, what distinguishes a growing society from a non-growing one?*

A What essentially distinguishes a growing society from a nongrowing one is its ability to produce and apply a regular flow of modern technology. Before this can happen, a great many prior changes must occur. There must be a prior revolution in agricultural productivity in order to supply food to the growing cities. There must be a big build-up of social overhead capital—schools, roads, health facilities, etc. And, usually, there must be some changes in production which will bring in more foreign exchange.

Q *In your recent book, "Stages of Economic Growth," you have described certain societies, where no sustained growth takes place, as "traditional" societies. What do such traditional societies have in common?*

A Traditional societies vary greatly from African tribes to the grand ebb and flow of the dynasties of China or the Roman Empire. These societies have not usually been static. Often they developed all the preconditions for growth "take-off"—except one. They improved their agriculture with irrigation. They built roads and other forms of social overhead capital. They engaged in trade and even did a certain amount of manufacturing. But what ultimately triggered their decline was the invariable absence of a scientific attitude toward the physical world, and a social and technical inability to *regularly* allocate first-rate talent to breaking the bottlenecks. In other words, they did not have a *flow* of modern technology.

From *Challenge* (May, 1960), pp. 30–37, a publication of tne Institute of Economic Affairs, New York University. Reprinted by permission.

W. W. Rostow is an economist who is best known for his theories of economic growth. After teaching for ten years at the Massachusetts Institute of Technology, he became in 1961 Chairman of the Policy Planning Council of the United States Department of State.

Q *And this was the fatal flaw?*

A The fatal flaw, yes. Of course, many patterns have marked the crises of these traditional societies, but behind them lay the fact that they could not break through into a stage of economic development where technology could substitute for adequate supplies of land and meet the requirements of a growing population.

Q *Does this mean that there was no possibility of a take-off before you had industrial technology?*

A That is right. While growth is not a function of modern technology, *sustained* growth is.

Q *What changes have to take place before a traditional society is ready for the take-off?*

A From the time that a traditional society is intruded upon from the outside and the time it is ready for its take-off, enormously complex and revolutionary changes—social, political, economic and psychological—have to take place. While there are certain uniformities in the problems —technical, social and psychological—that have to be faced, the lesson of history is that every case is unique. Some societies, such as Japan, have found it possible, for largely accidental reasons of social structure and culture, to make the changes necessary for take-off rather quickly. Others had to go through a most terrible torment, like China from the time of the Opium Wars down to 1949.

Powerful Spreading Effects of the New Technology

Q *Let us assume that a society has reached a stage where it is ready for the take-off. What is involved in getting it off the launching pad, as it were?*

A What is required is not only that modern technology be applied to some leading set of economic factors but, even more important, that the society react positively to the powerful spreading effects of this new technology. Let me give you an example. The take-offs of the United States, France and Germany during the mid-19th century, and those of Canada and Russia shortly before World War I, all stemmed from railroads. Now, the railway potentially leads to growth take-off because it has a number of very important "spread" effects. Railways set up a demand for coal, iron and heavy engineering industries. Railways spread out into the countryside and, if the countryside responds, they can accelerate agricultural specialization.

Q *But railways have not always resulted in an economic take-off.*

A No, they have not. In China, India and Argentina, the development of railways did not lead to a take-off. If the society, in the widest sense, does not actively respond, the building of railways will not have these self-generating effects. Society must be equipped with a set of institutions and values capable of responding to modern technology.

Q *What does this involve?*

A It involves several things. First, there must be a group of private or public entrepreneurs able and willing to exploit the new possibilities of productive activity or profit set in motion by the new technology. There must also be an adequate core of trained people who can perform the technical jobs necessary to exploit these opportunities. Finally, there must be a government which, either actively (as is true in most cases) or passively (as was the case in Britain in the late 18th-century cotton textile take-off), will do all that is necessary to encourage the technological breakthrough.

Q *If all this is done, the chances are that such technological developments will spread into other sectors of the economy.*

A Correct. Modern techniques can spread backward—that is, they can stimulate old industries in the way that the railways encouraged the coal and iron industries. They can spread laterally—by setting up requirements for new cities and new social overhead capital. But most important, they can spread forward by creating new industries. In this way, the steel industry came into its own as a result of the need for steel rails when it was discovered that iron rails wore out too fast. Now, the leading sector in the take-off has varied widely—from textiles in England to railroads in the United States and Germany, to timber in Sweden, to import substitution industries in Argentina and India. Each society will have its own set of leading sectors depending on its resources and on the stage in technological history when it comes into the game.

Q *Most of the take-offs we have discussed so far took place in the 19th century. But the technology required for a similar take-off in mid-20th-century Southeast Asia may be quite different. If the leading sectors are no longer, say, railroads, but mass irrigation and power projects, does this call for a larger government initiative during the take-off period?*

A Let us get one thing clear. No country—not even Britain during the 18th century—has ever been able to get itself ready for take-off without the government playing a very large role. That role has varied, of course. In the case of the U.S., government played an extremely important role. Prior to the Civil War, most of the social overhead capital was built by the state and local governments rather than by the federal government. While we had less of an agricultural problem than most countries, since we had ample supplies of good land, we did devise a public land policy especially to exploit this resource. Moreover, our land-grant colleges were a conscious act of federal policy designed to improve our agricultural technology. And, of course, we had a deliberate foreign exchange policy in the form of protective tariffs. Similarly, government played an extremely important role in the preconditioning of 19th-century Canada, Czarist Russia and Meiji Japan.

Q *So the underdeveloped countries today follow this same process?*

A Yes, but in a more extended form. Only very unhistorical economists can argue that government played no role in Western take-offs, or that what we are now witnessing in underdeveloped countries is something new and ideologically peculiar.

The Responsibility of Industrialization

Q *Well, what other factors may determine the extent of government intervention during the take-off period?*

A A lot depends on whether you have a solid commercial middle class ready to move in and assume the responsibility of industrialization. Where such a middle class did not exist, as in Japan, Turkey and Czarist Russia, governments often initially took a direct hand in stimulating industry. But, contrary to the expectations of ideologists, it is not true (outside of Communist countries) that governments never relinquish their hold on a particular industry. Governments which are not compulsively committed to economic control for power reasons often find that the public interest does not require them to maintain total ownership and operational control of the private fabricating sector. In fact, what we are rediscovering is that the public interest can be safeguarded by means other than having the government run industry, which, as many underdeveloped countries are beginning to find out, can be a great headache.

Q *Then the necessary degree of government intervention will vary with each society?*

A Of course. If, as was true with the Japanese and British, there is no very severe problem with social overhead transport capital because these islands have coastal shipping, the government's role in this area will be light. In countries like Russia and Canada, on the other hand, you had a very great transportation problem, and the government had to play a preponderant role. And the same variations exist in the fields of agriculture and foreign exchange. The extent of technically appropriate state intervention will vary with each situation.

Q *But, in the context of competitive coexistence, the growth rates themselves have become an important ideological issue. Will this not mean that even in societies where there is no ideological compulsion for state intervention, such as India, the initial performance of totalitarian societies may seem so impressive that the temptation to emulate totalitarian institutions may prove irresistible?*

A This is possible, but not very probable. I do not believe that people are quite as silly as professors sometimes are. What will matter in the competition between India and China, for example, is not whether the Indian growth rate matches the Chinese. If India, in the next decade, can move into a genuine take-off sufficient to give its people a real sense of improvement, if it can begin to make a dent on the unemployment problem, if it can improve agricultural productivity and provide her urban masses with a more stable food supply, I don't think Indians will care if they read in the newspapers that the Chinese GNP is increasing faster than theirs. A great deal—including, in my opinion, the fate of Communist China—hinges upon the Indian government's ability to give her people concrete evidence of material improvement.

Self-Sustained Growth Is Not a Smooth Process

Q *Let us assume that a country has successfully accomplished an economic take-off. Does this success assure it of permanent growth?*

A The answer to that is both yes and no. Certainly, no country that has once achieved a successful take-off has ever relapsed into stagnation or decline for more than a limited period. On the other hand, self-sustained growth is not a smooth process. Growth consists of a constant repetition of the take-off in the sense that leading economic sectors are constantly decelerating. Only by creatively introducing *new* leading sectors into the economy can we sustain over-all economic growth.

Q *Is the transition from one leading sector to another always smooth?*

A History is full of cases where certain leading sectors declined *before* a new set of leading sectors took hold. There was such a gap during the

1880s, for example, when railways could no longer lead growth in many countries. There was another such gap, at least in Western European history, during the interwar years when the potentialities for growth from the prevailing leading sectors—steel, steel ships, coal, iron and heavy chemicals—could no longer carry growth forward. At the same time, Western Europe was not quite able to adapt itself to the age of high mass consumption—that is, the age of automobiles, ball bearings, electricity, strip steel and gadgets. In fact, it was not until the 1950s that Europe finally moved into the same stage that we had already been in since the 1920s.

Q *But you believe that once a take-off has been achieved, new leading sectors will always emerge?*

A Well, that seems thus far to be the lesson of history.

Q *In your book you describe the U.S. as having reached the most highly developed stage of economic growth—the stage of high mass consumption. Can we expect other societies, like the Soviet Union, for example, to enter this stage irrespective of what their leaderships may desire?*

A In theory, I can see no reason why all cultures should choose to make the same use of a mature industrial machine and of modern technology that we do in the U.S. In the U.S., we have been able to see what happens in a society where 80 per cent of the people have cars and 70 per cent have their own houses. In the U.S., at least, people have opted for larger families and, perhaps, for a certain "retreat into leisure"—do-it-yourself projects, trips to national parks, long-playing records, and the like. But, there is nothing about the American choices which has been decreed by nature.

Symbols of Privacy and Mobility

Q *Still, wouldn't you say that increasing awareness that such a style of living is possible must have a political effect on the middle classes of more advanced Communist countries?*

A Well, my hunch is this. Once people enjoy a certain level of food, shelter and clothing, and have some measure of security, the two things they want next are privacy and mobility. Consider what the Russian middle class is now doing with its income. It, too, wants a *dacha* in the country and a *Moskvich* to get there—the perfect symbols for privacy and mobility. And the same thing is happening in Japan, except that there they ride Japanese motor scooters instead of automobiles. In fact, the trend may well turn out to be universal. Certainly, recent studies comparing consumption patterns here and in Western Europe show only trivial variations in demand once adjustments have been made for price and income differences.

Q *But countries like the Soviet Union are not free to follow consumer preferences in this matter.*

A That is true. While I believe that Communist countries would, if left free to follow consumer preferences, go the same way as the rest of the industrialized world, the major purpose of the Soviet government at present is to control the consumption process so as to prevent this from happening. This is not only a question of saving resources for capital equipment and armament. The mass automobile, for example, diverts resources for roads, gas stations and hamburger stands; it also provides a means whereby the Soviet citizen can obtain mobility and privacy. Khrushchev has formally announced that he does not intend to imitate the West in this matter. Instead of the private automobile, the Soviet government will go in for fleets of government-controlled taxi-cabs equipped, as was significantly explained to me, with transistor radios. In this way, the privacy involved in owning your own automobile will have been eliminated.

Q *Do you think that the Soviet government will get away with this?*

A My guess will be that it will—for perhaps a generation. But sooner or later the Russians will want to hit the road on their own with their families, just like the rest of the human race.

Q *If, as you say, the Soviet Union will move increasingly in the direction of more consumption—and more private property—won't this diversion of resources for private ends tend to limit the aggressiveness of Soviet policy?*

A To a very limited extent the official sanctioning of these consumption values may diminish the aggressiveness of the Soviet government. But, given the current Soviet growth rate, there is no reason why consumption cannot expand substantially without placing any limits on the resources available for military and political purposes. I believe that higher consumption in Soviet society can, in itself, make only a very minor contribution to world peace. Much more important, in this context, is the diffusion of power (both nuclear power and, beyond that, industrial power) into parts of the world which neither the U.S. nor Russia can control. If the free world maintains a strong stance, I believe it will gradually be driven home on the Russians that any dream they may have of world domination—and even ideological domination—is based on a rather hopeless illusion. For, in this matter, time is against her. In the end, Russia will have to accept her destiny as one substantial major power among a group of such powers in a world where domination is increasingly difficult.

Thank you, Professor Rostow.

CHAPTER

19

INEQUALITY, POVERTY, AND SOCIAL SECURITY

IN RECENT YEARS we have made only moderate progress toward reducing *inequalities* of income in the United States, but we have made substantial progress in raising the *average* of all incomes and in providing greater security for individuals and families. However, the problem of poverty is still with us, not so much because many people lack the food, clothing, and shelter necessary for survival, but because we now tend to define poverty in relative terms. The poverty-stricken are those who are deprived of the comforts, amenities, opportunities, and pleasures which most Americans take for granted. In "Poverty Amidst Affluence" each of six eminent social scientists discusses briefly a different aspect of the poverty problem.

In the last decade a great deal has been written about the problems of our Negro poor, whether in the rural South or in the slums of our great cities. That more than two-thirds of our poor are non-Negro is often forgotten. In our second selection *U. S. News & World Report* tells where the non-Negro poor are found, and discusses their attitudes and their problems.

40

Poverty Amidst Affluence

Excerpts published in the Monthly Labor Review from papers delivered at the West Virginia University Conference on Poverty Amidst Affluence, held in Morgantown, W. Va., on May 3-7, 1965.

Changing Concepts

Since the end of the Second World War, the conceptions of poverty and of social responsibility for it have changed so radically that the situation of the past has become almost irrelevant. An examination of the views and practices of the past is valuable, if at all, simply because it reveals a contrast so sharp that it illuminates the distance we have come in a relatively brief period.

The traditional belief that only starvation or the threat of it was a valid basis for social intervention limited the perception of the extent of poverty in the United States down almost to the end of the 19th century. Significantly, this democratic Nation was less responsive to the problem than most European countries at comparable stages of industrial development. The reasons were important.

A large proportion of the poor were either immigrants or Negroes and were therefore considered groups apart, toward which society did not bear full responsibility. The foreign-born had come of their own volition; they could go back if they wished; and they were better off than they had been in the places of their birth. The exclusion, by law, of newcomers likely to become a public charge created the assumption that those admitted had no claim upon communal assistance. As for the Negroes, a costly Civil War had liberated them; they were now to prove that they were worthy of their freedom.

A narrowing concept of community action dulled the awareness that poverty existed among the native white population also. Since aid was primarily a subject of voluntary philanthropic action, anything done for the poor was testimony to the goodness of the hearts of the charitable rather than the fulfillment of an obligation. There were acres of diamonds

From the *Monthly Labor Review,* July, 1965, pp. 836–840. Published by United States Department of Labor, Bureau of Labor Statistics, Washington, D.C.

in each man's garden; each was responsible for finding them. Failure was the result of laziness, wickedness, or lack of ability. The appearance of eugenic theories which accounted for dependency by congenital defects supplied the decisive element in this explanation.

The existence of empty land on the frontier and of open opportunities in the expanding cities provided just enough cases of success, of rags to a modest competence if not to riches, to lend plausibility to these assumptions. Insofar as they considered the problem in any general economic context, Americans took for granted a frame of reference of scarcity. There was no radical break with classical European social theory in this respect. But Americans could take pride in their exceptionalism. In the Old World, corrupt institutions and the lack of opportunity depressed the population in a hopeless poverty, of which the swarms of beggars were the visible evidence. In the United States, the Biblical injunction—"the poor always ye have with you"—remained valid; but the poor were the unworthy, unwilling or unable to better themselves. That the facts of the matter, even in the 19th century, contradicted this complacent view did not weaken its hold on the minds of the dominant groups in the society.

—Oscar Handlin
Winthrop Professor of History
Harvard University

Segregation of the Poor

Do the ways of the lowest socioeconomic segments of our society impede their entry into the mainstream of American life? Does poverty keep its tightest grip on those people for whom it has become a stabilized way of life?

Our basic question may be subdivided into three. First, do some aspects of lower-class culture interfere directly with the achievement of a better life? Let us be cautious about assuming that everything middle-class is superior. Who is to say that clearly differentiated husband and wife roles, such as typify working-class families, are better or worse than the loosely differentiated roles that mark professional families? Is there any virtue in belonging to clubs rather than to street-corner peer groups? Is it better to be Episcopalian? To suggest that one way of life may not be superior to another in all respects, though, is not to imply that all are equally valid. A proper criterion is whether that of the poor materially impedes their advancement. I believe that it does. The female-based household does very little to orient the growing boy toward the adult world of work or to a concept of family organization in which he might have a stable place. The street group, while useful in that it provides psychic satisfactions for its members, gives the growing boy values which too often are negative toward either education or "normal" adult responsibilities.

Next, is the discontinuity between the culture of the poor and the culture which dominates the larger community so great as to prevent ready passage from one to the other? There is no question that the deprived child starts school with a handicap which is rooted in the atmosphere and ethos of his home. He comes without the language skills, other preschool learning, or motivation that more favored children bring to the first grade, and he is less likely to have kindergarten. He may expect early failure because he cannot bridge the two culture worlds.

Finally, have residential patterns and variations in life styles and statuses given rise to a segregation of the poor which shuts them off from the norms and expectations of the larger community? There can be no doubt that such segregation exists. The extent to which it walls off the lowest income peoples from those of higher standing, and keeps the former from interacting with people with higher aspirations and attainments, is not known. Yet it is highly relevant. The surmounting of poverty requires that the people see the vision of a better life for themselves. They must come to feel the possibility that they, too, can move upward. It is not that a different life is not perceived, but rather that it is so often viewed as inaccessible.

—Harold A. Gibbard
Professor of Sociology
West Virginia University

Family Size and Poverty

The importance of family size as a determining factor in poverty was overlooked in the early analysis of poverty, which used a crude definition in terms of a family income of $3,000, regardless of family size. Subsequent and more comprehensive analysis has reinstated the large family as a potent factor in poverty. Large family size operates primarily to reduce the share of the family income available to meet each individual member's needs; but it also can operate in various ways to reduce the total family income, notably by preventing the mother from working.

A competitive free enterprise system will not (and cannot afford to) pay more for a productive service obtained from one source than it pays to another source, simply because the welfare of more individuals depends on that source. But if knowledge of the means of family limitation were universal, and resort to them socially sanctioned and encouraged, variations of family size would reflect rational choices stemming from differences in people's preferences as between higher consumption per head and more heads in the family, so that apart from families headed by incompetent adults there would be no genuine problem of poverty associated with variations in family size. It is the combination of a rational economic system and a largely irrational system of family size determination that underlies this part of the poverty problem.

Poverty due to discrimination is more widespread than might appear at first sight. The notion that discrimination is responsible for the greater incidence of poverty among nonwhites is a familiar one. But discrimination is also involved in the case of the aged poor, whom our society frequently forces to retire from remunerative work before their productive capacity and willingness to work are exhausted, and whom we are prepared to assist with public money only on condition that they do not work, or work only part-time for low wages. In a more subtle way, discrimination against the aged is involved in one of the causes of aged poverty, the erosion of the real value of people's savings by inflation; in allowing unions and corporations to raise wages and prices, we sacrifice the interests of past participants in the productive process to those of present participants. Furthermore, discrimination is at the root of the high incidence of poverty among households headed by women; for our society discriminates against the participation of women in the more remunerative employment opportunities in countless ways: Through giving women inferior educational opportunities, through restricting the job opportunities open to them and denying them promotion on equal terms with men, and through insisting that women with young children should remain home to look after them, which both prevents women from acquiring the employment experience necessary to command good jobs should they eventually have to support themselves, and prevents them from working, or from working full time, if they find themselves in the position of heading families with young children. Finally, I suspect that discrimination is partly responsible for the association of poverty with low levels of educational attainment, in the sense that a requirement of educational qualifications may frequently be less a matter of the necessity of the education than of a simple means of narrowing down the applicants that have to be considered to a manageable number.

—Harry G. Johnson
Professor of Economics
University of Chicago

Distinguishing Ends and Means

Confusion of ends and means is a near and present danger in the statement of the antipoverty goal. Antipoverty work should be distinguished from a generalized helping and doing good for people. Many people have trouble distinguishing the poverty problem from other problems such as unequal access to the protection of the laws, lack of education, lack of housing, lack of health services, delinquency and crime, limited citizen participation, spiritual and cultural deprivation, lack of fellowship, and geographic isolation. These problems are not exclusive to the poor—if government sets out to help the sick and disturbed, or those who need or want better housing, not only may the greater part of the help go to the nonpoor but it may do precious little to reduce poverty.

In instituting antipoverty programs there is a danger that these programs will be identified as "good things," that we may never get around to measuring whether the original end is being accomplished and, if so, whether the programs have had anything to do with it. The confusion is only somewhat lessened if we insist that the programs be of benefit to the poor exclusively. Poverty reduction does not mean merely "doing something for the poor" any more than economic growth means "doing something for business." There is value in continually relating means back to the end.

Students of poverty have long noted that the poor are different, alien, even barbarous (as George Bernard Shaw called them) and few have argued that poverty is character-building. But there has long been debate over the question put by Sir Benjamin Thompson in 1790:

> To make vicious and abandoned people happy, it has generally been supposed necessary to make them virtuous. But why not reverse this order? Why not make them first happy, and then virtuous?

Many remedies are in effect now, and the question is one of how far and how fast to extend them. Some critics have claimed that most of the contemporary American poor are not isolated and alienated and would respond favorably to better job opportunities or to more transfer payments. I suppose all are agreed that most of the "change the poor" remedies would be more effective if the poor were not so poor, and if they had clearer evidence that reform would lead to better employment prospects. But, also, all are agreed that some programs to change the attitudes, motivations, and potential productivity of the poor—and particularly of poor children—can make an independent contribution to a faster rate of poverty reduction, allowing for a time lag of one or two decades.

—Robert J. Lampman
Professor of Economics
University of Wisconsin

. . . .

Skills Development

Labor's functional share of national income has been rising. The demand for workers with high skills has been increasing at a higher rate than that for low skills. The incentive to increase skills has been strong and the supply of skills has been responding; for people have been investing much more than formerly to increase their skills.

A substantial part of poverty is a consequence of a number of disequilibria, among them these three:

1. The market for the skills that are required in agriculture has been long depressed. Although the labor force devoted to farming has declined by one-half since 1940, the market for these skills is still in serious disequilibrium. Older members of this labor force have had no real alternative but to settle for the depressed, salvage value of the skills they possess. In many farm areas the quality of elementary and secondary schooling has been and continues to be far below par, and thus the oncoming generation from these areas is ill prepared to take advantage of the strong market in other parts of the economy for high skills. Thus it should not come as a surprise that although farm families are presently a very small fraction of all U.S. families, they account for much of the observed poverty, and that many of the families in urban areas who are below the poverty line have recently come from our farms.

2. The market for the skills of Negroes has also been long depressed, and the poverty component here is large. This market has been intertwined with that of agriculture; and both on our farms and in our cities, there has been and continues to be much job discrimination.

3. The South is burdened with much more poverty than other regions, basically for three reasons: It is more dependent upon agriculture than the rest of the United States; the labor force in the South is more largely Negro than in the North and West, and in terms of marketable skills the Negroes in the South are even worse off than the Negroes in other regions; and relatively more of the whites in the labor force in the South have low skills than whites in other regions.

> —Theodore W. Schultz
> Professor of Economics
> University of Chicago

The Negative Income Tax

If reasonable rates of economic growth are maintained for another decade, the poverty gap will be so small that it will be foolish not "to take arms against [this small] sea of troubles, and by opposing, end them." A point will be reached—and it will come before 1975—when it will be possible by means of a negative income tax and a public works program to abolish economic poverty as that term is now defined.

The program might work something like this. Each family would have to file an income tax return. Those with incomes under $3,000 (the amount would vary by size of family) would be given the option of going to work on a public works project or participating in a training program for which they would receive payment at the rate of $3,000 a year. Exceptions would be made for the aged, disabled, and several other groups that would receive payment without working or training.

If such a program had been in existence in 1963 it would have involved the transfer of about $21 billion—about 3 percent of the gross national product—from the wealthiest 80 percent of the families to the poorest 20 percent. In 1963, about 9 million families had incomes under $3,000. If these families derived their entire support from the government, the cost would have been about $27 billion; however, they received about $6 billion in that year in the form of transfer payments. The net additional cost, therefore, would have been about $21 billion. There are, of course, other costs and benefits that enter into the equation; but let us postpone consideration of those items for the moment.

The application of the same proposal in 1975 would cost only about $13 billion (in 1962 purchasing power). This calculation is based on an assumed rate of growth of 4 percent a year in average family income. On this basis, only 5.7 million families would have incomes under $3,000 (in 1962 purchasing power) in 1975. If they derived all of their income from the government, the cost would be about $17 billion. This total, however, would include about $4 billion paid out under existing programs. The net additional cost, therefore, would be about $13 billion, or roughly 1 percent of the GNP in that year.

If the above calculations are correct, the great day may nearly be here when it will be possible for all Americans to have their basic physical needs met at currently acceptable standards without taking a pauper's oath and without losing dignity and self-respect. Economic poverty in the United States rests on a very weak foundation. Even if allowance is made for moderate increases in the poverty line, its ultimate defeat is only a matter of time—10 years or 20 at the most.

—Herman P. Miller
Institute of Government and Public Affairs
University of California at Los Angeles

41

How About the Non-Negro Poor?

from U. S. News & World Report

Poverty among Negroes is often given as a reason for riots which have rocked city after city of the United States.

The impression appears to be widespread that the nation's poor are mostly in Negro "ghettos," which, says a Negro psychologist, Dr. Kenneth B. Clark, "now represent a nuclear stockpile which can annihilate the very foundations of America."

Negroes are demanding—and getting—influential roles in antipoverty programs. "Poverty action" blocs in big cities are being organized by activists of the Negro-rights movement.

LO, THE POOR WHITES. Statistics of the Federal Government show, however, that there are more than twice as many poor whites as poor nonwhites in the U. S.

Also brought out is this fact: Descendants of the American Indians, who were holding the country when the white men arrived, are poorest of all —far worse off than Negroes.

In 1963, the last year for which details by color are available, the Social Security Administration reported that there were 23.9 million poor whites and 10.7 million poor nonwhites in this country.

Negroes make up about 92 per cent of the nonwhite population; American Indians, 2½ per cent. Japanese, Chinese, Filipinos and other nonwhites, among whom poverty is not a great problem account for the remaining 5½ per cent.

MEASURE OF POVERTY. The gauge of poverty used by the Government was income below about $3,100 a year for a four-person family. For an individual, the figure is $1,540.

No "insurrections" such as those staged by Negro mobs in Los Angeles, New York, Chicago, Philadelphia, Rochester and other cities have occurred among the non-Negro poor. In that category are, for example, the American Indians; Puerto Ricans in slums of New York City; Mexican-Americans in the Southwest; jobless whites in the nation's largest depressed area,

Reprinted from the October 4, 1965, issue of *U. S. News & World Report,* published at Washington, D.C.

Appalachia, and the "refugees" from Appalachia who live under conditions of dire poverty in Chicago and other cities.

Questions arise: How do these people differ from rioting Negroes in outlook and in "rights" and opportunities? What is their attitude toward society? Toward family responsibilities? Toward police? Are efforts made to organize them for "protests" against poverty?

To get answers, members of the staff of "U. S. News & World Report" investigated conditions and attitudes among the non-Negro poor in various parts of the country. Their reports follow.

AMERICAN INDIANS.   Without question, the American Indians are the most poverty-striken ethnic group found in the U. S.

Surviving now are about 550,000 Indians. Of these, an estimated 380,-000 live on or near reservations, with a median family income of $1,500 —less than half the median family income for Negroes, and about one fourth the median figure for all U. S. families.

Unemployment on most reservations runs 40 to 50 per cent. Indians lack the education and skills needed to compete for jobs. There are exceptions—such as the Indians of the Mohawk tribe who earn high pay as structural-steel workers. But the exceptions are few.

HOVELS, SHANTIES, SHACKS.   Nine out of 10 dwellings in which Indian families live on or adjacent to reservations—where summers usually are blistering hot, winters bleak and cold—are far below minimum standards for urban housing. They are hovels, shantylike hogans, tar-paper shacks.

Compared to non-Indian babies, the Indian child born on a reservation has only one half the chance of reaching his first birthday. Life expectancy for reservation-dwelling Indians is two thirds of the U. S. average.

Indians are not "wards of the Government." They are American citizens, free to work and live where they please. But efforts by the Government to "integrate" Indians by encouraging them to move to cities have not been very successful.

Of the estimated 170,000 who have left reservations to take jobs in cities and towns, not many have prospered. Most live in slums. About one third of the Indians who have been persuaded to relocate in cities wind up back on a reservation.

A PROUD RACE.   Unlike Negroes, Indians are not much interested in racial "integration." They are proud of their ancestry, willing to let the white man go his way while they go theirs.

Since most Indians find it hard to adjust to the white man's ways, those who do remain in cities tend to live close together. They do not complain of "segregation."

Indians, it is found, do have some advantages over poverty-stricken whites and Negroes. A number of special Government programs have been set up to aid Indians. Among such programs:

1. The U. S. Public Health Service provides complete medical attention for Indians on reservations. Indians who live nearby are eligible, too.

2. Education of most Indian children is wholly or partly subsidized by the Federal Government.

3. The Government manages the timber and mineral resources of Indian-owned lands, valued at 6 billion dollars. Some tribes—Navajos, for example—reap profits from oil, uranium and timber.

4. Some vocational training is provided and some assistance is given in finding jobs.

5. Special inducements are offered to employers who will locate plants near Indian reservations.

POVERTY NOT LICKED. In the last 15 years, more than 2 billion dollars has been spent by the Government to help Indians. This exceeds the total spent for that purpose in the preceding 150 years.

Yet, by and large, Indians remain desperately poor. Along with the problems of poverty, they sometimes find themselves discriminated against by whites in some parts of the West.

But no demonstrations are organized for "Indian rights."

PUERTO RICANS. Hundreds of thousands of Puerto Ricans have come north in search of a better life. Many, however, have been unable to escape from the clutches of poverty.

Among big cities, New York has the largest concentration of Puerto Ricans—about 750,000. Most of them are poor.

Problems faced by Puerto Ricans are described in a paper presented recently by three officers of the Puerto Rican Bar Association of New York:

"Seeking the pot of gold at the end of the rainbow, the Puerto Rican has gambled away his customs, norms and mores. He has accepted the challenge of living in a new environment which is regulated by different standards of behavior, many foreign to his own. He has thrust himself from a rural environment to a highly complex urban society, which has, as an added barrier, a different language of communication.

"The migrant Puerto Rican has inherited from earlier migrants to the urban metropolis of the United States the slum dwellings, the unskilled jobs, the high rate of unemployment, the prejudices and other maladies inherent in the lives of the poverty-stricken. . . ."

Many Puerto Ricans in New York City suffer the same privations that were blamed for Negro riots in the summer of 1964—rat-infested tenements, lack of job opportunities, a "ghetto" existence. Puerto Ricans, however, have not vented their frustrations in demonstrations and large-scale violence. Why?

Joseph Monserrat, a Puerto Rican whose job is to help fellow Puerto Ricans adjust to the pressures of big-city life, says this:

"One thing to remember about Puerto Ricans is that as yet we do not have ingrained in us the fact that we are a minority. In Puerto Rico, when you hear people talking about 'la minoria'—the minority—they are talking about the losing party in an election; they're not talking about a group of people."

PREFER TO NEGOTIATE.　The direct-action methods that militant Negro leaders advocate in drives to achieve gains for Negroes are shunned by most leaders of New York City's Puerto Ricans.

"Historically, we have been negotiators," one Puerto Rican commented. "We tend to feel that negotiation, rather than direct action, is a more appropriate approach to the solution of our problems."

From Julius Hernandez, who for years has been prominent in New York City's Puerto Rican community:

"Puerto Ricans haven't rioted because our attitude is different from that of the Negro. With us, racial prejudice is not a factor. The Puerto Rican just hasn't experienced it the way the Negro has.

"Also, we have strong family ties, a respect for the father and the older members of a family. I think that strong parental influence has been the main force in preventing disorderly outbursts by Puerto Ricans."

"Police brutality" is a charge often heard among Puerto Ricans, as among Negroes. But many Puerto Ricans, according to Mr. Hernandez, feel that "the police department is doing everything possible to achieve better relations."

MEXICAN-AMERICANS.　People with Spanish surnames—most of them Mexican-Americans—number more than 3.5 million in the five States where the census makes this distinction. The States are California, Texas, New Mexico, Arizona and Colorado.

A great many of these people are classed, by federal standards, as poor.

In California, they lag behind both whites and Negroes in education and housing.

Most authorities agree that anarchy of the type that erupted in the Los Angeles Negro district of Watts is not likely to explode among Mexican-Americans—although there have been clashes between gangs of Mexican-American youths and police in the past.

It is pointed out that in the Southwest, which was pioneered by Spanish-speaking explorers, the Spanish language still is widely used and found in historical and place names; as a result, many Mexican-Americans do not consider themselves in a minority group.

THEY FEEL THEY BELONG.　Also, a sociologist said, strong family ties give Mexican-Americans a "feeling of belonging," often lacking among impoverished Negroes. Attitudes toward religion, including opposition to divorce, are said to contribute to family unity.

Because his skin color does not set him apart, the Mexican-American usually is not subjected to overt discrimination. José Castorena, an employe of the California Fair Employment Practice Commission, says that "most Mexicans probably are able to find housing anywhere they can afford it." Antonio Rios, president of the Los Angeles County Community Service Organization, comments that "the Mexican group tends to mix with others very easily." This means, according to Cruz Reynosa, deputy director of the State FEPC, that "it is very easy to drop the Mexican ways."

Through the years, many Mexican-Americans in Los Angeles have felt, as one put it, that "the police are there to protect the white Anglo-Saxon community and to see that Negroes and Mexican-Americans don't get out of hand."

It is generally conceded, however, according to Mr. Rios, that, of late, "a better feeling exists between police and the Mexican-American community."

THE TEXAS WAY. Texas, which has more than 1.5 million Mexican-Americans, provides examples of the kind of assimilation that eliminates reasons for protests, demonstrations or riots.

San Antonio, for instance, is 45 per cent Mexican-American. Many of the city's "Latinos" are poor, but this does not cause tension.

"The Mexican-Americans here," said one, "don't take to the streets to protest something. As voters, they feel they can get better results at the polls."

"Success" stories seemingly have much to do with the nontruculent attitude of the Mexican-American poor. One such story was told recently by U. S. District Judge Reynaldo Garza, a Mexican-American who was appointed to the federal bench in 1961. The story was about a Mexican girl who entered the U. S. by swimming across the Rio Grande.

As Judge Garza told it—

"My family once hired a Mexican maid who had first come to my home as a wetback. She was dripping wet. I had to get her papers for her. Today, this maid and her husband live in Los Angeles, own an apartment and store, and the wife has a chauffeur to drive her around. Keep in mind that this was a little wetback who came to my house in 1946. Isn't that a success story? It's happening all over the country. Where else in the world would people have such opportunity?"

Negroes, Judge Garza said, should give the Civil Rights Acts of 1964 and 1965 "a chance to work." He added:

"I don't subscribe to the philosophy that we should placate people because they have been kept down too long. All wrongs can be righted within the framework of government."

POOR WHITES. Problems of poverty among Negroes have been dramatized again and again—not only in riots that have flared suddenly, but by massive "demonstrations," carefully organized.

There have been no "poor white" riots, however. No huge demonstrations have been organized to draw attention to the plight of poverty-stricken whites.

Millions of people in this category live in rural areas. Appalachia is one example, with its total of 1.2 million poor families.

Many millions more live in cities, most of them in neighborhoods that are congested and deteriorating, though not called "ghettos."

One of the largest concentrations of poor whites is in Chicago. An anti-poverty official there says that a majority are "refugees" from the mountain regions of Southern Appalachia.

A north-side Chicago neighborhood called Uptown has long been the "port of entry" for newcomers from Appalachia. The story of the poor whites of Uptown was told by Raleigh Campbell, executive director of the Council of the Southern Mountains, Inc., a private organization.

A WHITE EXODUS. When automation and the decline of coal mining hit Southern mountain areas after World War II, white inhabitants began to leave.

At first, Mr. Campbell said, they tended to move into such nearby cities as Cincinnati and Dayton, looking for unskilled or semiskilled jobs. There still are large numbers of poor-white mountain people in those cities. But in the last 10 years, as jobs became more and more scarce, many moved to larger cities, notably Chicago. They ran into the same problem—no jobs.

Thousands headed for Chicago's Uptown, where they might find kinfolk and old friends.

What are their problems? One, of course, is unemployment. Another is housing.

"The housing is unbelievable," Mr. Campbell said. "The people are crowded into small apartments. The furniture is old and dingy. Rents are extremely high. But the people live there because the apartments are available without leases and tenants can pay by the week."

Another problem is education. Many of the white parents are functionally or completely illiterate. This affects their children, who fall behind in school.

"Impoverished Negroes here are in some ways better off than the poor whites," Mr. Campbell said. "Negroes know the city and can take advantage of some of its services. They are urbanized. The poverty-stricken Southern white comes in with no idea of what to expect. He doesn't even know how to use public transportation here."

UNWANTED WELFARE. According to Mr. Campbell, the attitude of the mountain people toward welfare handouts appears to be unusual. He said:

"You hear that the hillbillies come to Chicago to get on the welfare rolls because they can make more from welfare than they can earn in the mountains. But the public-aid department says that fewer Appalachians are on welfare than other groups.

"Some of them in Chicago do finally give up and go on welfare. But many of them say 'No' to welfare and struggle on."

Do the Appalachians indicate any desire to organize and demonstrate?

No, said Mr. Campbell, adding:

"They have pride in their background and in each other. They try to help one another. Many of them are succeeding on their own, and then moving out."

Summing up, you find:

1. The non-Negro poor, for the most part, do not consider themselves oppressed or abused.

2. They are not organized to exert pressure or demonstrate. They have no such nationwide organizations as the National Association for the Advancement of Colored People, the Congress of Racial Equality, the Urban League.

3. The kind of resentment that sparks riots is not widespread among the non-Negro poor. The chief reason appears to be that a white person, no matter how poverty stricken, can move up the ladder more easily than a Negro.

20

LABOR RELATIONS AND THE PUBLIC WELFARE

No AREA IN OUR ECONOMY is the source of more problems than that which involves the relations between employers and organized labor. In our first selection a group of leading businessmen attempt to view unions objectively: their powers, their functions, and the problems which they create. In our second reading, "Unions and Politics," Jack Barbash surveys the historical stages by which unions have reached their present active participation in politics. He then describes and analyzes the nature of their political activities. He believes that American unionism now has a realistic and responsible conception of its political role, and that it has strengthened our democracy by diffusing political power and by challenging our economic system to share its favors more broadly.

42

The Businessman Looks at Unions

by the Research and Policy Committee
of the Committee for Economic Development

Unionism in America is very old—older than the Republic. Unions, when desired by the workers, have useful functions in our society and to perform these functions unions need certain kinds and degrees of power. Workers should be able to form unions of sufficient power to represent them effectively in negotiations with employers that affect terms and conditions of their employment. At the same time unions should not have so much power that they can injure or dominate consumers or workers, of whom the vast majority are not union members, or interfere with the growth and prosperity of the economy as a whole.

The problem is how to permit unions the powers they need to carry out their valuable, socially-beneficial, functions without allowing them power to injure others.

This statement presents an appraisal of the powers and performance of unions in America as they affect the national interest and offers recommendations for making the powers and conduct of unions more consistent with and conducive to the national interest.

This statement is written by a group of businessmen who employ labor and sell its product. Our experience as employers of labor undoubtedly influences our appraisal of the facts and our conception of the national interest. As we have worked on this statement we have been aware that this may be a source of bias. We have sought to guard against this danger by consulting with others of different backgrounds and by examining our own ideas with great care.

Under this title we reprint the "Introduction and Summary" of a Statement on National Policy published by the Committee for Economic Development (CED) in March, 1964, and called *Union Powers and Union Functions: Toward a Better Balance.* By permission of the CED, 711 Fifth Ave., New York, N. Y. 10022.

The CED is a voluntary organization of leading businessmen whose primary objective is to further the national welfare by bringing about a better understanding of the nature and functions of our free economy.

We offer this statement as a contribution to a national discussion in which many voices will be heard and should be heard. As an earlier contribution to this national discussion we arranged for the publication of a study "The Public Interest in National Labor Policy," by a group of outstanding experts. Our own conclusions agree in some respects with those of that study but differ on other important points.

It should be clear that we deal in this statement only with the conditions that exist where workers are organized in unions. The problems that exist in the more common, nonunion, situations are not treated here.

The Search for Balance

The problem of balancing powers and functions is not confined to unions; it exists for most institutions of our society, including business and government. A variety of means have been used to maintain balance —competition in the private economy, a mutually limiting relationship between government and the private economy, constitutional limitations on government, the balance of powers among branches of government and between the federal government and the states, the force of public opinion, and the voluntary exercise of power in a socially responsible way by those who have it. No once-for-all, permanent solution of the problem of power with respect to any major institution has been found. Instead we are continuously adapting the solutions to changing circumstances and objectives. Examples are changes in the relation between Congress and the Executive, or in the relations between the federal government and the states, or in the anti-trust laws.[1] This process has achieved a reasonable working balance between the powers and functions of the various power centers of the American society much of the time, although from time to time serious imbalances have emerged or at least been claimed.

The search for a suitable policy towards the powers of labor unions has a long history in the United States. We shall recall the highlights of that history only for the last thirty years. The passage of the Norris-LaGuardia Act in 1932, the National Industrial Recovery Act in 1933, and the National Labor Relations Act in 1935 marked a fundamental development in national policy. This legislation removed certain obstacles to the effective organization and operation of unions and established the right of workers to organize and bargain collectively, free of interference from their employer. It is significant that these laws came at the depth of the Great Depression of the 1930's, when mass unemployment and great economic distress were widely interpreted as evidence that the workings of the market place could not adequately protect the interest of workers.

[1] *The Public Interest in National Labor Policy.* By an Independent Study Group, Clark Kerr, Chairman. New York, Committee for Economic Development, 1961.

Union organization proceeded rapidly during the recovery of the late 1930's and during World War II. In 1930 less than 7 per cent of the labor force was organized in unions; by 1947 the proportion had risen to 25 per cent. With general acceptance of labor's right to organize, the violence that had once accompanied organizing efforts became much less frequent. In thousands of firms, unions and management came to mutually satisfactory arrangements for reaching and carrying out agreements governing terms and conditions of employment.

Despite these accomplishments, there was much concern, at the end of the War, with some aspects of unionism as it then existed. Some unions had attained power to close down a whole industry, or any part of it, by a strike, and by threatening to do so could gain wage increases without significant restraint by competition from other workers not represented by the union. In many firms and industries unions had obtained contracts which required union membership as a condition of employment, depriving some workers of freedom to choose whether or not to belong to a union and restricting employment opportunities by limiting union membership. A union representing employees in one firm could use its power there, through a secondary boycott,[2] to force organization of other firms. In some cases union policies were dominated by entrenched leadership that neither represented nor solicited the wishes of the union membership.

Realization of the extent of the powers that unions had acquired, highlighted by a number of nation-wide strikes and by local violence in the immediate postwar years, led to a search for ways to create a better balanced situation. The chief steps were taken in the Taft-Hartley Act of 1947 and the Landrum-Griffin Act of 1959. Among other things, this legislation:

a) Established a procedure by which a strike that threatened to create a national emergency could be postponed, by government action, for an 80-day "cooling-off" period.

b) Prohibited the "closed shop" (in which prior union membership is a condition for obtaining employment), established certain safeguards of workers' rights in a union shop (in which joining a union is a condition for retaining employment), and authorized the states to prohibit the union shop.

c) Limited the use of unfair labor practices, including secondary boycotts.

d) Required procedures favorable to more democracy within unions.

We believe that the national labor legislation adopted in the past generation, taken as a whole, has been constructive. To return to the situation

---

[2] Secondary boycotts and pressures attempt to induce workers or employers not directly involved in a labor dispute to cease doing business with the employer who has a dispute with the union.

which existed before 1932, or before 1947, or before 1959, would be highly undesirable. However, there is no reason to think that in the field of labor policy we have reached the best of possible worlds. Indeed, there is much evidence of concern in this country with excessive powers of labor unions.

Labor Organization and the National Interest

Unionism affects the national interest in many ways. It affects the economic performance of the nation—the rate of economic growth, the level of employment and unemployment, the stability of prices, and the distribution of income. It also has a fundamental influence upon the character of our society—on the freedom that individuals enjoy, on the equity of the relations among individuals and among groups, and on the role of government in relation to private institutions and individuals. There are wide differences among unions in their powers, structures, and policies; to generalize about American unions, therefore, is dangerous. Nevertheless, consideration of public policy toward organizations of labor must rest upon a judgment of the influences that unionism now exerts.

1. A basic characteristic of the American society is that we do not like to see people pushed around. As one aspect of this, we do not want workers to be subjected to arbitrary and indifferent treatment by employers with no defense except the threat to quit, a threat too costly to carry out in most cases. *Unions have played a large part directly and indirectly in making and applying equitable rules governing on-the-job relationships.*

To perform this function unions required a certain degree of power. Workers needed enough power relative to their employer to induce him, if necessary, to change his personnel practices. The value to the employees of many of the changes made was often overlooked by the employer. To bring about these changes, however, did not require unions to have the power that many of them now have. It did not require a union to have sufficient power in relation to the whole industry to impose large cost increases on the industry and its customers.

2. *That groups of people should organize to present their desires to the government and to work for adoption of government policies they favor is both legitimate and necessary in a democracy. For many interests of many workers this function is performed by labor unions.*

It is not necessary that the political interests of workers should be represented by organizations—i.e. labor unions—that also represent workers in collective bargaining. The other sectors of the economy, such as business and agriculture, are represented in the political process by associations that do not exercise collective bargaining power. In many other countries labor is politically represented by organizations which, while closely allied to unions, do not perform the economic functions of unions. The political representation of American labor by unions rather than by purely political organizations has disadvantages, including its tendency to give excessive weight to the interests of organized labor as compared with the interests of the large majority of American workers who are not union members. However, the system also has some advantages. It probably tends to focus attention of American labor on collective bargaining rather than on the effort to invoke the power of government to change conditions best left to private decision-making.

3. *The freedom of individuals to associate with each other, for almost any purpose, is one of the basic American freedoms. We value this freedom for its own sake and as a bulwark of other freedoms. The freedom of workers to associate in labor unions is, in general, guaranteed by present law and the union movement is an effective vehicle for the exercise of this freedom.* Nevertheless there are troublesome exceptions to this general principle. For the individual worker the significant freedom may not be the right to join or form "a" union but to join the particular union that is legally designated to represent him or that controls access to the employment which he seeks. Many unions are able to deny this right to workers seeking membership or employment, and some have done so, in order to limit the supply of their particular variety of labor skill, in order to discriminate against certain groups, or for other reasons.

Private association is a freedom, and private associations are legally protected because they are an expression of the voluntary choice of individuals. The freedom not to join a private association is equally precious and deserving of protection. This principle has substantial recognition in labor law. Nevertheless, in the 30 states where this is legal, unions have been able to use their power to obtain contracts requiring that all employees covered by the contract become union members. Employment may thus be denied to an individual if he does not join the union.

4. *A major accomplishment of American labor policy is the degree to which it has kept government out of the determination of specific employment conditions.* Government has undertaken to assure the ability of the private parties, singly or collectively, to deal with each other freely and without interference. The underlying philosophy has been that the government should not otherwise influence the decisions that are reached, and that the public interest in these decisions will be best served if they are made by the private parties directly involved. This philosophy in turn rests upon the belief that the power of both parties to collective bargaining will be limited by competitive forces which prevent their using their powers to the detriment of the wider public.

Nevertheless this principle has not been followed with complete consistency. *There seems to be danger of increasing government intervention to affect the consequences of collective bargaining.* This results in part from failure to draw a sharp line between government's proper role in assuring that collective bargaining can go on and government's interference with the substance of bargaining. But the danger results more seriously from the hard choice that arises if either or both of the private parties has excessive power, so that their freely-reached agreements cannot be assumed to serve the public interest.

5. *Probably the most visible consequence of unionism to many Americans is the occasional dramatic nation-wide or city-wide strike of a critical industry.* Strikes have been a source of inconvenience to almost everyone at some time and of hardship to many, and some firms have been forced out of business by them. But in relation to the size of the American economy, losses from strikes have been comparatively small.

6. *The stronger unions have been able to raise the incomes of their employed members, absolutely and relative to the incomes of other workers. In doing so they have been able to increase the percentage share of the nation's output received by their employed members and thus to reduce the percentage share received by the rest of the population. We do not believe that it is in the general interest for any group to have as much power as some unions do to force a redistribution of income in their favor by collectively withholding their productive services or threatening to do so.*

To raise the incomes of their members is, of course, one of the main objectives of unions. There is no reason to doubt that where unions are very strong, covering a whole industry or craft and substantially free of competition, they have succeeded in this objective.

The conclusion that strong unions have been able to gain for their employed members a larger share of the nation's output and thereby reduce the share received by other workers is not always obvious. For example, it might seem that all workers gain when strong unions gain because the winning of a wage increase by one of the stronger unions usually causes an increase in wages paid to other workers in the same company or in the same area. However, this is only one of the forces set in motion when one of the stronger unions wins a big wage increase. The big rise in wages or other labor costs won by a strong union for its members tends to limit employment in the industry covered by the union by raising its costs and forcing it to raise its prices if it can. The rise in prices restricts sales and the rise in labor costs intensifies the effort by that industry to save labor. Workers who might have been employed in the industry will have to seek work elsewhere and this will both retard wage increases elsewhere and probably leave some workers unemployed.

At the same time, the spreading effect of the big wage increase won by the stronger union will force up prices not only in the industry which it covers but also in other industries which are more or less forced to follow with wage increases. These higher prices will be paid by all workers, as consumers, and this will offset a large part of the gain in money income received by other workers and especially those whose wage increases were smallest.

This whole process is superimposed on the rise of real wage rates as real output per worker rises, which has been going on for a long time in the American economy—long before labor unions were important. As a result the wages of all workers rise, despite the increase in the share taken by employed members of the strong unions. The effect of the activity of strong unions has been to get their members a larger share, and to leave other people a smaller share, of the income gains resulting from the general increase in output per worker.

7. The preceding discussion has related to the effects of union activity on the distribution of the *real* national income. That discussion did not deal with the effects of union activity on the average level of prices.

It seems probable that union power contributes to a tendency for money wage rates and fringe benefit costs in general to rise more rapidly than productivity with the result that production costs on the average rise. In this situation the country would have a difficult choice between inflation and excessive unemployment, the most probable outcome being some of each. Fear of this possibility has led to increased government concern with the results of the collective bargaining process and increased government intervention in that process.

We can summarize our observations on the relation between labor organization and the national interest in the following way: Under present law unions are permitted and have attained sufficient power to act for workers in on-the-job relationships, to represent the interests of organized workers in the political process and, in general, to effectuate workers' freedom of association. These are valuable functions, in the national interest, and should be protected. On the other hand, the freedom of some workers to join or not to join a union and to seek employment has been restricted; some unions have been able to raise incomes of their employed members at the expense of other parts of the population, especially other workers; and there has been some contribution to the danger of inflation and unemployment.

We seek measures that will assure the continued performance of unions' useful functions while reducing the magnitude and danger of their adverse consequences and while limiting the extent of government intervention in labor relations. Concerned as we are about excessive union power, we are equally concerned about government power. One of the dangers we see in the growth of union power is the temptation it provides for assumption of more power by government.

Summary of Recommendations

For the purposes of this statement we divide the sources of union power into two parts. The first part is pure market power—the power of a group of workers to withhold their labor to win gains for themselves. The second part consists of a number of conditions, mainly defined by law, that affect the environment in which market power is used and the uses to which it can be put. Given the degree of market power a union has, the scale and character of its effects will be influenced by the countervailing measures employers may legally take, by the rigor and impartiality with which laws against violence are enforced, by the circumstances and purposes of government intervention in disputes, by the ability of unions to enforce or prevent membership of workers, and so on.

In the section of this statement which follows this summary we offer the following recommendations:

1. Every worker should have the right to decide freely to belong or not to belong to a union.

2. Racial or other discriminatory barriers to union membership, apprenticeship or employment should be eliminated. The equal right of all qualified workers to join the union in their trade or industry should be recognized by law. The right of any worker to belong to the union that represents him should not be denied except for nonpayment of dues or similar good cause.

3. United States courts should be authorized to issue a restraining order or injunction against unions in cases involving strikes in violation of a labor agreement, as they are now authorized to compel an employer to accept arbitration of disputes arising under agreements.

4. The right of employers, singly or collectively, to use the lockout in the bargaining process should not be diluted by the National Labor Relations Board (NLRB) or the courts. This right should be clarified in the law if necessary to avoid dilution. The employer's right to use the lockout is the counterpart of the union's right to strike.

5. There is need for legislation in most states aimed at limiting the use of union resources for political purposes.

6. The intent of Congress to outlaw pressure by a union against a party with whom it has no dispute (secondary boycott) should be carried out, and the law should be clarified if reasonable interpretation of the present language proves incapable of preventing evasions.

7. Laws against violence and the threat of violence, which tend to coerce through fear, should be respected and enforced in labor disputes by federal, state, and local authorities.

8. The present provisions in the Taft-Hartley Act for government action in national emergency disputes should be retained. The recent tendency toward increasing government intervention in the settlement of labor disputes, through "fact-finding" or the participation of high public officials or otherwise, except through mediation, should be halted.

9. Determination of the form and content of collective bargaining should be left to the parties. The present legal requirement to bargain "in good faith" should not be left as a vague demand for good conduct that will lead and has in fact led to uncertainty, confusion, excessive government intervention, and a morass of bureaucratic legislation—all detrimental to free collective bargaining.

The effect of this provision of law has been not to assure bargaining in good faith but to involve the NLRB in determining both how bargaining should be conducted and the substance of the bargain. In lieu of this provision, if there are any actions by either party that should be required or prohibited they should be specified in law. Deletion of the present legal requirement would not allow either party to escape bargaining, because bargaining results from the economic necessity of the parties to reach an agreement in order to continue production and employment.

10. Unfair labor practice cases should be handled in a more judicial way. The NLRB, which now handles them, should be given more of the attributes of a court, or jurisdiction over such cases should be transferred to a court especially designated for them.

These measures would, we believe, help to protect the rights of workers, defend the freedom of the collective bargaining process, and reduce certain legal inequalities between unions and employers without impairing the ability of unions to perform their proper functions. It is also necessary to consider possible steps going beyond these. The foregoing measures would leave essentially untouched the basic market power of unions, the power to withhold collectively the labor of all or most of the workers in a particular industry or craft, and the use of that power to determine compensation and conditions of employment.

Among the suggestions that have been advanced for dealing with excessive market power of unions are: limiting the size of a union to the employees of a single employer, prohibiting a union from bargaining with two or more competing employers and prohibiting collusion among unions dealing with competing employers, prohibiting industry-wide bargaining, prohibiting combinations among unions where the effect is substantially to lessen competition, and directing the appropriate government agency to take the effect on competition into account when certifying a particular union to represent a particular group of workers. All of these suggestions attempt to introduce a larger degree of competition into labor markets. An alternative approach is to prohibit the use of union power for certain specified purposes, including direct limitation of production, control of prices, and interference with the adoption of new production methods.

We are not prepared to make recommendations with respect to any of these suggestions. Some may be unnecessarily drastic, others may be ineffective. Some may put too much discretionary power in the hands of government, others may be impossible to administer. Better alternatives than any of these may be devised. Nevertheless, some of these suggestions, perhaps with modification, may on balance be desirable. More study will be required before responsible recommendations can be made.

The problem with which these suggestions attempt to deal is a real one. It is basically that in important parts of the economy the compensation and use of a basic productive resource—labor—is, with legal sanction, unduly insulated from the control and guidance of competition. To the extent that labor unions use their power to control the use of other resources, such as management ingenuity and new production methods, these too become unduly insulated from competition. This is a fact of profound significance in a society like ours, where private economic freedom is partly, though not solely, justified by competition, which limits power and directs private activity to the effective and economical provision of the goods and services demanded by the community.

43

Unions and Politics

by Jack Barbash

Workers organize and join unions to secure decent wages, equitable treatment on their jobs, and satisfaction in their work. Most workers see their union's role in politics as an extension of these work-site interests. The specific interaction between work-site organization and political organization is a function of a number of factors: specifically, the stage of industrial development, the way the organized work force is distributed between (roughly) skilled and unskilled workers, and the prevailing ideologies and ambitions of union leaders. All of these factors operate in the broader setting of a pluralistic democracy.

The American labor movement has come to its present political position in four stages. In the first stage a labor movement emerged among skilled workers who had not yet reconciled themselves to permanent wage-earner status in the emerging regime of capitalist industrialism. Their unions aimed, therefore, at fending off industrialism's fragmenting effect on their skills and job controls.

Beginning with the late 1820s local unions and central bodies sponsored a scattering of local labor parties espousing political and social reforms: for example, extension of education and elimination of imprisonment for debt. Later, unions were strongly influenced by various humanitarian and "utopian" movements. Whether working class politics or utopian visions, the union political expression at this time had one thing in common: it was a recoil from a burgeoning capitalism and a protest against a rationalized, atomized and competitive society. Even before Marx entered the scene, disaffected middle-class intellectuals articulated this protest and tried to channel the workers' anticapitalist, anti-industrial leanings into producers' cooperatives, currency reform, temperance and independent parties. The Knights of Labor marked the full flowering and then the decline of this sort of middle-class reform temper in American labor politics.

From *Challenge,* The Magazine of Economic Affairs, December, 1964, pp. 36–40. A publication of Challenge Communications, Inc., 475 Fifth Avenue, New York 10017. Reprinted by permission.
Jack Barbash is Professor of Labor Education and Economics at the University of Wisconsin.

The Industrial Revolution became the dominant feature of the economic landscape after the Civil War. And in the generation following, the workers reacted by constructing a labor movement based on national craft unionism strongly disposed toward job-control collective bargaining and against politics except as a marginal activity. The major issue in this period was between the socialists and the "pure and simple" trade unionists over political action. The pure and simple unionists opted for pressure group politics epitomized in the well-known "reward your friends and defeat your enemies" slogan, and such pressures as were exerted favored immediate job interests. The socialists argued for the labor movement's integral participation in a socialist or labor party.

The "pure and simple" trade unionists and the socialists made essentially the same assessment of capitalist industrialism—it was here to stay and therefore so was their position as workers here to stay. Emancipation would come from strengthening their collective response as workers, not from lifting themselves out from the working class. The "pure and simple" trade unionists learned it from their experience with state action in injunctions, boycotts and strikebreaking. The socialists learned it from the Communist Manifesto.

But the "pure and simple" trade unionists and the socialists derived different strategies from their common appraisal. The trade unionists, who were largely skilled workers, had no interest in replacing capitalism as long as they could moderate capitalism's employment impact on them. And because many unions of skilled workers could make the strategy of job control work, they had more confidence in their work-site power than in the outcome of their political power. The socialists hoped to destroy capitalist industrialism and replace it with socialist industrialism, and for this, class-conscious politics was a necessary extension of class-conscious economics.

World War I put an end to socialist influence in the labor movement and marked the beginning of stage three. The labor movement, dominated by the craft unions, pressed "pure and simple" unionism to the outer limits by opposing unemployment insurance or any kind of affirmative role for government policy.

Stage three was brought to a catastrophic close with the Great Depression of 1929. The Great Depression brought in the welfare state of the Roosevelt New Deal and statutory protection for unionism. Industrial unionism, both as of new unions and as the industrialization of the established craft unions, permeated the mass production sectors of the economy. Organized political and legislative activity acquired legitimacy as union function and the reign of pure and simple unionism was over. In 1937 John L. Lewis set out the rationale which still prevails:

Better living standards, shorter working hours and improved employment conditions for their members cannot be hoped for unless legislative and other provisions be made for economic planning and for price, production and profit controls. Because of these fundamental conditions it is obvious to industrial workers that the labor movement must organize itself and exert itself not only in the economic field but also in the political arena.

John L. Lewis and the industrial unionists, learning from their experience with Roosevelt, abandoned the class theory of the state held both by the socialists and the "pure and simple" trade unionists. Lewis—to use him as the symbol of the new unionism—demonstrated that state power need not be polarized in one class or another, but that pressure groups could engage in political collective bargaining on particular issues, and that specifically workers could pressure for the use of government power in the interests of the workers with reasonable chances of success. This bargaining, they learned further, could be effective only if supported by an *organized* and continuing legislative and political effort.

In the present period unions represent only a minority of the work force directly, but the economic effects of collective bargaining are considered so important that the federal administration asserts a continuing public interest in the results of collective bargaining and establishes guidelines for wage negotiations.

If union wage policies now affect the nation's economic performance, the reverse is also true to an unparalleled degree—the nation's economic performance assumes significant meaning for the *union's* performance. The characteristics of the economic situation with special point for the labor movement are:

1. A public sector resting on a permanently high level of defense expenditure and on an expanding welfare state with full employment as its major responsibility.

2. A private sector with the main thrusts provided by capital investment, construction and consumer durables; after the post-World War II period subject to recessions, but unlike post-World War I, apparently *depression*-proof.

3. A steadily declining proportion of the labor force in "manualist" employments, the heartland of union strength—with technological change as the mainspring of this development.

For the economy as a whole, this is the period of the integrated economy with particular economic decisions subject as never before to the test of whether they advance or retard economic growth. In this setting no labor movement and no union can insulate themselves against the effects of their activities on public policy; nor can they escape the effects of public policy on the union. Politics and legislation have become central concerns of the contemporary union out of necessity rather than out of doctrine, and what follows represents the salient features of the labor movement's political and legislative response.

Collective bargaining power is the fulcrum for political power. Collective bargaining is still the overriding union function, having achieved a depth of penetration, scope and systematization unprecedented in American industrial relations history and unrivaled by collective bargaining anywhere else in the world.

The labor movement's approach to politics partakes variously of the pressure group and of the political party. It is the pressure group strategy aimed at the preservation of collective bargaining and institutional power that engages union activities most insistently. But the reach of the pressures which a labor union needs to exert in order to preserve collective bargaining and institutional power has expanded until it fuses into broad economic policy.

Labor's political action assumes something of the shape of a political party because there is an inclusive labor program taking in the whole range of public policy. The program is more than decor, representing an authentic guide to the labor movement's policies in practice, subject to the discount that some unions take the program less seriously than others and that some stress one part of the program more than others.

The influences acting on the labor movement to commit its forces to a comprehensive political program have come first from its own assessment of the fitness of things—that an institution of power and position in the society must go beyond being "a narrow pressure group"; and then from the expectations that the labor movement, having matured or arrived, must "take its place as an equal among the trustees of the society and the political system." [1]

The labor movement lacks only its own national electoral instrumentalities to make it a full-dress political party. This gap is partly filled by the national Democratic party and the Democratic parties in many non-Southern states. Now, the national Democratic party is surely not a labor party, but the unions are the single most important force in it and, subject to the usual qualifications, that force is mainly exerted in the direction of program. In contrast to the pure model of European labor politics, the American labor movement does not strive for class political power within the Democratic party or, for that matter, outside of it. The source of labor movement strength in the Democratic party is the effort, money, facilities and votes it will enlist in behalf of the party's candidates. There is a substantial involvement of local labor leaders in behalf of Republican candidates

---

[1] David B. Truman, "Labor's Responsibility in Public Affairs," *Labor's Public Responsibility,* National Institute of Labor Education, 1960, p. 109.

and prominent labor leaders identified as Republicans, but it is rare for the union to function as an institutional force in the Republican party.

The political interests of the labor movement are implemented by an internal organizational network consisting of, among other things, a Committee for Political Education (COPE), a legislative department and a technical staff secretariat specializing variously in economic policy, civil rights, social security and international affairs, all in the AFL-CIO headquarters. The network further consists of the full-time lobbyists of the AFL-CIO, political departments in several large international unions, state legislative representation and political activity units (local versions of COPE) in every state and in every city of any size and local union committees; the last-named may be something considerably less than they purport to be. The unions outside of the AFL-CIO but still considering themselves as part of the labor movement are also heavily involved in politics and legislation, whether it is the Railroad Brotherhoods, the Teamsters, the Miners, or the ideologically oriented Longshoremen or United Electrical Workers. Only perhaps the local independent unions which do not think of themselves as part of a labor movement express little or no political interest.

The organizational network engages in such activities as propaganda, education and training, lobbying, registration campaigns, applying manpower and money in behalf of candidates, and polling surveys. It shows up in such roles as caucuses at political conventions, political insiders within the parties, and as candidates and office holders.

The labor movement's political action is decentralized, following in this respect the decentralized character of the total movement and the decentralized character of the political system in which the unions must function. The political and legislative line of the AFL-CIO as a federation has no binding force on affiliates who do, in fact, run counter to the federation's position at various times—and to each other's positions.

Union political action has had at least three concrete effects on the political process:

1. It has increased working class participation in voting.

2. It has provided a training ground in the organizational skills of politics, a point of access to influence in the political party, and a feeling of self-confidence by workers in aspiring to political power.

3. Unions have provided the base of political strength for the welfare state program in the Democratic party and have confronted the Republican party with the need to moderate its tendency toward doctrinaire conservatism if the party is to be a mass party rather than an ideological party.

In respect to political programs beyond bread and butter the union effect has been mainly by way of support and re-enforcement. While the unions have been involved in the development of programs they have not been the initiating force in the creative stages of a program. Once a program is conceived in broad outline, however—and this is more true nationally and of course during Democratic administrations—the labor movement's technicians will be active participants in drafting, massing legislative support, and if the program is enacted, in maintaining a permanent vigil over its administration. If not enacted, then the labor movement will be the chief prod for another try. Minimum wages, "medicare," and social security are current cases in point.

For the left-oriented intellectual this limited reacting posture is a defect in the quality of labor's political performance; "reaching out for the stars" is more in keeping with labor as an historic *movement*. For the economist this political power, whether reactive or creative, only extends the labor movement's inflationary thrust from collective bargaining to legislation.

There is a substantial distance between the political commitment of the union leadership and of the rank and file. For the rank and file member politics has the re-enforcement of job rights as its main purpose. The widest perspective on political action is viewed by the federation leadership, and the angle of political vision narrows but also intensifies as the leadership moves closer to the actual work situation. This is probably in keeping with the political habits of the population at large.

The radical transformation that has taken place within a generation in the union concept and execution of political action has been obscured by what seems to be continued adherence to the Gompers "reward your friends and punish your enemies" maxim. Nonpartisanship in the present period is supported by a going political concern composed of labor leaders who "belong" in the circles of political power and who matter in the nation's politics. This was not so under the older pre-1933 nonpartisanship and is a difference in degree that becomes a difference in kind. . . .

The secular trend for the labor movement in politics is upward. The decisive element in the trend is the expanding economic role of government to deal with military security, inflation and unemployment, economic growth and social welfare. Price and wage restraints, full employment, poverty and "automation" are the ways in which these issues become politically meaningful for workers and unions. At this moment it is the limitations of collective bargaining in dealing with the employment consequences of technological change that is and will continue to be a major spur to union political action. Inasmuch as "automation" ties in with every major economic problem, the labor political program will continue to be wide-ranging.

Labor's political role will be accelerated by ideology, but in this case not so much by the labor movement's own ideology as the ideology of the liberal intellectual community. However labor leaders may deprecate liberal criticism and expectations, union leadership at the higher levels of union government has historically been sensitive and responsive to the liberal climate of opinion. The pressure which union leadership has been reacting to on such issues as civil rights, foreign aid and trade, has been the liberal's ideological pressure as much as, if not more than, the political pressures of the union constituency.

From the very origins of unionism, the middle-class intellectual as utopian, Marxian socialist, or contemporary liberal, has assigned the unions an historic mission which goes beyond the job interests of the union's constituents and makes it an instrumentality of progress in the larger social realm. Lenin was right, of course, when he said that "the working class, exclusively by its own effort, is able to develop only trade union consciousness." In the United States the liberal has almost completely rejected formal socialism but this has not deterred him from urging (and getting) a larger political responsibility from the labor movement—but not so large as would be sufficient for the liberal's conception of the union role. The source of the intellectual appeal to the labor leadership is that at bottom they both, even the narrowest "business" unionist, share the same sentiment of the unions as a social movement.

The restraining influence on the leader in enlarging the union scope is his membership which holds him close to job interests. This insight and the special way he put it is Selig Perlman's enduring contribution to union theory. Since Perlman wrote, the dimensions of job interests have expanded from the craft unionism which was Perlman's prototype, to the industry interest of the mass-production/industrial-union unionist.

A "business in politics" movement has developed recently as a counter-vailing force to the union in politics. Businessmen had just about begun to understand that the union as a system of power in the plant need not be subversive to the enterprise when the implications of union political power reached them. As the businessmen view it, the union as a system of power in the political society is fraught with the greatest danger to the free enterprise system as well as a challenge to their own long-held positions. What distinguishes this "business in politics" movement is its self-consciousness, for, in point of fact, business has never been out of politics in the United States or anywhere else.

The self-consciousness of business politics raises up for the union the threat of external aggression that has always been a powerful drive to union political action. Nothing quite imparts the zing and the sense of outrage to labor politics as do injunctions, Taft-Hartley laws, right-to-work laws, and now possibly the "business in politics" movement—if it ever amounts to anything. The really massive political efforts by the unions have always been mounted *against* something.

The Negro worker in the civil rights upsurge is moving out of the working class substratum into an assertive role in the main line of the manual working class and its unions. The politicalization of Negro workers will give the labor movement's politics a strong civil rights thrust for a long period ahead.

What will finally sustain politics as vital union function is the large extent to which the political interest has been institutionalized in the form of organizations, programs and specialized personnel; and institutions do tend to develop momentum on their own.

All the portents, then, are for a broader political scope and for a more systematic political performance by the labor movement. But there are no signs that the expanding political vision will come to include a labor party because, to put it summarily:

There is little or no rank and file sentiment for it.

The union leaders are strongly committed to the established political arrangements and they believe that they haven't done too badly under them.

Labor leaders have no confidence that they can bring their constituents along with them into a labor party.

The leaders fear the class isolation which would follow and that, in any case, a labor party would insure the selection of antiunion, reactionary forces.

Given the federal structure, the labor party could hardly expect to be more than a local institution.

Finally, American political parties are mass parties, not doctrinal parties, and they will ultimately take over the most viable parts of the labor party's program.

American unionism is emerging with a conception of its political role that is flexible, realistic and responsible: flexible because it is willing to experiment with both collective bargaining and legislative enactment and, as the situation demands, to have one complement the other; realistic because program has some relationship to capabilities; and responsible because the effective political goals go beyond parochial job interests and assert a serious union concern with the larger national and international community. Self-interest politics have not been by-passed but self-interest is moving away from catch-as-catch-can.

The wholesale effects of the labor movement in politics have been to strengthen democracy in two ways: (1) by diffusing political power but not polarizing it, and (2) by challenging our economic system to share its favors broadly. These effects may very well be the chief factors responsible for the viability of Western "capitalist democracy."

21

AGRICULTURE AND ITS PROBLEMS

ONE OF OUR MOST DIFFICULT economic problems in the United States is to develop satisfactory public policies for dealing with the "farm problem." Should we or should we not attempt to protect the incomes of farmers? And if we decide to protect them, what methods should we employ?

Galbraith believes that we have used the wrong methods of supporting farm prices and income, but that some kind of government support is needed. He maintains that it is highly desirable to preserve the family farm and thinks that this will require marketing and production controls, though he concedes that these will somewhat reduce the freedom of the farmer to do as he pleases.

Our second selection is by Charles B. Shuman, President of the American Farm Bureau Federation, which is by far the largest farm organization in the United States, including more than half of all farm families. Shuman's views are very different from those of Galbraith. He is bitterly opposed to government controls that limit the farmer's freedom. Though he has indicated elsewhere that he would not be opposed to very moderate price supports, what he primarily seeks is a return to free markets. He believes that a better day will come for agriculture when farmers are released from costly government restrictions and controls, and allowed to use their abilities to produce freely the things that consumers want.

44

Farm Policy: The Problem and the Choices

by John Kenneth Galbraith

In the last 20 years we have achieved something. We have come close to agreement on at least two of the underlying causes of the farm problem. We agree, first of all, that a remarkable technological and capital advance has remarkably increased output from given land and labor. A great many changes—improved machinery and tillage, more and better power, hybrids, plant foods, improved nutrition, and disease control—have all contributed to this result.

Secondly, there is agreement that this great increase in the efficiency of farm production and the resulting increase in output has occurred in a country which has a relatively low absorptive capacity. In the economist's language both the price elasticity and the income elasticity of farm products is small. Because of limited price elasticity an unusually large crop does not move readily and easily into use when there is a modest reduction in prices. For the generality of farm products only a large reduction in price will much expand consumption. Some are unresponsive to almost any likely movement. Needless to say, this makes price cutting a painful way of getting expanded consumption.

Such is the meaning of low price elasticity. Low income elasticity means that as the incomes of people rise—urban incomes in particular—they spend more on clothing, on transportation, on recreation, and on other things but not a great deal more on food. The meaning of this will be evident to everyone. While expanding prosperity and increasing purchasing power would be a cure for overproduction in other industries, they are not similarly the salvation for agriculture.

I now come to another and, in some respects, more vital cause of our farm difficulties. This is also one which is much less clearly perceived.

From address by John Kenneth Galbraith before the National Farm Institute, Des Moines, Iowa, February 14, 1958. Reprinted in *Congressional Record*, March 6, 1958, pp. 3109–3111. By permission.

John Kenneth Galbraith is Professor of Economics at Harvard University. He is the author of a number of books and was Ambassador to India under President Kennedy.

And much of what I have to say later on depends on a clear perception of this point.

Unlike most industry and unlike most parts of the labor market, agriculture is peculiarly incapable of dealing with the problems of expanding output and comparatively inelastic demand. This incapability is inherent in the organization of the industry. Agriculture is an industry of many small units. No individual producer can exercise an appreciable influence on price or on the amount that is sold. As a result, it is not within the power of any individual producer—and since there is no effective organization to this end, it is not within the power of the agricultural industry as a whole—to keep expanding farm output from bringing down prices and incomes. And given the inelasticity of these markets, a large increase in supply can obviously be the cause of great hardship and even demoralization.

All this, you will say (or some will say), is inevitable. It is the way things should be. This is the free market. This is competition. Perhaps so. But it is a behavior that is more or less peculiar to agriculture. In the last 30 or 40 years there have been important technological improvements in the manufacture of automobiles, trucks, and tractors. The moving assembly line, special-purpose machine tools of high speed and efficiency, and automation have all worked a revolution in these industries. Did it lead to a glut on the market and a demoralization of prices? Of course it did not. It did not because the individual companies, very fortunately for them and perhaps also for the economy, were able to control their prices and regulate their output. This is a built-in power; it goes automatically with the fact that there are comparatively few firms in these industries. The steel industry is currently running at some 60 percent of capacity because it cannot sell a larger output at a price which it considers satisfactory. This it accomplishes easily without the slightest fuss or feathers. If farmers had the same market power they could, if necessary, cut hog production back by 40 percent in order to defend, say, a $20 price.

The power to protect its market that is enjoyed by the corporation is also enjoyed in considerable measure by the modern union. Early in this century American workers worried, and not without reason, lest the large influx of European migrants would break down their wage scales. They were in somewhat the same position as the farmer watching the effect of a large increase in supply on his prices. But now the unionized worker is reasonably well protected against such competition. Even though the supply of labor may exceed the demand, he doesn't have to worry about his wages being slashed. He, too, has won a considerable measure of security in the market.

Thus it has come about that the farmer belongs to about the only group—certainly his is by far the most important—which is still exposed to the full rigors of the competitive market. Or this would be so in the absence of Government programs. Government price protection, viewed in this light, is, or at least could be, only the equivalent of the price security that the modern corporation and the modern trade union have as a matter of course. There is this important peculiarity of the farmer's position. Because of the comparatively small scale of his operations, his large numbers, and the fact that agricultural production is by its nature scattered widely over the face of the country, he can achieve a measure of control over supply and price only with the aid of the Government. If one wishes to press the point, the market power of the modern corporation—deriving as it does from the State-issued charter—and the market power of the modern union both owe much to the State. But their debt is rather more subtle and better disguised than that of the farmer to the Agricultural Marketing Service and the CCC. So it is overlooked or perhaps conveniently ignored.

The meaning of this argument is also clear. It means that those who talk about returning the farmer to a free market are prescribing a very different fate for him than when they talk about free enterprise for General Motors or free collective bargaining for labor. In the free market the corporation and the union retain their power over prices and output. The farmer does not. What is sauce for the corporation is sourdough for the farmer. In its recent report, *Toward a Realistic Farm Program,* the Committee for Economic Development says that farm programs must have the basic objective of bettering the condition of the commercial farmer by means consistent with free markets and the national well-being. This means inevitably the particular kind of free market which farmers have. To prescribe the same kind of market for GM, one would have to recommend splitting the company up into a hundred or a thousand automobile-producing units. None of these would have more influence than the average corn farmer on price; an improvement in technology would mean expanded ouput and lowered prices, and a glut of autos for all. And this recommendation applied to the labor market would mean the dissolution of unions. The CED is a highly responsible body. It would never think of making such silly recommendations for industry or labor. Yet this is what, in effect, it prescribes for the farmer when it asks that he be enabled to free himself from Government subsidy and control.

The special rigor with which the free market treats the farmer has always seemed to me self-evident. I have been struck by the general unwillingness to acknowledge it. While it is not usually fruitful or even wise to reflect on the reasons for the unwisdom of others, I do think some economists have resisted the idea for reasons essentially of nostalgia. Economic theory anciently assumed a market structure similar to that of agriculture. There were many producers selling in a market which none could influence or control. This was the classical case of free competition. There has been a natural hesitation to accept the conclusion that what was once (supposedly at least) the rule for all is now the rule only or chiefly for the farmer.

Also once we agree that the market operates with particular severity for the farmer we are likely to ask what should be done about it. The door is immediately opened to talk of Government programs. And that talk is not of temporary expedients but of permanent measures. Those who find such ideas abhorrent realize, perhaps instinctively, that to talk of free markets is the best defense.

I should also add that no one ever gets into trouble praising the virtues of the free market.

Finally, in recent times, the beneficence of unregulated markets has acquired some of the overtones of a religious faith. It is hinted, even though it is not quite said, that divinity is on the side of the free market. Support prices, although they may not be precisely the work of the devil, are utterly lacking in heavenly sanction. I must say I regard this whole trend of discussion not only as unfortunate but even as objectionable. I am not an expert in theology, but I doubt that providence is much concerned with the American farm program. Certainly it seems to me a trifle presumptuous for any mortal, however great or pious, to claim or imply that God is on his side. I would suggest that, following an old American tradition, we keep religion out of what had best be purely secular discussion.

I

It will be plain from the foregoing that expanding output, in the presence of inelastic demand, and in the absence of any internal capacity to temper the effect, can bring exceedingly painful and perhaps even disastrous movements in farm prices and incomes. And not only can it do so but on any reading of recent experience is almost certain to do so. And there is the further possibility that these effects may be sharpened by shrinking demand induced by depression. What should we do?

Within recent times, so it seems to me at least, we have come to understand more clearly the choice that confronts us. This choice rests on an increasingly evident fact of our agriculture. It is the very great difference in the ability of different classes of farmers to survive satisfactorily under the market conditions I have described. As I say, this is something of which we are only gradually becoming aware. Let me explain it in some detail.

For purposes of this explanation we may think of three classes of farmers in the United States. The first group are the subcommercial or subsistence farmers. These are the people who sell very little. Their situation is characteristic in the southern Appalachians, the Piedmont Plateau, northern New England hill towns, the cutover regions of the Lake States, and the Ozarks. Their income is inadequate less because prices are low than because they have so little to bring to market. It is plain that if these families are to have a decent income 1 of 2 things must happen. They must be assisted in reorganizing their farm enterprises so that their output is appreciably increased or they must find a better livelihood outside of agriculture. For the family grossing less than $1,000 or $1,500 from agriculture, of which there are still a great many in the United States, one or another of these remedies is inevitable. I doubt the wisdom of those who seek to make political capital out of statements of public officials which recognize this choice.

But it seems clear that we must now recognize two separate groups within the category that we are accustomed to call commercial farmers. We must distinguish the case of the very large commercial farm which, there is increasing evidence to show, has been able to return its operators a satisfactory income in recent years from that of the more conventional family enterprise which is in serious trouble. In the nature of things the dividing line here is not very sharp and it undoubtedly varies from one type of farming to another. But the growing income advantage of the large farm—the very large farm—is strongly indicated. It is shown by the trend toward farm consolidation. It is strongly suggested by farm management budgeting and programming studies. And it is borne out by the statistics. Speaking of commercial farms, Koffsky and Grove, of the United States Department of Agriculture, conclude in their recent testimony on agricultural policy for the Joint Economic Committee that between 1949 and 1954–55, although the evidence is not entirely conclusive, "net income on farms with an annual value of sales of $25,000 or more was fairly well maintained, while incomes of smaller operations, although still in the high-production category, showed substantial declines." That the large farms would even come close to maintaining their income in this period was highly significant.

We can conclude, I believe, that in many areas at least, modern technology has come to favor the large farm enterprise. Agriculture has become an industry where there are substantial economies of scale. The most successful units may, indeed, be very large by any past standards—in some areas the investment will be from half or three-quarters of a million dollars upward. This is an important point, for there is still more than a slight reluctance to admit of the size of these units and to explore the full extent of the change that is involved. We hear scholars, Professor Schultz among them, speak of the need for a further large-scale withdrawal of the human factor from commercial agriculture. But we hear less of the massive reorganization of the farm units which this withdrawal implies. The huge scale of the resulting units is not recognized—or this part of the conclusion is soft pedalled. Yet, if any fewer people run our farm plant it can only mean that each person is operating a far larger firm.

For let there be no mistake, an agriculture where the average unit has a capitalization of a half million dollars or upward will be very different, both in its social and economic structure, from the agriculture to which we are accustomed. Not many can expect to start with a small or modest stake and control a half million or million dollars of capital during their lifetime. If these are the capital requirements of the successful farm, we shall have to accept as commonplace the separation of management from ownership. Owner-operation will be confined, with rare exceptions, to those who were shrewd enough to select well-to-do parents. We shall develop in our agriculture what amounts to an aristocratic tradition. There will no doubt also be closer integration with industrial operations with capital borrowed from industry and with closer control by industry. Modern broiler feeding is a sign.

Perhaps this development will not be so bad. But we should face up to its full implications. Those who now talk about adjustments and reorganization of commercial agriculture are talking about means without facing up to results. Those who praise the free market and the family farm in one breath are fooling either themselves or their audience. As I have noted, it is the very large farm, not the traditional family enterprise, which from the evidence has much the greater capacity to survive.

We should also recognize that the adjustment to high capitalization agriculture will not be painless. It will continue to be very painful. And we should spare a thought for the trail of uprooted families and spoiled and unhappy lives which such adjustment involves. I would especially warn colleges, now interesting themselves in these problems, against using the word "adjustment" as though it described a neutral and painless process.

II

Suppose we do not wish an agriculture of large, highly capitalized units. What is the alternative? The alternative is to have a farm policy in which the smaller commercial farm—what we have long thought of as the ordinary family enterprise—can survive. Given the technological dynamic of agriculture, the nature of its demand and the nature of the market structure, we cannot expect this from the market. It will come only as the result of Government programs that are designed to enable the family enterprise to survive. It has to be a Government program. Self-organization by farmers, of which some people are now talking, to regulate supply and protect their incomes is a pipe dream. Those who advocate it only advertise their innocence of history, economics, and human nature and their refusal to learn from past failure. I also confess my skepticism of individual commodity programs now so much in fashion. I very much fear that they will prove to be only a way of magnifying the tendency of farmers to disagree with each other—a tendency that is exceedingly well-developed—and thus to insure no action of any kind. I also deplore the belief that is currently so popular that if everyone just thinks hard enough someone, someday, will come up with a brilliant new idea for solving the farm problem and insuring everyone an adequate income. That is not going to happen either. Farmers are reputed to be hardheaded people. But a surprising number still have a sneaking faith in magic. The soil bank should stand as a warning. The good ideas have already occurred to people. So, of course, have the bad ones.

Or, to be more precise, the choices in farm policy are not very great. Any policy must provide a floor under prices or under income. As I have said on other occasions, a farm policy that doesn't deal with these matters is like a trade union which doesn't bother about wages. There must be production or marketing controls and these must be strong enough to keep the program from being unreasonably expensive. They will also inevitably interfere somewhat with the freedom of the farmer to do as he pleases. Nothing is controlled if a man can market all that he pleases. But we should also bear in mind that life involves a choice between different kinds of restraints. Inadequate income also imposes some very comprehensive restraints on the farm family.

I have long felt that there is a right way and a wrong way to support farm prices and income and that since World War II we have shown an unerring instinct for the wrong course. Production payments, either generally or specially financed, would be far more satisfactory. And since payments can be denied to overquote production, they fit in far better with a system of production control. But this is another story.

III

The choice today is not the survival of American agriculture, or even its efficiency. The great and growing productivity shows that these are not in jeopardy. What is at stake is the traditional organization of this industry. We are in process of deciding between the traditional family enterprise of modest capitalization and widely dispersed ownership and an agriculture composed of much larger scale, much more impersonal, and much more highly capitalized firms. This is not an absolute choice. We shall have both types of farm enterprises for a long time to come. But a strong farm program will protect the traditional structure. The present trend to the free market will put a substantial premium on the greater survival power of the large enterprise.

My own preference would be to temper efficiency with compassion and to have a farm program that protects the smaller farm. But my purpose tonight is not to persuade you but to suggest the choice.

45

A Critical Look at Farm Policy

by Charles B. Shuman

For several years the voting delegates to Farm Bureau conventions have stated that:

> A major objective of Farm Bureau policy is to create conditions whereby farmers may earn and get a high per family real income in a manner which will preserve freedom and opportunity. We firmly believe that this objective can best be accomplished by preserving the market price system as the principal influence in allocating the use of farm resources. The American farmer is more capable than government of planning the use of his acreage and other productive resources.

The attainment of this objective will depend upon legislative action to take government out of its assumed role of supply and price manager and of equal importance—the development of organizational action programs which will help farmers take over the job of resource management. Government farm programs were originally accepted by farmers because they felt inadequate to cope with the increasingly complex, rapidly changing and highly competitive production and marketing situation. After using the farm program "crutch" for more than 30 years, it should not be surprising to discover that many farmers fear they cannot walk alone. However, it has been repeatedly demonstrated in the two-thirds of agriculture which has never been subjected to government controls that farmers can make greater progress in solving their problems by using their own resources than by turning to political nostrums.

Thirty years of experience has demonstrated that prosperity for American agriculture cannot be obtained by legislation—it is not a right but must be earned. In recognition of this truth, Farm Bureau members have turned to their organization for expanded programs of service and marketing. The overall objective of Farm Bureau's expanded program is similar to the original objectives of farm legislation—balancing supply with demand, expanding markets, stabilizing and improving prices, and reducing costs of

Excerpts from Mr. Shuman's address at the Annual Meeting of The Farm Bureau Federation December 13, 1965. Reprinted by permission.

Charles B. Shuman, an Illinois farmer, is President of the American Farm Bureau Federation.

production and marketing. Such ambitious objectives cannot be attained in a short time, but it must be remembered that we have wasted more than three decades in the search for a legislative short-cut. I am happy to report that during this year of 1965 we have made excellent progress toward improving the capacity to solve some of these problems through the Farm Bureau organization.

The net income of the family farm consists of volume produced on the farm multiplied by the price received, minus the cost of operation. The rapid acceptance by farmers of the new knowledge and better methods uncovered by scientific research have fairly well taken care of the volume item. The two difficult and highly variable factors in this income formula are production costs and market prices. While the individual farm operator can do much to influence both costs and prices, there are also great opportunities to attack these factors in an organized way. One of the first cost cutting services to be organized by Farm Bureau was the insurance service programs of the various states. . . .

[President Shuman then discusses briefly a number of other services organized by The Farm Bureau Federation for the benefit of its members.]

Administration Agricultural Policies

It is natural for many politicians to try to please or fool as many voters as possible. This may rationalize, but does not justify, the rather ridiculous attempts of the Administration to ride off in opposite farm policy directions at the same time. Last February President Johnson told Congress that "Our objectives must be for farmers to get improved income out of the market place with less cost to the government." Secretary of Agriculture Orville L. Freeman assured the House Committee on Agriculture that he has "every respect for the operation of the market—it can set values and quality differentials far better than government." This is a far cry from his previous description of the competitive market in agriculture as "the law of the jungle" and is not consistent with his market wrecking surplus dumping actions. In this same statement which referred to the superiority of the market system, the Secretary urged that Congress grant him greater authority to manipulate feed grain and wheat prices because if prices were allowed to go too far above the support level "you couldn't get farmers into the program."

Despite the "market price" line of the Administration, farmers are increasingly being forced to look to direct payments from the federal treasury for much of their net income. It is estimated that these payments will jump to 3.4 billion dollars next year and that this will be approximately 24 percent of net farm income. The market price system which is the most nearly perfect mechanism to translate consumer needs into the production of goods and services is being systematically destroyed by the dumping of government surplus stocks to depress prices and the substitution of payments for market returns. A slight but significant change in the feed grain section of the Agricultural Act of 1965 illustrates the market wrecking intent of the Administration. The loan rate for corn (support price) has been dropped five cents per bushel while the direct subsidy payment to farmers has been increased from 20 to 30 cents.

A further demonstration of the Administration's determination to destroy the market system is illustrated by the recent decision to dump government stocks of bread wheat on the market. The USDA explained its arbitrary price control action thus:

> ". . . The 1965 wheat crop is somewhat lower than average in protein content. As a result, higher quality bread wheat is attracting abnormally high market premiums which could be reflected in higher flour and bread prices."

Within 24 hours of this announcement, the Department of Agriculture was selling bread wheat from its tremendous stocks. The market reaction was equally swift and sharp. Cash prices for high protein wheat dropped as much as seven cents a bushel in two days on the Minneapolis market. The wheat farmer gets hit by a bad season and his only chance to get a higher price for his fewer bushels of high quality grain is dashed by government dumping.

The question can well be asked, "Who is the Department of Agriculture trying to help?" The Department is suddenly concerned about the possibility of a small increase in the cost of bread to consumers, yet last summer the same Department maintained that much larger wheat cost increases due to the "bread tax" would not increase consumer prices. At one time, the USDA was devoted to helping farmers improve their income—now it penalizes those who try to solve their own problems. Farm programs once offered rewards to those who went along with controls—now they penalize those who refuse to knuckle under. The time was when USDA reports were trustworthy—now we are told that the slightly lower Commodity Credit Corporation stocks are due to the control program despite the cut in 1964 production due to the drouth. When there is a big yield, as in 1965, it is due to unusually favorable weather, but when a drouth burns up the crop, the program is "working effectively." According to the Department, the feed grain program had nothing to do with excessive feeding that triggered the disastrous break in livestock prices in 1962, but the program is somehow responsible for the recent higher prices of hogs and cattle.

Agricultural Act of 1965

Administration spokesmen and those who echo the same propaganda line have gone all out to sell the Agriculture Act of 1965 as a change in direction—"much more of a free enterprise program"; "less cost to taxpayer"; "soundest and most effective ever enacted." The facts are that this four year continuation of the same old discredited schemes that have failed in the past will set a new high cost record of more than $18 billion. The feed grain program is continued despite the fact that a five year expenditure of $5 billion to cut production has brought about the highest production on record in 1965.

Senator Clinton P. Anderson (D) of New Mexico recently listed "a sampling of the agricultural disarray that has been created—or accentuated —by unsound government farm programs:

"Farm production greater than market needs has been encouraged.

"The use of synthetics has been increased.

"Important markets at home and abroad have been lost.

"Per unit costs have been increased as operations have been reduced in size, and resources have been forced into secondary uses.

"The value of allotments has been capitalized into higher land prices."

The "new" farm bill is almost certain to bring more of these disastrous results to farmers. The Administration will not be able to live with this complicated monstrosity for four years. It is good that President Johnson has appointed a "Commission" to study a new approach to solving farm problems—he will need that "new approach" soon.

Essentially, the "new" farm law is a money bill. It passes out cash by the scoop shovel method with few strings attached. One Ohio county Agricultural Stabilization and Conservation Service committee wrote a letter to local businessmen in which they appealed for support on a "money" basis.

"To the Businessmen of _____ County:

Gentlemen:
Within the past several weeks _____ County farmers have received $1,489,480.00 for diverting 23,298 acres on 740 farms under the 1965 Feed Grain Program and $325,767.00 for diverting 3,086 acres on 703 farms under the 1965 Wheat Program. This makes a total of $1,815,-247.00 for these two programs.

*   *   *

Most of this money will remain in _____ County to be spent in your stores, pay off mortgages in your banks, pay taxes for your schools, and support your churches.

*   *   *

In order to maintain the surplus which assures us of plenty of food for all at a price we can afford to pay, it seems only fair that the other 93% of the population help the 7% who are producing this abundance."

Notice this subtle cheap food pitch to consumers. And that the surplus is to be maintained! . . .

War on Hunger

While the Secretary of Agriculture is busily extolling the virtues of his "new" farm bill, another phalanx of the Great Society is energetically boosting an expanded food give away to "developing" nations as a substitute for crop control. This "war on hunger" idea is being touted as the answer to our surplus problem. The world population explosion is certainly a serious threat to those nations that have not succeeded in unleashing their food production potential. But, despite our tremendous agricultural productivity, the United States cannot feed the world. We need to inquire into the causes of hunger in a world that has ample resources to feed any foreseeable population level. Why does India, for example, continue to depend on food aid while a large acreage of arable land remains relatively unproductive?

Most competent observers agree that there are two major causes of the food deficit in certain nations—ignorance of better methods and lack of capital. As a result of the new knowledge developed by our agricultural research institutions and its rapid adoption by farmers with extension services and industry assistance, U. S. farmers have a vast technological know-how that we are willing to share with others. Agricultural experts and technical observers have been brought to this country in an endless stream with their expenses paid by our government to visit American farms so that they can copy our methods back home. Khrushchev came to Iowa to learn how to grow corn and yet, despite this assistance the Russians cannot feed themselves.

There must be some ingredient in our success formula that they have refused to copy. This essential that is in a large measure responsible for our productivity is the incentive system which has been so successful in generating an abundant supply of capital by American agriculture and business. Recent reports from Russia indicate that socialist planners are being forced to provide various economic incentives to stimulate greater production. The one common denominator that applies to virtually all of these hungry nations is their devotion to a socialist political-economic system—a government managed economy. It is increasingly apparent that socialist nations cannot use the knowledge, even when we give it to them. Socialism and hunger are irrevocably associated.

What can we do about this situation? The world does not need to starve if the underdeveloped areas can be induced to accept the incentive method of capital formation—competitive capitalism. Too often our foreign aid programs have been tied to social reform when the critical need was for economic reform. Further extension of food aid by the United States should be conditioned upon the willingness of the recipient country to replace government management of agriculture with a market price system. We should insist that they encourage private capital investment by permitting incentives, by checking inflation and by removing other obstacles to progress. Such a program would make it possible to gradually replace food aid with increased domestic production or commercial purchases financed by increases in their own exports. However, these reforms will take time and meanwhile the U. S. and other productive nations will undoubtedly continue to supply large quantities of food. Does this offer a way out of our government farm program dilemma?

Public Law 480 was enacted in 1954 and has been primarily a surplus disposal device, although it has been increasingly used for foreign aid. President Johnson has recently urged that the entire foreign aid program be reorganized and redirected. In this revision, the surplus disposal aspect should be discontinued and the food aid needs should be purchased on the domestic market at the going market price. These purchases of grain, cotton, dairy, livestock, fruit and vegetable products would quickly strengthen market prices and assure the resource adjustments needed. No allocation scheme or world food allotments would be necessary.

A reading between the lines of certain "scare" statements about the depletion of our surplus (down from $7 billion to $6 billion) would seem to indicate that some of the Food for Hunger promoters have in mind a plan to keep all of the USDA supply managers employed with a domestic allocation plan tied to international commodity agreements. If the market price is given the opportunity to respond to foreign aid demand it should be possible to discontinue the present control programs and price supports could be used only as originally intended—to stabilize marketing, not to fix prices.

Farm Bureau's recommendations on controls and price supports would be in harmony with a redirected foreign aid program. There could be huge reductions in farm program costs as direct payments to farmers should be ended, Commodity Credit Corporation losses eliminated, and large cuts made in administrative expenses. The Cropland Adjustment Program would be a convenient haven for those farmers who have no faith in the market price system or who are willing to "give up some of their freedom for a little security."

There are definite signs that Farm Bureau is winning its long battle to "move as rapidly as possible to the market system." If we were not winning, there would be no commission to study new approaches; the Secretary of Agriculture would not "have every respect for the operation of the market"; the feed-the-world boys would not be suggesting the purchase of needs "on the market."

The schemes to control production and fix prices have failed in their objective of balancing supply with demand and increasing net farm income. Faced with an unbroken record of failure, the frustrated government supply managers are willing to try almost anything. The principal architect of the Cochrane-Freeman supply management plan, Professor Willard

Cochrane, illustrates the depth of this frustration. In his recent book, "The City Man's Guide to the Farm Problem," Cochrane still insists that compulsory controls would solve our problems but he admits that farmers will not accept this much dictatorship. He then suggests that consideration be given to limiting new agricultural research to slow down technological advance and thus reduce farm production! Shades of the dark ages! Why not pass a law to forbid the use of fertilizer? Yes, Socialism and hunger are related.

There is other evidence that Farm Bureau is winning the struggle to return the controlled-subsidized crops to the market place. As each new government intervention scheme gets into difficulty, the usual tactic of those who favor a managed agriculture is to concoct a new end run plan to divert attention from the failure. It is quite encouraging to recap these efforts and to note the many times when Farm Bureau almost single handedly stopped the play. The Cochrane-Freeman bill to develop supply-management programs on a commodity-by-commodity basis was defeated by Congress in 1961. In 1962, turkey producers rejected a national marketing order after a furious campaign and the Congress rejected marketing quotas for feed grains, and direct payments for dairymen. A nationwide potato marketing order proposal was dropped after Farm Bureau helped organize the opposition. The big news in 1963 was the overwhelming rejection of the wheat certificate plan in a national referendum of wheat growers. The Congress passed a "voluntary" wheat certificate plan and a cotton "mill subsidy" payment plan in 1964. Both proved very costly and drastic revision was necessary in the Act of 1965. Second only to the wheat referendum, perhaps Farm Bureau's most important victory in recent years was attained last summer when the heavily pro-Administration Congress rejected the attempt to transfer much of the costs of the wheat and rice programs to consumers by imposing a "bread tax" and a "rice tax." If this "around end" maneuver had been successful it would have been possible to conceal the true cost of farm controls and subsidies and thus increase the possibility that their existence would be extended. Fortunately many consumers awakened in time to join farmers in a successful effort to stop the attempt.

The farming business can be good if we give farm families the opportunity and the incentive to use their abilities and resources to produce things that our customers want. I am confident that this better day will come soon because farmers are weary of costly government programs based on political and hereditary privilege. They are coming to learn that they have less to fear from progress based on change than from the bureaucratic management and low income that are certain to accompany a legislated status quo. Consumers, too, are seeing that farm legislation reaches into their lives to influence the cost and quality of their daily bread. A new day for agriculture cannot be denied. . . .

22

THE CONSUMER

THOUGH THE AVERAGE AMERICAN CONSUMER now has more income and purchasing power than ever before, to spend his income wisely was never more difficult. In "The Battered and Besieged Consumer" Sidney Margolius describes some of the factors that contribute to consumer ignorance and confusion. Television advertising proclaims as miracle products detergents and cosmetics that contain commonplace ingredients, but sell at inflated prices. Virtues that they do not have are claimed for drugs and medicines that are likewise sold at excessive prices. Easy credit is offered at rates that seem reasonable but that, when analyzed, prove to represent annual interest charges of 12 to 40 per cent or more.

Yet it is also true, as Margolius emphasizes, that government, schools, consumer organizations, and even business firms are making greater efforts than ever before to educate the consumer and, in various ways, to protect him from exploitation.

46

The Battered and Besieged Consumer

by Sidney Margolius

This is the era of the outraged consumer. Scandals have exploded into headlines with machine-gun regularity: short-weighting at meat counters; specious and sometimes even rigged television commercials; instances of private arrangements among sellers to fix prices; confusing credit fees; evasive packaging of foods and cleaners; cheapening of meats and many "convenience" foods by addition of water and other fillers, exaggerated prices for many goods, from vitamins to home improvements, sold by a stream of door-to-door canvassers.

Often you must pay $12 for a medicine that costs $1.20 to manufacture; true interest of 12 to 36 per cent a year on installment purchases, and sometimes more. You may have signed up for a food-freezer plan and later found you paid twice the usual price. For car insurance, you pay 40 to 50 cents of your dollar just for the insurer's expenses and profit. On an individual health insurance policy, you get a 50-50 break. Fifty per cent goes to the company and 50 to benefits.

But also, never before has there been as much public concern and practical effort to correct consumer problems. Unions, consumer cooperatives, credit unions, other community organizations and political leaders all are seeking solutions.

At least seven states already have appointed consumer counsels, advisory committees or consumer fraud bureaus. For the first time since the Roosevelt Administration, the need for consumer representation in the federal government has been given Presidential backing. Consumer associations have been formed in California, Maryland, Michigan, Missouri, New Jersey, New York and Ohio. Consumer-minded senators have proposed legislation to deflate drug prices and require lenders and installment sellers to reveal the true annual interest rates they charge. New laws now regulate use of

Reprinted by permission of the publisher, Pocket Books, Inc., from the book *The Consumer's Guide to Better Buying* by Sidney Margolius. Copyright 1942, 1947, 1951, 1953, ©, 1962 by Sidney Margolius.

Sidney Margolius has studied merchandise, selling practices, and consumer needs for many years. His syndicated newspaper columns have helped thousands of families to buy more for less.

chemicals in foods and cosmetics and require honest identification of textiles.

Too, federal agencies charged with protecting consumers recently have displayed a new alacrity. In the early Sixties, the Federal Trade Commission issued a record number of complaints against deceptive practices and actually four times as many antimonoply actions as in the average of the previous ten years. Similarly, the Food and Drug Administration has moved more swiftly and often against deceptively labeled packages and exaggerated nutritional and medical claims.

This burst of energy in agencies which had dragged their feet for some years is a measure not only of the extent of consumer exploitation but also of the clamor for more policemen, or at least faster ones, to patrol the consumer beat.

Ironically, a major reason both for the many consumer gouges today and for the growing interest in protecting you from deception is the greater purchasing power of working families. Unions have put more money into wage earners' pockets. Through more stable employment, they now are better credit risks.

But while many families have more money, they are not experienced in handling it. They still rely on the fairness of sellers as though the old personal relationships still existed in this era of mass retailing and chain banking. A Boston man returned to a dealer a food freezer he had partly paid for but found had not really reduced his family food bills. To his astonishment, he was ordered by a local court to pay a deficiency judgment to a finance company for the balance plus repossession costs. "But I relied on the seller's good sportsmanship," he told me indignantly.

Significantly, in this comparatively prosperous period there are more personal bankruptcies, and many more involving wage earners, than in the big depression of the 1930's. In 1962, 90 per cent of the 170,000 personal bankruptcies involved wage earners, compared to 35 per cent of the 70,000 in 1935.

The fact is, most people are better trained in earning than in spending. In earlier generations, girls were trained in homemaking while they waited to get married. Now they are schooled to be airline hostesses, secretaries, even atomic physicists, but not in how to run a budget or, sometimes, in how to buy a chicken that has not been cut up into parts first. Today's husbands have higher job skills, but often, little understanding of how to buy insurance or invest family money.

This is a hard-working generation, willing to build part or even all of its own homes, devoting great attention to bringing up its children, constantly improving the family's educational attainments. But it also is a naïve generation in regard to handling money.

Another reason for the buying confusion today is that goods have become more and more complex. You no longer just buy milk. It is homogenized, irradiated, vitamin enriched and so on. This more complicated milk costs more too, so you have to know which, if any, of the additions are worth the extra money. You no longer can buy a dress just because it looks attractive. You need to know whether it is Sanforized, resin treated, color fast and, if color fast, whether to sun and light or merely to water.

Products now are hidden behind packaging and brand names. Our mothers bought toilet soap or laundry soap as needed. It was unwrapped and anonymous. Now we are urged to buy not "soap" but Lifebuoy, Lux, Ivory, Dial, Camay and so on. Except for odor and wrapper, we would not know one from the other, but we are told one brand is good for holding on to friends and the other for holding on to husbands.

Since the advent of television, we have been subjected to a new onslaught of artful and persistent advertising, often diverting our money to purchases that are sometimes overpriced, sometimes unnecessary, and sometimes both.

A traditional slogan of merchandising men is: "Don't sell the steak; sell the sizzle." By this they mean they can sell us more goods by playing up emotional and psychological aspects than by plain facts about the merchandise itself. The result, as a leading psychologist recently wrote in the *Harvard Business Review,* is that today's buyer "is often vague about the actual price he pays for something; he has few standards for judging the quality of what he buys and at times winds up not using it anyway."

Even a federal judge, Luther A. Youngdahl, pointed out how successful emotional appeals are in persuading us to buy. "The men of Madison Avenue have sold shirts by depicting a man with an eye patch," he said; "they have sold soap by advertising it to be '99 and 44/100th per cent pure' without bothering to add the noun; they have sold brassieres by displaying a sleepwalker."

For example, food manufacturers have discovered that while boys like the traditional grainy peanut butter, more can be sold to girls if it is smooth, since smoothness in foods is understood to be more feminine. In fact, manufacturers made some brands so smooth, by adding vegetable oils and fats, that the Food and Drug Administration ruled that they no longer could be called peanut butter. One company then made a virtue of necessity by advertising: "Have you discovered the delicious difference between 'Jif' and peanut butter? . . . 'Jif Peanut Spread' is extra creamy. . . . To pure peanuts, 'Jif' adds an exclusive blend of smoothing ingredients."

But when you separate the sizzle from the steak, you find you are getting part low-priced vegetable shortening, not 100 per cent ground peanuts.

"Sizzle selling" has increased almost in direct proportion to the fact that many goods sold under different brand names increasingly are much alike in their basic ingredients. Frequently you may be convinced to buy one product over another simply because its maker is financially able to dominate the advertising for that type of goods, especially on television, or because of a particularly clever advertising campaign.

For example, Clorox outsells all other bleaches even though it costs 11 to 20 per cent more than the competing brands. Yet, if you merely look at the label, you will see that it is basically the same as Rose-X, Co-Op, Bright Sail, Grand Union and many other brands. As the labels show, if people would read them, all chlorine bleaches have the same active ingredient: 5.25 per cent sodium hypochlorite. In fact, a leading bleach manufacturer testified at an FTC hearing: "All bleaches are, chemically speaking, identical. They bear different trade names."

Similarly, Mr. Clean is the largest-selling of the liquid all-purpose detergents, even though it costs more than most of the others of this type and the "giant size" is only 28 ounces compared to the full quart of the others (although the Mr. Clean bottle is the same height).

Demonstrating the power of advertising to dominate markets and herd the buying public, the FTC reports that Procter & Gamble spent over seven million dollars to introduce Comet and within a few months had 37 per cent of the national market, about as much as Ajax, the older leading brand.

Or consider Ban, which stores reported had become the best-selling deodorant as the result of a particularly effective and persistent TV campaign—"Ban takes the worry out of being close." Actually, most deodorants have the same basic ingredient—aluminum salts, generally aluminum chlorhydroxide—even though some sell for two and three times as much as others.

Many people, if not most, have become so confused by the multiplicity of brand names and advertising claims that they are afraid to trust their own buying judgment or even official standards for products. In New York, District 65 of the Retail, Wholesale and Department Store Union has its own miniature shopping center for its members. It offers "District 65" aspirin at 12 cents per hundred. It also has available one of the most widely advertised brands, Bayer, for 60 cents instead of the usual 73. Both meet the same recognized standard for aspirin. But the expensive brand far outsells the low-cost one, reports Harry Winocur, pharmaceutical manager.

The combination of uninformed money-handling and the hard-sell inevitably has taken its toll of family aspirations. The result for many moderate-income families is empty prosperity and inability to make financial progress. Wage earners may buy such extreme gadgets as gold-plated percolators, as business newspapers report. But this represents merely a kind of frustrated buying, because the more worth-while objectives are still out of reach. A family can't afford the adequate house it needs, so it buys an $18.95 percolator.

Here are the modern selling pressures you particularly need to guard against, for they can erode your living standards seriously:

THE TV CHANNEL TO YOUR POCKETBOOK. The combination of sight and sound on TV has proved to be almost hypnotic in its power to persuade. Dr. Arthur Shapiro, Professor of Medicine at the State University of New York and a founder of the Institute for Research in Hypnosis, has said: "The smoking habit is being established and re-established all the time in advertisements everywhere . . . The man selling cigarettes on television is a spellbinder. His spiel is repetitious, suggestive, soothing, reassuring."

More evidence of the pocketbook power of TV has come from the Bureau of Labor Statistics. Its price checkers reported greatly increased consumption of deodorants, nail polish, lipstick, other toiletries, which they attributed to heavy TV advertising.

TV's dramatic ability to divert family income to unnecessarily expensive or simply unnecessary purchases has been based, in a number of cases on record, on actually rigged demonstrations. For example, the "distortion free" view through General Motors car windows was achieved by filming the scenery through an open window in a G.M. car. In another G.M. commercial, petroleum jelly was smeared on the competitor's glass. In the famous Palmolive Shave Cream sandpaper test, the "sandpaper" subsequently was proved to be sand affixed to a sheet of plastic. The purportedly inferior foil used in a TV demonstration for camparison with Alcoa Wrap was deliberately torn, and a dried-out-looking ham selected to dramatize the ineffectiveness of "ordinary wrap." That dried-out lather from "ordinary" shave creams shown to "prove" the superiority of Rise cream was not lather at all but a foaming agent which disappears rapidly. The moisture drops shown on Blue Bonnet margarine, but not on the competitive brand, proved to be artificial. And if you have been impressed by TV dog appetites, the president of Rival Packing Company has stated that "the normal technique in preparing dog food commercials is to use a starved dog."

MODERN MEDICINE MEN. Advertising of nonprescription medicine has become another frequent source of confusion and money waste, and one that in some instances can even damage health. Kenneth Wilson, president of the National Better Business Bureau, has said that the current use of advertising "to further medical quackery is a serious setback."

Among heavily advertised patent medicines are those sold to elderly people with claims of rejuvenating powers. Dr. Michael Dasco, a leading rehabilitation expert, has pointed out that such medicines generally contain vitamins and alcohol, and that the alcohol is cheaper at the liquor store and most people do not need the extra vitamins.

Television is especially convincing in the sale of drugs and patent medicines because it can show pseudoscientific demonstrations and actors who look and talk authoritatively like doctors, dentists and scientists. That is why you sometimes see or hear at the end of the commercial: "This is a dramatized message." This statement, in small print or a low voice, is a belated admission, if viewers really notice or understand it, that the advertiser has given a false impression.

One of the most worrisome areas of misleading "medical" promotion is products sold to arthritis sufferers. Deceitful advertising victimizes five million sufferers of arthritis of 250 million dollars a year, the Arthritis and Rheumatism Foundation estimates. "Glorified aspirins" such as Arthrycin have been the greatest problem among misrepresented drugs, and vibrating machines the most frequently misrepresented mechanical devices. The "glorified aspirins" typically cost three dollars for one hundred tablets compared to ordinary aspirin prices of 13 to 73 cents.

Another costly arthritis nostrum—Tri-Wunda—against which both the Food and Drug Administration and postal authorities have taken action, consists of a laxative, a vitamin formula and a concoction of acids—at a cost of $12.50 for a two-month supply. One vitamin-mineral compound with an extract of alfalfa, called Arth-Rite, was termed valueless for treating any kind of arthritis or rheumatism, by the FTC.

Rubbing compounds often are sold to arthritis and rheumatism sufferers by means of pseudoscientific jargon and exaggerated claims ("Next morning I felt like a boy again.") The fact is, such products give only temporary relief of the minor aches and pains of these ills.

Toothpaste advertising always has been one of the most troublesome areas. But with the advent of TV, toothpaste promotion has reached an even more susceptible audience—the nation's children.

Dr. Sholem Pearlman of the American Dental Association reports that in several Chicago schools, the Association showed posters of a child washing hands before eating and brushing teeth after eating. The youngsters said that certain TV characters, "in whom they evidently place a great deal of confidence, said you only have to brush once in the morning because the toothpaste had something in it that would protect your teeth all day."

One of the most confusing campaigns has been Gleem's, showing an exasperated housewife whose family simply can't brush after every meal. The Food and Drug Administration can't do anything (or at least has not tried) about commercials which may seem to indicate that a toothpaste may protect you all day, since on their package labels the toothpaste manufacturers do not make the same claim as in ads. The Gleem label merely says: "Contains GL-70 . . . Miracle Cleaner and Bacteria Fighter," and explains that "GL-70 is Procter & Gamble's trademark for the active ingredient, a blend of anionic sulfonates."

While "GL-70" may sound to the layman like a new miracle drug, anionic sulfonates are simply detergents. Gleem has no "miracle" or medical ingredient. All toothpastes have detergents of one kind or another.

Another big television success has been scored by Bufferin. Its price of $1.29 per hundred is the highest for any type of aspirin. Pharmacists report that it has become a big seller despite its high price, and despite the fact that most people do not get an upset stomach from ordinary aspirin and so don't need the additional antacid ingredients.

Similarly, the TV commercials say that your doctor recommends the ingredients in Anacin. This is true enough, but some people may get the impression "your doctor" recommends Anacin. What doctors really recommend, if they recommend this combination of ingredients, is APC tablets (aspirin-phenacetin-caffeine). A knowing person can buy APC tablets under their generic name from many drug and department stores and clinics that sell private-brand drugs, and for a hundred tablets pay only 59 to 79 cents, and sometimes as little as 39 cents, instead of $1.25 for Anacin or 75 cents for 50 APC tablets labeled Empirin.

TV commercials showing one aspirin dissolving more quickly, thus promising "faster relief" than others, particularly have been criticized by the New York County Medical Society's magazine. If one type or brand takes only one second to dissolve, and another perhaps four, there is no practical difference.

Besides pain relievers, two other types of product that have come into wide usage as the result of heavy advertising on TV and radio are digestants and sleeping preparations. The latter, sold without a prescription, are usually antihistamines, which make some people feel drowsy, Harry Winocur points out. These include such widely advertised brands as Sominex, Nytol, Dormin and Sleep-Eze, which usually cost about one dollar for 12 capsules. To show how high a price you pay for such products, private-brand antihistamine sleeping capsules of the same strength are sometimes sold for as little as 63 cents for 30 capsules. These capsules actually cost one and one quarter cents apiece at wholesale under their generic or scientific names.

If you have been buying such expensive brands, you can save money by asking your pharmacist what nonprescription sleep preparations he has similar to the advertised brands but at a reasonable charge. He will appreciate your reliance on his professional judgment rather than on that of an advertising agency.

The digestants are often ordinary products under a brand name. Alka-Seltzer, one of the biggest sellers, is mainly aspirin in an effervescent form. Several of the other brands combine such commonplace ingredients as sodium bicarbonate (baking soda), sodium carbonate and citric acid, sometimes with aspirin. Bicarbonate of soda, of course, is simply an old-time household remedy for indigestion.

The newest drive in self-medication products involves cold tablets. In 1962, the FTC announced a broad investigation of the growing number of preparations advertised for treatment of congestion, inflammation and other respiratory ills, to determine whether certain companies had misrepresented their effectiveness. In one action, the FTC charged that Vicks Double-Buffered Cold Tablets had been falsely advertised as curing or shortening the duration of a common cold.

You can judge the steepness of prices of such products when you understand that they are merely a combination of APC tablets or another form of aspirin, antihistamines and perhaps some vitamin C, as shown on the labels.

Another booming area is vitamin supplements, often sold door-to-door at such high prices as $14 for a month's supply, compared to $3 to $5 charged for similar supplements by your pharmacist and at other regular stores.

According to Dr. Morton J. Rodman, Rutgers University pharmacology professor, one danger of "distorted" TV medicine commercials is that use of some such products may "lull a seriously sick person into a false sense of security and delay [his] going to a doctor." In the case of products claiming to relieve acid stomach or "tired blood," such delay "may prevent early diagnosis of ulcers, cancer, tuberculosis or other ailments."

Some advertising men themselves are increasingly critical of misleading claims. Fairfax Cone, of the Foote, Cone & Belding agency, has said that "newspapers, magazines, TV and radio could clean up advertising with the next deadlines simply by demanding proof of claims." He asks: "How can three different headache remedies all work fastest?"

Broadcasters blame some of their advertisers for deceptive or offensive advertising, and also those doctors "who vouch for the reliability of unreliable proprietary drug advertising," Stockton Helffrich of the National Association of Broadcasters code office has stated.

THE HIGH PRICE OF CARELESS CREDIT.   One of the costliest drains on moderate-income families, often leading to genuine tragedy, is the unknowing use of credit. There are three great dangers to your family in the present tendency toward careless use of installment plans:

1. *The habitual use of the modern "revolving charge accounts" for buying on credit not only large items but even small items like clothing, traditionally bought for cash.*

For many young families, "permanent charge accounts," as some stores call them, have become a permanent new living expense. In the case of a family in the twenty-five to forty-five age group, which relies most heavily on credit, the typical $700 a year of installment debt would mean an extra expense for finance charges of over $100 a year. All surveys have shown that most families do not understand the true interest rates they pay on installment purchases and personal loans since finance charges usually are stated as monthly percentages or discount rates, not as annual rates. The true interest rates are usually 12 to 36 per cent.

2. *The encouragement to overbuy or buy unnecessarily expensive goods*

on credit plans, and thus undertake larger obligations than can be managed.

This is exactly what is happening to many young families today. It is not unusual for couples involved in buying and equipping a home, while raising a family, to incur installment payments of as much as 35 per cent of their income, compared to the 20 per cent normally considered safe. If the breadwinner's work week is cut back, these families are faced with the loss of their possessions, and even if employment remains steady, they must pare basic necessities such as food and medical care to uncomfortable and even risky levels.

Here is one example of how families have come to trust in the monthly-payment system. As you undoubtedly have observed, many sellers do not advertise the full price of merchandise, but say: "You can have this car for $50 a month"; "This washer costs only $1 a week"; "This house costs $95 a month."

A San Francisco man and his wife decided they could afford $60 a month for a station wagon. They told the dealer they also could put down a total of $750 with their trade-in and some cash. The dealer arranged for them to pay the balance at the rate of $60 a month for 10 months, then they would refinance and pay $60 for another 30 months. But they also had to agree to pay the dealer $60 on the side in 30 days and another $110 in the following 10 months.

"I didn't realize it at the time but the dealer was tricking me into an eighty-seven-dollar-a-month payment," the buyer later reported. "The next day I saw it more clearly and said I didn't want the car. They threatened to make me borrow the money from a finance company. I went through with the deal, figuring that I would pay $87 a month for only ten months. But the dealer did not tell me that I was paying $250 in interest for the ten-month period plus additional finance charges when I refinanced the balance for another 30 months. I don't have any money to hire a lawyer. The whole incident has put a terrific burden on me. The balance on the contract at time of purchase was $3,132."

But this man did everything wrong. With four children, and a fifth on the way, he could not afford that costly a car. Nor did he compare the price of the car and the amount of finance charge among other dealers and lenders. He had come to believe that the station-wagon way of life shown in the TV commercials and ads was really within grasp through the magic numerology of the monthly-budget plan. Probably, years of bitterly fought wage increases won by his union went down the drain in this one incident.

Behind the widespread, almost habitual use of credit buying today, is the strong push retailers and banks give to "revolving credit," "budget accounts," "junior charge accounts" and similar plans. Sears, Roebuck, for example, reports that about half its sales now are on credit. Spiegel, another large mail-order retailer, does about 90 per cent of its business on credit. Such traditional cash retailers as the large variety chains and discount stores now also offer credit. The fee for such revolving charge accounts is usually 1.5 per cent a month—a true annual rate of 18 per cent.

Another modern easy-credit plan is bank charge accounts, allowing you to charge at local stores and pay the bank monthly. One large New York bank reports it now has 36,000 such accounts. Many banks now also offer "check credit," in which they credit a loan to your account and [you] draw on it by check, repaying monthly. (This plan at least has the virtue of charging you interest only on the amount you actually draw.)

3. *The use of easy credit as a vehicle of overpricing by door-to-door salesmen and installment stores.*

Door-to-door installment selling of a wide variety of goods, from home improvement to fire alarm systems, has become big business. Some 3000 companies now have a million and a half salespeople out selling directly to consumers. The prices sometimes are two and three times those charged by stores for the same items.

For example, cap-type hair dryers advertised on TV have been sold widely by door-to-door firms at $19.95 to $24.95 for the same, or similar, models that stores sell for $10 to $12. The door-to-door sellers package the dryers in hatbox carrying cases so they look more expensive.

Religious articles often are used as "account openers." These often are elaborately framed pictures or plaques of a Biblical scene or figure, sometimes offered with a Bible as a "free" premium. The door-to-door firms charge from $10 to $30 for such pictures and plaques, and report that they are among their biggest sellers. Electric clocks framed with religious pictures, selling at $25, also are popular. . . .

In general, door-to-door firms mark up their goods 2½ to 3 times the wholesale price. The salesmen themselves get 25 per cent commission, and collection and bad-debt costs are reported to afford an additional 30 per cent. In comparison with the margin of 60 to 67 per cent of your dollar taken by door-to-door firms, retail stores take 20 to 40 per cent. (Some of the more conservative door-to-door firms selling cosmetics and housewares take a little lower margin—55 per cent.)

How can door-to-door firms get these high markups when people merely need to compare prices at the nearest stores? First, they exploit the convenience of buying at home, religious feeling or sympathy, or they play on impulse. For example, chord organs, an impulse item, are successfully sold door to door because people find it less embarrassing to try one at home than in a store.

Secondly, door-to-door firms offer special brand names, which hampers comparison. But the overriding reason is that the high price is obscured by the low monthly payments.

Increasingly, the telephone is used by installment sellers to find prospects.

Solicitors get leads, often by telling you that the company is having a huge clearance or a special sale, or that a friend said you were thinking about buying, for example, carpeting. A solicitor often makes 120 phone calls a day. The company then dispatches a salesman to the families who show signs of interest. Such operations are known as "boiler rooms," the name law-enforcement agencies used to apply to a roomful of telephone solicitors selling stocks or seeking donations to dubious charities. Now the technique is being used more and more to sell consumer goods. The boiler-room operators usually have no store or showroom.

This method has been used to sell dancing lessons, storm windows, awnings, freezers and other products, and most recently, carpets. The prices charged for carpeting sold by boiler rooms often are 30 to 40 per cent more than you would pay at a store. One leading operator has reported that he buys carpeting wholesale at $3.75 a square yard, adds $2 for padding and installation and $4 for his profit. The total of $9.75 in this example is known in the trade as the "par" price. The salesman then charges as much over par as he judges he can get. This particular boiler room limits its salesmen to $4 over par. Thus, families who buy this way may pay as much as $13.75 a yard. In contrast, stores sell the same carpeting for about $8 a square yard plus the cost of padding and installation, or about $10 complete. Some boiler rooms have sold carpeting that cost $2.50 wholesale for as much as $15 a square yard.

A *Home Furnishings Daily* reporter, Steven Sarich, interviewed a Chicago boiler-room operator and learned that 90 per cent of sales are on the installment plan. Chicago has become one of the hottest centers for this kind of selling, with boiler rooms there reaching families as far away as Gary, Hammond and other industrial towns in that region. Sarich reports that a leading operator says boiler rooms can outsell regular stores because their canvassers have "tenacity." Once in your home, they find you are easier to sell. There are no distractions as in stores to divert you from the salesman's "pitch." Boiler rooms sprout like weeds as salesmen learn the technique, then set up their own business. Their chief overhead is for phones.

In Detroit, hundreds of families paid door-to-door sellers as much as $30 a yard for what later proved to be inferior carpeting. But the sellers had turned over their contracts to a Detroit bank, which insisted on payment. The families picketed the bank, and agreed among themselves not to make further payments. Over a hundred of them went to the state capitol in Lansing, demanding protection against deceptive sellers and the banks and finance companies who underwrite their operations.

This verbatim report from a California housewife shows how such money-raiders set the snare and then close in for the kill, with every move precisely timed: "I was contacted on the phone. I said I would not be interested. The lady on the phone said I would be under no obligation but they would like to show us a garbage disposer for advertising purposes only, and our name had been chosen in this location. I still said I wouldn't be interested, but that evening a demonstrator called. He said he was not a salesman, just a demonstrator. We let him demonstrate. The deal is that you pay for the machine alone. No installation fee. Free soap for a year. Free service for a year. They also pay part of the cost of pumping the septic tank. My husband signed the contract. The disposer was installed the next morning at 8 o'clock. I asked the firm not to put the contract through the bank as I would use my own money to save the finance charge. The seller didn't wait but that same day was paid by the bank for the full amount of the contract—$339."

Actually, good-quality garbage-disposer units can be bought for $60 to $85, plus $20 to $25 for installation if there are no special problems.

Note that without the financing provided by respected banks and finance companies, many of today's credit rackets could never have flourished to the extent they have. One upstate New York bank financed $1,800,000 in food-freezer contracts for a single high-pressure promoter.

A persistent device for selling expensive appliances, home improvements, home fire alarm systems and sometimes cars is the referral or bonus plan.

One woman reported that she bought a home-cleaning system, including a vacuum, floor polisher and carpet sweeper, for $220 (with finance charge, $260). She was attracted by the company's "referral program," promising payments if she made sales-producing appointments for the salesman. Later, she wondered whether this would be fair to her friends. Then she began to question why she had paid so much for a vacuum cleaner. She consulted the Better Business Bureau and found they were critical of referral plans. Finally, she learned that one of the names on the list of people the salesman said had earned bonuses was that of a regional manager for the vacuum cleaner firm. The salesman had said this man was a milkman. It turned out that he *was*—five years before.

Some purported referral plan sellers have no intention of paying bonuses, Better Business Bureau records show. But even in those plans which have paid some, chances of earning part of the purchase price this way are both limited and undependable. In the vacuum cleaner plan described above, you get a bonus only if a sale is actually made, not merely for securing appointments. Your possible participation is limited to six months. Meanwhile, you have signed a conditional sales contract and must make your payments whether you make any successful referrals or not. . . .

Political Organization and Social Problems

23

THE ROLE OF GOVERNMENT

THERE HAVE BEEN a number of theories of the origin of government, some of them purely fictional. MacIver believes that government began in the primitive family, and that it developed gradually to meet the universal need of societies for regulation. He attempts to trace the development of government and law from their simple forms in primitive societies to their complex forms in modern multi-group societies.

47

Man and Government

by Robert M. MacIver

. . . Government is a phenomenon that emerges within the social life, inherent in the nature of social order. Man's social nature is a complex system of responses and of needs. In the relation of man to man everywhere there is the seed of government. It takes different institutional shapes according to the interplay of these relations. Sometimes, in the simplest communities, it has no ministers or agents, but is sufficiently maintained by the spontaneous reaction of the prevailing folk-myths. Always it is guarded by these myths, however elaborate the machinery through which it operates. Wherever man lives on the earth, at whatever level of existence, there is social order, and always permeating it is government of some sort. Government is an aspect of society.

Since we know of no more universal or more elemental form of society than the family, we can learn some primary lessons about the roots of government if we begin by observing how within that minimum society the rudiments of government are already present.

The Family as Realm

When we speak of government without a qualifying adjective we mean political government, the centralized organization that maintains a system of order over a community large or small. Political government is one form of social regulation, but by no means the only form. This point must be remembered when we raise questions about the origins of government. Regulation is a universal aspect of society. Society means a system of ordered relations. The system may be informal, folk-sustained, uncentralized, and without specific agencies, or it may be highly organized. But social regulation is always present, for no society can exist without some control over the native impulses of human beings. Political government

From Robert M. MacIver, *The Web of Government,* pp. 20–35, 61–71, 421–430 *passim.* Copyright 1947 by Robert M. MacIver and used with permission of The Macmillan Company.

Robert M. MacIver is Emeritus Professor of Political Science at Columbia University.

appears when social regulation is taken over or begins to be presided over by a central social agency.

At first the business of regulation is mainly a family concern, broadly protected by the custom of the inclusive group. To ascribe the beginnings of government to force or to contract or to some particular conjuncture is to ignore the fact that already in the family, the primary social unit, there are always present the curbs and controls that constitute the essence of government. Government is not something that is invented by the cunning or the strong and imposed on the rest. Government, however much exploitation of the weak by the strong it may historically exhibit, is much more fundamental than these explanations imply. It is the continuation by the more inclusive society of a process of regulation that is already highly developed within the family. . . .

The same necessities that create the family create also regulation. . . . The long dependence of the human young necessitates the establishment of some kind of control over sexual relations. There must be rules, and against so powerful an appetite, against the recklessness and the caprice of desire, these rules must be guarded by powerful sanctions. They must have back of them the authority of the community, bulwarked by such myths as the prevailing culture can devise against so formidable a danger.

Here is government in miniature and already government of a quite elaborate character. For sex is so closely inwrought with other concerns, and particularly with those of possession and inheritance, that its control carries with it a whole social code. The existence of the family requires the regulation of sex, the regulation of property, and the regulation of youth. . . .

So far as the child is concerned the imperium of the home is always absolute at the first, and only the length of time through which it holds undisputed sway differentiates in this respect one form of culture from another. For the child the magic of the law begins as soon as it becomes aware of others and of its relation to others. What is right and what is wrong, the things it must not do and the things it must do, are delivered to it from on high, as the law was delivered to Moses. It is so ordained, it is the eternal way of things. It is incorporated in the rites and religious observances of the community. Beyond it there is no other law.

It is easy then to see how "the habits pertaining to government" are bred in childhood, and how the family itself is always, for the child at least, a miniature political realm. . . .

From Family to State

Before we proceed to show how government grew up from its cradle in the family we shall pause over a matter of definition. . . . When we speak of the state we mean the organization of which government is the administrative organ. Every social organization must have a focus of admin-istration, an agency by which its policies are given specific character and translated into action. But the organization is greater than the organ. In this sense the state is greater and more inclusive than government. A state has a constitution, a code of laws, a way of setting up its government, a body of citizens.

Under certain social conditions, particularly in the simpler societies, it is not appropriate to speak of a state. The political structure may be embryonic or rudimentary. Similarly there may be no structure properly called a church, even though a religion prevails and there are special officers of religion, priests or prophets. The terms "state" and "church" apply to specific associational forms that emerge at a later stage, and char-acterize more complex societies. . . .

In the simplest societies we know the main locus of government is the family circle. This circle is more inclusive than the unitary family of mod-ern civilization. It is a primary kin-group fulfilling the functions essential to the family and many others besides. It has a definite head, whether the paterfamilias, the patriarch, the maternal uncle, or some other mem-ber. Within this circle the specific business of government is carried on. It makes and enforces the rules that are needed to meet the various con-tingencies that arise. Its ability to do so depends, of course, on the cus-toms that are common to a community composed of a number of such families. The community is held together by the understanding that each family exercises this role, and since the community is itself a more inclu-sive group of the kin there is an accepted mode in conformity to which the role is exercised. This mode is authoritative, as the result of the socio-psychological processes of adaptation that have worked continuously on the kin-group. But the authority is guarded by the rule of custom as it is applied by each family unit. The operations of government are not yet centralized. If there is a headman, or chief, he is not yet a ruler but only *primus inter pares,* a man of somewhat higher prestige or distinction. But his functions tend to increase as changes bring new problems, as the size of the community grows, as relationships with neighboring tribes become more difficult or more important, and so forth.

We cannot cope with the ramifications and vicissitudes of the process in which government became institutionalized, in which the state-form emerged. It is a process that begins before there is any light of history and it is one that is still far from being fulfilled. Under endlessly varied circumstances the "habits pertaining to government," which at first were centered in the family and the kin-circle, found a locus in the inclusive community. We must be content to take a few glimpses, perhaps sufficient to show the more obvious steps that led to the extension and centralization of authority.

Frequently we find that the government of a tribe or of a locality is in the hands of the "old men," or, in patriarchal society, of "the fathers." In many languages, as in our own, such expressions as "the elders," "the city fathers," "the seigniory," "the senate," and so forth, connote authority. It is easy to understand how the heads of families would come together to discuss and administer inter-family concerns, or perhaps first to settle some trouble or compose some quarrel arising between members of their respective households. In such meetings some patriarch, some forceful personality, would assume the role of leader. The meeting becomes a council, and the leader becomes its head, the chief.

As chief, he superintends the organization of the community for particular purposes, to carry on a trading expedition, to stage a festival or a ritual, to arrange a hunt, to reallocate lands, to seize some booty from a neighboring tribe, to defend the community against enemies. For these purposes the chief at length gathers about him a group of assistants or henchmen, a bodyguard. So he becomes elevated above the other "fathers." His prerogatives become gradually defined, his particular honors, his lion's share of the booty, the ceremonies proper to his office. Custom is always at work turning example into precedent and precedent into institution.

An important step in this process is the turning of chieftainship into hereditary office. An aggressive or ambitious leader is likely to use his prestige so as to favor the appointment of his son or near-of-kin as his successor. Thus one family is singled out from all the rest, the ruling family. With this elevation the distinction between chief and subjects is developed, the distance between the chief and the other "fathers" is widened, with consequent new accretions of ceremony and ritual to corroborate the change.

Along such lines the institutions of government must have developed, though with many variations. . . .

Government and Law

Without law there is no order and without order men are lost, not knowing where they go, not knowing what they do. A system of ordered relationships is a primary condition of human life at every level. More than anything else it is what society means. Even an outlaw group, a pirate ship, a robber gang, a band of brigands, has its own code of law, without which it could not exist. The picture of the "lawless savage," running wild in the woods, is wholly fictitious. The "savage" is never lawless, he clings to his own laws more tenaciously, more blindly, than does the civilized man. Only the completely *déraciné,* the man torn from his social environment, or the extreme sophisticate, or the tyrant who emerges in a time of confusion, can be described approximately as lawless. The law of the "savage" is not our law, and there is no law between him and the outsider—a situation that still exists, in times of war, for civilized peoples. The world has been, and up to the present has remained, a collocation of areas of lawfulness, communities with no law binding the one to the other.

To the primitive his law is sacred. It is unchallengeable. For him the law is not something made by chief or legislator or judge. It is timelessly ordained. He can no more disown it than he can disown his tribe. No chief can interfere with it, or he becomes lawless himself. It does not indeed follow that the primitive never disobeys his law, only that he rarely doubts and practically never disbelieves its rightfulness. A man may firmly believe in God, and still break under temptation what he believes to be God's commandments. The primitive finds ways of evading the law and under strong impulsion will directly violate it. But it is still the law of his life. It is not like our civilized law, a specialized body of *legal* rules. It is one with custom, it is the way of the folk, hallowed by tradition, breathing the very spirit of the folk. It is unwritten law, and that sometimes raises troubles, for on particular points the interpreters may differ. It has little or no legal form, and that sometimes causes difficulties, for, as has been said of the law of the Cheyenne Indians, its conclusions do not fall "into easily accessible patterns to draw minor trouble-festers to a head, and so to get them settled. This shows again and again in smoldering irritations over points of fact." But it is the firmament of order in society.

To the primitive his folk-law is not something men can make and remake. It is as much given to him as the earth he lives on. He scarcely recognizes it for what it is, a cultural product that changes imperceptibly with the changing culture. But of course Thomas Hobbes was right when he explained the law in human society is not like the law that rules the communities of ants or of bees. It is not in that sense "natural," not biologically determined but socially constructed, a folk-creation. Hence there is still the need for social sanctions. The errant member of the flocks must be disciplined, or his example will weaken respect for the law. Sometimes the folk itself is the sufficient guardian of its ways. The disrepute it attaches to the offender, the ostracism with which it penalizes more serious transgressions, or the direct punishment it inflicts when strongly aroused —as when the people turned against the offender Achan and "all Israel stoned him with stones"—these reactions serve in place of the machinery of law.

But, as we have seen, there is always leadership, even for the seemingly spontaneous responses of the folk. The habit of personal government that developed in every family circle would be enough, apart from other considerations, to stimulate the establishment of personal government over the larger community. At first the chief might merely settle disputes, but in doing so he was unconsciously changing and making law. The government thus set up, the chief or the council of elders, came easily to be regarded as the guardian of the folkways. It was in effect an executive and judicial authority, rather than a legislative one. Its direct law-making activity was at most minor, incidental, and sporadic. Occasionally, at a more advanced stage, the heroic figure of a "law-maker" appears, like Lycurgus or Solon or Hammurabi or Moses. But the Great Legislator is usually represented as being either a codifier of the laws or a prophet who receives them from God. . . .

In a modern society we distinguish between custom and law, and recognize that custom and other non-legal principles control a great sector of human behavior. In simple societies there is no clear-cut distinction between custom and law. The specific legal code, with its specific machinery of enforcement, has not yet developed. Consequently such government as existed was not regarded as making rules for the community, but only as administering its affairs, settling disputes, and guarding the folkways against the dangerous violator. Where, however, communities expanded in population and resources, where they extended their boundaries, through war or otherwise, and took under their dominion other groups or communities, where by reason of such conditions the tempo of social change was accelerated, and especially where serious conflicts and maladjustments arose between the more demarcated economic categories or social classes of the larger society, there the old-established folkways no longer gave the needed guidance. Government took on the job of *legislation*.

Often the strife between privileged classes and oppressed or exploited classes caused intolerable unrest and dissension. To allay it a whole new system of laws was necessary. This was the task to which the famous law-givers of the ancient world devoted themselves. In Athens, for example, when strife became acute between the oligarchic families or Eupatridae and the discontented population, Draco came forward with a system of ruthless penal laws that failed to achieve their purpose. Solon followed and abolished many of the privileges of the Eupatridae, setting up at the same time an entirely new apparatus of government. Later Cleisthenes appeared and sought to unify a still divided people by establishing a remarkably democratic constitution, giving to the citizen body as a whole the most complete right to control the entire policy of the state.

But neither the most famous law-giver nor the most powerful despot abrogated the general pattern of law-ways already existent among their peoples. The great law-giver was mostly concerned with reforming the constitution, the broad framework of government, the respective shares of different groups in the making of policy, the powers and privileges possessed by different classes of the community. The main body of laws and law-usages remained and, where necessary, was readjusted to the new order. The despot scarcely tampered with the laws at all. . . .

Not only in primitive society but also in the ancient civilizations and in the mediaeval world it was accepted doctrine that the ruler was subject to the laws, not above them, and that the body of laws was something scarcely touched by the fiat of authority. The law is the law of the community, not the law of the ruler. Sometimes the law was regarded as expressive of the will of God, as among the Hebrews; sometimes it was regarded as emanating from the whole people. . . .

The same doctrine held throughout the Middle Ages. It was differently oriented to correspond with the different social structure. The mediaeval king or emperor did not make laws or decrees of his mere pleasure, but with the consent of his council. His council was supposed to stand for the community. His authority was always presumed to be derived from the community, and, as Bracton put it, the law was the bridle of authority. Furthermore, the notion of natural law as the abiding model of human law prevailed in the thought of the times. And of course there was the constant admonition to the ruler that he was subject to the law of God. In the Middle Ages there was no lack of accepted ethical and religious standards to which political authority was "in principle" subject. It is true that the approach of practice to principle was often remote. Perhaps there has been no great period of history wherein ethical prescriptions were so clearly formulated and so universally espoused while yet the behavior of those in power seemed in effect regardless of them. "The king stands below the law of nature," "the prince cannot change the law of nature," "any act that violates the law of nature is null and void"—such expressions recur in the writings of mediaeval thinkers but they neither deterred princes from their ambitions nor protected the people from arbitrary power. Abstract rights could give small comfort against concrete wrongs. . . .

With the Renaissance we find the rise of another doctrine concerning the relation of government and law, a doctrine that in its fulfillment denied the older conception of the basis of order in society and at times shook and even cracked the whole firmament of law. This was the doctrine that set the ruler above the law and made his single will the very source of law. . . . Political thinkers of the sixteenth century in Western Europe, and particularly in France, were engaged in buttressing the authority of the king, since their age was weary of the old wars of feudal barons within the disunited realm and of the new and more embittered wars of religious sects that threatened to destroy whatever unity the realm still possessed. The solution was to elevate the monarch to a commanding height above all other men and leaders of men and to invest him with complete supremacy over them all. So the doctrine of sovereignty was re-devised and greatly amplified and elaborated. The king, formerly the defender of the community-made law, now became the supreme lord who gave its law to the community. Hitherto the king had owed, in the thought of learned and ignorant alike, his authority to the law; now the law owed its authority to him. . . .

But there was a serious flaw in the new doctrine, and it was manifest from the first. The sovereign was one, indivisible, omni-competent. What then of the claims of religion? There were many who on this ground resisted the new exaltation of the king. Among them was the great Jesuit leader, Suarez, who vindicated the autonomy of the spiritual realm against the state, asserting again the higher authority of the former and the right of men to wage war against tyrannical rulers. Where there were no religious divisions within the greater state the problem could be somehow met. The king could still be by God appointed, invested with the divine right of kings, entering into a concordat with the church and acting as defender of the faith. But how could the adherents of one faith accept as sovereign over their religious brotherhood a ruler of another faith? How could they accept the principle of the treaty of Augsburg, that the religion of the prince held for the territory over which he ruled? The religion of every group proclaimed that it was better to obey God than man. Only three years after Bodin's work on *The Republic* there appeared also in France the famous Huguenot treatise, *Vindiciae contra tyrannos,* the author of which asserted that the sovereign becomes a tyrant, whom it is the duty of the magistrates to resist, if his commands run counter to true religion and the law of God.

From the time of the Reformation the number of religious sects was on the increase. In some countries the ruler was Roman Catholic, in others he was Protestant. Everywhere there were religious groups that suffered persecution for their faith. The age had not yet discovered that the ruler need not meddle with the religion of his subjects or that it was unnecessary to make a particular religion a condition of civic rights or that, when citizens were divided by religious differences, the firmament of order was not weakened but on the contrary much strengthened if each group was free to worship in its own way or to worship its own God. The new myth of sovereignty blocked, instead of promoting, the solution of this sharpening issue.

Meanwhile, although the states of Western Europe—France, England, and Spain—consolidated the monarchy, making the throne strong against the crumbling claims of the feudal hierarchy, their internal order was threatened again and again by religious strife. Bodin's trust in the law of nature gave no comfort to oppressed minorities, subject to the omni-competent sovereignty of ruthless kings. He himself believed in tolerance and detested religious fanatacism. But his doctrine of sovereignty merely gave to a fanatical age a new doctrinal sword. The religious group that had the monarchy on its side was only too ready to attribute to the secular arm the defence of the faith. In this there was no difference between the reformist Luther or Melanchthon, the Presbyterian Calvin or Beza or Knox, the Anglican bishops who in their *Convocation Book* declared that any rebellion against king or magistrate, for any cause whatsoever, is "a sin very detestable against God," and the Catholic Bossuet.

When, as happened often enough, the situation was reversed and their own faith was persecuted, the same groups were apt to invoke the law of God against the tyrant, and to declare, with many scriptural supports, that "to obey man in any thing against God is unlawful and in plain disobedience." So wrote, for example, Christopher Goodman in his work *How Superior Powers Ought to be Obeyed*. So said Calvin and Knox regarding monarchs who professed other faiths than their own.

The Massacre of St. Bartholomew, the "English Terror" organized by Thomas Cromwell under Henry the Eighth, the persecution of Protestants under "Bloody Mary," and the numerous "wars of religion" high-lighted the omni-competence of sovereignty. Revolts of the middle economic classes, especially in England, began to increase the confusion that hitherto had centered in the religious issue. The old bases of authority were menaced, the firmament of order was threatened. A new kind of society was developing within the greater state, a society no longer, like feudal society, uni-centered in its faith nor uniform in its economic pattern. It was the dawn of modern multi-group society. The authoritarian order, whether the feudal type or the new type of royal absolutism, was no longer appropriate, could not much longer be maintained. But the doctrine of the new order was not yet developed. The idea of "toleration," as a concession to non-conformist faiths, was wholly inadequate. Men felt the need for a new basis of order but old traditions yielded slowly. . . .

The Multi-Group Society

Our main argument to this point is that the relation of man to the many groups and forms of organization to which he is more nearly or more distantly, more deeply or more superficially, attached is not solved by making one of these, whether the state or any other, the sole or inclusive object of his devotion, the one social focus of his being. . . .

The many cultural organizations of society have not and cannot have any one focus, cannot without losing their identity and their function be amalgamated and absorbed as mere departments of the state. Now we face the question of the inter-adjustment of all these organizations, and of the groups who maintain them, within the ordered yet free life of the community. Here is the essential problem of our multi-group society.

The full requirement of cultural liberty has rarely, if ever, been realized. In democratic countries it is now *politically* established. These countries have advanced far since the days when the king of one of them announced that he would "make the extirpation of the heretics his principal business." Gradually they passed from persecution to toleration and from toleration to the position that a man's religion is no concern of the state. The Edict of Nantes in 1598 was the first acknowledgment of a Roman Catholic government that "heretics" should be accorded civil rights, but even as late as 1776 the greatest of French radicals could assert that it was "impossible for men to live at peace with those they believe to be damned." In Protestant countries Roman Catholics were at length "tolerated," but it was only in 1819 that even England admitted them to citizenship. As for Jews, they have suffered longer and more grievously from persecution and the denial of civil rights than those who professed any other religion.

The principles set out in the First Amendment of the United States Constitution, that no law shall be enacted respecting an establishment of religion, has in effect been accepted by most democratic countries as well as by some others that cannot be placed in that category. But the problem of the multi-group society is not solved merely by the formal recognition of equality before the law. Such equality can exist while nevertheless minority groups or groups in an inferior economic or social position may be subject to such discrimination that they are practically excluded from participation in the life of the community. An outstanding example is the situation of the Negroes in the United States, particularly in the South. Other groups suffer discrimination to different degrees. The Jewish people are exposed to it but so in a measure are various ethnic groups, especially those of Eastern European countries, while yet stronger disabilities are applied against the Chinese, the Japanese, and the people of India. If we add to these groups the American Indians, the Filipinos, the Mexicans and other Latin-Americans we get the picture of a country constitutionally dedicated to the equality of men that nevertheless exhibits a complex pattern of rifts and fissures ramifying across the life of the community.

In different countries the problem takes different shapes. While in the United States minority groups are dispersed throughout the population, in some other countries they have a territorial locus, as in the Balkan area. Sometimes ethnic differences are associated with differences of religion. Often the disadvantaged groups occupy an inferior economic status. Not infrequently there is political as well as social and economic discrimination. This situation is found in its extreme form in colonial possessions, where the usual relation of majority and minority is reversed in favor of a dominant alien group.

Under all conditions the discrimination of group against group is detrimental to the wellbeing of the community. Those who are discriminated against are balked in their social impulses, are prevented from developing their capacities, become warped or frustrated, secretly or openly nurse a spirit of animosity against the dominant group. Energies that otherwise might have been devoted to constructive service are diverted and consumed in the friction of fruitless conflict. The dominant group, fearing the loss of its privileges, takes its stand on a traditional conservatism and loses the power of adapting itself to the changing times. The dominated, unless they are sunk in the worse apathy of sullen impotence, respond to subversive doctrines that do not look beyond the overthrow of the authority they resent. Each side conceives a false image of the other, denying their common humanity, and the community is torn asunder.

There is no way out of this impasse, apart from revolution, except the gradual readjustment of group relations in the direction of equality of opportunity—not merely legal equality. Since this readjustment requires the abandonment of habits and traditions, the breaking of taboos, the reconstruction of the distorted images cherished by each group of the other, and the recognition that the narrower interests and fears and prides that stimulate discrimination and prejudice are adverse to the common good and often empty or vain, its achievement can be effected only through the arduous and generally slow processes of social education. The sense of community, dissipated by the pervading specialization of interests, needs to be reinforced. The common values of the embracing culture need to be reasserted and again made vital. The provision of equality of opportunity will not of itself bring about any such result. It will serve chiefly by removing a source of division that stands obdurately in the way of social cohesion. Only when this obstacle is removed can the positive values of the multi-group society be cultivated—if we have the wisdom to seek and to find them.

The sense of the need of community, if not the sense of community, is still alive and seeks embodiment. It is witnessed to by men's devotion to the nation and by their attachment to some local community they feel— or once felt—to be their home. But these bonds do not satisfy the need, do not sufficiently provide the experience of effective solidarity. The nation is too wide and too diverse. The local community is too heterogeneous, if it is large, or too limited, if it is small. Often the attachment to it is nostalgic or merely sentimental. So the unit gropes for a more satisfying unity, seeking to recover the spirit of co-operative living that animated the uni-group society. Sometimes men seek to recover it by methods that would re-impose the old order on the new. They would restore the myth of the uni-group society; they would make the all-inclusive state the sufficient focus of our moral and spiritual being; they would even, as totalitarians, ruthlessly co-ordinate out of existence our cultural heterogeneity. But there is no road back. The course of civilization is as irreversible as time itself. We have left behind the one-room social habitation of our ancestors. We have built ourselves a house of many mansions. Somehow we must learn to make it ours.

24

DEMOCRACIES AND DICTATORSHIPS

CHANGE IS UNIVERSAL in human societies, and this applies to social ideologies and forms of government as much as to other aspects of culture. In our first selection, Carr traces the change from earlier forms of democracy to the "mass democracy" found in our present-day society. Because this is a new phenomenon—"a creation of the last half-century"—many new problems have entered the picture. He believes that making mass democracy work will require not only creative effort by responsible leaders, but a society educated to such a point as to close the gap between the electorate and the leaders.

Adlai Stevenson considers the possible future for democracy, and discusses the present-day challenges to the idea of government by the consent of the governed. He concludes, however, that democracy will ultimately prevail provided that we re-examine and adapt its principles to the changing needs of our times.

In opposition to democracy stands the totalitarian theory of government. Brewster explains why all totalitarian states are dictatorships, even though not all dictatorships are totalitarian.

48

From Individualism to Mass Democracy

by Edward Hallett Carr

The problem of political organization in the new society is to adapt to the mass civilization of the twentieth century conceptions of democracy formed in earlier and highly individualistic periods of history. The proclamation by the French revolution of popular sovereignty was a serious challenge to institutions which had grown up under quite different auspices and influences. It is no accident that Athenian democracy, which has been commonly regarded as the source and exemplar of democratic institutions, was the creation and prerogative of a limited and privileged group of the population. It is no accident that Locke, the founder of the modern democratic tradition, was the chosen philosopher and prophet of the eighteenth-century English Whig oligarchy. It is no accident that the magnificent structure of British nineteenth-century liberal democracy was built up on a highly restrictive property franchise. History points unmistakably to the fact that political democracy, in the forms in which it has hitherto been known, flourishes best where some of the people, but not all the people, are free and equal; and, since this conclusion is incompatible with the conditions of the new society and repugnant to the contemporary conscience, the task of saving democracy in our time is the task of reconciling it with the postulate of popular sovereignty and mass civilization.

Modern democracy, as it grew up and spread from its focus in western Europe over the past three centuries, rested on three main propositions: first, that the individual conscience is the ultimate source of decisions about what is right and wrong; second, that there exists between different individuals a fundamental harmony of interests strong enough to enable them to live peacefully together in society; third, that where action has to be taken in the name of society, rational discussion between individuals is the best method of reaching a decision on that action. Modern democracy

From *The New Society* by Edward Hallett Carr, pp. 61–79. Published by St. Martin's Press, Inc., New York, and Macmillan & Co. Ltd., London, 1957. Reprinted by permission.

Edward Hallett Carr is an English political scientist with a special interest in Soviet history. He has been in the diplomatic service, and is a fellow of Trinity College.

is, in virtue of its origins, individualist, optimistic and rational. The three main propositions on which it is based have all been seriously challenged in the contemporary world.

In the first place, the individualist conception of democracy rests on a belief in the inherent rights of individuals based on natural law. According to this conception, the function of democratic government is not to create or innovate, but to interpret and apply rights which already exist. This accounts for the importance attached in the democratic tradition to the rights of minorities within the citizen body. Decision by majority vote might be a necessary and convenient device. But individuals belonging to the minority had the same inherent rights as those belonging to the majority. Insistence on the rule of law, preferably inscribed in a written and permanent constitution, was an important part of the individualist tradition of democracy. The individual enjoyed certain indefeasible rights against the society of which he was a member; these rights were often regarded as deriving from a real or hypothetical "social contract" which formed the title-deeds of society. Just as the individualist tradition in *laissez-faire* economics was hostile to all forms of combination, so the individualist tradition in politics was inimical to the idea of political parties. Both in Athenian democracy and in eighteenth-century Britain, parties were regarded with mistrust and denounced as "factions."

The French revolution with its announcement of the sovereignty of the people made the first serious assault on this view of democracy. The individualism of Locke's "natural law" was replaced by the collectivism of Rousseau's "general will." Both Pericles and Locke had thought in terms of a small and select society of privileged citizens. Rousseau for the first time thought in terms of the sovereignty of the whole people, and faced the issue of mass democracy. He did so reluctantly; for he himself preferred the tiny community where direct democracy, without representation or delegation of powers, was still possible. But he recognized that the large nation had come to stay, and held that in such conditions the people could be sovereign only if it imposed on itself the discipline of a "general will."

The practical conclusion drawn from this doctrine, not by Rousseau himself, but by the Jacobins, was the foundation of a single political party to embody the general will. Its logical conclusions were still more far-reaching. The individual, far from enjoying rights against society assured to him by natural law, had no appeal against the deliverances of the general will. The general will was the repository of virtue and justice, the state its instrument for putting them into effect. The individual who dissented from the general will cut himself off from the community and was a self-proclaimed traitor to it. Rousseau's doctrine led directly to the Jacobin practice of revolution terror.

It would be idle to embark on a theoretical discussion of the rival merits of the two conceptions of democracy. Individualism is an oligarchic doctrine—the doctrine of the select and enterprising few who refuse to be merged in the mass. The function of natural law in modern history, though it is susceptible of other interpretations, has been to sanctify existing rights and to brand as immoral attempts to overthrow them. A conception based on individual rights rooted in natural law was a natural product of the oligarchic and conservative eighteenth century. It was equally natural that this conception should be challenged and overthrown in the ferment of a revolution that proclaimed the supremacy of popular sovereignty.

While, however, the beginnings of mass democracy can be discerned in the doctrines of Rousseau and in the practice of the French revolution, the problem in its modern form was a product of the nineteenth century. The Industrial revolution started its career under the banner of individual enterprise. Adam Smith was as straightforward an example as could be desired of eighteenth-century individualism. But presently the machine overtook the man, and the competitive advantages of mass production ushered in the age of standardization and larger and larger economic units. And with the mammoth trust and mammoth trade union came the mammoth organ of opinion, the mammoth political party and, floating above them all, the mammoth state, narrowing still further the field of responsibility and action left to the individual and setting the stage for the new mass society. It was the English Utilitarians who, by rejecting natural law, turned their backs on the individualist tradition and, by postulating the greatest good and the greatest number as the supreme goal, laid the theoretical foundation of mass democracy in Britain; in practice, they were also the first radical reformers.

Before long, thinkers began to explore some of the awkward potentialities of mass democracy. The danger of the oppression of minorities by the majority was the most obvious. This was discerned by Tocqueville in the United States in the 1830's and by J. S. Mill in England twenty-five years later. In our own time the danger has reappeared in a more insidious form. Soviet Russia has a form of government which describes itself as a democracy. It claims, not without some historical justification, to stem from the Jacobins who stemmed from Rousseau and the doctrine of the general will. The general will is an orthodoxy which purports to express the common opinion; the minority which dissents can legitimately be suppressed. But we are not concerned here with the abuses and excesses of the Soviet form of government. What troubles us is the question how far, in moving from the individualism of restrictive liberal democracy to the mass civilization of today, we have ourselves become involved in a conception of democracy which postulates a general will. The question is all around us today not only in the form of loyalty tests, avowed or secret, or committees on un-American activities, but also in the form of the closed shop and of increasingly rigid standards of party discipline.

In a speech made to a regional Labour party conference at the time of Mr. Aneurin Bevan's resignation in April, the Minister of Defence denounced "absence of loyalty" in the party: "The loyalty of our party," exclaimed Mr. Shinwell, "is superior to any exhibition of political private enterprise. . . . No person, I don't care who he is, can be allowed to interfere with the democratic structure of this party." Lenin used strikingly similar phrases at the Bolshevik party congress in March 1921. We have moved far from the conception of truth emerging from the interplay of divergent individual opinions. Loyalty has come to mean the submission of the individual to the general will of the party or group.

The second postulate of Locke's conception of society, the belief in a fundamental harmony of interests between individuals, equally failed to stand the test of time, and for much the same reason. Even more than natural law, the harmony of interests was essentially a conservative doctrine. If the interest of the individual rightly understood coincided with the interest of the whole society, it followed that any individual who assailed the existing order was acting against his own true interests and could be condemned not only as wicked, but as short-sighted and foolish. Some such argument was, for instance, often invoked against strikers who failed to recognize the common interest uniting them with their employers. The French revolution, an act of self-assertion by the third estate against the two senior estates of nobility and clergy, demonstrated—like any other violent upheaval—the hollowness of the harmony of interest; and the doctrine was soon also to be powerfully challenged on the theoretical plane.

The challenge came from two quarters. The Utilitarians, while not making a frontal attack on the doctrine, implicitly denied it when they asserted that the harmony of interests had to be created by remedial action before it would work. They saw that some of the worst existing inequalities would have to be reformed out of existence before it was possible to speak without irony of a society based on a harmony of interests; and they believed in increased education, and the true liberty of thought which would result from it, as a necessary preparation for establishing harmony. Then Marx and Engels in the *Communist Manifesto* took the class struggle and made out of it a theory of history which, partial though it was, stood nearer to current reality than the theory of the harmony of interests had ever done. Social and economic pressures resulting from the breakdown of *laissez-faire* illustrated in practice what Marx had demonstrated in theory.

But in Great Britain it was reformist Utilitarianism rather than revolutionary Marxism that set the pace. The flagrant absence of a harmony of interests between competing and conflicting classes more and more urgently called for state intervention. The state could no longer be content to hold the ring; it must descend actively into the arena to create a harmony which did not exist in nature. Legislation, hitherto regarded as an exceptional function required from time to time to clear up some misunderstanding or to rectify some abuse, now became normal and continuous. It no longer sufficed to interpret and apply rights conferred on the individual by the laws of nature. What was expected of the state was positive and continuous activity—a form of social and economic engineering. The substitution of a planned economy for *laissez-faire* capitalism brought about a radical transformation in the attitude towards the state. The functions of the state were no longer merely supervisory, but creative and remedial. It was no longer an organ whose weakness was its virtue and whose activities should be restricted to a minimum in the interests of freedom. It was an organ which one sought to capture and control for the carrying out of necessary reforms; and, having captured it, one sought to make it as powerful and effective as possible in order to carry them out. The twentieth century has not only replaced individualist democracy by mass democracy, but has substituted the cult of the strong remedial state for the doctrine of the natural harmony of interests.

The third main characteristic of Locke's conception of society—a characteristic which helped to give the eighteenth century its nicknames of the Age of Reason or the Age of Enlightenment—was its faith in rational discussion as a guide to political action. This faith provided the most popular nineteenth-century justification of the rule of the majority as the basis of democracy. Since men were on the whole rational, and since the right answer to any given issue could be discovered by reason, one was more likely, in the case of dispute, to find right judgment on the side of the majority than on the side of the minority. Like other eighteenth-century conceptions, the doctrine of reason in politics was the doctrine of a ruling oligarchy. The rational approach to politics, which encouraged leisurely argument and eschewed passion, was eminently the approach of a well-to-do, leisured and cultured class. Its efficacy could be most clearly and certainly guaranteed when the citizen body consisted of a relatively small number of educated persons who could be trusted to reason intelligently and dispassionately on controversial issues submitted to them.

The prominent rôle assigned to reason in the original democratic scheme provides perhaps the most convincing explanation why democracy has hitherto always seemed to flourish best with a restrictive franchise. Much has been written in recent years of the decline of reason, and of respect for reason, in human affairs, when sometimes what has really happened has been the abandonment of the highly simplified eighteenth-century view of reason in favour of a subtler and more sophisticated analysis. But it is none the less true that the epoch-making changes in our attitude towards reason provide a key to some of the profoundest problems of contemporary democracy.

First of all, the notion that men of intelligence and good will were likely by process of rational discussion to reach a correct opinion on controversial political questions could be valid only in an age when such questions were comparatively few and simple enough to be accessible to the educated layman. It implicitly denied that any specialized knowledge was required to solve political problems. This hypothesis was perhaps tenable so long as the state was not required to intervene in economic issues, and the questions on which decisions had to be taken turned on matters of practical detail or general political principles. In the first half of the twentieth century these conditions had everywhere ceased to exist. In Great Britain major issues of a highly controversial character like the return to the gold standard in 1925 or the acceptance of the American loan in 1946 were of a kind in which no opinion seriously counted except that of the trained expert in possession of a vast array of facts and figures, some of them probably not available to the public. In such matters the ordinary citizen could not even have an intelligent opinion on the question who were the best experts to consult. The only rôle he could hope to play was to exercise his hunch at the election by choosing the right leader to consult the right experts about vital, though probably still unformulated, issues of policy which would ultimately affect his daily life.

At this initial stage of the argument reason itself is not dethroned from its supreme rôle in the decision of political issues. The citizen is merely asked to surrender his right of decision to the superior reason of the expert. At the second stage of the argument reason itself is used to dethrone reason. The social psychologist, employing rational methods of investigation, discovers that men in the mass are often most effectively moved by non-rational emotions such as admiration, envy, hatred, and can be most effectively reached not by rational argument, but by emotional appeals to eye and ear, or by sheer repetition. Propaganda is as essential a function of mass democracy as advertising of mass production. The political organizer takes a leaf out of the book of the commercial advertiser and sells the leader or the candidate to the voter by the same methods used to sell patent medicines or refrigerators. The appeal is no longer to the reason of the citizen, but to his gullibility.

A more recent phenomenon has been the emergence of what Max Weber called the "charismatic leader" as the expression of the general will. The retreat from individualism seemed to issue at last—and not alone in the so-called totalitarian countries—in the exaltation of a single individual leader who personified and resumed within himself the qualities and aspirations of the "little man," of the ordinary individual lost and bewildered in the new mass society. But the principal qualification of the leader is no longer his capacity to reason correctly on political or economic issues, or even his capacity to choose the best experts to reason for him, but a good public face, a convincing voice, a sympathetic fireside manner on the radio; and these qualities are deliberately built up for him by his publicity agents.

In this picture of the techniques of contemporary democracy, the party headquarters, the directing brain at the centre, still operates rationally, but uses irrational rather than rational means to achieve its ends—means which are, moreover, not merely irrational but largely irrelevant to the purposes to be pursued or to the decisions to be taken.

The third stage of the argument reaches deeper levels. Hegel, drawing out the philosophical implications of Rousseau's doctrine, had identified the course of history with universal reason, to which the individual reason stood in the same relation as the individual will to Rousseau's general will. Individual reason had been the corner-stone of individualist democracy. Marx took Hegel's collective reason to make it the corner-stone of the new mass democracy. Marx purported to reject the metaphysical character of Hegel's thought. But, equally with Hegel, he conceived of history pursuing a rational course, which could be analysed and even predicted in terms of reason. Hegel had spoken of the cunning of reason in history, using individuals to achieve purposes of which they themselves were unconscious. Marx would have rejected the turn of phrase as metaphysical. But his conception of history as a continuous process of class struggle contained elements of determinism which revealed its Hegelian ancestry, at any rate on one side. Marx remained a thorough-going rationalist. But the reason whose validity he accepted was collective rather than individual.

Marx played, however, a far more important part in what has been called "the flight from reason" than by the mere exaltation of the collective over the individual. By his vigorous assertion that "being determines consciousness, not consciousness being," that thinking is conditioned by the social environment of the thinker, and that ideas are the superstructure of a totality whose foundation is formed by the material conditions of life, Marx presented a clear challenge to what had hitherto been regarded as the sovereign or autonomous reason. The actors who played significant parts in the historical drama were playing parts already written for them: this indeed was what made them significant. The function of individual reason was to identify itself with the universal reason which determined the course of history and to make itself the agent and executor of this universal reason. Some such view is indeed involved in any attempt to trace back historical events to underlying social causes; and Marx— and still more Engels—hedged a little in later years about the rôle of the individual in history. But the extraordinary vigour and conviction with which he drove home his main argument, and the political theory which he founded on it, give him a leading place among those nineteenth-century thinkers who shattered the comfortable belief of the Age of Enlightenment in the decisive power of individual reason in shaping the course of history.

Marx's keenest polemics were those directed to prove the "conditioned" character of the thinking of his opponents and particularly of the capitalist ruling class of the most advanced countries of his day. If they thought as they did it was because, as members of a class, "being" determined their "consciousness," and their ideas necessarily lacked any independent objectivity and validity. Hegel, as a good conservative, had exempted the current reality of the Prussian from the operation of the dialectic which had destroyed successively so many earlier historical forms. Marx, as a revolutionary, admitted no such absolute in the present, but only in the future. The proletariat, whose victory would automatically abolish classes, was alone the basis of absolute value; and collective proletarian thinking had thus an objectivity which was denied to the thinking of other classes. Marx's willingness, like that of Hegel, to admit an absolute as the culminating point of his dialectical process was, however, an element of inconsistency in his system; and, just as Marx was far more concerned to dissect capitalism than to provide a blue-print for socialism, so his use of the dialectic to lay bare the conditioned thinking of his opponents lay far nearer to his heart, and was far more effective, than his enunciation of the objective and absolute values of the proletariat. Marx's writings gave a powerful impetus to all forms of relativism. It seemed less important, at a time when the proletarian revolution was as yet nowhere in sight, to note his admission of absolute truth as a prerogative of the proletariat. The proletariat was for Marx the collective repository of Rousseau's infallible general will.

Another thinker of the later nineteenth century also helped to mould the climate of political opinion. Like Darwin, Freud was a scientist without pretensions to be a philosopher or, still less, a political thinker. But in the flight from reason at the end of the nineteenth century, he played the same popular rôle as Darwin had played a generation earlier in the philosophy of *laissez-faire*. Freud demonstrated that the fundamental attitudes of human beings in action and thought are largely determined at levels beneath that of consciousness, and that the supposedly rational explanations of those attitudes which we offer to ourselves and others are artificial and erroneous "rationalizations" of processes which we have failed to understand. Reason is given to us, Freud seems to say, not to direct our thought and action, but to camouflage the hidden forces which do direct it. This is a still more devastating version of the Marxist thesis of substructure and superstructure. The substructure of reality resides in the unconscious: what appears above the surface is no more than the reflexion, seen in a distorting ideological mirror, of what goes on underneath.

The political conclusion from all this—Freud himself drew none—is that any attempt to appeal to the reason of the ordinary man is waste of time, or is useful merely as camouflage to conceal the real nature of the process of persuasion; the appeal must be made to those subconscious strata which are decisive for thought and action. The debunking of ideology undertaken by the political science of Marx is repeated in a far more drastic and far-reaching way by the psychological science of Freud and his successors.

By the middle of the nineteenth century, therefore, the propositions of Locke on which the theory of liberal democracy were founded had all been subjected to fundamental attack, and the attack broadened and deepened as the century went on. Individualism began to give way to collectivism both in economic organization and in the forms and practice of mass democracy: the age of mass civilization had begun. The alleged harmony of interests between individuals was replaced by the naked struggle between powerful classes and organized interest groups. The belief in the settlement of issues by rational discussion was undermined, first, by recognition of the complex and technical character of the issues involved, later and more seriously, by recognition that rational arguments were merely the conditioned reflexion of the class interests of those who put them forward, and, last and most seriously of all, by the discovery that the democratic voter, like other human beings, is most effectively reached not by arguments directed to his reason, but by appeals directed to his irrational, subconscious prejudices. The picture of democracy which emerged from these criticisms was the picture of an arena where powerful interest-groups struggled for the mastery. The leaders themselves were often the spokesmen and instruments of historical processes which they did not fully understand; their followers consisted of voters recruited and marshalled for purposes of which they were wholly unconscious by all the subtle techniques of modern psychological science and modern commercial advertising.

The picture is overdrawn. But we shall not begin to understand the problems of mass democracy unless we recognize the serious elements of truth in it, unless we recognize how far we have moved away from the conceptions and from the conditions out of which the democratic tradition was born. From the conception of democracy as a select society of free individuals enjoying equal rights, and periodically electing to manage the affairs of the society, a small number of their peers, who deliberate together and decide by rational argument on the course to pursue (the assumption being that the course which appeals to the majority is likely to be the most rational), we have passed to the current reality of mass democracy. The typical mass democracy of today is a vast society of individuals, stratified by widely different social and economic backgrounds into a series of groups or classes, enjoying equal political rights the exercise of which is organized through two or more closely integrated political machines called parties. Between the parties and individual citizens stand an indeterminate number of entities variously known as unions, associations, lobbies or pressure-groups devoted to the promotion of some economic interest, or of some social or humanitarian cause in which keen critics usually detect a latent and perhaps unconscious interest.

At the first stage of the democratic process, these associations and groups form a sort of exchange and mart where votes are traded for support of particular policies; the more votes such a group controls the better its chance of having its views incorporated in the party platform. At the second stage, when these bargains have been made, the party as a united entity "goes to the country" and endeavours by every form of political propaganda to win the support of the unattached voter. At the third stage, when the election has been decided, the parties once more dispute or bargain together, in the light of the votes cast, on the policies to be put into effect; the details of procedure at this third stage differ considerably in different democratic countries in accordance with varying constitutional requirements and party structures. What is important to note is that the first and third stages are fierce matters of bargaining. At the second stage, where the mass persuasion of the electorate is at issue, the methods employed now commonly approximate more and more closely to those of commercial advertisers, who, on the advice of modern psychologists, find the appeal to fear, envy or self-aggrandizement more effective than the appeal to reason.

Certainly in the United States, where contemporary large-scale democracy has worked most successfully and where the strongest confidence is felt in its survival, experienced practitioners of politics would give little encouragement to the idea that rational argument exercises a major influence on the democratic process. We have returned to a barely disguised struggle of interest-groups in which the arguments used are for the most part no more than a rationalization of the interests concerned, and the rôle of persuasion is played by carefully calculated appeals to the irrational subconscious.

This discussion is intended to show not that mass democracy is more corrupt or less efficient than other forms of government (this I do not believe), but that mass democracy is a new phenomenon—a creation of the last half-century—which it is inappropriate and misleading to consider in terms of the philosophy of Locke or of the liberal democracy of the nineteenth century. It is new, because the new democratic society consists no longer of a homogeneous closed society of equal and economically secure individuals mutually recognizing one another's rights, but of ill coordinated, highly stratified masses of people of whom a large majority are primarily occupied with the daily struggle for existence. It is new, because the new democratic state can no longer be content to hold the ring in the strife of private economic interests, but must enter the arena at every moment and take the initiative in urgent issues of economic policy which affect the daily life of all the citizens, and especially of the least secure. It is new, because the old rationalist assumptions of Locke and of liberal democracy have broken down under the weight both of changed material conditions and of new scientific insights and inventions, and the leaders of the new democracy are concerned no longer primarily with the reflexion of opinion, but with the moulding and manipulation of opinion. To speak today of the defence of democracy as if we were defending something which we knew and had possessed for many decades or many centuries is self-deception and sham.

It is no answer to point to institutions that have survived from earlier forms of democracy. The survival of kingship in Great Britain does not prove that the British system of government is a monarchy; and democratic institutions survive in many countries today—some survived even in Hitler's Germany—which have little or no claim to be called democracies. The criterion must be sought not in the survival of traditional institutions, but in the question where power resides and how it is exercised. In this respect democracy is a matter of degree. Some countries today are more democratic than others. But none is perhaps very democratic, if any high standard of democracy is applied. Mass democracy is a difficult and hitherto largely uncharted territory; and we should be nearer the mark, and should have a far more convincing slogan, if we spoke of the need, not to defend democracy, but to create it.

In my second and third lectures I discussed two of the basic problems which confront the new society—the problem of a planned economy and the problem of the right deployment and use of our human resources. These problems are basic in the sense that their solution is a condition of survival. The old methods of organizing production have collapsed, and society cannot exist without bringing new ones into operation. But those problems might conceivably be solved—are even, perhaps, in danger of being solved—by other than democratic means: here the task of mass democracy is to meet known and recognized needs by methods that are compatible with democracy, and to do it in time. The central problem which I have been discussing today touches the essence of democracy itself. Large-scale political organizations show many of the characteristics of large-scale economic organization, and have followed the same path of development. Mass democracy has, through its very nature, thrown up on all sides specialized groups of leaders—what are sometimes called élites. Everywhere, in government, in political parties, in trade unions, in co-operatives, these indispensable élites have taken shape with startling rapidity over the last thirty years. Everywhere the rift has widened between leaders and rank and file.

The rift takes two forms. In the first place, the interests of the leaders are no longer fully identical with those of the rank and file, since they include the special interest of the leaders in maintaining their own leadership—an interest which is no doubt rationalized, but not always justly, as constituting an interest of the whole group. The leaders, instead of remaining mere delegates of their equals, tend in virtue of their functions to become a separate professional, and then a separate social, group, forming the nucleus of a new ruling class or, more insidiously still, being absorbed into the old ruling class. Secondly, and most important of all, there is an ever-increasing gap between the terms in which an issue is debated and solved among leaders and the terms in which the same issue is presented to the rank and file. Nobody supposes that the arguments which the leaders and managers of a political party or a trade union use among themselves in private conclave are the same as those which they present to a meeting of their members; and the methods of persuasion used from the public platform or over the radio will diverge more widely still. When the decision of substance has been taken by the leaders, whether of government, of party or of union, a further decision is often required on the best method of selling the decision. Broadly speaking, the rôle of reason varies inversely with the number of those to whom the argument is addressed. The decision of the leaders may be taken on rational grounds. But the motivation of the decision to the rank and file of the party or union, and still more to the general public, will contain a larger element of the irrational the larger the audience becomes. The spectacle of an efficient élite maintaining its authority and asserting its will over the mass by the rationally calculated use of irrational methods of persuasion is the most disturbing nightmare of mass democracy.

The problem defies any rough-and-ready answer. It was implicit in Lincoln's formula of government "of the people" (meaning, I take it, belonging to the people in the sense of popular sovereignty), "by the people" (implying, I think, direct participation in the business of government) and "for the people" (requiring an identity of interests between governors and governed only obtainable when such participation occurs). It was implicit in Lenin's much-derided demand that every cook should learn to govern and that every worker should take his turn at the work of administration. The building of nineteenth-century democracy was long and arduous. The building of the new mass democracy will be no easier. The historian can here only look back over the way we have come, and analyse the fundamental questions which are being presented to the coming generation. He may be able to throw some light on the nature of the answers that are required; but he cannot define or prescribe them.

For myself, it seems inconceivable that we can return to the individualist democracy of a privileged class; and, by the same token, we cannot return to the exclusively political democracy of the weak state exercising only police functions. We are committed to mass democracy, to egalitarian democracy, to the public control and planning of the economic process, and therefore to the strong state exercising remedial and constructive functions. On the fundamental rôle of reason I shall say something in my last lecture. Here I will say only that I have no faith in a flight into the irrational or in an exaltation of irrational values. Reason may be an imperfect instrument; and we can no longer take the simple view of its character and functions which satisfied the eighteenth and nineteenth centuries. But it is none the less in a widening and deepening of the power of reason that we must place our hope. Mass democracy calls just as much as individualist democracy for an educated society as well as for responsible and courageous leaders; for it is only thus that the gap between leaders and masses, which is the major threat to mass democracy, can be bridged. The task is difficult but not hopeless; and just as Great Britain has done more than any other country during the last five years to mark out new lines of social and economic advance, so I believe that she has better opportunities than any other country to lay the foundations of an educated mass democracy.

49

The Prospects for Democracy

by Adlai E. Stevenson

I said some ten years ago: "Self-criticism is the secret weapon of democracy. . . . We dare not just look back on great yesterdays. We must look forward to great tomorrows. What counts now is not just what we are *against,* but what we are *for. Who* leads us is less important than *what* leads us—what convictions, what courage, what faith. . . ."

We have all learned that modern technology can strengthen the despot's hand and the dictator's grasp—and for that reason, if no other, we know that democracy is more necessary now than it ever was. Of course, democracy is not self-executing. We have to make it work, and to make it work we have to understand it. Sober thought and fearless criticism are impossible without critical thinkers and thinking critics. Such persons must be given the opportunity to come together, to see new facts in the light of old principles, to evaluate old principles in the light of new facts, and by

From *Challenges to Democracy: The Next Ten Years,* edited by Edward Reed, Frederick A. Praeger, Publisher, 1963, pp. 229–239 *passim.* Copyright © 1963 by The Fund for the Republic, Inc. Reprinted by permission.

Adlai E. Stevenson was Governor of Illinois from 1949 to 1953, and later was twice Democratic candidate for President. From 1960 until his death he was United States Ambassador to the United Nations.

deliberation, debate, and dialogue to hammer out the consensus that makes democracy possible. And this, as we all know well, though some of us forget from time to time, requires intellectual independence, impenitent speculation, and freedom from political pressure. . . .

The study of democratic institutions—how to create them, how to sustain them, how to preserve them—will be necessary as long as men continue to seek faith in themselves, continue to harbor hope in their own capacity to progress, and cherish the charity that unites them in a common cause. And with the world undergoing such rapid change in geography, politics, and economics, the need to adapt our old and venerated institutions to the changes is urgent.

I suppose whether democracy can prevail in the great upheaval of our time is a valid question. Certainly, after 150 years of uninterrupted expansion of the idea of government by consent of the governed, it has recently met with mounting and formidable challenges all over the world from Fascist, Nazi, Communist authoritarians, and a variety of dictatorships. And we have good reason to know how clumsy, slow, inefficient, and costly it is compared with the celerity, certainty, and secrecy of absolutism. But the important thing is that it *has* survived. The important thing is that even the absolutists masquerade as democrats; even the military and quasi-military dictatorships strive in the name of democracy to manage the public business. And all of them say that authoritarianism is only a necessary transition to democracy.

Why? Because it is the most popular form of government yet devised; because it is, as it always has been, not only the prize of the steadfast and the courageous but the privilege of those who are better off; because, in short, as Jefferson said, it is "the only form of government which is not eternally at open or secret war with the rights of the people."

I have, therefore, no doubt that, distant as it may be for many people, it will ultimately prevail, that it will rewin lost ground, that it will expand its dominion—that it can withstand the winds that are blowing through the world—if, and I repeat if, we who are its custodians continually reexamine and adapt its principles to the changing needs of our changing times.

Years ago, Reinhold Niebuhr observed that "man's capacity for justice makes democracy possible; but man's inclination to injustice makes democracy necessary." And I suppose most of us, if we were asked to name the most profound issues at stake in the world today, would say the issues of freedom and democracy. We would say that the Western world, for all its errors and shortcomings, has for centuries tried to evolve a society in which the individual has enough legal, social, and political elbowroom to be not the puppet of the community but his own autonomous self.

And we would say, too, that the enemies of freedom, whatever the magnificent ends they propose—the brotherhood of man, the kingdom of saints, "from each according to his ability, to each according to his needs"—miss just this essential point: that man is greater than the social purposes to which he can be put. He must not be kicked about even with the most high-minded objectives. He is not a means or an instrument. He is an end in himself.

This, I take it, is the essence of what we mean by democracy—not so much voting systems or parliamentary systems or economic or legal systems —though they all enter in—as an irrevocable and final dedication to the dignity of man.

In this sense, democracy is perhaps mankind's most audacious experiment. This dignity, this equality of the human person, could hardly be further removed from the existential facts of human existence. There is precious little dignity, precious little equality, in our natural state. Most human beings have to spend their lives in utter vulnerability, all are murderable, all are torturable, and survive only through the restraint shown by more powerful neighbors. All are born unequal in terms of capacity or of strength. All are born to the inherent frailty of the human condition, naked and helpless, vulnerable all through life to the will of others, limited by ignorance, limited by physical weakness, limited by fear, limited by the phobias that fear engenders. It is not surprising that, given this basic defenselessness, the natural condition of man has not been far removed from Hobbes's definition of it as "nasty, brutish, and short."

For nearly 3,000 years, the political and social genius of what we can permissibly call "Western man" has struggled with these brute facts of our unsatisfactory existence. Ever since the Hebrews discovered personal moral responsibility, and the Greeks discovered the autonomy of the citizen, the effort has been made, with setbacks and defeats, with dark ages and interregnums, to create a social order in which weak, fallible, obstinate, silly, magnificent man can maintain his dignity and exercise his free and responsible choice.

The task has never been easy. Each step has been a groping in the dark, the dark of violence, of brute power, and of overweening arrogance. What we seek to defend today against new critics and new adversaries is essentially a great body of *experience,* not theories or untried ideals, but a solid mass of lived-through facts.

Equality before the law has been expanded and safeguarded by consultation and by representation—in other words, by the vote, which is not simply a device for peacefully changing government, although it is that too. It is not only a means of allowing the wearer to say where the shoe pinches. It is, in addition, a means of offsetting the natural inequalities that grow up in any society, however organized, as a result of the unequal endowment of people. The head of, say, General Electric has more means of influencing society than a small-town electrician. Against the advantage of brains and money, the vote is the only advantage the small man has. His voice, or vote, added to millions of other voices, offsets the accumulated power of society's entrenched positions. But equality before the law and the ballot box are only strands in the seamless robe in which all of our liberties are woven together; carelessly unravel one and the robe itself may come apart.

Another strand is enough social and economic opportunity for each man, even the poorest, to hold his dignity intact. The widest access to education and to training, equal opportunity for talent to find its niche, security of income and of work, the chance of health—all these belong to a social order of responsible and respected citizens. We no longer define democracy solely in political terms. The great effort in this century has been to work out its economic and social implications.

We are profoundly concerned with the extension of the concept of democracy—extension in depth, for we now believe that no human being, however lowly his occupation or poor his resources, can be excluded from the dignity of man; and extension in space, for the whole world is now a community, and we have to find ways in which the idea of a truly human society can be realized on a planetary scale. The two processes going forward simultaneously in every part of the globe make up the vast revolutionary ferment of our time. What we have to attempt today is the building of intercontinental forms of free community—certainly the most testing experiment of all those made so far by free men. Yet our past achievements give us the right to hope for future success.

One form of association already exists between virtually all of the nations of the globe; and, whatever work we may accomplish on a regional basis, the progress at the United Nations in the direction of a free society of equals must be part of our effort to extend the principle of liberty as the essential working principle of mankind.

How are we to set about this formidable task? There is one method that I most profoundly hope we shall avoid, and that is the method of self-righteous exhortation. We have, I fear, displayed an unattractive tendency to lecture new governments on their constitutional shortcomings and to point sometimes openly, sometimes implicitly, to the superior performance of the West. We can proudly admit that free government is a Western invention—by all odds its finest political achievement. But there are several things we must remember as well. We must remember that it took about eight centuries to develop these patterns of life in our own culture. We must remember that our form of democracy is the most subtle, the most sophisticated form of government in the world. Other more primitive, still developing peoples cannot be expected to master it overnight, but move toward it they will; and such institutions as the United Nations help to train their leadership in our ways. Moreover, new states always face appalling problems of readjustment, and we must be smart enough to recognize when and how these alien leaderships move our way.

If now we see in Africa single-party rule, dominated by one leader, with changing policies and political choice severely restricted, we should not hold up our hands in horror, but rather remember that this is not far from our politics of two centuries ago. We might even have the modesty to admit that in Northern Ireland and in the American South, for example, we, too, practice single-party government.

Where we have every right to express our alarm, however, is in the breakdown of constitutional protection by the law. The danger lies not so much in parliamentary failure as in judicial failure. Yet, even here, our alarm should be expressed in modest terms. In eighteenth century England a man could be hanged for stealing a sheep, and horrible ships took convicts to Australia for no more than petty larceny. Nor was Europe's recent Fascist experiment precisely a law-abiding mode of government.

No, the way ahead does not lie through sermonizing carried on by people whose own eyes are too full of beams to judge clearly the others' motes. It lies, rather, in a sustained effort to work out within the United Nations and in international partnerships the chief lines of advance toward a more coherent, a more viable world community with freedom as its working principle and constitutionalism as its political habit. No one is likely to underestimate the appalling complexities of this task, but the outlook must have seemed as daunting to the lawyers struggling against Stuart despotism or to the Founding Fathers attempting to turn federalism into a workable system. The task is indeed "piled high with difficulty." We should attempt it, therefore, with all the more vigor and clarity, and I would suggest that the three criteria that I have stressed in domestic democracy are relevant too to the global democracy we painfully must try to build.

Today, the first of all tasks is to restrain the nation-states from taking the law into their own hands; in other words, from using force to assert its will, or, in the final word, from making war. From domestic society we know that the only way to banish lawless violence and fratricidal strife is by accepting rules of peaceful change and adjustment and building an impartial peace force to enforce the peaceful solutions that are agreed. This, I take it, to be a task of the United Nations. However, some of our vast modern states are still like the medieval barons, too powerful to be controlled in their feudal fastnesses. But perhaps we have reached a first stage of restraint on arbitrary power. Troubled areas—Palestine, the Congo, Laos—are policed not by rivals whose rivalry would lead to war, but by an external and impartial third force.

Could we not extend the principle? Could we not aim at the policing by the United Nations of more and more areas in which the rival interests of powerful states threaten to clash? Global systems of restraint may still evade us, but history suggests that we can start from the particular instance and then extend the principle, and every area withdrawn from the naked arbitrament of force is an area saved for the constitutional working of a sane human society.

Does the second principle I have picked out, the procedure of equal voting, apply to the building of a free world society? The critics say that the new states, holding the balance of power by means of their combined vote, drive the United Nations on toward ferocious extremes of anti-colonialism and attempt to impose other imprudent policies on the great powers that must disrupt the whole organization. Meanwhile, the great foot the bill.

There is much to be said on this score. For the moment, let me say only that in world society the small nation—like the small man in domestic society—is most likely to be vulnerable. His equal voice, his capacity to unite it with other small voices, is a measure of protection against his inequality. We see the need for this countervailing power inside our states, so let us not be too quick to denounce it in the world at large.

There is a further reason for being cautious and patient about the workings inside the United Nations of the potential ex-colonial majority. If we turn to the third principle of democracy—equality of esteem, equal dignity, equal access to the social and economic possibilities of society—we find that the disproportions that distort true community inside our nations are present in world society, too. This Afro-Asian bloc—a misnomer, for, save on the colonial issue, there is no bloc—represents most of the world's most truly underpriviledged peoples. If they cling to their United Nations status, the reason is that, as citizens of our planet, they have not yet much else to cling to. Pushed to the first outskirts of modernity by Western investment and trade, emancipated before they have received either the training or the powers of creating wealth that are needed for a modern society, they are caught between two worlds, the powerful, affluent expanding world of the developed "North" and the traditional, pretechnological, largely poor world of the underdeveloped "South."

This division in world society is a great obstacle to the expansion of the confidence and the community the world needs for a truly human society. And it threatens to become worse if such experiments as the European Common Market or the Atlantic Community prove to be, vis-à-vis the less fortunate parts of the world, a rich man's club, exclusive in its commerce, its investments, its arrangements, and its interests. The gap exists. We must not make it worse.

What can we do? I would like to suggest two lines to follow if we in this generation are to make our full contribution to the advance of world democracy.

I know there is much dissatisfaction about economic assistance, about foreign aid, much feeling that it is wasted, that it never achieves a break-through, that it dribbles down thousands of unspecified drains and ratholes. Yet, just so did the Victorians talk about tax money devoted to lifting the standard of the very poor in early industrial society. There were the "good poor," who said "please" and "thank you" and touched their forelocks. Then there were the "bad poor," who kept coal in the bath tub. But over a couple of generations, it was the raising of all this unfortunate mass of humanity that turned Western society into the first social order in history in which everyone could expect something of an equal chance.

After ten years, we are only at the beginning of this experiment in inter-national aid. We are learning greatly. We see the relevance of some policies, the supreme obstacles offered by others. We discriminate more. We are learning to be better givers.

Our second task is harder. It is harder for us than for any other member of the world's wealthy elite. It is to see that the last vestiges of discrimina-tion inside our own society are speedily abolished. It is no use talking of ourselves as the "vanguard of freedom and of democracy" while any of our fellow Americans can be treated like a James Meredith at the University of Mississippi. Must we not, as lovers of freedom, and as, too often, self-styled prophets of the free way of life, sometimes lapse into a shamed silence when we even have to talk about social injustice let alone deal with it—one hundred years after the Emancipation Proclamation?

I must end as I began. The essence of democracy is the dignity of man. We shall create a free world order on no other basis. If we attack Com-munism—as we must—for its contempt for political dignity, we must as unrelentingly attack lapses in social dignity.

It sometimes seems to me as though running through all of the great issues of the day—the anticolonial revolution, the political contest with Communism, the unification of Europe, the clamor of poorer lands for advance—there runs the underlying desire for some lasting realization of the dignity of man, man with a measure of political autonomy, man with the economic elbowroom to live above the torturing doubts of food and of work, man with the dignity to look his neighbor in the face and to see a friend. Isolate the problems, measure their magnitude, measure our progress in dealing with them—and you have my answer to the question of what the prospects for democracy are around the world. . . .

50

The Totalitarian Theory of the State

by R. Wallace Brewster

RECENCY OF THE APPLICATION OF TOTALITARIAN THEORY. Not until the present century was an attempt made to apply the totalitarian theory of the state. Although its *philosophy* is rooted in the past, never before was it worked out so completely and tried in actual operation. The totalitarian idea found its fullest expression in Italy and Germany under the direction of the Fascist and Nazi Parties, respectively, following World War I. The Japanese government easily adapted many established fascist ideas and practices and cooperated fully with the totalitarian countries of the Western world until defeated at the close of World War II. Japan retained, however, some elements of a non-totalitarian nature which made it a rather poor example of totalitarian theory. Russia and her satellites, too, can be classed as supporters of totalitarian theories and practices as well as Spain.

Because totalitarian theory was best exemplified in Italy and Germany, we shall use them as illustrations of totalitarian doctrines. There were some differences between the Italian and German versions, but they were relatively incidental matters of emphasis. Technically, we speak of Italian Fascism and German Nazism, but in general practice the single term "fascism" is applied to both, a usage that will be followed here.

Russia will not be used here as an example of totalitarian theory because of the confusion between basic Marxian communism and the interpretations of it made in Russia by Lenin and his successors. The task of adjusting theory and practice needed to explain the nature of Soviet totalitarianism is too long for the space available. Then, too, Marx never glorified the state as did the exponents of fascism. In fact, he asserted that the state is an evil and predicted that it would eventually "wither away" after a communist society had been established following the liquidation of the old order. Not only the failure of the Russian state to "wither away" but the use as well as totalitarian practices on a scale perhaps even greater

From *Government in Modern Society* by R. Wallace Brewster, pp. 98–99, 102–103, *passim*. Reprinted by permission of Houghton Mifflin Company. Copyright 1958.

R. Wallace Brewster is Professor of Political Science at Pennsylvania State University.

than in fascist Germany and Italy, complicates the problem of description. One leading analyst of Soviet institutions indicates how impossible it is for Soviet leaders to follow the Marxian theory of the state. "The 'withering away' thesis in Soviet ideology is conspicuous by its irrelevance . . . and the thesis that the state will wither away once capitalist encirclement is liquidated cannot be taken seriously."

In this connection, a study of various totalitarian systems, both fascist and communist, by two Harvard scholars, Carl J. Friedrich and Z. K. Brzezinski, led them to conclude that a common pattern exists throughout all of them. They are: an official ideology, a one-party governing system, a terroristic secret police, a monopoly on communication, exclusive access to weapons, and a nationally planned economy. It represents what William Ebenstein calls a "way of life" which characterizes totalitarian society. . . .

WHY DICTATORSHIP IS ESSENTIAL. The totalitarian state leaves no room for democratic liberalism with its insistence on rule by the "people." The masses are held to be incapable of deciding what is best for themselves, to say nothing of the national welfare. Furthermore, the people do not know what the state's will is. Parties merely represent hostile groups which tear the nation asunder and reduce the efficiency of group activity. There must be only one party representing the united nation.

In the place of bungling government by talk, they say, a government of action must be established which is clothed with the unlimited authority to make decisions *for* the people. Mussolini once summed it up by saying that "Fascism denies that the majority, by the simple fact that it is a majority, can direct human society; it denies that numbers alone can govern by means of a periodical consultation, and it affirms the immutable, beneficial, and fruitful inequality of mankind, which can never be permanently leveled through the mere operation of a mechanical process such as universal suffrage." [1]

Effective governmental action, it is asserted, can be assured only through a leader clothed with unlimited powers and responsible legally to no one. He is the sole source of authority in the state; neither the legislature nor the courts can limit anything he does. His successor is designated by him and not elected. His will is the law under the fiction that it embodies the will of all members of the nation. This omnipotent power of the chief executive of the state is absolutely necessary for the good of the nation; anything less would mean the best interests of the people could not be served. Since anything benefiting the nation is good and anything injuring it is bad, dictatorship is morally necessary. A . . . quotation from a Nazi is illustrative:

> The Führer is the bearer of the people's will; he is independent of all groups, associations, and interests, but he is bound by laws which are

[1] Benito Mussolini, *The Political and Social Doctrine of Fascism*, p. 9.

inherent in the nature of his people. . . . The Führer is no "representative" of a particular group whose wishes he must carry out. He is no "organ" of the state in the sense of a mere executive agent. He is rather himself the bearer of the collective will of the people. In his will the will of the people is realized. He transforms the mere feelings of the people into a conscious will. . . . Thus it is possible for him, in the name of the true will of the people which he serves, to go against the subjective opinions and convictions of single individuals within the people if these are not in accord with the objective destiny of the people. . . . He shapes the collective will of the people within himself and he embodies the political unity and entirety of the people in opposition to individual interests. . . .[2]

The fact that Fascist and Nazi doctrines call for a dictatorial (autocratic) form of government as an absolute essential does not mean that all countries which have dictatorships are necessarily totalitarian in their philosophy. By the same token, dictatorship does not necessarily mean the existence of a totalitarian state. There have been many dictatorships which did not represent totalitarian states, ranging from those of Alexander the Great, through Caesar, on to Napoleon. The same can be said for many Latin-American dictatorships. In other words, all totalitarian states have a dictatorial form of government but not all dictatorships operate within a totalitarian state.

[2] Ernest Rudolf Huber, *Constitutional Law of the Greater German Reich*, quoted in *National Socialism*, pp. 34–36.

CHAPTER

25

DEMOCRATIC GOVERNMENT
IN AMERICA

THE FEDERALIST PAPERS are a classic series of essays on the nature of
the government of the United States as outlined in the Constitution. They
were written in 1787 and 1788, when ratification of the Constitution was
under consideration by the States. The authors were Alexander Hamilton,
James Madison, and John Jay. In Number 14 Madison argues that, in
spite of the wide territory covered, union of the thirteen states as proposed
in the Constitution is both practical and desirable. In Number 37 Madison
presents the major difficulties faced by those who drew up the Constitution,
and explains the necessity for making many compromises.

J. William Fulbright finds that government by the people is possible
but difficult to achieve. He seeks a reconstructed philosophy of self-government, accepting the weaknesses as well as the strengths of human nature.
Such a philosophy must, he assumes, place heavy emphasis on the development of the human capacity for rational, moral choice. Charles Frankel
agrees that classical democratic theory badly needs revision, but he is
more optimistic about the future of democracy for he believes that we
behave a lot better than our theory leads us to suspect.

51

Excerpts from "The Federalist"

by James Madison

An Objection Drawn from the Extent of Country Answered [NO. 14]

We have seen the necessity of the Union, as our bulwark against foreign danger; as the conservator of peace among ourselves; as the guardian of our commerce, and other common interests; as the only substitute for those military establishments which have subverted the liberties of the old world; and as the proper antidote for the diseases of faction, which have proved fatal to other popular Governments, and of which alarming symptoms have been betrayed by our own.

All that remains, within this branch of our inquiries, is to take notice of an objection that may be drawn from the great extent of country which the Union embraces. A few observations on this subject, will be the more proper, as it is perceived, that the adversaries of the new Constitution are availing themselves of a prevailing prejudice, with regard to the practicable sphere of republican administration, in order to supply, by imaginary difficulties, the want of those solid objections, which they endeavour in vain to find. . . .

As the natural limit of a democracy, is that distance from the central point, which will just permit the most remote citizens to assemble as often as their public functions demand, and will include no greater number than can join in those functions: so the natural limit of a republic, is that distance from the centre, which will barely allow the representatives of the people to meet as often as may be necessary for the administration of public affairs. Can it be said, that the limits of the United States exceed this distance? It will be said by those who recollect, that the Atlantic coast is the longest side of the Union; that, during the term of thirteen years, the representatives of the States have been almost continually assembled; and that the members, from the most distant States, are not chargeable

---

James Madison took a leading part in drawing up the Constitution of the United States at the Constitutional Convention of 1787. He was later Secretary of State under Jefferson, and from 1809 to 1817 he served as the fourth President of the United States.

with greater intermissions of attendance, than those from the States in the neighborhood of Congress. . . .

Favourable as this view of the subject may be, some observations remain, which will place it in a light still more satisfactory.

In the first place, it is to be remembered, that the general Government is not to be charged with the whole power of making and administering laws: its jurisdiction is limited to certain enumerated objects, which concern all the members of the republic, but which are not to be attained by the separate provisions of any. The subordinate Governments, which can extend their care to all those other objects, which can be separately provided for, will retain their due authority and activity. Were it proposed by the plan of the Convention, to abolish the Governments of the particular States, its adversaries would have some ground for their objection; though it would not be difficult to show, that if they were abolished, the general Goverment would be compelled, by the principle of self preservation, to reinstate them in their proper jurisdiction.

A second observation to be made is, that the immediate object of the Federal constitution, is to secure the Union of the thirteen primitive States, which we know to be practicable; and to add to them such other States, as may arise in their own bosoms, or in their neighbourhoods, which we cannot doubt to be equally practicable. The arrangement that may be necessary for those angles and fractions of our territory, which lie on our northwestern frontier, must be left to those whom further discoveries and experience will render more equal to the task.

Let it be remarked, in the third place, that the intercourse throughout the Union will be daily facilitated by new improvements. Roads will everywhere be shortened, and kept in better order; accommodations for travellers will be multiplied and meliorated; an interior navigation on our eastern side, will be opened throughout, or nearly throughout, the whole extent of the Thirteen States. The communication between the western and Atlantic districts, and between different parts of each, will be rendered more and more easy, by those numerous canals, with which the beneficence of nature has intersected our country, and which art finds so little difficult to connect and complete.

A fourth, and still more important consideration, is, that as almost every State will, on one side or other, be a frontier, and will thus find, in a regard to its safety, an inducement to make some sacrifices for the sake of the general protection: so the States which lie at the greatest distance from the heart of the Union, and which of course may partake least of the ordinary circulation of its benefits, will be at the same time immediately contiguous to foreign nations, and will consequently stand, on particular occasions, in greatest need of strength and resources. It may be inconvenient for Georgia, or the States forming our western or northeastern borders, to send their representatives to the Seat of Government; but they would find it more so to struggle alone against an invading enemy, or even to support alone the whole expense of those precautions, which may be dictated by the neighbourhood of continual danger. If they should derive less benefit therefore from the Union in some respects, than the less distant States, they will derive greater benefit from it in other respects, and thus the proper equilibrium will be maintained throughout.

I submit to you, my fellow citizens, these considerations, in full confidence that the good sense which has so often marked your decisions, will allow them their due weight and effect; and that you will never suffer difficulties, however formidable in appearance, or however fashionable the error on which they may be founded, to drive you into the gloomy and perilous scenes into which the advocates for disunion would conduct you.

Concerning the Difficulties Which the Convention Must Have Experienced in the Formation of a Proper Plan [NO. 37]

Among the difficulties encountered by the Convention, a very important one must have lain, in combining the requisite stability and energy in government, with the inviolable attention due to liberty, and to the republican form. Without substantially accomplishing this part of their undertaking, they would have very imperfectly fulfilled the object of their appointment, or the expectation of the public: yet, it could not be easily accomplished, will be denied by no one who is unwilling to betray his ignorance of the subject. Energy in government, is essential to that security against external and internal danger, and to that prompt and salutary execution of the laws, which enter into the very definition of good government.

Stability in government is essential to national character, and to the advantages annexed to it, as well as to that repose and confidence in the minds of the people, which are among the chief blessings of civil society. An irregular and mutable legislation is not more an evil in itself, than it is odious to the people; and it may be pronounced with assurance, that the people of this country, enlightened as they are, with regard to the nature, and interested, as the great body of them are, in the effects of good government, will never be satisfied, till some remedy be applied to the vicissitudes and uncertainties, which characterize the State administrations. On comparing, however, these valuable ingredients with the vital principles of liberty, we must perceive at once, the difficulty of mingling them together in their due proportions. . . .

How far the Convention may have succeeded in this part of their work, will better appear on a more accurate view of it. From the cursory view here taken, it must clearly appear to have been an arduous part.

Not less arduous must have been the task of making the proper line of partition, between the authority of the General, and that of the State governments. Every man will be sensible of this difficulty, in proportion as he has been accustomed to contemplate and discriminate objects, extensive and complicated in their nature. The faculties of the mind itself have never yet been distinguished and defined, with satisfactory precision, by all the efforts of the most acute and metaphysical philosophers. Sense, perception, judgment, desire, volition, memory, imagination, are found to be separated, by such delicate shades and minute gradations, that their boundaries have eluded the most subtle investigations, and remain a pregnant source of ingenious disquisition and controversy. The boundaries between the great kingdoms of nature, and still more, between the various provinces, and lesser portions, into which they are subdivided, afford another illustration of the same important truth. The most sagacious and laborious naturalists have never yet succeeded, in tracing with certainty the line which separates the district of vegetable life, from the neighboring region of unorganized matter, or which marks the termination of the former, and the commencement of the animal empire. A still greater obscurity lies in the distinctive characters, by which the objects in each of these great departments of nature have been arranged and assorted.

When we pass from the works of nature, in which all the delineations are perfectly accurate, and appear to be otherwise only from the imperfection of the eye which surveys them, to the institutions of man, in which the obscurity arises as well from the object itself, as from the organ by which it is contemplated; we must perceive the necessity of moderating still further our expectations and hopes from the efforts of human sagacity. Experience has instructed us, that no skill in the science of government has yet been able to discriminate and define, with sufficient certainty, its three great provinces, the legislative, executive, and judiciary; or even the privileges and powers of the different legislative branches. Questions daily occur in the course of practice, which prove the obscurity which reigns in these subjects, and which puzzle the greatest adepts in political science. . . .

To the difficulties already mentioned, may be added the interfering pretensions of the larger and smaller States. We cannot err, in supposing that the former would contend for a participation in the Government, fully proportioned to their superior wealth and importance; and that the latter would not be less tenacious of the equality at present enjoyed by them. We may well suppose, that neither side would entirely yield to the other, and consequently that the struggle could be terminated only by compromise. It is extremely probable, also that after the ratio of representation had been adjusted, this very compromise must have produced a fresh struggle between the same parties, to give such a turn to the organization of the Government, and to the distribution of its powers, as would increase the importance of the branches, in forming which they had respectively obtained the greatest share of influence. There are features in the Constitution which warrant each of these suppositions; and as far as either of them is well founded, it shows that the Convention must have been compelled to sacrifice theoretical propriety to the force of extraneous considerations.

Nor could it have been the large and small States only, which would marshal themselves in oposition to each other on various points. Other combinations, resulting from a difference of local position and policy, must have created additional difficulties. As every State may be divided into different districts, and its citizens into different classes, which give birth to contending interests and local jealousies: so the different parts of the United States are distinguished from each other, by a variety of circumstances, which produce a like effect on a larger scale. And although this variety of interests, for reasons sufficiently explained in a former paper, may have a salutary influence on the administration of the Government when formed; yet everyone must be sensible of the contrary influence, which must have been experienced in the task of forming it.

Would it be wonderful if, under the pressure of all these difficulties, the Convention should have been forced into some deviations from that artificial structure and regular symmetry, which an abstract view of the subject might lead an ingenious theorist to bestow on a constitution planned in his closet, or in his imagination? The real wonder is, that so many difficulties should have been surmounted; and surmounted with an unanimity almost as unprecedented, as it must have been unexpected.

52

The Future of Democracy in America

by J. William Fulbright, with comments
by Charles Frankel

The question before us can be answered simply: Government by the people is possible but highly improbable. The difficulties of self-government are manifest throughout the world.

The history of political thought in the last century and a half is largely one of qualification, modification, and outright repudiation of the heady democratic optimism of the eighteenth century. "The play is still on," writes Carl Becker, "and we are still betting on freedom of the mind, but the outcome seems now somewhat more dubious than it did in Jefferson's time, because a century and a half of experience makes it clear that men do not in fact always use their freedom of speech and of the press in quite the rational and disinterested way they are supposed to."

The major preoccupation of democratic thought in our time has been its continuing and troubled effort to reconcile the irrefutable evidences of human weakness and irrationality, which modern history has so abundantly provided, with a political philosophy whose very foundation is the assumption of human goodness and reason. The dilemma has troubled all the free societies of the West, none more so than the United States, whose national experience until a generation ago seemed to represent the realization of classical democratic theory.

In addition to defects of concept and content, classic democratic thought is marked by a strikingly unhistoric spirit. It grandly and inexplicably conceived of democratic society as an organ created by a single act of human will and reason, ignoring the empirical lessons of the centuries of English history through which representative government had been tortuously evolving in the face of numberless obstacles and diversions. If Englishmen could fall prey to such delusions, it was far easier for Americans

From *Challenges to Democracy: The Next Ten Years*, edited by Edward Reed Frederick A. Praeger, Publisher, 1963, pp. 77–86, 89–93 *passim*. Copyright © 196. by The Fund for the Republic, Inc. Reprinted by permission.

J. William Fulbright is United States Senator from Arkansas.

Charles Frankel is Professor of Philosophy at Columbia University.

whose revolution lent some credence to the abstractions of rationalist philosophy.

The revolutionaries of 1776 inherited a society that was already the freest in the world. Its freedom was built on solid foundations of English traditions and constitutional principles, which formed the bedrock of future stability. The revolution was not directed against a feudal *ancien régime* but against the most liberal and progressive monarchy of Europe, whose "oppression" of the colonists had consisted in recent and limited infringements on *long-established* rights. The great advantage of America, said Alexis de Tocqueville in a profound insight, lay in not having had "to endure a democratic revolution."

The American experience has thus had the appearance but not the reality of a society built by fiat to the specifications of rationalist philosophy. We have been permitted the romance of imagining ourselves revolutionaries when in fact our democracy is the product of long tradition and evolution. The mischief of our rationalist illusion is that it leads to erroneous inferences about our own free society and about the prospects of government by the people elsewhere in the world. Most notably, it blinds us to the powerful limitations on human action imposed by history, to the incalculable difficulties of building a free society, and to the basic incapacity of man to create viable institutions out of the abstractions of pure reason. Society, said Edmund Burke, is indeed a contract, but "as the ends of such a partnership cannot be obtained in many generations, it becomes a partnership not only between those who are living, but between those who are living, those who are dead, and those who are to be born."

The descent from democratic optimism in Western political thought has been more than borne out by events. As a result of the great conflicts of the twentieth century, the world-wide dominance of the Western democracies has been lost. These conflicts and upheavals have thrown the democracies on the defensive and generated powerful strains within the free Western societies themselves. There has developed, writes Walter Lippmann, "a functional derangement of the relationship between the mass of the people and the government." "The people," he writes, "have acquired power which they are incapable of exercising, and the governments they elect have lost powers which they must recover if they are to govern."

The impact of mass opinion on vital issues of war and peace, in Lippmann's analysis, is to impose a "massive negative" at critical junctures when new courses of policy are needed. Lagging disastrously behind the movement of events, Lippmann contends, public opinion forced a vindictive peace in 1919, then refused to act against a resurgent Germany in the inter-war years, and finally was aroused to paroxysms of hatred and unattainable hopes in a second world war that need never have occurred. The impact of public opinion, says Lippmann, has been nothing less than a "compulsion to make mistakes."

For a politician who serves at the pleasure of his constituency, the course of prudence is to adhere to prevailing views. To be prematurely right is to court what, to the politician at least, is a premature retirement. We come at last to the ironic inversion of the classic democratic faith in the will of the people: Not only does public opinion fail to hold the politician to the course of wisdom and responsibility but, on the contrary, to take the right course requires a singular act of courage on the part of the politician. A few might share the Wilsonian view that "there is nothing more honorable than to be driven from power because one was right." Far more prevalent is the outlook of Lloyd George, who on more than one occasion quite candidly rejected proposals whose merit he conceded on the grounds that he did not wish to be "crucified" at home. In the Lloyd George view, which is a prototype—and not without some merit in my opinion—there is little glory and still less constructive purpose in being defeated for failing to do the impossible.

Can we reconstruct the excessively optimistic democratic thought of the eighteenth century into a chastened but more realistic philosophy of government by the people? I believe we can, and this belief, I think, is prevalent among the wisest of statesmen and scholars.

The philosophers of the Age of Reason emphasized the hopes and possibilities of a free society, but the strength and viability of democracy rests not only on its aspirations but also on its accommodations to the limitations of human wisdom, to man's inability to perceive the infinite. Democracy, Winston Churchill once said, is the worst form of government men have ever devised—except for every other form. Or in Jefferson's words: "Sometimes it is said that man cannot be trusted with the government of himself. Can he, then, be trusted with the government of others? Or have we found angels in the form of kings to govern him?"

If men are often irrational in their political behavior, it does not follow that they are *always* irrational and, what is more important, it does not follow that they are *incapable* of reason. Whether in fact a people's capacity for self-government can be realized depends on the character and quality of education. It seems to me an astonishing distortion of priorities that the American people and their government gladly spend billions of dollars for space exploration while denying desperately needed funds to their public schools. I do not believe that a society that has shamefully starved and neglected its public education can claim to have exploited its fullest possibilities and found them wanting.

The case for government by elites is irrefutable insofar as it rests on the need for expert and specialized knowledge. The average citizen is no more qualified for the detailed administration of government than the average politician is qualified to practice medicine or to split an atom. But in the choice of basic goals, the fundamental moral judgments that shape the life of a society, the judgment of trained elites is no more valid than the judgment of an educated people. The knowledge of the navigator is essential to the conduct of a voyage, but his special skills have no relevance to the choice of whether to take the voyage and where we wish to go.

The distinction, of course, is between means and ends. The experience of modern times shows us that when the passengers take over the navigation of the ship, it is likely to go on the rocks. This does not mean that their chosen destination is the wrong one or that an expert would have made a better choice, but only that they are unlikely to get there without the navigator's guidance.

The demonstrated superiority of democracy over dictatorship derives precisely from its refusal to let ruling elites make the basic moral decisions and value judgments of society. The core of classical democratic thought is the concept of free individuality as the ultimate moral value of human society. Stripped of its excessive optimism about human nature, the core of classic liberalism remains valid and intact. The value and strength of this concept are its promise of fulfillment for man's basic aspirations. The philosopher and the psychoanalyst agree that, whether it issues from reason or instinct, man's basic aspiration is for fulfillment as a free individual.

A reconstructed philosophy of self-government, accepting the weaknesses as well as the strengths of human nature, must place heavy emphasis on the development of the human *capacity* for rational moral choice. The challenge to public education is nothing less than to prepare the individual for self-government, to cultivate his capacity for free inquiry and his more humane instincts, to teach him *how* rather than *what* to think—in short, to sustain democracy by what Ralph Barton Perry has called "an express insistence upon quality and distinction."

A reconstructed philosophy of self-government must replace an ingenuous faith in human *nature* with a realistic faith in human *capacity,* recognizing that self-government, though the best form of political organization that men have devised, is also the most difficult. Democracy, in short, must come to terms with man's weaknesses and irrationalities while reaching out for the best that is in him.

Such a revised approach to democracy has certain implications for the way in which we organize our government and conduct its affairs. As Americans with our deeply rooted and fundamentally healthy distrust of government power, we might start by at least re-examining certain long-held convictions based on this distrust of power. We might at least consider the proposition, as expressed by Lord Radcliffe, that "liberty looked upon as the right to find and to try to realize the best that is in oneself is not something to which power is necessarily hostile," that, indeed, "such liberty may even need the active intervention of authority to make it possible."

To return to my metaphor, we must guard against allowing the navigator to determine our destination, but we must allow him to steer the ship without amateur supervision of every turn of the wheel. A political leader is chosen because of his supposed qualifications for his job. If he is qualified, he should be allowed to carry it out according to his own best judgment. If his judgment is found defective by his electors, he can and should be removed. His constituents, however, must recognize that he has a duty to his office as well as to them and that their duty in turn is to fill the office but not to run it. We must distinguish between the functions of *representation* and of *government, requiring* our elected leaders to represent us while *allowing* them to govern.

It may well be questioned whether the enormously complex and slow-moving procedures of the United States Government are adequate to meet both the dangers and opportunities of our foreign relations. Too often, decisions of principle are postponed or neglected and opportunities lost because of the obstacles to decision imposed by our policy processes. The source of this malady is the diffusion of authority between and within the executive and legislative branches and the accessibility of all of these centers of power to a wide variety of pressures and interests. The problem is compounded by the durable myth of Jacksonian democracy, the view that any literate citizen can do almost any job and that a democracy can do without a highly trained administrative elite.

"Foreign politics," wrote Tocqueville, "demand scarcely any of those qualities which a democracy possesses; and they require, on the contrary, the perfect use of almost all those faculties in which it is deficient. . . . A democracy is unable to regulate the details of an important undertaking, to persevere in a design, and to work out its execution in the presence of serious obstacles. It cannot combine its measures with secrecy, and it will not await their consequences with patience. These are qualities which more especially belong to an individual, or to an aristocracy."

My question is not whether we might wish to alter our traditional foreign policy-making procedures but whether in fact we have any choice but to do so in a world that obstinately refuses to conduct its affairs under Anglo-Saxon rules of procedure.

The source of an effective foreign policy under our system is Presidential power. There are major areas of foreign policy—those relating more to long-term problems than to immediate crises—wherein Presidential authority is incommensurate with Presidential responsibility as a result of the diffusion of power between executive and legislative branches and within the latter. The foreign policy powers of Congress under the Constitution enable it to implement, modify, or thwart the President's proposals but not itself to initiate or shape policy. These powers, moreover, are widely dispersed within Congress among autonomous committees, each under a chairman who owes little if anything in the way of political obligation to the President.

The defects of Congress as an institution reflect the defects of classic democratic thought. These pertain primarily to foreign policy. In domestic matters, it seems to me, the Congress is as well qualified to shape policy as the executive, and in some respects more so because of the freedom of at least some members from the particular electoral pressures that operate on the President. The frequency of elections and the local orientation of party organizations, however, do not encourage serious and sustained study of international relations. Congressmen are acutely susceptible to local and regional pressures and to the waves of fear and emotion that sometimes sweep over public opinion. The legislator, in short, is under constant and intense pressure to adhere to the prevailing tendencies of public opinion, however temporary and unstable.

Public opinion must be educated and led if it is to bolster a wise and effective foreign policy. This is pre-eminently a task for Presidential leadership because the Presidential office is the only one under our constitutional system that constitutes a forum for moral and political leadership on a national scale. Accordingly, I think that we must contemplate the further enhancement of Presidential authority in foreign affairs. The prospect is a disagreeable and perhaps a dangerous one, but the alternative is immobility and the paralysis of national policy in a revolutionary world, which can only lead to consequences immeasurably more disagreeable and dangerous.

The pre-eminence of Presidential responsibility is in no way an implied license for the legislator to evade national and international responsibility and to surrender to the pressures of local and parochial interest. I can find no better words to define this responsibility than those of Edmund Burke in his classic statement to his constituents at Bristol in 1774:

> Certainly, gentlemen, it ought to be the happiness and glory of a representative, to live in the strictest union, the closest correspondence, and the most unreserved communication with his constituents. Their wishes ought to have great weight with him; their opinion high respect; their business unremitted attention. It is his duty to sacrifice his repose, his pleasures, his satisfactions, to theirs; and, above all, ever, and in all cases, to prefer their interest to his own. But, his unbiased opinion, his mature judgment, his enlightened conscience, he ought not to sacrifice to you; to any man, or to any set of men living. These he does not derive from your pleasure; no, nor from the law and the constitution. They are a trust from Providence, for the abuse of which he is deeply answerable. Your representative owes you, not his industry only, but his judgment; and he betrays, instead of serving you, if he sacrifices it to your opinion.

As a freshman Senator in 1946, I attempted in a speech at the University of Chicago to define the proper role of the legislator in relation to his constituents, to the nation, and to his own conscience. After seventeen years I see no reason to alter the views I then expressed in these words:

The average legislator early in his career discovers that there are certain interests, or prejudices, of his constituents which are dangerous to trifle with. Some of these prejudices may not be of fundamental importance to the welfare of the nation, in which case he is justified in humoring them, even though he may disapprove. The difficult case is where the prejudice concerns fundamental policy affecting the national welfare. A sound sense of values, the ability to discriminate between that which is of fundamental importance and that which is only superficial, is an indispensable qualification of a good legislator. As an example of what I mean, let us take the poll-tax issue and isolationism. Regardless of how persuasive my colleagues or the national press may be about the evils of the poll tax, I do not see its fundamental importance, and I shall follow the views of the people of my state. Although it may be symbolic of conditions which many deplore, it is exceedingly doubtful that its abolition will cure any of our major problems. On the other hand, regardless of how strongly opposed my constituents may prove to be to the creation of, and participation in, an ever stronger United Nations Organization, I could not follow such a policy in that field unless it becomes clearly hopeless. . . .

In conclusion, I should like to reiterate the theme of these remarks: Government by the people, despite its failures and shortcomings, remains the one form of political organization that offers the promise of fulfillment for our highest aspirations. Although we have been compelled to qualify the unlimited optimism of classic democratic thought, we remain convinced that the core of that thought—the belief in the moral sanctity of the free mind and the free individual—remains the most valid of human philosophies. In Carl Becker's words: "Although we no longer have the unlimited and solvent backing of God or nature, we are still betting that freedom of the mind will never disprove the proposition that only through freedom of the mind can a reasonably just society ever be created."

Charles Frankel:

With Senator Fulbright, I agree that inherited democratic theory badly needs revision. My own view is that although we do not behave very well, we behave a lot better than our theory leads us to suspect. Inherited democratic theory leads us to criticize as diseases in contemporary democracy what are often very effective adjustments to the realities. I do not believe that the old theorists of democracy were quite as foolish and certainly not nearly as optimistic as Senator Fulbright suggests. James Madison, as one example, took for granted that the perpetual problem in all political systems is the problem of continued disagreement, continued rivalry, continued competition between interests, between persons, between opinions. Marxist theory would like to imagine that there is some magic, some alchemy, by which, in a future good society, this could be done away with. But if one assumes that disagreement or factionalism is in some way or other a fundamental desideratum of all sophisticated human societies, then some way for modifying and regulating these disagreements reasonably and peacefully has to be figured out. I think that classic democratic theory held these views and in this respect was very far from utopianism. . . .

Let me turn to the word "elite." I would point out, in the first place, that in the context of modern specialized expertise, and in the context of large bureaucratically organized government, the word "elite" is not used in its classic form. The word in its classic form stood for a class, a class with a homogeneous background and presumably a common social outlook. But today we talk about the "elite" as people who acquire positions of authority or of great advisory importance because of some specialized knowledge or some specialized kind of experience, and in this talk we habitually make certain assumptions that, when brought to the surface, can very quickly be shown to be erroneous.

One of the questions, for example, that is often raised is why the people with their passion and their foolishness should be allowed to rule and to get in the way of those who know better. An assumption here is that technical experts agree. This is just not so. Technical experts do not agree. Perhaps the range of disagreement is a little narrower than it is for the rest of us, but it is not the case that those who occupy "elite" positions in modern society—these technical experts—can be held to hold some one position. This is partly why I find Mr. Walter Lippmann's book on *The Public Philosophy* a little difficult to follow. He seems to assume throughout that the elite groups governing foreign policy would have an easy way of coming to agreement. I believe that there would be elites holding different points of view and that we would still need some mechanism for determining which set of leaders would regulate our policy.

A second assumption is that the decisions made in the political field by so-called "experts" or the "elite" are technical decisions. They are, but within extremely narrow limits. I can think of very few important political decisions that do not involve the weighing and assessing of evidence from a wide variety of different specialists. This means that even those who are experts in one field quickly become laymen the moment they move into another field. The view that expertise is a prerequisite for holding competent opinions on public affairs is one that does not disqualify only *some* of us "people." It disqualifies all of us. No one today can be an expert in all the fields that he should ideally be an expert in in order to make public decisions. What is called for in making public decisions, accordingly, is not omniscience or omnicompetent knowledge but something closer to wisdom, and common sense, and an understanding of when and where and for what reasons to rely on the advice of experts. This is all the more true where questions of morals are concerned, as Senator Fulbright rightly pointed out and as I should wish to underscore. There are no experts in morals.

The crucial problem for all of modern society in the light of this competition among elites is to work out some system for regulated competition, some system for choosing leaders, to govern the process. From a pragmatic point of view, I believe democracy is the system for choosing those who will lead.

This brings me to the question of the electorate. Insofar as the mass of the people are effectively involved in the political processes of their country, they are already organized in groups and are usually led by professional leaders. The political process is not in fact a process in which "they" are opposed to "we." It is a process in which some groups with leaders are "in" and other groups with leaders are "out." The most important modification that I would add to this too simple formula is that there are also some groups that are "way out"; that is to say, they are not in the competition at all.

One of the great features in the evolution of democracy has been the growth of a political community in which more and more groups of people have moved to an organized status and have become legitimate members of the political community, with leaders who could effectively voice their interests. At the present time, the United States is fighting that battle over the Negro groups, which are seeking to gain legitimacy and to have the same voice as the white groups. There is also the problem of reaching the unorganized, the invisible. Old people in the United States, for example, do not have effective organized representation. The interests of the urban groups are not effectively organized. It is often necessary for democratic government to take the lead in organizing the unorganized, in providing the voiceless with a voice; the problem of the relationship of the electorate to the elite is essentially, I think, a problem of association and organization.

With regard to the competence of citizens for self-government, these are the questions that seem to me relevant: Have they the requisite ability to judge human beings? Are they shrewd enough to tell the genuine article from the charlatan? Are they shrewd enough to tell the demagogue from the honest man? The obvious answer is "certainly not always"; very often, "no." But, over the history of democracy, there is pretty good evidence that the people have not made all that many mistakes. Moreover, they can choose only between the programs presented to them by their leaders, they can choose only between the candidates presented to them by the elite groups.

The electorate need not understand the details of the issues, but it must understand the general spirit, temper, and drift of the issues. It has to have some understanding of history; it has to have enough understanding of scientific method, enough understanding of intellectual discipline, to be able to see that arguments have come out of a certain context and have a certain background.

If I were to identify the most serious defect of received democratic theory, I would say it is the tendency to suppress the significance of leadership in a democracy. The crucial question is the recruitment and distribution of leaders. Are the best people in a given society willing to go into politics? Do they find the public life a satisfying and rich one? Is it too punishing? Is the morality or the code of politics one from which they would retreat? What is the distribution of leadership? Is the leadership of labor unions as talented, as educated, as the leadership of great corporations? Where are the leaders for those who are voiceless? Where are the moralists? Where, if you will, are the poets?

To return specifically to the problems of participation, I think the crucial issue is the way in which voluntary organizations and—not to avoid a dirty word that is not as dirty as we might think it—pressure groups are organized. In the next ten years, it seems to me, we shall have to move very strongly in the direction of guaranteeing rights to individuals within so-called voluntary organizations.

Another important issue is that of decentralization. I do not think decentralization will come in the United States without a plan. I think that only coordination of plans at a center is likely to produce the necessary *de*centralization that can give individuals the chance to work on the local and regional levels for issues with which they are competent to deal. There is no intrinsic virtue in participation as such. People have their own personal lives to live. If they do not wish to participate, they should not be asked to or forced to. But the tragedy of contemporary democracy is that many people wish to participate but cannot find the channel through which to make their voices heard and their energies felt.

This requires the application of what is perhaps America's greatest creation in politics, the federalist principle. A recent article on Switzerland said the success of that country resulted from the fact that people's liberties, particularly in small things, were regarded. I myself do not feel disenfranchised because I am not present every day while decisions about Cuba or something else are being discussed. I want the chance to choose the leaders who will make those decisions and to try to throw them out if I do not like their answers. But I would certainly feel disenfranchised if in my own neighborhood or in my own professional association I could not get up and speak and, if necessary, walk out, slamming the door loud enough so that others would know I had left. The sense of impotence at the local level is the crucial issue.

26

POLITICAL PARTIES AND ELECTIONS

ONE OF THE MOST COMMON CRITICISMS of the American political system is that the two major parties do not stand for anything. Their platforms, it is said, are similar and consist of vague generalities; their only real purpose is to win elections.

While this concept of our political parties is an exaggeration, it contains an important element of truth. Fischer, however, instead of regarding this lack of clear-cut division of major issues as a weakness, considers it one of the great elements of stability in our political system. He explains why, in his judgment, it protects the vital interests of divergent groups and minimizes conflict. As a result of it, he believes, when major government decisions are actually made they are usually supported by a "concurrent majority."

Arthur M. Schlesinger analyzes the historical significance of extremism in American politics. He optimistically concludes that the failure in the past of extremist movements in America means that they are not likely to fare better in the future. Devoted historically to the principles of fairplay and equal protection of the laws, the American people will not long support any group that tries to intimidate fellow citizens because of their personal or social views or ethnic background.

53

Government by Concurrent Majority

by John Fischer

Every now and then somebody comes up with the idea that the party system in American politics is absurd because our two great parties don't stand for clearly contrasting principles, and that we would be better off if we had a conservative party and a radical or liberal party. It is a persuasive argument, especially for well-meaning people who have not had much first-hand experience in politics. You have probably heard it; it runs something like this:

"Both of the traditional American parties are outrageous frauds. Neither the Republicans nor the Democrats have any fundamental principles or ideology. They do not even have a program. In every campaign the platforms of both parties are simply collections of noble generalities, muffled in the vaguest possible language; and in each case the two platforms are very nearly identical.

"Obviously, then, both parties are merely machines for grabbing power and distributing favors. In their lust for office they are quite willing to make a deal with anybody who can deliver a sizable block of votes. As a result, each party has become an outlandish cluster of local machines and special interest groups which have nothing in common except a craving for the public trough.

"This kind of political system"—so the argument runs—"is clearly meaningless. A man of high principles can never hope to accomplish anything through the old parties, because they are not interested in principle. Moreover, the whole arrangement is so illogical that it affronts every intelligent citizen.

"We ought to separate the sheep from the goats—to herd all the progressives on one side of the fence and all the conservatives on the other. Then politics really will have some meaning; every campaign can be fought over clearly defined issues. The Europeans, who are more sophisticated politically than we simple Americans, discovered this long ago,

From *Unwritten Rules of American Politics* by John Fischer, *Harper's Magazine,* November, 1948, pp. 27–36 *passim.* Reprinted by permission.

John Fischer is Editor-in-Chief of *Harper's Magazine* and Vice-President of Harper and Row, Publishers.

and in each of their countries they have arranged a neat political spectrum running from Left to Right."

This argument pops up with special urgency whenever a third party appears—Theodore Roosevelt's in 1912, Robert LaFollette's in 1924, or Henry Wallace's in 1948. And it sounds so plausible—at least on the surface—that many people have wondered why these splinter parties have always dwindled away after the election was over. Indeed, many veteran third-party enthusiasts have been able to account for their failure only by assuming a perverse and rock-headed stupidity among the American electorate.

There is, however, another possible explanation for the stubborn durability of our seemingly illogical two-party system; that it is more vigorous, more deeply rooted, and far better suited to our own peculiar needs than any European system would be; that it involves a more complex and subtle conception than the crude blacks and whites of the European ideological parties. There is considerable evidence, it seem to me, that our system—in spite of certain dangerous weaknesses—has on the whole worked out more successfully than the European. Perhaps it is the very subtlety of the American political tradition which is responsible for the almost universal misunderstanding of it abroad. . . . The most useful discussion of this tradition which I have come across is the work of John C. Calhoun, published nearly a century ago. Today of course he is an almost forgotten figure, and many people take it for granted that his views were discredited for good by the Civil War. . . .

Calhoun summed up his political thought in what he called the Doctrine of the Concurrent Majority. He saw the United States as a nation of tremendous and frightening diversity—a collection of many different climates, races, cultures, religions, and economic patterns. He saw the constant tension among all these special interests, and he realized that the central problem of American politics was to find some way of holding these conflicting groups together.

It could not be done by force; no one group was strong enough to impose its will on all the others. The goal could be achieved only by compromise—and no real compromise could be possible if any threat of coercion lurked behind the door. Therefore, Calhoun reasoned, every vital decision in American life would have to be adopted by a "concurrent majority"—by which he meant, in effect, a unanimous agreement of all interested parties. No decision which affected the interests of the slaveholders, he argued, should be taken without their consent; and by implication he would have given a similar veto to every other special interest, whether it be labor, management, the Catholic church, old-age pensioners, the silver miners, or the corngrowers of the Middle West.

Under the goad of the slavery issue, Calhoun was driven to state his doctrine in an extreme and unworkable form. If every sectional interest had been given the explicit, legal veto power which he called for, the government obviously would have been paralyzed. (That, in fact, is precisely what seems to be happening today in the United Nations.) It is the very essence of the idea of "concurrent majority" that it cannot be made legal and official. It can operate effectively only as an informal, highly elastic, and generally accepted understanding.

Moreover, government by concurrent majority can exist only when no one power is strong enough to dominate completely, *and then only when all of the contending interest groups recognize and abide by certain rules of the game.*

These rules are the fundamental bond of unity in American political life. . . . Under these rules every group tacitly binds itself to tolerate the interests and opinions of every other group. It must not try to impose its views on others, nor can it press its own special interests to the point where they seriously endanger the interests of other groups or of the nation as a whole.

Furthermore, each group must exercise its implied veto with responsibility and discretion; and in times of great emergency it must forsake its veto right altogether. It dare not be intransigent or doctrinaire. It must make every conceivable effort to compromise, relying on its veto only as a last resort. For if any player wields this weapon recklessly, the game will break up—or all the other players will turn on him in anger, suspend the rules for the time being, and maul those very interests he is trying so desperately to protect. That was what happened in 1860, when the followers of Calhoun carried his doctrine to an unbearable extreme. Much the same thing, on a less violent scale, happened to American business interests in 1933 and to the labor unions in 1947.

This is the somewhat elusive sense, it seems to me, in which Calhoun's theory has been adopted by the American people. But elusive and subtle as it may be, it remains the basic rule of the game of politics in this country—and in this country alone. Nothing comparable exists in any other nation, although the British, in a different way, have applied their own rules of responsibility and self-restraint.

It is a rule which operates unofficially and entirely outside the Constitution—but it has given us a method by which all the official and Constitutional organs of government can be made to work. It also provides a means of selecting leaders on all levels of our political life, for hammering out policies, and for organizing and managing the conquest of political power.

The way in which this tradition works in practice can be observed most easily in Congress. Anyone who has ever tried to push through a piece of legislation quickly discovers that the basic units of organization on Capitol Hill are not the parties, but the so-called blocs, which are familiar to everyone who reads a newspaper. There are dozens of them

—the farm bloc, the silver bloc, the friends of labor, the business group, the isolationists, the public power bloc—and they all cut across party lines. . . .

Now it is an unwritten but firm rule of Congress that no important bloc shall ever be voted down—under normal circumstances—on any matter which touches its own vital interests. Each of them, in other words, has a tacit right of veto on legislation in which it is primarily concerned. The ultimate expression of this right is the institution—uniquely American— of the filibuster in the Senate. Recently it has acquired a bad name among liberals because the Southern conservatives have used it ruthlessly to fight off civil rights legislation and protect white supremacy. Not so long ago, however, the filibuster was the stoutest weapon of such men as Norris and the LaFollettes in defending many a progressive cause.

Naturally no block wants to exercise its veto power except when it is absolutely forced to—for this is a negative power, and one which is always subject to retaliation. Positive power to influence legislation, on the other hand, can be gained only by conciliation, compromise, and endless horse-trading.

The farm bloc, for instance, normally needs no outside aid to halt the passage of a hostile bill. As a last resort, three or four strong-lunged states-men from the corn belt can always filibuster it to death in the Senate. If the bloc wants to put through a measure to support agricultural prices, however, it can succeed only by enlisting the help of other powerful special interest groups. Consequently, it must always be careful not to an-tagonize any potential ally by a reckless use of the veto; and it must be willing to pay for such help by throwing its support from time to time behind legislation sought by the labor bloc, the National Association of Manufacturers, or the school-teachers' lobby. . . .

This process of trading blocs of votes is generally known as log-rolling, and frequently it is deplored by the more innocent type of reformer. Such pious disapproval has no effect whatever on any practicing politician. He knows that log-rolling is a sensible and reasonably fair device, and that without it Congress could scarcely operate at all.

In fact, Congress gradually has developed a formal apparatus—the committee system—which is designed to make the log-rolling process as smooth and efficient as possible. There is no parallel system anywhere; the committees of Parliament and of the Continental legislative bodies work in an entirely different way.

Obviously the main business of Congress—the hammering out of a series of compromises between many special interest groups—cannot be conducted satisfactorily on the floor of the House or Senate. The meetings there are too large and far too public for such delicate negotiations. More-over, every speech delivered on the floor must be aimed primarily at the voters back home, and not at the other members of the chamber. Therefore,

Congress—especially the House—does nearly all its work in the closed sessions of its various committees, simply because the committee room is the only place where it is possible to arrange a compromise acceptable to all major interests affected.

For this reason, it is a matter of considerable importance to get a bill before the proper committee. Each committee serves as a forum for a particular cluster of special interests, and the assignment of a bill to a specific committee often decides which interest groups shall be recognized officially as affected by the measure and therefore entitled to a hand in its drafting. "Who is to have standing before the committee" is the technical term, and it is this decision that frequently decides the fate of the legislation.

Calhoun's principles of the concurrent majority and of sectional compromise operate just as powerfully, though sometimes less obviously, in every other American political institution. Our cabinet, for example, is the only one in the world where the members are charged by law with the representation of special interests—labor, agriculture, commerce, and so on. In other countries, each agency of government is at least presumed to act for the nation as a whole; here most agencies are expected to behave as servants for one interest or another. The Veterans' Administration, to cite the most familiar case, is frankly intended to look out for Our Boys; the Maritime Board is to look out for the shipping industry; the National Labor Relations Board, as originally established under the Wagner Act, was explicitly intended to build up the bargaining power of the unions.

Even within a single department, separate agencies are sometimes set up to represent conflicting interests. Thus in the Department of Agriculture under the New Deal the old Triple-A became primarily an instrument of the large-scale commercial farmers, as represented by their lobby, the Farm Bureau Federation; while the Farm Security Administration went to bat for the tenants, the farm laborers, and the little subsistence farmers, as represented by the Farmers Union. . . .

Calhoun's laws also govern the selection of virtually every candidate for public office. The mystery of "eligibility" which has eluded most foreign observers simply means that a candidate must not be unacceptable to any important special interest group—a negative rather than a positive qualification. A notorious case of this process at work was the selection of Mr. Truman as the Democrats' Vice Presidential candidate in 1944. As Edward J. Flynn, the Boss of the Bronx, has pointed out in his memoirs, Truman was the one man "who would hurt . . . least" as Roosevelt's running mate. Many stronger men were disqualified, Flynn explained, by the tacit veto of one sectional interest or another. Wallace was unacceptable to the business men and to many local party machines. Byrnes was distasteful to the Catholics, the Negroes, and organized labor. Rayburn came from the wrong part of the country. Truman, however, came from a border state, his labor record was good, he had not antagonized the conservatives, and—as Flynn put it—"he had never made any 'racial' remarks. He just dropped into the slot. . . ."

The stronghold of Calhoun's doctrine, however, is the American party —the wonder and despair of foreigners who cannot fit it into any of their concepts of political life.

The purpose of European parties is, of course, to divide men of different ideologies into coherent and disciplined organizations. The historic role of the American party, on the other hand, is not to divide but to unite. That task was imposed by simple necessity. If a division into ideological parties had been attempted, in addition to all the other centrifugal forces in this country, it very probably would have proved impossible to hold the nation together. The Founding Fathers understood this thoroughly; hence Washington's warning against "factions."

Indeed, on the one occasion when we did develop two ideological parties, squarely opposing each other on an issue of principle, the result was civil war. Fortunately, that was our last large-scale experiment with a third party formed on an ideological basis—for in its early days that is just what the Republican party was.

Its radical wing, led by such men as Thaddeus Stevens, Seward, and Chase, made a determined and skillful effort to substitute principles for interests as the foundations of American political life. Even within their own party, however, they were opposed by such practical politicians as Lincoln and Johnson—men who distrusted fanaticism in any form—and by the end of the Reconstruction period the experiment had been abandoned. American politics then swung back into its normal path and has never veered far away from it since. Although Calhoun's cause was defeated, his political theory came through the Civil War stronger than ever.

The result is that the American party has no permanent program and no fixed aim, except to win elections. Its one purpose is to unite the largest possible number of divergent interest groups in the pursuit of power. Its unity is one of compromise, not of dogma. It must—if it hopes to succeed —appeal to considerable numbers on both the left and the right, to rich and poor, Protestant and Catholic, farmer and industrial worker, native and foreign born.

It must be ready to bid for the support of any group that can deliver a sizable chunk of votes, accepting that group's program with whatever modifications may be necessary to reconcile the other members of the party. If sun worship, or Existentialism, or the nationalization of industry should ever attract any significant following in this country, you can be sure that both parties would soon whip up a plank designed to win it over.

This ability to absorb new ideas (along with the enthusiasts behind them) and to mold them into a shape acceptable to the party's standpatters is, perhaps, the chief measure of vitality in the party's leadership. Such ideas almost never germinate within the party itself. They are stolen— very often from third parties.

Indeed, the historic function of third parties has been to sprout new issues, nurse them along until they have gathered a body of supporters worth stealing, and then to turn them over (often reluctantly) to the major parties. A glance at the old platforms of the Populists, the Bull Moosers, and the Socialists will show what an astonishingly high percentage of their once-radical notions have been purloined by both Republicans and Democrats—and enacted into law. Thus the income tax, child-labor laws, minimum wages, regulation of railroads and utilities, and old-age pensions have all become part of the American Way of Life.

While each major party must always stand alert to grab a promising new issue, it also must be careful never to scare off any of the big, established interest groups. For as soon as it alienates any one of them, it finds itself in a state of crisis.

During the nineteen-thirties and -forties the Republicans lost much of their standing as a truly national party because they had made themselves unacceptable to labor. Similarly, the Democrats, during the middle stage of the New Deal, incurred the wrath of the business interests. Ever since Mr. Truman was plumped into the White House, the Democratic leadership has struggled desperately—though rather ineptly—to regain the confidence of business men without at the same time driving organized labor out of the ranks. It probably would be safe to predict that if the Republican party is to regain a long period of health, it must make an equally vigorous effort to win back the confidence of labor. For the permanent veto of any major element in American society means political death—as the ghosts of the Federalists and Whigs can testify.

The weaknesses of the American political system are obvious—much more obvious, in fact, than its virtues. These weaknesses have been so sharply criticized for the past hundred years, by a procession of able analysts ranging from Walter Bagehot to Thomas K. Finletter, that it is hardly necessary to mention them here. It is enough to note that most of the criticism has been aimed at two major flaws.

First, it is apparent that the doctrine of the concurrent majority is a negative one—a principle of inaction. A strong government, capable of rapid and decisive action, is difficult to achieve under a system which forbids it to do anything until virtually everybody acquiesces. In times of crisis, a dangerously long period of debate and compromise usually is necessary before any administration can carry out the drastic measures needed. The depression of the early thirties, the crisis in foreign policy which ended only with Pearl Harbor, the crisis of the Marshall program all illustrate this recurring problem.

This same characteristic of our system gives undue weight to the small but well-organized pressure group—especially when it is fighting *against* something. Hence a few power companies were able to block for twenty years the sensible use of the Muscle Shoals dam which eventually became the nucleus of TVA. An even more flagrant example is the silver bloc, representing only a tiny fraction of the American people. It has been looting the Treasury for a generation by a series of outrageous silver subsidy and purchase laws.

The negative character of our political rules also makes it uncommonly difficult for us to choose a President. Many of our oustanding political operatives—notably those who serve in the Senate—are virtually barred from a Presidential nomination because they are forced to get on record on too many issues. Inevitably they offend some important interest group, and therefore become "unavailable." Governors, who can keep their mouths shut on most national issues, have a much better chance to reach the White House. Moreover, the very qualities of caution and inoffensiveness which make a good candidate—Harding and Coolidge come most readily to mind—are likely to make a bad President.

An even more serious flaw in our scheme of politics is the difficulty in finding anybody to speak for the country as a whole. Calhoun would have argued that the national interest is merely the sum of all the various special interests, and therefore needs no spokesman of its own—but in this case he clearly was wrong.

In practice, we tend to settle sectional and class conflicts at the expense of the nation as a whole—with results painful to all of us. The labor troubles in the spring of 1946, for instance, could be settled only on a basis acceptable to *both* labor and management: that is, on the basis of higher wages *plus* higher prices. The upshot was an inflationary spiral which damaged everybody. Countless other instances, from soil erosion to the rash of billboards along our highways, bear witness to the American tendency to neglect matters which are "only" of national interest, and therefore are left without a recognized sponsor.

Over the generations we have developed a series of practices and institutions which partly remedy these weaknesses, although we are still far from a complete cure. One such development has been the gradual strengthening of the Presidency as against Congress. As the only man elected by all the people, the President inevitably has had to take over many of the policy-making and leadership functions which the Founding Fathers originally assigned to the legislators. This meant, of course, that he could no longer behave merely as an obedient executor of the will of Congress, but was forced into increasingly frequent conflicts with Capitol Hill.

Today we have come to recognize that this conflict is one of the most important obligations of the Presidency. No really strong executive tries to avoid it—he accepts it as an essential part of his job. If he simply tries to placate the pressure groups which speak through Congress, history writes him down as a failure. For it is his duty to enlist the support of many minorities for measures rooted in the national interest, reaching beyond their own immediate concern—and, if necessary, to stand up against the ravening minorities for the interest of the whole.

In recent times this particular part of the President's job has been made easier by the growth of the Theory of Temporary Emergencies. All of us —or nearly all—have come around to admitting that in time of emergency special interest groups must forego their right of veto. As a result, the President often is tempted to scare up an emergency to secure legislation which could not be passed under any other pretext. Thus, most of the New Deal bills were introduced as "temporary emergency measures," although they were clearly intended to be permanent from the very first; for in no other way could Mr. Roosevelt avoid the veto of the business interests.

Again, in 1939 the threat of war enabled the President to push through much legislation which would have been impossible under normal circumstances.

Because we have been so preoccupied with trying to patch up the flaws in our system, we have often overlooked its unique elements of strength. The chief of these is its ability to minimize conflict—not by suppressing the conflicting forces, but by absorbing and utilizing them. The result is a society which is both free and reasonably stable—a government which is as strong and effective as most dictatorships, but which can still adapt itself to social change.

The way in which the American political organism tames down the extremists of both the left and right is always fascinating to watch. Either party normally is willing to embrace any group or movement which can deliver votes—but in return it requires these groups to adjust their programs to fit the traditions, beliefs, and prejudices of the majority of the people. The fanatics, the implacable radicals cannot hope to get to first base in American politics until they abandon their fanaticism and learn the habits of conciliation. As a consequence, it is almost impossible for political movements here to become entirely irresponsible and to draw strength from the kind of demagogic obstruction which has nurtured both Communist and Fascist movements abroad.

The same process which gentles down the extremists also prods along the political laggards. As long as it is in a state of health, each American party has a conservative and a liberal wing. Sometimes one is dominant, sometimes the other—but even when the conservative element is most powerful, it must reckon with the left-wingers in its own family. At the moment the Republican party certainly is in one of its more conservative phases; yet it contains men who are at least as progressive as most of the old New Dealers. They, and their counterparts in the Democratic party, exert a steady tug to the left which prevents either party from lapsing into complete reaction.

The strength of this tug is indicated by the fact that the major New Deal reforms have now been almost universally accepted. In the mid-thirties, many leading Republicans, plus many conservative Democrats, were hell-bent on wiping out social security, TVA, SEC, minimum-wage laws, rural electrification, and all the other dread innovations of the New Deal. Today no Presidential aspirant would dare suggest the repeal of a single one of them. In this country there simply is no place for a hard core of irreconcilable reactionaries, comparable to those political groups in France which have never yet accepted the reforms of the French Revolution.

This American tendency to push extremists of both the left and right toward a middle position has enabled us, so far, to escape class warfare. This is no small achievement for any political system; for class warfare cannot be tolerated by a modern industrial society. If it seriously threatens, it is bound to be suppressed by some form of totalitarianism, as it has been in Germany, Spain, Italy, Russia, and most of Eastern Europe.

In fact, suppression might be termed the normal method of settling conflicts in continental Europe, where parties traditionally have been drawn up along ideological battle lines. Every political campaign becomes a religious crusade; each party is fanatically convinced that it and it alone has truth by the tail; each party is certain that its opponents not only are wrong, but wicked. If the sacred ideology is to be established beyond challenge, no heresy can be tolerated. Therefore it becomes a duty not only to defeat the enemy at the polls, but to wipe him out. Any suggestion of compromise must be rejected as treason and betrayal of the true faith. The party must be disciplined like an army, and if it cannot win by other means it must be ready to take up arms in deadly fact.

Under this kind of political system the best that can be hoped for is a prolonged deadlock between parties which are too numerous and weak to exterminate one another. The classic example is prewar France, where six revolutions or near-revolutions broke out within a century, where cabinets fell every weekend, and no government could ever become strong enough to govern effectively. The more usual outcome is a complete victory for one ideology or another, after a brief period of electioneering, turmoil, and fighting in the streets; then comes the liquidation of the defeated.

Because this sort of ideological politics is so foreign to our native tradition, neither Socialists, Communists, nor Fascists have ever been accepted as normal parties. So long as that tradition retains its very considerable vitality, it seems to me unlikely that any third party founded on an ideological basis can take root. The notion of a ruthless and unlimited class struggle, the concept of a master race, a fascist élite, or a proletariat which is entitled to impose its will on all others—these are ideas which are incompatible with the main current of American political life. The uncompromising ideologist, of whatever faith, appears in our eyes peculiarly "un-American," simply because he cannot recognize the rule of the concurrent majority, nor can he accept the rules of mutual toleration which are necessary to make it work. Unless he forsakes his ideology, he cannot even understand that basic principle of American politics which was perhaps best expressed by Judge Learned Hand: "The spirit of liberty is the spirit which is not too sure that it is right."

54

Extremism in American Politics

by Arthur M. Schlesinger

The presidential campaign of 1964 introduced the word "extremism" into our political vocabulary as a synonym for ultraconservatism, but the phenomenon itself is anything but new. Throughout our history it has lurked under the surface of public life, finding an escape hatch at more or less definite intervals. Psychologically the outbreaks have also borne striking resemblances, even though the professed objectives have shifted as occasion required. For these reasons a consideration of the leading examples should contribute to a better understanding of this recurring aspect of American politics.

Nearly a century and a half ago, in 1826, the abduction and presumed murder of one William Morgan of Batavia in western New York set off a wave of popular hysteria that became a force in state and national affairs. Morgan, a bricklayer, was a Mason who had written a book exposing the order's secrets, and widespread report instantly attributed his disappearance to retaliation on the part of vengeful members. When four persons were found guilty just of the kidnaping and got off with light sentences, suspicion of the fraternity's covert control of the courts, and probably also of all other departments of the government, hardened into certainty. Incidentally, the most diligent search failed to yield any trace of "the martyr's" body. The mystery remains to this day.

From New York the excitement spread to New England and the Middle Atlantic states as well as inland to Ohio and Indiana. Antimasonic news-

---

From *Saturday Review,* November 27, 1965, pp. 21–25. Reprinted by permission of *Saturday Review* and Mrs. Arthur M. Schlesinger.

The late Arthur M. Schlesinger was Professor of History at Harvard University, a well-known writer on historical topics, and a champion of civil liberties.

papers and magazines sprang up to fan the flames. Traveling lecturers denounced the "hydra-headed monster." Churches expelled Masonic preachers and laymen. Many lodges disbanded; in New York State alone their number dropped from 600 in 1826 to 50 in 1834. The Antimasons successfully ran candidates in local and state elections; several legislatures banned extrajudicial oaths; and Rhode Island and Pennsylvania required all secret societies henceforth to reveal their proceedings in annual reports.

In the national arena, politicians like Thurlow Weed and William H. Seward in New York and Thaddeus Stevens in Pennsylvania, seeking to oust President Jackson and the Democratic party from power in 1832, seized on the furor to consolidate a nationwide opposition. In doing so, however, they injected other issues and wrenched the movement so far from its original purpose that William Wirt, the Antimasonic nominee, failed to condemn the order in his letter of acceptance. Though both Jackson and Henry Clay, the National Republican candidate, were active or former Masons, Wirt received only Vermont's seven electoral votes, while his rivals won 219 and 49 respectively.

The party then soon flickered out. The reason, according to a committee of the Pennsylvania legislature, was that "It envies the possessors of office. It is ignorant. It absurdly denounces as a mysterious institution full of guilt and blood a society of which . . . ten or fifteen thousand of our most useful, intelligent, and eminent citizens of all parties are members." Probably more decisive was the fact that questions of crucial national importance such as the tariff and the United States Bank had arisen to give the voters something more tangible to worry about.

Already events were setting the stage for a new exhibition of frenzy. Oddly enough, these alarmists saw no danger in mystic brotherhoods and in due course donned the cloak of secrecy themselves. Their fear arose from the large inflow of Irish and Germans into the United States in the 1830s and 1840s, with the Irish in particular arousing wide hostility. As Catholics they seemed to menace America's traditional Protestantism, and as a copious supply of cheap labor they jeopardized the living standards of native workers. Rumors also coursed far and fast of "Romish" plots to subvert the public schools and even the republic itself.

The popular reaction was swift and tempestuous. In 1834 a mob burned down a convent school in Charlestown, Massachusetts, and later years saw rioting, often attended with bloodshed as well as incendiarism, in New York, Philadelphia, Detroit, Louisville, and elsewhere. Anti-Catholic lecturers and periodicals flourished. In 1836 a pretended ex-nun, Maria Monk, published her *Awful Disclosures* of imagined immorality and infanticide in a convent, which sold 300,000 copies before the Civil War. Even Samuel F. B. Morse, the portraitist, and inventor of the telegraph, took up arms against Rome with his *Foreign Conspiracy against the Liberties of the United States* (1834) and later tracts.

In the ensuing decade the nativists formed secret fraternal organizations to further the cause, such as the Order of United Americans, the Junior Order of United American Mechanics, and the Order of the Star-Spangled Banner. The last band, established in 1849 and the most militant of the lot, in turn set afoot the American or Know-Nothing party. The Know Nothings, popularly so dubbed because they denied to inquirers knowledge of the party's existence, demanded the exclusion of all foreign-born from office ("Americans must rule America"), a twenty-one-year naturalization period for voting, and the rigid separation of church and state. Aided by the nationwide consternation over the revival of the slavery controversy by the Kansas-Nebraska Act in 1854, and conducting no public campaign, they carried Massachusetts, Pennsylvania, and Delaware in the fall elections, also sent seventy-some supporters to Congress, and a year later captured five more states.

Exhilarated by these successes, the Know Nothings in 1856 nominated a national standard-bearer, the Whig ex-President Millard Fillmore, thereby bringing the historic Whig party to an end. By now, however, feeling throughout the country had reached such a pitch over the sectional question that the Know Nothings themselves could no longer ignore it, and it opened serious rifts in their conventions. Although Fillmore mustered nearly a quarter of all the popular votes, they were so scattered as to win only Maryland's eight electoral ones. Another fledgling party, the Republican, founded expressly to curb the expansion of slavery, obtained a much larger popular support and the 114 electoral votes of eleven states. Though it, too, lost to the Democrats, it could look confidently to the future. The Know Nothings shortly passed into oblivion.

How potent a force they might have become had the sectional issue not intruded no one can say. Yet, as the Antimasonic movement showed and later evidence confirmed, such conflagrations in America have always quickly burned themselves out. While the Know-Nothing convulsion was still at its height, the politically observant Horace Greeley declared it would "vanish as suddenly as it appeared." And the Indiana Congressman George W. Julian, writing after the fact, undoubtedly expressed the sober second thought of the electorate in terming it "a horrid conspiracy against decency, the rights of man, and the principle of human brotherhood."

The next great outbreak of fear and hate occurred after the Civil War, this time in the conquered South. The remaking of race relations by Congress in the measures known as Reconstruction had distorted the section's traditional pattern of life beyond recognition. The slaves were now not only free but were voters and officeholders helping run the reconstituted state governments to the exclusion of the old master class. For ingrained believers in white supremacy this reversed the natural order of things and meant the region's "Africanization."

With no relief to be expected from a Northern-controlled Congress or at the polls, the aroused whites formed clandestine societies of resistance. The Ku Klux Klan, the best known, started in 1866 at the little town of Pulaski in southern Tennessee as a social club of returned Confederate veterans who for fun rode about the countryside after dark, masked and clad in white on white-sheeted horses. But when the weird proceedings were seen to excite the superstitious dread of Negroes, the members, taking advantage of the fact, visited insubordinate blacks and their white allies at dead of night to warn them to desist or decamp. The Pulaski example gave birth to imitators in other parts of Tennessee and in other Southern states, and in April 1867 a secret gathering at Nashville combined the units or "dens" under the name of the Invisible Empire of the South, with officers bearing awesome titles.

As time went on, violence became the chief reliance. Victims might now be beaten, maimed, or murdered. Criminal bands, too, adopted the eerie disguise for purposes of loot or private vengeance. In Louisiana alone, federal records show that 1,885 persons suffered injury or death during the 1868 Presidential election year. The situation was already well out of hand when in January 1869 the "Grand Wizard" of the order decreed its dissolution. This action, however, only worsened conditions, for many of the dens refused to comply and the departure of the more responsible members gave the lawless elements full rein. Besides, scores of similar organizations had meanwhile sprung up, notably the Knights of the White Camelia, which, independently of the Klan, operated in the region from Texas to the Carolinas under the nominal control of a supreme council in New Orleans. The total number involved in these underground activities has been estimated at 550,000, though obviously the exact figure can never be known.

No other American extremist movement, before or since, has so brazenly defied the federal authority. Accordingly this has been the only instance (prior to the sporadic resistance to the school-desegregation decision of 1954 and the later civil rights acts) to bring down the might of the national government. In 1870 and 1871 Congress in successive laws empowered President Grant to end the societies with armed force if necessary and to appoint supervisors when required to assure Negroes full voting rights in federal elections. Soon hundreds of accused were arrested, United States troops reappeared in the South, and for a time the writ of habeas corpus was suspended in nine South Carolina counties. Consequently "Ku Kluxing" virtually ceased early in 1872. By then, however, the resourceful whites had learned they could frighten Negroes away from the polls by the mere threat of maltreatment. Later on, of course, when the South recovered full control of its affairs, they secured the same end by intricate election laws and the falsifying of returns.

The flare-up of intolerance to follow originated in the Midwest, being the handiwork of an anti-Catholic secret society, the American Protective Association. Founded in 1887 by one Henry F. Bowers, a lawyer of Clinton, Iowa, the APA reflected not only the ancient Protestant hostility to Catholicism but also, more directly, rural dislike of the rapidly growing cities, where the bulk of the Catholics resided, as well as urban resentment of the economic competition due to the mounting immigration from the papist countries of Southern and Eastern Europe. Every initiate swore to oppose "the diabolical work of the Roman Catholic Church" and, specifically, to hire or vote for none of its communicants or condone their appointment as teachers in the public schools.

As the membership spread east and west through the land, the principal features of the earlier Know-Nothing agitation were reproduced and expanded. "Escaped nuns" and "ex-priests" recited their shocking tales. Anti-Catholic weeklies and pamphlets whipped up passion. Forged documents, including an alleged encyclical commanding the faithful to "exterminate all heretics" on a given day in 1893, exposed Rome's designs against democratic Protestant America. A whispering campaign reported the collecting of arms in Catholic church basements. Mob violence likewise erupted, a Boston collision in 1895 causing the death of one man and the injury of many others. As a dismayed contemporary said of the APA, "In the name of freedom it stabs freedom in the dark; in the name of Christianity . . . it uses the weapons of the devil."

The members as a rule operated within the fold of the Republican party, since Irish Catholics comprised a mainstay of the Democrats. Assisted by self-styled patriotic societies with similar aims, the APA helped win many city and a number of state elections, contributed to William McKinley's victory in his race for governor of Ohio in 1893, and claimed 100 supporters in Congress the following year. At its peak in late 1894 it probably numbered 100,000 persons, with the greatest concentration in the Middle West. By the 1896 Presidential campaign, however, the bitter strife of the major parties over free silver and Bryanism obliterated the "Catholic menace" from the voters' minds, and the order disappeared from view.

The first outburst of zealotry in the present century was a throwback to both the Ku Klux Klan and the American Protective Association. Indeed, the new organization appropriated the name and methods of the Reconstruction body besides being itself Southern-born. Established in 1915 at Atlanta by William J. Simmons, an erstwhile itinerant preacher, it pledged its members to eliminate from political life all but white native-born Protestants. "By some scheme of Providence," Simmons declared, "the Negro was created a serf." Georgia already had a record of leading the Union in the number of its colored lynchings.

Because of the distracting effects of World War I, however, the resuscitated Klan made little headway until peace returned. Then alarm over the prospective deluging of the country by impoverished and perhaps revolutionary comers from devastated Europe caused it to extend rapidly through the South and Midwest, with strong outposts elsewhere as well; and in course of doing so it added animosity toward Jews to the older hatred of Negroes, Catholics, and immigrants. The anti-Semitism, long dormant but never before an overt issue, rested avowedly on a set of fraudulent documents of obscure Russian origin, *The Protocols of the Elders of Zion.* These allegedly unveiled a plot to assert Jewish predominance of the entire globe. As regards the United States, a contributor in the Klan organ, *The Searchlight,* offered to prove that Jews were already engaged in inciting the Afro-Americans to a race war. He indeed avowed he had "never met a disloyal American who failed to be either foreign-born or a Semitic." Men so thinking turned a deaf ear when the *Oklahoma Leader* rebuked this "new sort of Christianity that would flog Christ for being a Jew and a foreigner."

The night-riding Klansmen in ghostly attire, dotting the landscape as they went with fiery crosses, employed threats, beatings, arson, and murder against their victims, white and colored, and these unfortunates in due course came to include upholders even of such causes as the League of Nations, evolution, and birth control. In 1922 the organization entered politics, dominating for a time the states of Ohio, Indiana, Oklahoma, Arkansas, Texas, California, and Oregon with spokesmen in Congress. It wielded enough influence in the 1924 Democratic convention to deny the Presidential nomination to Alfred E. Smith, the Catholic governor of New York. A year later 40,000 Klansmen paraded down Washington's Pennsylvania Avenue. At its zenith the membership supposedly embraced between four and five million.

As in past instances of the kind, however, popular revulsion to brute force and lawlessness set in, hastened by revelations of financial and other misdoings of the leaders. In Indiana the scandals sent a "Grand Dragon," a Congressman, the mayor of Indianapolis, and various lesser officials to prison. Even before this, legislation in New York, Michigan, Minnesota, Iowa, Texas, and some other states had banned masked brotherhoods. Further evidence of the decline appeared in the Democratic nomination of Al Smith in 1928, and the same year saw the United States Supreme Court, in a case appealed from New York, denounce the Klan for "conduct inimical to personal rights and welfare" in taking the law secretly into its hands.

Of greener memory is the scaremongering associated with the term McCarthyism. This affair, different from its predecessors, was largely the work of one man operating from an important position in the federal government under the protection of Congressional immunity. As in the other episodes particular circumstances facilitated his success. The public, only recently recovered from the shock of World War II, faced with dread new perils to peace from the postwar aggressions of the Soviet Union on neighboring states, its acquisition of the atom bomb, and disclosures of several instances of Communist infiltration of the United States Government. On top of all these, America's springing to arms to save Korea from Communism brought the danger vividly home to every segment of the population.

Senator Joseph R. McCarthy of Wisconsin, hitherto an inconspicuous figure, seized the opportunity to exploit the anxieties apparently in a compulsive desire to win national prominence. Starting in 1950 he recklessly accused federal officials, high and low, of connivance with Russia. He charged that the State Department was knowingly harboring scores of card-carrying Communists. As chairman of a Senate committee he further assailed in public hearings persons of unblemished probity in the military and foreign services, wrecking their reputations and ruining their careers. When General Eisenhower ran for President in 1952, even that popular hero omitted from a speech a tribute to George C. Marshall out of deference to the Wisconsin Senator who had branded the army chief of staff in World War II and later Secretary of State as a party to a "conspiracy, the worldwide web of which had been spun in Moscow."

Through the nation at large as well as in Congress, McCarthy, in the troubled state of the popular mind, rallied an impassioned following regardless of party. Though many people privately denounced his methods, only the bravest dared speak out lest they, too, be pilloried for disloyalty. In due time, however, the public grew tired of the cries of "Wolf! Wolf!" when not one of McCarthy's accusations produced a court conviction. Violations of the constitutional rights of citizens came to loom larger than unsupported allegations of treason. The United States Senate itself administered the final blow when in December 1954 it adopted a resolution condemning McCarthy by the overwhelming vote of sixty-seven to twenty-two.

What did this series of extremist movements have in common? Their basic kinship lay in the purpose to deny to fellow citizens sacrosanct constitutional safeguards, whether freedom of religion, speech, and association, due process of law, the right of suffrage, or other guarantees. It is easy therefore to regard the upsurges as un-American. But, had they really been so, they would not all have been indigenous in origin and gathered the strength they did. The truth is that they reveal an aspect of the national character we tend to forget: the presence of impulses and forces which, though usually latent, are never dead and spring into life when conditions prove favorable.

Moreover, those affected, however credulous they may seem in retrospect, were by and large well-meaning persons believing earnestly that they were fighting dragons that threatend catastrophe to themselves and the country. This gave many of them a dedicated sense of participating for the first time in decisions of vital public concern. As soon, however, as the cause demonstrated vote-getting promise, politicians cannily used it to advance their personal fortunes. Only two of the movements, however, generated national parties, and neither outlasted the single campaign. The rest bored from within one or the other or both of the established organizations.

The goals they sought naturally varied according to the special circumstances, but these were always unmistakably set forth, since people are more easily aroused when offered cure-alls for their worries. Xenophobia and Negrophobia received the highest priority. Ironically enough, the initial provocation, Antimasonry, made so transitory an impression that the later insurgencies commonly themselves assumed the form of oath-bound orders.

Emotion was the mainspring of all of them. "Grand Wizard" Simmons of the second Ku Klux Klan undoubtedly spoke for the lot in saying, "The Klan does not believe that the fact that it is emotional and instinctive, rather than coldly intellectual, is a weakness. All action comes from emotion, rather than from ratiocination." With this conviction the leaders freely resorted to misrepresentation, distortion, and the Big Lie; and their overwrought followers responded by persecuting persons who offered opposition. Bodily harm and arson or, in the case of the McCarthy paroxysm, character assassination constituted their notion of serving the public good instead of the slow and (to them) highly suspect workings of the law.

These repressive movements occurred with a certain regularity, as though a people noted for hard common sense in day-to-day doings had to break loose from time to time when dealing with public matters. About twenty years separated the crests of the four waves in the last century, and thirty years in the two of the present one, thus suggesting that the intervals are growing longer. Despite these differences, however, the outcome was in every case the same, for each upon reaching its peak speedily declined, as if the public, surprised at itself, suddenly recovered its balance. Only once did federal legislation enter in as a factor. The United States is an undoctrinaire country, jealous for the rights and liberties of the individual; and if the testimony of history counts for anything, no movement built on prejudice is ever likely to gain more than a temporary hold.

Against this background the extremism of the Goldwater candidacy should be viewed. Superficially it surpassed all its forerunners by capturing the national convention of one of the two great parties and dictating its nominees and platform. The dramatic victory, however, resulted from the failure of the moderate or progressive Republicans to unite their strength against a determined and well-organized minority. The tail wagged the dog. When Goldwater declared in his acceptance speech, "Extremism in the defense of liberty is no vice. Moderation in the pursuit of justice is no virtue," one of his unsuccessful rivals expressed the general sentiment of the party in sternly rejoining, "To extol extremism—whether 'in defense of liberty' or 'in pursuit of justice'—is dangerous, irresponsible, and frightening." The weeks that followed the convention saw massive Republican defections.

From the start, then, the new leaders lacked the broad base of party support from which they had expected to operate. Beyond this they confronted a difficulty which a knowledge of the earlier agitations could have helped them solve. They did not define with clarity the enemy they were fighting and thus denied their followers an effective recruiting cry. Goldwater, on the one hand, pleaded nostalgically for a return to simpler government and greater state autonomy and, on the other, demanded an aggressive foreign policy—two positions hard to reconcile. In addition, his appeal was confused by the vigorous backing of the John Birch Society and of the White Citizens Councils and scattered reincarnations of the Ku Klux Klan in the South. These groups, the first McCarthyistic and the others racist, advocated measures which Goldwater himself neither explicitly avowed nor disclaimed.

Finally, the Goldwater endeavor proved ill-timed. If these upheavals partake of a roughly cyclical character, as the evidence suggests, even a more ably conceived campaign could not have got very far in 1964, since not twenty or thirty years but only ten had elapsed since the previous eruption. As it was, Goldwater went down to disastrous defeat, winning only his home state of Arizona and five others in the South. Although these latter had usually been Democratic politically, they saw in his issue of states' rights a means of suppressing the Negroes' human rights. A polling organization, moreover, reported that three out of every four of the relatively few Republican votes he received nationally stemmed from party loyalty, not confidence in the man or his program.

The uniform failure of this procession of extremist movements, even when well managed, to make more than a fleeting impression in the past augurs that they will not fare better in the future. Efforts to intimidate or manhandle fellow Americans because of their personal or social views, or to achieve the same end through repressive legislation, can never hope to win the lasting favor of a people dedicated historically to the principles of fair play and the equal protection of the law.

27

GOVERNMENT FINANCE AND THE SOCIAL WELFARE

BARBARA WARD believes that in the United States far too much is spent by individuals on nonessentials, and far too little is spent by government on public services. She implies that, if defense expenditures cannot be reduced, ways must be found to raise taxes. Chamberlin, on the other hand, suggests that we have done rather well in providing more funds for public services. He points out that since the 1920's the total of spending by governments at all levels has risen much faster than the national income, and he fears that a further increase in taxes would discourage initiative and check economic growth.

The Chamberlin article was written in 1960. It is interesting to note that several years later there had been a further great increase of public spending. (See figures in brackets, inserted by the editors.) However, this was made possible not so much by increased tax rates as by an extraordinary expansion of national output and income, along with some deficit spending. Federal income-tax rates were actually reduced.

In our third selection, C. Northcote Parkinson, writing humorously but with underlying seriousness, propounds "Parkinson's Second Law." He suspects that increased government revenue is apt to mean more inefficiency and waste rather than more or better services, and he maintains that the total tax burden cannot be allowed to exceed certain limits without endangering the social structure.

55

The Gap Between Social Needs and Public Expenditures

by Barbara Ward

Every assessment of America's future economic problems will presumably begin with the most dynamic factor in the American community—the pounding birth rate. It is now a conservative estimate to expect a population of some 220 millions by 1975. If the three and four child family becomes the pattern of the future, the estimate should be considerably higher.

In any normal, responsible family the arrival of more children leads to a change in habits of spending. More money will be set aside for education, for health, for insurance, for housing. Parents cut down some less essential expenditure—smoking, perhaps, or drinking—or postpone desirable purchases—new drapes, a new automobile.

When, in the great family which is the nation, a cataract of new babies pours into the community, it would not be unreasonable to expect something of the same kind of shift in spending. Housing, health, education—these would claim more of the national income, a wide range of consumer goods rather less.

This reasonable assumption is, however, a little complicated by the fact that some of the higher expenditures made necessary by America's growing population come out of the public purse. The millions and millions of new houses which must be built when the babies born in the great upsurge of population in the early 1940's begin to marry and form their own homes will be financed in the main by the families themselves. But the streets, the water supplies, the sanitation, the urban and suburban amenities, the police and fire protection which help to turn four walls and a roof into a functioning unit in a civilized community must all come from tax money. Health payments and insurances will be mainly private, but much more public money will be needed for hospital-building and for

Reprinted from *Problems of United States Economic Development,* Vol. I, January 1958, published by The Committee for Economic Development, 711 Fifth Avenue, New York 22, New York.

Barbara Ward (Lady Jackson) is a well-known English economist and writer who for some years was on the staff of *The Economist.*

various forms of preventive medical services. Education, by the fundamental decision to provide all Americans with a free birthright of learning, must come to an overwhelming degree from public funds.

All this is obvious enough—although the scale of social expenditure the new families will make necessary almost certainly is not. But there are one or two other factors which affect the scale of necessary social capital. It is not only the rising population that swells the need. There is a heavy backlog of unsatisfied demand. Smaller expenditures during the depression, the enforced economy of the war years, have left the community with a legacy of obsolete schools, houses, hospitals, and indeed whole urban areas, which, with the passage of each year, calls more urgently for replacement and lengthens the list of necessary new construction.

To give only the most fateful instance—that of education—the position today is that in spite of building 50,000 new classrooms each year, the authorities are not keeping pace with the new entries to school. The deficit is growing by thousands every year, and today it stands at 75,000 classrooms. At the same time, perhaps 20 per cent of existing school buildings are strictly obsolete—a euphemism used to cover, in some cases, insanitary firetraps.

The steady increase in *density* of population also underlines the need for higher social expenditure. It may be that the cheapest method of housing the new millions is to leave private demand and the real estate and construction interests to surround existing urban centers with ring after ring of outward-growing suburbs. The nineteen-seventies may be not only the decade when America passes the 250 millions marks but when Boston is finally linked to Washington in one continuous "conurbation." To decentralize industry to smaller communities, to consider the creation of entirely new cities in growing areas such as the Pacific Northwest—such policies might well be more costly in terms of a whole range of urban and environmental services, but conceivably they might have some relevance to a basic American right, "the pursuit of happiness" and hence a basic economic necessity, a healthy and intelligent working force.

Implications such as these of a growing density of population may be hard to assess. But not all are so. It is clear that in the next decades, the most precious of all America's resources—pure water—must become steadily more costly as it becomes more scarce.

Can one make any estimate of the scale of need for social capital in the coming decades? The survey published by the Twentieth Century Fund in 1955 attempted a comprehensive assessment and carried its forecasts to 1960. Its conclusion was that in virtually every field of publicly-financed community need, there would be deficits in the 1960's. In terms of the 1950 dollar, these would run at the level of over $5 billions a year in education, over a billion for health and hospitals, nearly a billion for the preservation of natural resources, over a half a billion for sanitation and water supply, and another half billion for police, fire protection, and postal services. But these figures leave out another urgent social need—to bring American housing, with nearly two million sub-standard units, up to a reasonable level.

According to the estimates made in the Fund's Survey, a full housing program would entail a total capital outlay of between $80 and $90 billions. This figure does not include any estimate for urban redevelopment and new urban centers; nor does the Survey distinguish between public and private expenditure. But the cost of parts of the program, such as the acquisition of sites in slums and blighted areas and some low-cost housing, would certainly fall on the public authorities. The Survey makes no estimate of the public share but it would perhaps be not unreasonable to add between a quarter and a half billion extra dollars to the annual "general welfare" budget to cover publicly-financed housing and urban needs. The figure implies a spread of the program over two decades and allots to public funds one-eighth of the extra cost.

The Survey's figures thus suggest that America will enter the sixties with a gap between social need and actual public expenditure of the annual order of $9 billions—or even $11 billions if one includes social insurance. But this estimate is, in fact, too low. It is stated in 1950 dollars while the purchasing power of the dollar has shrunk 14% since 1950. The Survey's estimates of the growth of population have, like all other population estimates, proved too conservative. And the figures assumed no downward trend in public spending. Since 1953, however, federal expenditure on the general welfare—as a percentage of gross national product—has fallen from 10 to 6 per cent and this decline could offset the rise in tax yields from an expanding national income. Yet $9 billions is in all conscience high enough, much higher than any sum that is likely to be financed in present conditions.

The problem of meeting this social outlay must differ radically according to the trend—towards continued hostility or potential appeasement—in the world at large. The weight of personal income tax which seems in 1957 the burden the American voter resents most strongly is largely determined by defence and its related expenditures. If military and international outlays could return to the $17 billions spent in 1950, an extra $9 or $10 billions for the general welfare budget would still leave room for a vast abatement in taxation.

But there is no such prospect in sight. Must the conclusion therefore be that, with income and property taxes standing at what the voter feels to be the outside limit, and more rapid inflation threatened by any budgetary deficit, the fate of the American community in the next decades is, with its jet-propelled birth rate, to combine expansion in some types of consumption and well-being with a marked deterioration in others—better refrigerators in badly serviced houses, two car garages and two shift schools, good clothes and poor sanitation, enough alcohol but not enough water— the line being decided by the financial origin of the goods and services, the "tax dollar" resented and resisted, the private and personal dollar accepted and prized?

The answer cannot be given in economic terms. Unquestionably a community which spends more on cosmetics than on sanitation, eight or nine times as much on liquor as on water supplies, at least 25% more on automobiles, gasoline and auto-servicing than upon education, and which has almost doubled its cigarette smoking (per capita) in the last twenty years has some small margin of postponable personal consumption with which, even under cold war budgeting, it can ensure that the children of tomorrow are not, in a technological society demanding even higher standards of competence, worse schooled and taught than their grandparents. And, in spite of the growing place occupied by the sales tax in the structure of state taxation, the limit of this mode of transfer from the private to the public sector has probably not been reached.

The question whether some cuts in consumption could in fact secure more money for community needs is not, however, an economic problem. It depends upon the political decision of the voters.

Nor, if against all expectation, the cold war ceased and defence expenditure were more than halved, would the availability of social capital be an *economic* question. In terms of the maintenance of employment, the economic argument is strong in favour of maintaining a high level of public expenditure. Private spending by way of tax reduction could not expand on a scale sufficient to absorb an annual fall in public expenditure of $20 billions. A domestic program ready prepared for schools, hospitals, transportation and urban redevelopment is therefore the logical accompaniment of all serious attempts at disarmament.

But the program itself involves political, not economic decisions. If tomorrow's citizens believed education to be as essential to national survival as are today's weapons of defence, there would be no fear of a shortfall either in social capital or in high levels of employment. But democracy, in America or elsewhere, has not yet reached such a decision.

56

Truth vs. Myths

by William Henry Chamberlin

Hard it is for a fact to run down a myth, especially when that myth is entwined in a cliché.

The favorite current myth of U.S. "liberals" is that Federal and state governments in this country are shamefully poor, while American citizens are shamefully rich, that public spending is outrageously stinted while private spending soars on luxurious consumer goods. And this myth is just one of several weightless propositions that the American Left has long been firing at the nation. . . .

The leading myth of the moment is that Federal and state governments in America are somehow getting short-changed while individuals prosper.

The First National City Bank of New York, in its monthly Letter, subjects this picture to the test of facts and figures.

The results reveal what a good many Americans would have suspected without necessarily having all the relevant data at their finger tips. The share of public spending in the national income has been steadily and rapidly increasing, not only absolutely, but relatively. This share, representing the amount of Federal, state and local taxation, grew from 10.8% in the mid-1920's to 20.8% in 1940 and to 31% in the late Fifties.

A specific comparison with 1927 shows that Federal cash income is up more than 20 times, while personal disposable income (after taxes) has grown about four times and state and local revenue more than five times. Federal cash expenditures were $9.6 billion in 1940, $94.8 billion in the late Fifties [$120.5 billion in 1964—Eds.]; state and local expenditures in this period went up from $10.3 billion to $48.8 billion [$70.6 billion in 1964], and gross national product from $95.6 billion to $463.8 billion [$628.7 billion in 1964].

A favorite contention of those who would vastly increase public spending is that education is starved; some very loose, misleading and downright false comparisons have been drawn with Soviet education. Yet expenditures on education rose from $2.8 billion in 1940 to almost $17

From *The Wall Street Journal*, July 1, 1960, p. 4. Reprinted by permission.
William Henry Chamberlin has written several books and is an editorial correspondent and book reviewer for *The Wall Street Journal*.

billion in the late Fifties. Total public and private expenditure on education in the United States in 1959 was $22 billion [more than $33 billion in 1964], a figure unmatched, absolutely or on a per capita basis, anywhere in the world. . . .

The National City Bank Letter points to a vicious circle which develops when impoverishment through excessive taxation leads to a demand for more Government subsidies, which leads to more taxation which leads. . . . And it draws this sound conclusion from its array of facts and figures:

"There are beyond doubt some government programs suffering from lack of sufficient funds. If this is so, it is hardly because the people are too rich, or inadequately taxed, but because government is trying to do more things than it can handle with real competence. The real point at issue is how much farther—if at all—we can safely go toward discouraging individual initiative, self-reliance and industrious habits. The barrage of complaints over inadequate economic growth would seem to suggest that we need to concern ourselves more, rather than less, with the human aspirations that make the economy go."

It is good to have in convenient form the facts of vastly expanded taxation and steadily increasing proportions of Federal and state expenditure to refute the myth of America as a country where the individual citizen rolls in wealth while public authorities are denied essential funds.

57

Parkinson's Second Law

by C. Northcote Parkinson

An extremely wealthy man underwent an extremely serious operation at the hands of an extremely distinguished surgeon. Ten days afterwards the surgeon asked how his patient was progressing. "Doing fine," said the

From *The Law and the Profits* by C. Northcote Parkinson, pp. 2–8, 14–16, 242–246, *passim*. Boston, Houghton Mifflin Company, and London, John Murray (Publishers) Ltd. © Copyright 1960 by C. Northcote Parkinson. Reprinted by permission.

C. Northcote Parkinson is an English historian who has become well known for his books on Parkinson's laws. He has taught at several leading schools, including the Universities of Malaya, Illinois, and California.

nurse. "He has already been trying to date Nurse Audrey, a sure sign of convalescence."

"Nurse Audrey?" asked the surgeon quickly. "Is that the blond girl from Illinois?"

"No," the nurse assured him, "Nurse Audrey is the redhead from Missouri."

"In that case," said the surgeon, "the patient needs something to steady his pulse. I shall tell him what the operation cost."

The patient sobered down under this treatment and did some rapid calculations on the back of his temperature chart.

"Your fee of $4000," he finally concluded, "represents the proportion I retain from the last $44,500 of my income. To pay you without being worse off would mean earning another $44,500 more than last year; no easy task."

"Well," replied the surgeon, "you know how it is. It is only by charging you that much that I can afford to charge others little or nothing."

"No doubt," said the patient. "But the fee still absorbs $44,500 of my theoretical income—no inconsiderable sum. Might I ask what proportion of the $4000 you will manage to retain?"

It was the surgeon's turn to scribble calculations, as a result of which he concluded that his actual gain, after tax had been paid, would amount to $800.

"Allow me to observe," said the patient, "that I must therefore earn $44,500 in order to give you $800 of spendable income; the entire balance going to government. Does that strike you as a transaction profitable to either of us?"

"Well, frankly, no," admitted the surgeon. "Put like that, the whole thing is absurd. But what else can we do?"

"First, we can make certain that no one is listening. No one at the keyhole? No federal agent under the bed? No tape recorder in the—? Are you quite sure that we can keep this strictly to ourselves?"

"Quite sure," the surgeon replied after quickly opening the door and glancing up and down the corridor. "What do you suggest?"

"Come closer so that I can whisper. *Why don't I give you a case of Scotch and so call it quits?*"

"Not enough," hissed the surgeon, "but if you made it *two* cases . . . ?"

"Yes?" whispered the patient.

"And lent me your cabin cruiser for three weeks in September . . ."

"*Yes?*"

"We might call it a deal!"

"That's fine. And do you know what gave me the idea? I studied Parkinson's Law and realized that excessive taxation has made nonsense of everything!"

"Rubbish, my dear fellow. Parkinson's Law has nothing to do with taxation. It has to do with overstaffing—of which, by the way, this hospital provides some interesting examples. In parasitology, for—"

"Like all medical men, you are out of date. You are referring to Parkinson's *First* Law. I am referring to his *Second* Law."

"I must admit that I never heard of it. It concerns taxation, you say?"

"It concerns taxation. It also concerns you. Now, listen . . . listen carefully. *Expenditure rises to meet income!*"

Expenditure rises to meet income. Parkinson's Second Law, like the first, is a matter of everyday experience, manifest as soon as it is stated, as obvious as it is simple. When the individual has a raise in salary, he and his wife are prone to decide how the additional income is to be spent; so much on an insurance policy, so much to the savings bank, so much in a trust fund for the children. They might just as well save themselves the trouble, for no surplus ever comes into view. The extra salary is silently absorbed, leaving the family barely in credit and often, in fact, with a deficit which has actually increased. Individual expenditure not only rises to meet income but tends to surpass it, and probably always will.

It is less widely recognized that what is true of individuals is also true of governments. Whatever the revenue may be, there will always be the pressing need to spend it. But between governments and individuals there is this vital difference, that the government rarely pauses even to consider what its income is. Were any of us to adopt the methods of public finance in our private affairs, we should ignore the total of our income and consider only what we should like to spend. We might decide on a second car, an extension of the home, a motor launch as well as a yacht, a country place and a long holiday in Bermuda. All these, we should tell each other, are essential. It would remain only to adjust our income to cover these bare necessities; and if we economize at all, it will be in matters of taxation. A government by contrast, which applied the methods of individual finance to public expenditure would begin by attempting to estimate what its actual revenue should be. Given so much to spend, how much should be allocated to what? A federal government which decided upon this novel approach to the subject would be responsible for a revolution in public finance. It is the chief object of this book to suggest that such a revolution, of which we have seen some hint in California, is now generally overdue.

Governmental as opposed to individual income is historically linked with the incidence of war. In all systems of revenue there has always been provision for the temporary expenses of conflict. During a time of emergency, with our interests, our beliefs, our pride or even our existence at stake, we agree to pay almost anything as the price of victory. The war ends and with it the temporary expenses which everyone has seen to be more or less inevitable. In theory the revenue should fall to something like its previous level. In practice it seldom does. While the governmental income remains almost at its wartime level, peacetime expenditure rises to meet it. In times past the action of this law was slightly restrained, to be sure, by two considerations which no longer apply. In the first place, it was usually felt that taxes had to be reduced somewhat in time of peace in order to allow of their being raised again in time of war. During a century, however, when each successive war is judged to be the last, this theory finds no further support. In the second place, there are types of extravagance which yield only a diminishing return. To the provision of banquets and the enjoyment of dancing girls there is (eventually) a physical limit. The same is not true, unfortunately, of departmental and technical luxuriance. Economic and cultural advisers can multiply beyond the point at which concubines might be thought a bore; beyond the point even at which they might be thought unbearable. Financially as well as aesthetically, the situation has become infinitely worse.

In countries like Britain and the United States the initiative in public finance comes from subdepartments of government which decide each year on their needs for the year that is to come. After allowing for present costs and future developments the experienced civil servant adds 10 per cent to the total, assuming (not always correctly) that his bid will be challenged at some stage by the financial branch. Assuming, however, that the expected wrangle takes place, the added 10 per cent is deleted at departmental level when the combined estimate comes to be drawn up. To this estimate the head of the department adds 10 per cent again, assuming (not always correctly) that his bid will be challenged by the Treasury. After the expected dispute, the revised estimate is laid before the responsible Minister, in England the Chancellor of the Exchequer, who consolidates all the departmental demands in a grand total and decides how the revenue can be made to equal the expenditure. With the agreement of his colleagues, he presents the nation with the bill. Here is the sum total of what the government needs, and these are the taxes which the people will have to pay. . . .

To summarize the position, the public revenue is regarded as limitless and expenditure rises eternally to meet it, and the various devices which are supposed to check expenditure fail to do so, being wrongly conceived and imperfectly motivated. The problem is a serious one and would seem to merit our attention. What is to be done? The modern instinct is to frame new regulations and laws, of which there are already more than enough. The better plan, less fashionable today, is to remotivate the people actually concerned, penalizing the extravagance we now reward and rewarding the economy we now penalize. As a first step toward redirecting the flood, we need to reverse the whole process of government finance. Ministers should not begin by ascertaining what the departments need. They should begin by asking what the country can afford to spend. We do not base our personal budget on what our past extravagances have taught us to like but on the income we can fairly expect to receive. We do not, in short, plan to spend what we have not got. The same principle should apply to public as it does to individual finance. The first question to decide is the ratio between the revenue and the gross national product. What proportion of the national income should the government demand? What proportion of the individual's income can the government safely take? And what happens when that proportion is exceeded? Economists (with one notable exception) have fought shy of this problem, allowing it to be assumed that, where government expenditure is concerned, the sky is the limit. It is one aim of this book to suggest that there are other and lower limits; a limit beyond which taxation is undesirable, a limit beyond which it is dangerous and a limit (finally) beyond which it is fatal. And these limits are clearly indicated by both economic theory and historical fact. . . .

Conclusion

The first task of a government should be to decide upon the proportion which they can safely take of the national income. In time of emergency, with the national existence at stake, the proportion can be high. At other times it should be low, allowing scope for increase when a crisis should arise. What, in normal circumstances, should that proportion be?

History tells us that governments of the more remote past have tended to exact about 10 per cent of the people's income. We learn, further, that tax demands above that level have often driven people to emigrate, at least in circumstances where migration was possible. Where flight has been for some reason impracticable, taxes of 20 per cent or more have been collected without much difficulty. As against that, taxes rising from 33 to 50 per cent have been the occasion for revolt or the cause of ruin. Taxes fixed at these high levels have characterized regimes of dwindling importance, their decay in strength being accompanied by decline of their literature and arts. During the present century, levels of taxation have risen toward the point at which previous disaster has been known to occur. Populations which have become largely literate are exposed to modern methods of tax collection which are based upon their literacy and upon their inability to escape. Democracy has given political power to those who, taxed themselves at the lower rate, will gladly support the penal taxation of the wealthy. The result has been the disproportionate or progressive system of direct taxation by which fortunes are largely confiscated. Taxation of this kind can be pushed to any extreme and there is at present no accepted level at which its upper limit can be fixed. It is currently assumed, rather, that the amount of revenue to be raised will be related in some way to the estimated total of public expenditure.

The drawback in thus attempting to adjust revenue to expenditure is that all expenditure rises to meet income. Parkinson's Second Law, a matter of common knowledge so far as the individual's finances are concerned, is also applicable to the government. But whereas the individual's expenses rise to meet and perhaps exceed an income level which is at least known, government expenditure rises in the same way toward a maximum that has never been defined; toward a ceiling that is not there. It rises, therefore, unchecked, toward levels which past experience has shown to be disastrous. In several modern countries the symptoms of approaching catastrophe are already obvious; and in none more so than in Britain. But this is not a matter in which Americans can afford to feel complacent. They are moving in the same direction even if they have not gone as far. They too have failed to fix a limit beyond which taxation must not go.

Where should the peacetime limit be drawn? It should be fixed at 20 per cent of the national income, well short of the point (25 per cent) at which the tax will cause inflation and further from the point (30 per cent) at which a country's international influence must begin to decline. From such a peacetime level the taxes can be safely raised in time of war, provided only that they are reduced again when the conflict ends. The perpetual danger, however, is that the wartime tax level will be afterwards maintained—peacetime expenditure having risen to meet it—with long-term disaster as the inevitable sequel.

To any such proposal as this, limiting national expenditure to the amount which the country can afford, there will be opposition from those who fear a reduction in the social services which they would rather see developed. How are low taxes compatible with the Welfare State? Will not cheaper government be worse? The answer is that cheaper government is better. The effect of providing government with unlimited funds is merely to clog the wheels of administration with useless officials and superfluous paper. All that we buy with higher taxes is additional administrative delay.

There are directions in which greater public expense would be fully justified—as, for instance, in the rebuilding of our obsolete cities—but this is no argument for heavier taxation. Funds for this and for every other enlightened purpose could be made available through the elimination of waste. Like taxation, waste has its origin in war. It continues after peace is made, and especially in the channels of expenditure which war has opened up. It continues as a torrent of needless expense, as a toil erosion of the deadliest kind. Waste is the enemy. It is the spectacle of public waste that seems to justify, if it does not cause, the widespread avoidance (or even evasion) of tax. It is the spectacle of public extravagance which seems to justify, if it does not cause, the nation-wide fashion in individual indebtedness. Toward serving the nobler purposes of the state, while at the same time easing the burden of taxes, an essential step is to eliminate waste; and the waste not merely of material but of talent and of time. But nothing of this sort is possible unless the whole process of public finance is reversed. There can be no economy while the public revenue is made roughly equal to the sum of the departmental demands. Economy must begin with fixing the revenue as a proportion of the national income and informing each department of the total expenditure it must not exceed. With every incentive to internal economy and with automatic dismissal following every deficit, we should soon find that much can be done with little and more, very often, can be done with less. Put an absolute limit to the revenue and then let expenditure rise to meet it. These are the profits of experience and from these profits we should derive our law.

PART

V

International Relations

28

THE WORLD COMMUNITY OF NATION-STATES

WHAT MAKES A GROUP OF PEOPLE into a nation? How are nationalism and patriotism fostered? In the first selection Schuman traces the origins of the modern nation-state, at the same time describing vividly the emotion-laden cult of patriotism which gives nations so much of their individuality, vitality, and power.

Galbraith finds that there is a chronic mood of contentment among those who advise the President on United States foreign policy. The instinct is to continue present policies without reconsideration whether they are right, wrong, or possibly disastrous. This contrasts with the attitude of those in government toward domestic affairs, in respect to which innovation is welcomed. Galbraith sees a great need for reconsidering many of our foreign policies in order to adjust them to the political realities of the present-day world.

58

The Making of Nations

by Frederick L. Schuman

> *National patriotism is the firm conviction that the best country in the world is the one you happened to be born in.*
>
> G. B. SHAW

> *Universal conscript military service, with its twin brother universal suffrage, has mastered all Continental Europe—with what promises of massacre and bankruptcy for the 20th Century!*
>
> HIPPOLYTE ADOLPHE TAINE
> *Les Origines de la France contemporaine, 1891.*

The major political trait of the peoples of the Western State System is their devotion to the "nations" into which they have got themselves divided. The Western peoples and their Oriental and African imitators are keenly aware of themselves as "nationals" of particular nation-states, already in existence or striving to be born. Millions are influenced more in their emotions and behavior by a sense of national solidarity and fellow feeling with their fellow nationals than by their racial, religious, economic, esthetic, or recreational interests. This becomes most apparent in wartime, when governments demand and usually receive unswerving and undivided allegiance. But war merely brings to the surface and makes plain through pathological exaggeration what already exists in peace: an almost universal disposition to place the nation before all other human groupings.

Education for Citizenship

The cult and creed of patriotism are instilled into people in every nation by an elaborate process of inculcation. Nationalism is close to the heart of the cultural heritage handed down from generation to generation in every modern society. Upon the eager minds of little children, as upon a blank slate, are written at an early age the large characters of "mother," "home,"

By permission from *International Politics* by Frederick L. Schuman, pp. 336–341, 370–371 *passim.* Copyright, 1958. McGraw-Hill Book Company, Inc.
Frederick L. Schuman is Professor of Government at Williams College.

"heaven," "flag," "fatherland," and "patriotism." The first impressions of the Great Society outside the family, the neighborhood, and the kindergarten are associated with national emblems, heroes, and myths. Every child in the Western world, before he has learned how to read and write his national language, has learned how to respond to the gaily colored banner which is the flag of his fatherland, to the stirring rhythm of the song which is his national anthem, to the names and legends of the great nation-builders who are revered as men like gods. Awe, reverence, and enthusiasm toward the nation-state and its symbols are inculcated from infancy.

Next comes the primer, with its quaint little tales of national glory and achievement, and then the elements of national history and geography. In later childhood there is nationalistic history with a vengeance, patriotic exercises, Flag Day celebrations, festivals and fun for Independence Day, or Constitution Day, or Bastille Day, or Guy Fawkes Day. Puberty brings membership in the Boy Scouts or the Girl Scouts, outings and parties and training in citizenship. In adolescence the young citizen becomes acquainted with the alien tongues and customs of enemies and strangers. He studies the national literature, the national history, the national *Kultur*. He becomes politically conscious and emotionally inspired by a fuller appreciation of his identity with his fatherland. *La Patrie* becomes father, mother, mistress, or lover in the heart of the youthful patriot; he (or she) is taught to swear undying allegiance to that which is more sacred even than truth, honor, or life itself. And at length, in early adulthood, comes, in most lands, military service for the young man, romantic attachments to soldier-lovers for the young woman, the right to vote and pay taxes, and a deep sense of loyalty and devotion to that half-real, half-mystical entity which is the nation-state.

The techniques of civic education through which this result is attained have been analyzed in many States by scores of assiduous scholars. The initiation rites of the tribe or clan through which the rising generation is made a participant in the social group are repeated with elaborate variation in the educational processes of every modern nation. Youth is conditioned to allegiance—no longer to the tribe, the clan, the class, the caste, the province, or the city, but to the nation, which demands an allegiance above all other allegiances and a loyalty requiring, if need be, the supreme sacrifice on the altar of patriotism. What youth has been taught, age seldom forgets—and all modern States are nations of patriots whose rulers may ordinarily rely upon the unswerving devotion of the great masses of the citizens to the mighty traditions of the national past. Each State thus develops and enriches its own personality by perpetually recreating itself in its own image. Each State perpetually models its figures of earth and gets them more and more to its liking. Each State becomes symbolized as an anthropomorphic deity to which are attributed the national virtues and vices, the national achievements and frustrations. Each patriot, like a new Narcissus, is enthralled by the beauty of his own image, which he sees reflected in the national mirror; and he feels himself to be one with the nation.

The Genesis of Modern Patriotism

An understanding of the process of manufacturing patriots, however, does not in itself serve to explain why national patriotism has come to occupy such an all-pervading place in Western culture. Hans Kohn, ablest contemporary student of modern nationalism, points out that the new creed "as we understand it, is not older than the second half of the 18th Century." Early tribalism in Israel and Athens gave way to a universalism which has persisted almost (but not quite) to our own times. The great "national" leaders and writers of the Enlightenment, degraded to the stature of tribal patriots by later generations, were nothing of the kind. Frederick the Great made a Frenchman President of the Prussian Royal Academy and declared himself content to have lived in the age of Voltaire. Johann Gottfried Herder denounced Prussia, praised Czechs and Russians, and proclaimed: "The human race is one whole; we work and suffer, sow and harvest, each for all." Hans Kohn concludes:

> Nationalism, taking the place of religion, is as diversified in its manifestations and aspirations, in its form and even its substance as religion itself. . . . Yet in all its diversities it fulfills one great task—giving meaning to man's life and justifying his noble and ignoble passions before himself and history, lifting him above the loneliness and futilities of his days, and endowing the order and power of government, without which no society can exist, with the majesty of true authority. . . . [But] nationalism is only a passing form of integration, beneficial and vitalizing, yet by its own exaggeration and dynamism easily destructive of human liberty. . . . From Jerusalem and Athens shine also the eternal guiding stars which lift the age of nationalism above itself, pointing forward on the road to deeper liberty and to higher forms of integration.

It seems probable that conflicts among culturally divergent populations played a significant role in producing within each community that sense of its own identity, that feeling of solidarity and common interest, that conception of the personality or ego of the group which is of the essence of national patriotism. Contacts of war would seem to be most effective in producing the type of group cohesion which lies behind nationalism. No emotion unifies a group so readily as hatred for a common enemy. International relations in the formative period of nationalism were for the most part those of war. Anglo-Saxon England attained unity for the first time when Alfred the Great rallied his subjects to resist the Danish invasion. Norman England was already an embryonic national State, with a Government of considerable authority and a population increasingly impressed with its "Englishness" by virtue of chronic conflicts with Scots, Irish, and French. In France, provincialism gave way to a common consciousness of "Frenchness" in the course of the Hundred Years' War, when its inhabitants at last organized themselves for effective resistance against English invaders and found a fitting symbol of the cause in the person of Jeanne d'Arc. In Spain, constant warfare against the Moors gave birth to Spanish nationalism and produced that blending of patriotic sentiment and crusading Catholicism which became its distinctive characteristic. In every case nationalism was born of war against alien groups.

All the later nationalisms between the 15th Century and the 20th were similarly born of conflicts between societies already differing from one another in language, religion, and institutions and made more aware of these differences by increased contacts with aliens. Dutch nationalism attained full flower in the long war against Spanish rule of the Netherlands. Swiss nationalism emerged out of conflicts with Austria. Sweden became a nation through struggles with Russians and Poles and Germans. American nationalism was generated by the War of the Revolution. In the 19th Century, Italian nationalism won unity for Italy as a result of common resistance to foreign invasion and common conflicts with Austria. The German nation became a unified State through battles with Danes, Austrians, and Frenchmen, after the "War of Liberation" earlier in the century converted Prussians, Bavarians, Swabians, and Wurtembergers into "Germans." The peculiarly intense nationalism of the Balkan peoples was the product of armed revolt against the Turks and of the presence within the Peninsula of many divergent groups, each of which became aware of itself through contact and conflict with neighbors. Irish, Turkish, Japanese, Indian, and Chinese nationalisms were likewise products of conflict against alien rulers, alien invaders, or alien foes across the frontier.

This suggests that the process whereby a community acquires a sense of its own identity and national personality bears a certain resemblance to the process whereby an individual growing up in society acquires a self, or ego, of his own. Social psychologists are generally agreed that an individual growing up to biological maturity in complete isolation from his fellows would not have a human "personality." The individual becomes humanized by social interaction with his fellows. His innate impulses are inhibited, directed, and conditioned through social pressure—until his personality becomes, in the language of the psychoanalyst, a fusion of instinctive biological drives (the "Id"), the conscious thinking and acting self (the "Ego"), and the unconscious controls and repressions of Id and Ego drives (the "Super-Ego"). The individual becomes aware of himself and develops distinctive personality traits by "taking the role of the other," by socialized experience with other persons.

Similarly, a nation acquires its ego by contacts with other nations. It becomes acutely aware of its own identity to the degree to which such contacts are intimate, rich, and varied. Contacts of war would seem to promote national solidarity more effectively than contacts of peace, for war requires cooperation in the interest of self-preservation. It dramatizes the flags, songs, slogans, traditions, and leaders which give unity to the group and distinguish it from other groups. National patriotism is the most complete expression of ethnocentrism. Its devotees are imbued with an intense consciousness of the collective personality of the national community, and this collective personality emerges out of social interaction between divergent groups not dissimilar to those between single human beings which produce and enrich the individual personality. The history of this process remains to be written by social psychologists with historical training or by historians who are also social psychologists.

The Cult of the Tribal Gods

Nationalists everywhere exalt the nation-state as the highest form of social organization. The national community must achieve political independence. It must incorporate within its frontiers all peoples speaking the language and having the culture of the national society. It must compel conformity to the dominant language and culture on the part of alien groups within its frontiers. It must attain unity, uniformity, solidarity. It must assert its rights vigorously and protect its interests energetically in contacts with other national groups. It is the all in all, the *ne plus ultra,* the final and perfect embodiment of social living for all loyal patriots. It is beyond good and evil, right or wrong; for its interests are supreme and paramount, and all means toward its greater glory and power are justified by the end. "A true nationalist places his country above everything; he therefore conceives, treats, and resolves all pending questions in their relation to the national interest." His object is "the exclusive pursuit of national policies, the absolute maintenance of national integrity, and a steady increase of national power—for a nation declines when it loses military might." To the patriot the nation-state is a great goddess to be worshipped, to be loved, to be served—and all sacrifices in her service are noble and heroic. She calls out to her worshippers:

> Lord! Let the beautiful ships which are on their way to our Africa arrive safely at their port. Grant that our soldiers on the sunny roads on the other side of the sea have fortune as their guiding star and glory as their goal. Grant that they may crown with fresh laurels the old, glorious flags of Vittorio Veneto, which now wave under the tropic sky. Let the culture of the new Rome of Mussolini fuse with that of Caesar's Rome to a poem of greatness. Let the Italian Empire dreamed of by our great men and our martyrs become reality in the near future. Lord! Let our lives, if Mother Italy demand it, become a joyful sacrifice on the altar

of Thy holy and just Will. [Prayer for the Ballila Boys, *L'Azione coloniale,* Rome, 1935.]

[Again,] as a spokesman of one of the newest (and oldest) nationalisms of our time, Ilya Ehrenburg to the Red Army, 1943:

> Together with you marches the frail little girl, Zoya, and the stern marines of Sevastopol. Together with you march your ancestors who welded together this land of Russia—the knights of Prince Igor, the legions of Dmitri. Together with you march the soldiers of 1812 who routed the invincible Napoleon. Together with you march Budenny's troops, Chapayev's volunteers, barefooted, hungry and all conquering. Together with you march your children, your mother, your wife. They bless you! . . . Soldier, together with you marches Russia! She is beside you. Listen to her winged step. In the moment of battle, she will cheer you with a glad word. If you waver, she will uphold you. If you conquer, she will embrace you. . . .

The New Nationalisms

Imitation, someone observed once upon a time, is the sincerest form of flattery. The national patriots of the North Atlantic communities painfully discovered in the middle years of the 20th Century that their prolonged and highly successful efforts to impose their power upon the "lesser breeds" were no longer successful in the face of the revolt of the victims. These, in turn, found no better way to resist their erstwhile masters than the way of copying Western nationalism and adapting it to their own purposes. In this wise, the Western cult of the nation-state has become in our time the universal faith of all mankind, with all of its glories, frustrations, and aberrations, plus some unique features of achievement and failure in the making of nations attributable to the legacy of colonialism and to the special circumstances of the human condition among those long disinherited and still impoverished.

Take a world map or, better, a globe, and trace a long line eastward and southeastward from the coast of Africa south of Gibraltar to the equatorial islands northwest of Australia. Along this line, if we exclude China, dwell almost 800,000,000 people, or nearly one-third of the human race—thinly scattered in the deserts and coastal plains of North Africa and the Levant, and densely crowded in the lush plains of southern and southeastern Asia and in what Westerners once called the "Spice Islands." Among these peoples African and Asian nationalisms, faithfully imitating earlier European prototypes, have come to full flower in our era. The peoples of the region thus delineated have nothing in common, linguistically, culturally, and religiously—and nothing in common politically save a common rebellion against Western rule. The followers of the faith of Islam, to be sure, are to be found along the line all the way from Morocco to

Indonesia. But Islam was never a unity nor is it now. Its disciples are interspersed along our perimeter of demarcation with millions of Christians and Jews and with many millions of Hindus and Buddhists.

Yet all the inhabitants of this vast expanse, intercepted by 20° north latitude, have more in common than they know. They know, indeed, very little beyond their local problems, fears, and hopes, for almost all of them are illiterate, ignorant, poor, and miserable as were all their ancestors for ages past. Many among them are peasants, still exploited by landlords in the ancient "feudal" pattern of human relations. In our time all are animated, dimly or brightly, with new dreams of a better life begotten by Western example. Whether their dreams are capable of fulfillment is a problem best deferred. Here it is in order to note that all these peoples have been moved by misery and resentment to adopt Western nationalism as a weapon against the West.[1]

59

Foreign Policy: The Stuck Whistle

by John Kenneth Galbraith

. . . Those on whom a President relies who are professionally concerned with domestic matters invariably want action. They do not praise continuity in our approach to Negro voting, the Appalachian plateau, or the control of crime. But in foreign policy a mood of chronic contentment prevails. Here the official instinct is to continue present policies, whether right, wrong, or potentially disastrous. It seeks continuity in our Canadian and Mexican relationships, which work well. Equally, it accepts continuity

From *The Atlantic Monthly,* February, 1965, pp. 64–67, *passim.* Copyright © 1965, by The Atlantic Monthly Company, Boston, Massachusetts, 02116. Reprinted with permission by the publisher and the author.

John Kenneth Galbraith is Professor of Economics at Harvard University. He is the author of a number of books and was United States ambassador to India under President Kennedy.

[1] Professor Schuman wrote this about 1957, just before the emergence of many new nations among the Negro peoples south of the Sahara Desert.

in policies toward Southeast Asia, China, the arms race, which aren't working at all or are certain to be a source of further deep trouble. Here change is the sort of annoying thing that restless outsiders are always proposing. They are a nuisance.

In domestic policy we also know that controversy is the price of change. We don't expect to get medical care for the aged without arousing the wrath of the American Medical Association. No one supposed that the Civil Rights Act would win applause from Strom Thurmond. We think little of a public official who prefers his personal peace to the controversy that is inherent in progress. But with foreign policy, again there is a difference. Where the world's newest nuclear power is involved, we rather expect those in charge to be fearful about arousing the ghosts of the China lobby or the communicants of the John Birch Society. Certainly they cannot afford to be thought soft on Communism, Castro, or the Panama Canal. Most conferences in the State Department—here I speak with the precision of firsthand knowledge—are not devoted to assessing the wisdom of a particular policy. They are concerned with what will be said on Capitol Hill. Everyone vastly prefers a foreign enemy to a domestic one.

At home a liberal is a man with a predisposition to change. In foreign policy his function is to use his liberal reputation to bless whatever is being done.

There is no reason why our foreign policy should be the natural stronghold of conservatism or contentment. And in foreign policy as well as in domestic policy, there cannot be progress without controversy. There is now great need for bringing our foreign policy abreast of the times, and even more, for bringing it abreast of simple necessity and of what, accordingly, we end up doing.

I also venture to think that the American people are in a mood for change. . . .

They want improved performance on our side. They will live with danger, but they also want serious efforts to mitigate it. They expect there will be disorder, tension, and conflict, but they want imaginative efforts to reduce them. They know of the problems of the poor countries and the danger of explosive population growth. They want to be assured, not that our efforts are inexpensive, but that they are serious and effective. . . .

I have served happily and instructively with the Department of State. It includes among its members perhaps the most intelligent and responsible servants that any government has ever had. The younger men who have come into the service since World War II command special respect—they are liberal, well educated, and anxious for the kind of change being here discussed. My difference is not with persons but with performance. In handling labor relations, protecting natural resources, developing the technology of defense and deterrence, exploring space, and guiding the economy, we regard the federal government with confidence. Competent management is assumed. But in the field of foreign policy, our expectations are much lower. Here we are inured to setbacks, misfortunes, sudden changes of direction, and desperate efforts to retrieve error. When things go badly, it is only fair to attribute something to the difficulty of the problem. But if things continue to go badly, it makes good sense to search for deeper causes.

The first cause of trouble is an ancient tendency to base policy on official convenience and belief—what Senator Fulbright calls "myth"—rather than on the underlying reality. What is convenient is usually what is being done or not done. This gets defended in speeches, before congressional committees, and in conferences. The persuasion is excellent; the only problem is that the reality is different and the leadership accordingly is in the wrong direction. Then, alas, comes the day of reckoning when the reality must be recognized and the price must be paid. Error has to be confessed and an escape plotted at the point when all the exits have been painted in. As a result, we give a maximum impression of political infirmity, both at home and abroad. This is a formidable bill. Let me suggest particulars.

The fulcrum of our foreign policy is our relation with the Soviet Union. Here the problem is less one of a change of policy than one of affirming the policy we actually follow. This, however, is no small step.

According to tradition and the official litany, our relations with the Soviets are implacably hostile. Warnings of the comprehensively adverse intentions of the Soviets come from the Department almost automatically. There is a fine simplicity about reducing everything to a simple opposition of interests. It shows one has no illusions. It implies membership in a kind of inner foreign-policy club going back to the Truman Administration. It also avoids trouble. The domestic anti-Communist crusaders are rather rough-spoken people. The litany of total conflict flows over into the news columns and editorial pages, and is fed back to the Department.

Yet the reality, as most lucid people have recognized since the Eisenhower Administration, is that the preservation of peace—not of our way of life but of life itself—depends on a tacit understanding with the Soviet Union. This understanding is the fruit not of charity, softheartedness, or goodness of soul; it is the product of the most elementary self-interest. Its elements are also reasonably clear. We are careful not to confront each other in Berlin, the rest of Europe, the Middle East, or Cuba in such fashion that the other country has no alternative but to fight. That would be to destroy both. We both keep up the threshold on the employment of nuclear weapons; they are not things to be employed casually against people or trees in Laos or Albania. We both resist the proliferation of these weapons. We are both conscious of the dangers of nuclear accident and take appropriate precautions. We both support the United Nations, not as a final solution of the world's problems, but as a shock absorber and alternative to what otherwise would be bilateral monopoly of world affairs by the two great powers. These are formidable points of agreement. They are also very serviceable. In their absence, the peace would not last a month. . . .

The clash between litany and reality showed itself in classic form in the matter of the UN assessments to pay for peacekeeping forces in the Congo and elsewhere. Our legal position on this was strong. It is also true that the actions which cost the money generally served our interests. For many months last year secondary officials in the State Department, guided by the litany, issued regular rescripts to the Soviets promising that they would be thrown out of the organization unless they paid. (The UN bureau of the State Department in Washington has a certain local reputation for the humorlessness with which it accepts the litany and the priestly diligence and solemnity with which it grinds out telegrams, statements, and speeches for its highly indifferent audiences.) Right-wing critics of the Department and all who dislike the United Nations and would like to see us pay for none of it were well pleased. But as the day of reckoning approached, the ultimate understanding—which was that we and the Soviets both agree on remaining in the UN—came into view. We did not want them to go. The press turned a little sour. Also it doubtless occurred to some people that a President just returned to office on a platform of peace and prosperity might be reluctant to begin by presiding over the dissolution of the United Nations. At more responsible levels of government a search began for some promising avenue of retreat and compromise. Soon we were agreeing with some haste to an understanding according to which there would be no voting at all and the Russians would stay. Eventually, one supposes, a more satisfactory compromise will be found. . . .

To base policy on the reality not only avoids recurrent backdown and retreat; it also allows forward movement. A frozen policy cannot exploit opportunity; it is frozen in all directions. And fear of criticism at home is unlikely to be combined with self-confidence abroad. If Roosevelt had feared doing business with Stalin and had been sensitive to the criticism of the American right, then more virulent than now, there would have been no UN. The greatest diplomatic success of the Kennedy years was the partial test-ban agreement. It was negotiated by Averell Harriman, who has a long record of self-confidence in dealing with the Soviets and is singularly indifferent to domestic criticism about his being soft on Communism.

I don't suggest that Soviet polemics have come to an end. We shall have to answer them as we shall have to continue to defend our position where our interests are in conflict. But we can no longer afford the illusion or language of total conflict. We must be clear that our policy is based on a vital area of understanding and agreement.

The unwillingness to accommodate policy to reality, with the consequence that we regularly find ourselves painted into a corner, is not, of course, confined to the Soviet Union. Renegotiation of the Panama Canal Treaty was in order long ago. The first response of the Department to trouble there a year ago was to appease the bitter-enders by proclaiming the treaty sacrosanct. The trouble was blamed on Communists. Now the treaty is to be renegotiated.

Similarly, the American people will be prepared for changes in the structure of NATO if we accept as the basis of our policy the fact that Europeans are far less dependent on the United States than they were fifteen years ago, and that also, as the result of lessened tension, they are far less subject to the cohesive influence of fear. This independence and lowered tension were things we sought and obtained. But we must accommodate to their consequences. We convert success into failure when we make NATO not a means to an end but an end in itself.

The military alliances which John Foster Dulles sponsored or negotiated in the Middle East and Southeast Asia were always of somewhat dubious value and even more questionable wisdom. From the beginning they caused friction with the countries which were not members; now they are becoming increasingly unpopular in the countries which adhere to them. . . . Instead of holding on to these arrangements as though they were immortal, the time has come for friendly re-examination while it is still between friends.

Our avowed policy toward the poor countries is based broadly on the notion that economic assistance and technical support will bring a fairly early takeoff toward economic self-support. Everyone in a position of consequence now knows that this will not happen; in some places it will not be possible to prevent further deterioration. And in India, Pakistan, Egypt, and a number of other countries we can no longer escape the terrible reality of the population explosion. We cannot abandon the efforts that are the only hope for improvement. Our only course is to abandon the facile promises and face the facts. Otherwise, having promised too much too soon, we will have more disillusionment and more disappointment, and we won't be doing the things that need to be done.

Finally, there is China. It fell to me two years ago to be our executive when the dispute between China and India broke into open war. The policies which we concerted with the Indians and the British and which combined support to the Indians with a clear indication of our disinterest in promoting a war in those distant mountains passed through my hands. I had some part in forming them. They worked; at the point of their main attack in the Northeast Frontier Agency, the Chinese returned to their previous lines. I cite all this not to serve my own vanity but to urge my credentials. I am in no need of sermons from those who say we must stand firm, must never underestimate the Chinese menace.

But our China policy has been on dead center now for fifteen years.

During that time we have had an ingenious succession of s̲
thought or explain why nothing should be done: the first n̲
they cannot shoot their way into the United Nations; recognit̲
sion to the UN are not a reward for bad behavior; they shou̲
ever they are doing in Africa; membership in the UN is no̲
of good behavior—although it is not clear that anyone ever suggested it
was. What passes for an American policy on China is really an effort to
devise plausible explanations for inaction and plausible reasons for urging
other countries to support us therein. Some of the latter may well be among
the world's better exercises in meretricious eloquence. Unfortunately, everyone between here and Nepal knows that the real reason for our position is
domestic politics.

We must have a new effort. The integrity of Taiwan is an obvious condition. The permanent seat in the Security Council for Taipei is not. Neither
Taiwan nor China has a better right to this seat than, say, India. The proper
course is to seek a reorganization of the Council. Without postponing other
steps, we should certainly make a prompt effort on travel and trade. Among
other advantages this would mean that we would no longer be impelled to
invest diplomatic effort in largely futile efforts petitioning to our friends
in Europe and Asia to refrain from trading with, or lending money to, or
sometimes even speaking to, the Chinese.

It is of course possible that the Chinese do not wish to come into the
world. But if we make an effort now there is at least a chance that a decade
hence China, with its nuclear arms, will be somewhat responsible to world
opinion and hence will become a more responsible member of the world
community. Acceptance of the test ban and control of delivery systems will
at least become possible. If no steps are taken—if we do not take the
initiative, and if we reject all Chinese proposals as propaganda—then we
can be sure that things will be no better and very likely will become much
worse. That is what the proponents of continuing inaction urge. The present
policy is not one of strength. It is one of surrender to internal weakness.

We are impatient of progress on domestic policy because these matters
are close to home. And excuses for inaction are easily identified as such.
We must become equally suspicious of those who try to sweep our foreign-
policy problems under the rug.

We have also learned here at home that the future does not lie with
the hard-nosed men who declare that nothing can be done or that we should
defend the status quo in Mississippi or Harlem with a gun. We must
realize that things are not much altered when we go abroad. There too
one must either anticipate change or be its victim.

29

INTERNATIONAL ECONOMIC
RELATIONS

IN THE MODERN WORLD, partly as a result of improvements in transportation and communication, and partly as the result of two world wars and the rise of communism, international economic relations have become increasingly important and increasingly complex.

In our first selection Joseph Frankel reviews briefly the various ways in which government controls of international economic relations can be, and are, used as instruments of foreign policy. In "Kuwait: A Super-Affluent Society," Fakhri Shehab describes how a very small Arab state has tried to meet the problems created by a great inflow of wealth from the sale of its oil in world markets. One of the interesting things which Kuwait has done is to set up a substantial foreign aid program in order to strengthen its political position in relation to the larger Arab states which are its neighbors.

60

Economic Controls and Foreign Policy

by Joseph Frankel

Economic instruments differ from diplomacy and propaganda in that they are not necessarily directly operated by governments. Indeed, in the nineteenth century, international trade which was dominated by the City of London gave the appearance of being divorced from politics and completely autonomous—although as E. H. Carr has forcibly pointed out in *The Twenty Years' Crisis,* this illusion was due only to Britain's unchallenged naval supremacy. In the twentieth century, the close connection between international politics and economics has been re-established. Private interests are still paramount in the international trade of western Powers, but clearly under close governmental direction. In communist and largely also in new, under-developed countries, trade is conducted by governmental agencies.

The other characteristic peculiar to economic instruments is their great advance towards internationalization. As soon as the governments had assumed economic powers, they began to yield them to international institutions. Western trade is circumscribed by the provisions of the General Agreement on Trade and Tariffs (GATT), manipulation of exchange rates of national currencies by the membership of the International Fund; members of the European Economic Community and of its eastern counterpart, the COMECON, have surrendered much of their economic sovereignty to these organizations. There are two reasons why the economic instruments are being internationalized in advance of others. First, considerable economic advantages are secured. Second, although the close connexion between economics and politics is now fully appreciated, the direct and immediate impact of economic internationalization on state sovereignty is considerably less than would be the impact of internationalization of such politically sensitive elements as armaments. Anyway, for the time being, while the most important economic institutions include only

From Joseph Frankel, *International Relations,* Galaxy Book, Oxford University Press, New York, 1964, pp. 138–144. Reprinted by permission of Oxford University Press (Home University Library Series), London, England.

Joseph Frankel is a British political scientist who is Professor of Politics at the University of Southampton.

western states, the problems arising from their existence have not been politically grave.

Economic instruments are widely employed both in peace and war; in peacetime international trade and assistance are most important, in wartime and during the cold war various measures of economic warfare are employed.

To some extent all countries must engage in international trade in order to obtain some goods which they cannot produce at home, and to sell others with the proceeds of which they can pay for their imports. Beyond this indispensable minimum, international trade provides the benefits of an international division of labour under which the various goods can be obtained from the most efficient and therefore cheapest producer. Free trade, which was actively pursued by Britain between 1846 and 1932, meant to the British an economically most efficient world-wide arrangement. To other countries it meant a perpetuation of a situation in which they had little chance of developing their own industries in open competition with the established, more efficient British exporters.

Protective tariffs, the most important instrument for controlling international trade, thus arose mainly for economic reasons, to shelter budding domestic industries from foreign competition. These industries, however, were desired not only for economic welfare but also for general political purposes, as an element of state-power. The Great Depression, which began in 1929, brought in its train an enormous increase in protective tariffs and also in other devices to keep out imports, such as quantitative controls (quotas) and currency restrictions.

Apart from this protective role, tariffs serve to secure better terms of trade through reciprocal arrangements but they can be used also for more clearly political purposes, as bargaining weapons in negotiations and as instruments of retaliation. Here the element of size and of relative importance in the foreign trade of the country concerned is decisive. The main buyers of a country's produce or the main suppliers of its vital imports are obviously influential. The Southern States used their position as the major suppliers of cotton for the Lancashire industry in their endeavour to secure British support during the American Civil War; the Austrians were able to bring Serbia to heel through declining to buy her pigs during the so-called "Pig War" in 1905; Britain exercised a similar pressure on Ireland through the "tariff war" of 1932–36; Hitler dominated eastern Europe in the late thirties by offering the only available large-scale market for its agricultural exports—he enjoyed a position which approached monopoly.

Through a deliberate policy, international trade can be directed within a group of states to enhance its economy but also to reinforce its political coherence, for instance in the various colonial systems or in the communist bloc or the European Economic Community today.

The present trend towards the liberalization of international trade and the establishment of international economic institutions have greatly reduced the freedom of the states to control their trade individually. Within the blocs, individual control is being superseded by an institutionalized co-operation; inter-bloc trade can be more suitably discussed under the heading of economic warfare.

For a long time investment in foreign countries was private and for economic purposes. It has continued to be so from the time of the great banking houses of the Fuggers in the sixteenth century, or the Rothschilds after the Napoleonic Wars, to the industrial empires and the great oil companies of our own generation. These investments were not divorced from politics, and the national governments encouraged or discouraged them to suit their political aims, but the usual form of direct governmental intervention is assistance and not investment. In all periods economically weak allies had to be buttressed by military supplies and political loans or grants, but since the last war grants have surpassed all precedents. By the colossal expenditure of over 20,000 million dollars, especially through the Marshall Plan, the Americans have helped to restore the economies and to modernize the armed forces of western Europe. They have been dispensing money for military support and for economic aid also outside Europe; at present funds are flowing out at the annual rate of 3–4,000 million dollars. In the mid-fifties the Russians began to offer large-scale economic assistance, and their competition with the Americans has become an important feature of the cold war. Sometimes the Superpowers court the same governments, for instance those in Afghanistan or Egypt. More often they support governments inclined more to them: thus the Americans have been helping the Philippines, South Vietnam and Formosa while the Russians have been supporting the Fidel Castro government of Cuba. All the colonial Powers, especially France and Britain, have given considerable assistance to their colonies and ex-colonies.

Even in peacetime the unfriendly purpose of economic policies can justify their classification as economic warfare. Such is the boycott of trade which is usually conducted by the people rather than the government, but which may have governmental support—one example is the Chinese boycott of British and Japanese goods in the inter-war period. Or it may be an action against the currency of another state, as in London in 1923 when the French occupied the Ruhr against the wishes of the British.

A state may resort to "dumping" in order to dislocate production and the world markets—thus in 1958 the Soviet Union resold, with disruptive results, quantities of Chinese tin at a price below that paid to the Chinese. Economic warfare can take also the form of the closing and opening of markets. In 1960, when the Americans became convinced of the hostility of the Castro Government in Cuba, they gradually brought to a halt the imports of Cuban sugar which had enjoyed a privileged market in their country; as a counter-move in economic warfare, in order to stabilize a régime hostile to the United States, the communist bloc stepped in and offered new markets for this sugar.

In wartime a belligerent may resort to 'pre-emption' of vital strategic materials from neutrals in order to deny them to the adversary, as the British tried to do in the last war with Spanish copper and Turkish chrome.

The best-established war-measure is naval blockade. Britain has been employing it ever since the times of Elizabeth I, it played an important part in the Napoleonic and the two World Wars, and is still by no means obsolete. The effectiveness of economic measures gave rise to the idea of "economic sanctions" which were embodied in the League of Nations Covenant as a promising expedient for curbing aggression without military intervention. The League applied such sanctions only once, against Italy in 1935 for her aggression against Ethiopia. The sanctions failed but probably only because the members were half-hearted in their support. In 1951 the United Nations decided in favour of economic sanctions against Communist China, in 1962 it was moving towards such sanctions against Katanga, and, in 1963, against South Africa.

The cold war has led to many measures which can be called economic warfare. Each bloc tries to deprive its opponent of the supplies of strategically important materials and products. Communist international trade is rigidly controlled, and the Americans have been making strenuous but not fully successful attempts to curb western exports of 'strategic' materials to the communist bloc.

61

Kuwait: A Super-Affluent Society

by Fakhri Shehab

Stretching over some 6,000 square miles of the hard, gravelly and waterless northeast corner of the Persian Gulf, Kuwait has been thrust from oblivion into sudden prominence by her hidden wealth and the creative

From *Foreign Affairs*, April, 1964, pp. 461–474. Copyright by Council on Foreign Relations, Inc., New York. Reprinted by permission.

Mr. Shehab is Professor of Middle Eastern Studies, St. Anthony's College, Oxford University, England.

enius of Western enterprise and technology. In less than two decades, since he first shipment of oil left her shores, material riches have changed the ace of her barren territory, and Kuwait is now experiencing a host of omplex social, political and economic problems which are shaking her ssentially tribal and primitive structure. The purpose of this essay is to iscuss the nature of the challenge presented by this transitional phase nd to examine Kuwait's response to it. But in order to appreciate the magitude of the task that confronts this city-state, the reader must first know omething of the static society that used to exist and of the main events hat have so radically transformed it into what it is now.

Present-day Kuwait was reportedly founded in the early eighteenth entury by tribesmen driven from their home in inner Arabia by warring insmen. The tiny fishing village they founded offered few and meagre esources; but its very austerity was perhaps its main asset. For the rigorus physical environment rendered the individual tough, imaginative, enterrising and excellent in team-work. These qualities have, for over two enturies, distinguished the Kuwaitis as the Gulf's most successful businessnen, sailors and sea-farers.

Broadly speaking, Kuwait was comprised of three main groups: a ruling amily, an oligarchy of merchants and a working class—mostly fishermen, earl-divers and shipbuilders. Of these groups, the second has been by ar the most powerful and dynamic social force. It was the merchants' nterprising spirit that provided the ruling family with their meagre income 1 the shape of customs duties and provided employment for the rest of he community. A triple social structure still exists in Kuwait, although, as ve shall see, new circumstances are altering it.

This small community needed peace first and foremost to enable it to ke out a living, and, in the two and a half centuries since they settled on he Gulf, the Kuwaitis have had no more than two internal crises involving erious violence, and only a few skirmishes with neighboring tribes. Crimes f violence are almost unknown and even litigation is a rare indulgence. ˌs with individuals, so with the state: the desire for peace eminently haracterizes Kuwait's relations with her neighbors—a monumental diplonatic feat considering the struggle for power that divides the Arab tates.

Of governmental organization Kuwait possessed little more than the raditional tribal type in which power was vested in an autocratic ruler, ʻho, in conformity with tradition, was chosen from among members of the ubah family for his superior personal qualities. The choice of a new uler was usually regarded as a family affair; and while clearly it was no emocracy, this primitive political system allowed the Kuwaiti wide freeoms of action and expression. Regard for tradition made public opinion n important political force. Hence, it was the general practice for the uler to consult the elders of the community on matters involving serious

decisions. Law and order were maintained in a simple and unceremoniou
way in accordance with Islamic law as modified by tribal usage and loca
custom. Internal security was preserved by a small bodyguard, and i
times of emergency external security was the responsibility of all able
bodied men (and sometimes women). Education was confined to a fev
primitive and privately run semi-religious institutions and not until 191
did the town notables organize the first elementary school. As for healtl
services, Kuwait's first hospital was not opened until well after her o
had begun to flow, in 1949.

This tribal structure held sway until 1937 when popular endeavors t
modernize it finally led to the election of the short-lived Legislative Assem
bly whose only legacy was the creation of certain government department
with broadly defined functions. These departments formed Kuwait's basi
administrative framework until 1962, when constitutional government wa
introduced.

Import duties, varying between 4 and 6 percent, constituted the mai
source of public revenue. The scope of the government operations may b
seen from the fact that in 1938–39 public revenue totaled some £60,00(
(approximately $290,000), of which nearly two-thirds came from impor
duties and the rest from miscellaneous dues and fees, plus a small royalt
paid by the Kuwait Oil Company following the discovery, though not th
actual extraction, of oil. This primitive financial system drew no distinc
tion between public domain or revenue, on the one hand, and the ruler'
personal estate and income on the other. At this stage, the city-state ha
hardly emerged as an independent and recognizable entity and the ruler
still resembling a tribal chieftain, combined with his basic responsibilitie
of maintaining law and order the traditional and costly functions of triba
hospitality.

As for the private sector, pearling and seafaring together absorbed th
majority of Kuwait's labor force (estimated at some 8,000 to 10,000 men)
It is said that average earnings in pearling hardly exceeded 100 rupees (jus
over $35 at the prewar rate) for a season of three to four months. Thi
was often supplemented by seafaring, which brought in an additional 15(
or 200 rupees for an expedition of some six months. Exceptionally, ar
enterprising man could add to these two sources of income by trading, anc
might make a profit of some 100 or 200 rupees. Thus, at best, average
family earnings from various sources barely touched 500 rupees (rathe
less than $180) a year. Assuming an average family of five, these calcula
tions would suggest an average personal annual income of some 10(
rupees (roughly about $35). As for an unskilled laborer, he barely man
aged to reach subsistence level. His daily wage was not more than a
half rupee, and employment was rarely available throughout the year
These conditions were far worse than those then obtaining in the agrariar
communities of Iran or Iraq.

I

Today such conditions exist only in memory, for Kuwait now is a land of superlatives. It is the largest oil producer in the Middle East and the fourth largest in the world; it boasts the world's largest oil port where the world's largest tankers are loaded in record time; at 62 billion barrels, its proved oil reserves are the largest in the world; and the magnitude of its oil receipts in relation to the size of the native population is such that even if all other sources of income in both the private and public sectors are disregarded, the annual revenue per citizen amounts to K.D. 1,200 (Kuwait Dinar = U.S. $2.8).

In sharp and dramatic contrast with the austerity of former times, Kuwait's current foreign trade statistics list an extraordinarily wide range of luxury goods transported by sea, land and air from some 60-odd countries, at an annual expenditure averaging in recent years nearly $300,000,-000, or about $825 per inhabitant. More impressive still is the present-day expenditure on fresh water distillation and power supply which costs the state not less than $140 per inhabitant, while every tree and shrub that decorates her thoroughfares and public squares costs an average of some $250 a year. As for social services, a welfare state of unsurpassed munificence has suddenly emerged. Expenditure on health and education and other benefits (mostly in pecuniary forms) has placed this tiny state on a higher level than some of the most sophisticated societies in the world; for in the fiscal year 1961–62 it reached some $240 per inhabitant as compared with $210 in the U.K. and slightly less in Sweden.[1]

What has been the impact of the sudden explosion of wealth upon this primitive society? In less than two decades the whole face of Kuwait has changed beyond recognition. But behind the spectacular physical change lie fundamental problems which have rarely, if ever, been faced by an affluent community before.

One basic question has always been asked: how long is it going to last? The Kuwaitis are quite alive to the precariousness of their riches. Anxiety over the future dominates their thoughts and many of their actions. It is evident in the attempt to build up their social capital, to set up an organized public service and to foster rapid industrial development; it is evident in the determined effort to accumulate foreign reserves; and, above all, it is evident in the desire to achieve all this in a desperately short time. Haste is, indeed, the order of the day.

But growth is a function of time and the hurried transformation of Kuwait from the poor, obscure and stagnant society it used to be into one of uncommon complexity and sophistication has proved challenging and, at times, even dangerous.

[1] Both the British and the Swedish figures include payments by the private sector in the form of employers' and employees' contributions.

Oil receipts began to accrue in 1946. In the early stages no more than rudimentary physical planning of the town was needed. The sharp increase in revenue in 1951 made clear that planning required expert advice, and foreign consultants were engaged for this purpose. Subsequently, a group of five engineering firms was engaged to carry out the work on a cost-plus basis. It was soon discovered, however, that this procedure pushed up costs unduly and left much room for abuse, and it was abandoned. It was realized that the task of building could not be simply farmed out to foreign contractors. Responsibility for planning and executing a development program was then entrusted to the Public Works Department. This was a tribute to the courage of the government, considering Kuwait's small population and the acute shortage of trained personnel.

Paucity of population is not necessarily associated with economic backwardness; the shortage of trained people is. The presence of both in a setting of extreme wealth makes the story of Kuwait unique. The earliest population figures available for those years are from the first census of 1957. They give Kuwait's total indigenous labor force as being 23,977, all between 15 and 60 years of age. By far the largest group (over 19,000) was composed of those with either no training at all or with only minimal professional qualifications. Another group, designated "professionals and technologists" and totaling some 4,000, includes only one chemist, one geologist, two physicians, two author-journalists, eight accountants and 156 clergymen.

The government's difficulties thus can hardly be exaggerated. To ensure control of its own affairs, it gave preference to its own citizens; and if suitable Kuwaitis were not available preference went to other Arab citizens and only in the last resort to non-Arabs. With abundant financial resources and in the absence of a strong civil service tradition, there soon evolved an administrative machine which was vast, complicated, cumbersome and not always guided by the highest ethical standards.

This created more problems for the state than it solved. Since all top administrative and executive jobs were reserved for citizens, the responsibility for final decisions invariably lay with them; the presence of the foreign technician or adviser did not help much. The Kuwaiti policy-maker was still called upon daily to evaluate highly technical, and not infrequently conflicting, proposals which ranged from the choice of some complex electronic equipment for an ultra-modern telephone system to the assessment of the chemical components of local soils as factors affecting the choice of road-construction techniques. As the great majority of Kuwaiti executives came to their new responsibilities unprepared, vital decisions were often deferred, and when they were made, showed the pressure of vested interests.

There was also the problem of the mere volume of the new business. At the start, far too many projects were undertaken and as time went on the number increased. The demands on the limited time of the Kuwaiti executives and policy-makers grew correspondingly, resulting in insufficient guidance from the top. This shortage of leadership in Kuwait was alarming, since it involved the one thing that could not be imported from abroad.

Meanwhile, business was offering unlimited scope for success and, to the qualified few, its attraction was too powerful to be resisted. Some sort of a compromise had therefore to be devised to eliminate this competition, and it was found by permitting civil servants to run their own businesses side-by-side with their public offices. This concession caused immense harm. It overtaxed the limited time and energy of those in key positions, strained their allegiance to the state, exposed them to grave temptations and meant that the public service ceased to be considered a career. Senior appointments were generally accepted for prestige reasons, mostly by those who lacked distinction; and employment in the lower echelons was regarded more or less as a sinecure, or as a means of channeling a certain amount of the wealth to the average citizen.

These factors have led to such overcrowding in the public service that salaries and wages now create a very serious drain on the treasury. The city-state at present has on its payroll no less than 53,000 men and women, both indigenous and aliens, excluding those in the armed forces, at an annual cost of nearly $168,000,000. This means that every three citizens are being served by one public servant at an average cost of about $1,120 per citizen.

This, then, was one of the results of the second phase of the experiment. It raised public expenditures for administration to an incredible level. It placed in positions of great responsibility either men of an older generation, whose views and standards were hopelessly outdated, or very young persons, who lacked the required experience; and it put a heavy strain on their loyalties. Further, it eliminated competitive selection for the public service and thus encouraged complacency in the new generation and a tendency to judge performance by local standards alone.

II

It was only natural that the new wealth should create a demand for services hitherto unknown in the country. The resulting problem was made especially acute by the ambitious projects planned by the government, and its determination to carry them out all at once. Inevitably, a uniquely attractive market for labor was created and a flood of skilled and unskilled workers flocked from the four corners of the globe, but mostly from neighboring countries. This influx created new problems. The ethnic and political composition of this immigrant labor was heterogeneous, though the largest proportion (about 70 percent) were Arabs. Their social habits, cultures, creeds and, above all, political leanings were numerous and widely divergent.

Moreover, by far the largest group of these aliens (73 percent) were males mostly between 15 and 50 years of age, which meant that they were transient immigrants.[2] It is this transient population that provides the bulk of Kuwait's skilled labor and 78 percent of her unskilled workers. It is they who supply the city-state with her teachers, doctors, architects, engineers and administrative and managerial personnel. They are the makers of her laws, the builders of her industry and the founders of her financial institutions. So pervasive has been their influence that there is hardly an aspect of national life which does not bear their mark. It affects the Kuwaitis choice of fashion, architecture and interior decoration; their cultural and artistic interests; their entertainments and dietetic habits; and even their colloquial Arabic, which has considerably changed under the influence of the newcomers.

Yet this all-powerful community of aliens has no permanent ties with the host country. Their services will apparently continue to be in demand indefinitely; yet the individuals themselves are constantly changing and are regarded by their hosts as changeable. This situation has inevitably led to a lack of continuity in planning and performance as well as to a sense of instability among the resident aliens, discernible in their behavior and their attitudes to the state.

The ephemeral status of the members of this community is especially marked among manual and menial workers. Grim unemployment in neighboring countries has driven tens of thousands of these men to search for a living in this rich oasis. But in turn the unlimited supply of labor has inevitably depressed wages to the point where the now derelict and nearly forgotten "iron law" may be seen in full swing. At present an unskilled laborer in Kuwait makes between nine and twelve shillings a day (about $1.25 to $1.65). This is generally higher than average earnings in the region; but the advantage is lost in a country where most goods are imported, where major imports are controlled by oligopolies and where rents and utilities are inordinately high. The result is that families are often left at home, and the wage-earner's remittances to his dependents reduce him to hardly more than subsistence. Thus the fate of thousands of aliens is to live in squalid hovels, indefinitely separated from their homes and families, desperate for employment; they have exchanged the best of their working years for wages that can just keep them and their dependents alive. Against the background of superabundance and prodigality existing in Kuwait, the wide gulf between the two segments of the population is not only indefensible but is bound to engender social resentment and instability.

Nor is this all. The remittances of the resident aliens are a permanent

2 This fact is reflected in the number of air travelers, which in recent years has reached some 230,000 annually, or more than 70 percent of the total population.

drain on the national income. The extent of it cannot be ascertained, but is conservatively estimated at some $120,000,000 a year. If this labor force could be persuaded to strike roots in Kuwait, this drain on national wealth would be minimized and the base of the economy would be broadened. This viewpoint is gaining recognition, but not fast enough.

Finally, the growing size of this foreign labor force has suddenly awakened the Kuwaitis to the fact that they are about to become a minority in their own country. According to the 1961 population census, they barely exceed half the total. This would be serious enough in any country, let alone in one so small, underpopulated and rich, and where the indigenous community lacks all the vital technical skills.

III

The discovery that it was being swamped by aliens alarmed Kuwait and prompted defensive measures. Foremost among these was the naturalization decree of 1959 and its amendment in 1960. This legislation, a landmark in Kuwait's history, confined Kuwaiti citizenship to residents in Kuwait prior to 1920, to their descendants in the male line and to foreign women upon marriage to Kuwaitis. For Arabs, naturalization is now possible only after 10 years of residence, and for non-Arabs after 15 years, commencing, in both cases, from the date of the amending decree. Moreover, only 50 persons are to be granted citizenship in any one year. Exceptions to this general rule are that Arabs in residence before 1945, and foreigners before 1930, as well as other Arab nationals who have performed outstanding services to the state, may be granted citizenship without waiting.

The legislation also confined certain basic rights and privileges to the citizen class. All imports and retail trades and all contractual business are either limited to Kuwaiti nationals or have to be transacted through Kuwaiti agents. In the civil service, pension rights, permanent tenure and certain key executive positions are exclusive privileges of citizens. The entry of aliens into some professions such as medicine and law, where not many citizens could compete for a long time to come, is restricted to a stringent licensing system.

A unique feature of this transformation is the ingenious device evolved to diffuse the new wealth among the citizen class through public expenditure. As we have seen earlier, the distinction between public income and property and the ruler's income or property was unknown in Kuwait. Gradually, as budgetary practices and controls were introduced, all public receipts were paid into the Exchequer.[3] Since the process was confined at first to annual disbursements and receipts of money, control of the public

---

[3] However, this new practice does not include Kuwait's substantial reserves which still remain with the Bank of England in the name of His Highness the Emir.

land was overlooked; and so long as realty was not of great economic significance the oversight was not serious. But then real estate prices rocketed.
Meanwhile, large tracts of worthless desert had been seized and fenced in
by those who had either the foresight or foreknowledge to anticipate the
coming public projects; and they subsequently were compensated handsomely by the state. With a rapid turnover of land and in the absence of
legislation covering the acquisition of land for public uses, the cost to the
Treasury was fantastic.

The process within the city itself differed somewhat from that outside
the old city wall. Land was purchased in excess of what was actually
required for public projects, and the surplus was later sold back to the
public, often at a fraction (estimated at 4 percent) of its cost to the
Treasury. Enormous private fortunes were amassed by both selling to,
and buying from, the state. It has been estimated that between 1957 and
1962 close to $840,000,000 of public money was spent on land.

This huge expenditure would have been justified on the grounds that
it engendered economic activity and diffused a large portion of the new
wealth, were it not that in fact only a limited amount was piped into the
local economy. By far the larger part was remitted abroad either directly,
or indirectly through the banking system. Further, the wealth was not
spread evenly, the greater part going to those at the top of the social
pyramid, even though, because of the small size of the indigenous community, a fair amount did go also to the masses. It now is argued that unless
the process is continued, large-scale bankruptcies will wreck the economy,
since substantial bank advances have been made to merchants who are said
to have invested them in land. It is difficult to ascertain whether this is
true; but banking statistics show that advances to Kuwaiti residents (about
$110,600,000 toward the end of 1963) represent just over 40 percent of
total visible imports—a fact that hardly bears out the argument. Yet the
practice continues unabated despite serious warning by government advisers
and the recommendation of the World Bank.

The process of diffusing the new wealth was not confined, however, to
land purchases. Social security benefits and state aid in most generous and
varied forms, free medical treatment and scholarships for training abroad,
the granting of free building sites and loans at very low interest—all were
made available to the citizen as his birthright.

IV

The effects of these measures on Kuwait must be evaluated from two
standpoints: the response they evoked from the aliens and the impact they
had on the citizen class.

That they have been effective in achieving their aim is obvious enough.
They have introduced a sharp distinction between the two classes of society

and they have reserved to the citizens all the fruits of the windfall of riches (with the lion's share going to a relatively small group within this class). Little else can be said in favor of these measures. They have permanently estranged and embittered the most efficient and indispensable element in the community—the resident alien. Uprooted, often separated from his family, insecure and unsettled, he has now become envious and resentful. With little or no hope of being permanently integrated into the community, he is left without any sense of allegiance to Kuwait.

Let us look now at the impact of these protective and restrictive measures on the citizens for whom they were devised. An immediate consequence was the reversal of the old order that made the state and members of the ruling family dependent on the merchants, for now it was the latter who sought favors from the state. They wanted not only compensation for land but also the preservation of their commercial interests. While the state has been strengthened by its financial independence and has become less susceptible to pressures from this group, the change was not an unmixed blessing, considering that the government is not dependent upon popular consent for its annual income.

Further, the ease with which wealth has been acquired has impaired the enterprise of the mercantile class and made them dependent on the state. Hardly any worthwhile financial or industrial venture which deviates from the established pattern is ever attempted by Kuwaiti entrepreneurs (of whom there are, in any case, very few) unless it is assured of state financing, protection or guarantee. Conversely, private capital can be forthcoming to excess when an expatriate entrepreneur, acting with state coöperation, comes forward with new ideas for investment.

Developments are disturbing, too, at the other end of the social scale. Here the state's compensatory payments were naturally less extensive, since the property involved was mainly private dwelling houses. The money received was promptly spent, usually on prestige items or travel abroad. When this spurt was over, the common citizen was assured a modest income from a minor government sinecure, and various state benefits, plus a small private income from, say, a taxi or a tiny retail store—the whole accepted in much the same spirit as that of a pensioner receiving his dole.

Originally intended to preserve the identity of the old community, reserve the bulk of the new wealth for its citizens and protect them against the intruding aliens, these measures have inadvertently forced competition out of national life and made Kuwait an insular society. The elimination of competition now probably presents the most serious social danger facing Kuwait. Young people have lost their perspective, their urge to acquire knowledge, their acceptance of discipline. As a result, the drive, diligence and risk-taking that characterized the old Kuwaiti are no more. At both ends of the social scale the new citizen is content to enjoy a life of leisure and inertia, and is unwilling that this happy state of affairs should be disturbed. Protected, pampered, lavishly provided for and accountable to no one, he lives in a world of make-believe.

Another serious threat is posed to Kuwaiti society by the social vacuum which these measures have created. By relegating the traditionally dynamic classes to a position of only titular authority at the apex of the social pyramid or else to one of passive contentment, they have placed a premium on inertia and prevented the rise of an indigenous and dynamic middle class. The vacuum thus created is naturally filled by watchful and enterprising aliens.

The people attracted to Kuwait by its new wealth were of varied backgrounds, experiences and standards of conduct. The avarice and intrigues of many of them have brought bitter disillusionment to the Kuwaiti. Consequently, traditional Kuwaiti behavior is changing and men for whom the spoken word used to have the sanctity of a written contract have become instinctively suspicious of strangers and new ideas.

Further, the magnitude of the new wealth has given money and material possessions an importance and their owners a sense of power hitherto unknown. Naturally this has resulted in false perspectives. Ostentatious consumption, prodigal expenditure, idleness and pleasure-seeking are common; frugality, moderation and enterprise have become the antiquated virtues of a bygone age.

Finally, and most important of all, the new wealth has assumed such proportions that it is beginning to threaten the very concept of the state. This is because the lavish welfare benefits and privileges have entailed no effort or sacrifice on the part of the public, which sees no need to contribute to a state whose chief problem is what to do with its income. A fundamental principle in the relationship between state and citizen has therefore been jeopardized—namely, that in exchange for protection and benefits, the citizen has a duty to serve it and to make necessary sacrifices for it. The idea of the state as a communal institution demanding service, sacrifice and devotion, and as an embodiment of political and social ideas, exists today in the minds and hearts of a very few and exceptional Kuwaitis.

V

This tiny city-state: prodigal, complacent, short of technical skills, unperturbed by the acquisitiveness of its upper classes, the torpor of its common citizens and the savage rivalry among its resident aliens—what chance has it of survival in a poor, covetous and unstable region?

First it must be noted that most major events in the Middle East are influencd by external and regional forces; the survival of political régimes does not solely depend on their own economic or social merits. However the record of Kuwait's achievements is such that (barring the unexpected) one may suppose that disruptive forces from outside will encounter there an exceptional degree of viability and resilience.

Kuwait entered the modern era of welfare and technology with very few handicaps from her past. Unfettered by rigid traditions or conventions, she was free to experiment and adopt institutions and practices best suited to her own circumstances. Naturally anyone willing to follow the rough path of trial and error must be prepared to pay the price; Kuwait was willing and has done so. This willingness to experiment with new ideas gives the state both dynamism and flexibility not often found in old societies. Kuwait is not stagnant, nor has her social fabric as yet assumed final form. Her social and economic legislation is constantly revised and improved; her public services are being reorganized and streamlined; her city planning is being reviewed.

There is, further, a feeling on the part of the indigenous community that its present privileged position can be preserved only by total and unqualified domestic solidarity. Solidarity among the Kuwaitis is a time-honored tradition, and the recent waves of immigration have so strengthened the need for it that any deviation is now simply inconceivable. This was plainly demonstrated in 1961 when the entire community rallied around the Emir in the face of Kassem's threats; all past rancor was forgotten as autocratic rule was wisely replaced by constitutional government.

Despite the shortcomings and dangers attending the rapid transformation of a primitive society into one of great sophistication, certain fundamental traits in the character of the individual Kuwaiti remain unimpaired. He still remains tolerant, placid, and, above all, devoted to and proud of his freedom. These qualities explain why differences of opinion continue to be settled by debate and not violence; why the fundamental freedoms of speech and the press are respected; why censorship and the secret police—two monumental features in every Arab state—do not figure in Kuwait's political life, and have no impact on the thoughts or actions of her people. It is fortunate that the drafting of the constitution should have been completed during this period of Kuwait's history when these qualities are still a salient feature of the Kuwaiti personality.

There remains one more item on this balance sheet which calls for special mention, namely Kuwait's attitude toward the massive, woeful and demoralizing poverty outside her boundaries.

Here again, Kuwait's perspicacity and high-mindedness have been extraordinary. Transcending all the animosities and feuds of contemporary Arab politics, she has single-handedly set up the most enduring and constructive institution ever attempted by a small state. This is the Kuwait Fund for the Economic Development of the Arab Countries, with capital resources totaling altogether K.D. 300,000,000 ($840,000,000). This institution has been established to make loans to other Arab states to enable

them to carry out projects directly useful in developing their economies. I
is a permanent well-administered organization with clearly defined objectives and intelligent criteria for evaluating projects. It stands out as a monu-
ment to Kuwait's foresight and generosity. It also marks a turning point in
her development as a state, for it demonstrates that she recognizes her
responsibilities and is willing and able to live up to them. Within less than
two years of its inception, the Fund has already lent $19,600,000 to the
Sudan for the modernization of its railways; $21,000,000 to Jordan for
agricultural and industrial projects; and $18,200,000 to Tunisia; beside
substantial sums pledged to Algeria, the Yemen and the U.A.R.

Naturally, Kuwait is very proud of her achievements; but in determining
her fate her own assessment of her performance is far less important than
the opinion of her neighbors. Whether or not her extravagance will be
excused because of her generosity, only time will tell. What is certain is
that she can justify her survival as a political entity in this age of regional
internationalism only by serving effectively and impartially as a distributor
of substantial economic aid to her neighbors. Herein lies Kuwait's present
raison d'être. In order to maintain her independent identity she will have
to pursue her plans for economic aid with a zeal induced by the knowledge
that it is an essential part of her struggle for survival.

30

NATIONALISM, IMPERIALISM, AND COMMUNIST EXPANSION

IN "A NEW LOOK AT NATIONALISM" Hans Kohn sees in the hyper-nationalism of the twentieth century a force that deepens antagonisms and threatens individual liberty and the universality of human culture. He notes that though extreme nationalism and imperialism are waning in the West, they have taken a new lease on life in the communist worlds and the countries which have newly emerged from colonialism.

In his discussion of China's strategic aims Morton Halperin maintains that, in spite of bellicose talk, the Peking regime subordinates foreign policy to such domestic objectives as preserving the regime and achieving economic and industrial growth. It hopes to increase its dominance in Asia and ultimately to regain Formosa, but has no intention of risking an atomic war with the United States because it is fully aware of our military power and knows that such a war would be disastrous for China. However, as Chinese power grows, it will create more and more problems for both Russia and the West.

62

A New Look at Nationalism

by Hans Kohn

. . . . The late great Dutch historian J. Huizinga wrote in his last work, *Geschonden Wereld,* that "nationalism, the exaggerated and unjustified tendency to emphasize national interests, has produced in our time the abominable fruit of hypernationalism, the curse of this century." It was in this very century that many new nationalisms and nation-states have come into being, filled with the spirit of the age. Thus nationalism has become a powerful political threat not only to international peace but also to human freedom, perhaps the most powerful threat because nationalism in our time by far excels other appeals to human emotions—social or religious appeals—by its impact on masses and individuals alike. Communist Marxism, originally an a-national and anti-national movement, had to take this into account and has lately developed into a new kind of national socialism. Nationalism today unleashes forces which deepen antagonisms and hallow them by appeals to an idealized and over-sentimentalized past. Thus nationalism has tended to become what it originally had not been, a threat to individual liberty and to the universality of human culture.

After the First World War many peoples were "liberated" and created independent nations. Often these peoples had rightful complaints about the inequality of their status and the curtailment of their individual freedom. But before the First World War, following the example set by Britain in Ireland, South Africa, and India, the trend all over the earth went in the direction of greater equality of status and of growing recognition of individual rights. The creation of the new nation-states in 1918 in many cases reversed this trend. Nationalities which had demanded release from oppression became oppressors themselves, and sometimes worse oppressors, as soon as they were independent. Innumerable disputes about historical and natural frontiers sprang up. National traditions and national interests were idolized and absolutized at the expense of concern for neighbor and consideration for mankind. In the new nation-states racially closely

From *The Virginia Quarterly Review,* vol. 32 (Summer, 1956), pp. 321–332. Reprinted by permission.
Hans Kohn is Emeritus Professor of History at City College, New York.

related peoples felt oppressed, Ukrainians in Poland, Slovaks in Czecho-slovakia, Croats in Serb-controlled Yugoslavia. Poland had bitter frontier disputes with Lithuania, Germany, Czechoslovakia, Russia—the frontiers of Yugoslavia and Italy, of Hungary and Rumania, of Bulgaria and Yugo-slavia were "bleeding" wounds and "unredeemed" populations continued to clamor for independence. This continued nationalist temper in central and eastern Europe helped in almost all the countries to undermine the respect for individual liberty: the deep hostility among the new nation-states facilitated German expansion first, Russian expansion later. The new Europe after 1918 offered the spectacle neither of peace nor of the progress of liberty and human civilization. The great hopes of Mazzini and Woodrow Wilson in national self-determination as a vehicle for democracy and harmony among peoples were not realized.

Twenty-five years later, nationalism became the dominant emotional force all over the globe. Nationalism is in itself neither good nor bad, as little as capitalism, socialism, or imperialism are. It would be disastrous to rational thought and individual liberty to regard a rethinking of nation-alism or capitalism as a prelude to a sophisticated justification of exploita-tion or domination. But neither is it to be supposed—a position toward which modern British and North American humanitarian sensitivity inclines —that the underdog in a given situation is right and morally superior. There is no easy general rule. Phenomena of utmost complexity and variety, capi-talism and socialism, nationalism and imperialism, differ in content and consequences with historical circumstances. But two paradoxical situations emerge from the study of nationalism. Thanks to its rapid spread all over the globe, the peoples of the earth are beginning to build, at least out-wardly, their life on similar foundations of nationalism, of popular edu-cation, of industrialization. Modern schools and machines, the forms of popular elections, the emancipation of women, and the idea of national loyalty and service to the nation have penetrated everywhere. Modern inventiveness has afforded the technical means to a degree unimaginable a few decades ago for making cultural interdependence and intercourse even easier than economic interdependence. But at the same time peoples newly awakened to nationalism have begun to stress and to overstress their self-hood and independence, their cultural particularities and self-sufficiency. In the age of the awakening or the revolt of the masses, collective passions and utopian expectations have centered around the newly awakened nation-alism to such a degree that ever new barriers disrupt the international community.

The other paradoxical situation is presented by the fact that nation-alism is more or less on the wane in the lands of its origin, in the West, where the peoples are seeking ways for supra-national political organiza-tion and ever closer cultural integration, and this at the very time when nationalism has grown to a fever pitch in Eastern Europe and in Asia.

The same is true of Marxian socialism. Marx lived in England and he found his first great mass following in Germany. But today socialism in these countries as throughout the West has more or less openly abandoned Marxism as its theoretical foundation and its practical guide. The discrepancy between Marxian theory of the middle of the nineteenth century and the surrounding Western reality of the middle of the twentieth century has become too glaring. Only in the lands outside the Western historical community has Marxism tremendously gained in influence and prestige, a process which no Marxist at the end of the last century would have thought possible. And these two paradoxical developments are seen in one when we realize that nowhere is the emphasis on national sovereignty and its sanctity today as strong as in Communist society. In this atmosphere of paradoxical and unexpected developments strange myths are produced and uncritically accepted by the West. There were in history many predatory empires whose road was destructive of civilization and freedom. But there were other empires which with all their glaring human —all too human—shortcomings formed a protective shield under which peace and culture, freedom and law could grow. The Roman Empire of the second century and the British Empire of the later nineteenth century belonged to this category. It was the strength of these empires which made these two centuries the relatively happiest which mankind has known in its long story of devastating wars and lamentable misfortunes.

Communism uses today anti-imperialism and nationalism as two of its strongest ideological weapons in the war against freedom. Communist propaganda profits from the fact that many Western intellectuals have accepted Lenin's strange theory that imperialism is the product of late capitalism, that capitalist nations are by necessity imperialist, and that imperialism means above all economic exploitation. The Soviet Union or Communist China being by definition anti-capitalist must therefore be by definition anti-imperialist and free from exploitation. All these wondrous definitions cover up a reality in which Ukrainians and Georgians, Latvians and Uzbeks are oppressed to a degree hardly reached anywhere else in modern times, whole peoples are uprooted and transplanted as they were in the Assyrian Empire, and Tibet and the Mohammedan peoples of Sinkiang are refused their independence and even not allowed to voice their desire for it. Communist and Asian nationalist mythology have fused in propagating the fairy tale that imperialism is a special vice of the white man. Even Professor Toynbee's Reith Lectures on "The World and the West" seem to accept the legend of Russia and Asia as the victims of Western aggressiveness. In reality the West has been attacked by Asian forces throughout the longer part of recorded history, from the Persian wars against Greece to the Second Siege of Vienna by the Turks in 1683. But it has not been in history a question of European against non-European peoples. There has been always oppression within Europe. And Asian and African peoples are as human as the European peoples are: they fought and exterminated each other, and enslaved and exploited each other, before and after the coming of the white man to those continents. The imperialist and nationalist conflicts among Asians and Africans will go on after the last vestiges of the relatively short Western imperial rule have disappeared. Yet the brief contact with modern Western civilization has vitalized the stagnant civilizations of Asia and Africa, has reinvigorated them and aroused in them a desire for liberty and human dignity, as contact with the same Western civilization had done a century before in Russia.

The myths about capitalist imperialism and the virtues of nationalism have brought many Asians to deny the existence of Soviet imperialism and of national independence movements in Communist or Asian empires. Little sympathy is expressed for the struggle of the Soviet nationalities or of the South Moluccans who demand their independence from Indonesia, or for the Karen national defense movement in Burma. The Indonesian government has repressed native insurgent forces in North Sumatra and in parts of Java and Celebes with a ruthlessness which would have been severely condemned in Western countries if it had been done by Western imperial administrations. Nor is this a tale of recent woes. Burmese conquerors have from the twelfth to the eighteenth centuries repeatedly invaded Thailand, destroyed the Thai capitals and led part of the population as slaves into captivity. Burma's threat to Thailand ended only when Britain imposed her rule upon Burma. Nor did the Thai kings refrain from military conquests in Laos. Similarly, racial superiority complexes are nothing peculiar to the white race. They are ethically reprehensible and politically unwise wherever they appear. But group superiority feelings are in different forms a general human failure.

The Manchu conquerors of China enforced strict racial segregation and prohibited all intermarriage. Japanese colonial administrators imitated and outdid the exterior trapping of the quickly vanishing caste of British colonials. The Mohammedans in Chinese northwestern territories fought valiantly in many uprisings for independence until the ghastly repressions in the nineteenth century drowned all their efforts in an ocean of blood. A moral superiority complex based on an inverse racialism and on bitter resentments can produce intellectually and ethically unsound attitudes. Imperialism is today on the wane in the West, but it may be reviving outside the West, shunning the name, preserving the substance. To many observers India's attitude to Kashmir reveals no respect for national self-determination nor an absolute horror for imperial considerations. The Indians have taken over Britain's "advisory role" in Nepal and like all "advisors" they are not too welcome. Chinese throughout southeast Asia and Indians in East Africa and Surinam show little inclination to integrate with the natives of the countries of their residence: potentially some of them present the danger which the Auslandsdeutshe presented not so long ago.

Cultural freedom can only exist if intellectual life is guided by an effort at critical and objective thinking. The greatest threat to such thinking, and therefore to cultural freedom, was represented centuries ago by authoritarian and absolutized religion. Today it is represented by nationalism, above all in its over-resentful or semi-totalitarian forms. But everywhere in the free world, outside the confines of Communist rule and perhaps even there under cover, the critical forces which were born in the seventeenth century in northwestern Europe are at work to combat the exclusivism and egocentrism of modern nationalism. None has spoken more strongly against the cult of one's own nation or nationalism than Vladimir Solovyev in Russia or Rabindranath Tagore in India, both men deeply rooted in the spiritual tradition of their community and yet wide open to the critical insights of the West. Everywhere most of us have allowed our thinking to be channeled into widely accepted stereotypes about nationalism and its relation to liberty. In this time of mental and verbal confusion when general political terms have become so emotionally fraught that they cover disparate realities, we have to start rethinking many concepts in their historical context and in their concrete application. One of the chief concepts about which this rethinking has to be done in the interest of human freedom and of the possibility of cultural intercourse and universal rationality is the concept of nationalism.

63

China's Strategic Outlook

by Morton Halperin

Chinese foreign policy objectives have been and continue to be subordinated to domestic objectives; i.e. the major and overriding objectives of the Peking régime have been and continue to be the preservation of the régime and economic growth and industrialisation of the society. If one looks at Chinese behaviour since 1949 and at the allocation of the Chinese

Reprinted by permission from *China and the Peace of Asia,* edited by Alastair Buchan, Frederick A. Praeger, Inc., Publishers, 1965, pp. 95, 99, 101, 102, 104–105, 106–108 *passim.*

Morton Halperin is Associate Professor of Government at Harvard University.

udget since 1949, one finds a very clear priority given to internal goals
nd to the preservation of the régime. Defence budgets have been modest,
ertainly by the image that one generally has of a very militant and mili-
ary China, and even by general standards of expenditures on defence.
he defence spending appears to be defensively oriented—that is largely
owards the object of defending Chinese territory, against a Chinese Nation-
list invasion or perhaps an American invasion, rather than towards offen-
ve operations which would involve heavy emphasis on air power. . . .

[Nevertheless] the Chinese see the world as in a very difficult crisis
tuation at the moment, with the change in Soviet policy threatening the
iternational Communist movement and threatening to bring about an
bandonment of the attempt to expand the area of Communism, creating
hat to them is the most serious problem of the current period—how to
aintain the international Communist movement, how to push forward
ith the attempt to expand Communism in face of a revisionist régime
the Soviet Union.

In contrast to this sense of urgency is the very strong feeling now in
eking that the permanence of the Chinese Communist régime has been
ssured. . . .

There is a widespread view that the Chinese do not understand nuclear
ar, that they do not fear nuclear war, and in fact even desire nuclear war,
id that they lack an appreciation of the realities of the nuclear age.
his is however a completely false picture of the Chinese. It's a pic-
re that has largely been spread by the Soviet Union because it happens
fulfil various Soviet objectives—in particular convincing the West that
wants a *détente* because it has these lunatics on its border. If one in fact
oks at what the Chinese say, if one looks at what the Chinese have done
various crisis situations, it becomes abundantly clear that the Chinese
ew is that nuclear war would in fact be a great disaster for the world and
particular for China and the Communist régime. They have no illusion
at the leaders of Communist China as well as the industrialisation of
hina which they've carried out could not be destroyed in a rather small
clear war. And they have no doubt that it would be a great disaster for
hina. . . .

There has been, we are told, a major revision in the Soviet outlook
war, so that they believe that nuclear war is no longer fatally inevitable.
his is not as great a change as has sometimes been presented, but what-
er kind of change it is the Chinese have also accepted it. The Chinese
ive very explicitly accepted the notion that nuclear war is not inevitable.
ar is inevitable, various kinds of wars of national revolution, wars be-
een capitalist societies, are inevitable; but nuclear war between the
ommunist *bloc* and the Capitalist *bloc* is not inevitable. Where the Chinese
ffer from the Russians is in their view on how to prevent nuclear war.
he Chinese argue that if one wants peace, one must prepare for war,

that the way to prevent nuclear war with the West is to build up the n
tary strength of the Communist *bloc,* to build up the will and determinat
of the Communist *bloc.* This means at least two things. It means
Soviets should strive for superiority over the United States in nuclear for
and not accept a dangerous inferiority, and it means that the Soviets sho
help the Chinese to become a nuclear power, because the more nucl
powers there are in the socialist camp, the easier it is to deter the Uni
States. It means also that one does not emphasise one's fear of nucl
war, that one does not emphasise the danger of nuclear war, or the
portance of *détente* or disarmament. The Chinese argue that disarmam
is not attainable as long as there are capitalist countries, that to empha
disarmament is to expose one's fear of nuclear war and to make nuc]
war thereby more, rather than less, likely because one encourages
opponent to push since he believes that you do fear nuclear war. . . .

The Chinese now see nuclear weapons as important to them to incre
their power within the Communist world. They feel that if they are «
going to successfully challenge the current régime in Moscow they
have to do it on a basis of increased power, and in particular nuclear pov
Finally the Chinese see nuclear weapons as of some marginal value in s
port of their political objectives in Asia as a background threat aga
Asian countries.

Turning to the question of the role of conventional forces as an ins
ment of Chinese foreign policy the dominant factor that comes out is
very strong Chinese desire to avoid major conventional war. There
two reasons for this: first is the economic cost involved in preparing
a major conventional war, the amount of equipment and training wl
would be necessary, and the economic cost of participating in the v
both in terms of resources used and in terms of possible destruction
addition, probably as important, perhaps more important, is the reco
tion that any large scale build-up of forces runs the dangers of provol
an American attack. The Chinese have been willing to use very lim
kinds of military force for very specific purposes in the Taiwan Sti
and on the Sino-Indian border.

They have used major force only in two kinds of situations: first w
they felt there was no danger of intervention by an outside power—in
Tibet situation where they felt quite correctly that nobody would pre
them from committing what is the clearest case of overt aggression in
post-war period. The other case occurred when Peking felt the alterna
of not using major military force was more dangerous than engaging in
kind of encounter in Korea.

The Chinese view revolutionary war as the major means of sprea
Communist influence and Chinese influence in the world. This largely st
from their own historical experience, the fact that this was the mean
power in China, this is the kind of life that all the rulers of China had l

th over the decades prior to 1949 and it is the method which they know
d which they feel can be successful. They have also had some further
perience in Vietnam and Cuba and to some extent in Algeria, which
s tended to lend support to the Chinese notion that the way to expand,
e way to overthrow capitalism, is by the use of wars of national liberation
nich can overthrow a régime or a party much more powerful than the
volutionaries. . . .

The Chinese are much more interested in supporting wars of national
eration in areas far from China than they are in areas around the
ninese borders, with the exception of Vietnam. The Vietnam situation
s to be understood in the light of the independent position of the North
etnamese régime. This is the major factor explaining the pushing of the
volutionary war in Vietnam (and of the war in Laos). This action does
t fit in with the Chinese preferred strategy, and if left to themselves, or
they had full control of the North Vietnamese, the Chinese would not
pushing nearly as hard as the North Vietnamese are. Apart from Indo-
nina, the major Chinese emphasis on wars of national liberation is in
eas far from China, in which this is the only means of extending Com-
unist control and Chinese control. In these areas there is no danger of
e war spilling over into China as there is in the case of Indo-China and
there would be on other parts of their border; and there is no historical
ninese interest, and no historical pattern of control by China.

In the border areas the major Chinese emphasis is not on revolutionary
ar but on the use of military pressure, on the use of the threat of military
rce, combined with political techniques; leading towards a Chinese at-
npt to dominate the countries on their border, to establish hegemony
er them by a combination of military pressure and political gestures,
omises and threats. One finds a pattern of policy in Burma, in Nepal, in
ambodia, in which the Chinese go through the stage of concluding a treaty
fining the boundary, a treaty of friendship aiming at gradual establishment
Chinese hegemony in the foreign policy field over these countries. There
s been no attempt even to exploit local situations which might make
ssible the Communisation of these countries in the short run. They are
epared to work with the groups in power, to accept curbs on the Com-
unist parties and on the overseas Chinese in these countries.

The reasons for this are quite clear. The Chinese are in effect pursuing
historical pattern of Chinese policy towards these areas. They feel
rrectly that they can get the degree of control that they want over these
untries, the elimination of American bases, the elimination of American
luence, the establishment of Chinese influence, without the régimes
coming Communist. Even if they were successful in establishing Com-
unist régimes, this would increase very substantially their economic
ligations towards these countries, their political obligations, without
inging them much in return. They recognize that the attempt to establish

Communist régimes all over their periphery would probably lead to much greater willingness on the part of at least some of the countries to accept American bases and American support and might ultimately lead to American intervention and attack on China. They recognize in other words that they are much better off with a string of neutralist régimes rather than in effect splitting the countries with the United States and having some Chinese satellites and some countries which have American bases and an American alliance system. They would much prefer them all to be neutral and they recognize that this probably requires some degree of restraint on their part combined with rather vigorous action.

What can be said about, in conclusion, the Chinese long-run view? Where do they think things are going in terms of their major objectives? Where do they see the world being in ten, fifteen or twenty years? Most important to them is what they see occurring in the establishment of China as a major world power and as a major nuclear power. The Chinese believe that they have successfully survived the internal crises of the early sixties and they are back on the road towards economic development and industrialisation, although it's a very long road. They see China ultimately emerging as a major world nuclear power.

Peking sees following from this the establishment of Chinese hegemony in Asia, the elimination of American bases and the recognition by all Asian countries of the dominance of China. They also clearly see the destruction of the Republic of China and the incorporation of Taiwan into the Peking régime, although they have no clear notion of how this is going to come about. They accept the fact that the United States will continue to be their major enemy and that there is no possibility of any settlement with the United States. To seek a *détente* would be dangerous and meaningless, and they simply have to resign themselves to the fact that for the indefinite future they face a major enemy in the United States. . . .

China will remain, then, a tough, calculating, anti-*status quo* power with a good appreciation of what goes on in the world, a good understanding of American objectives and policies, and the objectives and policies of other countries. With growing power, and ultimately nuclear power, she will pose an increasing threat to Western interests and to Russian interests over the foreseeable future.

31

THE SEARCH FOR PEACE

TODAY IT IS GENERALLY CONCEDED that a major war with atomic weapons would bring destruction of life and property on a scale never before dreamed of. As yet, however, we have found no very dependable formula for making certain that such a war will not occur.

In commenting on Pope John's encyclical "Pacem in Terris," Norman Cousins praises the Pope for putting the interests of all mankind above those of any one religious group by extending his hand to the Communist leaders and asking their cooperation in maintaining peace. Robert McAfee Brown also praises the Pope for extending the hand of good will to all mankind, but he feels that the Pope failed to recognize the practical difficulties of eliminating reliance on force. We can only hope, says Brown, that he was right in his belief that nations can be brought to rely not on equality of arms, but on mutual trust.

In the next selection Burnham attacks the theory that Communism need no longer be taken seriously; that such liberalizing developments have taken place within it that Communist countries are now motivated almost wholly by national interest and not by Communist ideology. He notes the subversive and revolutionary activities they have fostered in Cuba, Zanzibar, South Vietnam, and other countries.

Finally, Boris Souvarine argues that from Stalin to Brezhnev Communist foreign policy has been to maintain unrelenting pressure against the non-Communist world by intimidation and the fomenting of revolution. He maintains that the only thing the Communists respect is force, and that in spite of threats they will in no case risk provoking the United States to the point of nuclear war.

64

Comments on Pope John's "Pacem in Terris"

1. The Outstretched Hand by Norman Cousins
2. Agenda for Men of Good Will by Robert McAfee Brown

1. The Outstretched Hand

The political parties men serve, the flags they salute, the fraternities they maintain, the holy books they revere or abjure—all these have suddenly become of intermediate significance alongside the positions men take on the question of war or peace in a nuclear age. For there are only two groupings of ultimate consequence on earth. One grouping consists of those who give thought to the implications of nuclear war and are willing to look and build beyond national sovereignty in order to avert it. The other grouping regards nuclear force primarily as a form of advanced military weaponry at the call of the national sovereign state. All other groupings or parties, whatever their formal designations—Socialists, Communists, Democrats, Republicans, Christian Democrats, etc.—have only limited relevance in the human situation today and, for all their prominence or fury, are rapidly becoming vestigial.

The first grouping knows that the business of peace has become the most important business in the world. Within that grouping is an almost limitless diversity of backgrounds and affiliations. But they constitute a world peace party. The ties that bind them are literally the strongest in the world, for they are concerned with human destiny.

Of all the implications of nuclear force, therefore, none is more compelling and critical to religious leaders than the fact that nuclear war would only superficially be a war between nations. Essentially, as they see it, it would be a war against God. For it is the work of God and not of man alone that is now in jeopardy. The precariously balanced conditions that

From *Saturday Review*, February 13, 1965, pp. 20–23 *passim*. Reprinted with permission of *Saturday Review;* the authors; and in the case of the Brown article, the Center for the Study of Democratic Institutions, Santa Barbara, California.

Norman Cousins, editor of *Saturday Review* for many years, is now Vice-President and Director of the McCall Corporation.

Robert McAfee Brown is Professor of Religion at Stanford University.

make life on this planet possible—not solely human life but life in general —these conditions can now be smashed or altered. Man's works of art, his cities, his cathedrals, and his homes are palpable, personal, replaceable. But his genes and his basic nature belong to a higher design and are not his to expunge or assail.

Once this is understood it no longer seems inexplicable or politically naïve that the head of the Catholic Church, for almost half a century a world rallying point of anti-Communism, should have addressed himself directly to the political head of the Soviet Union in the cause of peace. Indeed, Pope John XXIII did more than that: he held out his hand. He did so in good faith and trust and with the expectation that the gesture would be reciprocated. In so doing, he demonstrated the power that lies within the humanness of humanity.

The policy of the outstretched hand was not just a manifestation of Christian spirit, or a supreme confidence in the power of goodness to awaken goodness, or a summons to the in-dwelling God in the name of a common humanity. The outstretched hand was the product of a supreme awareness of a new dimension in world affairs that affected the human future. It was also an act of responsibility at a time when man's differences were rapidly becoming the combustibles of a nuclear conflagration.

It may be asked whether Pope John's Christian message was comprehensible to Nikita Khrushchev. I had the privilege in April 1963 of bringing from the Vatican to the Kremlin an advance copy of "Pacem in Terris," officially translated into Russian in Rome. Chairman Khrushchev listened very carefully as I called attention to some of the key ideas in the encyclical. At several points in the text, especially in those sections dealing with the specific responsibilities of statesmen in a nuclear age, Mr. Khrushchev nodded in agreement.

The Chairman responded by saying he was profoundly impressed by Pope John's dedication to peace. He knew that Pope John was critically ill and that not much time was remaining to him. The Chairman said he was moved that the Pope insisted on devoting his remaining strength to an attempt to save humanity; this could not help but inspire even those who had regarded themselves as polar opposites from Catholicism. . . .

When I reported to Pope John on the mission to Moscow, I found him most pleased by Khrushchev's response to his call upon world leaders for responsibility and restraint and for an end to nuclear terror. The Pope said he had deliberately avoided polemics against the Soviet Union in recent years because of his belief that meaningful and useful communication would at some time be critically essential. Besides, he added, it was much too late for denunciations; there was time only to try to prevent an unspeakable holocaust. Moreover, he was not forgetting what he himself had seen of the Russian people during his earlier service as an Apostolic Delegate.

He did not believe that their essential religiosity had been destroyed. They were a warm and wonderful people and he knew they could be reached.

The Pope said he was grateful that his appeal for peace had had a considerable effect on Chairman Khrushchev and the Russian people during the week of the Cuban crisis; this was a good sign. He had no way of knowing during Cuba week whether his appeal would make any difference; even so, he said, it was important to try. He could not take the responsibility for withholding any moral power he might possess. And when his appeal was given prominent attention inside the Soviet Union, he felt this faith had been justified.

The main point here, of course, is that Pope John had succeeded where the so-called political realists had failed. He was able to crack through the supposedly impenetrable shell of political determinism. Since the most important cause on earth to Pope John was to make this planet safe and fit for sacred man, he did not allow himself to believe that any doors were closed to him in the pursuit of this purpose. Nor did he admit that apparent obstructive evil, even when personified, could not be pierced.

What is at stake today is not primarily Christian civilization or Islamic civilization or Jewish civilization or Hindu civilization or any other but the civilization and life of man. It is not man's particularized beliefs but his own uniqueness that counts. For what threatens him is the loss of the basic conditions that make life meaningful and purposeful. To the extent that any religion speaks only in behalf of its own interests, to the extent that it places itself above or apart from the whole, it jeopardizes its own interests and injures the whole.

In no religious document of our time is there a more profound awareness that peace is the one overriding issue and challenge of our age than in "Pacem in Terris." Its call for an end to the nuclear arms race came in the middle of the struggle to achieve a nuclear test ban and must be credited with a major role in the successful completion of that treaty. But the central historic significance of "Pacem in Terris" may lie in the fact that the spirit of ecumenicalism went beyond the need to attain Christian unity to the need to safeguard and ennoble human destiny.

2. Agenda for Men of Good Will

The fact that a papal encyclical, usually addressed solely to Roman Catholics should provide the basis for extended discussion by non-Catholics as well is a good symbol of the extended area of dialogue opened up by the author of the encyclical, Pope John XXIII. And a Protestant's first reaction must be one of gratitude that the encyclical is addressed to *him* as well as to "the Venerable Brothers the Patriarchs, Primates, Archbishops,

Bishops and Other Local Ordinaries. . . ." Pope John rightly saw that "peace on earth" is not a peculiarly Catholic topic, and so—for the first time in Roman Catholic history—he addressed a papal letter not only to his own flock but also to ". . . All Men of Good Will."

Perhaps the most crucial [area with which the Pope deals is] the question of the use of force. Do the facts of the atomic era make it possible any longer to speak of "the responsible use of force?" Pope John would seem to reply in the negative. Public authority, he declares, "must be set up by common accord and not imposed by force." The presence of atomic weapons only underlines the futility of force in international relations: ". . . it is hardly possible to imagine that in the atomic era war could be used as an instrument of justice."

The most detailed treatment of the problem, of course, is found in the paragraphs dealing with disarmament. Taking issue with the presence of atomic weapons as constituting a deterrent, Pope John states emphatically "that the arms race should cease; that the stockpiles which exist in various countries should be reduced equally and simultaneously by the parties concerned; that nuclear weapons should be banned; and that a general agreement should eventually be reached about progressive disarmament and an effective method of control." The only basis for true peace "consists not in equality of arms but in mutual trust alone."

There can be no quarrel, of course, with the desirability of these aims. The questions to be raised center on the means for achieving them. There is a long gap, to cite only one point, between the desire for disarmament and the effecting of disarmament. And one of the crucial problems is the problem of determining the criteria to be employed by the various nations during that long interval as they seek to order their relations with one another. The encyclical, in jumping rapidly to the desirability of disarmament, is less than clear in helping to discover such criteria; in its justifiable fear about the ravages of atomic destruction it underplays the need to discern means and limits and ways in which power is to be exercised responsibly in the present. Although we may agree that "any human society that is established on relations of force must be regarded as inhuman," we are faced with the fact that through our lifetimes at least we will live in a world where the use of force, and the threat of the use of force, do not evaporate simply because they are called "inhuman." The delineation of guidelines at this difficult point, of the responsible use of force precisely while we are attempting to find ways of outlawing force, is surely the major task. . . .

When Pope John urges that "the true and solid peace of nations consists not in equality of arms but in mutual trust alone," and then immediately adds, "We believe that this can be brought to pass," one can only hope fervently that he is right. . . .

65

Is Communism Folding Up?

by James Burnham

Hardly anyone except J. Edgar Hoover and the John Birch Society takes Communism seriously any longer. To be called an "anti-Communist" is almost excuse enough for a libel suit. All enlightened persons know that nationalism has proved itself to be the dominant political reality of our time, and that "communism," "fascism," "socialism," "Castroism," "Nkrumahism," "Baathism" and maybe even "democracy" are only up-to-date masks for my nationalism or yours. De Gaulle states more bluntly what Mao, Brezhnev, Tito, Nasser and LBJ do. International diplomacy and politics continue to be just that—diplomacy and politics "among nations." George Kennan has been right all along in insisting that you deal with "Russia" just as diplomats have always dealt with dynamic, expansive nations, by checking threatened aggressions, proposing treaties and compromises, constructing alliances, seeking balances of power. It's silly and paranoid to get into a sweat over a mythical "communism." We're happy to come to terms with good communisms like Tito's and Gomulka's and for that matter the Kremlin's, but we'll still keep a sharp eye on bad communism like Mao's and maybe Castro's; and we're hoping Ho's communism will end up with the Goods.

The case for ignoring Communism can be put persuasively; has, in fact, been put persuasively enough to become the premise of the official policy of the U. S. Government. It has been a good many years since Voice of America, Radio Free Europe, USIA brochures or movies, speeches of U. S. representatives or approved indoctrination courses within U. S. agencies dabbled in anti-Communism. Nor is this a merely rhetorical limitation. It has been a good many years, also, since official policy was deliberately anti-Communist: officially, the U. S. aim is encouragement of "positive" and "liberalizing" developments within Communist nations, mutual disarmament, trade and cultural exchange, and above all accommodation, co-

From *National Review,* July 27, 1965, p. 631. Reprinted by permission of *National Review,* 150 East 35th Street, New York, N. Y. 10016.

James Burnham was for many years Professor of Philosophy at New York University. He is the author of many books, and has been a senior editor of *National Review* for the past ten years.

existence and "convergence" with the Soviet Union. This rhetoric and policy make sense only if the currently prevailing opinion is correct that Communism need not be taken seriously.

The Surd in the Woodpile

Let us assume the Kennan-de Gaulle-Morgenthau-Lippmann approach: Communism is unimportant; nations in their concrete geographical settings are the real historical counters. On this assumption the idea of national interest becomes the key both to what governments do and to what they ought to do. There is, for example, a ready and intelligible explanation why Russia should want a band of compliant states between its own territories and Western Europe, and this Moscow got by shrewd exploitation of Germany's defeat. Similarly, it is clear that Russia's interest leads to attempts at political penetration of the Middle East and to the search for warm-water outlets.

But with all the strains on its available resources, what Russian national interest can explain massive intervention in the Caribbean and central America, in Venezuela and Cuba and Colombia—to cite only a few of the Latin American areas where large-scale activities directed and financed from Russia have lately been going on? Or in Indonesia, which has got a billion dollars worth of military and economic aid from Russia over the past decade? Or in Algeria, Zanzibar, Ghana and Burma? Or, for that matter, in almost every nation through the guidance and subvention of internal political movements?

These operations can be explained by "nationalism" and the Russian "national interest" only if we stretch those terms into meaninglessness. And in truth, Messrs. Kennan, Morgenthau, Lippmann & Co. go on to contradict their own premise by assuring us that in reality there is no major conflict of national interest between the U. S. and Russia.

Whence, then, all the trouble? Simply because the rulers of the Kremlin and the White House don't listen to Kennan, Morgenthau and Lippmann?

What the Kennans, etc., say is true enough (this is what gives it plausibility), but true only in one historical dimension of a multi-dimensional reality. They fail, a Marxist would say, to comprehend dialectics: fail to realize that simultaneously in our age there is taking place an international competition of national states and empires (new and old), as in the past several centuries, *and also* an unprecedented revolutionary struggle that is world-wide and civilization-deep. The Soviet leadership functions simultaneously as, in the first dimension, a national government, and, in the second, a command echelon in the revolutionary army. The actual course of Soviet-directed activity (and the activity of every other "national communism") is a synthesis (borrowing again from the dialectic) of the two functions, but only the first of these appears within prevailing U. S. doc-

trine. Without reference to the second function you cannot make sense o.
what the Russians (*i.e.,* revolutionaries who happen to be Russian) have
been doing in Colombia, Indonesia, Venezuela, Zanzibar and Cuba.

President Johnson's hard military actions in Vietnam and Santo Domingo
can be convincingly motivated only within the second dimension—as
counter-revolutionary operations in the world struggle against revolutionary
Communism. This is why they are disapproved by Kennan, Morgenthau
Lippmann and de Gaulle, for whom that dimension does not exist. It is
also why the critics have had the best of the public argument with the
spokesmen for the Administration, since the spokesmen, too, are unable
or unwilling to recognize the second dimension.

66

The Communist Threat and
How to Meet It

by Boris Souvarine

Ever since 1925 when Stalin first used the words peaceful cohabitation
and then peaceful co-existence to define the foreign policy that he had
inherited from Lenin, the policy has never varied in its essentials. It still
continues, even under the Western name of the cold war, although changed
circumstances have changed its aspect. From Stalin to Khrushchev and on
through Brezhnev, it has meant maintaining an unrelenting pressure against
the non-Communist world—but only to the brink of general war, not beyond.

The truth of this has been demonstrated over and over again, in sharp

From *Atlas* Magazine, September 1965, pp. 159–161. Translated and reprinted
by *Atlas* magazine from *Le Contrat Social* (Paris). Copyright © 1965 Aspen Pub
lishing Company, Inc. Reprinted by permission.

Boris Souvarine is a Russian Socialist who was one of the secretaries of the Third
Internationale. He broke with the Communists after the death of Lenin. His *Life*
of Stalin, written a quarter of a century ago, has become a classic. He now lives
in Paris and spends much of his time writing on current Soviet affairs.

ontradistinction to the ideas generally held among business leaders, government officials and the higher reaches of Western society (and that the unthinking general public, under the influence of the mass media, inevitably shares). For more than twenty years the threat of a third world war has weighed heavily on the attitude that the Western nations take toward the communist enemy. It has encouraged the West to confine itself to military preparedness while Moscow and Peking and their satellites have seized the revolutionary initiative everywhere without exposing the instigators of these pernicious activities to definitive reprisals. The formidable arms and armies of pseudo-Communist militarism may justify the military preparations of the Atlantic world. Nevertheless, the utter inertia of the democracies seems inconceivable, especially now that the ideological imperialism of oriental despotism is gaining ground in Asia, Africa and Latin America by applying its all too familiar methods of infiltration, corruption and subversion, fomenting trouble everywhere—here by guerrilla action, there by riots and in the next place through local wars.

Up to now, this intellectual and political inertia could only be accounted for on the basis that the prospect of armed conflict overshadowed the politico-psychological struggles carried out unceasingly and unswervingly on long-distance instructions from Moscow and Peking, from Cairo and Havana. These struggles sap and undermine the precarious order that the victors over totalitarianism vainly endeavor to strengthen and solidify. The warnings that Khrushchev and Mao have poured forth, their appeals, their constant threats of armed intervention, always with the implication that the third world war lurks just around the corner have been accepted unquestioningly at face value by London, Paris and other capitals. The irresponsible press that shocks its readers in order to boost circulation constantly invokes the fear of atomic war and creates a state of mind that readily accepts Communist blackmail. Nevertheless twenty years of threats have brought forth nothing bearing any resemblance to the final cataclysm. It's all talk.

The course of events in Vietnam in recent months should dissipate once and for all the false conceptions that have hamstrung all too long the strictly defensive tactics that have been adopted to answer the victorious efforts of the nations that pretend to be Communist. The Americans, who alone seem capable of checking the invasion of the peninsula of Indochina and the threat to all Southeast Asia up to the Indian border, have decided very late in the day to resort to large-scale measures, although they are still not striking at the heart or head of the enemy. For they are using only their air force and their navy against the implacable guerrillas.

The only thing the Communists respect is force. Defending a position that is essential to the security of the free world, Uncle Sam is like a man attacked by a swarm of wasps and limits himself to stinging back. He fights

with his own weapons, but only with part of them. He steps up his effor
in the hope of convincing Hanoi, Peking and Moscow that it is fooli
to use the Vietcong as a weapon of aggression. It seems unlikely that
will gain the upper hand; but that does not entitle those whose princip
make them his allies but who, in point of fact, are divided and faint-heart
to give him outdated advice, much less to express displeasure and even
blame him. The Communists alone are responsible for the present state
affairs.

It would seem that the powers that be in Washington have finally unde
stood that teaching the enemy a lesson (the only kind he understand
does not entail the slightest risk of a world war, contrary to what Stali
lackeys and their allies and supporters of every stamp have been parroti
for the past twenty years. President Kennedy put men in the White Hou
the State Department and the United Nations who are now conducting t
kind of military counter-offensive best designed to discourage Commun
imperialism and neo-colonialism. The worst mistake they could make wou
be to justify the fears of those compatriots of theirs who see a repetiti
of the classic formula of too little and too late.

The only thing the Communists respect is force. They will persevere
their designs on Vietnam as long as they are given any reason to assume th
future benefits will outweigh present losses. They will compromise to ga
some temporary advantage, but they will remain determined to renoun
nothing while preparing new means of achieving their ends. If they neg
tiate, it will be with the intention of somehow violating whatever agreeme
they reach, as they have always violated treaties to which they have sign
their names. Which means that force—necessary as it is to compel the
respect—does not offer a complete solution. Another kind of war is sprea
ing through the world, side by side with the application of force, a ruthle
war known as peaceful co-existence or cold war and the Western demo
racies will never win it with pianists and dancers.

In response to the military action of combined American and Sou
Vietnamese forces, the Chinese and the Russians will repeat their usu
threats, warnings and appeals, knowing that their blackmail will be echo
by their dupes and supporters in Europe and America, in Asia ar
Africa. . . .

More or less involuntary volunteers and specialists in handling mode
equipment have undoubtedly already gone to North Vietnam. Certainly ant
aircraft equipment will soon be on its way, but it will not counterbalan
American power provided political defeatism does not block its full appl
cation. The truth is that third world war threats amount to nothing b
dreary demonstrations staged in front of embassies and legations that fly th
American flag, endless declarations and eternal petitions with the usu
signatures—in short the whole shabby bag of tricks that go to make u
peaceful co-existence.

The only thing the Communists respect is force. What is more, they 1 in no case risk provoking the United States to the point of nuclear war. e men who now shape American strategy have made up their minds. . . . But force will not prevail unless it puts into action ideas that generate orce of their own.

PART

VI

The Shape of the Future

67

The Human Condition: Prologue

by Hannah Arendt

In 1957, an earth-born object made by man was launched into the universe, where for some weeks it circled the earth according to the same laws of gravitation that swing and keep in motion the celestial bodies—the sun, the moon, and the stars. To be sure, the man-made satellite was no moon or star, no heavenly body which could follow its circling path for a time span that to us mortals, bound by earthly time, lasts from eternity to eternity. Yet, for a time it managed to stay in the skies; it dwelt and moved in the proximity of the heavenly bodies as though it had been admitted tentatively to their sublime company.

This event, second in importance to no other, not even to the splitting of the atom, would have been greeted with unmitigated joy if it had not been for the uncomfortable military and political circumstances attending it. But, curiously enough, this joy was not triumphal; it was not pride or awe at the tremendousness of human power and mastery which filled the hearts of men, who now, when they looked up from the earth toward the skies, could behold there a thing of their own making. The immediate reaction, expressed on the spur of the moment, was relief about the first "step toward escape from men's imprisonment to the earth." And this strange statement, far from being the accidental slip of some American reporter, unwittingly echoed the extraordinary line which, more than twenty years ago, had been carved on the funeral obelisk for one of Russia's great scientists: "Mankind will not remain bound to the earth forever."

Such feelings have been commonplace for some time. They show that men everywhere are by no means slow to catch up and adjust to scientific discoveries and technical developments, but that, on the contrary, they have outsped them by decades. Here, as in other respects, science has realized and affirmed what men anticipated in dreams that were neither wild nor idle. What is new is only that one of this country's most respectable

Reprinted from *The Human Condition* by Hannah Arendt by permission of The University of Chicago Press. © 1958 by The University of Chicago.

Hannah Arendt is an author and political scientist. She has been Visiting Professor at such leading schools as the University of California, Princeton, and Columbia.

newspapers finally brought to its front page what up to then had been buried in the highly non-respectable literature of science fiction (to which, unfortunately, nobody yet has paid the attention it deserves as a vehicle of mass sentiments and mass desires). The banality of the statement should not make us overlook how extraordinary in fact it was; for although Christians have spoken of the earth as a vale of tears and philosophers have looked upon their body as a prison of mind or soul, nobody in the history of mankind has ever conceived of the earth as a prison for men's bodies or shown such eagerness to go literally from here to the moon. Should the emancipation and secularization of the modern age, which began with a turning-away, not necessarily from God, but from a god who was the Father of men in heaven, end with an even more fateful repudiation of an Earth who was the Mother of all living creatures under the sky?

The earth is the very quintessence of the human condition, and earthly nature, for all we know, may be unique in the universe in providing human beings with a habitat in which they can move and breathe without effort and without artifice. The human artifice of the world separates human existence from all mere animal environment, but life itself is outside this artificial world, and through life man remains related to all other living organisms. For some time now, a great many scientific endeavors have been directed toward making life also "artificial," toward cutting the last tie through which even man belongs among the children of nature. It is the same desire to escape from imprisonment to the earth that is manifest in the attempt to create life in the test tube, in the desire to mix "frozen germ plasm from people of demonstrated ability under the microscope to produce superior human beings" and "to alter [their] size, shape and function"; and to wish to escape the human condition, I suspect, also underlies the hope to extend man's life-span far beyond the hundred-year limit.

This future man, whom the scientists tell us they will produce in no more than a hundred years, seems to be possessed by a rebellion against human existence as it has been given, a free gift from nowhere (secularly speaking), which he wishes to exchange, as it were, for something he has made himself. There is no reason to doubt our abilities to accomplish such an exchange, just as there is no reason to doubt our present ability to destroy all organic life on earth. The question is only whether we wish to use our new scientific and technical knowledge in this direction, and this question cannot be decided by scientific means; it is a political question of the first order and therefore can hardly be left to the decision of professional scientists or professional politicians.

While such possibilities still may lie in a distant future, the first boomerang effects of science's great triumphs have made themselves felt in a crisis within the natural sciences themselves. The trouble concerns the fact that the "truths" of the modern scientific world view, though they can be demonstrated in mathematical formulas and proved technologically, will no longer lend themselves to normal expression in speech and thought. The moment these "truths" are spoken of conceptually and coherently, the resulting statements will be "not perhaps as meaningless as a 'triangular circle,' but much more so than a 'winged lion'." (Erwin Schrödinger). We do not yet know whether this situation is final. But it could be that we, who are earth-bound creatures and have begun to act as though we were dwellers of the universe, will forever be unable to understand, that is, to think and speak about the things which nevertheless we are able to do. In this case, it would be as though our brain, which constitutes the physical, material condition of our thoughts, were unable to follow what we do, so that from now on we would indeed need artificial machines to do our thinking and speaking. If it should turn out to be true that knowledge (in the modern sense of know-how) and thought have parted company for good, then we would indeed become the helpless slaves, not so much of our machines as of our know-how, thoughtless creatures at the mercy of every gadget which is technically possible, no matter how murderous it is.

However, even apart from these last and yet uncertain consequences, the situation created by the sciences is of great political significance. Wherever the relevance of speech is at stake, matters become political by definition, for speech is what makes man a political being. It we would follow the advice, so frequently urged upon us, to adjust our cultural attitudes to the present status of scientific achievement, we would in all earnest adopt a way of life in which speech is no longer meaningful. For the sciences today have been forced to adopt a "language" of mathematical symbols which, though it was originally meant only as an abbreviation for spoken statements, now contains statements that in no way can be translated back into speech. The reason why it may be wise to distrust the political judgment of scientists *qua* scientists is not primarily their lack of "character"—that they did not refuse to develop atomic weapons—or their naïveté—that they did not understand that once these weapons were developed they would be the last to be consulted about their use—but precisely the fact that they move in a world where speech has lost its power. And whatever men do or know or experience can make sense only to the extent that it can be spoken about. There may be truths beyond speech, and they may be of great relevance to man in the singular, that is, to man in so far as he is not a political being, whatever else he may be. Men in the plural, that is, men in so far as they live and move and act in this world, can experience meaningfulness only because they can talk with and make sense to each other and to themselves.

Closer at hand and perhaps equally decisive is another no less threatening event. This is the advent of automation, which in a few decades probably will empty the factories and liberate mankind from its oldest and most natural burden, the burden of laboring and the bondage to necessity.

Here, too, a fundamental aspect of the human condition is at stake, but the rebellion against it, the wish to be liberated from labor's "toil and trouble," is not modern but as old as recorded history. Freedom from labor itself is not new; it once belonged among the most firmly established privileges of the few. In this instance, it seems as though scientific progress and technical developments had been only taken advantage of to achieve something about which all former ages dreamed but which none had been able to realize.

However, this is so only in appearance. The modern age has carried with it a theoretical glorification of labor and has resulted in a factual transformation of the whole of society into a laboring society. The fulfilment of the wish, therefore, like the fulfilment of wishes in fairy tales, comes at a moment when it can only be self-defeating. It is a society of laborers which is about to be liberated from the fetters of labor, and this society does no longer know of those other higher and more meaningful activities for the sake of which this freedom would deserve to be won. Within this society, which is egalitarian because this is labor's way of making men live together, there is no class left, no aristocracy of either a political or spiritual nature from which a restoration of the other capacities of man could start anew. Even presidents, kings, and prime ministers think of their offices in terms of a job necessary for the life of society, and among the intellectuals, only solitary individuals are left who consider what they are doing in terms of work and not in terms of making a living. What we are confronted with is the prospect of a society of laborers without labor, that is, without the only activity left to them. Surely, nothing could be worse.

To these preoccupations and perplexities, this book does not offer an answer. Such answers are given every day, and they are matters of practical politics, subject to the agreement of many; they can never lie in theoretical considerations or the opinion of one person, as though we dealt here with problems for which only one solution is possible. What I propose in the following is a reconsideration of the human condition from the vantage point of our newest experiences and our most recent fears. This, obviously, is a matter of thought, and thoughtlessness—the heedless recklessness or hopeless confusion or complacent repetition of "truths" which have become trivial and empty—seems to me among the outstanding characteristics of our time. What I propose, therefore, is very simple: it is nothing more than to think what we are doing.

"What we are doing" is indeed the central theme of this book. It deals only with the most elementary articulations of the human condition, with those activities that traditionally, as well as according to current opinion, are within the range of every human being. For this and other reasons, the highest and perhaps purest activity of which men are capable, the activity of thinking, is left out of these present considerations. Systematically, therefore, the book is limited to a discussion of labor, work, and action, which forms its three central chapters. Historically, I deal in a last chapter with the modern age, and throughout the book with the various constellations within the hierarchy of activities as we know them from Western history.

However, the modern age is not the same as the modern world. Scientifically, the modern age which began in the seventeenth century came to an end at the beginning of the twentieth century; politically, the modern world, in which we live today, was born with the first atomic explosions. I do not discuss this modern world, against whose background this book was written. I confine myself, on the one hand, to an analysis of those general human capacities which grow out of the human condition and are permanent, that is, which cannot be irretrievably lost so long as the human condition itself is not changed. The purpose of the historical analysis, on the other hand, is to trace back modern world alienation, its twofold flight from the earth into the universe and from the world into the self, to its origins, in order to arrive at an understanding of the nature of society as it had developed and presented itself at the very moment when it was overcome by the advent of a new and yet unknown age.

68

Pope John's Revolution:
Secular or Religious?

by H. Stuart Hughes

Four years ago I put together an essay in which I tried to assess the achievements and prospects of Christian Democracy in contemporary Europe. The verdict was mostly negative: the achievements seemed to lie in the past, and the prospects for the future to be troubled by what I discerned as a growing neoclericalism. The essay ended on a note of well-wishing to my Catholic friends, both in my own country and abroad, whom

From *Commonweal*, a weekly journal of opinion edited by Catholic laymen, December 10, 1965, pp. 301–303. Reprinted by permission.

H. Stuart Hughes, the author of *The United States and Italy* and other works, is Professor of History at Harvard University.

I depicted as struggling against heartbreaking odds to give their faith a more flexible form that would bring them closer to agnostic "humanists" like myself.

At the very moment these sentiments were being penned, Pope John's "revolution" began. The two years from the publication of *Mater et Magistra* in May, 1961, to the Pope's death just a few weeks after his second great encyclical, *Pacem in Terris,* had appeared, surely rank as the most extraordinary that the Church has lived through since the sixteenth century. At the time . . . and I suspect that the same was true of many American Catholics . . . I did not quite appreciate how great the change had been. Not until the unprecedented explosion over religious liberty at the end of the third session of the Council last year did some of us fully realize the depth of Catholic response to the breath of innovation. We were not surprised by the vigor of the progressive leaders of the hierarchy . . . their names and past records were already familiar to us . . . what we had not anticipated was the size and the vociferousness of the majority behind them. From that point on, no fair-minded commentator, of whatever faith or lack thereof, could question the extent or the sincerity of the movement for *aggiornamento* within the Church.

Now a Catholic historian, E. E. Y. Hales, whose professional qualifications put the stamp of authenticity on his findings, has told us in a book, *Pope John and His Revolution* (Doubleday), that Pope John's was unquestionably a true revolution. He adds, however, that this revolution was not quite what most of its supporters have imagined. The Pope and the progressive majority in the Council were not invariably in harmony: although both stressed the concept of *aggiornamento,* they understood the term rather differently. John, particularly in the last year of his life, put the emphasis on succoring all humanity beyond the confines of Catholicism; "he seemed less preoccupied with the visible Church than with the world as a whole." The progressive prelates were more concerned with the reform of Catholicism itself; their introduction of vernaculars into the liturgy, for example, went expressly against John's announced intention.

Such distinctions, like the freely-ranging debates within the Council itself, are all to the good in the continuing process of educating those non-Catholics who persist in regarding the Church as a monolith. But they suggest the difficulties in arriving at a global assessment of the achievements of Pope John and of the Council he summoned. It is easy to stand on the sidelines cheering for the forces of light: this is the congenial but mentally slack stance of a number of American Protestant observers (the Jews have generally remained more detached). It is another matter to try to discover the long-term implications of reforms of such magnitude—and even perhaps to find something beyond obscurantism in the attitude of the conservative opposition.

What I like about Mr. Hales' distinction between Pope and Council is that it enables us to see the "revolution" under a number of guises which do not always go along together. The word *aggiornamento*—like that other favorite expression of Pope John's, *vogliamoci bene* ("let us wish each other well")—has a saving vagueness about it that permits every individual to read into it the content he prefers. In John's case, the governing principle seems to have been impatience with the note of "alarm and admonition" in the pronouncements of his predecessors, a sense that the Church and the world had had "enough definitions and condemnations" and a predilection for discovering the positive and the good even among the Church's ostensible enemies. Such an attitude was a logical outgrowth of nearly thirty years' diplomatic experience in non-Catholic countries or in a scarcely Catholic nation like France; one of John's greatest contributions was to bring into the mainstream of Church policy the special combination of realism, intellectual distinction, and spirtuality characteristic of a country in which Catholics are by far the strongest faith but still outnumbered by the unbelievers.

As Pope, then, John knew how to work to maximum effect in an alien or predominantly secular environment; in understanding the outside world he did not labor under the illusions or handicaps of his more exclusively Italianate predecessors. The result was the openness and the gift for finding virtue in apparent evil that enchanted those who came into contact with him. At the same time, these qualities were perfectly compatible with an unscholarly understanding of theology and (which is less well known) a basic conservatism about the faith itself and the internal discipline of the clergy and religious.

Looking Beyond Catholics

Pope John's own revolution, particularly as embodied in *Pacem in Terris,* his final testament, can be regarded by a non-Catholic as more secular than strictly religious. It was concerned with the two concentric circles beyond that of Catholics themselves—with Christians not in communion with Rome, and still more with those of other faiths or no faith at all, including atheists and Communists. To the radically secular world, John brought tidings of good will: for the first time in Papal history he expressed a clear preference for the democratic form of government; he embraced "a new concept of the duties of the state" which "many would call socialism"; he gave his blessing to the United Nations as the embryo of a world authority (an endorsement echoed by Pope Paul on his visit to New York); he welcomed the new nations of Asia and Africa, laying down without qualification that "there are no inferior peoples, no inferior races . . . only a duty incumbent upon those who have to assist those who have not"; he condemned nuclear war as an illicit means even for attaining a just end; and to preserve the peace he preached the necessity of extending the hand of understanding to Communist regimes. These he argued, should be judged by their fruits and not by their surface professions: they might teach a false philosophy, but this should not prevent Christians from working with them toward "some external good."

An exhilarating ideological platform: how many American Catholics (or for that matter, non-Catholics) would undertake to campaign for office on it? One of the great merits of Mr. Hales' book is its exposition of how thoroughgoing was the change Pope John proposed in the Church's relations to the secular world. We can understand the terror and scandal of the *bien-pensants:* something had happened almost as dreadful as André Gide's satiric vision of a Masonic anti-pope enthroned in the Vatican.

At the same time, John's international and social proposals seem to have occasioned less alarm among the conservatives in the Curia than another type of innovation which might strike an outsider as rather more palatable. (We learn with amazement that Cardinal Ottaviani has recently declared himself against nuclear war.) Perhaps it is, as Mr. Hales reminds us, that in its sessions subsequent to Pope John's death the Council shifted its emphasis and that much of his international program has been quietly interred. There is also the more significant possibility—frequently overlooked by liberal Catholics—that members of the hierarchy may be simultaneously venturesome on public policy and strict integralist in matters of the faith.

Pope John's ecumenical sweep extended way beyond the confines of Christianity. The views of Cardinal Bea, John's chief organizational supporter in this endeavor, were of necessity more closely focussed on the Christian community. But here—partly for the very reason that the subject matter was nearer to home—the potential effects were even more profoundly unsettling. It was one thing to teach new duties to secular sovereigns in terms of a Christian morality literally understood: this was a lesson that the medieval Popes had long since preached to kings and emperors. It was quite another matter—and far less familiar—to suggest to the Catholic faithful that the Church itself did not have a monopoly of the truth.

It was fitting, then, that the Council's most dramatic debates should have been those concerned with religious liberty, and the outside world was right in regarding the Fathers' stand on this issue as the touchstone of their whole achievement. Religious liberty had been dear to Pope John's heart—but it had not been what he had stressed most at the end of his life. In actual historical sequence, the declaration on freedom of belief (or of non-belief) was peculiarly the achievement of the Council's reforming majority—and of Pope Paul, whose final and decisive alignment with the reformers redeemed all his hesitations along the way.

Degrees of Toleration

It is at this point that the non-Catholic, and more particularly the agnostic, schooled in relativism, plural explanations, and self-doubt, needs to make a supreme effort of sympathetic imagination. He has to try, despite himself, to understand what it means for Catholics of the old school to accept the notion of toleration as a good in itself rather than just a practical adaptation to a lesser evil. If belief is free, then, as Mr. Hales suggests, the liberal Catholics of the nineteenth century have been proved right and Pius IX wrong. So much may not be too hard to swallow. But what if the new definition also means (something that Mr. Hales does *not* say) that the "Modernists" of the early twentieth century have been rehabilitated and St. Pius X disavowed? This would be a far more serious matter. For some of those whom the Papal condemnation of 1907 grouped under the term "Modernist" were as relaxed as Unitarians in their attitude to dogma. Will it now be permissible for the doctrine of the Church to be reinterpreted at will in symbolic, historical, or relativist terms? To me, such is the implication of the Council's declaration on religious liberty. For if non-Catholics are to be allowed to seek religious truth according to their own lights, how can the same privilege be withheld from those within the fold?

Under the guidance of Pope John and the Council, the Church went forth to meet the modern world. The encounter has only just begun—and there is no guarantee that the Church will have the upper hand. The forces of secularism are more numerous, wealthier, and better-educated than those of Catholicism (or even of Christianity as a whole). They do not argue with the Church any longer: they greet it with a shrug of the shoulders, or at best with an uncomprehending smile. The world into which the inquiring young Catholic is urged to venture has little comprehension of his faith: it threatens to seduce him not so much by material blandishments (such as the Church has traditionally warned against) as through a process of absorption and adaptation and dilution by imperceptible stages. In this situation, I can understand the anguish of Pope Paul and feel sympathy for a frankness in revealing his perplexities which in its own way is as human as John's. It is a fearful thing to have in one's hands a two-thousand-year-old deposit of faith and to tremble with doubt that one may be risking it all in a single decade of unbridled innovation.

Of necessity people like myself enthusiastically support the great reforms of the past four years. They bring us closer to our Catholic friends and to the lost Christianity in which we were reared and for which many of us still grieve. Pope John, we feel, was a "primitive Christian"—that is, he took his gospel quite literally and more particularly what it had to say about human love and fellowship. The Christians' doctrine of love has always been both their greatest treasure and their prime difficulty. Most of the time, as our Jewish friends warn us, it has proved to be psychologically impracticable; most of the time it has induced only hypocrisy. From the sense of this yawning gap between the ideal and the actual arose the radical disaffection that led so many of us as young adolescents to abandon any formal religious affiliation. Then suddenly—decades later—there appeared in the most unlikely place, on Peter's throne itself, a man for whom the old dream was both real and practical. We have still not recovered from the shock.

We—those outside the Church—are likely to assess Pope John's legacy and the work of the Council in some such simple terms as these: will they give reality at last to the Christians' ancient profession of love for all mankind? I think that on balance they will: in this respect I am more optimistic than Mr. Hales, who reserves his judgment on the future. And I am similarly convinced that some time within the next generation the Church will surmount the great stumbling-block of its present position on birth control: I cannot see how over the long term it can reconcile a faith based on love with a stand that condemns millions to want and despair. But I am less sanguine than Mr. Hales seems to be about whether such a great change can take place within the framework of the Church as it has been traditionally understood. I find the conservatives in the Italian and Spanish hierarchies not wholly in the wrong when they warn of the perils ahead. I do *not* believe that Catholicism will cease to exist. But I think it quite possible that the post-Johannine Church—at least the Church of the educated—will become so private, so personal, so enmeshed in the vocabulary and concepts of the secular world as to be almost unrecognizable as the Catholicism of the past. Whether this will be a loss or a gain is for members of the faith alone to decide.

69

The Economic Revolution

by Barbara Ward

Three quarters of the human race today is involved in a vast movement of revolutionary economic upheaval. They are attempting to modernize their economies—to move from the old patterns of static agriculture and limited commerce which made up the general pattern of the human economy for millennia on to the new productive, dynamic economy of modern industry, technology and science. The change is not so much a matter of choice as of stark necessity. Everywhere among the emergent peoples, populations are doubling every generation or so. Resources must at least keep pace if even present standards are to be maintained—and these, incidentally, allow each person an average income of no more than $120 a year. If life is to be a little more secure and healthy, a little better nourished, housed and clothed, a trebling of resources would hardly be sufficient. But there is no possibility of such expansion under the old economic methods. Static agriculture has only one means of growth—to take in more land. But in most of Asia there is no more land. Unless economic methods are radically recast, the outcome in the next forty years must be deepening misery, anarchy and despair.

This world-wide revolution of economic modernization is one in which the wealthy West is fundamentally involved. It was in the Atlantic area that the revolution began. It was under western influence that the first impact of the new methods reached the other continents and determined decisively the conditions under which they in their turn would seek to modernize their economies. Thus to ignore or to be indifferent to the present world-wide movement of economic change would be the equivalent of canceling at least 300 years of western experience. Worse, it would entail withdrawal from the greatest contemporary human effort to remold society and remake the face of the earth. And it is a fact of history that those who seek to withdraw from its great experiments usually end by being overwhelmed in them.

From *The Saturday Evening Post*, May 14, 1960, pp. 43, 52, 57–58, *passim*. Reprinted by permission of the author.
Barbara Ward (Lady Jackson) is a well-known English economist and writer who for some years was on the staff of *The Economist*.

We cannot fix a date for the origins of the modern economic revolution. A hundred different conditions, influences and decisions set it in motion, and the changes came cumulatively over several centuries. In part, it was rooted in medieval Europe's constitutional development which gave the merchant what he never had in the Orient—status, security and inducements to save. Calvinism played its part, teaching that hard work in pursuit of profit was blessed by God and that money so earned should be saved, not spent in luxury. The scientific temper of the eighteenth century encouraged progressive landowners and aspiring artisans to experiment with new methods of production. In Britain toward the end of the eighteenth century all these separate streams—of acquisitiveness, of work, of invention—had begun to flow together into that flood of economic and technological change which we loosely call the Industrial Revolution.

The men who made this revolution did not know what they were doing in any general sense. Each pursued his own interest and profit, and the sum of interests made up the working of the system. But with our hindsight we can disentangle the essential principles, the changes without which dynamic growth is impossible—the preconditions, therefore, of modernization anywhere else.

The two most important principles underlying the revolution of economic growth are productivity and saving. Productivity results from any method which helps men to produce more goods for the same output of effort and resources. The decisive changes in productivity in Britain's early industrial revolution were better agricultural methods and the application of a new form of power—steam from coal—to machines made by new processes of iron founding. The new machines began to flood the market with cheaper consumer goods—which incidentally wiped out handicrafts imported from Asia. Expanding trade created the need for better transport, bigger towns and harbors. New industrial techniques called for steadily increasing education.

These were the first steps. Since then invention has multiplied a thousandfold the effect of every instrument of growth. Above all, vast new sources of energy have been discovered—electricity, the atom. But the basic requirements of modernization have not changed. Now, as then, they are better farming, more education, "infrastructure"—roads, power, port —and industrialization.

All these techniques of greater production depend upon saving—that is, upon the postponement of consumption. In the eighteenth century Coke of Holkham postponed direct returns on his farms when he experimented with crop rotation. The fourfold increase in output paid him back handsomely and provided capital for further ventures. Similarly, when the duke of Bridgewater built the first canal to Lancashire, he took laborers and materials away from the immediate tasks of farming. When, as result of the saving on transport, the price of coal in Manchester was halved, resources were available to recompense the duke and to provide for further experiment. John Wilkinson used his savings—and other people's—all his life to pioneer new methods of iron founding and new uses for cast iron. One result was the steam engine and the first fundamental revolution in energy, that greatest of all sources of productivity.

Even the most primitive economies save a little—putting aside seed corn for the next harvest. Perhaps 5 per cent of national income is saved in this way. Economists reckon that, as a general rule, when the level of productive saving has reached about 15 per cent of national income, the economy has reached the point of "break-through" and can generate each year enough savings to insure the expansion of both savings and consumption in the future. This process—the process of self-sustaining growth—is the ultimate objective of all developing economies today.

One can see that it works in a cumulative way. The more techniques of progress there are—better methods, more powerful machines, more skilled labor—the easier it is to save. Yet there is always a period during which the original investments have to be made. Consumption is postponed for the first investment in better farming, for the first machines, for the first expansion in power. As a general rule, increases in capital at this stage have come from agriculture because in all pre-industrial societies farming is the occupation of nearly 90 per cent of the people. And the chances are that the process will entail great hardships for them. Saving is, after all, not-consuming. Farming people in a static economy are not, in general, very rich. Their surpluses are small. If they are to consume less and send off their surplus to the towns, they are likely to be poorer, unless—as in America and later in Japan—farming is actually expanding at the time of the transfer.

Nor is this the end of the difficulties inherent in beginning to save. If in Britain after 1810 all the output of the new machines had been consumed at once by the thousands of workers herding into the new industrial cities, there would have been no margin for further expansion. The organizers of the new wealth—the rising industrialists, the bankers, the landowners—kept the surplus created by the machines and devoted it to increased investment. In Britain between 1820 and 1860, little of the new production directly benefited the bulk of the workers. It was not until the system was fully established and goods began to pour out from the new processes—and workers themselves were beginning to organize and bargain for better wages—that a general rise in living standards began.

Since then Britain's national income has increased on the average by more than 3 per cent a year; and this is the general figure for the industrial West. In recent decades the pace has even quickened a little owing to higher levels of investment, both public and private, and new methods in technology. Today, therefore, the harsh times of original saving are quite forgotten. America's 176,000,000 people enjoy a national income of nearly $500,000,000,000. For years now 15 per cent and more of this income has been set aside for further investment while the citizens' own consumption has steadily increased. But in free Asia, in Africa and Latin America more than 1,000,000,000 people have a total income of only $120,000,000,000. Take 15 per cent of this for investment, and every form of consumption has to be cut. Saving is as harsh a discipline as it was in Britain in the 1850's. In fact, it is harsher, for the pressure of population is greater and the task of cutting consumption correspondingly more drastic.

It is in the context of these early grinding days of forced saving that we can best grasp both the origins and the continued appeal of Communism. All Marx's thinking was conditioned by the grim conditions of early industry in Britain. His contemporaries, as we have seen, had no very clear picture of the forces molding the new economy—nor apparently had Marx. He saw that a vast release of productive forces was taking place and gave the industrialists credit for it. But his attention and energy were fixed on the appalling conditions of the workers, and he denounced, like an ancient Hebrew prophet, the ugly fact of exploitation.

In part, he was right. The organizers of the new wealth were undoubtedly rewarding themselves handsomely—as commissars were to do a century later. But he missed the other facet of their policy—that the saving sweated from the workers provided the necessary capital for extending the whole base of the economy. In fact, Marx did not grasp *how* in practical terms a modern industrial society had to be built. He assumed that the *bourgeoisie* would first look after that; then the workers would take over a functioning machine once their deepening misery had driven them to revolt. There are thus no blueprints in *Das Kapital* for a modern economy, and when in 1917 the Communists found themselves with the whole of Russia on their hands, it was to their own pragmatism, not to Communist theory, that they had to look for guidance.

Russia had some beginnings of modernization. But the country was flattened by war and revolution. The first efforts of Communism—turning the factories over to the workers—made the confusion worse. In 1921 Lenin in fact decreed a modified acceptance of the market economy, hoping that peasants and traders would get the economy somehow back into motion. But by this time a fully integrated industrial society existed in the West which could be copied. The tremendous armaments built up by governments in the First World War showed what central direction could do to accelerate heavy industry and to mobilize the people's savings and work. It was Stalin's fateful achievement to use total state power to transpose to Russia the techniques of production evolved in the industrial West. The first Five Year Plan and its successors established the "infrastructure" and the heavy industry of a modern advanced economy by government fiat. At the same time it set in motion the vast schemes for education which would keep trained manpower in step with the machines. At first technicians and engineers were borrowed from abroad. But within a decade Russian development was self-sufficient. The break-through had been achieved—and at horrifying cost.

Communist Russia could not, any more than could capitalist Britain, avoid the iron necessity of beginning to save. There had to be capital— for the new sources of energy, the new factories, the new machines—and only the people at large could do the saving. But driven by his totalitarian daemon, Stalin pushed the percentage of national income devoted to saving far above the western figure. He compelled the Russians to save not 15 but 25 to 30 per cent of the fruits of their labors. Nor was this the end of the matter. Fearing an independent peasantry, he forced the farms to deliver their entire surplus to the government. They revolted, killed their animals and starved during the terrible imposition of collective farming. Far from agricultural techniques improving, output actually fell. But relentlessly the saving went on. Conditions in Russian farms and Russian cities were more appalling than in Victorian slums. Consumption was less, the "trickle down" even slower. For a decade at least, the great foes of exploitation exploited their own people as no capitalist had ever done, and squeezed out of them the last kopeck of saving.

But this is only one side of the story. Russian modernization was accomplished at breakneck speed. It had advanced far enough by 1941 to withstand Hitler's invasion. It achieved prodigies of postwar reconstruction. It has driven expansion onward at a rate of some 7 per cent a year. In four decades it has come within sight of America's military and industrial power. Today, even consumption is at last improving. To the peoples in emergent lands the speed and vigor of the transformation, accomplished in so few decades, is a matter of hope as well as fear. The times of iron discipline and ruthless saving in Russia are receding. What is more in evidence today is the growth and power. Inevitably the Soviet achievement seems to present an alternative to the slower traditional western method of reaching the point of "economic break-through." Among the preindustrial societies of today, China has already chosen the Russian route. And few other governments can hope to escape indefinitely from the dilemma of this choice.

The western nations are more or less aware of how much they, too, have at stake in the decision. If a third of the human race despaired of the open society with its flexible experimental methods and mild disciplines, and chose instead the iron path of total Communist control, the balance of freedom in the world would be perilously upset. Not only would the emergent peoples lose their liberty. The West itself might suffer from that loss of nerve and breakdown. in confidence which occurs when societies have the impression that their ways are not the ways of the future—that history is leaving them behind.

What is perhaps less clearly realized is the extent to which the West has influenced and, if it will, can still influence the outcome. The conditions today under which the emergent peoples are trying to modernize their economies have been brought about almost entirely by western policies and western influence. As late as 1939 most of the world was still controlled either by settlers of European stock—as in all of America— or by the colonial rulers of the same origin. In Asia, it is true, the westerners came out to trade, and it was only where local authority collapsed—as in Java and India—that they took over political control. But their economic influence undermined Manchu power in China, and Japan could not have resisted them after 1850 if it had not forcefully westernized itself. In short, western control or western influence determined virtually the entire pattern of development in Asia from the seventeenth century to the end of the last war. Africa in the last hundred years has similarly been under total western domination.

The western contribution to the four levers of modernization proved uneven. Peasant agriculture remained static, and the new plantations mainly benefited western interests. Modern education began—especially in India —but in 1936 there were still only 516 university students among Java's 40,000,000 people. A start was made on infrastructure, roads, railways, ports and power—again, India led the rest—but industrialization lagged far behind.

At this point we reach one of the consequences of the western impact which, though unintended, may have given a decisive setback to Asian development. Until the nineteenth century China and India were exporters to Europe of manufactures—hand-loom textiles, silks, pottery. In addition, peasant income all through the vast countryside was supplemented by local handicrafts. In Britain such centers of artisan enterprise were often the starting points of mechanized industry. In Japan after 1870, they were to prove so again as thousands of small workshops were moving to production with power and machines. But in India and China as the nineteenth century developed, this widespread preindustrial system of manufacture was wiped out by the flooding in of machine-made textiles and gadgets from the West. Local centers were extinguished. Peasant income fell. Indigenous growth ceased. Later in the century, modern factory industry began; but often, as in China, it was overwhelmingly foreign. In India, given Britain's doctrines of free trade and *laissez-faire,* Indian enterprise did not secure full tariff protection until after the First World War. Industrialization was thus slow in spreading and would have been even slower if two world wars had not hastened it a little.

The small extent to which modernization was encouraged by western colonial control can best be illustrated by the opposite experience of Japan, the one Asian country to exclude the westerners. After 1870, a policy of thoroughgoing modernization was carried through by the Japanese themselves. A land reform gave the peasant a stake in production, extension services helped him to increase output by 50 per cent between 1870 and 1910. Most of this surplus was transferred to the towns, where the state expanded roads and ports, railways and power, began a drive for universal literacy, sent young men overseas to train, established industries, sold back the big concerns to the clans—the Zaibatsu—and encouraged cottage industry to supplement them. Every lever of modernization was thus brought into service, and in a few decades the Japanese economy was within sight of self-sustaining growth, saving enough each year to increase the volume of savings thereafter—and this in spite of a population which was increasing as rapidly as any in Asia.

We cannot fairly assess the western impact without this background of population pressure. China already had a vast population and gross rural poverty when western economic influence became predominant after 1850. But in India and Java it was western control that helped the spurt. A hundred years of peace probably doubled India's population between 1800 and 1900. In Java the numbers grew from just over 3,000,000 in 1795 to nearly 30,000,000 by 1914. In the twentieth century, sanitation and medical services began to speed the rate of growth. Keeping pace with this increase would have required measures as vigorous as those of Japan to insure that economy and population grew together, each kind of growth stimulating the other as it did in the West. But under the impact of partial modernization—which best sums up Asia's western inheritance—population growth in most of the Asian countries began to accelerate before the economy had reached a position of self-sustaining growth. And this is perhaps the most fateful of all the legacies from the West.

Saving, it must be repeated, means not-consuming. The more mouths there are to feed in a static economy, the harder it is to postpone consumption. The only answer is to save more drastically and thus achieve growth. But how can this drastic saving be done when—after a century of rapid growth in population, combined with economic stagnancy—percapita income has sunk to the margin? How can a government increase savings to 15 per cent of national income if—as in India—the citizen's average income is only sixty dollars? This is the dilemma which most of Asia has inherited from the West. And this is the dilemma which could lead—as it has done in China—to the choice of the Communist alternative. In Communist discipline, in Communist techniques of forced accumulation, in Communist readiness to wring the last ounce of saving from the countryside, there seems to be a possible escape from the Asian impasse.

Equally the dilemma of saving could give the key to an effective western policy. The broad aim over the next two or three decades should be to bring the flow of investment in the emergent lands up to the level needed for self-sustaining growth. Thereafter there would continue to be foreign investment on a normal business basis; but the period of emergency help, designed to overcome the obstacles created by partial modernization, would have to come to an end.

If the present position is taken as a starting point, one can broadly estimate that the emergent peoples in the free world—1,000,000,000 of them —with their annual income of about $120,000,000,000, manage to save the 5 per cent traditional in static economies. To this $6,000,000,000 is added each year about $3,000,000,000 of outside capital, public and private. These figures are roughly half of what is needed. But they cannot be doubled immediately because the local people lack the margins for tougher saving and because the ground is not yet prepared—in public utilities, in transportation, in technical training—to absorb a sudden startling increase from outside.

The process is essentially long term. But a reasonable aim might be to double the flow of capital from outside over the next two decades. If this extra injection of saving—of the order of $6,000,000,000 a year, both public and private—were used to increase local skills and infrastructure, domestic capacity to save would certainly increase, although a doubling of the level is perhaps too optimistic. But even if domestic savings increased by 50 per cent over the ten years, the next decade would open with total savings at least within sight of the goal of 15 per cent of national income. The second decade could complete the transformation of the local economies, and thereafter special assistance would taper off.

Such a scheme is, of course, no more than a statement of intent. The actual content of the program would vary from country to country and region to region, and would reflect the varying degrees of modernization achieved during the period of direct western control or influence.

Since the old colonial governments were not very active in the field of basic agriculture, most underdeveloped areas require at least a quintupling of expenditure on the land so that men and resources can be transferred from it to other sectors without imposing Stalinlike controls. Education, particularly in Africa, also needs really ambitious expansion. On the other hand, the colonial record of infrastructure is normally more lavish. Roads, railways, public utilities exist. It is usually a question not of starting from scratch, but of extending an existing system sufficiently to permit a frontal attack upon industrialization. Infrastructure is, incidentally, pre-eminently an area for public investment, since private enterprise is not attracted by the low returns over long periods which public services provide.

The sphere of private enterprise now as in the past is likely to be the development of raw materials for export and all the myriad forms of industry—processing plants, consumer goods—which expanding wealth can support.

Not all the emergent peoples are ready for all these policies at once, but where—as in India—much of the infrastructure in both men and services already exists, investment plans can be more immediate and ambitious, and outside assistance can be mobilized on a larger scale. In fact, India might well be made the model of a speedy, efficient, co-ordinated effort of internal investment and outside help. In spite of their desperate poverty, the Indians have increased their domestic savings by 50 per cent in the last decade and hope to have doubled the annual rate by 1966. Even so, it still falls below the 15 per cent needed for self-sustaining growth. If, however, outside capital from all sources—public, private, international, national—could reach $1,000,000,000 a year during the third Five Year Plan, the point of break-through would be in sight at the end of the period; and the largest free community in Asia, in which live 40 per cent of the free world's emergent peoples, would have demonstrated that without totalitarian discipline, without the suppression of freedom or the imposition of forced saving on a murderous scale, an underdeveloped land can achieve full modernization and the possibility of sustained growth.

There is one proviso to this hope. At some point in the next decades there must be a check to the rate at which India's population is increasing—a need of which the Indian Government is well aware. But, in fact, the connection between rapid economic development and a more stable birth rate is exceedingly close. In a desperately poor society the birth of many children is an insurance against tragic rates of infantile mortality and, in some measure, an economic investment as well. It is only when parents, convinced of the chance of better health and rising standards, can hope to give their children surer prospects of survival and nurture, that they will feel inclined to raise a smaller family. It need hardly be stressed that in a free society, whatever measures are pursued by government, the decisive choice rests with the parents. Thus—as in the West —a measure of economic advance and expectation is virtually a precondition of a slackening in the population's rate of growth.

A target therefore may be set for the western nations of $5,000,000,000 to $6,000,000,000 a year in investment of all forms—public and private, from national and international agencies—with an immediate plan to allot $1,000,000,000 of this sum each year to India's crucial experiment in growth. That such an aim is easily within the West's resources requires little demonstration. It is no more than 1 per cent of the combined national incomes of the western nations; and since the recent rate of growth of these incomes is of the order of 4 per cent a year, to allot 1 per cent to a world investment project requires no diversion of resources. It merely entails a slight postponement in the rate at which consumption is actually increasing. To call this a strain or a sacrifice is an abuse of language.

But the mere availability of resources will not determine the result. The fundamental political question has to be decided—whether or not the western powers accept the need for a sustained, long-term policy of world investment and world growth. The arguments from self-interest seem overwhelming. We are beginning—after a decade of uncertainty—to see that the direct political appeal of Communism is on the wane. Hungary and Tibet are reminders that Communism can be the stalking horse of a new form of imperial control. Communism's chief appeal is therefore social and economic—that it can throw out the landlords, revolutionize agriculture, build industries at breakneck speed and achieve modernization in a decade. To people caught in the impasse between saving and rising population, its techniques of forced accumulation can still appeal—unless there is an alternative, the alternative of western aid. Sustained world investment is thus a fundamental weapon in the struggle against Communist expansion. . . .

But more than national security is at stake. In this century, owing to the work of historians and archivists, of archaeologists and explorers, we know more than men have ever known about the fate of civilizations. Our western forefathers could take their society for granted as the end product of a unique historical progress in which, little by little, the inventiveness and faith of free men had come to set up a world society under western influence and control. Today we know that progress is at best a fluctuating line; and that along the march of humanity many proud experiments in political organization, many essays in empire, many great and affluent societies have foundered by the way. We know, too, that again and again they failed not from an inherent lack of means and resources, but from something more subtle—a failure of the spirit, a loss of nerve or faith or inner control. . . .

There is no greater defeat for a man or a society than to set a great experiment in motion and then to abandon it before it is half done. The modernization of the world is such an experiment. Casually, unconsciously, but with deadly effectiveness, western man all round the globe destroyed the traditional gods and the ancient societies with his commerce and his science. Now that the old world is dead, is he to make no special effort to bring the new world to life? He has plowed up the continents and scattered the seeds of new methods and hopes and ambitions. Is he indifferent to the harvest? Does it mean nothing to him if great areas of the world, where western influence has been predominant, emerge from this tutelage unable to return to the old life, yet unfitted for the new? It is hard to believe that the future could ever belong to men demonstrating irresponsibility on so vast a scale.

But the greatest challenge is also the simplest. The element above all others which western man has brought into history is the belief in its moral dimensions. When one considers the rise and fall of empires, the predatory imperialism, the violence, the irrational destructiveness which has marked so much of mankind's story, one is tempted to see in it only "sound and fury, signifying nothing." But in the Christian, rational and humane tradition of the West, the attempt has been made to rescue wider and wider areas of human existence from the tyranny of man's grasping, irrational and violent instincts—and a fundamental element in this search for moral order, of which Communism itself is a perverted by-product, is the belief that men should not prey on other men but that they are, in very truth, their brother's keeper.

In the past this principle has been limited by the few resources available in any society for active help. Private charity could lessen misery, but the levers of economic growth were not available for a frontal attack on poverty itself. The Industrial Revolution has removed this inhibition. Within western society the principle that the wealthier, luckier and healthier should assist the less privileged to acquire the education and well-being needed to advance themselves—the principle of general welfare—has brought about a wider and wider sharing of the new wealth.

Today resources exist in such abundance that a world-wide extension of the principle of welfare is physically possible. All that is lacking is the political decision to do so. Is it possible that a society which boasts of its humanity and its Christian inspiration should ignore the challenge? Is it conceivable that such a society, having done so, should deserve to survive?

70

Planning for the Year 2000

by J. Bronowski

London

A specter is haunting the Western world—yes, today as in 1848. But it is no longer the one that was paraded in the Communist Manifesto. Today the name of the specter is automation.

In every industrial country, men are looking with alarm at the installation of new automatic machines. They see the machines taking over work which, until a few years ago, seemed to need the most delicate human judgment. For the new machines do not merely replace the brute power of the muscle—machines have been doing that for nearly 200 years, ever since first the water wheel and then the steam engine were brought into the factory. The new machines are beginning to replace a gift which is neater and more specifically human: the ability of the eye to measure, of the hand to adjust, of the brain to compare and to choose. When the Luddites smashed factory engines in 1811, they were fighting, hopelessly, against their mere physical power, which dwarfs the strength and with it the output of a man. But the specter of automation points its long shadow at his intellect.

In the United States as in England, and in most industrial countries, the automatic control of machine operations has gone farthest in the making of motor cars. This may be because, whenever anybody wants a car, everybody wants one; and alas, it is equally true that whenever anybody does not want a car, then all at once nobody wants one. That is, the motor industry is peculiarly sensitive to good times and to bad times; and in England, it was putting in automatic machines just when the times turned abruptly from good to bad. The result was panic among employers, a bitter but divided strike by the workmen, and bewilderment (heavily lathered with platitudes) in the Government. No one is clear whether the dispute reached back to automation, or was merely a by-product of the credit

From *The Nation,* March 22, 1958, pp. 248–250. Reprinted by permission.

J. Bronowski lives in England and is a lecturer who broadcasts frequently on radio. Trained as a mathematician at Cambridge, during World War II he did statistical research on the economic effects of bombing. Since 1959 he has been Director General of Process Development for the National Coal Board of Great Britain.

squeeze; and was the strike a protest against *any* dismissal of workers, or only against their sudden dismissal?

Questions like these are never answered in the day-to-day of politics. A compromise is reached, a crisis is settled for the moment; and when the next crisis comes, we suddenly find that what had been a midnight compromise has become a permanent principle. For example, the strike of Britain's auto workers was settled by paying some of them compensation for the loss of their jobs. This is a new principle in English industry. Is it really good government, is it good sense, to invent such a principle on the spur of the moment in order to get on with the export of motor cars?

There are political thinkers who believe that it *is* good sense, or at least that it is inevitable, that issues are decided in this way. They say that all acts of state are particular acts, and that they do not conform to a principle but rather, one by one, combine to form the principle which wise historians read into them after the event. It is useless, these thinkers say, to ask statesmen in advance whether men who are displaced by machines should or should not be paid compensation: that will be decided at the historical moment when the change comes, almost by accident, by the strength of the two sides, and by the social backing they can muster.

But surely it is possible for men, even if they are historians, to be wise before the event. I think that there are some changes in the structure of our society which can be foreseen now. It can be foreseen that in the year 2000 more people will do one kind of job and fewer will do another; that one kind of thing will be valued and another will not. That is, we can draw now the bony skeleton of any industrial society in the year 2000. It may be a world society or a city state; it may live in a settled peace or still under the threat of war; it may be democratic or totalitarian. Whatever it is, I believe that life in it will have certain large features.

First, it is of course plain that everyone will have at his elbow several times more mechanical energy than he has today. The population of the world must be expected nearly to double itself by the year 2000. But the rate at which energy is being added, particularly in the industrial countries, is much faster than this. The four billion people who will be alive in the year 2000 will not all have the energy standard of Western Europe today, where every inhabitant commands the mechanical equivalent of about five tons of coal a year. But they can be expected to average about half this standard—say, the equivalent each of two tons of coal a year.

The use of energy per head is closely linked with the standard of living, and the rise that I have forecast is therefore in itself the mark of a massive advance in living standards. But more than the crude figures, it is the whereabouts, the distribution of this energy that is significant. Most energy of this kind is generated in electric-power stations, and today these stations run, nearly all of them, on coal. The real difficulty in getting energy to Central India or Northern Australia or the Copper Belt in Africa is the difficulty of carrying coal there. In the year 2000, the greater part of the world's electrical energy will be generated from nuclear fuels. A nuclear fuel such as uranium or heavy hydrogen is over a million times more concentrated than coal; one ton of it does the work of more than a million tons of coal. Therefore it will be possible to carry the fuel, and to generate the energy, wherever it is wanted. There will no longer be a reason for the great industrial concentrations in the Ruhr, in Northern England, and in the Eastern United States. And what is as important, it will at last be as simple to have energy for agriculture as for industry.

Second, there will be advances in biological knowledge as far-reaching as those that have been made in physics. For fifty years now, we have been dazzled by a golden rain of exciting and beautiful discoveries about matter and energy—the electron, the quantum, relativity, the splitting of the atom, the proton, the neutron, the mesons—the bright list seems to have no end. But do not let us be blinded by them to the work which has been done in the last twenty years in the control of disease and of heredity. We are only beginning to learn what happens when we use a selective killer of weeds or breed a new strain of corn, when we feed anti-biotics to pigs or attack a cattle pest. That is, we are only beginning to learn that we can control our biological environment as well as our physical one. For the year 2000, this will be critical. Starvation has been prophesied twice to a growing world population: by Malthus about 1800, by Crookes about 1900. It was headed off the first time by taking agriculture to America, and the second time by using the new fertilizers. In the year 2000, starvation will be headed off by the control of the diseases and the heredity of plants and animals—by shaping our own biological environment.

And third, I come back to the haunting theme of automation. The most common species in the factory today is the man who works or minds a simple machine—the operator. By the year 2000, he will be as extinct as the hand-loom weaver and the dodo. The repetitive tasks of industry will be taken over by the machines, as the heavy tasks have been taken over long ago; and mental tedium will go the way of physical exhaustion. Today we still distinguish, even among repetitive jobs, between the skilled and the unskilled; but in the year 2000, all repetition will be unskilled. We simply waste our time if we oppose this change; it is as inevitable as the year 2000 itself—and just as neutral.

But its implications go very deep. For it will displace the clerk as well as the fitter; and the ability to balance a ledger will have no more value, or social status, than driving a rivet. This is the crux in the coming of automation, that it will shift the social standing of those who do different kinds of work. And this is why these speculations about the year 2000 are in place: because the shift is already going on, and it is our business to foresee now where it is certain to take us.

In themselves, the changes I have described will not determine whether by the year 2000 Africa will become industrialized, whether the nations will still be testing bombs, or whether we shall live under totalitarianism or under democracy. They will not even determine whether we shall live in large communities or small ones.

This last point is odd and easily overlooked, but I think that it is important. For 200 years now, it has been the rule that, as a nation has grown in industrial strength (and with it in industrial complexity), so more and more of its workers have had to move together into large cities. In the sixteenth century, Queen Elizabeth I of England passed laws to prevent the growth of London, yet today Greater London houses nearly one-fifth of the population of Britain, and carries on about a quarter of all her industries. The same process of industrial concentration has been at work in France, in Germany and in America.

There are several forces which prompt this process. One is the hunger of industry for power; and in the past, power has been cheap only where it has been made on a massive scale. A second force has been the growing specialization of agriculture. And a third has been the sheer physical need to have large numbers of people to handle manually semi-finished goods through the many stages of manufacture.

Not one of these reasons need have force fifty years from now. The atomic-power plant need not be large; if it can reasonably drive a submarine now, it can reasonably power a community then. In the same way, biological control of the heredity and the disease of plants and animals will make it possible in the year 2000 to grow our food in smaller units. But potentially the most powerful influence on the size of future communities, of course, is the coming of automatic machines. They make it possible for a few men to take a complex product such as a drug or an engine through all the stages of its manufacture. By using automatic machines, quite small communities can live in the elaborate world of industry; and they can do so either as the makers of some one product for a nation or, what is more difficult, as units which are self-contained and self-sufficient.

I have stressed the change which is possible in the size of the community, because this happens to be an historical subject as well as a critical one. Back in the 1820s, the pioneer of an idealistic socialism in Britain, Robert Owen, insisted that the industrial revolution of his day ought in the end to lead to smaller, not larger, communities. He hoped that societies of between 1,000 and 1,500 people, working co-operatively, could survive, and he actually founded some in America. In the setting of his time, Robert Owen was premature; but he was not wrong. There are now industrial developments which open the way to smaller communities, if we choose to take that way. Atomic energy and automation are among them; and so are the radio-telephone and the helicopter and the microfilm, because they all help to make it possible for the man in the village to be physically and intellectually as well equipped as the man in the metropolis. The size of the future community really depends only on the rarest skill which it needs to support on the spot—the surgeon, the brilliant teacher, or the matinee idol. Fifty years from now, a community of 10,000 may well be large enough to afford that.

But what such a community cannot afford is the unskilled worker. The atomic-power plant, the agricultural station, the automatic factory—none of them has a place for him. In the small community, each unskilled man is a heavy burden.

In a profound sense, therefore, the choice ahead of us is this: If between now and the year 2000, we can, step by step, turn the men who now do our repetitive work into men with individual skills, then we have a prospect of living in small and homogeneous communities. But if we remain with a large reservoir of unskilled men, then society will continue to move towards larger and larger concentrations.

To my mind this is a profound political choice; it is the choice which we must make now, every day, in a hundred tiny actions. We are about to have introduced, day by day, here and there, another and another automatic machine. One will do the work of ten typesetters, another will displace a hundred auto workers; and soon, a third will take the place of a thousand clerks. I have said repeatedly that automation today is coming to do the work of the brain, and therefore is taking the place of the white collar worker. If these men are permanently reduced to unskilled work, they will become the material for a new army of Brownshirts. Hitler's squads were recruited in just this way, from unemployed men whose collars had once been white.

That is already the danger in the short term. And it remains a danger in the long term, too, threatening the generations ahead of us. If we allow the survival of a permanent reservoir of unskilled workers, then we do two things: we insure that our cities will get larger and larger; and we connive at a permanent war in society between the skilled and the unskilled. It seems to me most likely that a society of this kind, concentrated in large units and divided between top dogs and under dogs, will fall into a totalitarian form of government. I do not need to look to the year 2000 for that; George Orwell looked only so far as 1984, and saw it.

Technical foresight is a necessity; our political actions depend on it. And they do not depend on taking the short view; they depend on the long

view, on looking far beyond the years of which we can speak positively—
they depend on seeing the large features of a future whose detail is still
unformed. We cannot escape the large bony features: atomic energy, biological control, automation. But the body of society is not all bone; a
good many different bodies clothe that skeleton. It is possible on that
skeleton to have either a totalitarian or a democratic society. I think that
it can be foreseen that the future society will be totalitarian if it contains
many unskilled men working in large cities, and will be democratic if it
consists of skilled men working in small communities.

Changes toward one or another of these future schemes are not brought
about by some instant illumination, a thunderclap of universal conversion.
They are brought about by our small daily acts, if we know in what direction
we are trying to act. And I have given two general directions to which
we should bend whatever we do, whenever we have the choice.

71

The Future As History

by Robert L. Heilbroner

I. A Recapitulation

We have been concerned with the great currents by which the future
environment is being shaped and formed. Now it is time to step back, and
in the light of the historic outlook, to consider again a question with which
we began our investigations. This is our *state of mind* about the future—
the philosophy of expectations with which we orient ourselves to its challenges, and beyond them, to the sweep of history itself.

This selection is the concluding chapter (Chapter IV) from *The Future As History*
by Robert L. Heilbroner. Copyright © 1959, 1960 by Robert L. Heilbroner. Reprinted by permission of Harper & Row, Publishers, and the author. Reprinted for
distribution in the British Commonwealth by permission of the William Morris
Agency, Inc., agent for the author.

Robert L. Heilbroner is an economist, lecturer, and writer. His best-known work,
The Worldly Philosophers, is often used in colleges as an introduction to the history
of economic thought. This book, beginning with Adam Smith, gives brief accounts
of the lives and theories of the leading economists of the English classical school.

In the past, as we know, we have approached the future with the sustaining beliefs of a philosophy of optimism. That is, we have always conceived of the future in terms of its benignity, its malleability, its compatibility with our hopes and desires. But if our preceding pages have had any purpose, it has been to demonstrate the inadequacy of this belief today. It is no longer possible for America to commit itself trustingly into the hands of a deity of history whose agent forces are comfortably circumscribed and comfortingly familiar. If one thing is certain it is that history's forces have reached a power utterly unlike that of our sheltered past, and that the changes those forces portend are very different from the propitious historic transformations they brought about in our past.

Let us briefly recapitulate what some of those changes are likely to be:

1. As a consequence of the new weapons technology we have not only lost our accustomed military security, but also any possibility of enforcing a military "solution" to the problem of communism. The weapons stalemate has thus magnified the influence of the non-military determinants of the central struggle of our times. The "historic forces" of politics and economics, of technologies and ideologies, are therefore of crucial importance in the resolution of this contest.

2. The trend of these forces is not an encouraging one. In the huge continents to the East and South we have witnessed an explosive awakening of hitherto ignored or abused peoples, who now seek a rapid redress of their age-old grievances. This has led the underdeveloped nations into a desperate effort for economic development—an effort which, in the environment of underdevelopment, turns naturally in the direction of economic collectivism. There are strong possibilities that this collectivism will veer far to the left, whether or not it falls directly under communist hegemony. It is likely as well to discard the frail structures of democracy, and to maintain its morale by an exaggerated nationalism. Finally, we must not ignore the possibility that American economic growth, by widening the gap between the underdeveloped peoples and ourselves, may place America at the focus of the frustration and resentments which economic development is likely at first to generate.

3. At the same time, the drift of Western society is itself away from the traditional forms of capitalism. In all nations, including our own, a framework of "socialist" planning is replacing the unregulated market mechanism. In Europe this drift into planning is made more significant by the fact that European capitalism, unlike American, is not a self-assured and unchallenged social order.

4. However, within our own nation there are strong tendencies which move us away from the traditional, and now perhaps nostalgic idea of

American society. One of these is the rampant technological and scientific development which marks our time. This development manifests itself in a proliferation of institutions needed to "support" the increasingly dependent individual, and in the rise of bureaucratic apparatuses needed to control the technological machinery itself. The rise of the welfare state, on the one hand, and of the military bureaucracy, on the other, are instances of the manner in which technology is enforcing a socialization of life.

5. There are also visible other tendencies which are transforming our society, particularly in its economic aspect. There is a strong likelihood that a radical redefinition of the limits of public economic activity will be enforced by the pressure of events. Over the near future this is likely to be provided in disguised form by the enlarging military sector, but in the longer run we shall probably be forced to find civilian outlets to replace the military. Somewhat further ahead lies the still more difficult problem of providing internal economic discipline in a society in which the usual market control mechanisms are increasingly weakened by widespread social abundance.

6. All these collective trends are accelerated by our main historic movement—our growth. The problem then is the degree to which our blind economic momentum makes it impossible to respond effectively to the technological, political, and economic forces which are bringing about a closing-in of our historic future. This is a question to which dogmatic answers cannot be given. But it must be pointed out that an effective control over the historic forces of our times would require changes not only in the structure of power but in the common denominator of values, which do not seem likely to occur, at least for a considerable period.

The probabilities, in other words, are that "history" will go against us for a long time, and that the trend of events, both at home and abroad, will persist in directions which we find inimical and uncongenial. It would be foolish to pretend to a degree of prescience about the future which no amount of analysis can provide, or to be doctrinaire about the evolution of events. Yet surely, to hope for the best in a situation where every indication leads us to expect a worsening, is hardly the way to fortify ourselves against the future. Optimism as a philosophy of historic expectations can no longer be considered a national virtue. It has become a dangerous national delusion.

But if our optimism fails and misleads us, what shall we put in its place? How shall we prepare ourselves for the oncoming challenges of the future? What might be the character of a philosophy suited to our times? These are the deeply meaningful questions to which we now turn.

2. The Failures of Optimism

It may help us to formulate answers to these questions if we ask ourselves what it has been about the recent past for which optimism as a philosophy of historic expectations has failed to prepare us. The answer is explicit in the theme of this book. It is an outlook on the future *as history*.

This is not to say that optimism does not contain—albeit tacitly—an estimate of the future "as history." We have already endeavored to show its roots in the technological, political, and economic forces that have generated modern history, and its unconscious assumptions about the automatic progress which those forces effect. But what is missing from the philosophy of optimism is a conscious recognition of the special circumstances of history from which it arose and about which it generalizes. It is a failure to see itself as the product of a unique and sheltered historic experience which could not be enlarged into a model for all historic experience irrespective of its setting.

As a result, optimism has misled us in two particulars. First, it has caused us to overestimate the degree of our freedom in history. Because it mirrors an historic experience in which our conscious efforts to "make" history coincided with and were aided by the movement *of* history, optimism has given us the notion that history is only, or largely, the product of our volitions. Thus it has deluded us as to our power when the forces of history run not with, but counter to, our designs. It has filled us with a belief that everything is possible, and has made it not a sign of wisdom but a suspicion of weakness to think in terms of what is impossible.

Secondly, optimism has given us a simplistic idea of the forces of history. Assessing those forces in terms of their eighteenth- and nineteenth-century manifestations, it has failed to alert us to the possibility that the identical basic forces, in another environment, might lead to very different results from those which we assume to be their natural outcome. Thus the philosophy of optimism has presented the idea of technical progress solely in terms of the enhancement of man's productive powers—which was indeed its outstanding attribute in the past—rather than in terms of the social repercussions of technology which may well be its principal impact upon us in the present and future. Similarly, the optimistic outlook has taught us that the impetus of popular political aspiration leads naturally to the development of democratic governments, as it did in the cradle of history in which it was nurtured, but has failed to alert us as to the turning which those self-same aspirations can take—and have already taken—in an environment in which the preconditions for Western parliamentary democracy are totally absent. Finally, in the terms of the optimistic philosophy, the consequences of economic progress have been perhaps the most artlessly conceived of all. Quite aside from whether it correctly judged the outcome of the internal mechanics of capitalism, the optimistic outlook made economic advancement itself an unambiguous and self-evident social goal—a point of view which, however justified by the conditions of insufficiency of the nineteenth century, entirely obscures the new problems, both of organization and of values, which the achievement of abundance itself brings into being.

Thus if we are to suggest the attributes of a philosophy of expectations better adapted to our times than that of optimism, we shall have to explore more fully the two main areas in which optimism is deficient. First we shall have to ask: What is possible at this moment in our history? What are the limits of intervention into, what are the "necessities" of the historic process? Secondly, we shall have to inquire: What attributes of the forces of history are neglected by the philosophy of optimism? How can we prepare for their unexpected and often unwelcomed repercussions? In a word, how can we think about the future as history?

3. The Limits of the Possible

Everyone who considers the first of these questions—what is "possible" and "impossible" in history—soon comes up against a classic dilemma. This is the dilemma of "free will"—or in terms of the historic process, of determinism versus historic freedom. It is the dilemma of choosing between a world where everything is "possible" and therefore where nothing can be counted on, including the most basic necessities for the continuance of the human community; and a world where nothing is possible, and therefore where nothing can be hoped for except that which is inevitably and immutably fixed and beyond alteration. It is a choice between history as chaos and history as a prison.

This is a dilemma which still exercises philosophers and historians. But the dilemma has more to do with the limitations of abstract thought than with the experience of history itself. For when we turn to the living reality of history, we do not encounter a dilemma, but a *problem*—which is a very different thing. And this problem is not to formulate the meaning of historic freedom in general and forever, but to determine in the light of the actualities of the moment how much of history lies within our grasp and how much lies beyond.

Once we approach the matter in this direct and pragmatic fashion, the idea of what is "possible" in history presents itself intelligibly enough before us. We then find ourselves confronted, as a condition of life, with a situation which may be logically awkward but which is not at all awkward as a fact. This is the coexistence of freedom and necessity in history— the simultaneous existence of its glacial imperturbability, its "laws," its "necessities" on the one hand, and its "freedom," its openness, its amenability to our wills on the other.

The point at which we can divide freedom from necessity also comes to us with reasonable clarity. We all know that there are some historic events—such as, for instance, the internal politics of Soviet rule—which it is virtually impossible for us to affect. We recognize another class of events that lie directly—or at least to an important degree—within the scope of our control and responsibility. The "possibility" of war, for instance, is a matter in which we are quite sure that our free decisions play an immense and probably determinative role—all the more so, since so many aspects of the "historic" situation clearly set the stage for war.

This is, however, only one way of assessing what is historically possible for us. For what we deem to be "historic events" by no means exhausts the aspects of change and development in history. As Karl Popper reminds us, "There is no history of mankind, there is only an indefinite number of histories of all kinds of aspects of human life"; [1] and when we turn to those aspects of history with which this book has been primarily concerned— the aspects of social change rather than of immediate political conflict— we find our possibilities of history-making sharply curtailed. In our society, the "history" of technological progress and penetration, or the "history" of political belief and economic development are not facets of human life which we normally subject to "history-making" decisions. In general we allow these aspects of history to follow their autonomous courses, and to evolve by their unguided interactions. Thus we limit our idea of what is possible in history by excluding from our control the forces of history themselves.

This is a very different situation from that which obtains in a more collectivistic society. The enormous national effort of Russian growth or the wholesale alterations in the social structure of China are instances of historic change whose possibility was initially discounted by observers who had in mind the limitations of historic intervention in our own kind of society. The point, then, is that there are no fixed and immutable limits to what is historically possible. Rather, different organizations of society define for themselves the limits of what is and what is not within reach of conscious history-making choice. Authoritarian societies, as a generality, have a much more comprehensive direction of the "forces" of history than open societies. On the other hand, open societies, through their democratic apparatus, retain a wider degree of control over the course of their "heroic" history, i.e., over the policies of their leaders.

4. The Possibilities Before America

What does this imply for the "possibility" of altering the historic outlook that lies before us?

To the extent that we are concerned with those aspects of the future

[1] *The Open Society* (London, 1952), vol. II, p. 270.

which will be molded by the anonymous forces of technology, political ideology, and economic evolution, we must accept the conclusion that the possibilities of major intervention are not great. For the portents of the future spring, in the main, from underlying pressures of ideologies and from the fixed structures of institutions whose conscious manipulation does not now lie within the reach of our accepted "history-making" powers. Of course we can make small changes in the superstructure of our institutions. But if, for example, we really want to undo the "creeping socialism" of our time, we should have to do more than legislate away our institutions of social welfare and economic control. To remove these institutions without removing the massive technology and the economic instability which have produced them would only be to open the way for a social explosion which would probably swing even further leftward. Essentially, the only way to halt the creep of "socialism" is to return to an atomistic economy with small-scale technical and economic units, and with a wholly different climate of political and social beliefs. This it is obviously impossible for us to attempt, without a degree of historic intervention which is entirely alien to our social philosophy.

It may even be that with the most violent assault upon "history," with the most revolutionary intervention into institutions and ideologies, it would still not be possible to reverse the basic direction of our historic momentum. In our time, we have seen extraordinary attempts to reshape the social forces of history, and extraordinary results in imposing a heroic, revolutionary will upon social history.[2] Yet the changes which were inaugurated were in nearly every instance in accord with the drift and temper of world history as a whole. There has been no successful revolution against the forces of technology, of popular political aspiration, and of socialism, although it is obvious that the slogans of "democracy" and "socialism" have been put to cruel use. No revolutionary has been able to preach anti-industrialism, or the inequality of classes, or the ideals of capitalism. Gandhi, who came closest to being an exception insofar as his dislike of technology was concerned, was nonetheless unable to keep India closed off from modern technology. The few nations which have sought to stand against the political trend—like Spain—have been in a state of exhaustion and have had no subsequent important historic development. There have been few major revolutions since 1945 which have not flown the banners of socialism.

Thus there seems indeed to be a basic character to world civilization in our times from which no vital historic effort can depart very far in its essentials, and the fact that even revolutions have had to conform to this pattern makes it unlikely in the extreme that a non-revolutionary society, such as our own, will succeed in resisting it. To what ultimate ends this

---

[2] For an excellent discussion of this problem in general, cf. Sidney Hook, *The Hero in History* (Boston, 1943), esp. Chap. XII.

"inevitable" direction of historic forces may carry society we do not know, for such questions take us far beyond the horizon of the "given" historic situation. What may be the final impact of science and technology on civilization, the end effect of our egalitarian political ideals, or the ultimate organization of collectivism, we do not know. All that we do know is that, for the moment, these general historic tendencies are firmly in the saddle, and that short of the profoundest change in the character of our civilization, or an incalculable redirection of events, they bid fair to dominate the social environment of the future.

But the fact that the *main direction* of historic movement is too deeply rooted to be turned aside does not mean that our future is therefore caught in a deterministic vise. It is not just necessity, but a mixture of necessity and freedom which, as always, confronts us as a condition of historic existence. If the idea of the future as history tells us what it is not "possible" for our kind of society to do, it also makes clear what *is* possible.

For example, the spreading hegemony of scientific technology may be an inescapable general tendency of our times, but the social consequences which we have previously discussed do not follow as an inescapable corollary. They are largely the result of *non-intervention* before the historic closing-in of science and technology. But non-intervention is not the only possible response to this historic force. It is rather a kind of abdication before the problem itself. It leads us to ignore the very thought that there may exist other controls over the technological revolution than the economic calculus which is at present our main device for regulating its admission into our lives. One need hardly say that a society which consistently ignored considerations of economics would seriously jeopardize its own well-being. But this does not mean that a society cannot, however imperfectly, attempt to weigh the non-economic advantages and disadvantages, the non-economic costs and benefits that seem likely to accrue from major alterations in its technological apparatus, and allow these considerations to balance, offset—and on occasion, even to veto—the guide of profitability. Thus the actual impact of science and technology on our social existence will depend not merely on the presence of these overriding forces in our age, but on the influence which we *unavoidably* exert on their social application—including the passive influence of permitting economic criteria to exert their sway largely unchallenged.

The same general conclusion is true with respect to the possibilities of influencing the other main forces which affect our future. There is little doubt, for instance, of the overwhelming power of popular aspirations in the underdeveloped nations, or of the likelihood that those aspirations, in the frustrating conditions of underdevelopment, will lead toward economic collectivism and political dictatorship. But the fact that there is very little we can do about this is very different from saying that we therebefore have no control over this aspect of the future. On the contrary, it is only by understanding the "inevitable" outlook that we can hope to devise policies which have some chance of exerting a lasting and positive effect on the course of economic development. Similar alternatives confront us in dealing with the trend of all industrialized nations, ourselves included, toward some form of economic collectivism. To continue to set ourselves adamantly against this trend is to minimize rather than maximize our possible historic influence. The possibility poised by history is not that of denying the advent of planning, but of seizing control of it to assure the kind of collective economic responsibility we want.

Thus the outlook on the future as history does not pave the way for an attitude of passivity and still less for defeatism. Those who would reject the idea of the "inevitable" future for these reasons are in fact more likely to object to the bold measures to which it points as the only means of rescuing our future from the category of "inevitable fate." It is unquestionably true that the exercise of such historic control is fraught with risk. *But so is the exercise of non-control.* The issue is not the simple and clearcut one of a greater or lesser freedom. It is the difficult and clouded choice of a subservience to the necessities imposed by the forces visibly at work in our midst, or the perilous freedom of an exercise of historic control over ourselves.

How we shall behave in the face of this difficult choice of historic paths, it is not easy to say. Whether in the end we shall remain passive before the enveloping changes of history, or attempt to adapt our institutions so as to minimize their impact, is a question whose answer inevitably involves subjective biases. The degree to which the "common sense," the "basic instincts" of the people can be relied upon, the flexibility and farsightedness of the powers that be—these are matters about which purely objective judgments are impossible. All that one can say is that the challenges are very subtle; that the requisite changes in institutions, while not revolutionary, are nonetheless very great; and that the required degree of farsightedness is correspondingly high. Thus it is not difficult to conclude that the possibilities of historic intervention will not, in fact, be put to use. A critic who assesses the American scene in terms of its alertness to the underlying challenges of our times can scarcely fail to be struck by the general poverty of the prevailing outlook: the men of wealth and power, mentally locked within their corporate privileges; the middle classes, more Bourbon than the Bourbons; the working classes, unable to formulate any social program of purpose beyond "getting theirs"; the academicians, blind to the irrationalities of the society they seek to rationalize.

Yet it is one of the disconcerting facts of an open society that it offers so many opportunities for facile generalizations and so little sure ground for generally valid ones. As long as there is still visible in American society a continuing evidence of new thought and dissent, a self-control with respect

to the use of political power, and above all, a nagging awareness that all
is not right, it would be arrogant and unjust to shrug away our future as
a hopeless cause. There are, after all, great traditions of responsibility and
social flexibility in America. In them there may yet reside the impetus to
seize the historic possibilities before us, and to make those changes which
may be necessary if the forces of history are not to sweep over us in an
uncontrolled and destructive fashion. But it is useless to hope that this will
happen so long as we persist in believing that in the future toward which
we are blindly careening everything is "possible," or that we can escape
the ultimate responsibility of defining our limits of possibility for ourselves.

5. The Idea of Progress

In our last section we have been concerned with the problems of historic
possibility and impossibility, of freedom and necessity, which a philosophy
of optimism tends to obscure. Now we must turn to a second shortcoming
of our traditional outlook on history. This is the tendency of our philosophy
to present the workings of the forces of history in an overly simplified
manner—a manner which has entirely failed to prepare us for the actual
turnings which history has taken. If we are to sum up the shortcoming in
a phrase it would be this: *The optimistic philosophy equates the movement
of history's forces with the idea of progress.*

Whether there is such a thing as "progress" in history depends, of course,
on what we mean by the word. It is clear enough that there has been,
particularly in the last three centuries, a steady and cumulative accretion
of technical virtuosity and scientific knowledge which permits us to speak
of "progress" in these fields in a fairly specific sense. One particularly
important aspect of this progress has been the measurable lengthening
of the longevity of man and the improvement of his capacity to alleviate
his bodily ills. A second instance of definable progress has been in the
rise of the level of well-being of the masses in the West—although this can
be said to be more than offset by an actual decline, over the last century,
of the "well-being" of the teeming masses of the East. A third instance, less
easily indexed, but no less demonstrable in the large, is the historic progress
from a society in which man is born into his status toward a society in
which he is able to define his status for himself.

It is with these aspects of the forces of history that optimism identifies
progress, and so long as the meaning of "progress" is restricted to such
reasonably definable movements, there can be no objection to the word.
But it is also apparent that we cannot generalize from these specific concepts of progress to the larger idea of an all-embracing progress of "society."
There is no reason to believe that today's private morality, level of social
ethics, and general nobility of public ideals are in any sense superior to
much of the recorded past, if indeed they are equal to the best of American

Revolutionary times or to the heights reached in the golden ages of Greece and Rome. Our cultural and aesthetic public existence is hardly at an historic high point. And if, with all his gains in health, well-being, or status, the average person is "happier," more serenely or creatively engaged in life than in the past, this is not apparent in the happiness, serenity, or creativity of our age. We often imagine that "life" is much better today than, say, in the Dark Ages, but this depends very much on whose lives we conjure up in these two periods. After all, we live at a time when German brutality reached what may be, statistically, a record for the systematic extermination of life, and when Russian despotism at its worst took us back to the level of morality of the crueler Biblical kings.

Yet these somber considerations do not dispose of the idea of progress. Rather they raise the question: Why is it that the forces of history, which are indisputably the carriers of potentially beneficial political and economic and technological change, have not resulted in a corresponding improvement in the human condition? What are the attributes of these forces, as agents of change, which the optimistic philosophy glosses over? Let us try to identify some of these attributes which are omitted in the optimistic notion of progress.

6. The Inertia of History

Because we live in a time of great change, and because our philosophy of optimism makes us expectant of and receptive to change, we may easily overlook a deeply important aspect of historic development. This is its quality of inertia. It is a quality which is manifest not only in resistance to change—although that is one of its more important aspects—but in the viscosity which is imparted to history because people tend to repeat and continue their ways of life as long as it is possible for them to do so.

We do not usually call inertia to mind when we seek the great molding forces of history. And yet this humble characteristic is responsible for more of "history" than all the campaigns, the movements, the revolutions we readily call to mind. The simple, but quintessential fact that human beings persist in living their lives in familiar ways, which are the only ways they know how, is the very lifeline of social continuity itself.

This inertia which exerts so powerful a drag on history undoubtedly has its biological and psychological roots. But it is more than just an "innate" human characteristic. It is also the outcome of the historic social condition of man. For the persistence of habit acts as a protective reflex for the overwhelming majority of men who know very little except that life is a fragile possession, and that tried and true ways, however onerous, have at least proved capable of sustaining it. A mulish perseverance in old ways is not without reason when life is lived at the brink of existence where a small error may spell disaster. An instance in point was provided some years ago when a team of United Nations agricultural experts sought in vain to persuade Turkish farmers to improve their crops by removing the stones from their fields. Finally a few of the younger ones consented—whereupon, to the chagrin of the experts, their yields promptly *declined*. In the arid climate of Turkey, the stones had served the function of helping to retain the scanty moisture in the soil.[3]

Inertia shows itself as well in a general reluctance to embrace new social ideas. Reformers throughout history have deplored the tenacity with which the privileged classes have clung to their prerogatives—even when it was no longer in their "best interests" to do so. This is not so surprising when we view the enormous gulf which has normally separated the privileged and the unprivileged. What is far more striking is the difficulty which reformers have had in making even the most miserable and oppressed classes "see" the inequity of their lot, and in persuading them to rise in protest. The fact that our historic glance is easily caught by a few *jacqueries* obscures the fact that revolutions are remarkable in history not for their frequency but for their rarity, even though the "normal" condition of man has always been harsh enough to warrant revolutionary sentiments. We must conclude that whenever it has been possible the human being has *wished* to believe in the rightness and fixity of the situation in which he has found himself.

The inertia of ideologies as well as of institutions is often taken as a lamentable fact. It is the despair of the social engineer, the *bête noir* of the utopian planner. Nonetheless we must remember that there is a constructive role which this inertia also plays. A society without ideological inertia would live from instant to instant in peril of a fatal turning. The fixity of our voting habits, our customary beliefs, our stubbornly held ideas, even when these are wrong, serves a purpose in protecting and stabilizing the community. The reformer who despairs because people will not listen to reason forgets that it is this same suspicion of change which helps to prevent people from heeding the Pied Pipers for whom society never lacks. We may make progress only by freeing ourselves from the rut of the past, but without this rut an orderly society would hardly be possible in the first place.

This historic undertow of inertia warns us against facile conceptions of "progress" in two respects. In the first place it disabuses us of the notion of the "ease" of social change. For most of the world's peoples, who have known only the changelessness of history, such a stress on the difficulty of change would not be necessary. But for ourselves, whose outlook is conditioned by the extraordinary dynamism of our unique historic experience, it is a needed caution. Contrary to our generally accepted belief, change is not the rule but the exception in life. Whether it is imposed from above or imposes itself from below, change must reckon with the reluc-

---

[3] *Cultural Patterns and Technical Change,* ed. Margaret Mead (New York, 1955), p. 186.

tance of humankind to relinquish habits not only of a lifetime, but of life itself. This is the reason why even such enormous transformations as those we have dealt with in this book are slow, stretched out over generations, invisible from one day to the next.

Second, the drag of inertia warns us against the overestimation of the effects of change. The optimistic conception of progress calls our attention to the sweeping improvements which can be brought about by technology or democracy or economic advance. All that is certainly true as far as it goes. No one can doubt the capacity of history's forces to legislate beneficial changes in society. But there is a level of social existence to which these forces penetrate last and least. This is the level at which "society" is visible only as the personal and private encounters of each of us with his fellow man. It is the level at which life is *lived,* rather than the level at which it is abstractly conceived.

Here, at this final level of personal experience, the inertia of history is most apparently manifest. It is here that the revolutionary, having brought about tremendous changes in "society," comes to grips with the petty irritations of inefficient colleagues and apathetic clerks, of the "human factor" which like sand in a machine, has wrecked so many well-planned enterprises. It is not that revolutions, or the more gradual changes of historic evolution, make these daily frictions of life any worse. It is rather that so much of life remains the same, regardless of the new boundaries in which it is contained.

In this grinding persistence of the "human factor" lies the reason for much of the disillusion which so frequently follows a passionate attempt to bring about social progress. As Ignazio Silone has written: "Political regimes come and go; bad habits remain." [4] The underlying sameness of life, the reassertion of old established ways, of "bad habits," is an aspect of history which must not be lost to sight amid the more dramatic changes of the superstructure of society. An appreciation of the fact of human inertia must not lead us to understate the extent to which change is possible in society, but it should caution us against identifying this change with the equivalent "progress" of human life at a fundamental level.

7. The Heritage of the Human Condition

We have seen that optimism misleads us with respect to the possibilities of "progress" because it tends to underestimate the difficulty and to overestimate the consequences of historic change. But it compounds that shortcoming with a second and perhaps even more important failure. This is its lack of realism as to our starting point in the making of history. It is its failure to confront truthfully and unflinchingly the condition of the human being as it now exists.

[4] "The Choice of Comrades," *Voices of Dissent* (New York, 1958), p. 325.

Optimism tacitly views that condition in a favorable light. The very assumption that the growth of technical skill, political equality, or economic well-being will automatically lead to "progress"—rather than to increased destructiveness, heightened social disorder, or vulgar opulence—already takes for granted an environment in which rationality, self-control, and dignity are paramount social attributes.

But this is hardly the impression one gets from an examination of the panorama of human existence. If there is such a thing as an average human being, he is to be found among the majority of mankind which lives in the continents of the East and South. The chasm which divides the average life on these continents from our own is so wide that we can barely imagine existence on the other side. To be an Indian villager, a Chinese peasant, an African mine-worker is to be in a human condition whose dark and narrow confines cannot be penetrated by a Western mind.

But life on our side of the chasm is also very far from presenting a heartening vista. In the United States, for example, preventable disease and even deformity are still widespread. Mental aberration identifiably touches a tenth of the population. Criminality, in various social forms from murder to tax evasion, is prevalent among all classes. The urban environment in which life is mainly lived is crowded, often unspeakably ugly, and in its spreading slums, vicious. The average education is barely adequate to allow the population to cope with the technological complexities of the age, and insufficient to allow all but a few to understand them. Large numbers of families do not know or care how to raise their children, as witness the epidemic incidence of juvenile disorders.

The list could be extended without difficulty. But what characterizes many, if not all of these degradations of life, is that they are unnecessary. Most of them could be vastly alleviated by a sustained and wholehearted effort. Yet such an effort—as to whose immense "value" all would agree—seems impossible to undertake. Indeed, the very suggestion that these areas of need should carry an absolutely overriding priority, taking precedence over any and all more "profitable" activities, smacks of a suspicious radicalism. We are simply not concerned, beyond a mild lip-service, with mounting an all-out effort to raise the level of national health or civic virtue, or mass living conditions or average education or upbringing. Looking at some of the institutions we nourish and defend, it would not be difficult to maintain that our society is an immense stamping press for the careless production of underdeveloped and malformed human beings, and that, whatever it may claim to be, it is not a society fundamentally concerned with moral issues, with serious purposes, or with human dignity.

The point, however, is not to berate ourselves for our obvious failure to produce anything like a "good society." The point is rather that, with all its glaring and inexcusable failures, the United States is still probably the most favored and favorable place on earth for a child to be born and to grow up.

These melancholy facts must assume their rightful place in any evaluation of the prospects for "social progress." For in such a social atmosphere the forces of history do not lead automatically in the direction which optimism assumes. In an atmosphere of neglect of and indifference to human capabilities, it is not at all surprising that technology should result in the trivialization of life and the stultification of work. It is certainly not remarkable that, in the harsh and primitive setting of underdevelopment, popular political aspirations press toward extreme and violent "solutions" to the problems of underdevelopment; nor that, in the more advanced societies, they mold society in the image of the mediocrity of mind and sentiment they represent. Nor, given the prevalence of physical poverty in the backward nations and of psychological poverty in all nations, is the pre-eminence of materialistic drives and goals to be wondered at. In sum, today as in the past, the half-educated, half-emancipated state of human society assures that there will be a long continuation of the violence, the instability, the blatant injustice, which are the most grievous aspects of the human tragedy. This is the true heritage of the human condition, and its bitter legacy.

What is perhaps the most sorrowful aspect of this tragedy is that its victims are chosen arbitrarily and at random. There is no guilt or innocence, no measure of culpability or responsibility in the fate meted out by a world which is still more brute than man. Those who fall in wars do not "start" the wars. The victims of Hitler or Stalin were not those who raised these dictators to power. Nor will there be a fine balancing of accounts when the crimes of South Africa eventually exact their terrible retribution, or when the indignities of the American South work their full damage to the American social fabric. In a world in which conscious morality can be regarded with derision, and reason with suspicion, this random toll of social tragedy cannot be avoided. It is the consequence of a situation in which, as Albert Camus writes in *The Fall:* "We cannot assert the innocence of anyone, whereas we can state with certainty the guilt of all."

To raise these dark thoughts is not to sermonize that man is "wicked" or to avoid the conclusion that some men are much more guilty than others. Neither is it to maintain that there is no hope for a betterment of the human condition. On the contrary, there is today a greater long-term prospect for such betterment than humanity has ever known before. But the heritage of the past is too deep to be overcome in a matter of a few generations. It will be a long while until the human condition has been substantially improved. Not to face up to this fact with compassion and concern is only to cringe before reality. And while this should urge us on with all the strength at our command to support every effort to improve the condition of man, it cannot but chasten us as to the reasonable expectations of the "progress" which that condition will permit.

8. The Ambiguity of Events

In the very idea of progress, as we commonly accept it, is contained the notion of goals. We strive for specific objectives, located in the future, and imagine that each objective gained is a recognizable step toward "progress." As a result we find ourselves confounded when, having reached an objective, what we encounter is not the "progress" we anticipated but a new set of problems stemming from the very advance itself.

This disconcerting aspect of experience can be described as the ambiguity of events. By this we mean that every event in history has a Janus-like quality—one face which regards the past, and one which looks ahead; one aspect which is the culmination of what has gone before, and another which is the point of departure for what is to follow.

Simplistic ideas of progress see only the near face of events when they look to the future. Hence such views of the future typically underrate its complexities. They do not consider that the solution of one problem is only the formulation of the next. What an awareness of the ambiguity of events thus subtracts from the optimistic view of progress is the luxury of believing that progress is a simple pyramiding of success. The two-sided nature of future events does not deny that our problems may be our opportunities but it asserts with equal conviction that our opportunities may become our problems.

There is no more dramatic example of this than the impact on world history of that most "unambiguous" of all evidences of progress: the development of modern medicine. It is not necessary to spell out the enormous benefits which medical science has brought to mankind. Yet no assessment of the over-all impact of modern medicine on our age can ignore the fact that it has also been the "cause" of an immense amount of additional suffering in the world. By its success in reducing the scourges of mass disease and infant mortality, the "progress" of medical science has crowded the already overpopulated villages and cities of Asia and South America with still more mouths, and has thus aggravated the very human suffering it set out to relieve.

Needless to say, not every instance of progress cancels itself out in so direct and distressing a fashion as this. The point, rather, is that progress does not merely consist in the surmounting of a previous problem, but inherently consists in the emergence of a new problem which, although different, may be quite as grave as the old. In the course of this book, for example, we have seen such new problems emerging from the advance of technology or from the achievement of abundance in our own society.

These new problems do not gainsay the advances which technology or economic growth bring us. But it may well be that the consequences of our technological captivity, or the control problems of economic abundance will be just as humanly crushing as the problems of insufficiency or technical inadequacy from whose solution they emerged. There is no reason to believe that the successive problems of "progress" pose easier challenges; indeed it is probable that the overcoming of the "simpler" problems of poverty and disease opens the doors on progressively more profound, elusive, and insoluble human dilemmas.

Marx and Hegel called this ambiguous aspect of progress the dialectic of history. Marx, however, brought his dialectical analysis to a halt with the achievement of communism as the "terminus" of the history of class struggle. Ironically enough, it is probable that there is no aspect of future history which today more desperately needs dialectical clarification than the achievement of the communist—or for the West, the socialist—goal. It is clear that as the "near side" of socialism approaches, it is the "far side" which becomes of ever greater interest and importance. To consider socialism as a "goal" of social history is to fall prey to the optimistic delusion that goals are milestones in history from which the next stage of development promises to be "easier" or unambiguously "better" than the past. To rid oneself of this comforting notion is not to lessen one's ardor to resolve the difficulties of the present, but to arm oneself realistically for the continuance of the human struggle in the future.

9. The Grand Dynamic of History

Is there then no possibility for progress?

As it must by now be clear, much depends on what one means by the question. If by "progress" we mean a fundamental elevation in the human estate, a noticeable movement of society in the direction of the ideals of Western humanism, a qualitative as well as a quantitative betterment of the condition of man, it is plain that we must put away our ideas of progress over the foreseeable vista of the historic future. For whereas there is no question but that the forces of our time are bringing about momentous and profound changes, it is only optimistic self-deception to anticipate, or even to wish for, the near advent of a perceptibly "better" world as a result. Taking into account the human condition as it now exists, the laggard slowness with which improvements in institutions are followed by improvements in "life," the blurred and ambiguous fashion in which history passes from problem to problem, it is certain enough that the tenor of world history will remain much as it is for a long while to come.

Indeed, from the point of view of the West and especially of America, it may seem to be deterioriating. As we have seen through the pages of this book, many of the tendencies of world history are likely to manifest themselves to us as a worsening of the outlook. We may well be tempted to interpret this growing intractability of the environment as the metamorphosis of progress into retrogression.

Against this dark horizon it is hardly possible to cling to the sanguine hopes and complacent expectations of the past. And yet if we can lift our gaze beyond the confines of our own situation, it is possible to see that every one of these changes is essential and inescapable if the present condition of humankind is to be surpassed. Until the avoidable evils of society have been redressed, or at least made the target of the wholehearted effort of the organized human community, it is not only premature but presumptuous to talk of "the dignity of the individual." The ugly, obvious, and terrible wounds of mankind must be dressed and allowed to heal before we can begin to know the capacities, much less enlarge the vision, of the human race as a whole.

In the present state of world history the transformations which are everywhere at work are performing this massive and crude surgery. We have dwelt sufficiently in the preceding pages on the violence and cruelty, the humanly deforming aspects of the changes about us. Now we must see that in their ultimate impact on history it is the positive side of these great transformations which must be stressed. However unruly the revolution of the underdeveloped nations, it is nonetheless the commencement of a movement away from the squalor and apathy which three-quarters of the human race still consider to be life. With all its disregard for Western standards of justice and liberty, the forced march of communism is nevertheless retreading the essential, but now forgotten path of early industrial development of the West. Whatever its capacity for the destruction or the diminution of man, the perfection and application of industrial technology is withal the only possible escape from the historic indenture of man. And no matter what its difficulties, the painful evolution beyond present-day capitalism is indispensable if those nations which have gained the benefits of material wealth are now to cope rationally with its administration.

Thus the blind and often brutal impact of the historic forces of our day can still be said to point in the direction of optimism and of progress. Only in our present situation, the West is no longer the spearhead of those forces, but their target. What is at bottom a movement of hope and well-being for the inarticulate and inadequate masses of mankind is a fearful threat of the delicate and now gravely exposed civilization of the articulate and advanced few.

No member of the Western community who loves its great achievements and who has enjoyed the inestimable value of its liberties and values can confront this outlook of history without anguish. Of all those who will feel the blows of the future, none will suffer more than the heirs of the long tradition of Western humanism, and none will more acutely feel the delays and the recession of "progress" as the world endures its protracted ordeal.

More aware than the rising masses of the world of the destination to which their inchoate revolution may hopefully carry them, it is the humanist spirits of the West who will feel most betrayed by the violence and excess which will likely accompany its course. Ever hopeful of the re-entry of the communist nations into the Western community of thought, it is the Western intellectuals and idealists who will bear the full agony of watching for and waiting for signs of change which may be very long in coming. Alive to the immense potential benefits of the technical virtuosity of their age, it is again the guardians of the humanist tradition who will most despair at its continued misapplication; just as it will be they rather than the masses who will wish for a more responsible form of economic society and who will chafe at the continuance of the old order.

This prospect of disappointment and delay may give rise to a tragedy greater than the tragic events of history itself. This would be the disillusion of Western thought and the abandonment of its hopes for and its distant vision of progress. It would be the surrender of the very ideals of the West before the crushing advent of history, and the adoption of an indifference, or worse, a cynicism before the march of events.

If this tragedy is to be avoided, the West will have need of two qualities: fortitude and understanding. It must come to see that because this is not a time of fulfillment does not mean that it is a time of waste. It is rather a time when the West must take upon itself a new and more difficult role in history than in the past: not that of leading in the van of history's forces under the banner of progress, but that of preserving from the ruthless onslaught of history's forces the integrity of the very idea of progress itself.

Particularly for Americans will this long period of abeyance provide a test of the spirit. Accustomed by our historic training to expect a mastery over events which is no longer possible, we are apt to interpret the intransigence of history as a kind of personal betrayal rather than as a vast and impersonal process of worldwide evolution. Thus there is the danger that we may abandon our optimism for a black and bitter pessimism, or for a kind of "heroic" defiance.

But neither pessimism nor defiance, any more than optimism, will give us the fortitude and understanding we require. For this we need an attitude which accepts the outlook of the historic future without succumbing to false hopes or to an equally false despair; a point of view which sees in the juggernaut of history's forces both the means by which progress painfully made in the past may be trampled underfoot, and the means by which a broader and stronger base for progress in the future may be brought into being.

Such an attitude may retain its kernel of optimism. But more is needed for the display of stoic fortitude than a residual faith in the idea of progress. Above all there is required an understanding of the grand dynamic of history's forces in preparing the way for eventual progress. There is needed a broad and compassionate comprehension of the history-shaking transformations now in mid-career, of their combined work of demolition and construction, of the hope they embody and the price they will exact. Only from such a sense of historic understanding can come the strength to pass through the gauntlet with an integrity of mind and spirit.

What is tragically characteristic of our lives today is an absence of just such an understanding. It is very difficult while America and the West are at bay to feel a sense of positive identification with the forces that are preparing the environment of the future. Less and less are we able to locate our lives meaningfully in the pageant of history. More and more do we find ourselves retreating to the sanctuary of an insulated individualism, sealed off in our private concerns from the larger events which surround us.

Such an historic disorientation and disengagement is a terrible private as well as public deprivation. In an age which no longer waits patiently through this life for the rewards of the next, it is a crushing spiritual blow to lose one's sense of participation in mankind's journey, and to see only a huge milling-around, a collective living-out of lives with no large purpose than the days which each accumulates. When we estrange ourselves from history we do not enlarge, we diminish ourselves, even as individuals. We subtract from our lives one meaning which they do in fact possess, whether we recognize it or not. We cannot help living in history. We can only fail to be aware of it. If we are to meet, endure, and transcend the trials and defeats of the future—for trials and defeats there are certain to be—it can only be from a point of view which, seeing the future as part of the sweep of history, enables us to establish our place in that immense procession in which is incorporated whatever hope humankind may have.